Women and Men Political Theorists

ENLIGHTENED CONVERSATIONS

Edited by
KRISTIN WATERS

Women and Men Political Theorists

Women and Men Political Theorists

ENLIGHTENED CONVERSATIONS

Edited and with Critical Introductions by

Kristin Waters

BLACKWELL
Publishers

Copyright © Blackwell Publishers Ltd 2000; editorial matter and organization © Kristin Waters 2000

First published 2000

2 4 6 8 10 9 7 5 3 1

Blackwell Publishers Inc.
350 Main Street
Malden, Massachusetts 02148
USA

Blackwell Publishers Ltd
108 Cowley Road
Oxford OX4 1JF
UK

Library of Congress Cataloging-in-Publication Data

Women and men political theorists: enlightened conversations/edited by Kristin Waters.
     p.   cm.
  Includes bibliographical references and index.
  ISBN 0–631–20979–4 (hb: alk.paper)—ISBN 0–631–20980–8 (pb: alk.paper)
  1. Feminist theory—Political aspects.   2. Political science. I. Waters, Kristin.

  HQ1190. W655 2000
  320′.01—dc21   99-049054

British Library Cataloguing in Publication Data

A CIP catalogue record for this book is available from the British Library.

Typeset 10 on 11.5pt Sabon
by Kolam Information Services Pvt. Ltd, Pondicherry, India

Printed in Great Britain by MPG Books, Bodmin, Cornwall
This book is printed on acid-free paper.

Contents

Acknowledgments

My own understanding of the canonical works of modern philosophy originates in the teaching and mentoring of the late William Lensing of Bard College, a philosopher who instilled in me respect for tradition and endless fascination with the ideas and arguments of modern philosophy. His knowledge and love of the discipline have been enduring gifts.

A handful of women in the Women's Studies Faculty Group at Clark University in the 1980s provided a new model of scholarship and collegiality. They introduced me to the practice of feminism, and changed my approach to academic endeavors. Pamela Wright's humor and intellect were radical forces. Cynthia Enloe, in myriad ways, created the model of teaching and working together in Women's Studies, a model characterized by immense energy, unbounded good will, and inventive techniques for creation *ex nihilo* – since the resources at that time were meager or non-existent. She guided the Clark Women's Studies Faculty Group past the landmines and around the obstacles of curricular tradition. Serena Hilsinger's brilliance as we team-taught the first Women's Studies capstone seminar, using works from Aristotle, Wollstonecraft, and Mill alongside the works of Charlotte Brontë, Jean Rhys, and Michele Cliff, may have provided the original paradigm for audacious juxtapositions. Lois Brynes' eye-rolling challenge when I opined that there were no women writers to teach in Modern Philosophy provided some of the impetus to prove myself wrong. Zena Sochor's steady competence and consistent support provided a clear-eyed view of the demands of academic life, and a model of how to meet those demands with equanimity. She is greatly missed.

In the early to mid-1980s, I taught a traditional course in political theory in Philosophy at Clark, which served Political Science majors as well. Later, when I taught the course for the Government Department, my newly raised consciousness became frustrated with the standard texts and I was grateful for the departmental support and the freedom to teach the texts that I pleased. Then and there I cobbled together a set of readings that became the prototype for this book.

As a strong believer that faculty should occasionally become students again, those occasions when I did so myself geometrically increased my understanding in certain fields. I am especially appreciative to faculty who allowed me to attend their seminars: Ann Ferguson's *Feminist Theory* course at the University of Massachusetts, Lois Brynes' *Meadows and Wastelands* at Clark University, Evelyn Fox Keller's *Women and Science* at MIT, and Patricia Williams' *Women and Notions of Property* at Harvard University. These women and many, many others are pioneers in transforming the curriculum in many different fields.

In Lois Brynes' course, I had the privilege of meeting Diane Bell, who was then the Henry Luce Professor of Religion, Economics, and Social Justice at the College of the Holy Cross. This meeting was the beginning of a lively and ongoing dialogue about feminist theory, especially feminist epistemology. It was also the beginning of an outstanding collegial relationship. Diane is now Professor of Anthropology and Director of Women's Studies at George Washington University.

The original book proposal was hatched at Clark Psychology professor Rachel Falmagne's breakfast table, in conversation with Linda Nicholson of the State University of New York (Albany), both of whom have provided ongoing encouragement. Cynthia Enloe gave me guidance in structuring the proposal. I have received helpful comments from Robert Douglas, Lewis Gordon, Alison Jaggar, Richard Schmidt, and Karsten Struel. Many other people have read and commented on versions of the chapter introductions: Diane Bell, Debbie Fisher, SunHee Gertz, Ed O'Reilly, Dan Shartin, and Karen Turner. I have also received generous support from Ann Bookman, and from Gene McCarthy, who gave me access to his personal library of African American literature. SunHee Gertz provided guidance throughout. The assistance of Mary Boliver has been invaluable.

When Part VI was in crisis, it was Professor Carol Conaway of Holy Cross who argued that Frederick Douglass was an original philosophical thinker whose work had been seriously ignored, and deserved inclusion in the volume. Lewis Gordon of the Pembroke Center at Brown University originated the suggestion of pairing Anna Julia Cooper with John Stuart Mill, noting the connections between Cooper's "What Are We Worth" and Mill's *Utilitarianism* and *Political Economy*. I've benefited from a number of conversations with both Carol and Lewis over the course of the project.

The proposal and several chapters of this book were written as part of a project while I was Visiting Research Professor in Women's Studies at Clark University. I wish to thank the generosity of this program for providing the opportunity for research, and especially Joanne Ljungberg for encouragement over the years. Blackwell Publishers provided me with a grant to support the completion of this project, for which I am very grateful. At Blackwell, Susan Rabinowitz found merit in the original proposal, Ken Provencher helped to shepherd the manuscript through the process, and Margaret Aherne provided skillfull and cheerful editing.

A number of libraries have provided resources, including the Truro Public Library at Cape Cod, Massachusetts, and especially the Goddard Library of Clark University and the Dinand Library at Holy Cross. In finding the writings of Mary Astell, I am especially thankful to the Watkinson Library at Trinity College, Hartford, the Shakespeare Folger Library in Washington, D.C., and the American Theological Library Association of Evanston, Illinois.

Three books in particular set the stage early for this work, and I am grateful to their authors for having written them. Dale Spender's *Women of Ideas and What Men Have Done to Them, From Aphra Behn to Adrienne Rich* should be essential reading for anyone interested in women in western thought. Details of the lives and work of hundreds of women writers appear on these pages. In particular, this is where I first read about Mary Astell and Matilda Joslyn Gage. In contrast to Spender's more popular (but nonetheless scholarly) work is Alison Jaggar's *Feminist Politics and Human Nature*. This book transforms western political theory and should be assigned reading for every modern political theory course. One ignores it at one's peril. It provides in exquisite detail all the major arguments of modern political theory, from Locke to Rawls, by way of Rousseau, Marx, Engels, Mill and other major writers, and the feminist critique. The third major influence was Patricia Hill Collins' *Black Feminist Thought*, which created a sea change of thinking about feminist political theory, and especially about the contributions of Black women and of epistemology.

Any undertaking of this kind, above and beyond other professional duties, absorbs substantial time and energy which, in my case, might otherwise have been devoted to my family life – a devotion which I take very seriously. It is one thing to ask those who are close to you to make space for a few evenings here and a few weekends there, but to request special dispensation for the better part of two years stretches beyond the limit of what one can reasonably request. I have had the good fortune to be sustained by the tolerance, care, and intelligence of my husband, Ed, and the companionship, humor, and affection of my extraordinary family including Ed, and our children, Colin and Jiaqi.

Introduction

Non-traditional interlopers to the practice of political theory-building are faced with a history that is full of lacunae, loose ends, and false starts, one that is incomplete and perplexing. New approaches include various forms of feminism, area studies, and post-colonial theory. These newer theories may well lack the elegance of traditional studies or canonical works, which are marked by a penchant for internal consistency with systems rather than by a resonance with historical events. But what these new theories lose in elegance they often make up for in vigor. Fueled by the vitality of new material, fresh conceptual tools and the excitement of discovery, new approaches are gaining scholarly recognition and a place in the curriculum.

The first step for theoretical development in reclamation projects such as this one is to *create a space* for new work. Marginalized views have been left out of traditional political narratives, a practice that feminists label "silencing" or "erasure." When mainstream scholars refuse to acknowledge the existence of alternative works, or devalue them, or ridicule their authors, existing works can simply disappear. This anthology makes a step toward bringing non-traditional political theory into the discourse. It is one element in the larger international endeavor to transform traditional curricula.

Throughout the modern period, from the seventeenth to the twentieth century, men and women have engaged in a dialogue about issues in political theory. But part of that dialogue has been occluded – the voices especially of women and minorities, and of others who have opposed the dominant ideologies. Women political thinkers have written, not just about women and "women's issues," but about all the central issues of political theory. Mary Wollstonecraft wrote about citizenship and inequality; Mercy Otis Warren addressed the dispute between republicanism and federalism. Like John Stuart Mill, African American Maria W. Stewart addressed how free speech and action affect liberty. Shifting focus from the central subject – in this case modern democratic man, striving for freedom and the good of society – to the "other," variously identified, is alone a monumental task. Writers from the margins have long observed the failures of a substitutional approach. A simple shift to the modern democratic woman, or the Black man striving for freedom and liberty, is likely to obliterate genuine structural differences between marginal and centrally located groups. Only through a careful understanding of non-traditional philosophical and historical sources can a more complete – less partial and distorted – view of political philosophy be attained.[1] Only through an understanding of the particular historical and social conditions of disempowered groups can their own political circumstances be acknowledged and honored.

Standpoint epistemologies privilege the theoretical frameworks generated from different social locations as the starting point for knowledge about politics and everyday life.[2] They require an openness to different ways of structuring problems, to admitting new concepts and new connections, to allowing topics that we thought were "not political theory" to be considered as such. This is because the easiest way to remarginalize different thought is to exclude it definitionally: "This isn't politics, isn't philosophy, isn't literature." As Patricia Hill Collins argues:

> Curriculum operates very much like "theory" does in the academy. Like the Curriculum, theory cuts both ways. Social theory in particular can serve either to reproduce existing power relations or to foster social and economic justice.[3]

Groups other than the dominant ones must be recognized for producing and authorizing theory. The challenge is to find ways to address both new, or newly available, material, and also to draw connections with traditional work so that the classical and newly considered works together can produce a coherent understanding, one which furthers rather than impedes interpretations of political theory that promote a just society.

This anthology pairs major political writings of men and women in the modern period, providing substantial primary source material for study in research and in political theory courses. The book is intended to create bridges in several directions. It links women and men writers of the seventeenth through the twentieth centuries, ending the typical occlusion of certain texts and recreating the dialogues that took place, historically, over issues in political theory and practice. The book also bridges concepts by contemporary writers, especially feminists, and concepts by earlier women and feminist writers. It aims to clarify the conceptual lineage of political ideas, and in some cases reveal a continuity of thought. Finally, it connects contemporary feminist writers and traditional theorists by exposing a body of critical literature that contests modern liberal theory. The concepts of liberty, government restraint, social good, civic virtue, and the role of the state are contested but shared in this bringing together of minds.

The Introduction to Part I provides slightly more historical grounding than later chapters because the historical events in seventeenth-century England set the stage for the versions of western political theory under discussion here. John Locke and Mary Astell were both major participants in the intellectual ferment of their times. I have included some detail about Locke's and Astell's lives, and in general I have followed the principle that where current access to information about a writer's work is limited by the small quantity of available secondary literature, more material should be provided than in the chapters where there is substantial secondary literature available to the reader.

Part II introduces the work of Jean-Jacques Rousseau and Mary Wollstonecraft. Because the underlying principle for the volume as a whole is to find pairs, or in the case of Part VI, a *set* of writings that resonate with each other, themes offer a better match than strict chronological ordering. Rousseau's writings preceded Wollstonecraft's by several decades, but his influence on her was profound. Her *Vindication of the Rights of Woman*, which appears in Part II, was published two years *after* her *Vindication of the Rights of Men*, which appears in Part III, but intellectually the former is the partner of Rousseau's work while the latter is the partner of Burke's *Reflections*. The reader is therefore introduced to Wollstonecraft's second *Vindication* first, which, as long as the chronology is understood, makes for a more logical set of pairings.

Wollstonecraft's iconoclastic, even scandalous, life has been subject to intense scrutiny over time, and even capitalized on by political theorist and popular novelist William Godwin, to whom she was married for less than a year before her death. In his *Memoirs of the Author of a Vindication of the Rights of Woman*, he found a best-seller that earned him a substantial sum for a number of years.[4] I have refrained from saying much about Wollstonecraft's personal life, for the very reason that it has so often overshadowed her political theory. But I also encourage the interested reader to undertake a responsible study of her fascinating life through some of the better biographies – *after* reading her political treatises.[5]

Issues of federalism and anti-federalism had not loomed large for me prior to doing the research for this text. But as I read more about Mercy Otis Warren, it sparked in me an interest in James Madison and the *Federalist Papers* as well. These issues seemed to me so alive today in the disputes between conservatives and liberals in the United States, but also in some of the issues taken up in the current debates about European union, and the efforts worldwide to achieve new nationhoods based on ethnicity. Curiously, these disputes are often characterized as "political" rather than "philosophical," meaning that they are partisan and not intellectually substantial. I think a careful look at Warren and Madison's work against a contemporary framework will reveal otherwise and show that issues of the nature and extent of local or regional autonomy have important implications in political theory.

The pairing of John Stuart Mill and Maria W. Stewart found in Part V was the one that sparked my interest in this project. The identity of topic and disjunction of circumstance were irresistible. Although they never met, like Locke and Astell, and Wollstonecraft and Rousseau, I could imagine Stewart and Mill engaging in conversation – in a heated dialogue about topics of common interest.

I discovered in my research that in the nineteenth century numerous African American men contributed to political theory in the United States, and have been ignored or forgotten: Martin Delany, Alexander Crummell, Henry Highland Garnet, and David Walker are a few.[6] Frederick Douglass was an obvious choice for this volume because his substantial writings are extensively collected and there is a (too) small but available secondary literature on his work. It was my original intent to include some of the writings of Susan B. Anthony and Elizabeth Cady Stanton, until I remembered Matilda Joslyn Gage, a more substantial intellectual (as opposed to activist) than Stanton or Anthony. As I began to think of Part VI in late twentieth century terms – in terms of a matrix of oppression structured initially by attention to race, gender, and class – the logic of combining Douglass, Gage, and Karl Marx seemed compelling. In these writers the three sorts of oppressions, all of central concern in the mid-eighteenth century, are juxtaposed to reveal the complexities of simultaneous and overlapping systems of domination.

In the final chapter I had thought to include something other than a second selection from Mill. Cooper's prose is so extraordinarily strong and rich that Mill's seems mechanical in contrast, and the connections were not immediately obvious, as they were with Stewart. But the intellectual connections became more apparent. The two shared an interest in liberty for African Americans, education, equality for women, and utilitarian theory. Both had a vision of progress for humanity fueled by similar ideals.

I remain convinced that political theory will be taught in a completely different way in the future; that this collection, which is now innovative and ground-breaking, will appear obvious decades from now. I look forward to the day when the more obscure among my selections will command a substantial secondary literature and serve up many competing volumes – scholarly editions heavily annotated with collations from different editions, student volumes with standardized spellings, usages, and clear explanatory notes. For now we must be content making use of the available primary source material.

There is a symbiotic relationship between theory and practice – between how we think and what we do. Perhaps even more than we typically understand, theory informs practice and contributes to the creation of social institutions and everyday actions. The oppositional writings in the modern period have contributed, not just to theory and practice in politics, but also to science, social science, and humanistic studies. By embracing new sources and their theories we have the opportunity to reassess the canon – in a sense to breathe new life into the old narratives and to create new ones. This book should contribute to that project in political theory, and perhaps provide a model for work in other disciplines as well.

Notes

1 See the introduction to S. Harding and M. Hintikka, *Discovering Reality: Feminist Perspectives on Epistemology, Metaphysics, and Philosophy of Science* (Dordrecht: D. Reidel, 1983).
2 See Sandra Harding's *The Science Question in Feminism* (Ithaca: Cornell University Press, 1986) and *Whose Science? Whose Knowledge?* (Ithaca: Cornell University Press, 1991) for thorough and thoughtful discussions of standpoint epistemologies.
3 Patricia Hill Collins, *Fighting Words: Black Women and the Search for Justice* (Minneapolis: University of Minnesota Press, 1998), p. xi.
4 William Godwin, *Memoirs of the Author of a Vindication of the Rights of Woman* (London: J. Johnson and G. G. and J. Robinson, 1798).
5 Eleanor Flexnor, *Mary Wollstonecraft: A Biography* (New York: Coward, McCann and Geohegan, 1972), Emily Sunstein, *A Different Face* (New York: Harper and Row, 1975), Claire Tomalin, *The Life and Death of Mary Wollstonecraft* (New York: Weidenfeld and Nicolson, 1974), Ralph Martin Wardle, *Mary Wollstonecraft, A Critical Biography* (Lincoln: University of Nebraska Press, 1966), Gary Kelly, *Revolutionary Feminism: The Mind and Career of Mary Wollstonecraft* (New York: St. Martin's Press, 1996), and Godwin's *Memoirs* are some of the many biographies. All must be read with a critical eye.
6 See for example L. Litwack and A. Meier, eds., *Black Leaders of the Nineteenth Century* (Chicago: University of Illinois Press, 1991), and J. H. Bracey, Jr., A. Meier, and E. Rudwick, *Black Nationalism in America* (New York: Bobbs Merrill, 1970).

PART I

Sources of Political Authority:

JOHN LOCKE AND MARY ASTELL

Absolute Arbitrary Power, or Governing with *settled standing laws*, can neither of them consist with the ends of Society and Government.[1]

Locke, Two Treatises of Government

In 1649, seventeen-year-old John Locke was a pupil at London's Westminster School, when, within earshot of the students, crowds let out an audible gasp as King Charles I was beheaded. It is difficult to imagine what kind of impact the king's execution would have had on a young man. In Locke's case, popular imagery suggests a person who nursed a lifelong dislike of strong measures, one who applied logic and common sense to difficult problems, including those of a political or metaphysical kind. Whatever diverse forces contributed to the formation of Locke's intellect, the result is clear. He is credited with creating the most enduring Enlightenment legacies – liberal political theory with its reverence for freedom and equality – and its progeny – liberal constitutions and representative governments adopted worldwide.

During the 1640s, Great Britain endured years of civil war. Pitting Oliver Cromwell's republicans against the supporters of monarchy and King Charles I, the rival sides fought over issues of religious toleration and the seat of sovereignty. One source of the dispute lay in the failure of the official Anglican church to tolerate dissenting Protestant views including the more radical sects such as the Levellers, Quakers, and Diggers.[2] A second source was Charles' refusal to submit to parliamentary power, which led Parliament to declare sovereignty for itself. Exasperated by the king's internal deceptions, reversals, and duplicitous dealings with foreign powers, the House of Commons tried Charles I and found him guilty of treason for "levying war against parliament and the Kingdom of England." Charles' execution signaled that the civil wars were drawing to a close, but as a central theme of political inquiry, concerns about the sources of political authority were just gathering momentum in western Europe.

After the beheading of Charles I and the ultimate defeat in battle of Charles II, Oliver Cromwell ruled as Lord Protector. During that time Britain was a Commonwealth, but one that was a military state; the ideals of republicanism were suborned to despotism in one of history's sadder democratic experiments. As one consequence, moderates on both sides seemed to accept the restoration of the monarchy in the person of the exiled Charles II in 1660. In the period that followed, the upper classes of London society immersed themselves in the great wit, plays, and poems of writers such as John Dryden, Alexander Pope, and Aphra Behn.[3]

During these times, Locke had an indifferent career at Christ Church, Oxford – not fond of the scholastic "hog shearing" (hair-splitting arguments) – studying meteorology, botany, and then medicine. Of this period, Locke scholar Peter Laslett says he was "urbane, idle, unhappy and unremarkable."[4] In 1666, Locke's fortunes changed when he met Anthony Ashley Cooper, later to be first earl of Shaftesbury, one of the most prominent and politically powerful men of his time. Locke performed a bizarre and apparently miraculous surgical operation on this ailing aristocrat. In doing so he found a patron and transformed his own prospects. Moving into Shaftesbury's residence, Exeter House, he acquired through this connection a number of political appointments including secretary of the colony of Carolina, for which he wrote a constitution.

It was a time of plots and counter-plots. The change of power from Charles II to James II created an atmosphere of uncertainty. Shaftesbury's newly formed Whig party was determined to remove James from the throne, by act of Parliament or by force. Shaftesbury, imprisoned in the Tower for several months in 1681, was then implicated in the Rye House assassination plot and fled to Holland in 1683, where he died soon after. A close associate of the Shaftesbury circle and Whig party politicians, Locke found himself in a dangerous position. By royal order he was removed from his position at Oxford, where in later years "the developed originality of his thought menaced the curriculum."[5] After the great burning of books in the Bodleian Library Quadrangle, the last ever in England, Locke left Oxford for ever and also sought refuge in Holland. His fortunes changed again when, in 1688, James was permanently deposed, and replaced on the throne by his Anglican sister, Mary, and her husband, William of Orange. Locke and his Whig associates had helped to arrange this "Glorious Revolution" and Locke himself escorted the new queen as they sailed from Holland to England.

[Locke] went much further towards revolution and treason than his earlier biographers knew, anxious as they were to present him as a man of unspotted personal and political virtue.[6]

Locke's *Two Treatises of Government* were published anonymously in 1689, and for centuries were taken as a *post facto* defense of the Glorious Revolution. But in the 1960s, Laslett argued that these texts were written in the dangerous days between 1679 and 1683, as Shaftesbury and political philosopher Algernon Sidney were imprisoned in the Tower for their Whig activities. Laslett notes that lists of books in Locke's library, made as he moved from place to place, included with his political texts a volume entitled *Morbus Gallicus* (literally "the French disease" – syphilis, in the xenophobic phraseology of English physicians). Laslett posits that this title was a double-entendre code for another "French disease" – despotism, and that the book was in fact the *Two Treatises*, disguised to protect Locke from the fate of his patron. Published during the Whig ascendancy, this political tract would have been written a decade earlier when the same views were clearly treasonous. The text may have been sanitized to mask its origins, and some of its "philosophical", that is, highly general character, would have derived from the expurgation of political particulars relating to anti-Jacobite maneuvers. One vital feature of Laslett's claim is that Locke, long characterized as the father of liberalism, the philosopher who was above the politics of his day, was in fact deeply enmeshed in Whig plotting and politics.

Locke's *Essay Concerning Human Understanding* was published in the same year, and along with the *Two Treatises* is accorded high standing in western thought. Soon after these publications, Locke went to live in the home of Sir Francis and Lady Damaris Masham (daughter of Neo-Platonist Ralph Cudworth) where he continued to write and to be visited by such luminaries as Isaac Newton and Samuel Clark. He died there in 1704.

> [Mary Astell was] "wholly wrapt up in Philosophical Metaphysical & Theological & indeed all kinds of Divine Speculations...[whose] life and doctrine [were] exactly conformable unspotted and all of a piece."[7]
>
> *George Ballard*

As pleased as Locke had been about the installation of Mary and William of Orange as queen and king of Great Britain, so to such a degree was Mary Astell appalled as she grew to understand these politics. From the point of view of representative government, William and Mary were elected, in the sense of chosen by representatives to lead the nation. An act of Parliament made legal the "settlement" of the crown. From the point of view of a hereditary monarchy, James II, deposed from the throne, was the true hereditary heir.

Mary Astell's father was a Newcastle coal merchant, a member of the Guild of Hostmen which had many privileges in controlling the burgeoning industry. Linking medieval economic arrangements with emerging modern capitalism, the coal industry in England presents a fascinating case of hereditary power in a merchant's trade.[8] The Hostmen, whose charter was granted by Elizabeth in 1600, mingled with the upper social classes. Coal interests in Newcastle supported the crown in the civil wars, and for the elite, Charles I had become a martyr figure. He was not, as the Dissenting view would have it, an inept, duplicitous traitor willing to sell his country to other countries in order to maintain absolute power.

This is the setting into which Mary Astell was born, in 1666, during the restoration of the Stuart monarchy, Parliament, and the Church of England. High social position was small comfort to Astell and her mother. When Astell was twelve her father died, leaving the family to rely on the generosity of other Hostmen. Under the tutelage of her uncle, Ralph Astell, an Anglican curate who was eventually expelled from his position because of drunkenness in the pulpit, Mary Astell showed an early aptitude for study, reading Milton and Spenser, and learning the theories of the Cambridge Platonists, including Ralph Cudworth. Against Thomas Hobbes' *Leviathan*, these philosophers argued a spiritualist metaphysics and rationalist philosophy which posited a mystical union of faith and reason.

As a young woman Astell became deeply depressed about her material circumstances.[9] She had no dowry. Her pride and her class consciousness persuaded her not to marry into another, "lower" social class, or to become a governess or teacher.

> *Nature permits not me the common way,*
> *By serving Court, or State, to gain*
> *That so much valued trifle, Fame*[10]

Thus she mused in one of the many poems she wrote throughout her life. She was acutely aware of her lack of opportunity, an awareness which only heightened as the years passed. But maturity led her to change her views – that not "Nature," but *society* kept her from fully developing her extensive talents. Astell was extremely pious throughout her life. She took her joy from intellectual activity, which was deeply entwined with her Anglican faith. Her material needs were sparse, but real.

Since Henry VIII had "dissolved" the monasteries in the 1540s and created himself head of the Anglican church, there were no longer cloistered places where women like herself who had few financial resources could go to live a quiet, studious life. She mourned this loss, at first privately and then publicly in her first published writing, *A Serious Proposal to the Ladies*. But before she could put pen to paper to argue her views she had to make for herself a suitable position in the world in the absence of any social institution designed for that purpose. And she did a most extraordinary thing. Astell gathered what funds she could, left her mother, and took the stagecoach to London. Desperately in need of a patron, she wrote a plea to the Archbishop of Canterbury, who had just been released from the Tower. Astell's intelligent support of Anglicanism must have appealed to the Archbishop, who gave her money and contacts and, according to her biographer Ruth Perry, may have provided her with an introduction to her future publisher, Rich Wilkin, who was "a resolute champion of monarchy."[11]

The Reflector is happily of the Feminine gender[12]
Mary Astell, Some Reflections upon Marriage

In spite of her ongoing financial difficulties, Astell pursued her philosophical labors, which "suited her abstract mind... [and] satisfied her abstemious and intellectual character."[13] Another unsolicited letter propelled her as a participant into the world of philosophical and political discourse. This time she wrote to John Norris, a renowned Platonist whom she admired "as the thinker who criticized Locke for relegating God to an unimportant role in the way human sensations build into ideas."[14] She boldly sparred with Norris, beginning a spirited correspondence centering on "her belief in the immaterial intellect, which had no gender and was the essential feature of human nature," which Perry interprets as "at the heart of her feminism... fed by her highly politicized sense of power relations between governments and constituencies."[15]

By 1694 she had published *A Serious Proposal to the Ladies*, her closely reasoned plea for a women's college, and in the next year her correspondence with Norris, *Letters Concerning the Love of God*, came into print. *A Serious Proposal* was critiqued by Lady Damaris Masham, who at an earlier time might have applauded her work. But by that time, Locke was residing in Lady Masham's household and her sympathies to views like Astell's had diminished. About this time Astell also published *Some Reflections upon Marriage*, in which she develops a novel and compelling argument against the dissolution of marriage contracts and of civil government.

At the turn of the century Astell became a lively participant in the pamphlet wars of the day, engaging in dispute with Daniel Defoe and with Addison and Steele. Their journal *The Tatler*, which provided a high-profile forum for political and literary ideas, referred to Astell as "Madonella." In quick succession she wrote several more lengthy pamphlets: *Moderation Truly Stated, A Fair Way with Dissenters and Their*

Patrons, An Impartial Enquiry into the Causes of Rebellion and Civil War in this Kingdom, and *Bart'lemy Fair.*

Astell's great vision was nearly achieved when she was promised an endowment of £10,000 (a huge sum in those days) for her Women's College, either by Lady Elizabeth Hastings or by Princess Anne. But Bishop Burnet dissuaded the donor, ostensibly on the political grounds that a scheme to support what seemed like a nunnery was dangerously papist. The real motives are hard to discern. One can only wonder how different our worlds of learning and practice would have been if women had had standing in universities in the early eighteenth century, instead of two hundred years later in the twentieth century. In a move of social policy worthy of close scrutiny, the feminism of the 1660s–1690s was converted to an impulse to mild social reform in the 1700s. Instead of becoming the Dean of a women's university, Astell conceived, established, and headed the Chelsea Charity School for Girls, devoted to putting some small polish on the lower classes, rather than to teaching theology or philosophy to those who had been traditionally excluded from educational opportunities.

Mary Astell had many great friendships in her life, including Lady Elizabeth Hastings, and literary feminist Lady Mary Wortley Montagu. Friendship, especially female friendship, constituted an important element of her thinking and her life. She thought deeply about relationships between women, and she and her circle created an informal system of support that crossed class lines and included the multi-dimensions of personal, educational, religious, and financial assistance.

Always a private and modest person, at the end of her life only the severe pain of her breast cancer convinced her to undergo a crude mastectomy. Astell's philosophical beliefs assured her that the afterlife, in the absence of the contingency of the body, might afford her the kind of equality denied her in life. She died in 1731. A philosophical mystery corresponds to the rediscovery of Mary Astell's writing. For years, philosophers have wondered why there were no systematic contemporary responses to Locke's great works of philosophy. It now appears that Locke's major critic at the end of the seventeenth century, virtually unknown today, was the well-known Mary Astell.[16]

LOCKE'S POLITICAL THEORY

[I]n the beginning, all the world was *America*.[17]

Borrowing Thomas Hobbes' justificatory strategy, Locke begins his work with the "state of nature," a hypothetical or historical condition from which one could argue to a civil society, a strategy used in twentieth-century political theory by John Rawls.[18] State-of-nature theory provides a kind of social psychology whereby one uncovers certain aspects of human behavior, or natural laws which reveal the rights and responsibilities that accrue to human beings. Hobbes' concept of persons issuing from state-of-nature theory was one of violent individuals who come together in a place where life was famously "nasty, brutish and short." More optimistic, Locke viewed the state of nature as one in which benign individuals possessed a right of self-preservation against occasional violence, and which was a state of freedom and equality where people as rational agents could get along. The role of reason was vital. The Enlightenment ideal posited reason as the source of what are now called human rights. In the abstract, the humanity granted by reason applied to all people equally, even women, people of different races, and the poor. But the transition of natural rights from a universal application to propertied English men only, occurs in the course of argument quickly, seamlessly, and invisibly, and thus is rendered "natural." The parallel between Locke and Hobbes ends with their argumentative methods, for Hobbes' derivation of absolutism from individualism is one of Locke's prime targets. In contrast, Locke argues against absolutism, entwining the theories of Richard Hooker and Thomas Aquinas which invoke a sovereign power limited by moral constraints, constitutional traditions, and responsibility to the community.

Original to Locke is his treatment of property rights as the paradigm of rights found in the state of nature. Locke created a theory of the legitimate acquisition of private property whereby several conditions for ownership must be fulfilled. One must (a) mix one's labor with the property, (b) in doing so improve or increase the value of the property, and (c) benefit oneself and others (that is, increase the common good):[19]

> Whatsoever then he removes out of the State that Nature hath provided, and left it in, he hath mixed his Labour with and joyned to it something that is his own and thereby makes it his Property.[20]

Rights in the state of nature include, fundamentally, a right of self-preservation. A right of executive power which, like the others, belonged to all equally, is transferred to the state in civil society, and formed the basis for Locke's justification of representative government. A right of all to punish also converts to the state in civil society and foreshadows the judicial arm of government. Elements of some of these rights are transferred to a legitimate power in the state, but retained as potential by the individual to combat abuse of power. With his individualism, his theory of property rights, acquisition and ownership, and self-legislation, Locke is helping to create capitalist theory as well as the modern theories of representative democracy and civil authority. Curiously, several of these premises lead logically in two directions – to modern liberal theory and to modern socialist theory. But that is another tale. (See Part VI.)

Civil Society

> Men being, as has been said, by Nature, all free, equal and independent, no one can be put out of this Estate, and subjected to the Political Power of another, without his own *consent.*[21]

For Locke, the chief problems with the state of nature are its inconvenience and inefficiency, when a duly constituted civil society could perform the duties of protecting citizenry more effectively than if each were performing this task himself. Further, cooperation has economic benefits, and these several benefits caused men to come together in a social contract of tacit consent to enjoy civil society. Locke's view is that sovereignty is seated in the subject, not in the monarch.[22] His position is in contrast with and serves as a rebuttal to the purported final words of Charles I before his execution. Claiming that he had desired the freedom and liberty of the people, Charles averred:

"but I must tell you that...[the people's] liberty and freedom consists in having government...It is not their having a share in government; that is nothing appertaining to them. A subject and a sovereign are clean different things."[23]

Between Locke, the republican, and Astell, the monarchist, this difference about the source of authority is one of the most profound.

A Prototype Bill of Rights

Central to Locke's contributions to political theory are his restrictions on the sovereign power imposed upon the legislature. Natural rights transformed into law create restrictions on what the legislature can do, even in the name of creating common good. These protections form the signal feature of modern constitutions, and find an early expression in the United States Constitution. The limits posed by Locke include an injunction *against* arbitrary power or laws, and *for* the rule of law for the common good. The government must protect private property, including limiting taxation (taxation by consent only), and not transferring power away from the people as a way of overriding these restrictions.

Locke's argument proceeds in an eminently readable way, from the state of nature to civil society; from natural and property rights to the establishment of a representative government designed to protect (certain of) its individual members; from an authoritative structure to the institutional restraints on that structure; from the overreaching of those restraints to the dissolution of government. Locke elegantly effected a shift from authoritarian hierarchical power to power invested in individuals, especially in those poised to create capital and all of its manifestations.

ASTELL'S THEORY

[Descartes'] radical epistemology put women on a theoretical par with men.[24]

A study of Mary Astell's philosophy is not for the faint of heart. Her political views have an affinity with those of Hobbes and Edmund Burke in their common defenses of monarchy, but she differs from Hobbes, criticizing his mechanistic individualism and atheism, which were anathema to her. Her feminism, or protofeminism, foreshadows certain aspects of radical feminism and even the separatist feminism of the late twentieth century. Her arguments about political foundations are radical-conservative and monarchical, but suggest (the danger of) arguments used today by postmodern writers against liberal foundationalism. She did not hold a high opinion of men. She wrote ostensibly for a female audience and both excoriated and was excoriated by the glib and witty writers of her day – Addison, Steele, and Defoe. She was a formidable intellect about whom there is tantalizingly little current scholarship and vast room for further study.

Her biographer Ruth Perry writes that both of the new radical epistemologies of the time, rationalism and empiricism, enabled women like Mary Astell to think of themselves as rational creatures situated in the Enlightenment ideology of human achievement. The rationalism of Descartes held that intellectual introspection could find truth, and the empiricism of Locke and Bacon found that one could "collect and record natural curiosities, peer through microscopes and telescopes and describe what she saw there."[25] In principle, both of these new methodologies were available to women in ways that authority-based medieval epistemologies were not. The democratic impulses of the century rubbed off on women, and while the franchise was not yet in sight, education and increased opportunities were. One writer observes that the "Cartesian philosophy fostered an introspective psychology, a radical consciousness of self–important to the growth of feminism – by its insistence on the thinking *I* as the touchstone of all knowledge and even existence."[26] Then, as today, new epistemologies created a radical shift which enabled new kinds of understanding to flourish.

> [P]erhaps I have said more than most Men will thank me for, I cannot help it, for how much soever I may be their friend and humble servant, I am more a friend to Truth.[27]

Astell's first book had the intriguing title of *A Serious Proposal to the Ladies, for the Advancement of their True and Greatest Interest, By a Lover of Her Sex*. The work begins with the Enlightenment premise that women have the same potential for reasoning as men and proceeds to argue the need (intellectually, economically, and socially) for a college for women. One of the early "second wave" feminists to revive Mary Astell's work is the Australian feminist Dale Spender. Spender's thesis is that counter-hegemonic theories such as feminism historically have difficulty gathering a head of steam and creating lasting social change because the dominant ideologies periodically erase them. Thus, they need to be reinvented by each succeeding generation. In the case of Mary Astell, despite her wide audience in the late seventeenth century, it is not a certainty even that she was read by another ardent feminist, Mary Wollstonecraft, in the late eighteenth century. And, until very recently, her work has been nearly invisible.

Spender credits Astell with formulating an early account of patriarchy as a system in which men claim control over women, physically, spiritually, and intellectually. A goal of Astell's is to reclaim women for themselves. Spender also attributes to Astell an early formulation of the concept of "victim blaming," that women are "blamed" for social arrangements that men devise. As Astell says:

> Women are from their very infancy debarred those advantages, with the want of which they are afterwards reproached, and nursed up in those vices which will hereafter be upbraided to them.[28]

Astell's serious proposal is to establish a women's college, where women could take up intellectual pursuits, tend to spiritual needs, and be protected from the problems associated with male control: forced domestic service, sexual exploitation, and domestic violence. The college would be funded by charitable subscription, and could be less expensive than the dowries required in marriage. She argues that women and men are made by God for the same purposes, and with the same intellect. Abstract thinking is what differentiates humans from animals. Since God has made nothing in vain, it follows that women should use their intellect.[29] The *Serious Proposal* was well received generally, and led her to write and publish *Part II*, which is a work on methodology, designed particularly for women to help them individually improve their learning, in the absence of an educational institution.

In 1700 she published *Some Reflections upon Marriage, Occasion'd by the Duke and Duchess of Mazarine's Case*. This work, about the divorce suit of her Chelsea neighbor, reveals Astell in all her complexity. The case was wildly famous, with many published accounts of the trial. The Duke of Mazarine, whose name was taken from the French cardinal who was the Duchess Hortense Mazarine's guardian, was a notorious brute and abusive husband.[30] His wife fled his abuses and the case wound up in court. Not just a commentary on marriage, this work is primarily a political critique. In it, Astell deftly inverts the analogy between the marriage contract and the social contract, used in different ways by Locke and Hobbes.

A Careful Argument

For the sake of argument, Astell hypothesizes the truth of Locke's claim that the sovereignty of the monarch is not absolute, and argues by analogy that the sovereignty of the husband is not absolute, something few writers including Locke were willing to claim. Using this device she exposes the excesses of marital abuse perpetrated by the Duke of Mazarine on his wife. In a remarkable twist, however, Astell concludes that Hortense Mazarine made a vow before God to obey her husband, and the vow may not be broken. God is the foundational authority. It is heinous that the husband should behave in such a way, but the proper response to unreasonable power is passive obedience – a term used by Tories and "high flyers" to describe the proper response to objectionable political authority. In other words, the Dissenters should have practiced passive obedience, not revolt, towards the Stuart monarchs.

Following the analogy, Astell reasons that if divorce in marriage is not justified, so neither is "divorce" in civil government. God is the foundational authority for the power of the monarch and passive obedience is required even in cases of the most blatant abuse.

> Because God made all Things for himself, and a rational mind is too noble a being to be made for the sake and service of any creature. The service she at any time becomes obliged to pay to a man, is only a business by the bye. Just as it may be any man's business and duty to keep hogs; he was not made for this, but if he hires himself out to such an employment, he ought conscientiously to perform it.[31]

A woman fool enough to marry a man must obey him as she might be obliged to "tend the pigs." Her argument contains another clever twist leading to her most radical conclusion. Astell argues *for* political authority: men must submit to the state, women must submit to men. In this there is only one loophole. Women may refuse to marry. Astell strongly advocated *not* marrying, getting out from under the authority of men, staying celibate:

> ... If a Wife's case be as it is here represented, it is not good for a Woman to Marry, and so there's an end of the Human Race. But this is no fair consequence, for all that can justly be inferr'd from hence, is that a woman has no mighty obligations to the Man who makes love to her, she has no reason to be fond of being a wife, or to reckon it a piece of Preferment when she is taken to be a Man's Upper-Servant: it is no advantage to her in this World, if rightly manag'd it may prove one as to the next.[32]

She realizes that taken to its conclusion (i.e. if all women followed this path) it would be the end of the human race, but seeing that as an unlikely outcome, she strongly recommends a separate woman's sphere. Astell perceives what much later comes to be critiqued, especially by socialist feminist writers, as the "public/private distinction" in liberalism and uses it to her advantage.[33] These writers argue that by creating a public world of legal action and protection for men and a private sphere for women, men can exclude women from legal redress and protection and can be physically abusive, take sexual advantage, and exact slave or servile work conditions for women, who have no recourse to the state. This analysis would apply to women who are under male power.

Astell's view is that the public sphere – the state – is not the proper sphere for women. Theirs is not to engage in politics or statecraft. So women who choose not to marry are in a kind of Lockean state of perfect freedom (although she would not call it that!) with no cause to be concerned with state authoritarianism or spousal control. Such women can have intellectual lives, go about their daily business, develop female friendships, and engage in religious devotion. Women like herself, so long as they have some small means of support, are truly free. This view foreshadows current arguments by Mary Daly, who dismisses the male sphere as "necrophiliac" and who exalts "woman-identified" culture as having a special and harmonic relationship with the world.[34] Astell's work also resonates with that of poet and essayist Adrienne Rich, who argues for woman-centered education.[35] Of course, Astell herself was deeply engaged with the prevailing male intellectual culture. But she had a profound vision of the benefits of a highly developed women's culture to society and especially to women.

In 1703 Astell published *Moderation Truly Stated*, a reply to arguments for "occasional conformity," the practice of Dissenters attending Anglican services once a year to make themselves eligible to hold office. In *An Impartial Enquiry into the Causes of Rebellion and Civil War in this Kingdom: An Examination of Dr. Kennett's Sermon, Jan. 31. 1703/4* (1704), she expresses outrage that a minister of the church would use the day commemorating Charles I's execution as an excuse to criticize the church and monarchy. Contrary to received wisdom, she argues that Dissenting views are more dangerous than papist ones. Her next pamphlet was *A Fair Way with the Dissenters and Their Patrons Not Writ by Mr. L. [eslie], or any other Furious Jacobite, whether Clergyman or Layman; but by a very moderate person and Dutiful Subject to the Queen*. This was a reply to Defoe's pamphlet *The Shortest Way with the Dissenters*, a heavy satire which proposes the total destruction of all non-Anglicans. In *A Fair Way* she argues for the destruction of Dissenters, but as a political party devoted to factionalizing and working against stability and order.

The Christian Religion, As Profess'd by a Daughter of the Church of England was written as a reply to Locke's philosophy, and its political implications. Political scientist Patricia Springborg identifies a systematic critique of Locke's three major principles: a principle of self-preservation, a right of freedom from heritable encumbrance, and a principle of government based on popular consent.[36] In *A Fair Way*, Astell uncovers serious problems with Locke's justification of a "rogue government" which she compares with a highwayman. She notes that in Locke the right of conquest is denied to the monarch but asserted with respect to the people. Just as anti-foundationalists of the late twentieth century gradually lay bare arguments for first principles, so does Astell argue that all social institutions are contingent. Her very different purpose is to justify dynastic transition through a religious foundation, but it raises honest questions about the sources of political authority.

Another important feature, especially of her first two books, *A Serious Proposal* and *Some Reflections upon Marriage*, is Astell's insistence that women have "an oblique angle of vision" from the standard or dominant one. This foreshadows a central innovation of twentieth-century feminism. An epistemological approach known as feminist standpoint epistemologies rejects the notion of a single logical point from which knowledge is generated. Instead, this view argues that one's subject position, social location, race, gender, and class position, and other factors as well, influence the creation of knowledge.[37] As Astell puts it in *Some Reflections upon Marriage*:

> Allow us then as many glasses as you please to help our sight, and as many good arguments as you can afford to convince our understanding; but don't exact, we beseech you, to affirm that we see such things as are only the discovery of men who have quicker senses; or that we understand, and know what we have by hear-say only; for to be so excessively complaisant, is neither to see nor to understand.[38]

Astell's work is important for standpoint epistemology, first, because she proposes an early version of this theory, and second, because she herself provides a distinctly seventeenth-century feminist standpoint which serves as an excellent counterpoint to the standard accounts of early modern political theory.

Locke, Astell, and Political Philosophy

Locke's philosophy and its systematic critique are the bricks and mortar of modern western political thought, from conservative and liberal to socialist and communitarian theories. Locke's theory is the standard against which other theories are drawn, measured, and compared. Jean-Jacques Rousseau's identification of the ills of modern society with the privatization of property is affirmed against Locke's elevation of indefeasible property rights. Mill and Marx both understood and were students of Locke's modern liberal theories.

A work that synthesizes socialist and feminist criticisms of liberal theory derived from Locke is Alison Jaggar's *Feminist Politics and Human Nature*.[39] Jaggar provides a comprehensive synthetic critique of modern liberalism. Drawing on the critical history of modern liberal theory, she identifies two salient features of liberalism, what she calls normative dualism and abstract individualism. Normative dualism issues from the liberal conception that human beings have a dual metaphysical ontology: they are composed of mental and physical components – minds and bodies. Medieval and classical Greek metaphysics did not posit a clear separation of these two sorts of being, avoiding the problems posed by oppositional dualities. Further, the Enlightenment period, in its view of reason as the essential human element, valued the mind more highly than the body. Ecofeminists such as Carolyn Merchant argue that this ideal which placed human reason above and in power and control over the physical, whether it be human bodies or the earth and the natural world, had disastrous results through the industrial revolution to the present in promoting harm to the physical environment. Women have long been troublesomely connected with nature. How can we revalue the physical and assert women's (and human) connections without relegating women to "naturally determined roles" and assigning positions that preclude rationality as a quality of women? As Merchant says:

celebrations of the connection between women and nature contain an inherent contradiction. If women overtly identify with nature and both are devalued in modern Western
culture, don't such efforts work against women's prospects for their own liberation? Is
not the conflation of woman and nature a form of essentialism?[40]

Jaggar explains that Enlightenment (and contemporary) mind/body dualisms are
normative because they value the rational more highly than the physical. Insofar as
women are not seen as primarily rational, but rather as primarily physical, they are
devalued, and viewed as something to be controlled rather than as beings exercising
rationality. Thus, a seemingly neutral abstract premise underlying liberal theory will
have the real-world consequence of devaluing women both in their traditional
activities and in innovative ones.

Jaggar identifies a second problem with liberalism – its abstract individualism, a
position which attributes rationality to *individuals*, rather than groups. Synthesizing
the work of many social and feminist theorists, Jaggar challenges the presocial
construction of individuals, a premise questioned, for example, by writers as diverse
as Marx, in his social theory, and Wittgenstein in the private language arguments.
She recounts both empirical and conceptual arguments against individualism, that
cognitions and emotions are socially and contextually constructed, not innate and
presocial; and that meaning and interpretation are social and cannot be made sense
of in individual isolation.

Astell's political thought presents the opposite situation from Locke's. Instead of
an immense standing literature, her "erasure" has been so complete that there is no
substantial secondary literature critiquing her work, only a few excellent, but iso-
lated, articles.[41] And yet Patricia Springborg argues that Astell's work is nothing less
than a systematic critique of Locke's whole philosophy. Curiously, the received
wisdom from Laslett and other prominent scholars is that Locke's political theory
was fundamentally inconsistent with his metaphysics and epistemology. Yet, Perry
and Springborg view Locke holistically. Springborg says that Astell's is

> a Locke who until recently has been eclipsed by the Locke of the American Revolution,
> the Locke of possessive individualism (or of the political economists) and other post-
> Enlightenment Lockes. Astell's Locke, in fact, provides a test of authenticity that only
> very recent scholarship has met. For this reason, perhaps her pioneering critique was for
> so long overlooked. The issues on which it focuses are Anglicanism, trinitarianism, and
> the settlement of 1688; contracts, oaths, and political allegiance; biblical patriarchalism
> and the claims of dynastic monarchy; and the rights of freeborn Englishmen versus the
> ancient constitution.[42]

In another critical exposition of Astell's theories, Ruth Perry argues that Astell
"thought the doctrine of individualism selfish and asocial and was suspicious of
the way genetic theories of citizenship beginning with a 'state of nature' erased the
social and political meaning of maternity."[43] Perry argues that the Enlightenment
and "glorious Revolution were times for reasserting male authority" and that Locke
effected a "paradigm shift" from a political world populated by men and women
involved in a web of familial and sexual interconnections to an all-male world based
solely on contractual obligation.[44]

Future scholarship on Astell will no doubt add substantially to the traditional
assessments of political theory. The investigation of liberal conceptions of freedom
and equality lay at the heart of any evaluation of western political philosophy, and in

western cultures, liberalism has exercised a profound influence, earning for itself the need for both sympathetic and critical accounts. Astell's critique of Locke raises serious questions about the sources of political authority, social contract theory, the legitimacy of revolutionary transfers of authority, and foundationalism not based on a higher power. Her original theories contribute ideas about education, marriage, a gender division of culture, religion, and political power. Considering Locke and Astell together recontextualizes the origins of liberal theory and may provide a less distorted account than one that views political theory only through the lenses of later times.

Notes

1 John Locke, *Two Treatises of Government*, p. 36 of this volume.
2 See Elizabeth Potter, "Locke's Epistemology and Women's Struggles," in Bat-Ami Bar On, ed., *Modern Engendering: Critical Feminist Readings in Modern Western Philosophy* (Albany: SUNY Press, 1994). Focusing on Locke's epistemology, Potter underscores the three-way (not two-way) political struggle of seventeenth-century England, between the Tories, the Whigs, and the radicals. She notes that the radicals were the true egalitarians and that "the mob" were lower-class men *and* women, many of whom engaged in actions not dreamed of by middle- and upper-class women. The Leveller Lilbourne remarked that "Every particular and individual man and woman that ever breathed ... are and were by nature all equal and alike in power, dignity, authority and majesty, none of them having (by nature) any authority over one ... another" (p. 31). Women adopted political power through demonstrations against high prices and poor economic conditions; they petitioned for the release of their leaders, who were political prisoners. Women served as foot soldiers in Cromwell's new model army. Using the Quaker model, Potter argues for an epistemology based on community knowledge rather than on the individual.
3 Aphra Behn wrote and had produced seventeen plays on the London stage. She wrote thirteen novels, of which *Oroonoko*, an abolitionist novel, is the best known. She was a spy, a feminist, and a writer whose work was almost completely forgotten until the 1980s. See Dale Spender, *Women of Ideas* (London: Routledge and Kegan Paul Ltd., 1982).
4 Locke, *Two Treatises of Government*, p. 31.
5 Ibid., p. 35. It is interesting to note this historical precedent for disputes regarding what readings are canonical, and should be included in the curriculum.
6 Ibid., p. 44.
7 From a letter by Astell biographer George Ballard written in 1746, quoted in Ruth Perry, *The Celebrated Mary Astell: An Early English Feminist* (Chicago: University of Chicago Press, 1986), pp. 52–3. Astell, of course, was no more above party politics than was Locke.
8 Ibid., p. 30.
9 It is instructive to note the patterns of depression especially among women writers, who find their material circumstances overly constraining. Feminist, sociologist, and economist Charlotte Perkins Gilman explores this problem in her novella *The Yellow Wallpaper.*
10 Perry, *The Celebrated Mary Astell*, p. 403.
11 Ibid., p. 68.
12 Mary Astell, *Some Reflections upon Marriage*, p. 46 of this volume.
13 Perry, *The Celebrated Mary Astell*, p. 73.
14 Ibid., p. 73.
15 Ibid., p. 79.

16   Patricia Springborg, "Mary Astell (1666–1731), Critic of Locke," *American Political Science Review*, 89:3 (1995), pp. 621–33. See also Springborg's introduction to *The Political Writings of Mary Astell* (Cambridge: Cambridge University Press, 1996).

17   Locke, *Two Treatises of Government*, p. 343.

18   John Rawls, *A Theory of Justice* (Cambridge, MA: Harvard University Press, 1971). (See Part V of this volume.)

19   See Kristin Waters, *Robert Nozick and the Demands of Libertarianism* (University Microfilms) for a discussion of Locke's development of capitalism, further articulation of his theory of acquisition, and problems with each element of this formulation. It is important also to recall that Locke attaches an important proviso to the acquisition of property: that property taken out of the common is legitimately acquired only if enough and as good is left for others.

20   Locke, *Two Treatises of Government*, p. 27 of this volume.

21   Ibid., p. 33.

22   A view which perhaps finds its best twentieth-century expression in the legal theory of H. L. A. Hart.

23   *Encyclopedia Britannica*, vol. 5, "Charles I" (Chicago: 1950), p. 270.

24   Perry, *The Celebrated Mary Astell*, p. 70.

25   Ibid.

26   Joan K. Kinnaird, "Mary Astell: Inspired by Ideas," in Dale Spender, ed., *Feminist Theorists: Three Centuries of Key Women Thinkers* (New York: Pantheon, 1983), p. 33.

27   Astell, *Some Reflections upon Marriage*, p. 54 of this volume.

28   Astell, *A Serious Proposal*, p. 40 of this volume.

29   Perry, *The Celebrated Mary Astell*, pp. 60–70.

30   The cardinal was the second most powerful man in France under French King Louis XIV. In *The Celebrated Mary Astell*, Perry elaborates on the Duke's abuses: "The duke proved an impossible husband. A religious fanatic, he woke his young wife in the middle of the night to tell her his visions and forbade her to nurse the baby on fast days. Sexually obsessed, he mutilated the magnificent statues at the Palais Mazarine and splashed paint on the nudes to make them 'decent.' He wanted to forbid his farmers to milk cows because it looked so obscene, and he once considered sawing off the teeth of his young daughters to make them unattractive and thus to protect them from future sexuality."

31   Astell, *Some Reflections upon Marriage*, p. 47 of this volume.

32   Ibid., p. 54.

33   See Alison M. Jaggar, *Feminist Politics and Human Nature* (Totowa, NJ: Rowman and Allenheld, 1983) for an especially clear treatment of this issue.

34   Mary Daly, *Gyn/Ecology: The Metaethics of Radical Feminism* (Boston: Beacon Press, 1978).

35   Adrienne Rich, *On Lies, Secrets and Silence: Selected Prose, 1966–1978* (New York: W. W. Norton & Co., 1979).

36   Springborg, "Mary Astell (1666–1731), Critic of Locke."

37   For discussions of standpoint epistemologies, see Diane Bell, "Yes, Virginia, There is a Feminist Ethnography: Reflections from Three Australian Fields," in *Gendered Fields: Women, Men and Ethnography*, ed. D. Bell. P. Caplan and W. Karim (London: Routledge, 1993); Patricia Hill Collins, *Black Feminist Thought: Knowledge, Consciousness and the Politics of Empowerment* (New York: Routledge, 1991); and Sandra Harding, *The Science Question in Feminism* (Ithaca: Cornell University Press, 1986).

38   Astell, *Some Reflections upon Marriage*, in Springborg, *The Political Writings of Mary Astell*, p. 10.

39   Jaggar, *Feminist Politics and Human Nature*, p. 43.

40   Carolyn Merchant, *Death of Nature: Women, Ecology and the Scientific Revolution* (New York: Harper and Row, 1980), p. xvi.

41 The entire 1950 *Encyclopedia Britannica* entry on Mary Astell says: "English author, was born at Newcastle-on-Tyne. She published, in 1697, a work entitled *A Serious Proposal*... A scheme of hers for an Anglican sisterhood, which was favorably entertained by Queen Anne, was frustrated by Bishop Burnet. Mary Astell was attacked in the *Tatler* (No. 52) under the name of Madonella."

42 Springborg, "Mary Astell (1666–1731), Critic of Locke," p. 624.

43 Ruth Perry, "Mary Astell and the Critique of Possessive Individualism," *Eighteenth Century Studies*, 23:4 (1990), p. 448.

44 Ibid., pp. 449–50.

The Second Treatise of Government

JOHN LOCKE

CHAPTER I

§1. It having been shewn in the foregoing discourse,

1. That *Adam* had not, either by natural right of fatherhood, or by positive donation from God, any such authority over his children, or dominion over the world, as is pretended:

2. That if he had, his heirs, yet, had no right to it:

3. That if his heirs had, there being no law of nature nor positive law of God that determines which is the right heir in all cases that may arise, the right of succession, and consequently of bearing rule, could not have been certainly determined:

4. That if even that had been determined, yet the knowledge of which is the eldest line of *Adam's* posterity, being so long since utterly lost, that in the races of mankind and families of the world, there remains not to one above another, the least pretence to be the eldest house, and to have the right of inheritance:

All these premises having, as I think, been clearly made out, it is impossible that the rulers now on earth should make any benefit, or derive any the least shadow of authority from that, which is held to be the fountain of all power, *Adam's private dominion and paternal jurisdiction*; so that he that will not give just occasion to think that all government in the world is the product only of force and violence, and that men live together by no other rules but that of beasts, where the strongest carries it, and so lay a foundation for perpetual disorder and mischief, tumult, sedition and rebellion, (things that the followers of that hypothesis so loudly cry out against) must of necessity find out another rise of government, another original of political power, and another way of designing and knowing the persons that have it, than what Sir *Robert Filmer* hath taught us.

§2. To this purpose, I think it may not be amiss, to set down what I take to be political power; that the power of a *magistrate* over a subject may be distinguished

John Locke. *Two Treatises of Government.* Originally published in 1689–90.

from that of a *father* over his children, a *master* over his servant, a *husband* over his wife, and a *lord* over his slave. All which distinct powers happening sometimes together in the same man, if he be considered under these different relations, it may help us to distinguish these powers one from another, and shew the difference betwixt a ruler of a common-wealth, a father of a family, and a captain of a galley.

§3. *Political power*, then, I take to be a *right* of making laws with penalties of death, and consequently all less penalties, for the regulating and preserving of property, and of employing the force of the community, in the execution of such laws, and in the defence of the common-wealth from foreign injury; and all this only for the public good.

CHAPTER II: OF THE STATE OF NATURE

§4. To understand political power right, and derive it from its original, we must consider, what state all men are naturally in, and that is, a *state of perfect freedom* to order their actions, and dispose of their possessions and persons, as they think fit, within the bounds of the law of nature, without asking leave, or depending upon the will of any other man.

A *state* also *of equality*, wherein all the power and jurisdiction is reciprocal, no one having more than another; there being nothing more evident, than that creatures of the same species and rank, promiscuously born to all the same advantages of nature, and the use of the same faculties, should also be equal one amongst another without subordination or subjection, unless the lord and master of them all should, by any manifest declaration of his will, set one above another, and confer on him, by an evident and clear appointment, an undoubted right to dominion and sovereignty.

§5. This *equality* of men by nature, the judicious *Hooker* looks upon as so evident in itself, and beyond all question, that he makes it the foundation of that obligation to mutual love amongst men, on which he builds the duties they owe one another, and from whence he derives the great maxims *of justice* and *charity*. His words are,

> The like natural inducement hath brought men to know that it is no less their duty, to love others than themselves; for seeing those things which are equal, must needs all have one measure; if I cannot but wish to receive good, even as much at every man's hands, as any man can wish unto his own soul, how should I look to have any part of my desire herein satisfied, unless myself be careful to satisfy the like desire, which is undoubtedly in other men, being of one and the same nature? To have any thing offered them repugnant to this desire, must needs in all respects grieve them as much as me; so that if I do harm, I must look to suffer, there being no reason that others should shew greater measure of love to me, than they have by me shewed unto them: my desire therefore to be loved of my equals in nature, as much as possible may be, imposeth upon me a natural duty of bearing to them-ward fully the like affection; from which relation of equality between ourselves and them that are as ourselves, what several rules and canons natural reason hath drawn, for direction of life, no man is ignorant. [*Richard Hooker*, Ecclesiastical Polity *(1594), Bk I, Ch. VIII.*]

§6. But though this be a *state of liberty*, yet *it is not a state of licence*: though man in that state have an uncontroulable liberty to dispose of his person or possessions, yet he has not liberty to destroy himself, or so much as any creature in his possession, but where some nobler use than its bare preservation calls for it. The *state of nature* has a law of nature to govern it, which obliges every one: and reason, which is that law, teaches all mankind, who will but consult it, that being all *equal and independent*, no one ought to harm another in his life, health, liberty, or possessions: for men being all the workmanship of one omnipotent, and infinitely wise maker; all the servants of one sovereign master, sent into the world by his order, and about his business; they are his property, whose workmanship they are, made to last during his, not one another's pleasure: and being furnished with like faculties, sharing all in one community of nature, there cannot be supposed any such *subordination* among us, that may authorize us to destroy one another, as if we were made for one another's uses, as the inferior ranks of creatures are for our's. Every one, as he is *bound to preserve himself*, and not to quit his station wilfully, so by the like reason, when his own preservation comes not in competition, ought he, as much as he can, *to preserve the rest of mankind*, and may not, unless it be to do justice on an offender, take away, or impair the life, or what tends to the preservation of the life, the liberty, health, limb, or goods of another.

§7. And that all men may be restrained from invading others rights, and from doing hurt to one another, and the law of nature be observed, which willeth the peace and *preservation of all mankind*, the *execution* of the law of nature is, in that state, put into every man's hands, whereby every one has a right to punish the transgressors of that law to such a degree, as may hinder its violation: for the *law of nature* would, as all other laws that concern men in this world, be in vain, if there were no body that in the state of nature had a *power to execute* that law, and thereby preserve the innocent and restrain offenders. And if any one in the state of nature may punish another for any evil he has done, every one may do so: for in that *state of perfect equality*, where naturally there is no superiority or jurisdiction of one over another, what any may do in prosecution of that law, every one must needs have a right to do.

§8. And thus, in the state of nature, *one man comes by a power over another*; but yet no absolute or arbitrary power, to use a criminal, when he has got him in his hands, according to the passionate heats, or boundless extravagancy of his own will; but only to retribute to him, so far as calm reason and conscience dictate, what is proportionate to his transgression, which is so much as may serve for *reparation* and *restraint*: for these two are the only reasons, why one man may lawfully do harm to another, which is that we call *punishment*. In transgressing the law of nature, the offender declares himself to live by another rule than that of reason and common equity, which is that measure God has set to the actions of men, for their mutual security; and so he becomes dangerous to mankind, the tye, which is to secure them from injury and violence, being slighted and broken by him. Which being a trespass against the whole species, and the peace and safety of it, provided for by the law of nature, every man upon this score, by the right he hath to preserve mankind in general, may restrain, or where it is necessary, destroy things noxious to them, and so may bring such evil on any one, who hath transgressed that law, as may make him repent the doing of it, and thereby deter him, and by his example others, from doing the like mischief. And in the case, and upon this ground, *every man hath a right to punish the offender, and be executioner of the law of nature.* [...]

§10. Besides the crime which consists in violating the law, and varying from the right rule of reason, whereby a man so far becomes degenerate, and declares himself to quit the principles of human nature, and to be a noxious creature, there is commonly *injury* done to some person or other, and some other man receives damage by his transgression: in which case he who hath received any damage, has, besides the right of punishment common to him with other men, a particular right to seek *reparation* from him that has done it: and any other person, who finds it just, may also join with him that is injured, and assist him in recovering from the offender so much as may make satisfaction for the harm he has suffered.

§11. From these *two distinct rights*, the one of *punishing* the crime *for restraint*, and preventing the like offence, which right of punishing is in every body; the other of taking *reparation*, which belongs only to the injured party, comes it to pass that the magistrate, who by being magistrate hath the common right of punishing put into his hands, can often, where the public good demands not the execution of the law, *remit* the punishment of criminal offences by his own authority, but yet cannot *remit* the satisfaction due to any private man for the damage he has received. That, he who has suffered the damage has a right to demand in his own name, and he alone can remit: the damnified person has this power of appropriating to himself the goods or service of the offender, *by right of self-preservation*, as every man has a power to punish the crime, to prevent its being committed again, *by the right he has of preserving all mankind*, and doing all reasonable things he can in order to that end: and thus it is, that every man, in the state of nature, has a power to kill a murderer, both to *deter* others from doing the like injury, which no reparation can compensate, by the example of the punishment that attends it from every body, and also to secure men from the attempts of a criminal, who having renounced reason, the common rule and measure God hath given to mankind, hath, by the unjust violence and slaughter he hath committed upon one, declared war against all mankind, and therefore may be destroyed as a *lion* or a *tyger*, one of those wild savage beasts, with whom men can have no society nor security: and upon this is grounded that great law of nature, *Whoso sheddeth man's blood, by man shall his blood be shed*. And *Cain* was so fully convinced, that every one had a right to destroy such a criminal, that after the murder of his brother, he cries out, *Every one that findeth me, shall slay me*; so plain was it writ in the hearts of all mankind. [...]

§13. To this strange doctrine, *viz.* That *in the state of nature every one has the executive power* of the law of nature, I doubt not but it will be objected, that it is unreasonable for men to be judges in their own cases, that self-love will make men partial to themselves and their friends: and on the other side, that ill nature, passion and revenge will carry them too far in punishing others; and hence nothing but confusion and disorder will follow, and that therefore God hath certainly appointed government to restrain the partiality and violence of men. I easily grant, that *civil government* is the proper remedy for the inconveniencies of the state of nature, which must certainly be great, where men may be judges in their own case, since it is easy to be imagined, that he who was so unjust as to do his brother an injury, will scarce be so just as to condemn himself for it: but I shall desire those who make this objection, to remember, that *absolute monarchs* are but men; and if government is to be the remedy of those evils, which necessarily follow from men's being judges in their own cases, and the state of nature is therefore not to be endured, I desire to know what kind of government that is, and how much better it is than the state of nature, where one man, commanding a multitude, has the liberty to be judge in his own case, and may do to all his subjects whatever he pleases, without the least liberty to any one to question or controul those who execute his pleasure? and in whatsoever he doth, whether led by reason, mistake or passion, must be submitted to? much better it is in the state of nature, wherein men are not bound to submit to the unjust will of another: and if he that judges, judges amiss in his own, or any other case, he is answerable for it to the rest of mankind.

§14. It is often asked as a mighty objection, *where are*, or ever were there any *men in such a state of nature?* To which it may suffice as an answer at present, that since all princes and rulers of *independent* governments all through the world, are in a state of nature, it is plain the world never was, nor ever will be, without numbers of men in that state. I have named all governors of *independent communities*, whether they are, or are not, in league with others: for it is not every compact that puts an end to the state of nature between men, but only this one of agreeing together mutually to enter into one community, and make one body politic; other promises, and compacts, men may make one with another, and yet still be in the state of nature. The promises and bargains for truck, &c. between the two men in the desert island, mentioned by *Garcilasso de la Vega*, in his history of *Peru*; or between a *Swiss* and an *Indian*, in the woods of *America*, are binding to them, though they are perfectly in a state of nature, in reference to one another: for truth and keeping of faith belongs to men, as men, and not as members of society. [...]

CHAPTER III: OF THE STATE OF WAR

§16. The *state of war* is a state of *enmity* and *destruction*: and therefore declaring by word or action, not a passionate and hasty, but a sedate settled design upon another man's life, *puts him in a state of war* with him against whom he has declared such an intention, and so has exposed his life to the other's power to be taken away by him, or any one that joins with him in his defence, and espouses his quarrel; it being reasonable and just, I should have a right to destroy that which threatens me with destruction: for, *by the fundamental law of nature, man being to be preserved* as much as possible, when all cannot be preserved, the safety of the innocent is to be preferred: and one may destroy a man who makes war upon him, or has discovered an enmity to his being, for the same reason that he may kill a *wolf* or a *lion*; because such men are not under the ties of the commonlaw of reason, have no other rule, but that of force and violence, and so may be treated as beasts of prey, those dangerous and noxious creatures, that will be sure to destroy him whenever he falls into their power.

§17. And hence it is, that he who attempts to get another man into his absolute power, does thereby *put himself into a state of war* with him; it being to be understood as a declaration of a design upon his life: for I have reason to conclude, that he who would get me into his power without my consent, would use me as he pleased when he had got me there, and destroy me too when he had a fancy to it; for no body can desire to *have me in his absolute power*, unless it be to compel me by force to that which is against the right of my freedom, i.e. make me a slave. To be free from such force is the only security of my preservation; and reason bids me look on him, as an enemy to my preservation, who would take away that *freedom* which is the fence to it; so that he who makes an *attempt to enslave* me, thereby puts himself into a state of war with me. He that, in the state of nature, *would take away the freedom* that belongs to any one in that state, must necessarily be supposed to have a design to take away every thing else, that *freedom* being the foundation of all the rest; as he that, in the state of society, would take away the *freedom* belonging to those of that society or common-wealth, must be supposed to design to take away from them every thing else, and so be looked on as *in a state of war*.

§18. This makes it lawful for a man to *kill a thief*, who has not in the least hurt him, nor declared any design upon his life, any farther than, by the use of force, so to get him in his power, as to take away his money, or what he pleases, from him; because using force, where he has no right, to get me into his power, let his pretence be what it will, I have no reason to suppose, that he, who would *take away my liberty*, would not, when he had me in his power, take away every thing else. And therefore it is lawful for me to treat him as one who has *put himself into a state of war* with me, *i.e.* kill him if I can; for to that hazard does he justly expose himself, whoever introduces a state of war, and is aggressor in it.

§19. And here we have the plain *difference between the state of nature and the state of war*, which however some men have confounded, are as far distant, as a state of peace, good will, mutual assistance and preservation, and a state of enmity, malice, violence and mutual destruction, are one from another. Men living together according to reason, without a common superior on earth, with authority to judge between them, is *properly the state of nature*. But force, or a declared design of force, upon the person of another, where there is no common superior on earth to appeal to for relief, *is the state of war*: and it is the want of such an appeal gives a man the right of war even against an *aggressor*, tho' he be in society and a fellow subject. Thus a *thief*, whom I cannot harm, but by appeal to the law, for having stolen all that I am worth, I may kill, when he sets on me to rob me but of my horse or coat; because the law, which was made for my preservation, where it cannot interpose to secure my life from present force, which, if lost, is capable of no reparation, permits me my own defence, and the right of war, a liberty to kill the aggressor, because the aggressor allows not time to appeal to our common judge, nor the decision of the law, for remedy in a case where the mischief may be irreparable. Want of a common judge with authority, puts all men in a state of nature: force without right, upon a man's person, makes a state of war, both where there is, and is not, a common judge.

§20. But when the actual force is over, the *state of war ceases* between those that are in society, and are equally on both sides subjected to the fair determination of the law; because then there lies open the remedy of appeal for the past injury, and to prevent future harm: but where no such appeal is, as in the state of nature, for want of positive laws, and judges with authority to appeal to, the state of war once begun, continues, with a right to the innocent party to destroy the other whenever he can, until the aggressor offers peace, and desires reconciliation on such terms as may repair any wrongs he has already done, and secure the innocent for the future; nay, where an appeal to the law, and constituted judges, lies open, but the remedy is denied by a manifest perverting of justice, and a barefaced wresting of the laws to protect or indemnify the violence or injuries of some men, or party of men, *there* it is hard to imagine any thing but *a state of war*: for where-ever violence is used, and injury done, though by hands appointed to administer justice, it is still violence and injury, however coloured with the name, pretences, or forms of law, the end whereof being to protect and redress the innocent, by an unbiassed application of it, to all who are under it; where-ever that is not *bona fide* done, *war is made* upon the sufferers, who having no appeal on earth to right them, they are left to the only remedy in such cases, an appeal to heaven.

§21. To avoid this *state of war* (wherein there is no appeal but to heaven, and wherein every the least difference is apt to end, where there is no authority to decide between the contenders) is one great reason of men's putting themselves into society, and quitting the state of nature: for where there is an authority, a power on earth, from which relief can be had by *appeal*, there the continuance of the *state of war* is excluded, and the controversy is decided by that power. [...]

CHAPTER IV: OF SLAVERY

§22. The *natural liberty* of man is to be free from any superior power on earth, and not to be under the will or legislative authority of man, but to have only the law of nature for his rule. The *liberty of man*, in society, is to be under no other legislative power, but that established, by consent, in the common-wealth; nor under the dominion of any will, or restraint of any law, but what that legislative shall enact, according to the trust put in it. Freedom then is not what Sir *Robert Filmer* tells us, *Observations, A. 55. a liberty for every one to do what he lists, to live as he pleases, and not to be tied by any laws:* but *freedom of men under government* is, to have a standing rule to live by, common to every one of that society, and made by the legislative power erected in it; a liberty to follow my own will in all things, where the rule prescribes not; and not to be subject to the inconstant, uncertain, unknown, arbitrary will of another man: as *freedom of nature* is, to be under no other restraint but the law of nature.

§23. This *freedom* from absolute, arbitrary power, is so necessary to, and closely joined with a man's preservation, that he cannot part with it, but by what forfeits his preservation and life together: for a man, not having the power of his own life, *cannot*, by compact, or his own consent, *enslave himself* to any one, nor put himself under the absolute, arbitrary power of another, to take away his life, when he pleases. No body can give more power than he has himself; and he that cannot take away his own life, cannot give another power over it. Indeed, having by his fault forfeited his own life, by some act that deserves death; he, to whom he has forfeited it, may (when he has him in his power) delay to take it, and make use of him to his own service, and he does him no injury by it: for, whenever he finds the hardship of his slavery outweigh the value of his life, it is in his power, by resisting the will of his master, to draw on himself the death he desires.

§24. This is the perfect condition of *slavery*, which is nothing else, but *the state of war continued, between a lawful conqueror and a captive*: for, if once *compact* enter between them, and make an agreement for a limited power on the one side, and obedience on the other, the *state of war and slavery* ceases, as long as the compact endures: for, as has been said, no man can, by agreement, pass over to another that which he hath not in himself, a power over his own life.

I confess, we find among the *Jews*, as well as other nations, that men did sell themselves; but, it is plain, this was only to *drudgery, not to slavery:* for, it is evident, the person sold was not under an absolute, arbitrary, despotical power: for the master could not have power to kill him, at any time, whom, at a certain time, he was obliged to let go free out of his service; and the master of such a servant was so far from having an arbitrary power over his life, that he could not, at pleasure, so much as maim him, but the loss of an eye, or tooth, set him free, *Exod.* xxi.

CHAPTER V: OF PROPERTY

§25. Whether we consider natural *reason*, which tells us, that men, being once born, have a right to their preservation, and consequently to meat and drink, and such other things as nature affords for their subsistence: or *revelation*, which gives us an account of those grants God made of the world to *Adam*, and to *Noah*, and his sons, it is very clear, that God, as king *David* says, *Psal.* cxv. 16. *has given the earth to the children of men;* given it to mankind in common. But this being supposed, it seems to some a very great difficulty, how any one should ever come to have a *property* in any thing: I will not content myself to answer, that if it be difficult to make out *property*, upon a supposition that God gave the world to *Adam*, and his posterity in common, it is impossible that any man, but one universal monarch, should have any *property* upon a supposition, that God gave the world to *Adam*, and his heirs in succession, exclusive of all the rest of his posterity. But I shall endeavour to shew, how men might come to have a *property* in several parts of that which God gave to mankind in common, and that without any express compact of all the commoners.

§26. God, who hath given the world to men in common, hath also given them reason to make use of it to the best advantage of life, and convenience. The earth, and all that is therein, is given to men for the support and comfort of their being. And tho' all the fruits it naturally produces, and beasts it feeds, belong to mankind in common, as they are produced by the spontaneous hand of nature; and no body has originally a private dominion, exclusive of the rest of mankind, in any of them, as they are thus in their natural state: yet being given for the use of men, there must of necessity be *a means to appropriate* them some way or other, before they can be of any use, or at all beneficial to any particular man. The fruit, or venison, which nourishes the wild *Indian*, who knows no inclosure, and is still a tenant in common, must be his, and so his, *i.e.* a part of him, that another can no longer have any right to it, before it can do him any good for the support of his life.

§27. Though the earth, and all inferior creatures, be common to all men, yet every man has a *property* in his own *person:* this no body has any right to but himself. The *labour* of his body, and the *work* of his hands, we may say, are properly his. Whatsoever then he removes out of the state that nature hath provided, and left it in, he hath mixed his *labour* with, and joined to it something that is his own, and thereby makes it his *property*. It being by him removed from the common state nature hath placed it in, it hath by this *labour* something annexed to it, that excludes the common right of other men: for this *labour* being the unquestionable property of the labourer, no man but he can have a right to what that is once joined to, at least where there is enough, and as good, left in common for others.

§28. He that is nourished by the acorns he picked up under an oak, or the apples he gathered from the trees in the wood, has certainly appropriated them to himself. No body can deny but the nourishment is his. I ask then, when did they begin to be his? when he digested? or when he eat? or when he boiled? or when he brought them home? or when he picked them up? and it is plain, if the first gathering made them not his, nothing else could. That *labour* put a distinction between them and common: that added something to them more than nature, the common mother of all, had done; and so they became his private right. And will any one say, he had no right to those acorns or apples, he thus appropriated, because he had not the consent of all mankind to make them his? Was it a robbery thus to assume to himself what belonged to all in common? If such a consent as that was necessary, man had starved, notwithstanding the plenty God had given him. We see in *commons*, which remain so by compact, that it is the taking any part of what is common, and removing it out of the state nature leaves it in, which *begins the property;* without which the common is of no use. And the taking of this or that part, does not depend on the express consent of all the commoners. Thus the grass my horse has bit; the turfs my servant has cut; and the ore I have digged in any place, where I have a right to them in common with others, become my *property*, without the assignation or consent of any body. The *labour* that was mine, removing them out of that common state they were in, hath *fixed* my *property* in them.

§29. By making an explicit consent of every commoner, necessary to any one's appropriating to himself any part of what is given in common, children or servants could not cut the meat, which their father or master had provided for them in common, without assigning to every one his peculiar part. Though the water running in the fountain be every one's, yet who can doubt, but that in the pitcher is his only who drew it out? His *labour* hath taken it out of the hands of nature, where it was common, and belonged equally to all her children, and *hath* thereby *appropriated* it to himself.

§30. Thus this law of reason makes the deer that *Indian*'s who hath killed it; it is allowed to be his goods, who hath bestowed his labour upon it, though before it was the common right of every one. And amongst those who are counted the civilized part of mankind, who have made and multiplied positive laws to determine *property*, this original law of nature, for the *beginning of property*, in what was before common, still takes place; and by virtue thereof, what fish any one catches in the ocean, that great and still remaining common of mankind; or what ambergrise any one takes up here, is by the *labour* that removes it out of that common state nature left it in, *made* his *property*, who takes that pains about it. And even amongst us, the hare that any one is hunting, is thought his who pursues her during the chase: for being a beast that is still looked upon as common, and no man's private possession; whoever has employed so much *labour* about any of that kind, as to find and pursue her, has thereby removed her from the state of nature, wherein she was common, and hath *begun a property*. [...]

§32. But the *chief matter of property* being now not the fruits of the earth, and the beasts that subsist on it, but *the earth itself;* as that which takes in and carries with it all the rest; I think it is plain, that *property* in that too is acquired as the former. *As much land* as a man tills, plants, improves, cultivates, and can use the product of, so much is his *property*. He by his labour does, as it were, inclose it from the common. Nor will it invalidate his right, to say every body else has an equal title to it; and therefore he cannot appropriate, he cannot inclose, without the consent of all his fellow-commoners, all mankind. God, when he gave the world in common to all mankind, commanded man also to labour, and the penury of his condition required it of him. God and his reason commanded him to subdue the earth, *i.e.* improve it for the benefit of life, and therein lay out something upon it that was his own, his labour. He that in obedience to this command of God, subdued, tilled and sowed any part of it, thereby annexed to it something that was his *property*, which another had no title to, nor could without injury take from him.

§33. Nor was this *appropriation* of any parcel of *land*, by improving it, any prejudice to any other man, since there was still enough, and as good left; and more than the yet unprovided could use. So that, in effect, there was never the less left for others because of his inclosure for himself: for he that leaves as much as another can make use of, does as good as take nothing at all. No body could think himself injured by the drinking of another man, though he took a good draught, who had a whole river of the same water left him to quench his thirst: and the case of land and water, where there is enough of both, is perfectly the same.

§34. God gave the world to men in common; but since he gave it them for their benefit, and the greatest conveniencies of life they were capable to draw from it, it cannot be supposed he meant it should always remain common and uncultivated. He gave it to the use of the industrious and rational, (and *labour* was to be *his title* to it;) not to the fancy or covetousness of the quarrelsome and contentious. He that had as good left for his improvement, as was already taken up, needed not complain, ought not to meddle with what was already improved by another's labour: if he did, it is plain he desired the benefit of another's pains, which he had no right to, and not the ground which God had given him in common with others to labour on, and whereof there was as good left, as that already possessed, and more than he knew what to do with, or his industry could reach to. [...]

§37. This is certain, that in the beginning, before the desire of having more than man needed had altered the intrinsic value of things, which depends only on their usefulness to the life of man; or had *agreed, that a little piece of yellow metal*, which would keep without wasting or decay, should be worth a great piece of flesh, or a whole heap of corn; though men had a right to appropriate, by their labour, each one of himself, as much of the things of nature, as he could use: yet this could not be much, nor to the prejudice of others, where the same plenty was still left to those who would use the same industry. To which let me add, that he who appropriates land to himself by his labour, does not lessen, but increase the common stock of mankind: for the provisions serving to the support of human life, produced by one acre of inclosed and cultivated land, are (to speak much within compass) ten times more than those which are yielded by an acre of land of an equal richness lying waste in common. And therefore he that incloses land, and has a greater plenty of the conveniencies of life from ten acres, than he could have from an hundred left to nature, may truly be said to give ninety acres to mankind: for his labour now supplies him with provisions out of ten acres, which were but the product of an hundred lying in common. I have here rated the improved land very low, in making its product but as ten to one, when it is much nearer an hundred to one: for I ask, whether in the wild woods and uncultivated waste of *America*, left to nature, without any improvement, tillage or husbandry, a thousand acres yield the needy and wretched inhabitants as many conveniencies of life, as ten acres of equally fertile land do in *Devonshire*, where they are well cultivated?

Before the appropriation of land, he who gathered as much of the wild fruit, killed, caught, or tamed, as many of the beasts, as he could; he that so imployed his pains about any of the spontaneous products of nature, as any way to alter them from the state which nature put them in, *by* placing any of his *labour* on them, did thereby *acquire a propriety in them*: but if they perished, in his possession, without their due use; if the fruits rotted, or the venison putrified, before he could spend it, he offended against the common law of nature, and was liable to be punished; he invaded his neighbour's share, for he had *no right, farther than his use* called for any of them, and they might serve to afford him conveniencies of life. [...]

§40. Nor is it so strange, as perhaps before consideration it may appear, that the *property of labour* should be able to over-balance the community of land: for it is *labour* indeed that *puts the difference of value* on every thing; and let any one consider what the difference is between an acre of land planted with tobacco or sugar, sown with wheat or barley, and an acre of the same land lying in common, without any husbandry upon it, and he will find, that the improvement of *labour* *makes* the far greater part of the value. I think it will be but a very modest computation to say, that of the *products* of the earth useful to the life of man nine tenths are the *effects of labour:* nay, if we will rightly estimate things as they come to our use, and cast up the several expences about them, what in them is purely owing to *nature*, and what to *labour*, we shall find, that in most of them ninety-nine hundredths are wholly to be put on the account of *labour*. [...]

§51. And thus, I think, it is very easy to conceive, without any difficulty, *how labour could at first begin a title of property* in the common things of nature, and how the spending it upon our uses bounded it. So that there could then be no reason of quarrelling about title, nor any doubt about the largeness of possession it gave. Right and conveniency went together; for as a man had a right to all he could employ his labour upon, so he had no temptation to labour for more than he could make use of. This left no room for controversy about the title, nor for incroachment on the right of others; what portion a man carved to himself, was easily seen; and it was useless, as well as dishonest, to carve himself too much, or take more than he needed.

CHAPTER VI: OF PATERNAL POWER

§52. It may perhaps be censured as an impertinent criticism, in a discourse of this nature, to find fault with words and names, that have obtained in the world: and yet possibly it may not be amiss to offer new ones, when the old are apt to lead men into mistakes, as this of *paternal power* probably has done, which seems so to place the power of parents over their children wholly in the *father*, as if the *mother* had no share in it; whereas, if we consult reason or revelation, we shall find, she hath an equal title. This may give one reason to ask, whether this might not be more properly called *parental power?* for whatever obligation nature and the right of generation lays on children, it must certainly bind them equal to both the concurrent causes of it. [...]

§53. Had but this one thing been well considered, without looking any deeper into the matter, it might perhaps have kept men from running into those gross mistakes, they have made, about this power of parents; which, however it might, without any great harshness, bear the name of absolute dominion, and regal authority, when under the title of *paternal power* it seemed appropriated to the father, would yet have founded but oddly, and in the very name shewn the absurdity, if this supposed absolute power over children had been called *parental*; and thereby have discovered, that it belonged to the *mother* too: for it will but very ill serve the turn of those men, who contend so much for the absolute power and authority of the *fatherhood*, as they call it, that the mother should have any share in it; and it would have but ill supported the *monarchy* they contend for, when by the very name it appeared, that that fundamental authority, from whence they would derive their government of a single person only, was not placed in one, but two persons jointly. But to let this of names pass.

§54. Though I have said above, *Chap. II. That all men by nature are equal*, I cannot be supposed to understand all sorts of *equality: age or virtue* may give men a just precedency: *excellency of parts* and *merit* may place others above the common level: *birth* may subject some, and *alliance* or *benefits* others, to pay an observance to those to whom nature, gratitude, or other respects, may have made it due: and yet all this consists with the *equality*, which all men are in, in respect of jurisdiction or dominion one over another; which was the *equality* I there spoke of, as proper to the business in hand, being that *equal right*, that every man hath, *to his natural freedom*, without being subjected to the will or authority of any other man.

§55. *Children*, I confess, are not born in this full state of *equality*, though they are born to it. Their parents have a sort of rule and jurisdiction over them, when they come into the world, and for some time after; but it is but a temporary one. The bonds of this subjection are like the swaddling clothes they are wrapt up in, and supported by, in the weakness of their infancy: age and reason as they grow up, loosen them, till at length they drop quite off, and leave a man at his own free disposal. [...]

§63. The *freedom* then of man, and liberty of acting according to his own will, is *grounded on* his having *reason*, which is able to instruct him in that law he is to govern himself by, and make him know how far he is left to the freedom of his own will. To turn him loose to an unrestrained liberty, before he has reason to guide him, is not the allowing him the privilege of his nature to be free; but to thrust him out amongst brutes, and abandon him to a state as wretched, and as much beneath that of a man, as their's. This is that which puts the *authority* into the *parents* hands to govern the *minority* of their children. God hath made it their business to employ this care on their offspring, and hath placed in them suitable inclinations of tenderness and concern to temper this power, to apply it, as his wisdom designed it, to the children's good, as long as they should need to be under it. [...]

CHAPTER VII: OF POLITICAL OR CIVIL SOCIETY

§77. God having made man such a creature, that in his own judgment, it was not good for him to be alone, put him under strong obligations of necessity, convenience, and inclination to drive him into *society*, as well as fitted him with understanding and language to continue and enjoy it. The *first society* was between man and wife, which gave beginning to that between parents and children; to which, in time, that between master and servant came to be added: and though all these might, and commonly did meet together, and make up but one family, wherein the master or mistress of it had some sort of rule proper to a family; each of these, or all together, came short of *political society*, as we shall see, if we consider the different ends, ties, and bounds of each of these.

§78. *Conjugal society* is made by a voluntary compact between man and woman; and tho' it consist chiefly in such a communion and right in one another's bodies as is necessary to its chief end, procreation; yet it draws with it mutual support and assistance, and a communion of interests too, as necessary not only to unite their care and affection, but also necessary to their common off-spring, who have a right to be nourished, and maintained by them, till they are able to provide for themselves.

§79. For the end of *conjunction, between male and female*, being not barely procreation, but the continuation of the species; this conjunction betwixt male and female ought to last, even after procreation, so long as is necessary to the nourishment and support of the young ones, who are to be sustained by those that got them, till they are able to shift and provide for themselves. This rule, which the infinite wise maker hath set to the works of his hands, we find the inferior creatures steadily obey. In those viviparous animals which feed on grass, the *conjunction between male and female* lasts no longer than the very act of copulation; because the teat of the dam being sufficient to nourish the young, till it be able to feed on grass, the male only begets, but concerns not himself for the female or young, to whose sustenance he can contribute nothing. But in beasts of prey the *conjunction* lasts longer: because the dam not being able well to subsist herself, and nourish her numerous off-spring by her own prey alone, a more laborious, as well as more dangerous way of living, than by feeding on grass, the assistance of the male is necessary to the maintenance of their common family, which cannot subsist till they are able to prey for themselves, but by the joint care of male and female. The same is to be observed in all birds, (except some domestic ones, where plenty of food excuses the cock from feeding, and taking care of the young brood) whose young needing food in the nest, the cock and hen continue mates, till the young are able to use their wing, and provide for themselves.

§80. And herein I think lies the chief, if not the only reason, *why the male and female in mankind are tied to a longer conjunction* than other creatures, *viz.* because the female is capable of conceiving, and *de facto* is commonly with child again, and brings forth too a new birth, long before the former is out of a dependency for support on his parents help, and able to shift for himself, and has all the assistance is due to him from his parents: whereby the father, who is bound to take care for those he hath begot, is under an obligation to continue in conjugal society with the same woman longer than other creatures, whose young being able to subsist of themselves, before the time of procreation returns again, the conjugal bond dissolves of itself, and they are at liberty, till *Hymen* at his usual anniversary season summons them again to chuse new mates. Wherein one cannot but admire the wisdom of the great Creator, who having given to man foresight, and an ability to lay up for the future, as well as to supply the present necessity, hath made it necessary, that *society of man and wife should be more lasting*, than of male and female amongst other creatures; that so their industry might be encouraged, and their interest better united, to make provision and lay up goods for their common issue, which uncertain mixture, or easy and frequent solutions of conjugal society would mightily disturb. [...]

§86. Let us therefore consider a *master of a family* with all these subordinate relations of *wife, children, servants*, and *slaves*, united under the domestic rule of a family; which, what resemblance soever it may have in its order, offices, and number too, with a little common-wealth, yet is very far from it, both in its constitution, power and end: or if it must be thought a monarchy, and the *paterfamilias* the absolute monarch in it, absolute monarchy will have but a very shattered and short power, when it is plain, by what has been said before, that the *master of the family* has a very distinct and differently limited *power*, both as to time and extent, over those several persons that are in it; for excepting the slave (and the family is as much a family, and his power as *paterfamilias* as great, whether there be any slaves in his family or no) he has no legislative power of life and death over any of them, and none too but what a *mistress of a family* may have as well as he. And he certainly can have no absolute power over the whole *family*, who has but a very limited one over every individual in it. But how a *family*, or any other society of men, differ from that which is properly *political society*, we shall best see, by considering wherein *political society* itself consists. [...]

§89. Where-ever therefore any number of men are so united into one society, as to quit every one his executive power of the law of nature, and to resign it to the public, there and there only is a *political, or civil society*. And this is done, where-ever any number of men, in the state of nature, enter into society to make one people, one body politic, under one supreme government; or else when any one joins himself to, and incorporates with any government already made: for hereby he authorizes the society, or which is all one, the legislative thereof, to make laws for him, as the public good of the society shall require; to the execution whereof, his own assistance (as to his own decrees) is due. And this *puts men* out of a state of nature *into* that of a *common-wealth*, by setting up a judge on earth, with authority to determine all the controversies, and redress the injuries that may happen to any member of the common-wealth; which judge is the legislative, or magistrates appointed by it. And where-ever there are any number of men, however associated, that have no such decisive power to appeal to, there they are still in *the state of nature*.

§90. Hence it is evident, that *absolute monarchy*, which by some men is counted the only government in the world, is indeed *inconsistent with civil society*, and so can be no form of civil-government at all: for the *end of civil society*, being to avoid, and remedy those inconveniencies of the state of nature, which necessarily follow from every man's being judge in his own case, by setting up a known authority, to which every one of that society may appeal upon any injury received, or controversy that may arise, and which every one of the society ought to obey; where-ever any persons are, who have not such an authority to appeal to, for the decision of any difference between them, there those persons are still *in the state of nature*; and so is every *absolute prince*, in respect of those who are under his *dominion*.

§91. For he being supposed to have all, both legislative and executive power in himself alone, there is no judge to be found, no appeal lies open to any one, who may fairly, and indifferently, and with authority decide, and from whose decision relief and redress may be expected of any injury or inconveniency, that may be suffered from the prince, or by his order: so that such a man, however intitled, *Czar*, or *Grand Seignior*, or how you please, is as much *in the state of nature*, with all under his dominion, as he is with the rest of mankind: for where-ever any two men are, who have no standing rule, and common judge to appeal to on earth, for the determination of controversies of right betwixt them, there they are still *in the state of nature*, and under all the inconveniencies of it, with only this woful difference to the subject, or rather slave of an absolute prince: that whereas, in the ordinary state of nature, he has a liberty to judge of his right, and according to the best of his power, to maintain it; now, whenever his property is invaded by the will and order of his monarch, he has not only no appeal, as those in society ought to have, but as if he were degraded from the common state of rational creatures, is denied a liberty to judge of, or to defend his right; and so is exposed to all the misery and inconveniencies, that a man can fear from one, who being in the unrestrained state of nature, is yet corrupted with flattery, and armed with power. [...]

CHAPTER VIII: OF THE BEGINNING OF POLITICAL SOCIETIES

§95. Men being, as has been said, by nature, all free, equal, and independent, no one can be put out of this estate, and subjected to the political power of another, without his own consent. The only way whereby any one divests himself of his natural liberty, and puts on the *bonds of civil society*, is by agreeing with other men to join and unite into a community for their comfortable, safe, and peaceable living one amongst another, in a secure enjoyment of their properties, and a greater security against any, that are not of it. This any number of men may do, because it injures not the freedom of the rest; they are left as they were in the liberty of the state of nature. When any number of men have so *consented to make one community or government*, they are thereby presently incorporated, and make *one body politic*, wherein the *majority* have a right to act and conclude the rest.

§96. For when any number of men have, by the consent of every individual, made a *community*, they have thereby made that *community* one body, with a power to act as one body, which is only by the will and determination of the *majority*: for that which acts any community, being only the consent of the individuals of it, and it being necessary to that which is one body to move one way; it is necessary the body should move that way whither the greater force carries it, which is the *consent of the majority*: or else it is impossible it should act or continue one body, *one community*, which the consent of every individual that united into it, agreed that it should; and so every one is bound by that consent to be concluded by the *majority*. And therefore we see, that in assemblies, impowered to act by positive laws, where no number is set by that positive law which impowers them, the *act of the majority* passes for the act of the whole, and of course determines, as having, by the law of nature and reason, the power of the whole.

§97. And thus every man, by consenting with others to make one body politic under one government, puts himself under an obligation, to every one of that society, to submit to the determination of the *majority*, and to be concluded by it; or else this *original compact*, whereby he with others incorporates into *one society*, would signify nothing, and be no compact, if he be left free, and under no other ties than he was in before in the state of nature. For what appearance would there be of any compact? what new engagement if he were no farther tied by any decrees of the society, than he himself thought fit, and did actually consent to? This would be still as great a liberty, as he himself had before his compact, or any one else in the state of nature hath, who may submit himself, and consent to any acts of it if he thinks fit. [...]

§122. But submitting to the laws of any country, living quietly, and enjoying privileges and protection under them, *makes not a man a member of that society* [...] Nothing can make any man so, but his actually entering into it by positive engagement, and express promise and compact. This is that, which I think, concerning the beginning of political societies, and that *consent which makes any one a member* of any common-wealth.

CHAPTER IX: OF THE ENDS OF POLITICAL SOCIETY AND GOVERNMENT

§123. If man in the state of nature be so free, as has been said; if he be absolute lord of his own person and possessions, equal to the greatest, and subject to no body, why will he part with his freedom? why will he give up this empire, and subject himself to the dominion and controul of any other power? To which it is obvious to answer, that though in the state of nature he hath such a right, yet the enjoyment of it is very uncertain, and constantly exposed to the invasion of others: for all being kings as much as he, every man his equal, and the greater part no strict observers of equity and justice, the enjoyment of the property he has in this state is very unsafe, very unsecure. This makes him willing to quit a condition, which, however free, is full of fears and continual dangers: and it is not without reason, that he seeks out, and is willing to join in society with others, who are already united, or have a mind to unite, for the mutual *preservation* of their lives, liberties and estates, which I call by the general name, *property*.

§124. The great and *chief end*, therefore, of men's uniting into common-wealths, and putting themselves under government, *is the preservation of their property*. To which in the state of nature there are many things wanting.

First, There wants an *established*, settled, known *law*, received and allowed by common consent to be the standard of right and wrong, and the common measure to decide all controversies between them: for though the law of nature be plain and intelligible to all rational creatures; yet men being biassed by their interest, as well as ignorant for want of study of it, are not apt to allow of it as a law binding to them in the application of it to their particular cases.

§125. *Secondly*, In the state of nature there wants *a known and indifferent judge*, with authority to determine all differences according to the established law: for every one in that state being both judge and executioner of the law of nature, men being partial to themselves, passion and revenge is very apt to carry them too far, and with too much heat, in their own cases; as well as negligence, and unconcernedness, to make them too remiss in other men's.

§126. *Thirdly*, In the state of nature there often wants *power* to back and support the sentence when right, and to *give* it due *execution*. They who by any injustice offended, will seldom fail, where they are able, by force to make good their injustice; such resistance many times makes the punishment dangerous, and frequently destructive, to those who attempt it.

§127. Thus mankind, notwithstanding all the privileges of the state of nature, being but in an ill condition, while they remain in it, are quickly driven into society. Hence it comes to pass, that we seldom find any number of men live any time together in this state. The inconveniencies that they are therein exposed to, by the irregular and uncertain exercise of the power every man has of punishing the transgressions of others, make them take sanctuary under the established laws of government, and therein seek *the preservation of their property*. It is this makes them so willingly give up every one his single power of punishing, to be exercised by such alone, as shall be appointed to it amongst them; and by such rules as the community, or those authorized by them to that purpose, shall agree on. And in this we have the original *right and rise of both the legislative and executive power*, as well as of the governments and societies themselves. [...]

CHAPTER XI: OF THE EXTENT OF THE LEGISLATIVE POWER

§134. The great end of men's entering into society, being the enjoyment of their properties in peace and safety, and the great instrument and means of that being the laws established in that society; the *first and fundamental positive law* of all common-wealths *is the establishing of the legislative* power; as the *first and fundamental natural law*, which is to govern even the legislative itself, *is the preservation of the society*, and (as far as will consist with the public good) of every person in it. This *legislative* is not only *the supreme power* of the common-wealth, but sacred and unalterable in the hands where the community have once placed it; nor can any edict of any body else, in what form soever conceived, or by what power soever backed, have the force and obligation of a *law*, which has not its *sanction from* that *legislative* which the public has chosen and appointed: for without this the law could not have that, which is absolutely necessary to its being a *law, the consent of the society*, over whom no body can have a power to make laws, but by their own consent, and by authority received from them; and therefore all the *obedience*, which by the most solemn ties any one can be obliged to pay, ultimately terminates in this *supreme power*, and is directed by those laws which it enacts: nor can any oaths to any foreign power whatsoever, or any domestic subordinate power, discharge any member of the society from his *obedience to the legislative*, acting pursuant to their trust; nor oblige him to any obedience contrary to the laws so enacted, or farther than they do allow; it being ridiculous to imagine one can be tied ultimately to *obey* any *power* in the society, which is not the *supreme*.

§135. Though the *legislative*, whether placed in one or more, whether it be always in being, or only by intervals, though it be the *supreme* power in every commonwealth; yet,

First, It is *not*, nor can possibly be absolutely *arbitrary* over the lives and fortunes of the people: for it being but the joint power of every member of the society given up to that person, or assembly, which is legislator; it can be no more than those persons had in a state of nature before they entered into society, and gave up to the community: for no body can transfer to another more power than he has in himself; and no body has an absolute arbitrary power over himself, or over any other, to destroy his own life, or take away the life or property of another. [...] *Legislative power* [...] is *limited to the public good* of the society. It is a power, that hath no other end but preservation, and therefore can never have a right to destroy, enslave, or designedly to impoverish the subjects. [...]

§136. *Secondly*, The *legislative*, or supreme authority, cannot assume to its self a power to rule by extemporary arbitrary decrees, but *is bound to dispense justice*, and decide the rights of the subject *by promulgated standing laws, and known authorized judges.* [...]

§137. Absolute arbitrary power, or governing without *settled standing laws*, can neither of them consist with the ends of society and government, which men would not quit the freedom of the state of nature for, and tie themselves up under, were it not to preserve their lives, liberties and fortunes, and by *stated rules* of right and property to secure their peace and quiet [...]

§138. *Thirdly*, The *supreme power cannot take* from any man any part of his *property* without his own consent: for the preservation of property being the end of government, and that for which men enter into society, it necessarily supposes and requires, that the people should *have property*, without which they must be supposed to lose that, by entering into society, which was the end for which they entered into it; too gross an absurdity for any man to own. *Men* therefore *in society having property*, they have such a right to the goods, which by the law of the community are their's, that no body hath a right to take their substance or any part of it from them, without their own consent: without this they have no *property* at all [...]

§141. *Fourthly*, The *legislative cannot transfer the power of making laws* to any other hands: for it being but a delegated power from the people, they who have it cannot pass it over to others. The people alone can appoint the form of the commonwealth, which is by constituting the legislative, and appointing in whose hands that shall be. [...]

§142. These are the *bounds* which the trust, that is put in them by the society, and the law of God and nature, have *set to the legislative* power of every common-wealth, in all forms of government.

First, They are to govern by *promulgated established laws*, not to be varied in particular cases, but to have one rule for rich and poor, for the favourite at court, and the country man at plough.

Secondly, These *laws* also ought to be designed *for* no other end ultimately, but *the good of the people*.

Thirdly, They must *not raise taxes* on the *property of the people, without the consent of the people*, given by themselves, or their deputies. And this properly concerns only such governments where the *legislative* is always in being, or at least where the people have not reserved any part of the legislative to deputies, to be from time to time chosen by themselves.

Fourthly, The *legislative* neither must *nor can transfer the power of making laws* to any body else, or place it any where, but where the people have.

CHAPTER XII: OF THE LEGISLATIVE, EXECUTIVE, AND FEDERATIVE POWER OF THE COMMON-WEALTH

[...] §154. If the *legislative*, or any part of it, be made up of *representatives* chosen for that time by the people, which afterwards return into the ordinary state of subjects, and have no share in the legislature but upon a new choice, this power of chusing must also be exercised by the people, either at certain appointed seasons, or else when they are summoned to it; and in this latter case, the power of convoking the legislative is ordinarily placed in the executive, and has one of these two limitations in respect of time: that either the original constitution requires their *assembling* and *acting* at certain intervals, and then the executive power does nothing but ministerially issue directions for their electing and assembling, according to due forms; or else it is left to his prudence to call them by new elections, when the occasions or exigencies of the public require the amendment of old, or making of new laws, or the redress or prevention of any inconveniencies, that lie on, or threaten the people. [...]

CHAPTER XIX: OF THE DISSOLUTION OF GOVERNMENT

§211. He that will with any clearness speak of the *dissolution of government*, ought in the first place to distinguish between the *dissolution of the society* and the *dissolution of the government*. That which makes the community, and brings men out of the loose state of nature, into *one politic society*, is the agreement which every one has with the rest to incorporate, and act as one body, and so be one distinct common-wealth. The usual, and almost only way whereby *this union is dissolved*, is the inroad of foreign force making a conquest upon them: for in that case, (not being able to maintain and support themselves, as *one intire* and *independent body*) the union belonging to that body which consisted therein, must necessarily cease, and so every one return to the state he was in before, with a liberty to shift for himself, and provide for his own safety, as he thinks fit, in some other society. Whenever the *society is dissolved*, it is certain the government of that society cannot remain. Thus conquerors swords often cut up governments by the roots, and mangle societies to pieces, separating the subdued or scattered multitude from the protection of, and dependence on, that society which ought to have preserved them from violence. The world is too well instructed in, and too forward to allow of, this way of dissolving of governments, to need any more to be said of it; and there wants not much argument to prove, that where the *society is dissolved*, the government cannot remain; that being as impossible, as for the frame of an house to subsist when the materials of it are scattered and dissipated by a whirl-wind, or jumbled into a confused heap by an earthquake.

§212. Besides this over-turning from without, *governments are dissolved from within*,

First, When the *legislative* is *altered*. Civil society being a state of peace, amongst those who are of it, from whom the state of war is excluded by the umpirage, which they have provided in their legislative, for the ending all differences that may arise amongst any of them, it is in their *legislative*, that the members of a common-wealth are united, and combined together into one coherent living body. This *is the soul that gives form, life, and unity*, to the common-wealth: from hence the several members have their mutual influence, sympathy, and connexion: and therefore, when the *legislative* is broken, or *dissolved*, dissolution and death follows: for the *essence and union of the society* consisting in having one will, the legislative, when once established by the majority, has the declaring, and as it were keeping of that will. The *constitution of the legislative* is the first and fundamental act of society, whereby provision is made for the *continuation of their union*, under the direction of persons, and bonds of laws, made by persons authorized thereunto, by the consent and appointment of the people, without which no one man, or number of men, amongst them, can have authority of making laws that shall be binding to the rest. When any one, or more, shall take upon them to make laws, whom the people have not appointed so to do, they make laws without authority, which the people are not therefore bound to obey; by which means they come again to be out of subjection, and may constitute to themselves a *new legislative*, as they think best, being in full liberty to resist the force of those, who without authority would impose any thing upon them. Every one is at the disposure of his own will, when those who had, by the delegation of the society, the declaring of the public will, are excluded from it, and others usurp the place, who have no such authority or delegation. [. . .]

§243. To conclude, The *power that every individual gave the society*, when he entered into it, can never revert to the individuals again, as long as the society lasts, but will always remain in the community; because without this there can be no community, no common-wealth, which is contrary to the original agreement: so also when the society hath placed the legislative in any assembly of men, to continue in them and their successors, with direction and authority for providing such successors, *the legislative can never revert to the people* whilst that government lasts; because having provided a legislative with power to continue for ever, they have given up their political power to the legislative, and cannot resume it. But if they have set limits to the duration of their legislative, and made this supreme power in any person, or assembly, only temporary; or else, when by the miscarriages of those in authority, it is forfeited; upon the forfeiture, or at the determination of the time set, *it reverts to the society*, and the people have a right to act as supreme, and continue the legislative in themselves; or erect a new form, or under the old form place it in new hands, as they think good.

CHAPTER 2

A Serious Proposal to the Ladies, for the Advancement of their True and Greatest Interest, By a Lover of Her Sex

MARY ASTELL

LADIES,

Since the Profitable Adventures that have gone abroad in the World have met with so great Encouragement, tho' the highest advantage they can propose, is an uncertain Lot for such matters as Opinion, not real worth, gives a value to; things which if obtain'd are as flitting and fickle as that Chance which is to dispose of them; I therefore persuade my self, you will not be less kind to a Proposition that comes attended with more certain and substantial Gain; whose only design is to improve your Charms and heighten your Value, by suffering you no longer to be cheap and contemptible. Its aim is to fix that Beauty, to make it lasting and permanent, which Nature with all the helps of Art cannot secure, and to place it out of the reach of Sickness and Old Age [...] This is a Matter infinitely more worthy your Debates, than what Colours are most agreeable, or what's the Dress becomes you best. Your Glass will not do you half so much service as a serious reflection on your own Minds, which will discover Irregularities more worthy your Correction, and keep you from being either too much elated or depress'd by the representations of the other. [...] No solicitude in the adornation of your selves is discommended, provided you employ your care about that which is really your *self*; and do not neglect that particle of Divinity within you, which must survive, and may (if you please) be happy and perfect, when it's unsuitable and much inferiour Companion is mouldering into Dust. Neither will any pleasure be denied you, who are only desir'd not to catch at the Shadow and let the Substance go. You may be as ambitious as you please, so you aspire to the best things; and contend with your Neighbours as much as you can, that they may not out do you in any commendable Quality. Let it never be said, That they

Mary Astell. *A Serious Proposal to the Ladies*. Originally published in 1696.

to whom pre-eminence is so very agreeable, can be tamely content that others shou'd surpass them in *this*, and precede them in a *better* World! [...] Let us learn to pride ourselves in something more excellent than the invention of a Fashion; And not entertain such a degrading thought of our own *worth*, as to imagine that our Souls were given us only for the service of our Bodies, and that the best improvement we can make of these, is to attract the Eyes of Men. We value *them* too much, and our *selves* too little, if we place any part of our desert in their Opinion; and don't think our selves capable of Nobler Things than the pitiful Conquest of some worthless heart. [...] Ladies, as to do nothing unworthy of you; so true to your Interest, as not to lessen your Empire and depreciate your Charms. Let not your Thoughts be wholly busied in observing what respect is paid you, but a part of them at least, in studying to deserve it. And after all, remember that Goodness is the truest Greatness; to be wise for your selves the greatest Wit; and *that* Beauty the most desirable which will endure to Eternity.

Pardon me the seeming rudeness of this Proposal, which goes upon a supposition that there's something amiss in you, which it is intended to amend. My design is not to expose, but to rectifie your Failures. To be exempt from mistake, is a privilege few can pretend to, the greatest is to be past Conviction and too obstinate to reform. Even the *Men*, as exact as they wou'd seem, and as much as they divert themselves with our Miscarriages, are very often guilty of greater faults, and such, as considering the advantages they enjoy, are much more inexcusable. But I will not pretend to correct their Errors, who either are, or at least *think* themselves too wise to receive Instruction from a Womans Pen. My earnest desire is, That you Ladies, would be as perfect and happy as 'tis possible to be in this imperfect state [...] One wou'd therefore almost think, that the wise disposer of all things, foreseeing how unjustly Women are denied opportunities of improvement from *without* has therefore by way of compensation endow'd them with greater propensions to Vertue and a natural goodness of Temper within, which if duly manag'd, would raise them to the most eminent pitch of heroick Vertue. Hither, Ladies, I desire you wou'd aspire, 'tis a noble and becoming Ambition, and to remove such Obstacles as lie in your way is the design of this Paper. We will therefore enquire what it is that stops your flight, that keeps you groveling here below, like *Domitian* catching Flies when you should be busied in obtaining Empires.

Altho' it has been said by Men of more Wit than Wisdom, and perhaps of more malice than either, that Women are naturally incapable of acting Prudently, or that they are necessarily determined to folly, I must by no means grant it; that Hypothesis would render my endeavours impertinent, for then it would be in vain to advise the one, or endeavour the Reformation of the other. Besides, there are Examples in all Ages, which sufficiently confute the Ignorance and Malice of this Assertion.

The Incapacity, if there be any, is acquired not natural; and none of their Follies are so necessary, but that they might avoid them if they pleas'd themselves. Some disadvantages indeed they labour under, and what these are we shall see by and by and endeavour to surmount; but Women need not take up with mean things, since (if they are not wanting to themselves) they are capable of the best. [...]

Women are from their very Infancy debar'd those Advantages, with the want of which they are afterwards reproached, and nursed up in those Vices which will hereafter be upbraided to them. So partial are Men as to expect Brick where they afford no Straw; and so abundantly civil as to take care we shou'd make good that obliging Epithet of *Ignorant*, which out of an excess of good Manners, they are pleas'd to bestow on us! [...]

That therefore Women are unprofitable to most, and a plague and dishonour to some men is not much to be regretted on account of the *Men*, because 'tis the product of their own folly, in denying them the benefits of an ingenuous and liberal Education, the most effectual means to direct them into, and to secure their progress in the ways of Vertue.

For that Ignorance is the cause of most Feminine Vices, may be instanc'd in that Pride and Vanity which is usually imputed to us, and which I suppose if throughly sifted, will appear to be some way or other, the rise and Original of all the rest. These, tho' very bad Weeds, are the product of a good Soil, they are nothing else but Generosity degenerated and corrupted. A desire to advance and perfect its Being, is planted by GOD in all Rational Natures, to excite them hereby to every worthy and becoming Action; for certainly next to the Grace of GOD, nothing does so powerfully restrain people from Evil and stir them up to Good, as a generous Temper. And therefore to be ambitious of perfections is no fault, tho' to assume the Glory of our Excellencies to our selves, or to Glory in such as we really have not, are. And were Womens haughtiness express'd in disdaining to do a mean and evil thing, wou'd they pride themselves in somewhat truly perfective of a Rational nature, there were no hurt in it. [...]

Whence is it but from ignorance, from a want of Understanding to compare and judge of things, to chuse a right End, to proportion the Means to the End, and to rate ev'ry thing according to its proper value, that we quit the Substance for the Shadow, Reality for Appearance, and embrace those very things which if we understood we shou'd hate and fly, but now are reconcil'd to, merely because they usurp the Name, tho' they have nothing of the Nature of those venerable Objects we desire and seek? [...]

Thus Ignorance and a narrow Education lay the Foundation of Vice, and Imitation and Custom rear it up. Custom, that merciless torrent that carries all before it, and which indeed can be stem'd by none but such as have a great deal of Prudence and a rooted Vertue. For 'tis but Decorous that she who is not capable of giving better Rules, shou'd follow those she sees before her, least she only change the instance and retain the absurdity. 'Twou'd puzzle a considerate Person to account for all that Sin and Folly that is in the World (which certainly has nothing in it self to recommend it) did not Custom help to solve the difficulty... 'Tis Custom therefore, that Tyrant Custom, which is the grand motive to all those irrational choices which we daily see made in the World, so very contrary to our *present* interest and pleasure, as well as to our Future. [...]

Add to this the hurry and noise of the World, which does generally so busy and pre-ingage us, that we have little time and less inclination to stand still and reflect on our own Minds. Those impertinent Amusements which have seiz'd us, keep their hold so well and so constantly buz about our Ears, that we cannot attend to the Dictates of our Reason... By an habitual inadvertency we render our selves incapable of any serious and improveing thought, till our minds themselves become as light and frothy as those things they are conversant about. [...]

And now having discovered the Disease and its cause, 'tis proper to apply a Remedy; single Medicines are too weak to cure such complicated Distempers, they require a full Dispensatory; and what wou'd a good Woman refuse to do, could she hope by that to advantage the greatest part of the World, and improve her Sex in knowledge and true Religion? I doubt not, Ladies, but that the Age, as bad as it is, affords very many of you who will readily embrace whatever has a true tendency to the Glory of GOD and your mutual Edification, to revive the ancient Spirit of Piety in the World and to transmit it to succeeding Generations. [...]

Now as to the Proposal, it is to erect a *Monastery*, or if you will (to avoid giving offence to the scrupulous and injudicious, by names which tho' innocent in themselves, have been abus'd by superstitious Practices,) we will call it a *Religious Retirement*, and such as shall have a double aspect, being not only a Retreat from the World for those who desire that advantage, but likewise, an Institution and previous discipline, to fit us to do the greatest good in it; such an Institution as this (if I do not mightily deceive my self) would be the most probable method to amend the present and improve the future Age. For here those who are convinc'd of the emptiness of earthly Enjoyments, who are sick of the vanity of the world and its impertinencies, may find more substantial and satisfying entertainments, and need not be confin'd to what they justly loath. Those who are desirous to know and fortify their weak side, first do good to themselves, that hereafter they may be capable of doing more good to others; or for their greater security are willing to avoid *temptation*, may get out of that danger which a continual stay in view of the Enemy, and the familiarity and unwearied application of the Temptation may expose them to; and gain an opportunity to look into themselves to be acquainted at home and no longer the greatest strangers to their own hearts. Such as are willing in a more peculiar and undisturb'd manner, to attend the great business they came into the world about, the service of GOD and improvement of their own Minds, may find a convenient and blissful recess from the noise and hurry of the World...

You are therefore Ladies, invited into a place, where you shall suffer no other confinement, but to be kept out of the road of sin: You shall not be depriv'd of your grandeur, but only exchange the vain Pomps and Pageantry of the world, empty Titles and Forms of State, for the true and solid Greatness of being able to despise them. You will only quit the Chat of insignificant people for an ingenious Conversation; the froth of flashy Wit for real Wisdom; idle tales for instructive discourses. The deceitful Flatteries of those who under pretence of loving and admiring you, really served their *own* base ends for the seasonable Reproofs and wholsom Counsels of your hearty wellwishers and affectionate Friends, which will procure you those perfections your feigned lovers pretended you had, and kept you from obtaining [...] In fine, the place to which you are invited is a Type and Antepast of Heav'n, where your Employment will be as there, to magnify GOD, to love one another, and to communicate that useful *knowledge*, which by the due improvement of your time in Study and Contemplation you will obtain, and which when obtain'd, will afford you a much sweeter and more durable delight, than all those pitiful diversions, those revellings and amusements, which now thro your ignorance of better, appear the only grateful and relishing Entertainments [...]

For since GOD has given Women as well as Men intelligent Souls, why should they be forbidden to improve them? Since he has not denied us the faculty of Thinking, why shou'd we not (at least in gratitude to him) employ our Thoughts on himself their noblest Object, and not unworthily bestow them on Trifles and Gaities and secular Affairs? Being the Soul was created for the contemplation of Truth as well as for the fruition of Good, is it not as cruel and unjust to preclude Women from the knowledge of the one as from the enjoyment of the other? Especially since the Will is blind, and cannot chuse but by the direction of the

Understanding; or to speak more properly, since the Soul always *Wills* according as she *Understands*, so that if she Understands amiss, she Wills amiss. And as Exercise enlarges & exalts any Faculty, so thro' want of using it becomes crampt & lessened; if therefore we make little or no use of our Understandings, we shall shortly have none to use; and the more contracted and unemploy'd the deliberating and directive Power is, the more liable is the elective to unworthy and mischievous options. [...] Let such therefore as deny us the improvement of our Intellectuals, either take up *his* Paradox, who said *that Women have no Souls*, which at this time a day, when they are allow'd to Brutes, wou'd be as unphilosophical as it is unmannerly, or else let them permit us to cultivate and improve them. There is a sort of Learning indeed which is worse than the greatest Ignorance: A Woman may study Plays and Romances all her days, and be a great deal more knowing but never a jot the wiser. Such a knowledge as this serves only to instruct and put her forward in the practice of the greatest Follies, yet how can they justly blame her who forbid, or at least won't afford opportunity of better? A rational mind *will* be employ'd, it will never be satisfy'd in doing nothing, and if you neglect to furnish it with good materials, 'tis like to take up with such as come to hand.

We pretend not that Women shou'd teach in the Church, or usurp Authority where it is not allow'd them; permit us only to understand our *own* duty, and not be forc'd to take it upon trust from others; to be at least so far learned, as to be able to form in our minds a true Idea of Christianity, it being so very necessary to fence us against the danger of these *last* and *perilous days*, in which Deceivers a part of whose Character is to *lead captive silly Women*, need not *creep into Houses* since they have Authority to proclaim their Errors on the *House top*. And let us also acquire a true Practical Knowledge such as will convince us of the absolute necessity of *Holy Living* as well as of *Right Believing*, and that no Heresy is more dangerous than that of an ungodly and wicked Life. And since the *French Tongue* is understood by most Ladies, methinks they may much better improve it by the study of Philosophy (as I hear the *French Ladies* do) *Des Cartes, Malebranche* and others, than by reading idle *Novels* and *Romances*. 'Tis strange we shou'd be so forward to imitate their Fashions and Fopperies, and have no regard to what really deserves our Imitation! And why shall it not be thought as genteel to understand *French Philosophy*, as to be accoutred in a *French Mode*? Let therefore the famous Madam *D'acier, Scudéry*; Etc. and our own incomparable *Orinda*, excite the Emulation of the English Ladies.

The Ladies, I'm sure, have no reason to dislike this Proposal, but I know not how the Men will resent it to have their enclosure broke down, and Women invited to tast of that Tree of Knowledge they have so long unjustly *Monopoliz'd*. But they must excuse me, if I be as partial to my own Sex as they are to theirs, and think Women as capable of Learning as Men are, and that it becomes them as well. For I cannot imagine wherein the hurt lies, if instead of doing mischief to one another, by an uncharitable and vain Conversation, Women be enabled to inform and instruct those of their own Sex at least; the Holy Ghost having left it on record, that *Priscilla* as well as her Husband, catechiz'd the eloquent *Apollos* and the great Apostle found no fault with her. It will therefore be very proper for our Ladies to spend part of their time in this Retirement, in adorning their minds with useful Knowledge. [...]

Farther yet, besides that holy emulation which a continual view of the brightest and most exemplary Lives will excite in us, we shall have opportunity of contracting

the purest and noblest Friendship; a Blessing, the purchase of which were richly
worth all the World besides! For she who possesses a worthy Person, has certainly
obtain'd the richest Treasure... Probably one considerable cause of the degeneracy
of the present Age, is the little true Friendship that is to be found in it; or perhaps you
will rather say that this is the effect of our corruption. The cause and the effect are
indeed reciprocal; for were the World better there wou'd be more Friendship, and
were there more Friendship we shou'd have a better World. But because *Iniquity
abounds*, therefore the *love of many* is not only *waxen cold*, but quite benumb'd and
perish'd. But if we have such narrow hearts, be so full of mistaken Self-love, so
unreasonably fond of our selves, that we cannot spare a hearty Goodwill to one or
two choice Persons, how can it ever be thought, that we shou'd well acquit our selves
of that Charity which is due to all Mankind? For Friendship is nothing else but
Charity contracted; it is (in the words of an admired Author) a kind of revenging our
selves on the narrowness of our Faculties, by exemplifying that extraordinary
Charity on one or two, which we are willing, but not able to exercise towards all.
And therefore 'tis without doubt the best Instructor to teach us our duty to our
Neighbour, and a most excellent Monitor to excite us to make payment as far as our
power will reach... That institution therefore must needs be highly beneficial, which
both disposes us to be Friends our selves and helps to find them. But by Friendship I
do not mean any thing like those intimacies that are abroad in the World, which are
often combinations in evil and at best but insignificant dearnesses, as little resembling true Friendship, as modern Practice does Primitive Christianity. But I intend by
it the greatest usefulness, the most refin'd and disinteress'd Benevolence, a love that
thinks nothing within the bounds of Power and Duty, too much to do or suffer for its
Beloved; And makes no distinction betwixt its Friend and its self, except that in
Temporals it prefers her interest. But tho' it be very desirable to obtain such a
Treasure, such a Medicine of Life as the wise man speaks, yet the danger is great
least being deceiv'd in our choice, we suck in Poyson where we expected Health. And
considering how apt we are to disguise our selves, how hard it is to know our own
hearts much less anothers, it is not advisable to be too hasty in contracting so
important a Relation; before that be done, it were well if we could look into the
very Soul of the beloved Person, to discover what resemblance it bears to our own,
and in this Society we shall have the best opportunities of doing so. There are no
Interests here to serve, no contrivances for another to be a stale to; the Souls of all the
Religious will be open and free, and those particular Friendships must be no
prejudice to the general Amity. [...]

And if after so many Spiritual Advantages, it be convenient to mention Temporals,
here Heiresses and Persons of Fortune may be kept secure from the rude attempts of
designing Men; And she who has more Money than Discretion, need not curse her
Stars for being expos'd a prey to bold importunate and rapacious Vultures. She will
not here be inveigled and impos'd on, will neither be bought nor sold, nor be forc'd
to marry for her own quiet, when she has no inclination to it, but what the being tir'd
out with a restless importunity occasions. Or if she be dispos'd to marry, here she
may remain in safety till a convenient Match be offer'd by her Friends, and be freed
from the danger of a dishonourable one. Modesty requiring that a Woman should
not love before Marriage, but only make choice of one whom she can love hereafter;
She who has none but innocent affections, being easily able to fix them where Duty
requires.

And though at first I propos'd to my self to speak nothing in particular of the employment of the Religious, yet to give a Specimen how useful they will be to the World, I am now inclin'd to declare, that it is design'd a part of their business shall be to give the best Education to the Children of Persons of Quality, who shall be attended and instructed in lesser Matters by meaner Persons deputed to that Office, but the forming of their minds shall be the particular care of those of their own Rank, who cannot have a more pleasant and useful employment than to exercise and encrease their own knowledge, by instilling it into these young ones, who are most like to profit under such Tutors. [...]

And when by the increase of their Revenue, the *Religious* are enabled to do such a work of Charity, the Education they design to bestow on the Daughters of Gentlemen who are fallen into decay will be no inconsiderable advantage to the Nation. For hereby many Souls will be preserv'd from great Dishonours and put in a comfortable way of subsisting, being either receiv'd into the House if they incline to it, or otherwise dispos'd of. It being suppos'd that prudent Men will reckon the endowments they here acquire a sufficient *Dowry*, and that a discreet and vertuous Gentlewoman will make a better Wife than she whose mind is empty tho' her Purse be full. [...]

But the men if they rightly understand their own interest, have no reason to oppose the ingenious Education of the Women, since 'twou'd go a great way towards reclaiming the men, great is the influence we have over them in their Childhood, in which time if a Mother be discreet and knowing as well as devout, she has many opportunities of giving such a *Form* and *Season* to the tender Mind of the Child, as will shew its good effects thro' all the stages of his Life. [...]

There is a sort of Bravery and Greatness of Soul, which does more truly ennoble us than the highest Title, and it consists in living up to the dignity of our Natures, being so sensible of our own worth as to think our selves too great to do a degenerate and unbecoming thing; in passing indifferently thro' Good and Evil Fortune, without being corrupted by the one or deprest by the other. For she that can do so, gives evidence that her Happiness depends not on so mutable a thing as this World; but, in a due subserviency to the Almighty, is bottom'd only on her own great Mind. [...] Whereas a wise and good Woman is useful and valuable in all Ages and Conditions: she who chiefly attends the *one thing needful*, the *good part which shall not be taken from her*, lives a cheerful and pleasant Life, innocent and sedate, calm and tranquil, and makes a glorious Exit; being translated from the most happy life on Earth, to unspeakable happiness in Heaven; a fresh and fragrant Name embalming her Dust, and extending its Perfume to succeeding Ages. Whilst the Fools, and the worst sort of them the wicked, live as well as die in Misery, go out in a snuff, leaving nothing but stench and putrefaction behind them.

To close all, if this *Proposal* which is but a rough draught and rude Essay, and which might be made much more beautiful by a better Pen, give occasion to wiser heads to improve and perfect it, I have my end. For imperfect as it is, it seems so desirable, that she who drew the Scheme is full of hopes, it will not want kind hands to perform and compleat it. But if it miss of that, it is but a few hours thrown away, and a little labour in vain, which yet will not be lost, if what is here offer'd may serve to express her hearty Good-will, and how much she desires your Improvement, who is Ladies, *Your very humble Servant*.

Some Reflections upon Marriage, Occasion'd by the Duke & Duchess of Mazarine's Case; Which is also Consider'd

INTRODUCTION

These Reflections being made in the Country, where the Book that occasion'd them came but late to Hand, the *Reader* is desir'd to excuse their Unseasonableness as well as other Faults; and to believe that they have no other Design than to Correct some Abuses, which are not the less because Power and Prescription seem to Authorize them. If any are so needlessly curious as to enquire from what Hand they come, they may please to know, that it is not good Manners to ask, since the Title-Page does not tell them: We are all of us sufficiently Vain, and without doubt the Celebrated Name of *Author*, which most are so fond of, had not been avoided but for very good Reasons: To name but one; *Who will care to pull upon themselves an Hornet's Nest?* [. . .]

But the *Reflector*, who hopes *Reflector* is not bad English, now Governor is happily of the feminine Gender, had as good or better have said nothing; For People by being forbid, are only excited to a more curious Enquiry [. . .], set out upon the Forlorn Hope, meaning no hurt to any body, nor designing any thing but the Publick Good, and to retrieve, if possible, the Native Liberty, the Rights and Privileges of the Subject.

Far be it from her to stir up Sedition of any sort, none can abhor it more; and she heartily wishes that our Masters wou'd pay their Civil and Ecclesiastical Governors the same Submission, which they themselves extract from their Domestic Subjects. Nor can she imagine how she any way undermines the Masculine Empire, or blows the Trumpet of Rebellion to the Moiety of Mankind. Is it by exhorting Women, not to expect to have their own Will in any thing, but to be entirely Submissive, when once they have made choice of a Lord and Master, tho' he happen not to be so Wise, so Kind, or even so Just a Governor as was expected? She did not indeed advise them to think his Folly Wisdom, nor his Brutality that Love and Worship he promised in his Matrimonial Oath, for this required a Flight of Wit and Sense much above her poor Ability, and proper only to Masculine Understandings. However she did not in any manner prompt them to Resist, or to Abdicate the Perjur'd Spouse, tho' the Laws of GOD and the Land make special Provision for it, in a case wherein, as is to be fear'd, few Men can truly plead Not Guilty.

Tis true, thro' Want of Learning, and of that Superior Genius which Men as Men lay claim to, she was ignorant of the *Natural Inferiority* of our Sex, which our Masters lay down as a Self-Evident and Fundamental Truth. She saw nothing in the Reason of Things, to make this either a Principle or a Conclusion, but much to the contrary; it being Sedition at least, if not Treason to assert it in this Reign. For if by the Natural Superiority of their Sex, they mean that every Man is by Nature superior to every Woman, which is the obvious meaning, and that which must be stuck to if they would speak Sense, it wou'd be a Sin in *any* Woman to have Dominion over *any* Man, and the greatest Queen ought not to command but to obey her Footman, because no Municipal Laws can supersede or change the Law of Nature; so that if the Dominion of the Men be such, the *Salique Law*, as unjust as *English Men* have ever thought it, ought to take place over all the Earth, and the most glorious Reigns in the *English, Danish, Castilian*, and other Annals, were wicked Violations of the Law of Nature!

If they mean that *some* Men are superior to *some* Women, this is no great Discovery; had they turn'd the Tables they might have seen that *some* Women are Superior to *some* Men. Or had they been pleased to remember their Oaths of Allegiance and Supremacy, they might have known that *One* Woman is superior to *All* the Men in these Nations, or else they have sworn to very little purpose. And it must not be suppos'd, that their Reason and Religion wou'd suffer them to take Oaths, contrary to the Law of Nature and Reason of things. [...]

That the Custom of the World has put Women, generally speaking, into a State of Subjection, is not deny'd; but the Right can no more be prov'd from the Fact, than the Predominancy of Vice can justifie it. A certain great Man has endeavour'd to prove by Reasons not contemptible, that in the Original State of things the Woman was the Superior, and that her Subjection to the Man is an Effect of the Fall, and the Punishment of her Sin. And that Ingenious Theorist Mr *Whiston* asserts, That before the Fall there was a greater equality between the two Sexes. However this be 'tis certainly no Arrogance in a Woman to conclude, that she was made for the Service of GOD, and that this is her End. Because GOD made all Things for Himself, and a Rational Mind is too noble a Being to be Made for the Sake and Service of any Creature. The Service she at any time becomes oblig'd to pay to a Man, is only a Business by the Bye. Just as it may be any Man's Business and Duty to keep Hogs; he was not Made for this, but if he hires himself out to such an Employment, he ought conscientiously to perform it. Nor can anything be concluded to the contrary from St. *Paul's* Argument, *I Cor. II* [...]neither from the Gradation the Apostle there uses, that *the Head of every Man is Christ, and that the Head of the Woman is the Man, and the Head of Christ is GOD*; It being evident from the Form of Baptism, that there is no natural Inferiority among the Divine Persons, but that they are in all things Coequal. The Apostle indeed adds, that *the Man is the Glory of God, and the Woman the Glory of the Man*, Etc. But what does he infer from hence? he says not a word of Inequality, or natural Inferiority, but concludes, that a Woman ought to Cover her head, and a Man ought not to cover his, and that *even Nature itself, teaches* us, that *if a Man have long hair it is a shame unto him*. Whatever the Apostle's Argument proves in this place, nothing can be plainer, than that there is much more said against the present Fashion of Men's wearing long Hair, than for that Supremacy they lay claim to. [...]And therefore St *Paul* thought it necessary to reprove them so severely in order to humble them, but this being done, he takes care in the Conclusion to set the matter on a right Foot, placing the two Sexes on a Level, to keep Men as much as might be, from taking those advantages which People who have strength in their hands, are apt to assume over those who can't contend with them. For, says he, *Nevertheless*, or notwithstanding the former Argument, *the Man is not without the Woman, nor the Woman without the Man, but all things of GOD*. The Relation between the two Sexes is mutual, and the Dependance Reciprocal, both of them Depending intirely upon GOD, and upon Him only; which one wou'd think is no great Argument of the natural Inferiority of either Sex. [...]

But what says the Holy Scripture? It speaks of Women as in a State of Subjection, and so it does of the *Jews* and *Christians* when under the Dominion of the *Chaldeans* and *Romans*, requiring of the one as well as of the other a quiet submission to them under whose Power they liv'd. But will any one say that these had a *Natural Superiority* and Right to Dominion? that they had a superior Understanding, or any Pre-eminence, except what their greater Strength acquir'd? Or that the other were subjected to their Adversaries for any other Reason but the Punishment of their sins, and in order to their Reformation? Or for the Exercise of their Vertue, and because the Order of the World and the Good of Society requir'd it?

If Mankind had never sinn'd, Reason wou'd always have been obey'd, there wou'd have been no struggle for Dominion, and Brutal Power wou'd not have prevail'd. But in the laps'd State of Mankind, and now that Men will not be guided by their Reason but by their Appetites, and do not what they *ought* but what they *can*, the Reason, or that which stands for it, the Will and Pleasure of the Governor is to be the Reason of those who will not be guided by their own, and must take place for Order's sake, altho' it shou'd not be conformable to right Reason. [...]So that since Women are acknowledg'd to have least Bodily strength, their being commanded to obey is in pure kindness to them and for their Quiet and Security, as well as for the Exercise of their Vertue. But does it follow that Domestic Governors have more Sense than their Subjects, any more than that other Governors have? We do not find that any Man thinks the worse of his own Understanding because another has superior Power; or concludes himself less capable of a Post of Honour and Authority, because he is not Prefer'd to it. How much time wou'd lie on Men's hands, how empty wou'd the Places of Concourse be, and how silent most Companies, did Men forbear to Censure their Governors, that is in effect to think themselves Wiser. Indeed Government wou'd be much more desirable than it is, did it invest the Possessor with a superior Understanding as well as Power. And if mere Power gives a Right to Rule, there can be no such thing as Usurpation; but a Highway-Man so long as he has strength to force, has also a Right to require our Obedience.

Again, if Absolute Sovereignty be not necessary in a State, how comes it to be so in a Family? or if in a Family why not in a State; since no Reason can be alledg'd for the one that will not hold more strongly for the other? If the Authority of the Husband so far as it extends, is sacred and inalienable, why not of the Prince? The Domestic Sovereign is without Dispute Elected, and the Stipulations and Contract are mutual, is it not then partial in Men to the last degree, to contend for, and practise that Arbitrary Dominion in their Families, which they abhor and exclaim against in the State? For if Arbitrary Power is evil in itself, and an improper Method of Governing Rational and Free Agents, it ought not to be Practis'd any where; Nor is it less, but rather more mischievous in Families than in Kingdoms, by how much 100000 Tyrants are worse than one. What tho' a Husband can't deprive a Wife of Life without being responsible to the Law, he may however do what is much more grievous to a generous Mind, render Life miserable, for which she has no Redress, scarce Pity which is afforded to every other Complainant. It being thought a Wife's Duty to suffer everything without Complaint. *If all Men are born free*, how is it that all Women are born slaves? as they must be if the being subjected to the *inconstant, uncertain, unknown, arbitrary Will* of Men, be the *perfect Condition of Slavery*? and if the Essence of Freedom consists, as our Masters say it does, in having a *standing Rule to live by*? And why is Slavery so much condemn'd and strove against in one Case, and so highly applauded, and held so necessary and so sacred in another?

Tis true that GOD told *Eve* after the Fall that *her Husband shou'd Rule over her*. And so it is that he told *Esau* by the mouth of *Isaac* his Father, that he shou'd serve his *younger Brother*, and shou'd in time, and when he was strong enough to do it, *break the Yoke from off his Neck*. Now why one Text shou'd be a Command any more than the other, and not both of them be Predictions only; or why the former shou'd prove *Adam's* natural Right to Rule, and much less every Man's, any more than the latter is a Proof of *Jacob's* Right to Rule, and of *Esau's* to Rebel, one is yet to learn? The Text in both Cases foretelling what wou'd be; but, in neither of them determining what ought to be. [...]

The World will hardly allow a Woman to say any thing well, unless as she borrows it from Men, or is assisted by them: But GOD Himself allows that the Daughters of *Zelophehad spake right*, and passes their Request into a Law. Considering how much the Tyranny shall I say, or the superior Force of Men, keeps Women from Acting in the World, or doing any thing considerable, and remembring withal the conciseness of the Sacred Story, no small part of it is bestow'd in transmitting the History of Women famous in their Generations: Two of the Canonical Books bearing the Names of those great Women whose Vertues and Actions are there recorded. *Ruth* being call'd from among the *Gentiles* to be an Ancestor of the Messiah, and *Esther* being rais'd up by GOD to be the great Instrument of the Deliverance and Prosperity of the Jewish Church. [...]

However, there are strong and prevalent Reasons which demonstrate the Superiority and Pre-eminence of the Men. For in the first place, Boys have much Time and Pains, Care and Cost bestow'd on their Education, Girls have little or none. The former are early initiated in the Sciences, are made acquainted with Antient and Modern Discoveries, they Study Books and Men, have all imaginable encouragement; not only Fame, a dry Reward now adays, but also Title, Authority, Power, and Riches themselves which purchase all things, are the Reward of their Improvement. The latter are restrain'd, frown'd upon, and beat, not *for* but *from* the Muses; Laughter and Ridicule that never-failing Scare-Crow is set up to drive them from the Tree of Knowledge. But if in spite of all Difficulties Nature prevails, and they can't be kept so ignorant as their Masters wou'd have them, they are star'd upon as Monsters, Censur'd, Envy'd, and every way Discourag'd, or at the best they have the Fate the Proverb assigns them, *Vertue is prais'd and starv'd*. And therefore since the coursest Materials need the most Curing, as every Workman can inform you, and the worst Ground the most elaborate Culture, it undeniably follows, that Men's Understandings are superior to Women's, for after many Years Study and Experience they become Wise and Learned, and Women are not Born so!

Again, Men are possess'd of all Places of Power, Trust and Profit, they make Laws and exercise the Magistracy, not only the sharpest Sword, but even all the Swords and Blunderbusses are theirs, which by the strongest Logic in the World, gives them the best Title to every thing they please to claim as their Prerogative; who shall contend with them? Immemorial Prescription is on their side in these parts of the World, Antient Tradition and Modern Usage! Our Fathers have all along both Taught and Practis'd Superiority over the weaker Sex, and consequently Women are by Nature inferior to Men, as was to be Demonstrated. An Argument which must be acknowledg'd unanswerable, for as well as I love my Sex, I will not pretend a Reply to *such* Demonstration!

Only let me beg to be inform'd, to whom we poor Fatherless Maids, and Widows who have lost their Masters, owe Subjection? It can't be to all Men in general, unless all Men were agreed to give the same Commands; do we then fall as Strays to the first who finds us? By the Maxims of some Men, and the Conduct of some Women one wou'd think so. But whoever he be that thus happens to become our Master, if he allows us to be Reasonable Creatures, and does not merely Compliment us with that Title, since no Man denies our Readiness to use our Tongues, it wou'd tend, I shou'd think, to our Master's advantage, and therefore he may be pleased to be advis'd to teach us to improve our Reason. But if Reason is only allow'd us by way of Raillery, and the secret Maxim is that we have none, or little more than Brutes, 'tis the best way to confine us with Chain and Block to the Chimney-Corner, which probably might save the Estates of some Families and the Honor of others.

I do not propose this to prevent a Rebellion, for Women are not so well united as to form an Insurrection. They are for the most part Wise enough to Love their Chains, and to discern how very becomingly they set. They think as humbly of themselves as their Masters can wish, with respect to the other Sex, but in regard to their own, they have a Spice of Masculine Ambition, every one wou'd Lead, and none will Follow. [...]

To conclude, if that GREAT QUEEN who has subdu'd the Proud, and made the pretended Invincible more than once fly before her; who has Rescu'd an Empire, Reduc'd a Kingdom, Conquer'd Provinces in as little time almost as one can Travel them, and seems to have Chain'd Victory to her Standard; who disposes of Crowns, gives Laws and Liberty to *Europe*, and is the chief Instrument in the Hand of the Almighty to pull down and to set up the Great Men of the Earth; [...] whilst she only reaps for her self the Lawrels of Disinteressed Glory, and the Royal Pleasure of doing Heroically; if this Glory of her own Sex and Envy of the other, will not think we need, or does not hold us worthy of, the Protection of her ever Victorious Arms, and Men have not the Gratitude for her sake at least, to do Justice to her Sex, who has been such a universal Benefactress to theirs: Adieu to the Liberties not of this or that Nation or Region only, but of the Moiety of Mankind! To all the great things that Women might perform, Inspir'd by her Example, Encourag'd by her Smiles, and supported by her Power! To their Discovery of New Worlds for the Exercise of her Goodness, New Sciences to publish her Fame, and reducing Nature itself to a Subjection to her Empire! [...] To the Women's tracing a new Path to Honor, in which none shall walk but such as scorn to Cringe in order to Rise, and who are Proof both against giving and receiving Flattery! In a word, to those Halcyon, or if you will *Millennium* Days, in which the Wolf and the Lamb shall feed together, and a Tyrannous Domination which Nature never meant, shall no longer render useless if not hurtful, the Industry and Understandings of half Mankind!

SOME REFLECTIONS UPON MARRIAGE

Curiosity, which is sometimes an occasion of Good, and too frequently of Mischief, by disturbing either our Own, or our Neighbour's Repose, having put me upon reading the *Duke and Dutchess* of Mazarine's *Case*; I thought an Afternoon wou'd not be quite thrown away in pursuing some Reflections that it occasion'd. The Name of *Mazarine* is considerable enough to draw the Eyes of the Curious, and when one remembers what a noise it once made in *Europe*, what Politick Schemes have been laid, what vast Designs brought about by the Cardinal that bore it; how well his measures were concerted for the Grandeur of that Nation into which he was transplanted, and that he wanted neither Power nor Inclination to establish his own Family and make it as considerable as any Subject's could possibly be, and what Honours and Riches he had heap'd together in order to this; one cannot but enquire how it comes about that he should be so defeated in this last design? and that those to whom he intrusted his Name and Treasure, should make a figure so very different from what might have been expected from them? [...]

The Dutchess of *Mazarine's* Name has spread perhaps as far as her Uncle's and one can't help wishing that so much Wit and Beauty, so much Politeness and Address, has been accompany'd and supported by more valuable and lasting Qualities; one cannot but desire that her Advocate instead of recriminating had clear'd the imputations laid on her, and that she her self, who says enough in her Memoirs to shew she was unfortunate, had said more to prove her self-discreet [...] she who was capable of being a great Ornament to her Family and Blessing to the Age she liv'd in, should only serve (to say no worse) as an unhappy Shipwrack to point out the dangers of an ill Education and unequal Marriage.

Monsieur *Mazarine* is not to be justified, nor Madam his Spouse excus'd. It is no question which is most Criminal, the having no Sense, or the abuse of a liberal Portion; nor any hard matter to determine who is most to be pity'd, he whom Nature never qualify'd for great things, who therefore can't be very sensible of great Misfortunes; or she, who being capable of every thing must therefore suffer more and be the more lamented. To be yok'd for Life to a disagreeable Person and Temper; to have Folly and Ignorance tyrannize over Wit and Sense; to be contradicted in every thing one does or says, and bore down not by Reason but Authority; to be denied ones most innocent desires, for no other cause but the Will and Pleasure of an absolute Lord and Master, whose Follies a Woman with all her Prudence cannot hide, and whose Commands she cannot but despise at the same time she obeys them; is a misery none can have a just Idea of, but those who have felt it. [...]

Had *Madam Mazarine's* Education made a right Improvement of her Wit and Sense, we should not have found her seeking Relief by such imprudent, not to say scandalous Methods, as the running away in Disguise with a spruce Cavalier, and rambling to so many Courts and Places, nor diverting her self with such Childish, Ridiculous, or Ill-natur'd Amusements, as the greatest part of the Adventures in her Memoirs are made up of. [...]

A Woman who seeks Consolation under Domestic troubles from the Gaieties of a Court, from Gaming and Courtship, from Rambling and odd Adventures, and the Amusements mixt Company affords, may Plaister up the Sore, but will never heal it; nay, which is worse, she makes it Fester beyond a possibility of Cure. She justifies the Injury her Husband has done her, by shewing that whatever other good Qualities she may have, Discretion, one of the Principal, is wanting. [...]

But Madam *Mazarine* is dead, may her Faults die with her; may there be no more occasion given for the like Adventures, or if there is, may the Ladies be more Wise and Good than to take it! Let us see then from whence the mischief proceeds, and try if it can be prevented; for certainly Men may be very happy in a Married State; 'tis their own fault if they are at any time otherwise. [...]

The Christian Institution of Marriage provides the best that may be for Domestic Quiet and Content, and for the Education of Children; so that if we were not under the tye of Religion, even the Good of Society and civil Duty would oblige us to what that requires at our Hands. [...]

But if Marriage be such a blessed State, how comes it, may you say, that there are so few happy Marriages? Now in answer to this, it is not to be wonder'd that so few succeed, we should rather be surpriz'd to find so many do, considering how imprudently Men engage, the Motives they act by, and the very strange Conduct they observe throughout.

For pray, what do Men propose to themselves in Marriage? What Qualifications do they look after in a Spouse? What will she bring is the first enquiry? How many Acres? Or how much ready Coin? Not that this is altogether an unnecessary Question, for Marriage without a Competency, that is, not only a bare Subsistence, but even a handsome and plentiful Provision, according to the Quality and Circumstances of the Parties, is no very comfortable Condition. They who marry for Love as they call it, find time enough to repent their rash Folly, and are not long in being convinc'd, that whatever fine Speeches might be made in the heat of Passion, there could be no *real Kindness* between those who can agree to make each other miserable. But as an Estate is to be consider'd, so it should not be the *Main*, much less the *Only* consideration, for Happiness does not depend on Wealth, *that* may be wanting, and too often is, where *this* abounds. He who Marries himself to a Fortune only, must expect no other satisfaction than that can bring him [...]

Thus, whether it be Wit or Beauty that a Man's in Love with, there's no great hopes of a lasting Happiness; Beauty with all the helps of Art is of no long date, the more it is help'd the sooner it decays, and he who only or chiefly chose for Beauty, will in a little time find the same reason for another Choice. Nor is that sort of Wit which he prefers of a more sure tenure, or allowing it to last, it will not always please. For that which has not a real excellency and value in it self, entertains no longer than the giddy Humour which recommended it to us holds; and when we can like on no just, or on very little Ground, tis certain a dislike will arise, as lightly and as unaccountably. And it is not improbable that such a Husband may in a little time by ill usage provoke such a Wife to exercise her Wit, that is, her Spleen on him, and then it is not hard to guess how very agreeable it will be to him. [...]

But do the Women never chuse amiss? Are the Men only in fault? that is not pretended; for he who will be just, must be forc'd to acknowledge, that neither Sex are always in the right. A Woman indeed can't properly be said to Choose, all that is allow'd her, is to Refuse or Accept what is offer'd. [...]

What then is to be done? How must a Man chuse, and what Qualities must encline a Woman to accept, that so our Marry'd couple may be as happy as that State can make them? This is no hard Question; let the Soul be principally consider'd, and regard had in the first Place to a good Understanding, a Vertuous Mind, and in all other respects let there be as much equality as may be. [...]

But how can a Man respect his Wife when he has a contemptible Opinion of her and her Sex? When from his own Elevation he looks down on them as void of Understanding, and full of Ignorance and Passion, so that Folly and a Woman are equivalent Terms with him? Can he think there is any Gratitude due to her whose utmost services he exacts as strict Duty? Because she was made to be a Slave to his Will, and has no higher end than to Serve and Obey him! Perhaps we arrogate too much to our selves when we say this Material World was made for our sakes; that its Glorious Maker has given us the use of it is certain, but when we suppose a thing to be made purely for our sakes, because we have Dominion over it, we draw a false Conclusion, as he who shou'd say the People were made for the Prince who is set over them, wou'd be thought to be out of his Senses as well as his Politicks. [...]

But how can a Woman scruple intire Subjection, how can she forbear to admire the worth and excellency of the Superior Sex, if she at all considers it? Have not all the great Actions that have been perform'd in the World been done by Men? Have not they founded Empires and overturn'd them? Do not they make Laws and continually repeal and amend them? Their vast Minds lay Kingdoms wast, no bounds or measures can be prescrib'd to their Desires. War and Peace depend on them, they form Cabals and have the Wisdom and Courage to get over all the Rubs which may lie in the way of their desired Grandeur. What is it they cannot do? They make Worlds and ruine them, form Systems of universal nature and dispute eternally about them; their Pen gives worth to the most trifling Controversie; nor can a fray be inconsiderable if they have drawn their Swords in't. All that the wise Man pronounces is an Oracle, and every Word the Witty speaks a Jest. It is a Woman's Happiness to hear, admire and praise them, especially if a little Ill-nature keeps them at any time from bestowing due Applauses on each other! And if she aspires no further, she is thought to be in her proper Sphere of Action, she is as wise and as good as can be expected from her!

She then who Marrys ought to lay it down for an indisputable Maxim, that her Husband must govern absolutely and intirely, and that she has nothing else to do but to Please and Obey. She must not attempt to divide his Authority, or so much as dispute it, to struggle with her Yoke will only make it gall the more, but must believe him Wise and Good and in all respects the best, at least he must be so to her. She who can't do this is no way fit to be a Wife, she may set up for that peculiar Coronet the ancient Fathers talk'd of, but is not qualify'd to receive that great reward, which attends the eminent exercise of Humility and Self-denial, Patience and Resignation, the Duties that a Wife is call'd to.

But some refractory Woman perhaps will say, how can this be? Is it possible for her to believe him Wise and Good who by a thousand Demonstrations convinces her and all the World of the contrary? Did the bare Name of Husband confer Sense on a Man, and the mere being in Authority infallibly qualifie him for Government, much might be done. But since a wise Man and a Husband are not Terms convertible, and how loth soever one is to own it, Matter of Fact won't allow us to deny, that the Head many times stands in need of the Inferior's Brains to manage it, she must beg leave to be excus'd from such high thoughts of her Sovereign, and if she submits to his Power, it is not so much Reason as Necessity that compels her.

Now of how little force soever this Objection may be in other respects, methinks it is strong enough to prove the necessity of a good Education, and that Men never mistake their true Interest more than when they endeavour to keep Women in Ignorance. Cou'd they indeed deprive them of their Natural good Sense at the same time they deny them the due improvement of it, they might compass their End; otherwise Natural Sense unassisted may run in to a false Track and serve only to punish him justly, who wou'd not allow it to be useful to himself or others. [...]

To wind up this matter, if a Woman were duly Principled and Taught to know the World, especially the true Sentiments that Men have of her, and the Traps they lay for her under so many gilded Compliments, and such a seemingly great Respect, that disgrace wou'd be prevented which is brought upon too many Families, Women would Marry more discreetly, and demean themselves better in a Married State than some People say they do. The foundation indeed ought to be laid deep and strong, she shou'd be made a good Christian and understand why she is so, and then she will be everything else that is Good. Men need keep no Spies on a Woman's Conduct, need have no fear of her Vertue, or so much as of her Prudence and Caution, were but a due sense of true Honour and Vertue awaken'd in her, were her Reason excited and prepar'd to consider the Sophistry of those Temptations which wou'd perswade her from her Duty; and were she put in a way to know that it is both her Wisdom and Interest to observe it; She would then duly examine and weigh all the Circumstances, the Good and Evil of a Married State, and not be surpriz'd with unforeseen Inconveniences, and either never consent to be a Wife, or make a good one when she does. This would shew her what Human Nature is, as well as what it *ought* to be, and teach her not only what she may justly expect, but what she must be Content with; would enable her to cure some Faults, and patiently to suffer what she cannot cure. [...]

Again, it may be said, if a Wife's case be as it is here represented, it is not good for a Woman to Marry, and so there's an end of [the] Human Race. But this is no fair Consequence, for all that can justly be inferr'd from hence, is that a Woman has no mighty Obligations to the Man who makes Love to her, she has no reason to be fond of being a Wife, or to reckon it a piece of Preferment when she is taken to be a Man's Upper-Servant; it is no advantage to her in this World, if rightly manag'd it may prove one as to the next. For she who Marries purely to do Good, to Educate Souls for Heaven, who can be so truly mortify'd as to lay aside her own Will and Desires, to pay such as intire Submission for Life, to one whom she cannot be sure will always deserve it, does certainly perform a more Heroic Action than all the famous Masculine Heroes can boast of, she suffers a continual Martyrdom to bring Glory to GOD and Benefit to Mankind, which consideration indeed may carry her through all Difficulties, I know not what else can, and engage her to Love him who proves perhaps so much worse than a Brute, as to make this Condition yet more grievous than it needed to be. She has need of a strong Reason, of a truly Christian and well-temper'd Spirit, of all the Assistance the best Education can give her, and ought to have some good assurance of her own Firmness and Vertue, who ventures on such a Trial; and for this Reason 'tis less to be wonder'd at that Women Marry off in hast, for perhaps if they took time to consider and reflect upon it, they seldom wou'd Marry.

To conclude, perhaps I've said more than most Men will thank me for, I cannot help it, for how much soever I may be their Friend and humble Servant, I am more a Friend to Truth. Truth is strong, and sometime or other will prevail, nor is it for their Honour, and therefore one wou'd think not for their Interest, to be Partial to themselves and Unjust to others. They may fancy I have made some discoveries which like *Arcana Imperii*, ought to be kept secret, but in good earnest, I do them more Honour than to suppose their lawful Prerogatives need any mean Arts to support them. If they have Usurpt, I love Justice too much to wish Success and continuance to Usurpations, which tho' submitted to out of Prudence, and for Quietness sake, yet leave every Body free to regain their lawful Right whenever they have Power and Opportunity. I don't say that Tyranny *ought*, but we find in *Fact*, that it provokes the Oppress'd to throw off even a Lawful Yoke that sits too heavy: And if he who is freely Elected, after all his fair Promises and the fine Hopes he rais'd, proves a Tyrant, the consideration that he was one's own Choice, will not render more Submissive and Patient, but I fear more Refractory. For tho' it is very unreasonable, yet we see 'tis the course of the World, not only to return Injury for Injury, but Crime for Crime; both Parties indeed are Guilty, but the Aggressors have a double Guilt, they have not only their own, but their Neighbours ruin to answer for.

As to the Female Reader, I hope she will allow I've endeavour'd to do her Justice, nor betray'd her Cause as her Advocates usually do, under pretence of defending it. A Practice too mean for any to be Guilty of who have the least Sense of Honour, and who do any more than meerly pretend to it. I think I have held the Ballance even, and not being conscious of Partiality I ask no Pardon for it. To plead for the Oppress'd and to defend the Weak seem'd to me a generous undertaking; for tho' it may be secure, 'tis not always Honourable to run over to the strongest party. And if she infers from what has been said that Marriage is a very Happy State for Men, if they think fit to make it so; that they govern the World, they have Prescription on their side, Women are too weak to dispute it with them, therefore they, as all other Governours, are most, if not only accountable, for what's amiss, for whether other Governments in their Original, were or were not confer'd according to the Merit of the Person, yet certainly in this case, if Heaven has appointed the Man to Govern, it has qualify'd him for it: So far I agree with her. But if she goes on to infer, that therefore if a Man has not these Qualifications where is his Right? That if he misemploys, he abuses it? And if he abuses, according to modern Deduction, he forfeits it, I must leave her there. A peaceable Woman indeed will not carry it so far, she will neither question her Husband's Right nor his Fitness to Govern; but how? Not as an absolute Lord and Master, with an Arbitrary and Tyrannical sway, but as Reason Governs and Conducts a Man, by proposing what is Just and Fit. And the Man who acts according to that Wisdom he assumes, who wou'd have that Superiority he pretends to, acknowledg'd Just, will receive no Injury by any thing that has been offer'd here. A Woman will value him the more who is so Wise and Good, when she discerns how much he excels the rest of his noble Sex; the less he requires, the more will he Merit that Esteem and Deference, which those who are so forward to exact, seem conscious they don't deserve. So then the Man's Prerogative is not at all infring'd, whilst the Woman's Privileges are secur'd; and if any Woman think her self Injur'd, she has a Remedy in reserve which few Men will Envy or endeavour to Rob her of, the Exercise and Improvement of her Vertue here, and the Reward of it hereafter.

An Impartial Enquiry into the Causes of Rebellion and Civil War

It was not till *Feb.* 27 that I met with Dr *Kennet's* Sermon.[1] Having heard it much commended, and finding it in a second Edition, I was inclined to Read, and for the same reasons to make some Remarks upon it. [...]

The Design of his Sermon and Enquiry, is, as it ought to be, to remove the *cursed Causes* of our Civil War, whatever they were, *and to prevent the like fatal Effects for the future*; which is the best way we know of *to attone for the past Iniquities*. The *leading Causes of this days Evil, improv'd by wicked Arts and Designs, were five*, according to the Doctor's Computation, tho' in reality all may be reduc'd to the

French Interest and *Alliance*, especially if you join to it *the Apprehensions and Fears of Popery thence arising*; for these *led on the Jealousies of Oppression and Illegal Power, which tended more and more to*, and *help'd to* produce the other two. So that upon the matter, the *French Alliance*, at least with the Fears of Popery attending it, was, in his account, the main Cause of the Civil Wars: and so the Dr. makes it expresly the rest being only a chain of Effects proceeding from it. [...]

But sure we of this Age, who have this dismal Tragedy so fresh in our Memories, must be the greatest Fools in nature, if we suffer our selves to be bubbled any more by Men of the same Principles, and by the same Artifices so often detected, and so justly abhorr'd. Have we not had Warnings enough to beware of those Miscreants, who set whole Nations on fire, only that their own despicable selves may be talk'd of, and that they may warm them at the Flame? Men who are equally ruinous to Prince and People, who effectually destroy the Liberties of the Subject under pretence of defending them; who bring in Popery, for they act by some of the very worst Popish Principles, whilst they rail against it! [...]

And, what was the thing they aim'd at, and at last unhappily effected? What but the Ruin of the Government in Church and State? The bringing *the Necks* of their Fellow Subjects, *Englishmen*, who *had the Spirit of a Free People!* under their own infamous *Yoke*, and *their Feet into* the most reproachful *Chains*, becoming themselves the Actors of those Arbitrary and Illegal Actions, which they had so loudly, and in great measure, falsly imputed to their Lawful Superiours. And the *Freeborn* People of *England*, for all their *Spirit of Honour and Genius to Liberty*, even those great *Fore-Fathers*, whose *Off-spring we are*, had the *disdain of serving* in the most slavish manner, and of wearing the heavy and shameful *Yoke* of some of the vilest of their Fellow Subjects: Till GOD was pleas'd to restore our Monarch, and with him the Exercise of our Religion, and the Liberties of the *English* Nation. But this is a common Story, which every body knows, and therefore the Doctor wou'd not lose his time upon't; only in my mind, and whatever might be in his, methinks the whole course of his Sermon inculcates this necessary Lesson, Beware of every one who wou'd draw you into *a necessity* of *believing*, that your *Liberties and Estates are in some danger*, who wou'd give you such a *Prospect*, and work you into such a *Persuasion*, and so draw you in by the old Cant of *Self-Preservation*, tho' they seem to demonstrate ever so great a *necessity*: Much more ought you to abhor being *drawn in* by the bare *meaning* of it, at least if you have any regard to real Self-Preservation, and think your Souls of greater moment than your Lives or Estates. Nay, even for the very Preservation of these Dear Lives of yours, since, if you dare believe our Lord himself, the surest way to save your Lives is to be ready to part with them; and the most likely way to lose them, is this unchristian Desire of saving them (St. *Matth.*, 8. 35.). For such Arts as those, the putting such *Thoughts* into the Heads of the *Good-natur'd English People*, was that which *seduc'd them into that Unnatural Rebellion*, which has had so many dismal Effects upon this Nation. [...]

Upon those Principles by which the Martyr lost his Head; since a good-natur'd People are prone to Compassion, and the Beheading of a King at his own Palace Gate, is so shocking an Action that Men can't but detest all the ways and means that tended thereunto; since the Memory of this is reviv'd every Year by a Solemnity; and which is yet worse, since my Lord *Clarendon* has so unluckily display'd the whole Contrivance, so that Men can't renew those Methods without being observ'd and countermin'd; and yet it may often happen to be necessary for a Man's Affairs to bring about a Revolution, either to piece his broken Fortunes, or to gratify his Ambition or Revenge, or to restore himself to the Posts he formerly enjoy'd, or for which he thinks himself best qualified; and tho' when a Prince does any irregular or disobliging Action this may be a good Pretence, yet a *Civil War* may be *indeed begun more out of Hatred to a Party,* who are, or who we fear may be uppermost, than out of *any Dissatisfaction* to the Prince: for these, and no doubt for other Reasons, 'tis highly necessary, the *Truth* which we have taught of late, the *Justice* we have practis'd, and *Charity,* which always begins at home, taking care in the first place to make our own Fortunes, are all of them nearly concern'd to keep this Fundamental Right in the Peoples view, *viz.* 'That Power is originally from the People, and that Princes are responsible to them for the exercise thereof.' The People must ever and anon be reminded as plainly as we dare, and as Prudence, the Humour of the Times, and the Service of the Cause will permit; that this Right has often been exercis'd; that there are many Precedents, or that the Suspicion, the very *Thought and Dread of Popery, Oppression, and Illegal Power,* the very *Prospect* that *their Liberties and Estates were in some Danger,* have drawn in their great Forefathers to stand upon their Guard, *meaning Self-preservation,* and that Princes, how sacred soever they be, must not think to *attempt* upon the Liberties of a Free People, without *bringing down Ruin and Confusion upon themselves.* [...]

Further, If it can be prov'd or insinuated, that King *Charles* I. deserv'd what he suffer'd, or at least that he gave too *just Occasion* for it, (for when one treats of Causes and Effects, it's usual to trace them up to the last Link, and fix there) this will make Princes cautious what *Counsels* they fall into, or what Ministers they use. Since *it is possible* (we have had more than one fatal Experiment) *that the Influence of others may bring a Suspicion upon Princes, when they themselves are Innocent; and in many Cases, a Suspicion artfully improv'd, shall work up as much Mischief as the real Guilt wou'd do.* 'Tis best therefore for Princes to be always Gracious to that Party which is apt to suspect, to imploy these, if they mean to fit quiet in their Thrones, so long at least, as till these Suspectors found greater Interest in removing them. For the other dull Souls, who are not apt to suspect, who are fitter for a *Yoke,* and not so uneasie under it, will rest contented.

Perhaps some *Few,* who want a *better Mind,* may *misapprehend* all This, improve it to *unreasonable Scandal, and industriously spread their Calumnies thro' all the Town,* as if this Doctrine were destructive of Government, and wou'd make the best Princes uneasie in it. But the Doctor has sufficiently provided against this, he has done Justice to the Martyr's Memory, in giving a fair Character of his Personal Vertues, and letting us know, that he meant well. He calls the *Civil War the Great Rebellion;* and the Murther of the King, *that Horrid Fact committed on the Lord's Anointed;* and we must not think so ill of the Reader's Understanding, as not to suppose him able to reconcile all this. But besides, the Doctor has laid in a sufficient Antidote against the Poison of Rebellious Principles, by the great Zeal he expresses *against Popery, that irreconcilable Enemy, not only to our Reform'd Faith and Worship, but to our Civil Rights, and Liberties, and Properties, to our Establish'd Laws, and to all our settled Constitution:* And by his Prayers, and earnest Endeavours, to keep it at a distance from us. [...]

But as Mr. *Foulis (History of the Popish Treasons and Usurpations)* very honestly tells us, 'If we allow that People may lawfully Rebel against Princes, and at the same time be Judges of the justness of the Reason; to be in Authority will be a Slavery, the Word Monarch absolute Nonsense, the King oblig'd to obey every man's Passion and

Folly; nor Peace nor Justice can be expected, the Nation being in a perpetual Hurly-burly every other day, as of late times, new Magistrates starting up by Strength of Policy: and he that's still uppermost of this *Leap-frog* Government, will extort Obedience, confirm'd by Oaths, from his suppos'd Subjects, which will ruin the Honest, and damn the rest with Perjury. Change, as a Novelty, at first is rather a Pleasure than Gain to the People, and at last a Burden and Ruin; and what a Factious People once resolve on, they will never want pretence of Reason, themselves being Judges.' – Certain I am, that Christian Religion does no where allow Rebellion; and if a Heathen and a Christian (*a Papist or a Protestant*) do the same Fault, it is not the Unbelief (*or Errors*) of the former, that makes him more wicked in the Act than the Religion of the latter; and he that bawls out the Liberty of Conscience and Loss of Religion to vindicate his Rebellion, has too much of Atheism in him, to be a true Christian. He is not indeed a Christian, and least of all the most Reform'd and Perfect Christian, who makes "that which shou'd have no Arms but Prayers and Tears, a Pretence to prove the Devil a Saint, and Treason an Article of Faith". [...]

And since our Constitution lodges the Legislative Power in the Prince and the Three Estates assembled in Parliament; as it is not in the Power of the Prince and one of the Houses, to Make or Abrogate any Law, without the Concurrence of the other House, so neither can it be Lawfully done by the Prince alone, or by the two Houses without the Prince. All such pretended Acts, and all the Consequences of them, being illegal and Void in themselves, without the Formality of a Repeal, as is evident to every honest Man, if he will but attend to common Sense, plain *English*, and the unalterable Reason of things. I hope then we shall hear no more of the People's Supremacy till these Good Men have got *the Act of Uniformity* Repeal'd. But, alas, what do Laws signifie to Rebels, who have Power to Break or Cunning to Evade them! For all sides must allow, that there are even yet many other Good Laws in force, which sufficiently condemn those Principles and Practices in which they glorys. [...]

But enough of this, which has no *meaning* but to shew, That King *Charles* I. did not Match with *France* against the Genius and Inclinations of his People: Neither did the King receive any Aid or Assistance from the *French* Interest, as the Doctor wou'd have us believe, but it is evident, that his Rebellious Subjects did; *Pym* himself being a *French* Pensioner; and the *Scots*, who were the first Incendiaries, keeping a Correspondence with *France*, and receiving Directions and Assistance from *Richelieu*.

Popery was the Cry 'tis true, but the Establish'd Church was the thing aim'd at; 'twas this they covenanted to destroy Root and Branch: The Tumults began with *No Bishops, No Bishops*, then no *Common Prayer*; and when they had the King at their Mercy, nothing wou'd satisfie them but *a course for attaining the just Ends*, (as they call'd them) *express'd in the solemn League and Covenant*; that is, the pulling down the Church, and the depriving the King of all his just and legal Rights. Nor wou'd even this have satisfy'd them, without the Destruction of his Person: And for what Reason? but because *they consider'd what themselves might suffer, if he shou'd come to Reign again*, as their own Historian *May* himself confesseth, saith my Author. Their Guilt indeed, was a strong and well-grounded *Apprehension*: But who might they thank for it? It was this that wou'd not suffer them to be quiet, when the King had redress'd all their pretended Grievances, mov'd every Shadow of Oppression, and granted them all that they had the confidence to ask.

The short is; The true and the principal Cause of that Great Rebellion, and that Horrid Fact which compleated it, and which we can never enough deplore, was this: Some Cunning and Self-ended Men, whose Wickedness was equal to their Craft, and their Craft sufficient to carry them thro' their Wickedness; these had *Thoughts* and *Meanings* to destroy the Government in Church and State, and to set up a Model of their own Invention, agreeable to their own private Interests and Designs, under the specious Pretences of the Peoples Rights and Liberties. They did not indeed speak out, and declare this at first, for that wou'd have spoil'd the Intrigue, every body wou'd have abhorr'd them; but a little Discernment might have found what they drove at. For to lessen and incroach upon the Royal Authority, is the only way to null it by degrees, as an ingenious Person observes upon this Occasion. [...]

If *Doubts* and *Suspicions*, a *Thought*, a *necessity of Believing*, a *Prospect* and *Persuasion*, a *Meaning* of *Self-Preservation*, or even Self-Preservation, when Life is really in Danger, can lessen the Guilt of this *Unnatural Rebellion*, and all the *Horrid Facts* it produc'd; what will they not excuse! He who robs upon the High-Way, has his *Prospects*, and *Persuasions*, and *Necessities*; and when he resists the Officers of Justice, he only *means Self-Preservation*. [...]

In the Name of Wonder, what do these People mean, who are at present so loud against Popery and Arbitrary Power! Tho' 'tis indeed no Wonder, for their Meaning is too plain and evident! When their Prince was not only in a League with some of the most rigid and persecuting Popish Princes, but even with the Pope himself: When Mass was as public, and as much frequented, as in any King's Reign since the Reformation, scarce excepting King *James* the Second's; when there were more perverted to the Romish Religion, and more considerable Persons, than were even in the Reign of a declar'd Papist, excepting those Worthy Patriots, who Apostatiz'd from GOD, to qualifie themselves to betray their King the more effectually; When our Protestant Religion and *English* Liberties were defended by Popish Hands, with Protestant Swords in them! then not a Fear, not a word of the Danger of Popery!

As little did we hear of *Illegal Acts* and *Arbitrary Power*, of *Oppression* and *Persecution*, in a Reign that tugg'd hard for a Standing Army in time of Peace; that had Interest to suspend the *Habeas Corpus* Act several times, tho' it be the great Security of the *English* Liberties; that outed 7 or 8 Reverend Prelates, the Ornament and Glory of the *English* Church, besides several of the inferiour Clergy, and Members of the Universities, and that only for *Conscience sake*, and because they cou'd not swallow such new Oaths, as they believ'd to be contrary to the old ones: And tho' 12 of them were thought so deserving, that there was a Provision made in their Favour, even by that Act that depriv'd them of their Freeholds and Subsistance, of their Rights as *English-men* and Ministers of GOD's Church, yet not one of them enjoy'd, in that Human, Charitable and Religious Reign! the Advantages which the *Body of the Good-natur'd* English *People* design'd them. [...]

But no sooner was her Majesty happily plac'd in the Throne of her Father, thro' GOD's great and most seasonable Mercy to an unworthy People, but all the old Clamours are reviv'd, tho' she has done nothing to Provoke, but every thing to Oblige them! Tho' her only fault, if Duty and Respect will allow that Expression, consists in too much of the Royal Martyr's Clemency and Goodness; Her Majesty's Reign having left us nothing to wish, but that she had less of K. *Charles* and more of the Spirit of Q. *Elizabeth*, since a Factious People can no way be kept in bounds, but by a sprightly and vigorous Exertion of just Authority. And what's the Reason of the present Clamours? What but that the Faction know that the Queen has an *English*

Heart; that she was not only Educated in our Episcopal Church, but that her Judgment confirms her in it; she is the Royal Martyr's Grand-daughter, the Lineal Heir of his Crowns and Vertues, and they have no hopes that she will betray the Church, under pretence of Defending it; which are Causes enow to alarm the Party! But sad Experience has taught us to decypher their Gibberish! we know too well, that in their Dialect *Popery* stands for the *Church of England*; the *Just* and *Legal Rights* of an English Monarch are call'd *Arbitrary Power*; by the *Privileges* of either *House*, they mean such exorbitant Power as may enable them to *Tyrannize* over their Fellow Subjects, nay over their very Sovereign; *Liberty of the People*, in their Language, signifies an unbounded Licentiousness, whereby they take upon them, whenever they think fit, to Oppose, or even to Remove their Governours, provided they are strong enough to compass their wicked purpose; and to be reproach'd by them for being in a *French Interest*, signifies neither more nor less, than to be a faithful Subject, able to smell out their Plots, and to counterwork their pernicious Designs.

To come then to account for the Causes of our deplorable Civil Wars, we may be allow'd to do it in this manner: Tho' Government is absolutely necessary for the Good of Mankind, yet no Government, no not that of GOD himself, can suit with their deprav'd and boundless Appetites. Few govern themselves by Reason, and they who transgress its Laws, will always find somewhat or other to be uneasie at, and consequently will ever desire, and as far as they can endeavour, to change their Circumstances. But since there are more Fools in the World than Wise Men, and even among those who pass for Wise, that is, who have Abilities to be truly so, too many abuse and warp their Understandings to petty and evil Designs, and to such Tricks and Artifices as appear the readiest way to attain them. Since Riches and Power are what Men covet, supposing these can procure them all they wish; Hopes to gain more, or at least to secure what one has, will always be a handle by which Humane Nature may be mov'd, and carry'd about as the cunning Manager pleases. And therefore of *Necessity* in all Civil Wars and Commotions, there must be some Knaves at the Head of a great many Fools, whom the other wheedle and cajole with many plausible Pretences, according to the Opportunity, and the Humour of those they manage. These are made to believe strange things of their Governours and their Arbitrary Designs, which wou'd surely take effect, did not the Prudence and Industry of those vigilant Patriots disappoint them. They discover Plots which themselves have made; they give up Liberties upon a valuable consideration, and when time shall serve, know how to procure to themselves the Honour of Retrieving them. And what do they ask of the People for all this Care and Trouble, and Public Spirit? only to stand by and assist them; to follow where they lead, and to depend upon their Wisdom and Honesty with an implicit Confidence? For they, good Men, are incapable of ill Intentions or selfish Designs! no, the Liberty of the People, and Good of the Nation, is all they contend for! Now under this *Prospect* and *Persuasion*, must not the People of *necessity* be drawn in, for *Self-Preservation*, and to support these fair Speakers! [...]

I will not pretend to justifie all the Actions of our Princes, but it is much more Difficult; nay, it is impossible to justifie, or honestly excuse the Behaviour of our People towards them. Tyranny and Oppression are no doubt a grievance; they are so to the Prince, as well as to the Subject. Nor shou'd I think a Prince wou'd fall into them, unless seduc'd by some of his Flattering Courtiers and Ambitious Ministers; and therefore our Law very Reasonably provides, that these, and these only, shou'd suffer for it. But are Sedition and Rebellion no Grievances? they are not less, perhaps more Grievous than Tyranny, even to the People; for they expose us to the Oppression of a multitude of Tyrants. And as *we here in this Nation* may have suffer'd by the former, so have we oftner and much more grievously by the latter. The accursed Roots of which are I fear still left among us, and there are but too many wicked ones who cultivate these Tares with the utmost Arts and Industry. May GOD inspire the Heart of his Vicegerent with the Spirit of Courage and Understanding, to restrain and keep under *all such workers of Iniquity, as turn Religion into Rebellion, and Faith into Faction.* That so She may never leave it in their power to prevail either against her Royal Person or her Good and Faithful Subjects, *or to triumph in the Ruin of GOD's Church* among us; seeing they have not fail'd upon occasion to give us [too] evident Proof, that when they have the Power to hurt, they never want the Inclination.

Note

1   In this pamphlet Astell is referring to a sermon given on the occasion of the anniversary of the execution of King Charles I, published as: White Kennett, *A Compassionate Enquiry into the Causes of the Civil War. In a Sermon Preached in the Church of St Botolph Aldgate, On January 31, 1704, the Day of the Fast of the Martyrdom of King Charles the First* (London, 1704).

The *Christian Religion,* As Profess'd by a DAUGHTER of the Church of *England* (Extracts)

SECTION 5: WOMEN AS WELL AS MEN

If GOD had not intended that Women shou'd use their Reason, He wou'd not have given them any, 'for He does nothing in vain.' If they are to use their Reason, certainly it ought to be employ'd about the noblest Objects, and in business of the greatest Consequence, therefore in Religion. That our God-fathers and God-mothers answer'd for us at the Font, was an act of Charity in them, and will be a great Benefit to us if we make a right use of it; but it will be *our* Condemnation if we are Christians merely upon this account, for that only can be imputed to a free Agent which is done with Understanding and Choice. A Christian Woman therefore must not be a *Child in Understanding*; she must serve GOD with *Understanding* as well as with *Affection*, must *love Him with all her Mind and Soul*, as well as *with all her Heart and Strength*; in a word, must perform *a reasonable Service* if she means to be acceptable to her Maker.

SECTION 139: THE ACCOUNT OF LOVE IN THAT DISCOURSE IS INCONSISTENT WITH THE LOVE OF ENEMIES, PARTICULARLY OF A PERSECUTOR

Suppose our Enemy is a Persecutor, and does invade that *Fundamental, Sacred and unalterable Law of Self- preservation*, as some call it, Persecution is *no way desirable* to us according to their Principles, and much less the Persecutor; so that *it is manifestly impossible and [contradictory] that we shou'd rejoice and take complaisance in him.* Now if we *Love our Neighbour as our selves, their Being and Well-being must necessarily be desirable to us.* But the Being and much less the Well-being of a Persecutor can't be desirable. A Persecutor who wou'd deprive us of our dear and desirable Estates, Offices and Employments, our dearer Lives perhaps, (over which we our selves *have no power*, therefore how shou'd he come by't, tho' we invested him with all the power we had, on condition he kept his compact?) and as we *say*, our dearest Religion! It is therefore utterly impossible, if the former Principles be true, and contrary to the Nature of things, to Love a Persecutor. We may wish him so well indeed, as to deprive him of the power to Persecute, we may tye his hands, or to make sure, work, throw him out if we are able, in great kindness to him and in a little to our selves without question! But none of this is Love, for according to our Author *Wishing well* is not *Loving*, tho' it may follow from Love. And besides it is not a little Paradoxical, and a Thought that none cou'd have fallen into but those free thinkers who are got above the *Alms Basket*, and the slavish Principles of former Christians, to suppose we wish well to a Man when we do him all the hurt we can! But to submit to and bear with a Persecutor, *the common Enemy and Pest of Mankind*, much more to delight, to rejoice, and take complaisance in him, is contrary to all Sense and Reason, to *our Just and Natural Rights*, and can go down with none but *such Servile Flatterers*, who wou'd have all *Men born to what their mean Souls has fitted them, Slavery.*

SECTION 312: WHEREIN SELF PRESERVATION CONSISTS

What then in *Self Preservation*, that Fundamental Law of Nature, as some call it, to which all other Laws, Divine as well as Human, are made to do Homage? And how shall it be provided for? Very well; for it does not consist in the Preservation of the Person or *Composite*, but in preserving the Mind from Evil, the Mind which is truly the Self, and which ought to be secur'd at all hazards. It is this *Self Preservation* and no other, that is a *Fundamental Sacred and Unalterable Law*, as might easily be prov'd were this a proper place; which Law he obeys, and he only, who will do or suffer any thing rather than Sin. *No Man having a power to deliver up this Preservation, or consequently the means of it, to the absolute Will and arbitrary Dominion of another, but has always a Right to Preserve what he has not a Power to part with*, as a certain Author says in another Case where it will not hold.

PART II

Enlightenment and Counter-Enlightenment:

THE OPPOSITIONAL ATTITUDES OF JEAN-JACQUES ROUSSEAU AND MARY WOLLSTONECRAFT

What, then, is the subject of this discourse? To mark ... the moment when, right taking
the place of violence, nature was subjected to the law.[1]
Jean-Jacques Rousseau, Discourse on the Origin of Inequality

Few writers present a more troubling aspect than Jean-Jacques Rousseau (1712–78),
and it can be said with some sense that he was "all things to all people," or rather,
quite different things to different people, including his various acquaintances,
successors, intellectual interpreters, victims, and admirers. Political philosophers
have long debated whether he was a great exponent of democratic theory or a
dangerous precursor of totalitarianism, and any student of his writing can find strong
evidence of his support of democracy, as well as sources of totalizing tendencies.

Equally troubling is his personal life, for while some consider Rousseau to have
been a person of deep-felt convictions, even the kindest critics are in awe of his
persistently quarrelsome character, his frequent dissembling, and his ill treatment of
friends and family. George Sabine, who interpreted political theory for several generations of political theory students, had this to say about the complex character and
political theory of Rousseau:

> [he] differed from his contemporaries in everything but his opinions: even when he used
> the same words, he meant something different. His character, his outlook on life, his
> scale of values, his instinctive reactions, all differed essentially from what the Enlight-
> enment regarded as admirable.[2]

His historical position places him far enough from the origins of religious, scientific,
and political change in the sixteenth and seventeenth centuries to enable him to reflect
critically on these new developments and to develop the oppositional Romantic
philosophy. His personal history places him in a position to reflect on the political
and religious circumstances of France and continental Europe.

The year 1715 marked the end of Louis XIV's half-century reign of absolute power in France. During his reign, the civic structures of local autonomous rule were reappropriated to the monarchy in a thorough consolidation of power. Across Europe monarchical reigns were marked by religious intolerance; Rousseau's own parents had fled to Geneva to escape religious persecution in France. The period of Rousseau's life corresponded with the events and circumstances leading from the constitutional struggles in Great Britain to the revolutions in France and the American colonies.

When Rousseau was born in Geneva in 1712, his mother, Suzanne Bernard, became ill from complications attending his birth and died from puerperal fever, an epidemic created by the new science's medical practices. The trend away from midwifery to medicalization had introduced practices that inadvertently promoted septicemia and caused literally thousands of deaths in childbirth.[3] Rousseau's father lacked success in his profession as a watchmaker, and after legal difficulties he fled Geneva, leaving his son in the care of the mother's relations. By Rousseau's own account, in his autobiographical *Confessions*, his experiences apprenticing to trades were not marked by success. So as a young man he came to lead the life of a vagabond, staying intermittently in various places, including what is now northern Italy, Switzerland, and France. The twelve years when he dwelled in Paris exerted a profound influence on his intellectual development.

Rousseau had several affairs and romantic attachments and formed many dependencies, most particularly with Madame de Warens, who contributed to his financial support for the better part of a decade. Raised to Calvinism, under the influence of M. de Warens he converted to Catholicism, but returned to Calvinism in a desultory way in his later years. In 1745 he began a relationship with a servant in his Parisian hotel, Theresa le Vasseur, with whom he had five children, all of whom he gave up to a foundling hospital as orphans, against the wishes of their mother.

Rousseau's intellectual awakening occurred when he responded to an advertisement for an essay contest sponsored by the Academy of Dijon. His submission, *A Discourse on Science and Art*, won first prize and was followed by another submission, the *Discourse on the Origin of Inequality* (1754), which, while not earning the accolades of the first essay, wielded a more profound influence on future political thought.

In his time Rousseau quarreled with the encyclopaedist Denis Diderot, the satirist François Voltaire, and the good-natured philosopher David Hume, to name only the more famous among those with whom he had friendships and differences. Edmund Burke thought him unprincipled and vain. Through the course of time, his difficult personality can only have been made more troubled by the genuine persecution he experienced in France, Geneva, and Bern as a result of his radical democratic and anti-absolutist political arguments. When Rousseau died, in Paris, he was debilitated both psychologically and physically, having led a most unusual and even fantastic life.

> The man of sensibility would be moved to tears by the sight of a single destitute peasant family, but would be cold to well-thought-out schemes for ameliorating the lot of peasants as a class.[4]
>
> *Bertrand Russell*

Rousseau's thought always reflects the tension between its related elements: the Enlightenment and the Romantic reaction against it. If the sensibility of the Romantic movement was in the air in eighteenth-century France, it nonetheless needed a unifying spirit and spirited champion, and no one was better suited than Rousseau. This movement, which can be traced into the twentieth century, began as the first major revolt against the ideals of the Enlightenment. Reason, science, and the life of the mind were put aside for an aesthetic based on violent and volatile individual emotional response. Science and logic represented a system of stultified manners, an attempt to remove man from a more natural state of human connection. Emotionality, especially sympathy and pity, were to form the basis of human action and response. Yet Rousseau also appealed to reason as the hallmark of the civil state.

Rousseau's political theory follows an evident progression. The earlier works, such as the *Discourses* and other essays, focus on the individual and romanticize the role of nature and the "natural man." But while Rousseau extols the virtues of the "noble savage" he also, like Locke, develops the concept of state-of-nature theory as an invention for considering man in a hypothetical pre-political condition. The excesses of Parisian society, and the fact that Rousseau himself was never comfortable with urbanity, led him to condemn the arts, sciences, and society of city life, and to extol the virtues of a Geneva-like city-state – small, homogenous, capable of governance by participation.

Balanced between the pre-political natural state and the bloated, corrupt metropolis, exemplified by Paris, is the family, situated in the small city-state. The family, located in the community, provides an intermediate and preferable stage between the state of nature and the overly developed life of the corrupt city. In *Émile* (1762), the education of the young man is crucial to Rousseau's political vision, supplying his self-conscious analogy to Plato's *Republic*, with its strong focus on education. With the guidance of his tutor, Émile is allowed to learn for himself, through experience, in preparation ultimately for understanding civil society.

In Rousseau's more mature writings, particularly *The Social Contract* (1762), the political ideal is not a naive and unreasonable state of innocence. Instead, Rousseau poses the much more complex question of how, and through what kind of community, man can find a form of governance that is both liberating and unifying. Because this emerges as one of the most central questions of political theory, Rousseau is justly famous. His answers are intriguing, compelling, and disturbing, and form a basis for modern political discourse.

> Man is born free and everywhere he is in chains. Anyone who thinks himself the master of others is no less a slave than they. How has this come about? I do not know. What can make it legitimate? I believe I can resolve this question.[5]
> *Rousseau*, The Social Contract

Rousseau was foremost an advocate of direct democracy, as opposed to a Lockean system of representative government, and it is this single feature that most connects Rousseau to the radical democratic traditions. Here we have the fullest statement of majoritarian democracy, unmoved by the problem of the tyranny of the majority over the minority, that so interested John Stuart Mill and others in the individualistic liberal tradition. His notion of the polity brought a unique understanding to the paradox of freedom, that is, to the problem of how an individual can retain freedom while submitting to the state, and he proposed a novel solution to this paradox. For Rousseau, the citizen of the state converts his individual will to the general will, as expressed by the laws of the majoritarian democracy. Because this will is directed to the good of society as a whole, it cannot be genuinely counter to individual will.

Expressed in terms of Kantian idealism, "obedience to the law is freedom;" we are tyrannized only by individuals, not by society itself. And the fullest expression of the individual is as a citizen of the state.

For Rousseau's scheme to work, society would have to meet certain requirements: it must be free from great inequalities of wealth, allow liberty under the law, provide material welfare, and create a system of public education.[6] In Rousseau's writing, the Romantic movement connects with political theory in its concern for liberty, but also with community (a concept later theorists developed into nationalism). His political thought is not utilitarian, no less is it liberal; he posits no clear separation of the individual and the state in his mature views.

In *Émile* especially, Rousseau outlines his ideas about the education of women and men. Here, his seeming misogyny rivals his misanthropy, and his unashamed expression of patriarchal ideals has made him a ready target for feminist critics. First and foremost was Mary Wollstonecraft. Wollstonecraft was several generations younger than Rousseau, and her life is considered in the next chapter, along with the events of her own time, including the American and French Revolutions. What follows is a consideration of her philosophy as it relates to Rousseau and the philosophical issues he raises.

> Women are everywhere in a deplorable state; for in order to preserve their innocence, as ignorance is courteously termed, truth is hidden from them, and they are made to assume an artificial character before their faculties have acquired any strength.[7]
> **Mary Wollstonecraft, A Vindication of the Rights of Woman**

Mary Wollstonecraft's social and political theory was influenced by Lockean ideals of reason and virtue, but she was also very much taken with the anti-Enlightenment romanticism of Rousseau's political vision. After all, "the romantic rebellion against its parent was in itself a proof of the filial relation..."[8] And like so many women writers through the ages, her intellectual awakening with regard to gender was occasioned by the disillusionment of discovering herself excluded from or ill-treated by the theories she most admired. Rousseau's response to the Enlightenment created the oppositional Romantic philosophy; Wollstonecraft's response to Rousseau created the first full expression of the oppositional modern feminist philosophy. They were kindred spirits and stark opponents.

Wollstonecraft's life and writing, in style and substance, were affected by the Romantic creed of emotional response. Indeed, her response to Rousseau's *Émile* is full of emotionality:

> But peace to [Rousseau's] Manes [spirit]! I war not with his ashes, but his opinions. I war only with the sensibility that led him to degrade woman by making her the slave of love.[9]

Wollstonecraft was attracted to the sensibility of Romanticism, but she clearly perceived the first philosophical truth apprehended by feminists in the modern period: if women's position in relation to men is to be improved, it must be done by acknowledging and arguing for the principle that women possess reason and that (by both classical and Enlightenment standards) reason is the *sine qua non* of being human, of being a full person situated within society, and ultimately of being a citizen. Ironically and significantly, she upbraids Rousseau for his lack of reason:

Why was Rousseau divided between ecstasy and misery?...the effervescence of his imagination produced both; but, had his fancy been allowed to cool, it is possible that he might have acquired more strength of mind.[10]

Rousseau suffered from the polarities created by the Cartesian split of mind and body, of reason and emotion, remarked by Wollstonecraft and analyzed two hundred years later by several writers, including Susan Bordo, when she critiques how "the spiritual and corporeal are now two distinct substances which share no qualities ... and are each defined precisely in opposition to each other."[11] Wollstonecraft and Rousseau both struggle with the dualisms of Enlightenment philosophy.

To understand Wollstonecraft's argument, one must first understand her strategy, and as is often the case for writers outside of the dominant tradition, her approach is oblique. Throughout her work, she cleverly provides two types of arguments, one that appeals to the dominant ideology and one that appeals to the subversive one. This should be read not as inconsistency, but as rhetorical strategy.[12] One kind of argument is that women who are educated to use their reason will be better wives and mothers. This argument adopts the Natural Complement Theory (NCT), also called "sexual dimorphism," that women and men are essentially different but complementary types of things, a view held by Kant, Rousseau, and many others. Sometimes held by present-day conservatives, the NCT often projects a "different but equal" character. Against the claim of equality, critics argue that in this theory the qualities valued most highly (for example, reason) are attributed to men while devalued qualities (for example, emotion) are attributed to women; thus, it would follow that women are not *complementary* but are *supplementary* to men.[13] In the NCT women are actively discouraged and even barred from certain types of social and political activities. By asserting that education to develop virtue and reason in women will enhance them in their supplemental roles, Wollstonecraft strategically makes the education and advancement of women appeal even to women's oppressors.

The more radical argument holds that there is inherent and not just instrumental value in women developing virtue and reason. Women can, in a real sense, be *equal* to men. Wollstonecraft's second approach, the equal-to-men argument, is quite subtle. She insists repeatedly in the text for an ontological comparison.

I still insist, that not only the virtue, but the *knowledge* of the two sexes should be the same in nature, if not in degree, and that women, considered not only as moral, but rational creatures, ought to endeavour to acquire human virtues (or perfections) by the *same* means as men, instead of being educated like a fanciful kind of *half* being – one of Rousseau's wild chimeras.[14]

For the two most crucial and fundamental Enlightenment categories – reason and virtue – women are the same *in kind* as men; *men and women have the same moral and rational nature*. In order to make this daring claim, Wollstonecraft is willing to make some concessions. First, she concedes (a trifle too quickly, perhaps) any claim to physical equality.[15] Second, she opines that these essential qualities – reason and virtue – are attributed to women in *lesser* degree than to men. Sameness in kind is so important to her case, that she is willing to concede that women may be less rational, and less virtuous than men, so long as they can dwell in the same ontological categories as men – the categories of rationality and virtue, which define one as human and citizen. In this light we can see not just the irony but the argumentative strategy contained in her scolding of Rousseau for being insufficiently rational. For if some women (like Wollstonecraft) are more rational than some men (like Rousseau), then the position that all women have a lesser degree of the same kind of rationality as men cannot be sustained, since in fact, some women have a greater degree of rationality than some men.[16]

Wollstonecraft is often identified as the perfect exponent of liberal feminism, but this characterization occludes the undeniably radical character of her claims. She was "liberal" in that liberalism was the radical theory of the day. She was liberal in that she championed equal rights. But her inclusion of women in the formula was radical, her views on universal education were radical, and her views on property and poverty were radical. What most attracted Wollstonecraft to Rousseau's writings were his views on equality – perhaps because of similarities in their social positions. Both were middle-class but without independent means of support. A major difference between the two was that while Rousseau was parasitic upon both male and female friends, Wollstonecraft was a supporter of others – her father, her lovers, her sister, and her friends.

Still, Rousseau's views on property and poverty appealed to Wollstonecraft. Inspired by Rousseau, she mounted an attack on the system of hereditary distinction and argued that the tendency to equality will increase both happiness and virtue. In her chapter on the "pernicious effects" of "unnatural distinctions" she detailed the many ways in which property corrupts. Property is transitory, and both its presence and absence can lead to vice – weakness in the wealthy, immorality in the poor, neglect in women, dissipation in men. She sees property as leading away from love and friendship, toward acrimony and war.

Property distinctions are codified by law, and law itself, along with custom, enforces unnatural distinctions. The legal system does this by denying freedom to women and the poor, enforcing a system of democracy that is a masquerade for tyranny, and supporting unfair tax laws. Many of these claims are given a fictional treatment in her novel *Maria, Or the Wrongs of Woman* (1798). Her most radical claims concern social policy. She derides the notion of representative government ("a convenient handle for despotism") when women are not included. And this more than a hundred years before the franchise for women was established in western nations. She argues that women should be physicians as well as nurses, that they should study politics and enter business. Her views on property and education are her most class-conscious and gender-neutral. The lengthy final chapter is devoted to arguing for a radical scheme for universal national education, applying across gender and class. She envisions co-educational day schools (not boarding schools) that are free from religious affiliation and teach the same curriculum to all students, at least part of the time.

CRITICAL DIRECTIONS

Traditional interpretations of Rousseauian theory follow two different paths. According to one he is a radical egalitarian:

> Rousseau's admirers extol the passion of his prose and the egalitarianism of his vision – an egalitarianism that far surpasses Locke's. He has been called the first modern writer on politics who was *of* the people; the submerged, inarticulate masses of the *petite*

bourgeoisie, the poor artisans and workingmen . . . for whom there was no room, and no hope, in the existing order of things.[17]

Most prior political theorists had come from privilege, and as a result, even those who had a vision of universal rights and freedom were oblivious to the full implications of their vision. Their abstract ideas were not intended to have concrete implications for all classes. In contrast, Rousseau was able to articulate a democratic vision for the common man. His defense of collectivism and of freedom, which finds expression in his conception of the community, clearly presages the socialism of Marx, Engels, Lenin, and others in the twentieth century.

It is remarkable to find that, as with Hegel, theorists on the opposite side of the spectrum also find much to admire in Rousseau. Conservative support of Rousseauian theory tends to focus on his defense of the patriarchal family, the gender roles played in it, and the family's central role in society. For example, Allan Bloom's critique of liberal democracy follows Rousseau in endorsing "natural differences" between men and women that, Bloom argues, necessitate the gender division of labor and other inequalities both in the family and in the civil sphere.[18] In Rousseau's retreat from urbanization and his critique of "progress," theorists on the right find a comforting tendency to conserve traditions.

Among contemporary theorists, including Lynda Lange, Genevieve Lloyd, Carole Pateman, and Nancy Tuana, numerous writers identify and criticize the patriarchalist tradition in Rousseau.[19] For example, in an early second-wave feminist analysis of political theory, Susan Moller Okin traces the systematic failure to accord equality and freedom to women in Plato, Aristotle, and Rousseau. She focuses on the functional roles attributed to women historically, and the failure to value women, as men are valued, in and of themselves.[20] Others trace patriarchal constraints on women and examine the consistency of gender-based arguments.

Another second-wave writer, Jane Roland Martin, suggests the need for a closer look at Rousseau's writing about female characters. For example, considering Sophie, in *Émile*, she investigates the use of a "gender-based theory of complementary traits" (the NCT) and the failure of this theory, when combined with his views on education and the division of labor, to produce a consistent account of the development of the citizen. She argues that to be a citizen and participate in the polity (in the general will), one must have other-regarding virtues. But as described by Rousseau, men educated along the lines of Émile have these virtues neither by nature nor by education. Women might be educated to have them, but in Rousseau's scheme, they aren't. So unlike Plato, who abolishes the family in the *Republic* as contrary to the aims of the state, Rousseau identifies the family as the site of political socialization essential for men to function in the polity. But according to Martin this cannot happen because men are educated to a dependency on women and women are educated only to the interests of the family. According to Martin, Wollstonecraft argues in contrast for the rationality of women and then provides an alternative construction in which women are educated to both domestic duties and citizenship. Instead of creating a polarizing split between the public and private spheres, Wollstonecraft carefully integrates these activities, and in doing so she abolishes some of the tensions that seem insurmountable in Rousseau's theory. Fresh concepts of both "woman" and "citizen" emerge.[21]

One troublesome quality of the *Vindication* noted by the modern reader is the degree to which Wollstonecraft berates women for their behavior and status. She holds women at least partially accountable for their "inferior position," blaming it on frivolity, vanity, shallowness, and a hoard of other vices that she attributes to women. What lies behind this persistent theme? Is she attempting to mollify a male audience by shifting the blame to women? Is she issuing a wake-up call to women to take responsibility for themselves? Is she targeting the class distinctions which cultivate a mindless affect among the wealthy? Each of these considerations may contribute to Wollstonecraft's approach, but another possibility underlies these. Earlier I articulated two arguments taken up by Wollstonecraft, first, that women are different from and complementary to men, and second, that women are equal to men in ways relevant to citizenship in the state. The first argument places women in an inferior, instrumental or supplemental position. The second, "equal-to-men" argument attempts to place women on a par with men where men both serve as model for human beings, persons, or citizens and are simultaneously gendered as male. Unlike Mary Astell (see Part I), Matilda Joslyn Gage (see Part VI), or Anna Julia Cooper (see Part VII), who value women independently, Wollstonecraft apparently adopts a male model of humanity, and then despairs as to women's ability to attain this ideal. Models for equality have serious implications, especially in the law, and among current scholars, Catharine MacKinnon, Deborah Rhode, and Wendy W. Williams have recognized the flaws in creating a standard or model for what it is to be a person, human being, or citizen based on what it is to be a man.[22]

A final contemporary critique comes from Iris Marion Young, who holds that "Rousseau's political philosophy is the paradigm of the ideal of the civic public" in response against the diverse, particularized public of eighteenth-century Europe.[23] According to Young, the civic public maintained as republican ideals "the universal and impartial point of view of reason, standing opposed to and expelling desire, sentiment, and the particularity of needs and interests." Man's need for emotionality and desire was to be satisfied in the private sphere over which women were moral guardians. For Young, this means a privatizing of all kinds of particularity, "differences of race and culture, the variability and heterogeneity of needs" in an effort to achieve "unity and coherence" in the public realm.[24] Young questions the whole project of achieving public unity and stability through the use of abstract reason and instead argues for a participatory democracy which honors and uses difference as a virtue, not as something to be suppressed and confined.

Rousseau and Wollstonecraft are a particularly apt pair. Both were personally subject to emotionality and taken with the Romantic sensibility, which they both used to create compelling rhetorical styles and moving political arguments. Both were sufficiently subject to the allure of reason in its golden age to feature this mighty abstraction in a prominent position. In acknowledging both reason and emotion they each confront one of the more troubling oppositions of modern theory. They share radical ideas about property and an opposition to the dominant ideology, contributing significantly to both the creation, and the critique, of modern political theory.

Notes

1   Jean-Jacques Rousseau, *Discourse on the Origin of Inequality*, p. 77 of this volume.
2   George Sabine, *A History of Political Theory*, 3rd edn. (London: George G. Harrap & Co., 1963), p. 575.
3   Particularly, the new professionals were performing autopsies on cadavers and then going directly, without washing, to deliveries. See Adrienne Rich, *Of Woman Born: Motherhood as Experience and Institution* (New York: W. W. Norton & Co., 1976) for an

analysis of the effects of patriarchal practices on childbearing, but also Carl G. Hempel, *The Philosophy of Natural Science* (Englewood Cliffs, NJ: Prentice-Hall, 1966) for a discussion of Ignaz Semmelweis' work on childbed or puerperal fever. Mary Wollstonecraft was another casualty of such practices.

4 Bertrand Russell, *A History of Western Philosophy* (New York: Simon and Schuster, 1945), p. 676.

5 Jean-Jacques Rousseau, *On the Social Contract*, trans. Donald A. Cress (Indianapolis: Hackett, 1983), p. 17.

6 Sabine, *A History of Political Theory*, p. 586.

7 Mary Wollstonecraft, *A Vindication of the Rights of Woman*, p. 105 of this volume.

8 *Encyclopedia of Philosophy* (New York: Macmillan Publishing Co., 1967): "romanticism," vols. 7 and 8, p. 207.

9 Wollstonecraft, *A Vindication of the Rights of Woman*, p. 112 of this volume.

10 Ibid.

11 Susan Bordo, "The Cartesian Masculinization of Thought and the Seventeenth-Century Fight for the Feminine," in Bat Ami Bar On, ed., *Modern Engendering: Critical Feminist Readings in Modern Western Philosophy* (Albany: SUNY Press, 1994), p. 5. But see also *The Flight to Objectivity: Essays on Cartesianism and Culture* (Albany: SUNY Press, 1987).

12 The strategy is comparable to that of male writers of the Enlightenment, who were shaking off theological in favor of scientific arguments. To curry favor, and not incur the wrath of the religious powers, arguments would often run in pairs. The first would be a theological argument, the second a more rigorous scientific one. Far from being consistent, the arguments were often conflicting, or even contradictory. One finds this in both Locke and Newton.

13 See Kristin Waters, "Women in Kantian Ethics: A Failure at Universality," in Bat Ami Bar On, ed., *Modern Engendering: Critical Feminist Readings in Modern Western Philosophy*, and Ann Ferguson, "Androgyny as an Ideal for Human Development," in *Feminism and Philosophy*, ed. Mary Vetterling-Braggin et al. (Totowa, NJ: Rowman and Allenheld, 1977).

14 This volume, p. 103.

15 See the discussion of Alison Jaggar's account of normative dualism in Part I. For Wollstonecraft, women's supposed physical inferiority to men is natural but increased by social factors. This accords with normative dualism, that component of Enlightenment ontologies that value the mental over the physical. So for Wollstonecraft, conceding physical inferiority is not such a loss. Contemporary readers may not wish to make this concession.

16 Another way to view her argumentative strategies is to see the first as largely utilitarian (educating women produces the greatest overall happiness). The second approach is deontological and secures rights for (men and women) individuals regardless of the usefulness of doing so.

17 William Ebenstein, *Great Political Thinkers: Plato to the Present* (New York: Holt, Rinehart, and Winston, 1965), p. 494.

18 Jean-Jacques Rousseau, *Émile*, trans. Allan Bloom (New York: Basic Books, 1979).

19 Genevieve Lloyd, *The Man of Reason: "Male" and "Female" in Western Philosophy* (Minneapolis: University of Minnesota Press, 1984); Carole Pateman, *The Sexual Contract* (Stanford: Stanford University Press, 1988); Lynda Lange, "Women and Rousseau's Democratic Theory: Philosopher Monsters and Authoritarian Equality," in Bat Ami Bar On, ed., *Modern Engendering: Critical Feminist Readings in Modern Western Philosophy*; and Nancy Tuana, *Woman and the History of Philosophy* (New York: Paragon House, 1992).

20 Susan Moller Okin, *Women in Western Political Thought* (Princeton: Princeton University Press, 1979).

21 Jane Roland Martin, *Reclaiming a Conversation: The Ideal of an Educated Woman* (New Haven: Yale University Press, 1985).

22 See Catharine A. MacKinnon, *Feminism Unmodified: Discourses on Life and Law* (Cambridge, MA: Harvard University Press, 1987); Wendy W. Williams, "The Equality Crisis: Some Reflections on Culture, Courts, and Feminism," in *Feminist Legal Theory: Readings in Law and Gender*, ed. Katharine T. Bartlett and Rosanne Kennedy (Boulder: Westview Press, 1991); and Deborah L. Rhode, "Gender Difference and Gender Disadvantage," *Women and Politics*, 10:2 (1990).

23 Iris Marion Young, *Justice and the Politics of Difference* (Princeton: Princeton University Press, 1990), p. 108.

24 Ibid., p. 111.

CHAPTER 3

Discourse on the Origin of Inequality

JEAN-JACQUES ROUSSEAU

To
The Republic
of Geneva

Magnificent, Most Honored and Sovereign Lords:
Convinced that only a virtuous man may bestow on his homeland those honors which it can acknowledge, I have labored for thirty years to earn the right to offer you public homage. And since this happy occasion supplements to some extent what my efforts have been unable to accomplish, I believed I might be allowed here to give heed to the zeal that urges me on, instead of the right that ought to have given me authorization. Having had the good fortune to be born among you, how could I meditate on the equality which nature has established among men and upon the inequality they have instituted without thinking of the profound wisdom with which both, felicitously combined in this state, cooperate in the manner that most closely approximates the natural law and that is most favorable to society, to the maintenance of public order and to the happiness of private individuals? In searching for the best maxims that good sense could dictate concerning the constitution of a government, I have been so struck on seeing them all in operation in your own, that even if I had not been born within your walls, I would have believed myself incapable of dispensing with offering this picture of human society to that people which, of all peoples, seems to me to be in possession of the greatest advantages, and to have best prevented its abuses.

If I had had to choose my birthplace, I would have chosen a society of a size limited by the extent of human faculties, that is to say, limited by the possibility of being well governed, and where, with each being sufficient to his task, no one would have been forced to relegate to others the functions with which he was charged; a state where, with all private individuals being known to one another, neither the obscure maneuvers of vice nor the modesty of virtue could be hidden from the notice and the judgment of the public, and where that pleasant habit of seeing and knowing one another turned love of homeland into love of the citizens rather than into love of the land.

Jean-Jacques Rousseau. *Discourse on the Origin of Inequality*, trans. Donald A.Cress (Indianapolis, Ind. and Cambridge, Mass.: Hackett, 1992). Reprinted by permission of Hackett Publishing Co., Inc. All rights reserved.

I would have wanted to be born in a country where the sovereign and the people could have but one and the same interest, so that all the movements of the machine always tended only to the common happiness. Since this could not have taken place unless the people and the sovereign were one and the same person, it follows that I would have wished to be born under a democratic government, wisely tempered.

I would have wanted to live and die free, that is to say, subject to the laws in such wise that neither I nor anyone else could shake off their honorable yoke: that pleasant and salutary yoke, which the most arrogant heads bear with all the greater docility, since they are made to bear no other.

I would therefore have wanted it to be impossible for anyone in the state to say that he was above the law and for anyone outside to demand that the state was obliged to give him recognition. For whatever the constitution of a government may be, if a single man is found who is not subject to the law, all the others are necessarily at his discretion. And if there is a national leader and a foreign leader as well, whatever the division of authority they may make, it is impossible for both of them to be strictly obeyed and for the state to be well governed.

I would not have wanted to dwell in a newly constituted republic, however good its laws may be, out of fear that, with the government perhaps constituted otherwise than would be required for the moment and being unsuited to the new citizens or the citizens to the new government, the state would be subject to being overthrown and destroyed almost from its inception. For liberty is like those solid and tasty foods or those full-bodied wines which are appropriate for nourishing and strengthening robust constitutions that are used to them, but which overpower, ruin and intoxicate the weak and delicate who are not suited for them. Once peoples are accustomed to masters, they are no longer in a position to get along without them. If they try to shake off the yoke, they put all the more distance between themselves and liberty, because, in mistaking for liberty an unbridled license which is its opposite, their revolutions nearly always deliver them over to seducers who simply make their chains heavier. [...]

I would have searched for a country where the right of legislation was common to all citizens, for who can know better than they the conditions under which it suits them to live together in a single society? But I would not have approved of plebiscites like those of the Romans where the state's leaders and those most interested in its preservation were excluded from the deliberations on which its safety often depended, and where, by an absurd inconsistency, the magistrates were deprived of the rights enjoyed by ordinary citizens.

On the contrary, I would have desired that, in order to stop the self-centered and ill-conceived projects and the dangerous innovations that finally ruined Athens, no one would have the power to propose new laws according to his fancy; that this right belonged exclusively to the magistrates; that even they used it with such caution that the populace, for its part, was so hesitant about giving its consent to these laws, and that their promulgation could only be done with such solemnity that before the constitution was overturned one had time to be convinced that it is above all the great antiquity of the laws that makes them holy and venerable; that the populace soon holds in contempt those laws that it sees change daily; and that in becoming accustomed to neglect old usages on the pretext of making improvements, great evils are often introduced in order to correct the lesser ones.

Above all, I would have fled, as necessarily ill-governed, a republic where the people, believing it could get along without its magistrates or permit them but a precarious authority, would imprudently have held on to the administration of civil affairs and the execution of its own laws. Such must have been the rude constitution of the first governments immediately emerging from the state of nature, and such too was one of the vices which ruined the republic of Athens.

But I would have chosen that republic where private individuals, being content to give sanction to the laws and to decide as a body and upon the recommendation of their leaders the most important public affairs, would establish respected tribunals, distinguish with care their various departments, annually elect the most capable and most upright of their fellow citizens to administer justice and to govern the state; and where, with the virtue of the magistrates thus bearing witness to the wisdom of the people, they would mutually honor one another. Thus if some fatal misunderstandings were ever to disturb public concord, even those periods of blindness and errors were marked by indications of moderation, reciprocal esteem, and a common respect for the laws: presages and guarantees of a sincere and perpetual reconciliation.

Such, MAGNIFICENT, MOST HONORED, AND SOVEREIGN LORDS, are the advantages that I would have sought in the homeland that I would have chosen for myself. And if in addition providence had joined to it a charming location, a temperate climate, a fertile country and the most delightful appearance there is under the heavens, to complete my happiness I would have desired only to enjoy all these goods in the bosom of that happy homeland, living peacefully in sweet society with my fellow citizens, and practicing toward them (following their own example), humanity, friendship, and all the virtues; and leaving behind me the honorable memory of a good man and a decent and virtuous patriot. [...]

May you all, MAGNIFICENT, MOST HONORED AND SOVEREIGN LORDS, deign to receive with the same goodness the respectful testimonies of the interest I take in your common prosperity. If I were unfortunate enough to be guilty of some indiscreet rapture in this lively effusion of my heart, I beg you to pardon it as the tender affection of a true patriot, and to the ardent and legitimate zeal of a man who envisages no greater happiness for himself than that of seeing all of you happy.

With the most profound respect, I am, MAGNIFICENT, MOST HONORED AND SOVEREIGN LORDS, your most humble and most obedient servant and fellow citizen.

Jean-Jacques Rousseau

Chambéry
12 June 1754

PREFACE

Of all the branches of human knowledge, the most useful and the least advanced seems to me to be that of man; and I dare say that the inscription on the temple at Delphi alone contained a precept more important and more difficult than all the huge tomes of the moralists. Thus I regard the subject of this discourse as one of the most interesting questions that philosophy is capable of proposing, and unhappily for us, one of the thorniest that philosophers can attempt to resolve. For how can the source of the inequality among men be known unless one begins by knowing men themselves? [...]

For it is no light undertaking to separate what is original from what is artificial in the present nature of man, and to have a proper understanding of a state which no longer exists, which perhaps never existed, which probably never will exist, and yet about which it is necessary to have accurate notions in order to judge properly our own present state. He who would attempt to determine precisely which precautions to take in order to make solid observations on this subject would need even more philosophy than is generally supposed; and a good solution of the following problem would not seem to me unworthy of the Aristotles and Plinys of our century: *What experiments would be necessary to achieve knowledge of natural man? And what are the means of carrying out these experiments in the midst of society?* Far from undertaking to resolve this problem, I believe I have meditated sufficiently on the subject to dare respond in advance that the greatest philosophers will not be too good to direct these experiments, nor the most powerful sovereigns to carry them out. It is hardly reasonable to expect such a combination, especially with the perseverance or rather the succession of understanding and good will needed on both sides in order to achieve success. [...]

Leaving aside therefore all the scientific books which teach us only to see men as they have made themselves, and meditating on the first and most simple operations of the human soul, I believe I perceive in it two principles that are prior to reason, of which one makes us ardently interested in our well-being and our self-preservation, and the other inspires in us a natural repugnance to seeing any sentient being, especially our fellow man, perish or suffer. It is from the conjunction and combination that our mind is in a position to make regarding these two principles, without the need for introducing that of sociability, that all the rules of natural right appear to me to flow; rules which reason is later forced to reestablish on other foundations, when, by its successive developments, it has succeeded in smothering nature.

In this way one is not obliged to make a man a philosopher before making him a man. His duties toward others are not uniquely dictated to him by the belated lessons of wisdom; and as long as he does not resist the inner impulse of compassion, he will never harm another man or even another sentient being, except in the legitimate instance where, if his preservation were involved, he is obliged to give preference to himself. By this means, an end can also be made to the ancient disputes regarding the participation of animals in the natural law. For it is clear that, lacking intelligence and liberty, they cannot recognize this law; but since they share to some extent in our nature by virtue of the sentient quality with which they are endowed, one will judge that they should also participate in natural right, and that man is subject to some sort of duties toward them. It seems, in effect, that if I am obliged not to do any harm to my fellow man, it is less because he is a rational being than because he is a sentient being: a quality that, since it is common to both animals and men, should at least give the former the right not to be needlessly mistreated by the latter.

This same study of original man, of his true needs and the fundamental principles of his duties, is also the only good means that can be used to remove those multitudes of difficulties which present themselves regarding the origin of moral inequality, the true foundations of the body politic, the reciprocal rights of its members, and a thousand other similar questions that are as important as they are poorly explained.

In considering human society from a tranquil and disinterested point of view it seems at first to manifest merely the violence of powerful men and the oppression of the weak. The mind revolts against the harshness of the former; one is inclined to deplore the blindness of the latter. And since nothing is less stable among men than those external relationships which chance brings about more often than wisdom, and which are called weakness or power, wealth or poverty, human establishments appear at first glance to be based on piles of shifting sand. It is only in examining them closely, only after having cleared away the dust and sand that surround the edifice, that one learns to respect its foundations. [...]

Learn whom God has ordered you to be, and in what part of human affairs you have been placed.

[* * * * *]

QUESTION
Proposed by the Academy of Dijon
What is the Origin of Inequality
Among Men, and is it Authorized
by the Natural Law?

DISCOURSE ON THE ORIGIN AND FOUNDATIONS OF INEQUALITY AMONG MEN

It is of man that I have to speak, and the question I am examining indicates to me that I am going to be speaking to men, for such questions are not proposed by those who are afraid to honor the truth. I will therefore confidently defend the cause of humanity before the wise men who invite me to do so, and I will not be displeased with myself if I make myself worthy of my subject and my judges.

I conceive of two kinds of inequality in the human species: one which I call natural or physical, because it is established by nature and consists in the difference of age, health, bodily strength, and qualities of mind or soul. The other may be called moral or political inequality, because it depends on a kind of convention and is established, or at least authorized, by the consent of men. This latter type of inequality consists in the different privileges enjoyed by some at the expense of others, such as being richer, more honored, more powerful than they, or even causing themselves to be obeyed by them.

There is no point in asking what the source of natural inequality is, because the answer would be found enunciated in the simple definition of the word. There is still less of a point in asking whether there would not be some essential connection between the two inequalities, for that would amount to asking whether those who command are necessarily better than those who obey, and whether strength of body or mind, wisdom or virtue are always found in the same individuals in proportion to power or wealth. Perhaps this is a good question for slaves to discuss within earshot of their masters, but it is not suitable for reasonable and free men who seek the truth.

Precisely what, then, is the subject of this discourse? To mark, in the progress of things, the moment when, right taking the place of violence, nature was subjected to the law. To explain the sequence of wonders by which the strong could resolve to serve the weak, and the people to buy imaginary repose at the price of real felicity. [...]

Part One

However important it may be, in order to render sound judgments regarding the natural state of man, to consider him from his origin and to examine him, so to speak, in the first embryo of the species, I will not follow his nature through its successive developments.[...]I will suppose him to have been formed from all time as I see him today: walking on two feet, using his hands as we use ours, directing his gaze over all of nature, and measuring with his eyes the vast expanse of the heavens.

When I strip that being, thus constituted, of all the supernatural gifts he could have received and of all the artificial faculties he could have acquired only through long progress; when I consider him, in a word, as he must have left the hands of nature, I see an animal less strong than some, less agile than others, but all in all, the most advantageously organized of all. I see him satisfying his hunger under an oak tree, quenching his thirst at the first stream, finding his bed at the foot of the same tree that supplied his meal; and thus all his needs are satisfied.

When the earth is left to its natural fertility and covered with immense forests that were never mutilated by the axe, it offers storehouses and shelters at every step to animals of every species. Men, dispersed among the animals, observe and imitate their industry, and thereby raise themselves to the level of animal instinct, with the advantage that, whereas each species has only its own instincts, man, who may perhaps have none that belongs to him, appropriates all of them to himself, feeds himself equally well on most of the various foods which the other animals divide among themselves, and consequently finds his sustenance more easily than any of the rest can.

Accustomed from childhood to inclement weather and the rigors of the seasons, acclimated to fatigue, and forced, naked and without arms, to defend their lives and their prey against other ferocious beasts, or to escape them by taking flight, men develop a robust and nearly unalterable temperament. Children enter the world with the excellent constitution of their parents and strengthen it with the same exercises that produced it, thus acquiring all the vigor that the human race is capable of having. Nature treats them precisely the way the law of Sparta treated the children of its citizens: it renders strong and robust those who are well constituted and makes all the rest perish, thereby differing from our present-day societies, where the state, by making children burdensome to their parents, kills them indiscriminately before their birth.

Since the savage man's body is the only instrument he knows, he employs it for a variety of purposes that, for lack of practice, ours are incapable of serving. And our industry deprives us of the force and agility that necessity obliges him to acquire. If he had had an axe, would his wrists break such strong branches? If he had had a sling, would he throw a stone with so much force? If he had had a ladder, would he climb a tree so nimbly? If he had had a horse, would he run so fast? Give a civilized man time to gather all his machines around him, and undoubtedly he will easily overcome a savage man. But if you want to see an even more unequal fight, pit them against each other naked and disarmed, and you will soon realize the advantage of constantly having all of one's forces at one's disposal, of always being ready for any event, and of always carrying one's entire self, as it were, with one. [...]

There are other, more formidable enemies, against which man does not have the same means of self-defense: natural infirmities, childhood, old age, and illnesses of all kinds – sad signs of our weakness, of which the first two are common to all animals, with the last belonging principally to man living in society. On the subject of childhood, I even observe that a mother, by carrying her child everywhere with her, can feed it much more easily than females of several animal species, which are forced to be continually coming and going, with great fatigue, to seek their food and to suckle or feed their young. It is true that if a woman were to perish, the child runs a considerable risk of perishing with her. But this danger is common to a hundred other species, whose young are for quite some time incapable of going off to seek their nourishment for themselves. And although childhood is longer among us, our lifespan is also longer; thus things are more or less equal in this respect, although there are other rules, not relevant to my subject, which are concerned with the duration of infancy and the number of young. Among the elderly, who are less active and perspire little, the need for food diminishes with the faculty of providing for it. And since savage life shields them from gout and rheumatism, and since old age is, of all ills, the one that human assistance can least alleviate, they eventually die without anyone being aware that they are ceasing to exist, and almost without being aware of it themselves. [...]

So far I have considered only physical man. Let us now try to look at him from a metaphysical and moral point of view.

In any animal I see nothing but an ingenious machine to which nature has given senses in order for it to renew its strength and to protect itself, to a certain point, from all that tends to destroy or disturb it. I am aware of precisely the same things in the human machine, with the difference that nature alone does everything in the operations of an animal, whereas man contributes, as a free agent, to his own operations. The former chooses or rejects by instinct and the latter by an act of freedom. Hence an animal cannot deviate from the rule that is prescribed to it, even when it would be advantageous to do so, while man deviates from it, often to his own detriment. Thus a pigeon would die of hunger near a bowl filled with choice meats, and so would a cat perched atop a pile of fruit or grain, even though both could nourish themselves quite well with the food they disdain, if they were of a mind to try some. And thus dissolute men abandon themselves to excesses which cause them fever and death, because the mind perverts the senses and because the will still speaks when nature is silent.[...]

But if the difficulties surrounding all these questions should leave some room for dispute on this difference between man and animal, there is another very specific quality which distinguishes them and about which there can be no argument: the faculty of self-perfection, a faculty which, with the aid of circumstances, successively develops all the others, and resides among us as much in the species as in the individual. [...]

Savage man, left by nature to instinct alone, or rather compensated for the instinct he is perhaps lacking by faculties capable of first replacing them and then of raising him to the level of instinct, will therefore begin with purely animal functions. Perceiving and feeling will be his first state, which he will have in common with all animals. Willing and not willing, desiring, and fearing will be the first and nearly the only operations of his soul until new circumstances bring about new developments in it.

Whatever the moralists may say about it, human understanding owes much to the passions, which, by common consensus, also owes a great deal to it. It is by their activity that our reason is perfected. We seek to know only because we desire to find enjoyment; and it is impossible to conceive why someone who had neither desires nor fears would go to the bother of reasoning. The passions in turn take their origin from our needs, and their progress from our knowledge. For one can desire or fear things only by virtue of the ideas one can have of them, or from the simple impulse of nature; and savage man, deprived of every sort of enlightenment, feels only the passion of this latter sort. His desires do not go beyond his physical needs. The only goods he knows in the universe are nourishment, a woman and rest; the only evils he fears are pain and hunger. I say pain and not death because an animal will never know what it is to die; and knowledge of death and its terrors is one of the first acquisitions that man has made in withdrawing from the animal condition. [...]

But without having recourse to the uncertain testimony of history, does anyone fail to see that everything seems to remove savage man from the temptation and the means of ceasing to be savage? His imagination depicts nothing to him; his heart asks nothing of him. His modest needs are so easily found at hand, and he is so far from the degree of knowledge necessary to make him desire to acquire greater knowledge, that he can have neither foresight nor curiosity. The spectacle of nature becomes a matter of indifference to him by dint of its becoming familiar to him. It is always the same order, always the same succession of changes. He does not have a mind for marveling at the greatest wonders; and we must not seek in him the philosophy that a man needs in order to know how to observe once what he has seen everyday. His soul, agitated by nothing, is given over to the single feeling of his own present existence, without any idea of the future, however near it may be, and his projects, as limited as his views, hardly extend to the end of the day. Such is, even today, the extent of the Carib's foresight. In the morning he sells his bed of cotton and in the evening he returns in tears to buy it back, for want of having foreseen that he would need it that night. [...]

Whatever these origins may be, it is clear, from the little care taken by nature to bring men together through mutual needs and to facilitate their use of speech, how little she prepared them for becoming habituated to the ways of society, and how little she contributed to all that men have done to establish the bonds of society. In fact, it is impossible to imagine why, in that primitive state, one man would have a greater need for another man than a monkey or a wolf has for another of its respective species; or, assuming this need, what motive could induce the other man to satisfy it; or even, in this latter instance, how could they be in mutual agreement regarding the conditions. I know that we are repeatedly told that nothing would have been so miserable than man in that state; and if it is true, as I believe I have proved, that it is only after many centuries that men could have had the desire and the opportunity to leave that state, that would be a charge to bring against nature, not against him whom nature has thus constituted. But if we understand the word *miserable* properly, it is a word which is without meaning or which signifies merely a painful privation and suffering of the body or the soul. Now I would very much like someone to explain to me what kind of misery can there be for a free being whose heart is at peace and whose body is in good health? I ask which of the two, civil or natural life, is more likely to become insufferable to those who live it? We see about us practically no people who do not complain about their existence; many even deprive themselves of it to the extent they are able, and the combination of divine and human laws is hardly enough to stop this disorder. I ask if anyone has ever heard tell of a savage who was living in liberty ever dreaming of complaining about his life and of killing himself. Let the judgment therefore be made with less pride on which side real misery lies. On the other hand, nothing would have been so miserable as savage man, dazzled by enlightenment, tormented by passions, and reasoning about a state different from his own. It was by a very wise providence that the latent faculties he possessed should develop only as the occasion to exercise them presents itself, so that they would be neither superfluous nor troublesome to him beforehand, nor underdeveloped and useless in time of need. In instinct alone, man had everything he needed in order to live in the state of nature; in a cultivated reason, he has only what he needs to live in society.

At first it would seem that men in that state, having among themselves no type of moral relations or acknowledged duties, could be neither good nor evil, and had neither vices nor virtues, unless, if we take these words in a physical sense, we call those qualities that can harm an individual's preservation "vices" in him, and those that can contribute to it "virtues." In that case it would be necessary to call the one who least resists the simple impulses of nature the most virtuous. But without departing from the standard meaning of these words, it is appropriate to suspend the judgment we could make regarding such a situation and to be on our guard against our prejudices, until we have examined with scale in hand whether there are more virtues than vices among civilized men; or whether their virtues are more advantageous than their vices are lethal; or whether the progress of their knowledge is sufficient compensation for ills they inflict on one another as they learn of the good they ought to do; or whether, all things considered, they would not be in a happier set of circumstances if they had neither evil to fear nor good to hope for from anyone, rather than subjecting themselves to a universal dependence and obliging themselves to receive everything from those who do not oblige themselves to give them anything.

Above all, let us not conclude with Hobbes that because man has no idea of goodness he is naturally evil; that he is vicious because he does not know virtue; that he always refuses to perform services for his fellow men he does not believe he owes them; or that, by virtue of the right, which he reasonably attributes to himself, to those things he needs, he foolishly imagines himself to be the sole proprietor of the entire universe. Hobbes has very clearly seen the defect of all modern definitions of natural right, but the consequences he draws from his own definition show that he takes it in a sense that is no less false. [...] Benevolence and even friendship are, properly understood, the products of a constant pity fixed on a particular object; for is desiring that someone not suffer anything but desiring that he be happy? Were it true that commiseration were merely a sentiment that puts us in the position of the one who suffers, a sentiment that is obscure and powerful in savage man, developed but weak in man dwelling in civil society, what importance would this idea have to the truth of what I say, except to give it more force? In fact, commiseration will be all the more energetic as the witnessing animal identifies itself more intimately with the suffering animal. Now it is evident that this identification must have been infinitely closer in the state of nature than in the state of reasoning. Reason is what engenders egocentrism, and reflection strengthens it. Reason is what turns man in upon himself. Reason is what separates him from all that troubles him and afflicts him. Philosophy is what isolates him and what moves him to say in secret, at the sight of a suffering man, "Perish if you will; I am safe and sound." No longer can anything but danger to the entire society trouble the tranquil slumber of the philosopher and yank him from his bed. His fellow man can be killed with impunity underneath his window. He has merely to place his hands over his ears and argue with himself a little in order to prevent nature, which rebels within him, from identifying him with the man being assassinated. Savage man does not have this admirable talent, and for lack of wisdom and reason he is always seen thoughtlessly giving in to the first sentiment of humanity. When there is a riot or a street brawl, the populace gathers together; the prudent man withdraws from the scene. It is the rabble, the women of the marketplace, who separate the combatants and prevent decent people from killing one another.

It is therefore quite certain that pity is a natural sentiment, which, by moderating in each individual the activity of the love of oneself, contributes to the mutual preservation of the entire species. Pity is what carries us without reflection to the aid of those we see suffering. Pity is what, in the state of nature, takes the place of laws, mores, and virtue, with the advantage that no one is tempted to disobey its sweet voice. Pity is what will prevent every robust savage from robbing a weak child or an infirm old man of his hard-earned subsistence, if he himself expects to be able to find his own someplace else. Instead of the sublime maxim of reasoned justice, *Do unto others as you would have them do unto you*, pity inspires all men with another maxim of natural goodness, much less perfect but perhaps more useful than the preceding one: *Do what is good for you with as little harm as possible to others*. In a word, it is in this natural sentiment, rather than in subtle arguments that one must search for the cause of the repugnance at doing evil that every man would experience, even independently of the maxims of education. Although it might be appropriate for Socrates and minds of his stature to acquire virtue through reason, the human race would long ago have ceased to exist, if its preservation had depended solely on the reasonings of its members. [...]

Among the passions that agitate the heart of man, there is an ardent, impetuous one that renders one sex necessary to the other; a terrible passion which braves all dangers, overcomes all obstacles, and which, in its fury, seems fitted to destroy the human race it is destined to preserve. What would become of men, victimized by this unrestrained and brutal rage, without modesty and self-control, fighting everyday over the object of their passion at the price of their blood? [...]

Let us begin by distinguishing between the moral and the physical aspects of the sentiment of love. The physical aspect is that general desire which inclines one sex to unite with another. The moral aspect is what determines this desire and fixes it exclusively on one single object, or which at least gives it a greater degree of energy for this preferred object. Now it is easy to see that the moral aspect of love is an artificial sentiment born of social custom, and extolled by women with so much skill and care in order to establish their hegemony and make dominant the sex that ought to obey. Since this feeling is founded on certain notions of merit or beauty that a savage is not in a position to have, and on comparisons he is incapable of making, it must be almost non-existent for him. For since his mind could not form abstract ideas of regularity and proportion, his heart is not susceptible to sentiments of admiration and love, which, even without its being observed come into being from the application of these ideas. He pays exclusive attention to the temperament he has received from nature, and not the taste he has been unable to acquire; any woman suits his purpose.

Limited merely to the physical aspect of love, and fortunate enough to be ignorant of those preferences which stir up the feeling and increase the difficulties in satisfying it, men must feel the ardors of their temperament less frequently and less vividly, and consequently have fewer and less cruel conflicts among themselves. Imagination, which wreaks so much havoc among us, does not speak to savage hearts; each man peacefully awaits the impetus of nature, gives himself over to it without choice, and with more pleasure than frenzy; and once the need is satisfied, all desire is snuffed out.

Hence it is incontestable that love itself, like all other passions, had acquired only in society that impetuous ardor which so often makes it lethal to men. [. . .]

Let us conclude that, wandering in the forests, without industry, without speech, without dwelling, without war, without relationships, with no need for his fellow men, and correspondingly with no desire to do them harm, perhaps never even recognizing any of them individually, savage man, subject to few passions and self-sufficient, had only the sentiments and enlightenment appropriate to that state; he felt only his true needs, took notice of only what he believed he had an interest in seeing; and that his intelligence made no more progress than his vanity. If by chance he made some discovery, he was all the less able to communicate it to others because he did not even know his own children. Art perished with its inventor. There was neither education nor progress; generations were multiplied to no purpose. Since each one always began from the same point, centuries went by with all the crudeness of the first ages; the species was already old, and man remained ever a child. [. . .]

Part Two

The first person who, having enclosed a plot of land, took it into his head to say *this is mine* and found people simple enough to believe him, was the true founder of civil society. What crimes, wars, murders, what miseries and horrors would the human race have been spared, had some one pulled up the stakes or filled in the ditch and cried out to his fellow men: "Do not listen to this imposter. You are lost if you forget that the fruits of the earth belong to all and the earth to no one!" But it is quite likely that by then things had already reached the point where they could no longer continue as they were. For this idea of property, depending on many prior ideas which could only have arisen successively, was not formed all at once in the human mind. It was necessary to make great progress, to acquire much industry and enlightenment, and to transmit and augment them from one age to another, before arriving at this final stage in the state of nature. Let us therefore take things farther back and try to piece together under a single viewpoint that slow succession of events and advances in knowledge in their most natural order.

Man's first sentiment was that of his own existence; his first concern was that of his preservation. The products of the earth provided him with all the help he needed; instinct led him to make use of them. With hunger and other appetites making him experience by turns various ways of existing, there was one appetite that invited him to perpetuate his species; and this blind inclination, devoid of any sentiment of the heart, produced a purely animal act. Once this need had been satisfied, the two sexes no longer took cognizance of one another, and even the child no longer meant anything to the mother once it could do without her.

Such was the condition of man in his nascent stage; such was the life of an animal limited at first to pure sensations, and scarcely profiting from the gifts nature offered him, far from dreaming of extracting anything from her. But difficulties soon presented themselves to him; it was necessary to learn to overcome them. The height of trees, which kept him from reaching their fruits, the competition of animals that sought to feed themselves on these same fruits, the ferocity of those animals that wanted to take his own life: everything obliged him to apply himself to bodily exercises. It was necessary to become agile, fleet-footed and vigorous in combat. Natural arms, which are tree branches and stones, were soon found ready at hand. He learned to surmount nature's obstacles, combat other animals when necessary, fight for his subsistence even with men, or compensate for what he had to yield to those stronger than himself.

In proportion as the human race spread, difficulties multiplied with the men. Differences in soils, climates and seasons could force them to inculcate these differences in their lifestyles. Barren years, long and hard winters, hot summers that consume everything required new resourcefulness from them. Along the seashore and the riverbanks they invented the fishing line and hook, and became fishermen and fish-eaters. In the forests they made bows and arrows, and became hunters and warriors. In cold countries they covered themselves with the skins of animals they had killed. Lightning, a volcano, or some fortuitous chance happening acquainted them with fire: a new resource against the rigors of winter. They learned to preserve this element, then to reproduce it, and finally to use it to prepare meats that previously they devoured raw. [...]

Taught by experience that love of well-being is the sole motive of human actions, he found himself in a position to distinguish the rare occasions when common interest should make him count on the assistance of his fellowmen, and those even rarer occasions when competition ought to make him distrust them. In the first case, he united with them in a herd, or at most in some sort of free association, that obligated no one and that lasted only as long as the passing need that had formed it. In the second case, everyone sought to obtain his own advantage, either by overt force, if he believed he could, or by cleverness and cunning, if he felt himself to be the weaker.

This is how men could imperceptibly acquire some crude idea of mutual commitments and of the advantages to be had in fulfilling them, but only insofar as present and perceptible interests could require it, since foresight meant nothing to them, and far from concerning themselves about a distant future, they did not even give a thought to the next day. [...]

The first developments of the heart were the effect of a new situation that united the husbands and wives, fathers and children in one common habitation. The habit of living together gave rise to the sweetest sentiments known to men: conjugal love and paternal love. Each family became a little society all the better united because mutual attachment and liberty were its only bonds; and it was then that the first difference was established in the lifestyle of the two sexes, which until then had had only one. Women became more sedentary and grew accustomed to watch over the hut and the children, while the man went to seek their common subsistence. With their slightly softer life the two sexes also began to lose something of their ferocity and vigor. But while each one separately became less suited to combat savage beasts, on the other hand it was easier to assemble in order jointly to resist them.

In this new state, with a simple and solitary life, very limited needs, and the tools they had invented to provide for them, since men enjoyed a great deal of leisure time, they used it to procure for themselves many types of conveniences unknown to their fathers; and that was the first yoke they imposed on themselves without realizing it, and the first source of evils they prepared for their descendants. For in addition to their continuing thus to soften body and mind (those conveniences having through habit lost almost all their pleasure, and being at the same time degenerated into true needs), being deprived of them became much more cruel than possessing them was sweet; and they were unhappy about losing them without being happy about possessing them. [...]

Everything begins to take on a new appearance. Having previously wandered about the forests and having assumed a more fixed situation, men slowly came together and united into different bands, eventually forming in each country a particular nation, united by mores and characteristic features, not by regulations and laws, but by the same kind of life and foods and by the common influence of the climate. Eventually a permanent proximity cannot fail to engender some intercourse among different families. Young people of different sexes live in neighboring huts; the passing intercourse demanded by nature soon leads to another, through frequent contact with one another, no less sweet and more permanent. People become accustomed to consider different objects and to make comparisons. Imperceptibly they acquire the ideas of merit and beauty which produce feelings of preference. By dint of seeing one another, they can no longer get along without seeing one another again. A sweet and tender feeling insinuates itself into the soul and at the least opposition becomes an impetuous fury. Jealousy awakens with love; discord triumphs, and the sweetest passion receives sacrifices of human blood.

In proportion as ideas and sentiments succeed one another and as the mind and heart are trained, the human race continues to be tamed, relationships spread and bonds are tightened. People grew accustomed to gather in front of their huts or around a large tree; song and dance, true children of love and leisure, became the amusement or rather the occupation of idle men and women who had flocked together. Each one began to look at the others and to want to be looked at himself, and public esteem had a value. The one who sang or danced the best, the handsomest, the strongest, the most adroit or the most eloquent became the most highly regarded. And this was the first step toward inequality and, at the same time, toward vice. From these first preferences were born vanity and contempt on the one hand, and shame and envy on the other. And the fermentation caused by these new leavens eventually produced compounds fatal to happiness and innocence.

As soon as men had begun mutually to value one another, and the idea of esteem was formed in their minds, each one claimed to have a right to it, and it was no longer possible for anyone to be lacking it with impunity. From this came the first duties of civility, even among savages; and from this every voluntary wrong became an outrage, because along with the harm that resulted from the injury, the offended party saw in it contempt for his person, which often was more insufferable than the harm itself. Hence each man punished the contempt shown him in a manner proportionate to the esteem in which he held himself; acts of revenge became terrible, and men became bloodthirsty and cruel. This is precisely the stage reached by most of the savage people known to us; and it is for want of having made adequate distinctions among their ideas or of having noticed how far these peoples already were from the original state of nature that many have hastened to conclude that man is naturally cruel, and that he needs civilization in order to soften him. On the contrary, nothing is so gentle as man in his primitive state, when, placed by nature at an equal distance from the stupidity of brutes and the fatal enlightenment of civil man, and limited equally by instinct and reason to protecting himself from the harm that threatens him, he is restrained by natural pity from needlessly harming anyone himself, even if he has been harmed. For according to the axiom of the wise Locke, *where there is no property, there is no injury.* [...]

The example of savages, almost all of whom have been found in this state, seems to confirm that the human race had been made to remain in it always; that this state is the veritable youth of the world; and that all the subsequent progress has been in appearance so many steps toward the perfection of the individual, and in fact toward the decay of the species. [...]

From the cultivation of land, there necessarily followed the division of land; and from property once recognized, the first rules of justice. For in order to render everyone what is his, it is necessary that everyone can have something. Moreover, as men began to look toward the future and as they saw that they all saw they had goods to lose, there was not one of them who did not have to fear reprisals against himself for wrongs he might do to another. This origin is all the more natural as it is impossible to conceive of the idea of property arising from anything but manual labor, for it is not clear what man can add, beyond his own labor, in order to appropriate things he has not made. It is labor alone that, in giving the cultivator a right to the product of the soil he has tilled, consequently gives him a right, at least until the harvest, and thus from year to year. With this possession continuing uninterrupted, it is easily transformed into property. When the ancients, says Grotius, gave Ceres the epithet of legislatrix, gave the name Thesmophories to a festival celebrated in her honor, they thereby made it apparent that the division of lands has produced a new kind of right: namely, the right of property, different from that which results from the natural law.

Things in this state could have remained equal, if talents had been equal, and if the use of iron and the consumption of foodstuffs had always been in precise balance. But this proportion, which was not maintained by anything, was soon broken. The strongest did the most work; the most adroit turned theirs to better advantage: the most ingenious found ways to shorten their labor. The farmer had a greater need for iron, or the blacksmith had a greater need for wheat; and in laboring equally, the one earned a great deal while the other barely had enough to live. Thus it is that natural inequality imperceptibly manifests itself together with inequality occasioned by the socialization process. Thus it is that the differences among men, developed by those of circumstances, make themselves more noticeable, more permanent in their effects, and begin to influence the fate of private individuals in the same proportion. [...]

Thus we find here all our faculties developed, memory and imagination in play, egocentrism looking out for its interests, reason rendered active, and the mind having nearly reached the limit of the perfection of which it is capable. We find here all the natural qualities put into action, the rank and fate of each man established not only on the basis of the quantity of goods and the power to serve or harm, but also on the basis of mind, beauty, strength or skill, on the basis of merit or talents. And since these qualities were the only ones that could attract consideration, he was soon forced to have them or affect them. It was necessary, for his advantage, to show himself to be something other than what he in fact was. Being something and appearing to be something became two completely different things; and from this distinction there arose grand ostentation, deceptive cunning, and all the vices that follow in their wake. On the other hand, although man had previously been free and independent, we find him, so to speak, subject, by virtue of a multitude of fresh needs, to all of nature and particularly to his fellowmen, whose slave in a sense he becomes even in becoming their master; rich, he needs their services; poor, he needs their help; and being midway between wealth and poverty does not put him in a position to get along without them. It is therefore necessary for him to seek incessantly to interest them in his fate and to make them find their own profit, in fact or in appearance, in working for his. This makes him two-faced and crooked with some, imperious and harsh with others, and puts him in the position of having to abuse everyone he needs when he cannot make them fear him and does not find it in his interests to be of useful service to them. Finally, consuming ambition, the zeal for raising the relative level of his fortune, less out of real need than in order to put himself above others, inspires in all men a wicked tendency to harm one another, a secret jealousy all the more dangerous because, in order to strike its blow in greater safety, it often wears the mask of benevolence; in short, competition and rivalry on the one hand, opposition of interest on the other, and always the hidden desire to profit at the expense of someone else. All these ills are the first effect of property and the inseparable offshoot of incipient inequality. [...]

Thus, when both the most powerful or the most miserable made of their strength or their needs a sort of right to another's goods, equivalent, according to them, to the right of property, the destruction of equality was followed by the most frightful disorder. Thus the usurpations of the rich, the acts of brigandage by the poor, the unbridled passions of all, stifling natural pity and the still weak voice of justice, made men greedy, ambitious and wicked. There arose between the right of the strongest and the right of the first occupant a perpetual conflict that ended only in fights and murders. Emerging society gave way to the most horrible state of war; since the human race, vilified and desolated, was no longer able to retrace its steps or give up the unfortunate acquisitions it had made, and since it labored only toward its shame by abusing the faculties that honor it, it brought itself to the brink of its ruin. *Horrified by the newness of the ill, both the poor man and the rich man hope to flee from wealth, hating what they once had prayed for.*

It is not possible that men should not have eventually reflected upon so miserable a situation and upon the calamities that overwhelm them. The rich in particular must have soon felt how disadvantageous to them it was to have a perpetual war in which they alone paid all the costs, and in which the risk of losing one's life was common to all and the risk of losing one's goods was personal. [...] Bereft of valid reasons to justify himself and sufficient forces to defend himself; easily crushing a private individual, but himself crushed by troops of bandits; alone against all and unable on account of mutual jealousies to unite with his equals against enemies united by the common hope of plunder, the rich, pressed by necessity, finally conceived the most thought-out project that ever entered the human mind. It was to use in his favor the very strength of those who attacked him, to turn his adversaries into his defenders, to instill in them other maxims, and to give them other institutions which were as favorable to him as natural right was unfavorable to him.

With this end in mind, after having shown his neighbors the horror of a situation which armed them all against each other and made their possessions as burdensome as their needs, and in which no one could find safety in either poverty or wealth, he easily invented specious reasons to lead them to his goal. "Let us unite," he says to them, "in order to protect the weak from oppression, restrain the ambitious, and assure everyone of possessing what belongs to him. Let us institute rules of justice and peace to which all will be obliged to conform, which will make special exceptions for no one, and which will in some way compensate for the caprices of fortune by subjecting the strong and the weak to mutual obligations. In short, instead of turning our forces against ourselves, let us gather them into one supreme power that governs us according to wise laws, that protects and defends all the members of the association, repulses common enemies, and maintains us in an eternal concord."

Considerably less than the equivalent of this discourse was needed to convince crude, easily seduced men who also had too many disputes to settle among themselves to be able to get along without arbiters, and too much greed and ambition to be able to get along without masters for long. They all ran to chain themselves, in the belief that they secured their liberty, for although they had enough sense to realize the advantages of a political establishment, they did not have enough experience to foresee its dangers. Those most capable of anticipating the abuses were precisely those who counted on profiting from them; and even the wise saw the need to be resolved to sacrifice one part of their liberty to preserve the other, just as a wounded man has his arm amputated to save the rest of his body.

Such was, or should have been, the origin of society and laws, which gave new fetters to the weak and new forces to the rich, irretrievably destroyed natural liberty, established forever the law of property and of inequality, changed adroit usurpation into an irrevocable right, and for the profit of a few ambitious men henceforth subjected the entire human race to labor, servitude and misery. [...]

As for paternal authority, from which several have derived absolute government and all society, it is enough, without having recourse to the contrary proofs of Locke and Sidney, to note that nothing in the world is farther from the ferocious spirit of despotism than the gentleness of that authority which looks more to the advantage of the one who obeys than to the utility of the one who commands; that by the law of nature, the father is master of the child as long as his help is necessary for him; that beyond this point they become equals, and the son, completely independent of the father, then owes him merely respect and not obedience; for gratitude is clearly a duty that must be rendered, but not a right that can be demanded. Instead of saying that civil society derives from paternal power, on the contrary it must be said that it is from civil society that this power draws its principal force. An individual was not recognized as the father of several children until the children remained gathered about him. The goods of the father, of which he is truly the master, are the goods that keep his children in a state of dependence toward him, and he can cause their receiving a share in his estate to be consequent upon the extent to which they will have well merited it from him by continuous deference to his wishes. Now, far from having some similar favor to expect from their despot (since they belong to him as personal possessions – they and all they possess – or at least he claims this to be the case), subjects are reduced to receiving as a favor what he leaves them of their goods. He does what is just when he despoils them; he does them a favor when he allows them to live. [...]

Thus it appears certain to me not only that governments did not begin with arbitrary power, which is but their corruption and extreme limit, and which finally brings them back simply to the law of the strongest, for which they were initially to have been the remedy; but also that even if they had begun thus, this power, being illegitimate by its nature, could not have served as a foundation for the rights of society, nor, as a consequence, for the inequality occasioned by social institutions.

Without entering at present into the investigations that are yet to be made into the nature of the fundamental compact of all government, I restrict myself, in following common opinion, to considering here the establishment of the body politic as a true contract between the populace and the leaders it chooses for itself: a contract by which the two parties obligate themselves to observe the laws that are stipulated in it and that form the bonds of their union. Since, with respect to social relations, the populace has united all its wills into a single one, all the articles on which this will is explicated become so many fundamental laws obligating all the members of the state without exception, and one of these regulates the choice and power of the magistrates charged with watching over the execution of the others. This power extends to everything that can maintain the constitution, without going so far as to change it. To it are joined honors that make the laws and their ministers worthy of respect, and, for the ministers personally, prerogatives that compensate them for the troublesome labors that a good administration requires. The magistrate, for his part, obligates himself to use the power entrusted to him only in accordance with the intention of the constituents, to maintain each one in the peaceful enjoyment of what belongs to him, and to prefer on every occasion the public utility to his own interest. [...]

The various forms of government take their origin from the greater or lesser differences that were found among private individuals at the moment of institution. If a man were eminent in power, virtue, wealth or prestige, he alone was elected magistrate, and the state became monarchical. If several men, more or less equal among themselves, stood out over all the others, they were elected jointly, and there was an aristocracy. Those whose fortune or talents were less disproportionate, and who least departed from the state of nature, kept the supreme administration and formed a democracy. Time made evident which of these forms was the most advantageous to men. Some remained in subjection only to the laws; the others soon obeyed masters. Citizens wanted to keep their liberty; the subjects thought only of taking it away from their neighbors, since they could not endure others enjoying a good they themselves no longer enjoyed. In a word, on the one hand were riches and conquests, and on the other were happiness and virtue.

In these various forms of government all the magistratures were at first elective; and when wealth did not prevail, preference was given to merit, which gives a natural ascendancy, and to age, which gives experience in conducting business and cool-headedness in deliberation. The elders of the Hebrews, the gerontes of Sparta, the senate of Rome, and even the etymology of our word *seigneur* show how much age was respected in former times. The more elections fell upon men of advanced age, the more frequent elections became, and the more their difficulties were made to be felt. Intrigues were introduced; factions were formed; parties became embittered; civil wars flared up. Finally, the blood of citizens was sacrificed to the alleged happiness of the state, and people were on the verge of falling back into the anarchy of earlier times. The ambition of the leaders profited from these circumstances to perpetuate their offices within their families. The people, already accustomed to dependence, tranquillity and the conveniences of life, and already incapable of breaking their chains, consented to let their servitude increase in order to secure their tranquillity. Thus it was that the leaders, having become hereditary, grew accustomed to regard their magistratures as family property, to regard themselves as the proprietors of the state (of which at first they were but the officers), to call their fellow citizens their slaves, to count them like cattle in the number of things that belonged to them, and to call themselves equals of the gods and kings of kings.

If we follow the progress of inequality in these various revolutions, we will find that the first stage was the establishment of the law and of the right of property, the second stage was the institution of the magistracy, and the third and final stage was the transformation of legitimate power into arbitrary power. Thus the class of rich and poor was authorized by the first epoch, that of the strong and the weak by the second, and that of master and slave by the third: the ultimate degree of inequality and the limit to which all the others finally lead, until new revolutions completely dissolve the government or bring it nearer to its legitimate institution. [...]

If this were the place to go into detail, I would easily explain how the inequality of prestige and authority becomes inevitable among private individuals, as soon as they are united in one single society and are forced to make comparisons among themselves and to take into account the differences they discover in the continual use they have to make of one another. These differences are of several sorts, but in general, since wealth, nobility or rank, power and personal merit are the principal distinctions by which someone is measured in society, I would prove that the agreement or conflict of these various forces is the surest indication of a well- or ill-constituted state. I would make it apparent that among these four types of inequality, since personal qualities are the origin of all the others, wealth is the last to which they are ultimately reduced, because it readily serves to buy all the rest, since it is the most immediately useful to well-being and the easiest to communicate. This observation enables one to judge rather precisely the extent to which each people is removed from its primitive institution, and of the progress it has made toward the final stage of corruption. I would note how much that universal desire for reputation, honors, and preferences, which devours us all, trains and compares our talents and strengths; how much it excites and multiplies the passions; and, by making all men competitors, rivals, or rather enemies, how many setbacks, successes and catastrophes of every sort it causes every day, by making so many contenders run the same course. I would show that it is to this ardor for making oneself the topic of conversation, to this furor to distinguish oneself which nearly always keeps us outside ourselves, that we owe what is best and worst among men, our virtues and vices, our sciences and our errors, our conquerors and our philosophers, that is to say, a multitude of bad things against a small number of good ones. Finally, I would prove that if one sees a handful of powerful and rich men at the height of greatness and fortune while the mob grovels in obscurity and misery, it is because the former prize the things they enjoy only to the extent that the others are deprived of them; and because, without changing their position, they would cease to be happy, if the people ceased to be miserable.

But these details alone would be the subject of a large work in which one would weigh the advantages and the disadvantages of every government relative to the rights of the state of nature, and where one would examine all the different faces under which inequality has appeared until now and may appear in ages, according to the nature of these governments and the upheavals that time will necessarily bring in its wake. We would see the multitude oppressed from within as a consequence of the very precautions it had taken against what menaced it from without. We would see oppression continually increase, without the oppressed ever being able to know where it would end or what legitimate means would be left for them to stop it. We would see the rights of citizens and national liberties gradually die out, and the protests of the weak treated like seditious murmurs. We would see politics restrict the honor of defending the common cause to a mercenary portion of the people. We would see arising from this the necessity for taxes, the discouraged farmer leaving his field, even during peacetime, and leaving his plow in order to gird himself with a sword. We would see the rise of fatal and bizarre rules in the code of honor. We would see the defenders of the homeland sooner or later become its enemies, constantly holding a dagger over their fellow citizens, and there would come a time when we would hear them say to the oppressor of their country: *"If you order me to plunge my sword into my brother's breast or my father's throat, and into my pregnant wife's entrails, I will do so, even though my right hand is unwilling."*

From the extreme inequality of conditions and fortunes, from the diversity of passions and talents, from useless arts, from pernicious arts, from frivolous sciences there would come a pack of prejudices equally contrary to reason, happiness and virtue. One would see the leaders fomenting whatever can weaken men united together by disuniting them; whatever can give society an air of apparent concord while sowing the seeds of real division; whatever can inspire defiance and hatred in the various classes through the opposition of their rights and interests, and can as a consequence strengthen the power that contains them all.

It is from the bosom of this disorder and these upheavals that despotism, by gradually raising its hideous head and devouring everything it had seen to be good and healthy in every part of the state, would eventually succeed in trampling underfoot the laws and the people, and in establishing itself on the ruins of the republic. The times that would precede this last transformation would be times of troubles and calamities; but in the end everything would be swallowed up by the monster, and the peoples would no longer have leader or laws, but only tyrants. Also, from that moment on, there would no longer be any question of mores and virtue, for wherever despotism, *in which decency affords no hope*, reigns, it tolerates no other master. As soon as it speaks, there is neither probity nor duty to consult, and the blindest obedience is the only virtue remaining for slaves.

Here is the final stage of inequality, and the extreme point that closes the circle and touches the point from which we started. Here all private individuals become equals again, because they are nothing. And since subjects no longer have any law other than the master's will, nor the master any rule other than his passions, the notions of good and the principles of justice again vanish. Here everything is returned solely to the law of the strongest, and consequently to a new state of nature different from the one with which we began, in that the one was the state of nature in its purity, and this last one is the fruit of an excess of corruption. Moreover, there is so little difference between these two states, and the governmental contract is so utterly dissolved by despotism, that the despot is master only as long as he is the strongest; and as soon as he can be ousted, he has no cause to protest against violence. The uprising that ends in the strangulation or the dethronement of a sultan is as lawful an act as those by which he disposed of the lives and goods of his subjects the day before. Force alone maintained him; force alone brings him down. Thus everything happens in accordance with the natural order, and whatever the outcome of these brief and frequent upheavals may be, no one can complain about someone else's injustice, but only of his own imprudence or his misfortune.

In discovering and following thus the forgotten and lost routes that must have led man from the natural state to the civil state; in reestablishing, with the intermediate positions I have just taken note of, those that time constraints on me have made me suppress or that the imagination has not suggested to me, no attentive reader can fail to be struck by the immense space that separates these two states. It is in this slow succession of things that he will see the solution to an infinity of moral and political problems which the philosophers are unable to resolve. He will realize that, since the human race of one age is not the human race of another age, the reason why Diogenes did not find his man is because he searched among his contemporaries for a man who no longer existed. Cato, he will say, perished with Rome and liberty because he was out of place in his age; and this greatest of men merely astonished the world, which five hundred years earlier he would have governed. In short, he will explain how the soul and human passions are imperceptibly altered and, as it were, change their nature; why, in the long run, our needs and our pleasures change their objects; why, with original man gradually disappearing, society no longer offers to the eyes of the wise man anything but an assemblage of artificial men and factitious passions which are the work of all these new relations and have no true foundation in nature. What reflection teaches us on this subject is perfectly confirmed by observation: savage man and civilized man differ so greatly in the depths of their hearts and in their inclinations, that what constitutes the supreme happiness of the one would reduce the other to despair. Savage man breathes only tranquillity and liberty; he wants simply to live and rest easy; and not even the unperturbed tranquillity of the Stoic approaches his profound indifference for any other objects. On the other hand, the citizen is always active and in a sweat, always agitated, and unceasingly tormenting himself in order to seek still more laborious occupations. He works until he dies; he even runs to his death in order to be in a position to live, or renounces life in order to acquire immortality. He pays court to the great whom he hates and to the rich whom he scorns. He stops at nothing to obtain the honor of serving them. He proudly crows about his own baseness and their protection; and proud of his slavery, he speaks with disdain about those who do not have the honor of taking part in it. What a spectacle for the Carib are the difficult and envied labors of the European minister! How many cruel deaths would that indolent savage not prefer to the horror of such a life, which often is not mollified even by the pleasure of doing good. But in order to see the purpose of so many cares, the words *power* and *reputation* would have to have a meaning in his mind; he would have to learn that there is a type of men who place some value on the regard the rest of the world has for them, and who know how to be happy and content with themselves on the testimony of others rather than on their own. Such, in fact, is the true cause of all these differences; the savage lives in himself; the man accustomed to the ways of society is always outside himself and knows how to live only in the opinion of others. And it is, as it were, from their judgment alone that he draws the sentiment of his own existence. It is not pertinent to my subject to show how, from such a disposition, so much indifference for good and evil arises, along with such fine discourse on morality; how, with everything reduced to appearances, everything becomes factitious and bogus: honor, friendship, virtue, and often even our vices, about which we eventually find the secret of boasting; how, in a word, always asking others what we are and never daring to question ourselves on this matter, in the midst of so much philosophy, humanity, politeness, and sublime maxims, we have merely a deceitful and frivolous exterior: honor without virtue, reason without wisdom, and pleasure without happiness. It is enough for me to have proved that this is not the original state of man, and that this is only the spirit of society, and the inequality that society engenders, which thus change and alter all our natural inclinations.

I have tried to set forth the origin and progress of inequality, the establishment and abuse of political societies, to the extent that these things can be deduced from the nature of man by the light of reason alone, and independently of the sacred dogmas that give to sovereign authority the sanction of divine right. It follows from this presentation that, since inequality is practically non-existent in the state of nature, it derives its force and growth from the development of our faculties and the progress of the human mind, and eventually becomes stable and legitimate through the establishment of property and laws. Moreover, it follows that moral inequality, authorized by positive right alone, is contrary to natural right whenever it is not combined in the same proportion with physical inequality: a distinction that is sufficient to determine what one should think in this regard about the sort of inequality that reigns among all civilized people, for it is obviously contrary to the law of nature, however it may be defined, for a child to command an old man, for an imbecile to lead a wise man, and for a handful of people to gorge themselves on superfluities while the starving multitude lacks necessities.

CHAPTER 4

A Vindication of the Rights of Woman with Strictures on Political and Moral Subjects

MARY WOLLSTONECRAFT

INTRODUCTION

After considering the historic page, and viewing the living world with anxious solicitude, the most melancholy emotions of sorrowful indignation have depressed my spirits, and I have sighed when obliged to confess, that either nature has made a great difference between man and man, or that the civilization which has hitherto taken place in the world has been very partial. I have turned over various books written on the subject of education, and patiently observed the conduct of parents and the management of schools; but what has been the result? – a profound conviction that the neglected education of my fellow-creatures is the grand source of the misery I deplore; and that women, in particular, are rendered weak and wretched by a variety of concurring causes, originating from one hasty conclusion. The conduct and manners of women, in fact, evidently prove that their minds are not in a healthy state; for, like the flowers which are planted in too rich a soil, strength and usefulness are sacrificed to beauty; and the flaunting leaves, after having pleased a fastidious eye, fade, disregarded on the stalk, long before the season when they ought to have arrived at maturity. – One cause of this barren blooming I attribute to a false system of education, gathered from the books written on this subject by men who, considering females rather as women than human creatures, have been more anxious to make them alluring mistresses than affectionate wives and rational mothers; and the understanding of the sex has been so bubbled by this specious homage, that the civilized women of the present century, with a few exceptions, are only anxious to inspire love, when they ought to cherish a nobler ambition, and by their abilities and virtues exact respect. [...]

Mary Wollstonecraft. *A Vindication of the Rights of Woman*. Originally published in 1792.

I am aware of an obvious inference: – from every quarter have I heard exclamations against masculine women; but where are they to be found? If by this appellation men mean to inveigh against their ardour in hunting, shooting, and gaming, I shall most cordially join in the cry; but if it be against the imitation of manly virtues, or, more properly speaking, the attainment of those talents and virtues, the exercise of which ennobles the human character, and which raise females in the scale of animal being, when they are comprehensively termed mankind; – all those who view them with a philosophic eye must, I should think, wish with me, that they may every day grow more and more masculine.

This discussion naturally divides the subject. I shall first consider women in the grand light of human creatures, who, in common with men, are placed on this earth to unfold their faculties; and afterwards I shall more particularly point out their peculiar designation. [...]

My own sex, I hope, will excuse me, if I treat them like rational creatures, instead of flattering their *fascinating* graces, and viewing them as if they were in a state of perpetual childhood, unable to stand alone. I earnestly wish to point out in what true dignity and human happiness consists – I wish to persuade women to endeavour to acquire strength, both of mind and body, and to convince them that the soft phrases, susceptibility of heart, delicacy of sentiment, and refinement of taste, are almost synonymous with epithets of weakness, and that those beings who are only the objects of pity and that kind of love, which has been termed its sister, will soon become objects of contempt.

Dismissing then those pretty feminine phrases, which the men condescendingly use to soften our slavish dependence, and despising that weak elegancy of mind, exquisite sensibility, and sweet docility of manners, supposed to be the sexual characteristics of the weaker vessel, I wish to shew that elegance is inferior to virtue, that the first object of laudable ambition is to obtain a character as a human being, regardless of the distinction of sex; and that secondary views should be brought to this simple touchstone. [...]

If then it can be fairly deduced from the present conduct of the sex, from the prevalent fondness for pleasure which takes place of ambition and those nobler passions that open and enlarge the soul; that the instruction which women have hitherto received has only tended, with the constitution of civil society, to render them insignificant objects of desire – mere propagators of fools! – if it can be proved that in aiming to accomplish them, without cultivating their understandings, they are taken out of their sphere of duties, and made ridiculous and useless when the short-lived bloom of beauty is over, I presume that *rational* men will excuse me for endeavouring to persuade them to become more masculine and respectable. [...]

CHAPTER I: THE RIGHTS AND INVOLVED DUTIES OF MANKIND CONSIDERED

In the present state of society it appears necessary to go back to first principles in search of the most simple truths, and to dispute with some prevailing prejudice every inch of ground. To clear my way, I must be allowed to ask some plain questions, and the answers will probably appear as unequivocal as the axioms on which reasoning is built; though, when entangled with various motives of action, they are formally contradicted, either by the words or conduct of men.

In what does man's pre-eminence over the brute creation consist? The answer is as clear as that a half is less than the whole; in Reason.

What acquirement exalts one being above another? Virtue; we spontaneously reply.

For what purpose were the passions implanted? That man by struggling with them might attain a degree of knowledge denied to the brutes; whispers Experience.

Consequently the perfection of our nature and capability of happiness, must be estimated by the degree of reason, virtue, and knowledge, that distinguish the individual, and direct the laws which bind society: and that from the exercise of reason, knowledge and virtue naturally flow, is equally undeniable, if mankind be viewed collectively.

The rights and duties of man thus simplified, it seems almost impertinent to attempt to illustrate truths that appear so incontrovertible; yet such deeply rooted prejudices have clouded reason, and such spurious qualities have assumed the name of virtues, that it is necessary to pursue the course of reason as it has been perplexed and involved in error, by various adventitious circumstances, comparing the simple axiom with casual deviations. [...]

The civilization of the bulk of the people of Europe is very partial; nay, it may be made a question, whether they have acquired any virtues in exchange for innocence, equivalent to the misery produced by the vices that have been plastered over unsightly ignorance, and the freedom which has been bartered for splendid slavery. The desire of dazzling by riches, the most certain pre-eminence that man can obtain, the pleasure of commanding flattering sycophants, and many other complicated low calculations of doting self-love, have all contributed to overwhelm the mass of mankind, and make liberty a convenient handle for mock patriotism. [...]

Such, indeed, has been the wretchedness that has flowed from hereditary honours, riches, and monarchy, that men of lively sensibility have almost uttered blasphemy in order to justify the dispensations of providence. [...]

Impressed by this view of the misery and disorder which pervaded society, and fatigued with jostling against artificial fools, Rousseau became enamoured of solitude, and, being at the same time an optimist, he labours with uncommon eloquence to prove that man was naturally a solitary animal. Misled by his respect for the goodness of God, who certainly – for what man of sense and feeling can doubt it! – gave life only to communicate happiness, he considers evil as positive, and the work of man; not aware that he was exalting one attribute at the expence of another, equally necessary to divine perfection.

Reared on a false hypothesis his arguments in favour of a state of nature are plausible, but unsound. I say unsound; for to assert that a state of nature is preferable to civilization, in all its possible perfection, is, in other words, to arraign supreme wisdom; and the paradoxical exclamation, that God has made all things right, and that error has been introduced by the creature, whom he formed, knowing what he formed, is as unphilosophical as impious. [...]

Rousseau exerts himself to prove that all *was* right originally: a crowd of authors that all *is* now right: and I, that all will *be* right. [...]

Society, therefore, as it becomes more enlightened, should be very careful not to establish bodies of men who must necessarily be made foolish or vicious by the very constitution of their profession.

In the infancy of society, when men were just emerging out of barbarism, chiefs and priests, touching the most powerful springs of savage conduct, hope and fear, must have had unbounded sway. An aristocracy, of course, is naturally the first form of government. But, clashing interests soon losing their equipoise, a monarchy and hierarchy break out of the confusion of ambitious struggles, and the foundation of both is secured by feudal tenures. This appears to be the origin of monarchical and priestly power, and the dawn of civilization. But such combustible materials cannot long be pent up; and, getting vent in foreign wars and intestine insurrections, the people acquire some power in tumult, which obliges their rulers to gloss over their oppression with a shew of right. Thus, as wars, agriculture, commerce, and literature, expand the mind, despots are compelled, to make covert corruption hold fast the power which was formerly snatched by open force. And this baneful lurking gangrene is most quickly spread by luxury and superstition, the sure dregs of ambition. The indolent puppet of a court first becomes a luxurious monster, or fastidious sensualist, and then makes the contagion which his unnatural state spread, the instrument of tyranny.

It is the pestiferous purple which renders the progress of civilization a curse, and warps the understanding, till men of sensibility doubt whether the expansion of intellect produces a greater portion of happiness or misery. But the nature of the poison points out the antidote; and had Rousseau mounted one step higher in his investigation, or could his eye have pierced through the foggy atmosphere, which he almost disdained to breathe, his active mind would have darted forward to contemplate the perfection of man in the establishment of true civilization, instead of taking his ferocious flight back to the night of sensual ignorance.

CHAPTER II: THE PREVAILING OPINION OF A SEXUAL CHARACTER DISCUSSED

To account for, and excuse the tyranny of man, many ingenious arguments have been brought forward to prove, that the two sexes, in the acquirement of virtue, ought to aim at attaining a very different character: or, to speak explicitly, women are not allowed to have sufficient strength of mind to acquire what really deserves the name of virtue. Yet it should seem, allowing them to have souls, that there is but one way appointed by Providence to lead *mankind* to either virtue or happiness.

If then women are not a swarm of ephemeron triflers, why should they be kept in ignorance under the specious name of innocence? Men complain, and with reason, of the follies and caprices of our sex, when they do not keenly satirize our headstrong passions and groveling vices. – Behold, I should answer, the natural effect of ignorance! The mind will ever be unstable that has only prejudices to rest on, and the current will run with destructive fury when there are no barriers to break its force. Women are told from their infancy, and taught by the example of their mothers, that a little knowledge of human weakness, justly termed cunning, softness of temper, *outward* obedience, and a scrupulous attention to a puerile kind of propriety, will obtain for them the protection of man; and should they be beautiful, every thing else is needless, for, at least, twenty years of their lives. [...]

How grossly do they insult us who thus advise us only to render ourselves gentle, domestic brutes! For instance, the winning softness so warmly, and frequently, recommended, that governs by obeying. What childish expressions, and how insignificant is the being – can it be an immortal one? who will condescend to govern by such sinister methods! 'Certainly,' says Lord Bacon, 'man is of kin to the beasts by his body; and if he be not of kin to God by his spirit, he is a base and ignoble creature!'

Men, indeed, appear to me to act in a very unphilosophical manner when they try to secure the good conduct of women by attempting to keep them always in a state of childhood. Rousseau was more consistent when he wished to stop the progress of reason in both sexes, for if men eat of the tree of knowledge, women will come in for a taste; but, from the imperfect cultivation which their understandings now receive, they only attain a knowledge of evil.

Children, I grant, should be innocent; but when the epithet is applied to men, or women, it is but a civil term for weakness. For if it be allowed that women were destined by Providence to acquire human virtues, and by the exercise of their under-standings, that stability of character which is the firmest ground to rest our future hopes upon, they must be permitted to turn to the fountain of light, and not forced to shape their course by the twinkling of a mere satellite. Milton, I grant, was of a very different opinion; for he only bends to the indefeasible right of beauty, though it would be difficult to render two passages which I now mean to contrast, consistent. But into similar inconsistencies are great men often led by their senses.

> 'To whom thus Eve with perfect beauty adorn'd.
> 'My Author and Disposer, what thou bidst
> 'Unargued I obey; So God ordains;
> 'God is thy law, thou mine: to know no more
> 'Is Woman's happiest knowledge and her praise.[1]

These are exactly the arguments that I have used to children; but I have added, your reason is now gaining strength, and, till it arrives at some degree of maturity, you must look up to me for advice – then you ought to *think*, and only rely on God.

Yet in the following lines Milton seems to coincide with me; when he makes Adam thus expostulate with his Maker.

> 'Hast thou not made me here thy substitute,
> 'And these inferior far beneath me set?
> 'Among unequals what society
> 'Can sort, what harmony or true delight?
> 'Which must be mutual, in proportion due
> 'Giv'n and receiv'd; but in disparity
> 'The one intense, the other still remiss
> 'Cannot well suit with either, but soon prove
> 'Tedious alike: of fellowship I speak
> 'Such as I seek, fit to participate
> 'All rational delight –[2]

In treating, therefore, of the manners of women, let us, disregarding sensual arguments, trace what we should endeavour to make them in order to co-operate, if the expression be not too bold, with the supreme Being.

By individual education, I mean, for the sense of the word is not precisely defined, such an attention to a child as will slowly sharpen the senses, form the temper, regulate the passions as they begin to ferment, and set the understanding to work before the body arrives at maturity; so that the man may only have to proceed, not to begin, the important task of learning to think and reason.

To prevent any misconstruction, I must add, that I do not believe that a private education can work the wonders which some sanguine writers have attributed to it. Men and women must be educated, in a great degree, by the opinions and manners of the society they live in. In every age there has been a stream of popular opinion that has carried all before it, and given a family character, as it were, to the century. It may then fairly be inferred, that, till society be differently constituted, much cannot be expected from education. It is, however, sufficient for my present purpose to assert, that, whatever effect circumstances have on the abilities, every being may become virtuous by the exercise of its own reason; for if but one being was created with vicious inclinations, that is positively bad, what can save us from atheism? or if we worship a God, is not that God a devil?

Consequently, the most perfect education, in my opinion, is such an exercise of the understanding as is best calculated to strengthen the body and form the heart. Or, in other words, to enable the individual to attain such habits of virtue as will render it independent. In fact, it is a farce to call any being virtuous whose virtues do not result from the exercise of its own reason. This was Rousseau's opinion respecting men: I extend it to women, and confidently assert that they have been drawn out of their sphere by false refinement, and not by an endeavour to acquire masculine qualities. [...]

Let it not be concluded that I wish to invert the order of things; I have already granted, that, from the constitution of their bodies, men seem to be designed by Providence to attain a greater degree of virtue. I speak collectively of the whole sex; but I see not the shadow of a reason to conclude that their virtues should differ in respect to their nature. In fact, how can they, if virtue has only one eternal standard? I must therefore, if I reason consequentially, as strenously maintain that they have the same simple direction, as that there is a God.

It follows then that cunning should not be opposed to wisdom, little cares to great exertions, or insipid softness, varnished over with the name of gentleness, to that fortitude which grand views alone can inspire.

I shall be told that woman would then lose many of her peculiar graces, and the opinion of a well known poet might be quoted to refute my unqualified assertion. For Pope has said, in the name of the whole male sex,

> 'Yet ne'er so sure our passion to create,
> 'As when she touch'd the brink of all we hate.'[3]

In what light this sally places men and women, I shall leave to the judicious to determine; meanwhile I shall content myself with observing, that I cannot discover why, unless they are mortal, females should always be degraded by being made subservient to love or lust.

To speak disrespectfully of love is, I know, high treason against sentiment and fine feelings; but I wish to speak the simple language of truth, and rather to address the head than the heart. To endeavour to reason love out of the world, would be to out Quixote Cervantes, and equally offend against common sense: but an endeavour to restrain this tumultuous passion, and to prove that it should not be allowed to dethrone superior powers, or to usurp the sceptre which the understanding should ever coolly wield, appears less wild. [...]

Let me reason with the supporters of this opinion who have any knowledge of human nature, do they imagine that marriage can eradicate the habitude of life? The woman who has only been taught to please will soon find that her charms are oblique sunbeams, and that they cannot have much effect on her husband's heart when they are seen every day, when the summer is passed and gone. Will she then have sufficient native energy to look into herself for comfort, and cultivate her dormant faculties? or, is it not more rational to expect that she will try to please other men; and, in the emotions raised by the expectation of new conquests, endeavour to forget the mortification her love or pride has received? When the husband ceases to be a lover – and the time will inevitably come, her desire of pleasing will then grow languid, or become a spring of bitterness; and love, perhaps, the most evanescent of all passions, gives place to jealousy or vanity. [...]

Women ought to endeavour to purify their heart: but can they do so when their uncultivated understandings make them entirely dependent on their senses for employment and amusement, when no noble pursuit sets them above the little vanities of the day, or enables them to curb the wild emotions that agitate a reed over which every passing breeze has power? To gain the affections of a virtuous man is affectation necessary? Nature has given woman a weaker frame than man; but, to ensure her husband's affections, must a wife, who by the exercise of her mind and body whilst she was discharging the duties of a daughter, wife, and mother, has allowed her constitution to retain its natural strength, and her nerves a healthy tone, is she, I say, to condescend to use art and feign a sickly delicacy in order to secure her husband's affection? Weakness may excite tenderness, and gratify the arrogant pride of man; but the lordly caresses of a protector will not gratify a noble mind that pants for, and deserves to be respected. Fondness is a poor substitute for friendship! [...]

Besides, the woman who strengthens her body and exercises her mind will, by managing her family and practising various virtues, become the friend, and not the humble dependent of her husband; and if she, by possessing such substantial qualities, merit his regard, she will not find it necessary to conceal her affection, nor to pretend to an unnatural coldness of constitution to excite her husband's passions. In fact, if we revert to history, we shall find that the women who have distinguished themselves have neither been the most beautiful nor the most gentle of their sex. [...]

A mistaken education, a narrow, uncultivated mind, and many sexual prejudices, tend to make women more constant than men; but, for the present, I shall not touch on this branch of the subject. I will go still further, and advance, without dreaming of a paradox, that an unhappy marriage is often very advantageous to a family, and that the neglected wife is, in general, the best mother. And this would almost always be the consequence if the female mind were more enlarged: for, it seems to be the common dispensation of Providence, that what we gain in present enjoyment should be deducted from the treasure of life, experience; and that when we are gathering the flowers of the day and revelling in pleasure, the solid fruit of toil and wisdom should not be caught at the same time. The way lies before us, we must turn to the right or left: and he who will pass life away in bounding from one pleasure to another, must not complain if he acquire neither wisdom nor respectability of character.

Supposing, for a moment, that the soul is not immortal, and that man was only created for the present scene, – I think we should have reason to complain that love, infantine fondness, ever grew insipid and palled upon the sense. Let us eat, drink, and love, for to-morrow we die, would be, in fact, the language of reason, the morality of life; and who but a fool would part with a reality for a fleeting shadow? But, if awed by observing the improbable powers of the mind, we disdain to confine our wishes or thoughts to such a comparatively mean field of action; that only appears grand and important, as it is connected with a boundless prospect and sublime hopes, what necessity is there for falsehood in conduct, and why must the sacred majesty of truth be violated to detain a deceitful good that saps the very foundation of virtue? Why must the female mind be tainted by coquetish arts to gratify the sensualist, and prevent love from subsiding into friendship, or compassionate tenderness, when there are not qualities on which friendship can be built? Let the honest heart shew itself, and *reason* teach passion to submit to necessity; or, let the dignified pursuit of virtue and knowledge raise the mind above those emotions which rather imbitter than sweeten the cup of life, when they are not restrained within due bounds. [...]

Gentleness of manners, forbearance and long-suffering, are such amiable Godlike qualities, that in sublime poetic strains the Deity has been invested with them; and, perhaps, no representation of his goodness so strongly fastens on the human affec-tions as those that represent him abundant in mercy and willing to pardon. Gentle-ness, considered in this point of view, bears on its front all the characteristics of grandeur, combined with the winning graces of condescension; but what a different aspect it assumes when it is the submissive demeanour of dependence, the support of weakness that loves, because it wants protection; and is forbearing, because it must silently endure injuries; smiling under the lash at which it dare not snarl. Abject as this picture appears, it is the portrait of an accomplished woman, according to the received opinion of female excellence, separated by specious reasoners from human excellence. Or, they kindly restore the rib, and make one moral being of a man and woman; not forgetting to give her all the 'submissive charms.'

How women are to exist in that state where there is to be neither marrying nor giving in marriage, we are not told. For though moralists have agreed that the tenor of life seems to prove that *man* is prepared by various circumstances for a future state, they constantly concur in advising *woman* only to provide for the present. Gentleness, docility, and a spaniel-like affection are, on this ground, consistently recommended as the cardinal virtues of the sex; and, disregarding the arbitrary economy of nature, one writer has declared that it is masculine for a woman to be melancholy. She was created to be the toy of man, his rattle, and it must jingle in his ears whenever, dismissing reason, he chooses to be amused. [...]

As a philosopher, I read with indignation the plausible epithets which men use to soften their insults; and, as a moralist, I ask what is meant by such heterogeneous associations, as fair defects, amiable weaknesses, &c.? If there be but one criterion of morals, but one archetype for man, women appear to be suspended by destiny, according to the vulgar tale of Mahomet's coffin; they have neither the unerring instinct of brutes, nor are allowed to fix the eye of reason on a perfect model. They were made to be loved, and must not aim at respect, lest they should be hunted out of society as masculine.

But to view the subject in another point of view. Do passive indolent women make the best wives? Confining our discussion to the present moment of existence, let us see how such weak creatures perform their part? Do the women who, by the attainment of a few superficial accomplishments, have strengthened the prevailing prejudice, merely contribute to the happiness of their husbands? Do they display their charms merely to amuse them? And have women, who have early imbibed notions of passive obedience, sufficient character to manage a family or educate children? So far from it, that, after surveying the history of woman, I cannot help, agreeing with the severest satirist, considering the sex as the weakest as well as the most oppressed half of the species. What does history disclose but marks of infer-iority, and how few women have emancipated themselves from the galling yoke of sovereign man? – So few, that the exceptions remind me of an ingenious conjecture respecting Newton: that he was probably a being of a superior order, accidentally caged in a human body. Following the same train of thinking, I have been led to imagine that the few extraordinary women who have rushed in eccentrical directions out of the orbit prescribed to their sex, were *male* spirits, confined by mistake in female frames. But if it be not philosophical to think of sex when the soul is mentioned, the inferiority must depend on the organs: or the heavenly fire, which is to ferment the clay, is not given in equal portions. [...]

Surely there can be but one rule of right, if morality has an eternal foundation, and whoever sacrifices virtue, strictly so called, to present convenience, or whose *duty* it is to act in such a manner, lives only for the passing day, and cannot be an accountable creature. [...]

If, I say, for I would not impress by declamation when Reason offers her sober light, if they be really capable of acting like rational creatures, let them not be treated like slaves; or, like the brutes who are dependent on the reason of man, when they associate with him; but cultivate their minds, give them the salutary, sublime curb of principle, and let them attain conscious dignity by feeling themselves only dependent on God. Teach them, in common with man, to submit to necessity, instead of giving, to render them more pleasing, a sex to morals.

Further, should experience prove that they cannot attain the same degree of strength of mind, perseverance, and fortitude, let their virtues be the same in kind, though they may vainly struggle for the same degree; and the superiority of man will be equally clear, if not clearer; and truth, as it is a simple principle, which admits of no modification, would be common to both. Nay, the order of society as it is at present regulated would not be inverted, for woman would then only have the rank that reason assigned her, and arts could not be practised to bring the balance even, much less to turn it. [...]

As to the argument respecting the subjection in which the sex has ever been held, it retorts on man. The many have always been enthralled by the few; and monsters, who scarcely have shewn any discernment of human excellence, have tyrannized over thousands of their fellow-creatures. Why have men of superiour endowments submitted to such degradation? For, is it not universally acknowledged that kings, viewed collectively, have ever been inferior, in abilities and virtue, to the same number of men taken from the common mass of mankind – yet, have they not, and are they not still treated with a degree of reverence that is an insult to reason? China is not the only country where a living man has been made a God. *Men* have submitted to superior strength to enjoy with impunity the pleasure of the moment – *women* have only done the same, and therefore till it is proved that the courtier, who servilely resigns the birthright of a man, is not a moral agent, it cannot be demonstrated that woman is essentially inferior to man because she has always been subjugated.

Brutal force has hitherto governed the world, and that the science of politics is in its infancy, is evident from philosophers scrupling to give the knowledge most useful to man that determinate distinction.

I shall not pursue this argument any further than to establish an obvious inference, that as sound politics diffuse liberty, mankind, including woman, will become more wise and virtuous.

CHAPTER III: THE SAME SUBJECT CONTINUED

Bodily strength from being the distinction of heroes is now sunk into such unmerited contempt that men, as well as women, seem to think it unnecessary: the latter, as it takes from their feminine graces, and from that lovely weakness the source of their undue power; and the former, because it appears inimical to the character of a gentleman.

That they have both by departing from one extreme run into another, may easily be proved; but first it may be proper to observe, that a vulgar error has obtained a degree of credit, which has given force to a false conclusion, in which an effect has been mistaken for a cause.

People of genius have, very frequently, impaired their constitutions by study or careless inattention to their health, and the violence of their passions bearing a proportion to the vigour of their intellects, the sword's destroying the scabbard has become almost proverbial, and superficial observers have inferred from thence, that men of genius have commonly weak, or, to use a more fashionable phrase, delicate constitutions. Yet the contrary, I believe, will appear to be the fact; for, on diligent inquiry, I find that strength of mind has, in most cases, been accompanied by superior strength of body, – natural soundness of constitution, – not that robust tone of nerves and vigour of muscles, which arise from bodily labour, when the mind is quiescent, or only directs the hands. [...]

I am aware that this argument would carry me further than it may be supposed I wish to go; but I follow truth, and, still adhering to my first position, I will allow that bodily strength seems to give man a natural superiority over woman; and this is the only solid basis on which the superiority of the sex can be built. But I still insist, that not only the virtue, but the *knowledge* of the two sexes should be the same in nature, if not in degree, and that women, considered not only as moral, but rational creatures, ought to endeavour to acquire human virtues (or perfections) by the *same* means as men, instead of being educated like a fanciful kind of *half* being – one of Rousseau's wild chimeras.

But, if strength of body be, with some shew of reason, the boast of men, why are women so infatuated as to be proud of a defect? Rousseau has furnished them with a plausible excuse, which could only have occurred to a man, whose imagination had been allowed to run wild, and refine on the impressions made by exquisite senses; – that they might, forsooth, have a pretext for yielding to a natural appetite without violating a romantic species of modesty, which gratifies the pride and libertinism of man.

Women, deluded by these sentiments, sometimes boast of their weakness, cunningly obtaining power by playing on the *weakness* of men; and they may well glory in their illicit sway, for, like Turkish bashaws, they have more real power than their masters: but virtue is sacrificed to temporary gratifications, and the respectability of life to the triumph of an hour. [...]

But should it be proved that woman is naturally weaker than man, whence does it follow that it is natural for her to labour to become still weaker than nature intended her to be? Arguments of this cast are an insult to common sense, and savour of passion. The *divine right* of husbands, like the divine right of kings, may, it is to be hoped, in this enlightened age, be contested without danger, and, though conviction may not silence many boisterous disputants, yet, when any prevailing prejudice is attacked, the wise will consider, and leave the narrow-minded to rail with thoughtless vehemence at innovation.

The mother, who wishes to give true dignity of character to her daughter, must, regardless of the sneers of ignorance, proceed on a plan diametrically opposite to that which Rousseau has recommended with all the deluding charms of eloquence and philosophical sophistry: for his eloquence renders absurdities plausible, and his dogmatic conclusions puzzle, without convincing, those who have not ability to refute them.

Throughout the whole animal kingdom every young creature requires almost continual exercise, and the infancy of children, conformable to this intimation, should be passed in harmless gambols, that exercise the feet and hands, without requiring very minute direction from the head, or the constant attention of a nurse. In fact, the care necessary for self-preservation is the first natural exercise of the understanding, as little inventions to amuse the present moment unfold the imagination. But these wise designs of nature are counteracted by mistaken fondness or blind zeal. The child is not left a moment to its own direction, particularly a girl, and thus rendered dependent – dependence is called natural.

To preserve personal beauty, woman's glory! the limbs and faculties are cramped with worse than Chinese bands, and the sedentary life which they are condemned to live, whilst boys frolic in the open air, weakens the muscles and relaxes the nerves. – As for Rousseau's remarks, which have since been echoed by several writers, that they have naturally, that is from their birth, independent of education, a fondness for dolls, dressing, and talking – they are so puerile as not to merit a serious refutation. That a girl, condemned to sit for hours together listening to the idle chat of weak nurses, or to attend at her mother's toilet, will endeavour to join the conversation, is, indeed, very natural; and that she will imitate her mother or aunts, and amuse herself by adorning her lifeless doll, as they do in dressing her, poor innocent babe! is undoubtedly a most natural consequence. For men of the greatest abilities have seldom had sufficient strength to rise above the surrounding atmosphere; and, if the page of genius have always been blurred by the prejudices of the age, some allowance should be made for a sex, who, like kings, always see things through a false medium.

Pursuing these reflections, the fondness for dress, conspicuous in women, may be easily accounted for, without supposing it the result of a desire to please the sex on which they are dependent. The absurdity, in short, of supposing that a girl is naturally a coquette, and that a desire connected with the impulse of nature to propagate the species, should appear even before an improper education has, by heating the imagination, called it forth prematurely, is so unphilosophical, that such a sagacious observer as Rousseau would not have adopted it, if he had not been accustomed to make reason give way to his desire of singularity, and truth to a favourite paradox.

Yet thus to give a sex to mind was not very consistent with the principles of a man who argued so warmly, and so well, for the immortality of the soul. – But what a weak barrier is truth when it stands in the way of an hypothesis! Rousseau respected – almost adored virtue – and yet he allowed himself to love with sensual fondness. His imagination constantly prepared inflammable fewel for his inflammable senses; but, in order to reconcile his respect for self-denial, fortitude, and those heroic virtues, which a mind like his could not coolly admire, he labours to invert the law of nature, and broaches a doctrine pregnant with mischief and derogatory to the character of supreme wisdom. [...]

I have, probably, had an opportunity of observing more girls in their infancy than J. J. Rousseau – I can recollect my own feelings, and I have looked steadily around me; yet, so far from coinciding with him in opinion respecting the first dawn of the female character, I will venture to affirm, that a girl, whose spirits have not been damped by inactivity, or innocence tainted by false shame, will always be a romp, and the doll will never excite attention unless confinement allows her no alternative. Girls and boys, in short, would play harmlessly together, if the distinction of sex was not inculcated long before nature makes any difference. – I will go further, and affirm, as an indisputable fact, that most of the women, in the circle of my observation, who have acted like rational creatures, or shewn any vigour of intellect, have accidentally been allowed to run wild – as some of the elegant formers of the fair sex would insinuate. [...]

Women are every where in this deplorable state; for, in order to preserve their innocence, as ignorance is courteously termed, truth is hidden from them, and they are made to assume an artificial character before their faculties have acquired any strength. Taught from their infancy that beauty is woman's sceptre, the mind shapes itself to the body, and, roaming round its gilt cage, only seeks to adorn its prison. Men have various employments and pursuits which engage their attention, and give a character to the opening mind; but women, confined to one, and having their thoughts constantly directed to the most insignificant part of themselves, seldom extend their views beyond the triumph of the hour. But were their understanding once emancipated from the slavery to which the pride and sensuality of man and their short-sighted desire, like that of dominion in tyrants, of present sway, has subjected them, we should probably read of their weaknesses with surprise. I must be allowed to pursue the argument a little farther.

Perhaps, if the existence of an evil being were allowed, who, in the allegorical language of scripture, went about seeking whom he should devour, he could not more effectually degrade the human character than by giving a man absolute power. [...]

It is time to effect a revolution in female manners – time to restore to them their lost dignity – and make them, as a part of the human species, labour by reforming themselves to reform the world. It is time to separate unchangeable morals from local manners. – If men be demi-gods – why let us serve them! And if the dignity of the female soul be as disputable as that of animals – if their reason does not afford sufficient light to direct their conduct whilst unerring instinct is denied – they are surely of all creatures the most miserable! and, bent beneath the iron hand of destiny, must submit to be a *fair defect* in creation. But to justify the ways of Providence respecting them, by pointing out some irrefragable reason for thus making such a large portion of mankind accountable and not accountable, would puzzle the subtilest casuist.

The only solid foundation for morality appears to be the character of the supreme Being; the harmony of which arises from a balance of attributes; – and, to speak with reverence, one attribute seems to imply the *necessity* of another. He must be just, because he is wise, he must be good, because he is omnipotent. For to exalt one attribute at the expence of another equally noble and necessary, bears the stamp of the warped reason of man – the homage of passion. Man, accustomed to bow down to power in his savage state, can seldom divest himself of this barbarous prejudice, even when civilization determines how much superior mental is to bodily strength; and his reason is clouded by these crude opinions, even when he thinks of the Deity. – His omnipotence is made to swallow up, or preside over his other attributes, and those mortals are supposed to limit his power irreverently, who think that it must be regulated by his wisdom. [...]

Let fancy now present a woman with a tolerable understanding, for I do not wish to leave the line of mediocrity, whose constitution, strengthened by exercise, has allowed her body to acquire its full vigour; her mind, at the same time, gradually expanding itself to comprehend the moral duties of life, and in what human virtue and dignity consist.

Formed thus by the discharge of the relative duties of her station, she marries from affection, without losing sight of prudence, and looking beyond matrimonial felicity, she secures her husband's respect before it is necessary to exert mean arts to please him and feed a dying flame, which nature doomed to expire when the object became familiar, when friendship and forbearance take place of a more ardent affection. – This is the natural death of love, and domestic peace is not destroyed by struggles to prevent its extinction. I also suppose the husband to be virtuous; or she is still more in want of independent principles. [...]

I wish to sum up what I have said in a few words, for I here throw down my gauntlet, and deny the existence of sexual virtues, not excepting modesty. For man and woman, truth, if I understand the meaning of the word, must be the same; yet the fanciful female character, so prettily drawn by poets and novelists, demanding the sacrifice of truth and sincerity, virtue becomes a relative idea, having no other foundation than utility, and of that utility men pretend arbitrarily to judge, shaping it to their own convenience.

Women, I allow, may have different duties to fulfil: but they are *human* duties, and the principles that should regulate the discharge of them, I sturdily maintain, must be the same. [...]

CHAPTER IV: OBSERVATIONS ON THE STATE OF DEGRADATION TO WHICH WOMAN IS REDUCED BY VARIOUS CAUSES

That woman is naturally weak, or degraded by a concurrence of circumstances, is, I think, clear. But this position I shall simply contrast with a conclusion, which I have frequently heard fall from sensible men in favour of an aristocracy: that the mass of mankind cannot be anything, or the obsequious slaves, who patiently allow themselves to be driven forward, would feel their own consequence, and spurn their chains. Men, they further observe, submit every where to oppression, when they have only to lift up their heads to throw off the yoke; yet, instead of asserting their birthright, they quietly lick the dust, and say, let us eat and drink, for to-morrow we die. Women, I argue from analogy, are degraded by the same propensity to enjoy the present moment; and, at last, despise the freedom which they have not sufficient virtue to struggle to attain. But I must be more explicit.

With respect to the culture of the heart, it is unanimously allowed that sex is out of the question; but the line of subordination in the mental powers is never to be passed over. Only 'absolute in loveliness,' the portion of rationality granted to woman, is, indeed, very scanty; for, denying her genius and judgment, it is scarcely possible to divine what remains to characterize intellect.

The stamen of immortality, if I may be allowed the phrase, is the perfectibility of human reason; for, were man created perfect, or did a flood of knowledge break in upon him, when he arrived at maturity, that precluded error, I should doubt whether his existence would be continued after the dissolution of the body. But, in the present state of things, every difficulty in morals that escapes from human discussion, and equally baffles the investigation of profound thinking, and the lightning glance of genius, is an argument on which I build my belief of the immortality of the soul. Reason is, consequentially, the simple power of improvement; or, more properly speaking, of discerning truth. Every individual is in this respect a world in itself. More or less may be conspicuous in one being than another; but the nature of reason must be the same in all, if it be an emanation of divinity, the tie that connects the creature with the Creator; for, can that soul be stamped with the heavenly image, that is not perfected by the exercise of its own reason? Yet outwardly ornamented with elaborate care, and so adorned to delight man, 'that with honour he may love,' the soul of woman is not allowed to have this distinction, and man, ever placed between her and reason, she is always represented as only created to see through a gross medium, and to take things on trust. But dismissing these fanciful theories, and considering woman as a whole, let it be what it will, instead of a part of man, the inquiry is whether she have reason or not. If she have, which, for a moment, I will take for granted, she was not created merely to be the solace of man, and the sexual should not destroy the human character.

Into this error men have, probably, been led by viewing education in a false light; not considering it as the first step to form a being advancing gradually towards perfection; but only as a preparation for life. On this sensual error, for I must call it so, has the false system of female manners been reared, which robs the whole sex of its dignity, and classes the brown and fair with the smiling flowers that only adorn the land. This has ever been the language of men, and the fear of departing from a supposed sexual character, has made even women of superiour sense adopt the same sentiments. Thus understanding, strictly speaking, has been denied to woman; and instinct, sublimated into wit and cunning, for the purposes of life, has been substituted in its stead.

The power of generalizing ideas, of drawing comprehensive conclusions from individual observations, is the only acquirement, for an immortal being, that really deserves the name of knowledge. Merely to observe, without endeavouring to account for any thing, may (in a very incomplete manner) serve as the common sense of life; but where is the store laid up that is to clothe the soul when it leaves the body?

This power has not only been denied to women; but writers have insisted that it is inconsistent, with a few exceptions, with their sexual character. Let men prove this, and I shall grant that woman only exists for man. I must, however, previously remark, that the power of generalizing ideas, to any great extent, is not very common amongst men or women. But this exercise is the true cultivation of the understanding; and every thing conspires to render the cultivation of the understanding more difficult in the female than the male world.

I am naturally led by this assertion to the main subject of the present chapter, and shall now attempt to point out some of the causes that degrade the sex, and prevent women from generalizing their observations.

I shall not go back to the remote annals of antiquity to trace the history of woman; it is sufficient to allow that she has always been either a slave, or a despot, and to remark, that each of these situations equally retards the progress of reason. The grand source of female folly and vice has ever appeared to me to arise from narrowness of mind; and the very constitution of civil governments has put almost insuperable obstacles in the way to prevent the cultivation of the female understanding: – yet virtue can be built on no other foundation! The same obstacles are thrown in the way of the rich, and the same consequences ensue. [...]

Ignorance is a frail base for virtue! Yet, that it is the condition for which woman was organized, has been insisted upon by the writers who have most vehemently argued in favour of the superiority of man; a superiority not in degree, but essence; though, to soften the argument, they have laboured to prove, with chivalrous generosity, that the sexes ought not to be compared; man was made to reason, woman to feel: and that together, flesh and spirit, they make the most perfect whole, by blending happily reason and sensibility into one character. [...]

I come round to my old argument; if woman be allowed to have an immortal soul, she must have, as the employment of life, an understanding to improve. And when, to render the present state more complete, though every thing proves it to be but a fraction of a mighty sum, she is incited by present gratification to forget her grand destination, nature is counteracted, or she was born only to procreate and rot. Or, granting brutes, of every description, a soul, though not a reasonable one, the exercise of instinct and sensibility may be the step, which they are to take, in this life, towards the attainment of reason in the next; so that through all eternity they will lag behind man, who, why we cannot tell, had the power given him of attaining reason in his first mode of existence. [...]

In tracing the causes that, in my opinion, have degraded woman, I have confined my observations to such as universally act upon the morals and manners of the whole sex, and to me it appears clear that they all spring from want of understanding. Whether this arise from a physical or accidental weakness of faculties, time alone can determine; for I shall not lay any great stress on the example of a few women who, from having received a masculine education, have acquired courage and resolution; I only contend that the men who have been placed in similar situations, have acquired a similar character – I speak of bodies of men, and that men of genius and talents have started out of a class, in which women have never yet been placed.

CHAPTER V: ANIMADVERSIONS ON SOME OF THE WRITERS WHO HAVE RENDERED WOMEN OBJECTS OF PITY, BORDERING ON CONTEMPT

The opinions speciously supported, in some modern publications on the female character and education, which have given the tone to most of the observations made, in a more cursory manner, on the sex, remain now to be examined.

Sect. I

I shall begin with Rousseau, and give a sketch of his character of woman, in his own words, interspersing comments and reflections. My comments, it is true, will all spring from a few simple principles, and might have been deduced from what I have already said; but the artificial structure has been raised with so much ingenuity, that it seems necessary to attack it in a more circumstantial manner, and make the application myself.

Sophia, says Rousseau, should be as perfect a woman as Emilius is a man, and to render her so, it is necessary to examine the character which nature has given to the sex.

He then proceeds to prove that woman ought to be weak and passive, because she has less bodily strength than man; and hence infers, that she was formed to please and to be subject to him; and that it is her duty to render herself *agreeable* to her master – this being the grand end of her existence. Still, however, to give a little mock dignity to lust, he insists that man should not exert his strength, but depend on the will of the woman, when he seeks for pleasure with her.

'Hence we deduce a third consequence from the different constitutions of the sexes; which is, that the strongest should be master in appearance, and be dependent in fact on the weakest; and that not from any frivolous practice of gallantry or vanity of protectorship, but from an invariable law of nature, which, furnishing woman with a greater facility to excite desires than she has given man to satisfy them, makes the latter dependent on the good pleasure of the former, and compels him to endeavour to please in his turn, *in order to obtain her consent that he should be strongest.* On these occasions, the most delightful circumstance a man finds in his victory is, to doubt whether it was the woman's weakness that yielded to his superior strength, or whether her inclinations spoke in his favour: the females are also generally artful enough to leave this matter in doubt. The understanding of women answers in this respect perfectly to their constitution: so far from being ashamed of their weakness, they glory in it; their tender muscles make no resistance; they affect to be incapable of lifting the smallest burthens, and would blush to be thought robust and strong. To what purpose is all this? Not merely for the sake of appearing delicate, but through an artful precaution: it is thus they provide an excuse before-hand, and a right to be feeble when they think it expedient.'[4]

I have quoted this passage, lest my readers should suspect that I warped the author's reasoning to support my own arguments. I have already asserted that in educating women these fundamental principles lead to a system of cunning and lasciviousness.

Supposing woman to have been formed only to please, and be subject to man, the conclusion is just, she ought to sacrifice every other consideration to render herself agreeable to him: and let this brutal desire of self-preservation be the grand spring of all her actions, when it is proved to be the iron bed of fate, to fit which her character should be stretched or contracted, regardless of all moral or physical distinctions. But, if, as I think, may be demonstrated, the purposes, of even this life, viewing the whole, be subverted by practical rules built upon this ignoble base, I may be allowed to doubt whether woman was created for man: and, though the cry of irreligion, or even atheism, be raised against me, I will simply declare, that were an angel from heaven to tell me that Moses's beautiful, poetical cosmogony, and the account of the fall of man, were literally true, I could not believe what my reason told me was derogatory to the character of the Supreme Being: and, having no fear of the devil before mine eyes, I venture to call this a suggestion of reason, instead of resting my weakness on the broad shoulders of the first seducer of my frail sex.

'It being once demonstrated,' continues Rousseau, 'that man and woman are not, nor ought to be, constituted alike in temperament and character, it follows of course that they should not be educated in the same manner. In pursuing the directions of nature, they ought indeed to act in concert, but they should not be engaged in the same employments: the end of their pursuits should be the same, but the means they should take to accomplish them, and of consequence their tastes and inclinations, should be different. [...] Here then we see a primary propensity firmly established, which you need only to pursue and regulate. The little creature will doubtless be very desirous to know how to dress up her doll, to make its sleeve-knots, its flounces, its head-dress, &c. she is obliged to have so much recourse to the people about her, for their assistance in these articles, that it would be much more agreeable to her to owe them all to her own industry. Hence we have a good reason for the first lessons that are usually taught these young females: in which we do not appear to be setting them a task, but obliging them, by instructing them in what is immediately useful to themselves. And, in fact, almost all of them learn with reluctance to read and write; but very readily apply themselves to the use of their needles. They imagine themselves already grown up, and think with pleasure that such qualifications will enable them to decorate themselves.'[5]

This is certainly only an education of the body; but Rousseau is not the only man who has indirectly said that merely the person of a *young* woman, without any mind, unless animal spirits come under that description, is very pleasing. To render it weak, and what some may call beautiful, the understanding is neglected, and girls forced to sit still, play with dolls and listen to foolish conversations; – the effect of habit is insisted upon as an undoubted indication of nature. I know it was Rousseau's opinion that the first years of youth should be employed to form the body, though in educating Emilius he deviates from this plan; yet, the difference between strengthening the body, on which strength of mind in a great measure depends, and only giving it an easy motion, is very wide.

Rousseau's observations, it is proper to remark, were made in a country where the art of pleasing was refined only to extract the grossness of vice. He did not go back to nature, or his ruling appetite disturbed the operations of reason, else he would not have drawn these crude inferences.

In France boys and girls, particularly the latter, are only educated to please, to manage their persons, and regulate their exterior behaviour; and their minds are corrupted, at a very early age, by the worldly and pious cautions they receive to guard them against immodesty. I speak of past times. The very confessions which mere children were obliged to make, and the questions asked by the holy men, I assert these facts on good authority, were sufficient to impress a sexual character; and the education of society was a school of coquetry and art. At the age of ten or eleven; nay, often much sooner, girls began to coquet, and talked, unreproved, of establishing themselves in the world by marriage.

In short, they were treated like women, almost from their very birth, and compliments were listened to instead of instruction. These, weakening the mind, Nature was supposed to have acted like a step-mother, when she formed this after-thought of creation. [...]

Men have superiour strength of body; but were it not for mistaken notions of beauty, women would acquire sufficient to enable them to earn their own subsistence, the true definition of independence; and to bear those bodily inconveniencies and exertions that are requisite to strengthen the mind.

Let us then, by being allowed to take the same exercise as boys, not only during infancy, but youth, arrive at perfection of body, that we may know how far the natural superiority of man extends. For what reason or virtue can be expected from a creature when the seed-time of life is neglected? None – did not the winds of heaven casually scatter many useful seeds in the fallow ground.

'Beauty cannot be acquired by dress, and coquetry is an art not so early and speedily attained. While girls are yet young, however, they are in a capacity to study agreeable gesture, a pleasing modulation of voice, an easy carriage and behaviour; as well as to take the advantage of gracefully adapting their looks and attitudes to time, place, and occasion. Their application, therefore, should not be solely confined to the arts of industry and the needle, when they come to display other talents, whose utility is already apparent.'[6]

'For my part, I would have a young Englishwoman cultivate her agreeable talents, in order to please her future husband, with as much care and assiduity as a young Circassian cultivates her's, to fit her for the Haram of an Eastern bashaw.'[7]

To render women completely insignificant, he adds – 'The tongues of women are very voluble; they speak earlier, more readily, and more agreeably, than the men; they are accused also of speaking much more: but so it ought to be, and I should be very ready to convert this reproach into a compliment; their lips and eyes have the same activity, and for the same reason. A man speaks of what he knows, a woman of what pleases her; the one requires knowledge, the other taste; the principal object of a man's discourse should be what is useful, that of a woman's what is agreeable. There ought to be nothing in common between their different conversation but truth.'[8] [. . .]

But, to complete the sketch. 'It is easy to be conceived, that if male children be not in a capacity to form any true notions of religion, those ideas must be greatly above the conception of the females [. . .]. As authority ought to regulate the religion of the women, it is not so needful to explain to them the reasons for their belief, as to lay down precisely the tenets they are to believe: for the creed, which presents only obscure ideas to the mind, is the source of fanaticism; and that which presents absurdities, leads to infidelity.'[9]

Absolute, uncontroverted authority, it seems, must subsist somewhere: but is not this a direct and exclusive appropriation of reason? The *rights* of humanity have been thus confined to the male line from Adam downwards. Rousseau would carry his male aristocracy still further, for he insinuates, that he should not blame those, who contend for leaving woman in a state of the most profound ignorance, if it were not necessary in order to preserve her chastity and justify the man's choice, in the eyes of the world, to give her a little knowledge of men, and the customs produced by human passions; else she might propagate at home without being rendered less voluptuous and innocent by the exercise of her understanding: excepting, indeed, during the first year of marriage, when she might employ it to dress like Sophia. 'Her dress is extremely modest in appearance, and yet very coquettish in fact: she does not make a display of her charms, she conceals them; but in concealing them, she knows how to affect your imagination. Every one who sees her will say, There is a modest and discreet girl; but while you are near her, your eyes and affections wander all over her person, so that you cannot withdraw them; and you would conclude, that every part of her dress, simple as it seems, was only put in its proper order to be taken to pieces by the imagination.'[10] Is this modesty? Is this a preparation for immortality? Again. – What opinion are we to form of a system of education, when the author says of his heroine, 'that with her, doing things well, is but a *secondary* concern; her principal concern is to do them *neatly.*'[11]

Secondary, in fact, are all her virtues and qualities, for, respecting religion, he makes her parents thus address her, accustomed to submission – 'Your husband will instruct you in *good time.*'[12]

After thus cramping a woman's mind, if, in order to keep it fair, he have not made it quite a blank, he advises her to reflect, that a reflecting man may not yawn in her company, when he is tired of caressing her.[13] What has she to reflect about who must obey? and would it not be a refinement on cruelty only to open her mind to make the darkness and misery of her fate *visible*? Yet, these are his sensible remarks; how consistent with what I have already been obliged to quote, to give a fair view of the subject, the reader may determine. [...]

Why was Rousseau's life divided between ecstasy and misery? Can any other answer be given than this, that the effervescence of his imagination produced both; but, had his fancy been allowed to cool, it is possible that he might have acquired more strength of mind. Still, if the purpose of life be to educate the intellectual part of man, all with respect to him was right; yet, had not death led to a nobler scene of action, it is probable that he would have enjoyed more equal happiness on earth, and have felt the calm sensations of the man of nature instead of being prepared for another stage of existence by nourishing the passions which agitate the civilized man.

But peace to his manes! I war not with his ashes, but his opinions. I war only with the sensibility that led him to degrade woman by making her the slave of love. [...]

CHAPTER VI: THE EFFECT WHICH AN EARLY ASSOCIATION OF IDEAS HAS UPON THE CHARACTER

Educated in the enervating style recommended by the writers on whom I have been animadverting; and not having a chance, from their subordinate state in society, to recover their lost ground, is it surprising that women every where appear a defect in nature? Is it surprising, when we consider what a determinate effect an early association of ideas has on the character, that they neglect their understandings, and turn all their attention to their persons?

The great advantages which naturally result from storing the mind with know-ledge, are obvious from the following considerations. The association of our ideas is either habitual or instantaneous; and the latter mode seems rather to depend on the original temperature of the mind than on the will. When the ideas, and matters of fact, are once taken in, they lie by for use, till some fortuitous circumstance makes the information dart into the mind with illustrative force, that has been received at very different periods of our lives. Like the lightning's flash are many recollections; one idea assimilating and explaining another, with astonishing rapidity. I do not now allude to that quick perception of truth, which is so intuitive that it baffles research, and makes us at a loss to determine whether it is reminiscence or ratiocination, lost sight of in its celerity, that opens the dark cloud. Over those instantaneous associ-ations we have little power; for when the mind is once enlarged by excursive flights, or profound reflection, the raw materials will, in some degree, arrange themselves. The understanding, it is true, may keep us from going out of drawing when we group our thoughts, or transcribe from the imagination the warm sketches of fancy; but the animal spirits, the individual character, give the colouring. Over this subtile electric fluid, how little power do we possess, and over it how little power can reason obtain! These fine intractable spirits appear to be the essence of genius, and beaming in its eagle eye, produce in the most eminent degree the happy energy of associating thoughts that surprise, delight, and instruct. These are the glowing minds that concentrate pictures for their fellow-creatures; forcing them to view with interest the objects reflected from the impassioned imagination, which they passed over in nature.

I must be allowed to explain myself. The generality of people cannot see or feel poetically, they want fancy, and therefore fly from solitude in search of sensible objects; but when an author lends them his eyes they can see as he saw, and be amused by images they could not select, though lying before them.

Education thus only supplies the man of genius with knowledge to give variety and contrast to his associations; but there is an habitual association of ideas, that grows 'with our growth,' which has a great effect on the moral character of mankind; and by which a turn is given to the mind that commonly remains throughout life. So ductile is the understanding, and yet so stubborn, that the associations which depend on adventitious circumstances, during the period that the body takes to arrive at maturity, can seldom be disentangled by reason. One idea calls up another, its old associate, and memory, faithful to the first impressions, particularly when the intellectual powers are not employed to cool our sensations, retraces them with mechanical exactness.

This habitual slavery, to first impressions, has a more baneful effect on the female than the male character, because business and other dry employments of the under-standing, tend to deaden the feelings and break associations that do violence to reason. But females, who are made women of when they are mere children, and brought back to childhood when they ought to leave the go-cart forever, have not sufficient strength of mind to efface the superinductions of art that have smothered nature. [...]

CHAPTER IX: OF THE PERNICIOUS EFFECTS WHICH ARISE FROM THE UNNATURAL DISTINCTIONS ESTABLISHED IN SOCIETY

From the respect paid to property flow, as from a poisoned fountain, most of the evils and vices which render this world such a dreary scene to the contemplative mind. For it is in the most polished society that noisome reptiles and venomous serpents lurk under the rank herbage; and there is voluptuousness pampered by the still sultry air, which relaxes every good disposition before it ripens into virtue.

One class presses on another; for all are aiming to procure respect on account of their property: and property, once gained, will procure the respect due only to talents and virtue. Men neglect the duties incumbent on man, yet are treated like demi-gods; religion is also separated from morality by a ceremonial veil, yet men wonder that the world is almost, literally speaking, a den of sharpers or oppressors.

There is a homely proverb, which speaks a shrewd truth, that whoever the devil finds idle he will employ. And what but habitual idleness can hereditary wealth and titles produce? For man is so constituted that he can only attain a proper use of his faculties by exercising them, and will not exercise them unless necessity, of some kind, first set the wheels in motion. Virtue likewise can only be acquired by the discharge of relative duties; but the importance of these sacred duties will scarcely be felt by the being who is cajoled out of his humanity by the flattery of sycophants. There must be more equality established in society, or morality will never gain ground, and this virtuous equality will not rest firmly even when founded on a rock, if one half of mankind be chained to its bottom by fate, for they will be continually undermining it through ignorance or pride.

It is vain to expect virtue from women till they are, in some degree, independent of men; nay, it is vain to expect that strength of natural affection, which would make them good wives and mothers. Whilst they are absolutely dependent on their husbands they will be cunning, mean, and selfish, and the men who can be gratified by the fawning fondness of spaniel-like affection, have not much delicacy, for love is not to be bought, in any sense of the words, its silken wings are instantly shrivelled up when any thing beside a return in kind is sought. Yet whilst wealth enervates men; and women live, as it were, by their personal charms, how can we expect them to discharge those ennobling duties which equally require exertion and self-denial. Hereditary property sophisticates the mind, and the unfortunate victims to it, if I may so express myself, swathed from their birth, seldom exert the locomotive faculty of body or mind; and, thus viewing every thing through one medium, and that a false one, they are unable to discern in what true merit and happiness consist. False, indeed, must be the light when the drapery of situation hides the man, and makes him stalk in masquerade, dragging from one scene of dissipation to another the nerveless limbs that hang with stupid listlessness, and rolling round the vacant eye which plainly tells us that there is no mind at home.

I mean, therefore, to infer that the society is not properly organized which does not compel men and women to discharge their respective duties, by making it the only way to acquire that countenance from their fellow-creatures, which every human being wishes some way to attain. The respect, consequently, which is paid to wealth and mere personal charms, is a true north-east blast, that blights the tender blossoms of affection and virtue. Nature has wisely attached affections to duties, to sweeten toil, and to give that vigour to the exertions of reason which only the heart can give. But, the affection which is put on merely because it is the appropriated insignia of a certain character, when its duties are not fulfilled, is one of the empty compliments which vice and folly are obliged to pay to virtue and the real nature of things.

To illustrate my opinion, I need only observe, that when a woman is admired for her beauty, and suffers herself to be so far intoxicated by the admiration she receives, as to neglect to discharge the indispensable duty of a mother, she sins against herself by neglecting to cultivate an affection that would equally tend to make her useful and happy. True happiness, I mean all the contentment, and virtuous satisfaction, that can be snatched in this imperfect state, must arise from well regulated affections; and an affection includes a duty. Men are not aware of the misery they cause, and the vicious weakness they cherish, by only inciting women to render themselves pleasing; they do not consider that they thus make natural and artificial duties clash, by sacrificing the comfort and respectability of a woman's life to voluptuous notions of beauty, when in nature they all harmonize.

Cold would be the heart of a husband, were he not rendered unnatural by early debauchery, who did not feel more delight at seeing his child suckled by its mother, than the most artful wanton tricks could ever raise; yet this natural way of cementing the matrimonial tie, and twisting esteem with fonder recollections, wealth leads women to spurn. To preserve their beauty, and wear the flowery crown of the day, which gives them a kind of right to reign for a short time over the sex, they neglect to stamp impressions on their husbands' hearts, that would be remembered with more tenderness when the snow on the head began to chill the bosom, than even their virgin charms. The maternal solicitude of a reasonable affectionate woman is very interesting, and the chastened dignity with which a mother returns the caresses that she and her child receive from a father who has been fulfilling the serious duties of his station, is not only a respectable, but a beautiful sight. So singular, indeed, are my feelings, and I have endeavoured not to catch factitious ones, that after having been fatigued with the sight of insipid grandeur and the slavish ceremonies that with cumberous pomp supplied the place of domestic affections, I have turned to some other scene to relieve my eye by resting it on the refreshing green every where scattered by nature. I have then viewed with pleasure a woman nursing her children, and discharging the duties of her station with, perhaps, merely a servant maid to take off her hands the servile part of the household business. I have seen her prepare herself and children, with only the luxury of cleanliness, to receive her husband, who returning weary home in the evening found smiling babes and a clean hearth. My heart has loitered in the midst of the group, and has even throbbed with sympathetic emotion, when the scraping of the well known foot has raised a pleasing tumult.

Whilst my benevolence has been gratified by contemplating this artless picture, I have thought that a couple of this description, equally necessary and independent of each other, because each fulfilled the respective duties of their station, possessed all that life could give. – Raised sufficiently above abject poverty not to be obliged to weigh the consequence of every farthing they spend, and having sufficient to prevent their attending to a frigid system of œconomy, which narrows both heart and mind. I declare, so vulgar are my conceptions, that I know not what is wanted to render this the happiest as well as the most respectable situation in the world, but a taste for literature, to throw a little variety and interest into social converse, and some superfluous money to give to the needy and to buy books. For it is not pleasant when the heart is opened by compassion and the head active in arranging plans of usefulness, to have a prim urchin continually twitching back the elbow to prevent the hand from drawing out an almost empty purse, whispering at the same time some prudential maxim about the priority of justice.

Destructive, however, as riches and inherited honours are to the human character, women are more debased and cramped, if possible, by them, than men, because men may still, in some degree, unfold their faculties by becoming soldiers and statesmen. [...]

The preposterous distinctions of rank, which render civilization a curse, by dividing the world between voluptuous tyrants, and cunning envious dependents, corrupt, almost equally, every class of people, because respectability is not attached to the discharge of the relative duties of life, but to the station, and when the duties are not fulfilled the affections cannot gain sufficient strength to fortify the virtue of which they are the natural reward. Still there are some loop-holes out of which a man may creep, and dare to think and act for himself; but for a woman it is an herculean task, because she has difficulties peculiar to her sex to overcome, which require almost superhuman powers.

A truly benevolent legislator always endeavours to make it the interest of each individual to be virtuous; and thus private virtue becoming the cement of public happiness, an orderly whole is consolidated by the tendency of all the parts towards a common centre. But, the private or public virtue of woman is very problematical; for Rousseau, and a numerous list of male writers, insist that she should all her life be subjected to a severe restraint, that of propriety. Why subject her to propriety – blind propriety, if she be capable of acting from a nobler spring, if she be an heir of immortality? Is sugar always to be produced by vital blood? Is one half of the human species, like the poor African slaves, to be subject to prejudices that brutalize them, when principles would be a surer guard, only to sweeten the cup of man? Is not this indirectly to deny woman reason? for a gift is a mockery, if it be unfit for use.

Women are, in common with men, rendered weak and luxurious by the relaxing pleasures which wealth procures; but added to this they are made slaves to their persons, and must render them alluring that man may lend them his reason to guide their tottering steps aright. Or should they be ambitious, they must govern their tyrants by sinister tricks, for without rights there cannot be any incumbent duties. The laws respecting woman, which I mean to discuss in a future part, make an absurd unit of a man and his wife; and then, by the easy transition of only considering him as responsible, she is reduced to a mere cypher.

The being who discharges the duties of its station is independent; and, speaking of women at large, their first duty is to themselves as rational creatures, and the next, in point of importance, as citizens, is that, which includes so many, of a mother. The rank in life which dispenses with their fulfilling this duty, necessarily degrades them by making them mere dolls. Or, should they turn to something more important than merely fitting drapery upon a smooth block, their minds are only occupied by some soft platonic attachment; or, the actual management of an intrigue may keep their thoughts in motion; for when they neglect domestic duties, they have it not in their power to take the field and march and counter-march like soldiers, or wrangle in the senate to keep their faculties from rusting.

I know that, as a proof of the inferiority of the sex, Rousseau has exultingly exclaimed, How can they leave the nursery for the camp! – And the camp has by some moralists been termed the school of the most heroic virtues; though, I think, it would puzzle a keen casuist to prove the reasonableness of the greater number of wars that have dubbed heroes. I do not mean to consider this question critically; because, having frequently viewed these freaks of ambition as the first natural mode of civilization, when the ground must be torn up, and the woods cleared by fire and sword, I do not choose to call them pests; but surely the present system of war has little connection with virtue of any denomination, being rather the school of *finesse* and effeminacy, than of fortitude.

Yet, if defensive war, the only justifiable war, in the present advanced state of society, where virtue can shew its face and ripen amidst the rigours which purify the air on the mountain's top, were alone to be adopted as just and glorious, the true heroism of antiquity might again animate female bosoms. – But fair and softly, gentle reader, male or female, do not alarm thyself, for though I have compared the character of a modern soldier with that of a civilized woman, I am not going to advise them to turn their distaff into a musket, though I sincerely wish to see the bayonet converted into a pruning-hook. I only recreated an imagination, fatigued by contemplating the vices and follies which all proceed from a feculent stream of wealth that has muddied the pure rills of natural affection, by supposing that society will some time or other be so constituted, that man must necessarily fulfil the duties of a citizen, or be despised, and that while he was employed in any of the departments of civil life, his wife, also an active citizen, should be equally intent to manage her family, educate her children, and assist her neighbours.

But, to render her really virtuous and useful, she must not, if she discharge her civil duties, want, individually, the protection of civil laws; she must not be dependent on her husband's bounty for her subsistence during his life, or support after his death – for how can a being be generous who has nothing of its own? or, virtuous, who is not free? The wife, in the present state of things, who is faithful to her husband, and neither suckles nor educates her children, scarcely deserves the name of a wife, and has no right to that of a citizen. But take away natural rights, and duties become null.

Women then must be considered as only the wanton solace of men, when they become so weak in mind and body, that they cannot exert themselves, unless to pursue some frothy pleasure, or to invent some frivolous fashion. What can be a more melancholy sight to a thinking mind, than to look into the numerous carriages that drive helter-skelter about this metropolis in a morning full of pale-faced creatures who are flying from themselves. I have often wished, with Dr. Johnson, to place some of them in a little shop with half a dozen children looking up to their languid countenances for support. I am much mistaken, if some latent vigour would not soon give health and spirit to their eyes, and some lines drawn by the exercise of reason on the blank cheeks, which before were only undulated by dimples, might restore lost dignity to the character, or rather enable it to attain the true dignity of its nature. Virtue is not to be acquired even by speculation, much less by the negative supineness that wealth naturally generates.

Besides, when poverty is more disgraceful than even vice, is not morality cut to the quick? Still to avoid misconstruction, though I consider that women in the common walks of life are called to fulfil the duties of wives and mothers, by religion and reason, I cannot help lamenting that women of a superiour cast have not a road open by which they can pursue more extensive plans of usefulness and independence. I may excite laughter, by dropping an hint, which I mean to pursue, some future time, for I really think that women ought to have representatives, instead of being arbitrarily governed without having any direct share allowed them in the deliberations of government.

But, as the whole system of representation is now, in this country, only a convenient handle for despotism, they need not complain, for they are as well represented as a numerous class of hard working mechanics, who pay for the support of royalty when they can scarcely stop their children's mouths with bread. How are they represented whose very sweat supports the splendid stud of an heir apparent, or varnishes the chariot of some female favourite who looks down on shame? Taxes on the very necessaries of life, enable an endless tribe of idle princes and princesses to pass with stupid pomp before a gaping crowd, who almost worship the very parade which costs them so dear. This is mere gothic grandeur, something like the barbarous useless parade of having sentinels on horseback at Whitehall, which I could never view without a mixture of contempt and indignation. [...]

But what have women to do in society? I may be asked, but to loiter with easy grace; surely you would not condemn them all to suckle fools and chronicle small beer! No. Women might certainly study the art of healing, and be physicians as well as nurses. And midwifery, decency seems to allot to them, though I am afraid the word midwife, in our dictionaries, will soon give place to *accoucheur*, and one proof of the former delicacy of the sex be effaced from the language.

They might, also, study politics, and settle their benevolence on the broadest basis; for the reading of history will scarcely be more useful than the perusal of romances, if read as mere biography; if the character of the times, the political improvements, arts, &c. be not observed. In short, if it be not considered as the history of man; and not of particular men, who filled a niche in the temple of fame, and dropped into the black rolling stream of time, that silently sweeps all before it, into the shapeless void called – eternity. – For shape, can it be called, 'that shape hath none?'

Business of various kinds, they might likewise pursue, if they were educated in a more orderly manner, which might save many from common and legal prostitution. Women would not then marry for a support, as men accept of places under government, and neglect the implied duties; nor would an attempt to earn their own subsistence, a most laudable one! sink them almost to the level of those poor abandoned creatures who live by prostitution. For are not milliners and mantua-makers reckoned the next class? The few employments open to women, so far from being liberal, are menial; and when a superiour education enables them to take charge of the education of children as governesses, they are not treated like the tutors of sons, though even clerical tutors are not always treated in a manner calculated to render them respectable in the eyes of their pupils, to say nothing of the private comfort of the individual. But as women educated like gentlewomen, are never designed for the humiliating situation which necessity sometimes forces them to fill; these situations are considered in the light of a degradation; and they know little of the human heart, who need to be told, that nothing so painfully sharpens sensibility as such a fall in life.

Some of these women might be restrained from marrying by a proper spirit or delicacy, and others may not have had it in their power to escape in this pitiful way from servitude; is not that government then very defective, and very unmindful of the happiness of one half of its members, that does not provide for honest, independent women, by encouraging them to fill respectable stations? But in order to render their private virtue a public benefit, they must have a civil existence in the state, married or single; else we shall continually see some worthy woman, whose sensibility has been rendered painfully acute by undeserved contempt, droop like 'the lily broken down by a plow-share.'

It is a melancholy truth; yet such is the blessed effect of civilization! the most respectable women are the most oppressed; and, unless they have understandings far superiour to the common run of understandings, taking in both sexes, they must, from being treated like contemptible beings, become contemptible. How many women thus waste life away the prey of discontent, who might have practised as physicians, regulated a farm, managed a shop, and stood erect, supported by their own industry, instead of hanging their heads surcharged with the dew of sensibility, that consumes the beauty to which it at first gave lustre; nay, I doubt whether pity and love are so near akin as poets feign, for I have seldom seen much compassion excited by the helplessness of females, unless they were fair; then, perhaps, pity was the soft handmaid of love, or the harbinger of lust. [...]

Those writers are particularly useful, in my opinion, who make man feel for man, independent of the station he fills, or the drapery of factitious sentiments. I then would fain convince reasonable men of the importance of some of my remarks, and prevail on them to weigh dispassionately the whole tenor of my observations. – I appeal to their understandings; and, as a fellow-creature, claim, in the name of my sex, some interest in their hearts. I entreat them to assist to emancipate their companion, to make her a *help meet* for them!

Would men but generously snap our chains, and be content with rational fellowship instead of slavish obedience, they would find us more observant daughters, more affectionate sisters, more faithful wives, more reasonable mothers – in a word, better citizens. We should then love them with true affection, because we should learn to respect ourselves; and the peace of mind of a worthy man would not be interrupted by the idle vanity of his wife, nor the babes sent to nestle in a strange bosom, having never found a home in their mother's. [...]

CHAPTER XII: ON NATIONAL EDUCATION

The good effects resulting from attention to private education will ever be very confined, and the parent who really puts his own hand to the plow, will always, in some degree, be disappointed, till education becomes a grand national concern. A man cannot retire into a desert with his child, and if he did he could not bring himself back to childhood, and become the proper friend and play-fellow of an infant or youth. And when children are confined to the society of men and women, they very soon acquire that kind of premature manhood which stops the growth of every vigorous power of mind or body. In order to open their faculties they should be excited to think for themselves; and this can only be done by mixing a number of children together, and making them jointly pursue the same objects.

A child very soon contracts a benumbing indolence of mind, which he has seldom sufficient vigour afterwards to shake off, when he only asks a question instead of seeking for information, and then relies implicitly on the answer he receives. With his equals in age this could never be the case, and the subjects of inquiry, though they might be influenced, would not be entirely under the direction of men, who frequently damp, if not destroy, abilities, by bringing them forward too hastily: and too hastily they will infallibly be brought forward, if the child could be confined to the society of a man, however sagacious that man may be.

Besides, in youth the seeds of every affection should be sown, and the respectful regard, which is felt for a parent, is very different from the social affections that are to constitute the happiness of life as it advances. Of these equality is the basis, and an intercourse of sentiments unclogged by that observant seriousness which prevents disputation, though it may not inforce submission. Let a child have ever such an affection for his parent, he will always languish to play and prattle with children; and the very respect he feels, for filial esteem always has a dash of fear mixed with it, will, if it do not teach him cunning, at least prevent him from pouring out the little secrets which first open the heart to friendship and confidence, gradually leading to more expansive benevolence. Added to this, he will never acquire that frank ingenuousness of behaviour, which young people can only attain by being frequently in society where they dare to speak what they think; neither afraid of being reproved for their presumption, nor laughed at for their folly. [...]

The only way to avoid two extremes equally injurious to morality, would be to contrive some way of combining a public and private education. Thus to make men citizens two natural steps might be taken, which seem directly to lead to the desired point; for the domestic affections, that first open the heart to the various modifications of humanity, would be cultivated, whilst the children were nevertheless allowed to spend great part of their time, on terms of equality, with other children.

I still recollect, with pleasure, the country day school; where a boy trudged in the morning, wet or dry, carrying his books, and his dinner, if it were at a considerable distance: a servant did not then lead master by the hand, for, when he had once put on coat and breeches, he was allowed to shift for himself, and return alone in the evening to recount the feats of the day close at the parental knee. His father's house was his home, and was ever after fondly remembered; nay, I appeal to many superiour men, who were educated in this manner, whether the recollection of some shady lane where they conned their lesson; or, of some stile, where they sat making a kite, or mending a bat, has not endeared their country to them?

But, what boy ever recollected with pleasure the years he spent in close confinement, at an academy near London? unless, indeed, he should, by chance, remember the poor scare-crow of an usher, whom he tormented; or, the tartman, from whom he caught a cake, to devour it with a cattish appetite of selfishness. At boarding-schools of every description, the relaxation of the junior boys is mischief; and of the senior, vice. Besides, in great schools, what can be more prejudicial to the moral character than the system of tyranny and abject slavery which is established amongst the boys, to say nothing of the slavery to forms, which makes religion worse than a farce? For what good can be expected from the youth who receives the sacrament of the Lord's supper, to avoid forfeiting half a guinea, which he probably afterwards spends in some sensual manner? Half the employment of the youths is to elude the necessity of attending public worship; and well they may, for such a constant repetition of the same thing must be a very irksome restraint on their natural vivacity. As these ceremonies have the most fatal effect on their morals, and as a ritual performed by the lips, when the heart and mind are far away, is not now stored up by our church as a bank to draw on for the fees of the poor souls in purgatory, why should they not be abolished? [...]

In order then to inspire a love of home and domestic pleasures, children ought to be educated at home, for riotous holidays only make them fond of home for their own sakes. Yet, the vacations, which do not foster domestic affections, continually disturb the course of study, and render any plan of improvement abortive which includes temperance; still, were they abolished, children would be entirely separated from their parents, and I question whether they would become better citizens by sacrificing the preparatory affections, by destroying the force of relationships that render the marriage state as necessary as respectable. But, if a private education produce self-importance, or insulate a man in his family, the evil is only shifted, not remedied.

This train of reasoning brings me back to a subject, on which I mean to dwell, the necessity of establishing proper day-schools.

But, these should be national establishments, for whilst school-masters are dependent on the caprice of parents, little exertion can be expected from them, more than is necessary to please ignorant people. Indeed, the necessity of a master's giving the parents some sample of the boys abilities, which during the vacation is shewn to every visitor, is productive of more mischief than would at first be supposed. For it is seldom done entirely, to speak with moderation, by the child itself; thus the master countenances falsehood, or winds the poor machine up to some extraordinary exertion, that injures the wheels, and stops the progress of gradual improvement. The memory is loaded with unintelligible words, to make a shew of, without the understanding's acquiring any distinct ideas; but only that education deserves emphatically to be termed cultivation of mind, which teaches young people how to begin to think. The imagination should not be allowed to debauch the understanding before it gained strength, or vanity will become the forerunner of vice: for every way of exhibiting the acquirements of a child is injurious to its moral character. [...]

The little respect paid to chastity in the male world is, I am persuaded, the grand source of many of the physical and moral evils that torment mankind, as well as of the vices and follies that degrade and destroy women; yet at school, boys infallibly lose that decent bashfulness, which might have ripened into modesty, at home.

And what nasty indecent tricks do they not also learn from each other, when a number of them pig together in the same bedchamber, not to speak of the vices, which render the body weak, whilst they effectually prevent the acquisition of any delicacy of mind. The little attention paid to the cultivation of modesty, amongst men, produces great depravity in all the relationships of society; for, not only love – love that ought to purify the heart, and first call forth all the youthful powers, to prepare the man to discharge the benevolent duties of life, is sacrificed to premature lust; but, all the social affections are deadened by the selfish gratifications, which very early pollute the mind, and dry up the generous juices of the heart. In what an unnatural manner is innocence often violated; and what serious consequences ensue to render private vices a public pest. Besides, an habit of personal order, which has more effect on the moral character, than is, in general, supposed, can only be acquired at home, where that respectable reserve is kept up which checks the familiarity, that sinking into beastliness, undermines the affection it insults.

I have already animadverted on the bad habits which females acquire when they are shut up together; and, I think, that the observation may fairly be extended to the other sex, till the natural inference is drawn which I have had in view throughout – that to improve both sexes they ought, not only in private families, but in public schools, to be educated together. If marriage be the cement of society, mankind should all be educated after the same model, or the intercourse of the sexes will never deserve the name of fellowship, nor will women ever fulfil the peculiar duties of their sex, till they become enlightened citizens, till they become free by being enabled to earn their own subsistence, independent of men; in the same manner, I mean, to prevent misconstruction, as one man is independent of another. Nay, marriage will never be held sacred till women, by being brought up with men, are prepared to be their companions rather than their mistresses: for the mean doublings of cunning will ever render them contemptible, whilst oppression renders them timid. So convinced am I of this truth, that I will venture to predict that virtue will never prevail in society till the virtues of both sexes are founded on reason; and, till the affections common to both are allowed to gain their due strength by the discharge of mutual duties.

Were boys and girls permitted to pursue the same studies together, those graceful decencies might early be inculcated which produce modesty without those sexual distinctions that taint the mind. Lessons of politeness, and that formulary of decorum, which treads on the heels of falsehood, would be rendered useless by habitual propriety of behaviour. Not, indeed, put on for visitors like the courtly robe of politeness, but the sober effect of cleanliness of mind. Would not this simple elegance of sincerity be a chaste homage paid to domestic affections, far surpassing the meretricious compliments that shine with false lustre in the heartless intercourse of fashionable life? But, till more understanding preponderates in society, there will ever be a want of heart and taste, and the harlot's *rouge* will supply the place of that celestial suffusion which only virtuous affections can give to the face. Gallantry, and what is called love, may subsist without simplicity of character; but the main pillars of friendship, are respect and confidence – esteem is never founded on it cannot tell what! [...]

When, therefore, I call women slaves, I mean in a political and civil sense; for, indirectly they obtain too much power, and are debased by their exertions to obtain illicit sway.

Let an enlightened nation then try what effect reason would have to bring them back to nature, and their duty; and allowing them to share the advantages of education and government with man, see whether they will become better, as they grow wiser and become free. They cannot be injured by the experiment; for it is not in the power of man to render them more insignificant than they are at present.

To render this practicable, day schools, for particular ages, should be established by government, in which boys and girls might be educated together. The school for the younger children, from five to nine years of age, ought to be absolutely free and open to all classes. A sufficient number of masters should also be chosen by a select committee, in each parish, to whom any complaint of negligence, &c. might be made, if signed by six of the children's parents. [...]

After the age of nine, girls and boys, intended for domestic employments, or mechanical trades, ought to be removed to other schools, and receive instruction, in some measure appropriated to the destination of each individual, the two sexes being still together in the morning; but in the afternoon, the girls should attend a school, where plain-work, mantua-making, millinery, &c. would be their employment.

The young people of superior abilities, or fortune, might now be taught, in another school, the dead and living languages, the elements of science, and continue the study of history and politics, on a more extensive scale, which would not exclude polite literature.

Girls and boys still together? I hear some readers ask: yes. And I should not fear any other consequence than that some early attachment might take place; which, whilst it had the best effect on the moral character of the young people, might not perfectly agree with the views of the parents, for it will be a long time, I fear, before the world will be so far enlightened that parents, only anxious to render their children virtuous, shall allow them to choose companions for life themselves.

Besides, this would be a sure way to promote early marriages, and from early marriages the most salutary physical and moral effects naturally flow. What a different character does a married citizen assume from the selfish coxcomb, who lives, but for himself, and who is often afraid to marry lest he should not be able to live in a certain style. Great emergencies excepted, which would rarely occur in a society of which equality was the basis, a man can only be prepared to discharge the duties of public life, by the habitual practice of those inferiour ones which form the man.

In this plan of education the constitution of boys would not be ruined by the early debaucheries, which now make men so selfish, or girls rendered weak and vain, by indolence, and frivolous pursuits. But, I presuppose, that such a degree of equality should be established between the sexes as would shut out gallantry and coquetry, yet allow friendship and love to temper the heart for the discharge of higher duties.

These would be schools of morality – and the happiness of man, allowed to flow from the pure springs of duty and affection, what advances might not the human mind make? Society can only be happy and free in proportion as it is virtuous; but the present distinctions, established in society, corrode all private, and blast all public virtue. [...]

Asserting the rights which women in common with men ought to contend for, I have not attempted to extenuate their faults; but to prove them to be the natural consequence of their education and station in society. If so, it is reasonable to suppose that they will change their character, and correct their vices and follies, when they are allowed to be free in a physical, moral, and civil sense.

Let woman share the rights and she will emulate the virtues of man; for she must grow more perfect when emancipated, or justify the authority that chains such a weak being to her duty. – If the latter, it will be expedient to open a fresh trade with Russia for whips; a present which a father should always make to his son-in-law on his wedding day, that a husband may keep his whole family in order by the same means; and without any violation of justice reign, wielding this sceptre, sole master of his house, because he is the only being in it who has reason: – the divine, indefeasible earthly sovereignty breathed into man by the Master of the universe. Allowing this position, women have not any inherent rights to claim; and, by the same rule, their duties vanish, for rights and duties are inseparable.

Be just then, O ye men of understanding! and mark not more severely what women do amiss, than the vicious tricks of the horse or the ass for whom ye provide provender – and allow her the privileges of ignorance, to whom ye deny the rights of reason, or ye will be worse than Egyptian task-masters, expecting virtue where nature has not given understanding!

Notes

1 *Paradise Lost*; IV. 634–8.
2 Ibid., VIII 381–92.
3 Alexander Pope, *Moral Essays*, II. 51–2.
4 Jean-Jacques Rousseau, *Émile*, trans. Barbara Foxley (London, 1911), p. 323.
5 Ibid., pp. 326, 331.
6 Ibid., p. 336.
7 Ibid., p. 337.
8 Ibid., p. 339.
9 Ibid., p. 340.
10 Ibid., pp. 356–7.
11 Ibid., p. 358.
12 Ibid., p. 359.
13 Ibid., p. 371.

PART III

Conservation or Revolution as the Path to Democratic Change:

EDMUND BURKE AND MARY WOLLSTONECRAFT

AN ICONOCLASTIC VOICE

... It is, sir, possible to render the poor happier in this world, without depriving them of the consolation which you gratuitously grant them in the next.[1]
Mary Wollstonecraft, A Vindication of the Rights of Men

Mary Wollstonecraft was thirty-one when Edmund Burke, near the end of a long career as a statesman of the Whig party, published his *Reflections on the Revolution in France* in 1790. In his time, he had preached tolerance toward the American Revolution, but he was virulent in his opposition to revolution in France. Within a month, Wollstonecraft penned her response, *A Vindication of the Rights of Men*, a closely written critique of Burke's conservatism. As the London journals took up the issue of Burke's pamphlet and Wollstonecraft's response, she moved from obscurity to fame in the heated debate over the political future of monarchism and the republican alternative.

Wollstonecraft was much experienced by a hard, daring life that included witnessing the French Revolution first-hand, watching from her window as Louis XVI was led to his execution, and fleeing its grislier developments as she and so many others became *persona non grata*. Her first-hand account is found in *An Historical and Moral View of the Progress of the French Revolution*. Her personal knowledge of the Revolution's excesses did not shake her principled conviction that large inequalities of property were wrong, nor did it diminish her devotion to democratic ideals.

Wollstonecraft grew up in a middle-class family, daughter of a violent father and an indifferent mother. She learned through those closest to her the cruelty and unfairness women could suffer. Her mother was emotionally distant from her, possibly a result of the abusive treatment by her father. Her dearest friend, Fanny

Blood, died of puerperal fever subsequent to childbirth. Her sister Eliza suffered a breakdown as a result of poor treatment by her overly controlling husband and Wollstonecraft engineered an escape for her. Through these experiences, the fact was driven home that English law provided no protection from violence for married women, nor any authority over their children, or indeed, themselves.

Self-educated, Wollstonecraft worked to support herself, her friends, and her relations, opening a school at Newington Green in London. Here she made the acquaintance of a number of Dissenting ministers who helped shape her intellectual development, including Dr. Richard Price and Joseph Priestley. When the school failed, she worked for a time as a governess in Ireland, where she first read Rousseau's *Émile*, and soon began in earnest her life as a writer. Back in London, she wrote *Thoughts on the Education of Daughters*, numerous reviews, mainly in the *Analytical Review*, translations, essays, and pamphlets.

Her most influential works are two tracts of political theory, *A Vindication of the Rights of Men* (1790) and *A Vindication of the Rights of Woman* (1792), both written prior to her residence in France. In Paris she associated with those who shared her revolutionary spirit: political pamphleteer Thomas Paine, English poet Helen Maria Williams, Manon Roland, who was executed during the reign of terror, and an American soldier, adventurer, and businessman, Gilbert Imlay, with whom she formed an attachment and had a child, Fanny Imlay. On leaving France, she travelled to Scandinavia with her young daughter, conducting Imlay's import business for him, and on returning she published *Letters Written During a Short Residence in Sweden, Norway and Denmark*. Back in London, her connections with Gilbert Imlay at an end, Wollstonecraft renewed old connections and established new ones. She was part of a circle of intellectual friends whose central figure was the publisher Joseph Johnson and which included William Blake, Thomas Paine, Mary Hays, and William Godwin, whom she married in 1797.

PRESERVE THE CURRENT STATE

We are resolved to keep an established church, an established monarchy, an established aristocracy, and an established democracy, each in the degree to which it exists, and in no greater.[2]

Edmund Burke, Reflections on the Revolution in France

Edmund Burke was born in Ireland and educated at Trinity College, Dublin. After an early law career in London, he became a minor man of letters and a politician. Burke's legacy in Parliament was chiefly as a member of the opposition Whig party where he was known for elaborate compromise and a reliance on modest reform and administration. He is heralded as the chief political theorist of modern conservatism. His theoretical contributions are of special interest since the later part of the twentieth century experienced a renewed vigor of conservatism, as political theory and as political practice.

Burke's *Reflections* is the quintessential conservative tract because it makes the argument that existing institutions, in this case England's constitutional monarchy, system of hereditary property, and established church, are good in and of themselves. He contends that the prevailing system of government is inherently good, and also extrinsically good, for a variety of reasons. The government has existed and functioned over a period of time, which lends to the institution many virtues. The mere fact of prolonged existence points to a certain functionality. Further, its evolution over time provides a built-in wisdom, and "the fruits of experience" are reflected in its design.

For Burke, stability itself is to be honored. He denies divine right but scoffs also at the notion of an elected assembly or Parliament that is supported neither by history nor by "right." His argument proceeds that British institutions carry with them the trappings of nobility and of the clergy and, therefore, deserve allegiance. Consider here his rhapsodic memory of Marie Antoinette, "glittering like the morning-star, full of life and splendor and joy."[3] The visible appearances of power and privilege instill in people honor and reverence for the institutions they represent, a proper attitude and sensibility. Activities that are disruptive of the status quo unbalance the machinery of government and disturb its efficient functioning.

THE REPUBLICAN RESPONSE

Wollstonecraft's *Vindication of the Rights of Men* is a work of great political importance. It comprises an original sustained critique of the conservative position, one that stands today as a challenge to this political position. It is historically the leading response to Burke's tract, and it introduces a gendered, or feminist, response to Burke that reveals inconsistencies in the conservative position.

Wollstonecraft's response to Burke's *Reflections* begins with a systematic questioning of his arguments. What is *inherently* good about conserving existing institutions? Is antiquity a good in itself? Are all institutions worth preserving merely because they are ancient or because they have a history? Are we to reverence "the rust of antiquity"? She repeatedly draws attention, as many contemporary feminists have, to the invocation of *nature* as an argument for preserving the status quo.[4] For how can we distinguish that which is natural from that which is constructed by the social environment in which it develops?

Wollstonecraft argues that we must distinguish between "the fruits of experience," that is, *learning* from the past, and an unthinking reverence for established practices, habits, and institutions. The fruits of experience may tell us, not just the wonders of the past, but the evil or inefficacy of entrenched practices, and they will not always (as Burke suggests) support the continuity of such practices. Thus, conservation and preservation are not in themselves sufficient as guiding principles for evaluating our institutions. We must, says Wollstonecraft in a Lockean mode, use *reason* to effect this evaluation. Wollstonecraft's strongest arguments are not in merely exposing what she perceives as the flaws of the conservative position. She is at her best when she combines criticism with a positive argument about the best sorts of institutions for creating states and citizens.

THE PARADOX OF CONSERVATISM

In the 1970s, political philosophers, among them Robert Nozick, helped revive libertarian theory, the radical right view that only the most minimal state is justified.[5] Ronald Reagan, as a conservative Republican, swept into the United States presidency in 1980 on the force of a renewed popularity of libertarian minimalism. Conservatism is the uneasy cousin of libertarianism, both views perched on the right and having intriguing intellectual connections and ruptures. The libertarian position derives from an extreme (and incomplete) reading of Lockean individualistic liberalism, that preserves in the state the rights found in Locke's state of nature, upholding personal liberty and transferring to the government only the function of universal protection. The conservative position shares the libertarian notion, with notable exceptions, that the state should not meddle in the affairs of the individual.

Conservative theory and practice are plagued by an apparent contradiction. Contemporary conservatives wish to limit the role played by government and preserve individual liberty, upholding the concept of negative freedom, or freedom from interference. Especially, the government should not meddle with property rights. And yet the backbone of conservatism is a deeply rooted sense of morality and virtue grounded in established religion and social practice. On these grounds, conservatives often argue for policies designed to "enforce morality," particularly sexual morality, and private behavior. The paradox is, how can the conservative position advocate governmental non-interference in property and governmental interference in morality at the same time?

The inconsistency is often explained in contemporary times by reference to *fiscal* and *social* conservatism, in which the position that maintains that the state should not interfere in individual affairs is torn asunder. The more internally consistent fiscal conservative position favors minimal taxation, minimal spending, and minimal redistribution of goods through social programs. Closer ideologically to libertarianism, this position is generally silent regarding other social issues. But most contemporary conservatives couple support for restrained taxation and spending with tough legal intervention on issues relating to family, sexuality, and the community. Can a Lockean principle of freedom from governmental interference be driving such seemingly inconsistent policies?

A way of explaining, but not of resolving, the paradox is by returning to the original conservative theorist, Edmund Burke. The term *conservative* arises from the sense that there is value in existing and ancient institutions, and that these should be *preserved* or *conserved*, like tomatoes or strawberries in a glass jar. For Burke, arguing in support of the English "Glorious" Revolution of 1688, and against the revolution in France of 1789, those institutions to be preserved were the constitutional monarchy, the system of hereditary property, the established church and its clergy, and the system of "chivalry" and morality that accompanied these institutions. Thus, originally, the stricture against meddling with hereditary property and supporting the prevailing moral codes were of a piece; all were part of the English (and French) social and political structure, which had evolved organically for historical reasons and *not by reason of political principle*. Particularly, it was easier to protect property rights and gain compliance from a large lower class by imposing a strict moral structure.

The scope of virtue or morality in the argument between Wollstonecraft and Burke almost exactly parallels the argument between liberals and conservatives in the twentieth century. For liberals, moral behavior consists in diminishing inequalities through systems for redistribution of goods: property, health care, child care, and access to democratic institutions. For conservatives, moral behavior focuses primarily on sexual behavior, and resides in an attitude of censure toward premarital sex, extramarital sex, homosexual sex, and social problems that are thought to issue from under-controlled sexuality: AIDS, welfare, state-funded medical care, and the taxation that is used to support these programs.

Burke was much opposed to abstract notions of rights and liberties. He was a political functionary who argued for restrained policy decisions as the key to wise government, originally with regard to the recalcitrant American colonies. So the original conservatism was not as grounded in an abstract principle, say, of non-interference as it was in a desire to preserve the status quo. Finding the historical roots of conservatism provides an explanation of how the political theory came to be, but it does not provide a theoretical solution to the conservative paradox.

POLITICAL VIRTUE: RACE, CLASS, AND GENDER

The central theme of Wollstonecraft's writing is the role of *virtue*, informed by reason and sensibility, in creating proper actions and practices. People must be *educated for virtue*; it is not innate. Virtue, for Wollstonecraft, primarily means eliminating unnatural inequalities in systems of property, politics, and gender. She grasps throughout that systems of domination and submission make for twisted relationships, be they public or private. Indeed, like contemporary feminists, she wishes to break down the very split between public and private morality, because how can democratic citizenship issue from domination in the private sphere?[6]

The primary aim of her argument in favor of virtue as a personal and civic quality is her case against *inequality*, which we find in three forms: as class inequality, as gender inequality, and as race inequality. Foremost in the *Vindication of the Rights of Men* is the argument about inequality of class. Institutions are designed for the few, those with *hereditary property*, and the many are sacrificed to them. To see how this works, notice the inconsistency of the laws with regard to justice and the natural rights of man. The landed gentry may place a decoy adjacent to a poor farmer's land, attracting birds that destroy the farmer's crops and livelihood, and the farmer has no recourse. But should the farmer poach upon the gentry's birds or deer, he may be sentenced to death. So the property of the rich has greater value than the lives and livelihood of the poor. Likewise, despite the claims of freedom and liberty, a poor person may be pressed into naval service and be stripped of his normal means of support. And yet the poor fight for the rights of the rich, for they have no property of their own to protect.

Wollstonecraft also addresses gender and race inequalities. Her arguments against gender inequality are mainly found in her second political tract, *A Vindication of the Rights of Woman*, but appear occasionally in this earlier work, as when she hopes that "the fine lady [might] become a rational woman." (These arguments are discussed extensively in Part II above.) The *Vindication of the Rights of Men* also uses the wrongs of slavery as a paradigm of the problem with conservatism. Our social and political history – our institutions and practices – support the slave trade. It is ingrained in the culture. But any reference to reason about the rights and dignity of man, and what is morally required of us, will inform our heads and hearts that slavery is wrong. Thus, she argues that conservative institutions and policies entrench a morally reprehensible practice and provide no argument for showing the wrongs of slavery. Only by reference to abstract principles of right, investigated through reason, will we reach the proper political and moral conclusions. Wollstonecraft's use of what feminist sociologist Patricia Hill Collins calls the matrices of oppression – race, sex, and class – to argue against inequality suggests a surprisingly strong link between this early feminist argument and contemporary ones.[7]

Further, established institutions are more likely to be draped in impressive or appealing trappings that hide the corruption of the underlying structure. Republican constitutions and political mechanisms cannot hide behind such trappings. In *A Vindication of Political Virtue*, political theorist Virginia Sapiro argues convincingly that Wollstonecraft was well aware of *appearance, image, and representation* in politics and in political writing.[8] Thus, Burke conveys the image of the revolutionaries in France as the harlot, sexually charged and out of control, executing their glittering queen. Wollstonecraft provides a contrasting image of classically adorned republicans, reflecting the simplicity of the new political systems. Wollstonecraft herself, in a move foreshadowing twentieth-century feminism, stopped powdering her hair and using adornments that she felt symbolized privilege over equality.

Burke became immensely popular after writing his *Reflections*; it became the crowning achievement of his career. The monarchs of Europe, from George III to Stanislaus of Poland to Catherine of Russia, sent him letters, medals, and honors. Wollstonecraft went on to achieve notoriety in her lifetime and authored perhaps the greatest feminist tract of all time. After a lengthy parliamentary career, Burke died on July 8, 1797, at the age of 78. Wollstonecraft died two months later, at the age of thirty-eight, from puerperal fever, a complication from childbirth.

Notes

1   Mary Wollstonecraft, *A Vindication of the Rights of Men*, p. 167 of this volume.
2   Edmund Burke, *Reflections on the Revolution in France*, p. 142 of this volume.
3   Ibid., p. 140.
4   See Evelyn Fox Keller's *Reflections on Gender and Science* (New Haven: Yale University Press, 1985) and Ruth Hubbard's *The Politics of Women's Biology* (New Brunswick: Rutgers University Press, 1990). These works address the scientific arguments, but many contemporary feminists make the more general argument against natural distinctions as a foundation for inequality.
5   Robert Nozick, *Anarchy, State and Utopia* (New York: Basic Books, 1974). See also Robert Paul Wolff, *A Defense of Anarchism* (Los Angeles: University of California Press, 1998).
6   See Alison Jaggar, *Feminist Politics and Human Nature* (Totowa, NJ: Rowman and Allenheld, 1983) for an especially clear treatment of this issue. See also the discussion in Part II above of Jane Roland Martin's analysis of Rousseau and Wollstonecraft's theories.
7   Patricia Hill Collins, *Black Feminist Thought: Knowledge, Consciousness and the Politics of Empowerment* (New York: Routledge, 1991).
8   Virginia Sapiro, *A Vindication of Political Virtue* (Chicago: University of Chicago Press, 1992).

CHAPTER 5

Reflections on the Revolution in France

EDMUND BURKE

You imagined, when you wrote last, that I might possibly be reckoned among the approvers of certain proceedings in France, from the solemn public seal of sanction they have received from two clubs of gentlemen in London, called the Constitutional Society, and the Revolution Society.

I certainly have the honor to belong to more clubs than one in which the Constitution of this kingdom and the principles of the glorious Revolution are held in high reverence; and I reckon myself among the most forward in my zeal for maintaining that Constitution and those principles in their utmost purity and vigor. It is because I do so that I think it necessary for me that there should be no mistake. Those who cultivate the memory of our Revolution, and those who are attached to the Constitution of this kingdom, will take good care how they are involved with persons who, under the pretext of zeal towards the Revolution and Constitution, too frequently wander from their true principles, and are ready on every occasion to depart from the firm, but cautious and deliberate, spirit which produced the one and which presides in the other. . . .

I flatter myself that I love a manly, moral, regulated liberty as well as any gentleman . . . But I cannot stand forward, and give praise or blame to anything which relates to human actions and human concerns on a simple view of the object, as it stands stripped of every relation, in all the nakedness and solitude of metaphysical abstraction. Circumstances (which with some gentlemen pass for nothing) give in reality to every political principle its distinguishing color and discriminating effect. The circumstances are what render every civil and political scheme beneficial or noxious to mankind. Abstractedly speaking, government, as well as liberty, is good; yet could I, in common sense, ten years ago, have felicitated France on her enjoyment of a government, (for she then had a government,) without inquiry what the nature of that government was, or how it was administered? Can I now congratulate the same nation upon its freedom? Is it because liberty in the abstract may be classed

Edmund Burke. *Reflections on the Revolution in France*. Originally published in 1790.

amongst the blessings of mankind, that I am seriously to felicitate a madman who has escaped from the protecting restraint and wholesome darkness of his cell on his restoration to the enjoyment of light and liberty? Am I to congratulate a highwayman and murderer who has broke prison upon the recovery of his natural rights? [...]

On the forenoon of the fourth of November last, Doctor Richard Price, a Non-Conforming minister of eminence, preached at the Dissenting meeting-house of the Old Jewry, to his club or society, a very extraordinary miscellaneous sermon, in which there are some good moral and religious sentiments, and not ill expressed, mixed up with a sort of porridge of various political opinions and reflections: but the Revolution in France is the grand ingredient in the caldron....

I looked on that sermon as the public declaration of a man much connected with literary caballers and intriguing philosophers, with political theologians and theological politicians, both at home and abroad. I know they set him up as a sort of oracle; because, with the best intentions in the world, he naturally *philippizes*, and chants his prophetic song in exact unison with their designs.

That sermon is in a strain which I believe has not been heard in this kingdom, in any of the pulpits which are tolerated or encouraged in it, since the year 1648 – when a predecessor of Dr. Price, the Reverend Hugh Peters, made the vault of the king's own chapel at St. James's ring with the honor and privilege of the saints, who, with the "high praises of God in their mouths, and a *two*-edged sword in their hands, were to execute judgment on the heathen, and punishments upon the *people*; to bind their *kings* with chains, and their *nobles* with fetters of iron." Few harangues from the pulpit, except in the days of your League in France, or in the days of our Solemn League and Covenant in England, have ever breathed less of the spirit of moderation than this lecture in the Old Jewry....

His doctrines affect our Constitution in its vital parts. He tells the Revolution Society, in this political sermon, that his Majesty "is almost the *only* lawful king in the world, because the *only* one who owes his crown to *the choice of his people*." As to the kings of *the world*, all of whom (except one) this arch-pontiff of the *rights of men*, with all the plenitude and with more than the boldness of the Papal deposing power in its meridian fervor of the twelfth century, puts into one sweeping clause of ban and anathema, and proclaims usurpers by circles of longitude and latitude over the whole globe, it behooves them to consider how they admit into their territories these apostolic missionaries, who are to tell their subjects they are not lawful kings. That is their concern. It is ours, as a domestic interest of some moment, seriously to consider the solidity of the *only* principle upon which these gentlemen acknowledge a king of Great Britain to be entitled to their allegiance.

This doctrine, as applied to the prince now on the British throne, either is nonsense, and therefore neither true nor false, or it affirms a most unfounded, dangerous, illegal, and unconstitutional position. According to this spiritual doctor of politics, if his Majesty does not owe his crown to the choice of his people, he is no *lawful* king. Now nothing can be more untrue than that the crown of this kingdom is so held by his Majesty. Therefore, if you follow their rule, the king of Great Britain, who most certainly does not owe his high office to any form of popular election, is in no respect better than the rest of the gang of usurpers, who reign, or rather rob, all over the face of this our miserable world, without any sort of right or title to the allegiance of their people. The policy of this general doctrine, so qualified, is evident enough. The propagators of this political gospel are in hopes their abstract principle (their principle that a popular choice is necessary to the legal existence of the sovereign magistracy) would be overlooked, whilst the king of Great Britain was not affected by it. In the mean time the ears of their congregations would be gradually habituated to it, as if it were a first principle admitted without dispute. [...]

At some time or other, to be sure, all the beginners of dynasties were chosen by those who called them to govern. There is ground enough for the opinion that all the kingdoms of Europe were at a remote period elective, with more or fewer limitations in the objects of choice. But whatever kings might have been here or elsewhere a thousand years ago, or in whatever manner the ruling dynasties of England or France may have begun, the king of Great Britain is at this day king by a fixed rule of succession, according to the laws of his country; and whilst the legal conditions of the compact of sovereignty are performed by him, (as they are performed,) he holds his crown in contempt of the choice of the Revolution Society, who have not a single vote for a king amongst them, either individually or collectively....

Whatever may be the success of evasion in explaining away the gross error of *fact*, which supposes that his Majesty (though he holds it in concurrence with the wishes) owes his crown to the choice of his people, yet nothing can evade their full explicit declaration concerning the principle of a right in the people to choose; which right is directly maintained and tenaciously adhered to. All the oblique insinuations concerning election bottom in this proposition and are referable to it. Lest the foundation of the king's exclusive legal title should pass for a mere rant of adulatory freedom, the political divine proceeds dogmatically to assert that, by the principles of the Revolution, the people of England have acquired three fundamental rights, all which, with him, compose one system and lie together in one short sentence, namely, that we have acquired a right:

(1)   to choose our own governors.
(2)   to cashier them for misconduct.
(3)   to frame a government for ourselves.

This new and hitherto unheard-of bill of rights, though made in the name of the whole people, belongs to those gentlemen and their faction only. The body of the people of England have no share in it. They utterly disclaim it. They will resist the practical assertion of it with their lives and fortunes. They are bound to do so by the laws of their country made at the time of that very Revolution which is appealed to in favor of the fictitious rights claimed by the Society which abuses its name.

These gentlemen of the Old Jewry, in all their reasonings on the Revolution of 1688, have a revolution which happened in England about forty years before, and the late French Revolution, so much before their eyes and in their hearts, that they are constantly confounding all the three together. It is necessary that we should separate what they confound. We must recall their erring fancies to the *acts* of the Revolution which we revere, for the discovery of its true *principles*. If the *principles* of the Revolution of 1688 are anywhere to be found, it is in the statute called the *Declaration of Right*....

This Declaration of Right ... is the corner-stone of our Constitution, as reinforced, explained, improved, and in its fundamental principles forever settled. It is called "An act for declaring the rights and liberties of the subject, and for *settling* the *succession* of the crown." You will observe that these rights and this succession are declared in one body, and bound indissolubly together.

A few years after this period, a second opportunity offered for asserting a right of election to the crown. On the prospect of a total failure of issue from King William, and from the princess, afterwards Queen Anne, the consideration of the settlement of the crown, and of a further security for the liberties of the people, again came before the legislature. Did they this second time make any provision for legalizing the crown on the spurious Revolution principles of the Old Jewry? No. They followed the principles which prevailed in the Declaration of Right, indicating with more precision the persons who were to inherit in the Protestant line. This act also incorporated, by the same policy, our liberties and an hereditary succession in the same act. Instead of a right to choose our own governors, they declared that the *succession* in that line (the Protestant line drawn from James the First), was absolutely necessary "for the peace, quiet, and security of the realm," and that it was equally urgent on them "to maintain a *certainty in the succession* thereof, to which the subjects may safely have recourse for their protection." Both these acts, in which are heard the unerring, unambiguous oracles of revolution policy, instead of countenancing the delusive, gipsy predictions of a "right to choose our governors," prove to a demonstration how totally adverse the wisdom of the nation was from turning a case of necessity into a rule of law.

Unquestionably, there was at the Revolution, in the person of King William, a small and a temporary deviation from the strict order of a regular hereditary succession; but it is against all genuine principles of jurisprudence to draw a principle from a law made in a special case and regarding an individual person. [...]

The succession of the crown has always been what it now is – an hereditary succession by law; in the old line it was a succession by the common law; in the new, by the statute law operating on the principles of the common law, not changing the substance, but regulating the mode and describing the persons. Both these descriptions of law are of the same force and are derived from an equal authority emanating from the common agreement and original compact of the state, *communi sponsione reipublicae*, and as such are equally binding on king and people, too, as long as the terms are observed and they continue the same body politic. [...]

A state without the means of some change is without the means of its conservation. Without such means it might even risk the loss of that part of the Constitution which it wished the most religiously to preserve. The two principles of conservation and correction operated strongly at the two critical periods of the Restoration and Revolution, when England found itself without a king. At both those periods the nation had lost the bond of union in their ancient edifice: they did not, however, dissolve the whole fabric. On the contrary, in both cases they regenerated the deficient part of the old Constitution through the parts which were not impaired....

On this principle, the law of inheritance had admitted some amendment in the old time, and long before the era of the Revolution.... This is the spirit of our Constitution, not only in its settled course, but in all its revolutions. Whoever came in, or however he came in, whether he obtained the crown by law or by force, the hereditary succession was either continued or adopted....

Do these new doctors of the rights of men presume to assert that King James the Second, who came to the crown as next of blood, according to the rules of a then unqualified succession, was not to all intents and purposes a lawful king of England, before he had done any of those acts which were justly construed into an abdication of his crown? If he was not, much trouble in Parliament might have been saved at the period these gentlemen commemorate. But King James was a bad king with a good title, and not an usurper....

No experience has taught us that in any other course or method than that of an *hereditary crown* our liberties can be regularly perpetuated and preserved sacred as our *hereditary right*. An irregular, convulsive movement may be necessary to throw off an irregular, convulsive disease. But the course of succession is the healthy habit of the British Constitution. [...]

The second claim of the Revolution Society is "a right of cashiering their governors for *misconduct*."...

No government could stand a moment, if it could be blown down with anything so loose and indefinite as an opinion of "*misconduct*." They who led at the Revolution grounded their virtual abdication of King James upon no such light and uncertain principle. They charged him with nothing less than a design, confirmed by a multitude of illegal overt acts, to *subvert the Protestant Church and State*, and their *fundamental*, unquestionable laws and liberties: they charged him with having broken the *original contract* between king and people. This was more than *misconduct*. A grave and overruling necessity obliged them to take the step they took, and took with infinite reluctance, as under that most rigorous of all laws. Their trust for the future preservation of the Constitution was not in future revolutions. The grand policy of all their regulations was to render it almost impracticable for any future sovereign to compel the states of the kingdom to have again recourse to those violent remedies....

The third head of right asserted by the pulpit of the Old Jewry, namely, the "right to form a government for ourselves," has, at least, as little countenance from anything done at the Revolution, either in precedent or principle, as the two first of their claims. The Revolution was made to preserve our *ancient* indisputable laws and liberties, and that *ancient* constitution of government which is our only security for law and liberty. If you are desirous of knowing the spirit of our Constitution, and the policy which predominated in that great period which has secured it to this hour, pray look for both in our histories, in our records, in our acts of Parliament and journals of Parliament, and not in the sermons of the Old Jewry, and the after-dinner toasts of the Revolution Society.... The very idea of the fabrication of a new government is enough to fill us with disgust and horror. We wished at the period of the Revolution, and do now wish, to derive all we possess as *an inheritance from our forefathers*. Upon that body and stock of inheritance we have taken care not to inoculate any scion alien to the nature of the original plant. All the reformations we have hitherto made have proceeded upon the principle of reference to antiquity...

Our oldest reformation is that of Magna Charta....

You will observe, that, from Magna Charta to the Declaration of Right, it has been the uniform policy of our Constitution to claim and assert our liberties as an *entailed inheritance* derived to us from our forefathers, and to be transmitted to our posterity – as an estate specially belonging to the people of this kingdom, without any reference whatever to any other more general or prior right. By this means our Constitution preserves an unity in so great a diversity of its parts. We have an inheritable crown, an inheritable peerage, and a House of Commons and a people inheriting privileges, franchises, and liberties from a long line of ancestors. In such a state of unbounded power, for undefined and undefinable purposes, the evil of a moral and almost physical inaptitude of the man to the function must be the greatest we can conceive to happen in the management of human affairs.

We know that the British House of Commons, without shutting its doors to any merit in any class, is, by the sure operation of adequate causes, filled with everything illustrious in rank, in descent, in hereditary and in acquired opulence, in cultivated talents, in military, civil, naval, and politic distinction, that the country can afford. But supposing, what hardly can be supposed as a case, that the House of Commons should be composed in the same manner with the *Tiers État* in France – would this dominion of chicane be borne with patience, or even conceived without horror? ...

After all, if the House of Commons were to have an wholly professional and faculty composition, what is the power of the House of Commons, circumscribed and shut in by the immovable barriers of laws, usages, positive rules of doctrine and practice, counterpoised by the House of Lords, and every moment of its existence at the discretion of the crown to continue, prorogue, or dissolve us? The power of the House of Commons, direct or indirect, is, indeed, great ... The power, however, of the House of Commons, when least diminished, is as a drop of water in the ocean, compared to that residing in a settled majority of your National Assembly. That assembly, since the destruction of the orders, has no fundamental law, no strict convention, no respected usage to restrain it. Instead of finding themselves obliged to conform to a fixed constitution, they have a power to make a constitution what shall conform to their designs. Nothing in heaven or upon earth can serve as a control on them. What ought to be the heads, the hearts, the dispositions, that are qualified, or that dare, not only to make laws under a fixed constitution, but at one heat to strike out a totally new constitution for a great kingdom, and in every part of it, from the monarch on the throne to the vestry of a parish? But

"Fools rush in where angels fear to tread."

You might, if you pleased, have profited of our example, and have given to your recovered freedom a correspondent dignity. Your privileges, though discontinued, were not lost to memory. Your Constitution, it is true, whilst you were out of possession, suffered waste and dilapidation; but you possessed in some parts the walls, and in all the foundations, of a noble and venerable castle. You might have repaired those walls; you might have built on those old foundations. Your Constitution was suspended before it was perfected; but you had the elements of a Constitution very nearly as good as could be wished. In your old states you possessed that variety of parts corresponding with the various descriptions of which your community was happily composed; you had all that combination and all that opposition of interests, you had that action and counteraction, which, in the natural and in the political world, from the reciprocal struggle of discordant powers draws out the harmony of the universe. These opposed and conflicting interests, which you considered as so great a blemish in your old and in our present Constitution, interpose a salutary check to all precipitate resolutions. They render deliberation a matter, not of choice, but of necessity; they make all change a subject of *compromise*, which naturally begets moderation; they produce *temperaments*, preventing the sore evil of harsh, crude, unqualified reformations, and rendering all the headlong exertions of arbitrary power, in the few or in the many, forever impracticable. Through that diversity of members and interests, general liberty had as many securities as there were separate views in the several orders; whilst by pressing down the whole by the weight of a real monarchy, the separate parts would have been prevented from warping and starting from their allotted places. [...]

There is no qualification for government but virtue and wisdom, actual or presumptive. Wherever they are actually found, they have, in whatever state, condition, profession, or trade, the passport of Heaven to human place and honor. Woe to the country which would madly and impiously reject the service of the talents and virtues, civil, military, or religious, that are given to grace and to serve it; and would condemn to obscurity everything formed to diffuse lustre and glory around a state! Woe to that country, too, that, passing into the opposite extreme, considers a low education, a mean, contracted view of things, a sordid, mercenary occupation, as a preferable title to command!...I do not hesitate to say that the road to eminence and power, from obscure condition, ought not to be made too easy, nor a thing too much of course. If rare merit be the rarest of all rare things, it ought to pass through some sort of probation. The temple of honor ought to be seated on an eminence. If it be opened through virtue, let it be remembered, too, that virtue is never tried but by some difficulty and some struggle.

Nothing is a due and adequate representation of a state, that does not represent its ability, as well as its property. But as ability is a vigorous and active principle, and as property is sluggish, inert, and timid, it never can be safe from the invasions of ability, unless it be, out of all proportion, predominant in the representation. It must be represented, too, in great masses of accumulation, or it is not rightly protected. The characteristic essence of property, formed out of the combined principles of its acquisition and conservation, is to be *unequal*. The great masses, therefore, which excite envy, and tempt rapacity, must be put out of the possibility of danger. Then they form a natural rampart about the lesser properties in all their gradations. The same quantity of property which is by the natural course of things divided among many has not the same operation. Its defensive power is weakened as it is diffused. In this diffusion each man's portion is less than what, in the eagerness of his desires, he may flatter himself to obtain by dissipating the accumulations of others. The plunder of the few would, indeed, give but a share inconceivably small in the distribution to the many. But the many are not capable of making this calculation; and those who lead them to rapine never intend this distribution.

The power of perpetuating our property in our families is one of the most valuable and interesting circumstances belonging to it, and that which tends the most to the perpetuation of society itself. It makes our weakness subservient to our virtue; it grafts benevolence even upon avarice. The possessors of family wealth, and of the distinction which attends hereditary possession, (as most concerned in it,) are the natural securities for this transmission. With us the House of Peers is formed upon this principle. It is wholly composed of hereditary property and hereditary distinction, and made, therefore, the third of the legislature, and, in the last event, the sole judge of all property in all its subdivisions. The House of Commons, too, though not necessarily, yet in fact, is always so composed, in the far greater part. Let those large proprietors be what they will, (and they have their chance of being amongst the best,) they are, at the very worst, the ballast in the vessel of the commonwealth. For though hereditary wealth, and the rank which goes with it, are too much idolized by creeping sycophants, and the blind, abject admirers of power, they are too rashly slighted in shallow speculations of the petulant, assuming, shortsighted coxcombs of philosophy....

Your leaders in France began by affecting to admire, almost to adore, the British Constitution; but as they advanced, they came to look upon it with a sovereign contempt. The friends of your National Assembly amongst us have full as mean an opinion of what was formerly thought the glory of their country. The Revolution Society has discovered that the English nation is not free....

These gentlemen value themselves on being systematic, and not without reason. They must therefore look on this gross and palpable defect of representation, this fundamental grievance, (so they call it,) as a thing not only vicious in itself, but as rendering our whole government absolutely *illegitimate*, and not at all better than a downright *usurpation*. Another revolution, to get rid of this illegitimate and usurped government, would of course be perfectly justifiable, if not absolutely necessary....

Something they must destroy, or they seem to themselves to exist for no purpose. One set is for destroying the civil power through the ecclesiastical; another for demolishing the ecclesiastic through the civil. They are aware that the worst consequences might happen to the public in accomplishing this double ruin of Church and State; but they are so heated with their theories, that they give more than hints that this ruin, with all the mischiefs that must lead to it and attend it, and which to themselves appear quite certain, would not be unacceptable to them, or very remote from their wishes. [...]

Far am I from denying in theory, full as far is my heart from withholding in practice, (if I were of power to give or to withhold,) the *real* rights of men. In denying their false claims of right, I do not mean to injure those which are real, and are such as their pretended rights would totally destroy. If civil society be made for the advantage of man, all the advantages for which it is made become his right. It is an institution of beneficence; and law itself is only beneficence acting by a rule. Men have a right to live by that rule; they have a right to justice, as between their fellows, whether their fellows are in politic function or in ordinary occupation. They have a right to the fruits of their industry, and to the means of making their industry fruitful. They have a right to the acquisitions of their parents, to the nourishment and improvement of their offspring, to instruction in life and to consolation in death. Whatever each man can separately do, without trespassing upon others, he has a right to do for himself; and he has a right to a fair portion of all which society, with all its combinations of skill and force, can do in his favor. In this partnership all men have equal rights; but not to equal things. He that has but five shillings in the partnership has as good a right to it as he that has five hundred pounds has to his larger proportion; but he has not a right to an equal dividend in the product of the joint stock. And as to the share of power, authority, and direction which each individual ought to have in the management of the state, that I must deny to be amongst the direct original rights of man in civil society; for I have in my contemplation the civil social man, and no other. It is a thing to be settled by convention.

If civil society be the offspring of convention, that convention must be its law. That convention must limit and modify all the descriptions of constitution which are formed under it. Every sort of legislative, judicial, or executory power are its creatures. They can have no being in any other state of things; and how can any man claim, under the conventions of civil society, rights which do not so much as suppose its existence – rights which are absolutely repugnant to it? One of the first motives to civil society, and which becomes one of its fundamental rules, is *that no man should be judge in his own cause*. By this each person has at once divested himself of the first fundamental right of uncovenanted man, that is, to judge for himself, and to assert his own cause. He abdicates all right to be his own governor. He inclusively, in a great measure, abandons the right of self-defence, the first law of Nature. Men cannot enjoy the rights of an uncivil and of a civil state together. That he may obtain justice, he gives up his right of determining what it is in points the most essential to him. That he may secure some liberty, he makes a surrender in trust of the whole of it.

Government is not made in virtue of natural rights, which may and do exist in total independence of it – and exist in much greater clearness, and in a much greater degree of abstract perfection: but their abstract perfection is their practical defect. By having a right to everything they want everything. Government is a contrivance of human wisdom to provide for human *wants*. Men have a right that these wants should be provided for by this wisdom. Among these wants is to be reckoned the want, out of civil society, of a sufficient restraint upon their passions. Society requires not only that the passions of individuals should be subjected, but that even in the mass and body, as well as in the individuals, the inclinations of men should frequently be thwarted, their will controlled, and their passions brought into subjection. This can only be done *by a power out of themselves*, and not, in the exercise of its function, subject to that will and to those passions which it is its office to bridle and subdue. In this sense the restraints on men, as well as their liberties, are to be reckoned among their rights. But as the liberties and the restrictions vary with times and circumstances, and admit of infinite modifications, they cannot be settled upon any abstract rule; and nothing is so foolish as to discuss them upon that principle.

The moment you abate anything from the full rights of men each to govern himself, and suffer any artificial, positive limitation upon those rights, from that moment the whole organization of government becomes a consideration of convenience. This it is which makes the constitution of a state, and the due distribution of its powers, a matter of the most delicate and complicated skill. It requires a deep knowledge of human nature and human necessities, and of the things which facilitate or obstruct the various ends which are to be pursued by the mechanism of civil institutions. The state is to have recruits to its strength and remedies to its distempers. What is the use of discussing a man's abstract right to food or medicine? The question is upon the method of procuring and administering them. In that deliberation I shall always advise to call in the aid of the farmer and the physician, rather than the professor of metaphysics.

The science of constructing a commonwealth, or renovating it, or reforming it, is, like every other experimental science, not to be taught *a priori*. Nor is it a short experience that can instruct us in that practical science; because the real effects of moral causes are not always immediate, but that which in the first instance is prejudicial may be excellent in its remoter operation, and its excellence may arise even from the ill effects it produces in the beginning. The reverse also happens; and very plausible schemes, with very pleasing commencements, have often shameful and lamentable conclusions. In states there are often some obscure and almost latent causes, things which appear at first view of little moment, on which a very great part of its prosperity or adversity may most essentially depend. The science of government being, therefore, so practical in itself, and intended for such practical purposes, a matter which requires experience, and even more experience than any person can gain in his whole life, however sagacious and observing he may be, it is with infinite caution that any man ought to venture upon pulling down an edifice which has answered in any tolerable degree for ages the common purposes of society, or on building it up again without having models and patterns of approved utility before his eyes. [...]

History will record, that, on the morning of the sixth of October, 1789, the king and queen of France, after a day of confusion, alarm, dismay, and slaughter, lay down, under the pledged security of public faith, to indulge nature in a few hours of respite, and troubled, melancholy repose. From this sleep the queen was first startled by the voice of the sentinel at her door, who cried out to her to save herself by flight – that this was the last proof of fidelity he could give – that they were upon him, and he was dead. Instantly he was cut down. A band of cruel ruffians and assassins, reeking with his blood, rushed into the chamber of the queen, and pierced with a hundred strokes of bayonets and poniards the bed, from whence this persecuted woman had but just time to fly almost naked, and, through ways unknown to the murderers, had escaped to seek refuge at the feet of a king and husband not secure of his own life for a moment.

This king, to say no more of him, and this queen, and their infant children, (who once would have been the pride and hope of a great and generous people,) were then forced to abandon the sanctuary of the most splendid palace in the world, which they left swimming in blood, polluted by massacre, and strewed with scattered limbs and mutilated carcasses. Thence they were conducted into the capital of their kingdom....

It is now sixteen or seventeen years since I saw the queen of France, then the Dauphiness, at Versailles; and surely never lighted on this orb, which she hardly seemed to touch, a more delightful vision. I saw her just above the horizon, decorating and cheering the elevated sphere she just began to move in – glittering like the morning-star, full of life and splendor and joy. Oh! what a revolution! and what an heart must I have, to contemplate without emotion that elevation and that fall! Little did I dream, when she added titles of veneration to those of enthusiastic, distant, respectful love, that she should ever be obliged to carry the sharp antidote against disgrace concealed in that bosom! little did I dream that I should have lived to see such disasters fallen upon her in a nation of gallant men, in a nation of men of honor, and of cavaliers! I thought ten thousand swords must have leaped from their scabbards to avenge even a look that threatened her with insult. But the age of chivalry is gone. That of sophisters, economists, and calculators has succeeded; and the glory of Europe is extinguished forever. Never, never more, shall we behold that generous loyalty to rank and sex, that proud submission, that dignified obedience, that subordination of the heart, which kept alive, even in servitude itself, the spirit of an exalted freedom! The unbought grace of life, the cheap defence of nations, the nurse of manly sentiment and heroic enterprise, is gone! It is gone, that sensibility of principle, that chastity of honor, which felt a stain like a wound, which inspired courage whilst it mitigated ferocity, which ennobled whatever it touched, and under which vice itself lost half its evil by losing all its grossness!

This mixed system of opinion and sentiment had its origin in the ancient chivalry; and the principle, though varied in its appearance by the varying state of human affairs, subsisted and influenced through a long succession of generations, even to the time we live in. If it should ever be totally extinguished, the loss, I fear, will be great. It is this which has given its character to modern Europe. It is this which has distinguished it under all its forms of government, and distinguished it to its advantage, from the states of Asia, and possibly from those states which flourished in the most brilliant periods of the antique world. It was this, which, without confounding ranks, had produced a noble equality, and handed it down through all the gradations of social life. It was this opinion which mitigated kings into companions, and raised private men to be fellows with kings. Without force or opposition, it subdued the fierceness of pride and power; it obliged sovereigns to submit to the soft collar of social esteem, compelled stern authority to submit to elegance, and gave a domination, vanquisher of laws, to be subdued by manners.

But now all is to be changed. All the pleasing illusions which made power gentle and obedience liberal, which harmonized the different shades of life, and which by a bland assimilation incorporated into politics the sentiments which beautify and soften private society, are to be dissolved by this new conquering empire of light and reason. All the decent drapery of life is to be rudely torn off. All the superadded ideas, furnished from the wardrobe of a moral imagination, which the heart owns and the understanding ratifies, as necessary to cover the defects of our naked, shivering nature, and to raise it to dignity in our own estimation, are to be exploded, as a ridiculous, absurd, and antiquated fashion.

On this scheme of things, a king is but a man, a queen is but a woman, a woman is but an animal – and an animal not of the highest order. All homage paid to the sex in general as such, and without distinct views, is to be regarded as romance and folly. Regicide, and parricide, and sacrilege, are but fictions of superstition, corrupting jurisprudence by destroying its simplicity. The murder of a king, or a queen, or a bishop, or a father, are only common homicide – and if the people are by any chance or in any way gainers by it, a sort of homicide much the most pardonable, and into which we ought not to make too severe a scrutiny.

On the scheme of this barbarous philosophy, which is the offspring of cold hearts and muddy understandings, and which is as void of solid wisdom as it is destitute of all taste and elegance, laws are to be supported only by their own terrors, and by the concern which each individual may find in them from his own private speculations, or can spare to them from his own private interests. In the groves of *their* academy, at the end of every vista, you see nothing but the gallows. Nothing is left which engages the affections on the part of the commonwealth. On the principles of this mechanic philosophy, our institutions can never be embodied, if I may use the expression, in persons – so as to create in us love, veneration, admiration, or attachment. But that sort of reason which banishes the affections is incapable of filling their place. These public affections, combined with manners, are required sometimes as supplements, sometimes as correctives, always as aids to law.... There ought to be a system of manners in every nation which a well-formed mind would be disposed to relish. To make us love our country, our country ought to be lovely. [...]

If it could have been made clear to me that the king and queen of France (those, I mean, who were such before the triumph) were inexorable and cruel tyrants, that they had formed a deliberate scheme for massacring the National Assembly, (I think I have seen something like the latter insinuated in certain publications,) I should think their captivity just. If this be true, much more ought to have been done, but done, in my opinion, in another manner. The punishment of real tyrants is a noble and awful act of justice; and it has with truth been said to be consolatory to the human mind. But if I were to punish a wicked king, I should regard the dignity in avenging the crime. Justice is grave and decorous, and in its punishments rather seems to submit to a necessity than to make a choice. [...]

We know, and it is our pride to know, that man is by his constitution a religious animal; that atheism is against, not only our reason, but our instincts; and that it cannot prevail long. But if, in the moment of riot, and in a drunken delirium from the hot spirit drawn out of the alembic of hell, which in France is now so furiously boiling, we should uncover our nakedness, by throwing off that Christian religion which has hitherto been our boast and comfort, and one great source of civilization amongst us, and among many other nations, we are apprehensive (being well aware that the mind will not endure a void) that some uncouth, pernicious, and degrading superstition might take the place of it.

For that reason, before we take from our establishment the natural, human means of estimation, and give it up to contempt, as you have done, and in doing it have incurred the penalties you well deserve to suffer, we desire that some other may be presented to us in the place of it. We shall then form our judgment.

On these ideas, instead of quarrelling with establishments, as some do, who have made a philosophy and a religion of their hostility to such institutions, we cleave closely to them. We are resolved to keep an established church, an established monarchy, an established aristocracy, and an established democracy, each in the degree it exists, and in no greater. I shall show you presently how much of each of these we possess. [...]

Society is, indeed, a contract. Subordinate contracts for objects of mere occasional interest may be dissolved at pleasure; but the state ought not to be considered as nothing better than a partnership agreement in a trade of pepper and coffee, calico or tobacco, or some other such low concern, to be taken up for a little temporary interest, and to be dissolved by the fancy of the parties. It is to be looked on with other reverence; because it is not a partnership in things subservient only to the gross animal existence of a temporary and perishable nature. It is a partnership in all science, a partnership in all art, a partnership in every virtue and in all perfection. As the ends of such a partnership cannot be obtained in many generations, it becomes a partnership not only between those who are living, but between those who are living, those who are dead, and those who are to be born. Each contract of each particular state is but a clause in the great primeval contract of eternal society, linking the lower with the higher natures, connecting the visible and invisible world, according to a fixed compact sanctioned by the inviolable oath which holds all physical and all moral natures each in their appointed place. [...]

When all the frauds, impostures, violences, rapines, burnings, murders, confiscations, compulsory paper currencies, and every description of tyranny and cruelty employed to bring about and to uphold this Revolution have their natural effect, that is, to shock the moral sentiments of all virtuous and sober minds, the abettors of this philosophic system immediately strain their throats in a declamation against the old monarchical government of France. When they have rendered that deposed power sufficiently black, they then proceed in argument, as if all those who disapprove of their new abuses must of course be partisans of the old – that those who reprobate their crude and violent schemes of liberty ought to be treated as advocates for servitude. [...]

Your government in France, though usually, and I think justly, reputed the best of the unqualified or ill-qualified monarchies, was still full of abuses. These abuses accumulated in a length of time, as they must accumulate in every monarchy not under the constant inspection of a popular representative. I am no stranger to the faults and defects of the subverted government of France; and I think I am not inclined by nature or policy to make a panegyric upon anything which is a just and natural object of censure. But the question is not now of the vices of that monarchy, but of its existence. Is it, then, true, that the French government was such as to be incapable or undeserving of reform, so that it was of absolute necessity the whole fabric should be at once pulled down, and the area cleared for the erection of a theoretic, experimental edifice in its place? All France was of a different opinion in the beginning of the year 1789. The instructions to the representatives to the States-General, from every district in that kingdom, were filled with projects for the reformation of that government, without the remotest suggestion of a design to destroy it. Had such a design been then even insinuated, I believe there would have been but one voice, and that voice for rejecting it with scorn and horror. Men have been sometimes led by degrees, sometimes hurried, into things of which, if they could have seen the whole together, they never would have permitted the most remote approach. When those instructions were given, there was no question but that abuses existed, and that they demanded a reform: nor is there now. In the interval between the instructions and the Revolution things changed their shape; and in consequence of that change, the true question at present is, whether those who would have reformed or those who have destroyed are in the right. [. . .]

Denying, as I am well warranted to do, that the nobility had any considerable share in the oppression of the people, in cases in which real oppression existed, I am ready to admit that they were not without considerable faults and errors. A foolish imitation of the worst part of the manners of England, which impaired their natural character, without substituting in its place what perhaps they meant to copy, has certainly rendered them worse than formerly they were. Habitual dissoluteness of manners, continued beyond the pardonable period of life, was more common amongst them than it is with us; and it reigned with the less hope of remedy, though possibly with something of less mischief, by being covered with more exterior decorum. They countenanced too much that licentious philosophy which has helped to bring on their ruin. There was another error amongst them more fatal. Those of the commons who approached to or exceeded many of the nobility in point of wealth were not fully admitted to the rank and estimation which wealth, in reason and good policy, ought to bestow in every country – though I think not equally with that of other nobility. The two kinds of aristocracy were too punctiliously kept asunder: less so, however, than in Germany and some other nations. [. . .]

If your clergy, or any clergy, should show themselves vicious beyond the fair bounds allowed to human infirmity, and to those professional faults which can hardly be separated from professional virtues, though their vices never can countenance the exercise of oppression, I do admit that they would naturally have the effect of abating very much of our indignation against the tyrants who exceed measure and justice in their punishment. I can allow in clergymen, through all their divisions, some tenaciousness of their own opinion, some overflowings of zeal for its propagation, some predilection to their own state and office, some attachment to the interest of their own corps, some preference to those who listen with docility to their doctrines beyond those who scorn and deride them. I allow all this, because I am a man who have to deal with men, and who would not, through a violence of toleration, run into the greatest of all intolerance. I must bear with infirmities, until they fester into crimes.

Undoubtedly, the natural progress of the passions, from frailty to vice, ought to be prevented by a watchful eye and a firm hand. But is it true that the body of your clergy had passed those limits of a just allowance? From the general style of your late publications of all sorts, one would be led to believe that your clergy in France were a sort of monsters: an horrible composition of superstition, ignorance, sloth, fraud, avarice, and tyranny. But is this true? Is it true that the lapse of time, the cessation of conflicting interests, the woeful experience of the evils resulting from party rage, have had no sort of influence gradually to meliorate their minds? Is it true that they were daily renewing invasions on the civil power, troubling the domestic quiet of their country, and rendering the operations of its government feeble and precarious? Is it true that the clergy of our times have pressed down the laity with an iron hand, and were in all places lighting up the fires of a savage persecution? Did they by every fraud endeavor to increase their estates? Did they use to exceed the due demands on estates that were their own? Or, rigidly screwing up right into wrong, did they convert a legal claim into a vexatious extortion? When not possessed of power, were they filled with the vices of those who envy it? Were they inflamed with a violent, litigious spirit of controversy? Goaded on with the ambition of intellectual sovereignty, were they ready to fly in the face of all magistracy, to fire churches, to massacre the priests of other descriptions, to pull down altars, and to make their way over the ruins of subverted governments to an empire of doctrine, sometimes flattering, sometimes forcing, the consciences of men from the jurisdiction of public institutions into a submission to their personal authority, beginning with a claim of liberty and ending with an abuse of power? [...]

When my occasions took me into France, towards the close of the late reign, the clergy, under all their forms, engaged a considerable part of my curiosity. So far from finding (except from one set of men, not then very numerous, though very active) the complaints and discontents against that body which some publications had given me reason to expect, I perceived little or no public or private uneasiness on their account. On further examination, I found the clergy, in general, persons of moderate minds and decorous manners: I include the seculars, and the regulars of both sexes. I had not the good fortune to know a great many of the parochial clergy: but in general I received a perfectly good account of their morals, and of their attention to their duties. With some of the higher clergy I had a personal acquaintance, and of the rest in that class a very good means of information. They were almost all of them persons of noble birth. They resembled others of their own rank; and where there was any difference, it was in their favor. They were more fully educated than the military noblesse – so as by no means to disgrace their profession by ignorance, or by want of fitness for the exercise of their authority. They seemed to me, beyond the clerical character, liberal and open, with the hearts of gentlemen and men of honor, neither insolent nor servile in their manners and conduct. They seemed to me rather a superior class – a set of men amongst whom you would not be surprised to find a Fénelon. I saw among the clergy in Paris (many of the description are not to be met with anywhere) men of great learning and candor; and I had reason to believe that this description was not confined to Paris. [...]

In every prosperous community something more is produced than goes to the immediate support of the producer. This surplus forms the income of the landed capitalist. It will be spent by a proprietor who does not labor. But this idleness is itself the spring of labor, this repose the spur to industry. The only concern for the state is, that the capital taken in rent from the land should be returned again to the industry from whence it came, and that its expenditure should be with the least possible detriment to the morals of those who expend it and to those of the people to whom it is returned.

In all the views of receipt, expenditure, and personal employment, a sober legis- lator would carefully compare the possessor whom he was recommended to expel with the stranger who was proposed to fill his place. Before the inconveniences are incurred which *must* attend all violent revolutions in property through extensive confiscation, we ought to have some rational assurance that the purchasers of the confiscated property will be in a considerable degree more laborious, more virtuous, more sober, less disposed to extort an unreasonable proportion of the gains of the laborer, or to consume on themselves a larger share than is fit for the measure of an individual – or that they should be qualified to dispense the surplus in a more steady and equal mode, so as to answer the purposes of a politic expenditure, than the old possessors, call those possessors bishops, or canons, or commendatory abbots, or monks, or what you please. The monks are lazy. Be it so. Suppose them no otherwise employed than by singing in the choir. They are as usefully employed as those who neither sing nor say – as usefully even as those who sing upon the stage. [...]

Whatever they are, I wish my countrymen rather to recommend to our neighbors the example of the British constitution than to take models from them for the improvement of our own. In the former, they have got an invaluable treasure. They are not, I think, without some causes of apprehension and complaint, but these they do not owe to their constitution but to their own conduct. I think our happy situation owing to our constitution, but owing to the whole of it, and not to any part singly, owing in a great measure to what we have left standing in our several reviews and reformations as well as to what we have altered or superadded. Our people will find employment enough for a truly patriotic, free, and independent spirit in guarding what they possess from violation. I would not exclude alteration neither, but even when I changed, it should be to preserve. I should be led to my remedy by a great grievance. In what I did, I should follow the example of our ancestors. I would make the reparation as nearly as possible in the style of the building. A politic caution, a guarded circumspection, a moral rather than a complexional timidity were among the ruling principles of our forefathers in their most decided conduct. Not being illuminated with the light of which the gentlemen of France tell us they have got so abundant a share, they acted under a strong impression of the ignorance and fallibility of mankind. He that had made them thus fallible rewarded them for having in their conduct attended to their nature. Let us imitate their caution if we wish to deserve their fortune or to retain their bequests. Let us add, if we please, but let us preserve what they have left; and, standing on the firm ground of the British constitution, let us be satisfied to admire rather than attempt to follow in their desperate flights the aeronauts of France.

I have told you candidly my sentiments. I think they are not likely to alter yours. I do know that they ought. You are young; you cannot guide but must follow the fortune of your country. But hereafter they may be of some use to you, in some future form which your commonwealth may take. In the present it can hardly remain; but before its final settlement it may be obliged to pass, as one of our poets says, "through great varieties of untried being," and in all its transmigrations to be purified by fire and blood.

I have little to recommend my opinions but long observation and much impartiality. They come from one who has been no tool of power, no flatterer of greatness; and who in his last acts does not wish to belie the tenor of his life. They come from one almost the whole of whose public exertion has been a struggle for the liberty of others; from one in whose breast no anger, durable or vehement, has ever been kindled but by what he considered as tyranny; and who snatches from his share in the endeavors which are used by good men to discredit opulent oppression the hours he has employed on your affairs; and who in so doing persuades himself he has not departed from his usual office; they come from one who desires honors, distinctions, and emoluments but little, and who expects them not at all; who has no contempt for fame, and no fear of obloquy; who shuns contention, though he will hazard an opinion; from one who wishes to preserve consistency, but who would preserve consistency by varying his means to secure the unity of his end, and, when the equipoise of the vessel in which he sails may be endangered by overloading it upon one side, is desirous of carrying the small weight of his reasons to that which may preserve its equipoise.

CHAPTER 6

A Vindication of the Rights of Men

MARY WOLLSTONECRAFT

Sir,

It is not necessary, with courtly insincerity, to apologise to you for thus intruding on your precious time, not to profess that I think it an honour to discuss an important subject with a man whose literary abilities have raised him to notice in the state. I have not yet learned to twist my periods, nor, in the equivocal idiom of politeness, to disguise my sentiments, and imply what I should be afraid to utter: if, therefore, in the course of this epistle, I chance to express contempt, and even indignation, with some emphasis, I beseech you to believe that it is not a flight of fancy; for truth, in morals, has ever appeared to me the essence of the sublime; and, in taste, simplicity the only criterion of the beautiful. But I war not with an individual when I contend for the *rights of men* and the liberty of reason. You see I do not condescend to cull my words to avoid the invidious phrase, nor shall I be prevented from giving a manly definition of it, by the flimsy ridicule which a lively fancy has interwoven with the present acceptation of the term. Reverencing the rights of humanity, I shall dare to assert them; not intimidated by the horse laugh that you have raised, or waiting till time has wiped away the compassionate tears which you have elaborately laboured to excite.

From the many just sentiments interspersed through the letter before me, and from the whole tendency of it, I should believe you to be a good, though a vain man, if some circumstances in your conduct did not render the inflexibility of your integrity doubtful; and for this vanity a knowledge of human nature enables me to discover such extenuating circumstances, in the very texture of your mind, that I am ready to call it amiable, and separate the public from the private character.

I know that a lively imagination renders a man particularly calculated to shine in conversation and in those desultory productions where method is disregarded; and the instantaneous applause which his eloquence extorts is at once a reward and a spur. Once a wit and always a wit, is an aphorism that has received the sanction of

Mary Wollstonecraft. *A Vindication of the Rights of Men*. Originally published in 1790.

experience; yet I am apt to conclude that the man who with scrupulous anxiety endeavours to support that shining character, can never nourish by reflection any profound, or, if you please, metaphysical passion. Ambition becomes only the tool of vanity, and his reason, the weather-cock of unrestrained feelings, is only employed to varnish over the faults which it ought to have corrected.

Sacred, however, would the infirmities and errors of a good man be, in my eyes, if they were only displayed in a private circle; if the venial fault only rendered the wit anxious, like a celebrated beauty, to raise admiration on every occasion, and excite emotion, instead of the calm reciprocation of mutual esteem and unimpassioned respect. Such vanity enlivens social intercourse, and forces the little great man to be always on his guard to secure his throne; and an ingenious man, who is ever on the watch for conquest, will, in his eagerness to exhibit his whole store of knowledge, furnish an attentive observer with some useful information, calcined by fancy and formed by taste.

And though some dry reasoner might whisper that the arguments were superficial, and should even add, that the feelings which are thus ostentatiously displayed are often the cold declamation of the head, and not the effusions of the heart – what will these shrewd remarks avail, when the witty arguments and ornamental feelings are on a level with the comprehension of the fashionable world, and a book is found very amusing? Even the Ladies, Sir, may repeat your sprightly sallies, and retail in theatrical attitudes many of your sentimental exclamations. Sensibility is the *manie* of the day, and compassion the virtue which is to cover a multitude of vices, whilst justice is left to mourn in sullen silence, and balance truth in vain.

In life, an honest man with a confined understanding is frequently the slave of his habits and the dupe of his feelings, whilst the man with a clearer head and colder heart makes the passions of others bend to his interest; but truly sublime is the character that acts from principle, and governs the inferior springs of activity without slackening their vigour; whose feelings give vital heat to his resolves, but never hurry him into feverish eccentricities.

However, as you have informed us that respect chills love, it is natural to conclude, that all your pretty flights arise from your pampered sensibility; and that, vain of this fancied pre-eminence of organs, you foster every emotion till the fumes, mounting to your brain, dispel the sober suggestions of reason. It is not in this view surprising, that when you should argue you become impassioned, and that reflection inflames your imagination, instead of enlightening your understanding.

Quitting now the flowers of rhetoric, let us, Sir, reason together; and, believe me, I should not have meddled with these troubled waters, in order to point out your inconsistencies, if your wit had not burnished up some rusty, baneful opinions, and swelled the shallow current of ridicule till it resembled the flow of reason, and presumed to be the test of truth.

I shall not attempt to follow you through 'horse-way and foot-path;' but, attacking the foundation of your opinions, I shall leave the superstructure to find a centre of gravity on which it may lean till some strong blast puffs it into the air; or your teeming fancy, which the ripening judgment of sixty years has not tamed, produces another Chinese erection, to stare, at every turn, the plain country people in the face, who bluntly call such an airy edifice – a folly.

The birthright of man, to give you, Sir, a short definition of this disputed right, is such a degree of liberty, civil and religious, as is compatible with the liberty of every other individual with whom he is united in a social compact, and the continued existence of that compact.

Liberty, in this simple, unsophisticated sense, I acknowledge, is a fair idea that has never yet received a form in the various governments that have been established on our beauteous globe; the demon of property has ever been at hand to encroach on the sacred rights of men, and to fence round with awful pomp laws that war with justice. But that it results from the eternal foundation of right – from immutable truth – who will presume to deny, that pretends to rationality – if reason has led them to build their morality and religion on an everlasting foundation – the attributes of God?

I glow with indignation when I attempt, methodically, to unravel your slavish paradoxes, in which I can find no fixed first principle to refute; I shall not, therefore, condescend to shew where you affirm in one page what you deny in another; and how frequently you draw conclusions without any previous premises: – it would be something like cowardice to fight with a man who had never exercised the weapons with which his opponent chose to combat, and irksome to refute sentence after sentence in which the latent spirit of tyranny appeared.

I perceive, from the whole tenor of your Reflections, that you have a mortal antipathy to reason; but, if there is any thing like argument, or first principles, in your wild declamation, behold the result: – that we are to reverence the rust of antiquity, and term the unnatural customs, which ignorance and mistaken self-interest have consolidated, the sage fruit of experience: nay, that, if we do discover some errors, our *feelings* should lead us to excuse, with blind love, or unprincipled filial affection, the venerable vestiges of ancient days. These are gothic notions of beauty – the ivy is beautiful, but, when it insidiously destroys the trunk from which it receives support, who would not grub it up?

Further, that we ought cautiously to remain for ever in frozen inactivity, because a thaw, whilst it nourishes the soil, spreads a temporary inundation; and the fear of risking any personal present convenience should prevent a struggle for the most estimable advantages. This is sound reasoning, I grant, in the mouth of the rich and short-sighted.

Yes, Sir, the strong gained riches, the few have sacrificed the many to their vices; and, to be able to pamper their appetites, and supinely exist without exercising mind or body, they have ceased to be men. – Lost to the relish of true pleasure, such beings would, indeed, deserve compassion, if injustice was not softened by the tyrant's plea – necessity; if prescription was not raised as an immortal boundary against innovation. Their minds, in fact, instead of being cultivated, have been so warped by education, that it may require some ages to bring them back to nature, and enable them to see their true interest, with that degree of conviction which is necessary to influence their conduct.

The civilization which has taken place in Europe has been very partial, and, like every custom that an arbitrary point of honour has established, refines the manners at the expence of morals, by making sentiments and opinions current in conversation that have no root in the heart, or weight in the cooler resolves of the mind. – And what has stopped its progress? – hereditary property – hereditary honours. The man has been changed into an artificial monster by the station in which he was born, and the consequent homage that benumbed his faculties like the torpedo's touch; – or a being, with a capacity of reasoning, would not have failed to discover, as his faculties unfolded, that true happiness arose from the friendship and intimacy which can only be enjoyed by equals; and that charity is not a condescending distribution of alms, but an intercourse of good offices and mutual benefits, founded on respect for justice and humanity.

Governed by these principles, the poor wretch, whose *inelegant* distress extorted from a mixed feeling of disgust and animal sympathy present relief, would have been considered as a man, whose misery demanded a part of his birthright, supposing him to be industrious; but should his vices have reduced him to poverty, he could only have addressed his fellow-men as weak beings, subject to like passions, who ought to forgive, because they expect to be forgiven, for suffering the impulse of the moment to silence the suggestions of conscience, or reason, which you will; for, in my view of things, they are synonymous terms.

Will Mr Burke be at the trouble to inform us, how far we are to go back to discover the rights of men, since the light of reason is such a fallacious guide that none but fools trust to its cold investigation?

In the infancy of society, confining our view to our own country, customs were established by the lawless power of an ambitious individual; or a weak prince was obliged to comply with every demand of the licentious barbarous insurgents, who disputed his authority with irrefragable arguments at the point of their swords; or the more specious requests of the Parliament, who only allowed him conditional supplies.

Are these the venerable pillars of our constitution? And is Magna Charta to rest for its chief support on a former grant, which reverts to another, till chaos becomes the base of the mighty structure – or we cannot tell what? – for coherence, without some pervading principle of order, is a solecism.

Speaking of Edward the IIId. Hume observes, that 'he was a prince of great capacity, not governed by favourites, not led astray by any unruly passion, sensible that nothing could be more essential to his interests than to keep on good terms with his people: yet, on the whole, it appears that the government, at best, was only a barbarous monarchy, not regulated by any fixed maxims, or bounded by any certain or undisputed rights, which in practice were regularly observed. The King conducted himself by one set of principles; the Barons by another; the Commons by a third; the Clergy by a fourth. All these systems of government were opposite and incompatible: each of them prevailed in its turn, as incidents were favourable to it: a great prince rendered the monarchical power predominant: the weakness of a king gave reins to the aristocracy: a superstitious age saw the clergy triumphant: the people, for whom chiefly government was instituted, and who chiefly deserve consideration, were the weakest of the whole.'

And just before that most auspicious aera, the fourteenth century, during the reign of Richard II. whose total incapacity to manage the reins of power, and keep in subjection his haughty Barons, rendered him a mere cypher; the House of Commons, to whom he was obliged frequently to apply, not only for subsidies but assistance to quell the insurrections that the contempt in which he was held naturally produced, gradually rose into power; for whenever they granted supplies to the King, they demanded in return, though it bore the name of petition, a confirmation, or the renewal of former charters, which had been infringed, and even utterly disregarded by the King and his seditious Barons, who principally held their independence of the crown by force of arms, and the encouragement which they gave to robbers and villains, who infested the country, and lived by rapine and violence.

To what dreadful extremities were the poorer sort reduced, their property, the fruit of their industry, being entirely at the disposal of their lords, who were so many petty tyrants!

In return for the supplies and assistance which the king received from the commons, they demanded privileges, which Edward, in his distress for money to prosecute the numerous wars in which he was engaged during the greater part of his reign, was constrained to grant them; so that by degrees they rose to power, and became a check on both king and nobles. Thus was the foundation of our liberty established, chiefly through the pressing necessities of the king, who was more intent on being supplied for the moment, in order to carry on his wars and ambitious projects, than aware of the blow he gave to kingly power, by thus making a body of men feel their importance, who afterwards might strenuously oppose tyranny and oppression, and effectually guard the subject's property from seizure and confiscation. Richard's weakness completed what Edward's ambition began.

At this period, it is true, Wickliffe opened a vista for reason by attacking some of the most pernicious tenets of the church of Rome; still the prospect was sufficiently misty to authorize the question – Where was the dignity of thinking of the fourteenth century?

A Roman Catholic, it is true, enlightened by the reformation, might, with singular propriety, celebrate the epoch that preceded it, to turn our thoughts from former atrocious enormities; but a Protestant must acknowledge that this faint dawn of liberty only made the subsiding darkness more visible; and that the boasted virtues of that century all bear the stamp of stupid pride and headstrong barbarism. Civility was then called condescension, and ostentatious almsgiving humanity; and men were content to borrow their virtues, or, to speak with more propriety, their consequence, from posterity, rather than undertake the arduous task of acquiring it for themselves.

The imperfection of all modern governments must, without waiting to repeat the trite remark, that all human institutions are unavoidably imperfect, in a great measure have arisen from this simple circumstance, that the constitution, if such an heterogeneous mass deserve that name, was settled in the dark days of ignorance, when the minds of men were shackled by the grossest prejudices and most immoral superstition. And do you, Sir, a sagacious philosopher, recommend night as the fittest time to analyze a ray of light?

Are we to seek for the rights of men in the ages when a few marks were the only penalty imposed for the life of a man, and death for death when the property of the rich was touched? when – I blush to discover the depravity of our nature – when a deer was killed! Are these the laws that it is natural to love, and sacrilegious to invade? – Were the rights of men understood when the law authorized or tolerated murder? – or is power and right the same in your creed?

But in fact all your declamation leads so directly to this conclusion, that I beseech you to ask your own heart, when you call yourself a friend of liberty, whether it would not be more consistent to style yourself the champion of property, the adorer of the golden image which power has set up? – And, when you are examining your heart, if it would not be too much like mathematical drudgery, to which a fine imagination very reluctantly stoops, enquire further, how it is consistent with the vulgar notions of honesty, and the foundation of morality – truth; for a man to boast of his virtue and independence, when he cannot forget that he is at the moment enjoying the wages of falsehood; and that, in a skulking, unmanly way, he has secured himself a pension of fifteen hundred pounds per annum on the Irish establishment? Do honest men, Sir, for I am not rising to the refined principle of honour, ever receive the reward of their public services, or secret assistance, in the name of *another*?

But to return from a digression which you will more perfectly understand than any of my readers – on what principle you, Sir, can justify the reformation, which tore up by the roots an old establishment, I cannot guess – but, I beg your pardon, perhaps you do not wish to justify it – and have some mental reservation to excuse you, to yourself, for not openly avowing your reverence. Or, to go further back; – had you been a Jew – you would have joined in the cry, crucify him! – crucify him! The promulgator of a new doctrine, and the violator of old laws and customs, that not melting, like ours, into darkness and ignorance, rested on Divine authority, must have been a dangerous innovator, in your eyes, particularly if you had not been informed that the Carpenter's Son was of the stock and lineage of David. But there is no end to the arguments which might be deduced to combat such palpable absurdities, by shewing the manifest inconsistencies which are necessarily involved in a direful train of false opinions.

It is necessary emphatically to repeat, that there are rights which men inherit at their birth, as rational creatures, who were raised above the brute creation by their improvable faculties; and that, in receiving these, not from their forefathers but, from God, prescription can never undermine natural rights.

A father may dissipate his property without his child having any right to complain; – but should he attempt to sell him for a slave, or fetter him with laws contrary to reason; nature, in enabling him to discern good from evil, teaches him to break the ignoble chain, and not to believe that bread becomes flesh, and wine blood, because his parents swallowed the Eucharist with this blind persuasion.

There is no end to this implicit submission to authority – some where it must stop, or we return to barbarism; and the capacity of improvement, which gives us a natural sceptre on earth, is a cheat, an ignis-fatuus, that leads us from inviting meadows into bogs and dung-hills. And if it be allowed that many of the precautions, with which any alteration was made, in our government, were prudent, it rather proves its weakness than substantiates an opinion of the soundness of the stamina, or the excellence of the constitution.

But on what principle Mr Burke could defend American independence, I cannot conceive; for the whole tenor of his plausible arguments settles slavery on an everlasting foundation. Allowing his servile reverence for antiquity, and prudent attention to self-interest, to have the force which he insists on, the slave trade ought never to be abolished; and, because our ignorant forefathers, not understanding the native dignity of man, sanctioned a traffic that outrages every suggestion of reason and religion, we are to submit to the inhuman custom, and term an atrocious insult to humanity the love of our country, and a proper submission to the laws by which our property is secured. – Security of property! Behold, in a few words, the definition of English liberty. And to this selfish principle every nobler one is sacrificed. – The Briton takes place of the man, and the image of God is lost in the citizen! But it is not that enthusiastic flame which in Greece and Rome consumed every sordid passion: no, self is the focus; and the disparting rays rise not above our foggy atmosphere. But softly – it is only the property of the rich that is secure; the man who lives by the sweat of his brow has no asylum from oppression; the strong man may enter – when was the castle of the poor sacred? and the base informer steal him from the family that depend on his industry for subsistence.

Fully sensible as you must be of the baneful consequences that inevitably follow this notorious infringement on the dearest rights of men, and that it is an infernal blot on the very face of our immaculate constitution, I cannot avoid expressing my surprise that when you recommended our form of government as a model, you did not caution the French against the arbitrary custom of pressing men for the sea service. You should have hinted to them, that property in England is much more secure than liberty, and not have concealed that the liberty of an honest mechanic – his all – is often sacrificed to secure the property of the rich. For it is a farce to pretend that a man fights *for his country, his hearth, or his altars*, when he has neither liberty nor property. – His property is in his nervous arms – and they are compelled to pull a strange rope at the surly command of a tyrannic boy, who probably obtained his rank on account of his family connections, or the prostituted vote of his father, whose interest in a borough, or voice as a senator, was acceptable to the minister.

Our penal laws punish with death the thief who steals a few pounds; but to take by violence, or trepan, a man, is no such heinous offence. – For who shall dare to complain of the venerable vestige of the law that rendered the life of a deer more sacred than that of a man? But it was the poor man with only his native dignity who was thus oppressed – and only metaphysical sophists and cold mathematicians can discern this insubstantial form; it is a work of abstraction – and a *gentleman* of lively imagination must borrow some drapery from fancy before he can love or pity a *man*. Misery, to reach your heart, I perceive, must have its cap and bells; your tears are reserved, very *naturally* considering your character, for the declamation of the theatre, or for the downfall of queens, whose rank alters the nature of folly, and throws a graceful veil over vices that degrade humanity; whilst the distress of many industrious mothers, whose *helpmates* have been torn from them, and the hungry cry of helpless babes, were vulgar sorrows that could not move your commiseration, though they might extort an alms. 'The tears that are shed for fictitious sorrow are admirably adapted,' says Rousseau, 'to make us proud of all the virtues which we do not possess.'

The baneful effects of the despotic practice of pressing we shall, in all probability, soon feel; for a number of men, who have been taken from their daily employments, will shortly be let loose on society, now that there is no longer any apprehension of a war.

The vulgar, and by this epithet I mean not only to describe a class of people, who, working to support the body, have not had time to cultivate their minds; but likewise those who, born in the lap of affluence, have never had their invention sharpened by a necessity are, nine out of ten, the creatures of habit and impulse.

If I were not afraid to derange your nervous system by the bare mention of a metaphysical enquiry, I should observe, Sir, that self-preservation is, literally speaking, the first law of nature; and that the care necessary to support and guard the body is the first step to unfold the mind, and inspire a manly spirit of independence. The mewing babe in swaddling-clothes, who is treated like a superior being, may perchance become a gentleman; but nature must have given him uncommon faculties if, when pleasure hangs on every bough, he has sufficient fortitude either to exercise his mind or body in order to acquire personal merit. The passions are necessary auxiliaries of reason: a present impulse pushes us forward, and when we discover that the game did not deserve the chace, we find that we have gone over much ground, and not only gained many new ideas, but a habit of thinking. The exercise of our faculties is the great end, though not the goal we had in view when we started with such eagerness.

It would be straying still further into metaphysics to add, that this is one of the strongest arguments for the natural immortality of the soul. – Every thing looks like a means, nothing like an end, or point of rest, when we can say, now let us sit down and enjoy the present moment; our faculties and wishes are proportioned to the present scene; we may return without repining to our sister clod. And, if no conscious dignity whisper that we are capable of relishing more refined pleasures, the thirst of truth appears to be allayed; and thought, the faint type of an immaterial energy, no longer bounding it knows not where, is confined to the tenement that affords it sufficient variety. – The rich man may then thank his God that he is not like other men – but when is retribution to be made to the miserable, who cry day and night for help, and there is no one at hand to help them? And not only misery but immorality proceeds from this stretch of arbitrary authority. The vulgar have not the power of emptying their mind of the only ideas they imbibed whilst their hands were employed; they cannot quickly turn from one kind of life to another. Pressing them entirely unhinges their minds; they acquire new habits, and cannot return to their old occupations with their former readiness; consequently they fall into idleness, drunkenness, and the whole train of vices which you stigmatise as gross.

A government that acts in this manner cannot be called a good parent, nor inspire natural (habitual is the proper word) affection, in the breasts of children who are thus disregarded.

The game laws are almost as oppressive to the peasantry as press-warrants to the mechanic. In this land of liberty what is to secure the property of the poor farmer when his noble landlord chooses to plant a decoy field near his little property? Game devour the fruit of his labour; but fines and imprisonment await him if he dare to kill any – or lift up his hand to interrupt the pleasure of his lord. How many families have been plunged, in the *sporting* countries, into misery and vice for some paltry transgression of these coercive laws, by the natural consequence of that anger which a man feels when he sees the reward of his industry laid waste by unfeeling luxury? – when his children's bread is given to dogs!

You have shewn, Sir, by your silence on these subjects, that your respect for rank has swallowed up the common feelings of humanity; you seem to consider the poor as only the live stock of an estate, the feather of hereditary nobility. When you had so little respect for the silent majority of misery, I am not surprised at your manner of treating an individual whose brow a mitre will never grace, and whose popularity may have wounded your vanity – for vanity is ever sore. Even in France, Sir, before the revolution, literary celebrity procured a man the treatment of a gentleman; but you are going back for your credentials of politeness to more distant times. – Gothic affability is the mode you think proper to adopt, the condescension of a Baron, not the civility of a liberal man. Politeness is, indeed, the only substitute for humanity; or what distinguishes the civilised man from the unlettered savage? and he who is not governed by reason should square his behaviour by an arbitrary standard; but by what rule your attack on Dr Price was regulated we have yet to learn. [...]

Blackstone, to whom Mr Burke pays great deference, seems to agree with Dr Price, that the succession of the King of Great Britain depends on the choice of the people, or that they have a power to cut it off; but this power, as you have fully proved, has been cautiously exerted, and might with more propriety be termed a *right* than a power. Be it so! – yet when you elaborately cited precedents to shew that our forefathers paid great respect to hereditary claims, you might have gone back to your favourite epoch, and shewn their respect for a church that fulminating laws have since loaded with opprobrium. The preponderance of inconsistencies, when weighed with precedents, should lessen the most bigotted veneration for antiquity, and force men of the eighteenth century to acknowledge, that our *canonized fore-fathers* were unable, or afraid, to revert to reason, without resting on the crutch of authority; and should not be brought as a proof that their children are never to be allowed to walk alone.

When we doubt the infallible wisdom of our ancestors, it is only advancing on the same ground to doubt the sincerity of the law, and the propriety of that servile appellation – OUR SOVEREIGN LORD THE KING. Who were the dictators of this adulatory language of the law? Were they not courtly parasites and worldly priests? Besides, whoever at divine service, whose feelings were not deadened by habit, or their understandings quiescent, ever repeated without horror the same epithets applied to a man and his Creator? If this is confused jargon – say what are the dictates of sober reason, or the criterion to distinguish nonsense?

You further sarcastically animadvert on the consistency of the democratists, by wresting the obvious meaning of a common phrase, *the dregs of the people*; or your contempt for poverty may have led you into an error. Be that as it may, an unprejudiced man would have directly perceived the single sense of the word, and an old Member of Parliament could scarcely have missed it. He who had so often felt the pulse of the electors needed not have gone beyond his own experience to discover that the dregs alluded to were the vicious, and not the lower class of the community.

Again, Sir, I must doubt your sincerity or your discernment. – You have been behind the curtain; and, though it might be difficult to bring back your sophisticated heart to nature and make you feel like a man, yet the awestruck confusion in which you were plunged must have gone off when the vulgar emotion of wonder, excited by finding yourself a Senator, had subsided. Then you must have seen the clogged wheels of corruption continually oiled by the sweat of the laborious poor, squeezed out of them by unceasing taxation. You must have discovered that the majority in the House of Commons was often purchased by the crown, and that the people were oppressed by the influence of their own money, extorted by the venal voice of a packed representation.

You must have known that a man of merit cannot rise in the church, the army, or navy, unless he has some interest in a borough; and that even a paltry exciseman's place can only be secured by electioneering interest. I will go further, and assert that few Bishops, though there have been learned and good Bishops, have gained the mitre without submitting to a servility of dependence that degrades the man. – All these circumstances you must have known, yet you talk of virtue and liberty, as the vulgar talk of the letter of the law; and the polite of propriety. It is true that these ceremonial observances produce decorum; the sepulchres are white-washed, and do not offend the squeamish eyes of high rank; but virtue is out of the question when you only worship a shadow, and worship it to secure your property.

Man has been termed, with strict propriety, a microcosm, a little world in himself. – He is so; – yet must, however, be reckoned an ephemera, or, to adopt your figure of rhetoric, a summer's fly. The perpetuation of property in our families is one of the privileges you most warmly contend for; yet it would not be very difficult to prove that the mind must have a very limited range that thus confines its benevolence to such a narrow circle, which, with great propriety, may be included in the sordid calculations of blind self-love.

A brutal attachment to children has appeared most conspicuous in parents who have treated them like slaves, and demanded due homage for all the property they transferred to them, during their lives. It has led them to force their children to break

the most sacred ties; to do violence to a natural impulse, and run into legal prostitution to increase wealth or shun poverty; and, still worse, the dread of parental
malediction has made many weak characters violate truth in the face of Heaven;
and, to avoid a father's angry curse, the most sacred promises have been broken. It
appears to be a natural suggestion of reason, that a man should be freed from
implicit obedience to parents and private punishments, when he is of an age to be
subject to the jurisdiction of the laws of his country; and that the barbarous cruelty
of allowing parents to imprison their children, to prevent their contaminating their
noble blood by following the dictates of nature when they chose to marry, or for any
misdemeanor that does not come under the cognizance of public justice, is one of the
most arbitrary violations of liberty.

Who can recount all the unnatural crimes which the *laudable, interesting* desire of
perpetuating a name has produced? The younger children have been sacrificed to the
eldest son; sent into exile, or confined in convents, that they might not encroach on
what was called, with shameful falsehood, the *family* estate. Will Mr Burke call this
parental affection reasonable or virtuous? – No; it is the spurious offspring of over-
weening, mistaken pride – and not that first source of civilization, natural parental
affection, that makes no difference between child and child, but what reason justifies
by pointing out superior merit.

Another pernicious consequence which unavoidably arises from this artificial
affection is, the insuperable bar which it puts in the way of early marriages. It
would be difficult to determine whether the minds or bodies of our youth are most
injured by this impediment. Our young men become selfish coxcombs, and gallantry
with modest women, and intrigues with those of another description, weaken both
mind and body, before either has arrived at maturity. The character of a master of a
family, a husband, and a father, forms the citizen imperceptibly, by producing a sober
manliness of thought, and orderly behaviour; but, from the lax morals and depraved
affections of the libertine, what results? – a finical man of taste, who is only anxious
to secure his own private gratifications, and to maintain his rank in society.

The same system has an equally pernicious effect on female morals. – Girls are
sacrificed to family convenience, or else marry to settle themselves in a superior rank,
and coquet, without restraint, with the fine gentleman whom I have already
described. And to such lengths has this vanity, this desire of shining, carried them,
that it is not now necessary to guard girls against imprudent love matches; for if
some widows did not now and then *fall* in love, Love and Hymen would seldom
meet, unless at a village church.

I do not intend to be sarcastically paradoxical when I say, that women of fashion
take husbands that they may have it in their power to coquet, the grand business of
genteel life, with a number of admirers, and thus flutter the spring of life away,
without laying up any store for the winter of age, or being of any use to society.
Affection in the marriage state can only be founded on respect – and are these weak
beings respectable? Children are neglected for lovers, and we express surprise that
adulteries are so common! A woman never forgets to adorn herself to make an
impression on the senses of the other sex, and to extort the homage which it is gallant
to pay, and yet we wonder that they have such confined understandings.

Have ye not heard that we cannot serve two masters? an immoderate desire to
please contracts the faculties, and immerges, to borrow the idea of a great philosopher, the soul in matter, till it becomes unable to mount on the wing of contemplation.

It would be an arduous task to trace all the vice and misery that arise in society from the middle class of people apeing the manners of the great. All are aiming to procure respect on account of their property; and most places are considered as sinecures that enable men to start into notice. The grand concern of three parts out of four is to contrive to live above their equals, and to appear to be richer than they are. How much domestic comfort and private satisfaction is sacrificed to this irrational ambition! It is a destructive mildew that blights the fairest virtues; benevolence, friendship, generosity, and all those endearing charities which bind human hearts together, and the pursuits which raise the mind to higher contemplations, all that were not cankered in the bud by the false notions that 'grew with its growth and strengthened with its strength,' are crushed by the iron hand of property!

Property, I do not scruple to aver it, should be fluctuating, which would be the case, if it were more equally divided amongst all the children of a family; else it is an everlasting rampart, in consequence of a barbarous feudal institution, that enables the elder son to overpower talents and depress virtue.

Besides, an unmanly servility, most inimical to true dignity of character is, by this means, fostered in society. Men of some abilities play on the follies of the rich, and mounting to fortune as they degrade themselves, they stand in the way of men of superior talents, who cannot advance in such crooked paths, or wade through the filth which *parasites* never boggle at. Pursuing their way straight forward, their spirit is either bent or broken by the rich man's contumelies, or the difficulties they have to encounter.

The only security of property that nature authorizes and reason sanctions is, the right a man has to enjoy the acquisitions which his talents and industry have acquired; and to bequeath them to whom he chooses. Happy would it be for the world if there were no other road to wealth or honour; if pride, in the shape of parental affection, did not absorb the man, and prevent friendship from having the same weight as relationship. Luxury and effeminacy would not then introduce so much idiotism into the noble families which form one of the pillars of our state: the ground would not lie fallow, nor would undirected activity of mind spread the contagion of restless idleness, and its concomitant, vice, through the whole mass of society. [...]

You further proceed grossly to misrepresent Dr Price's meaning; and, with an affectation of holy fervour, express your indignation at his profaning a beautiful rapturous ejaculation, when alluding to the King of France's submission to the National Assembly; he rejoiced to hail a glorious revolution, which promised an universal diffusion of liberty and happiness.

Observe, Sir, that I called your piety affectation. – A rant to enable you to point your venomous dart, and round your period. I speak with warmth, because, of all hypocrites, my soul most indignantly spurns a religious one; – and I very cautiously bring forward such a heavy charge, to strip you of your cloak of sanctity. Your speech at the time the bill for a regency was agitated now lies before me. – *Then* you could in direct terms, to promote ambitious or interested views, exclaim without any pious qualms – 'Ought they to make a mockery of him, putting a crown of thorns on his head, a reed in his hand, and dressing him in a raiment of purple, cry, Hail! King of the British!' Where was your sensibility when you could utter this cruel mockery, equally insulting to God and man? Go hence, thou slave of impulse, look into the private recesses of thy heart, and take not a mote from thy brother's eye, till thou hast removed the beam from thine own.

Of your partial feelings I shall take another view, and shew that following nature, which is, you say, 'wisdom without reflection, and *above it*' – has led you into great inconsistences, to use the softest phrase. When, on a late melancholy occasion, a very important question was agitated, with what indecent warmth did *you* treat a woman, for I shall not lay any stress on her title, whose conduct in life has deserved praise, though not, perhaps, the servile elogiums which have been lavished on the queen. But sympathy, and you tell us that you have a heart of flesh, was made to give way to party spirit and the feelings of a man, not to allude to your Romantic gallantry, to the views of the statesman. When you descanted on the horrors of the 6th of October, and gave a glowing, and, in some instances, a most exaggerated description of that infernal night, without having troubled yourself to clean your palette, you might have returned home and indulged us with a sketch of the misery you personally aggravated. [...]

Whether the glory of Europe is set, I shall not now enquire; but probably the spirit of romance and chivalry is in the wane; and reason will gain by its extinction.

From observing several cold Romantic characters I have been led to confine the term Romantic to one definition – false, or rather artificial, feelings. Works of genius are read with a prepossession in their favour, and sentiments imitated, because they were fashionable and pretty, and not because they were forcibly felt.

In modern poetry the understanding and memory often fabricate the pretended effusions of the heart, and romance destroys all simplicity; which, in works of taste, is but a synonymous word for truth. This Romantic spirit has extended to our prose, and scattered artificial flowers over the most barren heath; or a mixture of verse and prose producing the strangest incongruities. The turgid bombast of some of your periods fully proves these assertions; for when the heart speaks we are seldom shocked by hyperbole, or dry raptures.

I speak in this decided tone, because from turning over the pages of your late publication, with more attention than I did when I first read it cursorily over; and comparing the sentiments it contains with your conduct on many important occasions, I am led very often to doubt your sincerity, and to suppose that you have said many things merely for the sake of saying them well; or to throw some pointed obloquy on characters and opinions that jostled with your vanity.

It is an arduous task to follow the doublings of cunning, or the subterfuges of inconsistency; for in controversy, as in battle, the brave man wishes to face his enemy, and fight on the same ground. Knowing, however, the influence of a ruling passion, and how often it assumes the form of reason when there is much sensibility in the heart, I respect an opponent, though he tenaciously maintains opinions in which I cannot coincide; but, if I once discover that many of those opinions are empty rhetorical flourishes, my respect is soon changed into that pity which borders on contempt; and the mock dignity and haughty stalk, only reminds me of the ass in the lion's skin. [...]

In what respect are we superior to the brute creation, if intellect is not allowed to be the guide of passion? Brutes hope and fear, love and hate; but, without a capacity to improve, a power of turning these passions to good or evil, they neither acquire virtue nor wisdom. – Why? Because the Creator has not given them reason.

But the cultivation of reason is an arduous task, and men of lively fancy, finding it easier to follow the impulse of passion, endeavour to persuade themselves and others that it is most *natural*. And happy is it for those, who indolently let that heaven-lighted spark rest like the ancient lamps in sepulchres, that some virtuous habits, with which the reason of others shackled them, supplies its place. – Affection for parents, reverence for superiors or antiquity, notions of honour, or that worldly self-interest that shrewdly shews them that honesty is the best policy: all proceed from the reason for which they serve as substitutes; – but it is reason at second-hand.

Children are born ignorant, consequently innocent; the passions, are neither good nor evil dispositions, till they receive a direction, and either bound over the feeble barrier raised by a faint glimmering of unexercised reason, called conscience, or strengthen her wavering dictates till sound principles are deeply rooted, and able to cope with the headstrong passions that often assume her awful form. What moral purpose can be answered by extolling good dispositions, as they are called, when these good dispositions are described as instincts: for instinct moves in a direct line to its ultimate end, and asks not for guide or support. But if virtue is to be acquired by experience, or taught by example, reason, perfected by reflection, must be the director of the whole host of passions, which produce a fructifying heat, but no light, that you would exalt into her place. – She must hold the rudder, or, let the wind blow which way it list, the vessel will never advance smoothly to its destined port; for the time lost in tacking about would dreadfully impede its progress.

In the name of the people of England, you say, 'that we know *we* have made no discoveries; and we think that no discoveries are to be made in morality; nor many in the great principles of government, nor in the ideas of liberty, which were understood long before we were born, altogether as well as they will be after the grave has heaped its mould upon our presumption, and the silent tomb shall have imposed its law on our pert loquacity. In England we have not yet been completely emboweled of our natural entrails; we still feel within us, and we cherish and cultivate those inbred sentiments which are faithful guardians, the active monitors of our duty, the true supporters of all liberal and manly morals.' – What do you mean by inbred senti-ments? From whence do they come? How were they bred? Are they the brood of folly, which swarm like the insects on the banks of the Nile, when mud and putrefaction have enriched the languid soil? Were these *inbred* sentiments faithful guardians of our duty when the church was an asylum for murderers, and men worshipped bread as a God? when slavery was authorized by law to fasten her fangs on human flesh, and the iron eat into the very soul? If these sentiments are not acquired, if our passive dispositions do not expand into virtuous affections and passions, why are not the Tartars in the first rude horde endued with sentiments white and *elegant* as the driven snow? Why is passion or heroism the child of reflection, the consequence of dwelling with intent contemplation on one object? The appetites are the only perfect inbred powers that I can discern; and they like instincts have a certain aim, they can be satisfied – but improveable reason has not yet discovered the perfection it may arrive at – God forbid!

First, however, it is necessary to make what we know practical. Who can deny, that has marked the slow progress of civilization, that men may become more virtuous and happy without any new discovery in morals? Who will venture to assert that virtue would not be promoted by the more extensive cultivation of reason? If nothing more is to be done, let us eat and drink, for to-morrow we die – and die for ever! Who will pretend to say, that there is as much happiness diffused on this globe as it is capable of affording? as many social virtues as reason would foster, if she could gain the strength she is able to acquire even in this imperfect state; if the voice of nature was allowed to speak audibly from the bottom of the heart, and the *native* unalienable rights of men were recognized in their full force; if factitious merit

did not take place of genuine acquired virtue, and enable men to build their enjoyment on the misery of their fellow creatures; if men were more under the dominion
of reason than opinion, and did not cherish their prejudices 'because they were
prejudices?' I am not, Sir, aware of your sneers, hailing a millennium, though a state
of greater purity of morals may not be a mere poetic fiction; nor did my fancy ever
create a heaven on earth, since reason threw off her swaddling clothes. I perceive, but
too forcibly, that happiness, literally speaking, dwells not here; – and that we wander
to and fro in a vale of darkness as well as tears. I perceive that my passions pursue
objects that the imagination enlarges, till they become only a sublime idea that
shrinks from the enquiry of sense, and mocks the experimental philosophers who
would confine this spiritual phlogiston in their material crucibles. I know that the
human understanding is deluded with vain shadows, and that when we eagerly
pursue any study, we only reach the boundary set to human enquiries. – Thus far
shalt thou go, and no further, says some stern difficulty; and the *cause* we were
pursuing melts into utter darkness. But these are only the trials of contemplative
minds, the foundation of virtue remains firm. – The power of exercising our understanding raises us above the brutes; and this exercise produces that 'primary morality,' which you term 'untaught feelings.'

If virtue be an instinct, I renounce all hope of immortality; and with it all the
sublime reveries and dignified sentiments that have smoothed the rugged path of life:
it is all a cheat, a lying vision; I have disquieted myself in vain; for in my eye all
feelings are false and spurious, that do not rest on justice as their foundation, and are
not concentred by universal love.

I reverence the rights of men. – Sacred rights! for which I acquire a more profound
respect, the more I look into my own mind; and, professing these heterodox opinions, I still preserve my bowels; my heart is human, beats quick with human
sympathies – and I FEAR God!

I bend with awful reverence when I enquire on what my fear is built. – I fear that
sublime power, whose motive for creating me must have been wise and good; and I
submit to the moral laws which my reason deduces from this view of my dependence
on him. – It is not his power that I fear – it is not to an arbitrary will, but to unerring
reason I submit. – Submit – yes; I disregard the charge of arrogance, to the law that
regulates his just resolves; and the happiness I pant after must be the same in kind,
and produced by the same exertions as his – though unfeigned humility overwhelms
every idea that would presume to compare the goodness which the most exalted
created being could acquire, with the grand source of life and bliss.

This fear of God makes me reverence myself. – Yes, Sir, the regard I have for
honest fame, and the friendship of the virtuous, falls far short of the respect which I
have for myself. And this, enlightened self-love, if an epithet the meaning of which
has been grossly perverted will convey my idea, forces me to see; and, if I may
venture to borrow a prostituted term, to *feel*, that happiness is reflected, and that, in
communicating good, my soul receives its noble aliment. – I do not trouble myself,
therefore, to enquire whether this is the fear the *people* of England feel: – and, if it be
natural to include all the modifications which you have annexed – it is not.

Besides, I cannot help suspecting that, if you had the *enlightened* respect for
yourself, which you affect to despise, you would not have said that the constitution
of our church and state, formed, like most other modern ones, by degrees, as Europe
was emerging out of barbarism, was formed 'under the auspices, and was confirmed
by the sanctions, of religion and piety.' You have turned over the historic page; have

been hackneyed in the ways of men, and must know that private cabals and public feuds, private virtues and vices, religion and superstition, have all concurred to foment the mass and swell it to its present form; nay more, that it in part owes its sightly appearance to bold rebellion and insidious innovation. Factions, Sir, have been the leaven, and private interest has produced public good.

These general reflections are not thrown out to insinuate that virtue was a creature of yesterday: No; she had her share in the grand drama. I guard against misrepresentation; but the man who cannot modify general assertions, has scarcely learned the first rudiments of reasoning. I know that there is a great portion of virtue in the Romish church, yet I should not choose to neglect clothing myself with a garment of my own righteousness, depending on a kind donative of works of supererogation. I know that there are many clergymen, of all denominations, wise and virtuous; yet I have not that respect for the whole body, which, you say, characterizes our nation, 'emanating from a certain plainness and directness of understanding.' – Now we are stumbling on *inbred* feelings and secret lights again – or, I beg your pardon, it may be the furbished up face which you choose to give to the argument. [...]

The only way in which the people interfere in government, religious or civil, is in electing representatives. And, Sir, let me ask you, with manly plainness – are these *holy* nominations? Where is the booth of religion? Does she mix her awful mandates, or lift her persuasive voice, in those scenes of drunken riot and beastly gluttony? Does she preside over those nocturnal abominations which so evidently tend to deprave the manners of the lower class of people? The pestilence stops not here – the rich and poor have one common nature, and many of the great families, which, on this side adoration, you venerate, date their misery, I speak of stubborn matters of fact, from the thoughtless extravagance of an electioneering frolic. – Yet, after the effervescence of spirits, raised by opposition, and all the little and tyrannic arts of canvassing are over – quiet souls! they only intend to march rank and file to say YES – or NO.

Experience, I believe, will shew that sordid interest, or licentious thoughtlessness, is the spring of action at most elections. – Again, I beg you not to lose sight of my modification of general rules. So far are the people from being habitually convinced of the sanctity of the charge they are conferring, that the venality of their votes must admonish them that they have no right to expect disinterested conduct. But to return to the church, and the habitual conviction of the people of England.

So far are the people from being 'habitually convinced that no evil can be acceptable, either in the act or the permission, to him whose essence is good;' that the sermons which they hear are to them almost as unintelligible as if they were preached in a foreign tongue. The language and sentiments rising above their capacities, very orthodox Christians are driven to fanatical meetings for amusement, if not for edification. The clergy, I speak of the body, not forgetting the respect and affection which I have for individuals, perform the duty of their profession as a kind of fee-simple, to entitle them to the emoluments accruing from it; and their ignorant flock think that merely going to church is meritorious.

So defective, in fact, are our laws, respecting religious establishments, that I have heard many rational pious clergymen complain, that they had no method of receiving their stipend that did not clog their endeavours to be useful; whilst the lives of many less conscientious rectors are passed in litigious disputes with the people they engaged to instruct; or in distant cities, in all the ease of luxurious idleness.

But you return to your old firm ground. – *Art thou there, True-penny?* Must we swear to secure property, and make assurance doubly sure, to give your perturbed spirit rest? Peace, peace to the manes of thy patriotic phrensy, which contributed to deprive some of thy fellow-citizens of their property in America: another spirit now walks abroad to secure the property of the church. – The tithes are safe! – We will not say for ever – because the time may come, when the traveller may ask where proud London stood? when its *temples*, its laws, and its trade, may be buried in one common ruin, and only serve as a by-word to point a moral, or furnish senators, who wage a wordy war, on the other side of the Atlantic, with tropes to swell their thundering bursts of eloquence.

Who shall dare to accuse you of inconsistency any more, when you have so staunchly supported the despotic principles which agree so perfectly with the un-erring interest of a large body of your fellow-citizens; not the largest – for when you venerate parliaments – I presume it is not the majority, as you have had the presumption to dissent, and loudly explain your reasons. – But it was not my intention, when I began this letter, to descend to the minutiae of your conduct, or to weigh your infirmities in a balance; it is only some of your pernicious opinions that I wish to hunt out of their lurking holes; and to shew you to yourself, stripped of the gorgeous drapery in which you have enwrapped your tyrannic principles.

That the people of England respect the national establishment I do not deny; I recollect the melancholy proof which they gave, in this very century, of their *enlightened* zeal and reasonable affection. I likewise know that, according to the dictates of a *prudent* law, in a commercial state, truth is reckoned a libel; yet I acknowledge, having never made my humanity give place to Gothic gallantry, that I should have been better pleased to have heard that Lord George Gordon was confined on account of the calamities which he brought on his country, than for a *libel* on the queen of France.

But one argument which you adduce to strengthen your assertion, appears to carry the preponderancy towards the other side.

You observe that 'our education is so formed as to confirm and fix this impression, (respect for the religious establishment); and that our education is in a manner wholly in the hands of ecclesiastics, and in all stages from infancy to manhood.' Far from agreeing with you, Sir, that these regulations render the clergy a more useful and respectable body, experience convinces me that the very contrary is the fact. In schools and colleges they may, in some degree, support their dignity within the monastic walls; but, in paying due respect to the parents of the young nobility under their tutorage, they do not forget, obsequiously, to respect their noble patrons. The little respect paid, in great houses, to tutors and chaplains proves, Sir, the fallacy of your reasoning. It would be almost invidious to remark, that they sometimes are only modern substitutes for the jesters of Gothic memory, and serve as whetstones for the blunt wit of the noble peer who patronizes them; and what respect a boy can imbibe for a *butt*, at which the shaft of ridicule is daily glanced, I leave those to determine who can distinguish depravity of morals under the specious mask of refined manners. [...]

Reading your Reflections warily over, it has continually and forcibly struck me, that had you been a Frenchman, you would have been, in spite of your respect for rank and antiquity, a violent revolutionist; and deceived, as you now probably are, by the passions that cloud your reason, have termed your Romantic enthusiasm an enlightened love of your country, a benevolent respect for the rights of men. Your imagination would have taken fire, and have found arguments, full as ingenious as those you now offer, to prove that the constitution, of which so few pillars remained, that constitution which time had almost obliterated, was not a model sufficiently noble to deserve close adherence. And, for the English constitution, you might not have had such a profound veneration as you have lately acquired; nay, it is not impossible that you might have entertained the same opinion of the English Parliament, that you professed to have during the American war.

Another observation which, by frequently occurring, has almost grown into a conviction, is simply this, that had the English in general reprobated the French Revolution, you would have stood forth alone, and been the avowed Goliath of liberty. But, not liking to see so many brothers near the throne of fame, you have turned the current of your passions, and consequently of your reasoning, another way. Had Dr Price's sermon not lighted some sparks very like envy in your bosom, I shrewdly suspect that he would have been treated with more candour; nor is it charitable to suppose that any thing but personal pique and hurt vanity could have dictated such bitter sarcasms and reiterated expressions of contempt as occur in your Reflections.

But without fixed principles even goodness of heart is no security from inconsistency, and mild affectionate sensibility only renders a man more ingeniously cruel, when the pangs of hurt vanity are mistaken for virtuous indignation, and the gall of bitterness for the milk of Christian charity.

Where is the dignity, the infallibility of sensibility, in the fair ladies, whom, if the voice of rumour is to be credited, the captive negroes curse in all the agony of bodily pain, for the unheard of tortures they invent? It is probable that some of them, after the sight of a flagellation, compose their ruffled spirits and exercise their tender feelings by the perusal of the last imported novel. – How true these tears are to nature, I leave you to determine. But these ladies may have read your Enquiry concerning the origin of our ideas of the Sublime and Beautiful, and, convinced by your arguments, may have laboured to be pretty, by counterfeiting weakness.

You may have convinced them that *littleness* and *weakness* are the very essence of beauty; and that the Supreme Being, in giving women beauty in the most supereminent degree, seemed to command them, by the powerful voice of Nature, not to cultivate the moral virtues that might chance to excite respect, and interfere with the pleasing sensations they were created to inspire. Thus confining truth, fortitude, and humanity, within the rigid pale of manly morals, they might justly argue, that to be loved, women's high end and great distinction! they should 'learn to lisp, to totter in their walk, and nick-name God's creatures.' Never, they might repeat after you, was any man, much less a woman, rendered amiable by the force of those exalted qualities, fortitude, justice, wisdom, and truth; and thus forewarned of the sacrifice they must make to those austere, unnatural virtues, they would be authorized to turn all their attention to their persons, systematically neglecting morals to secure beauty. [...]

To say the truth, I not only tremble for the souls of women, but for the good natured man, whom every one loves. The *amiable* weakness of his mind is a strong argument against its immateriality, and seems to prove that beauty relaxes the *solids* of the soul as well as the body.

It follows then immediately, from your own reasoning, that respect and love are antagonist principles; and that, if we really wish to render men more virtuous, we must endeavour to banish all enervating modifications of beauty from civil society.

We must, to carry your argument a little further, return to the Spartan regulations, and settle the virtues of men on the stern foundation of mortification and self-denial; for any attempt to civilize the heart, to make it humane by implanting reasonable principles, is a mere philosophic dream. If refinement inevitably lessens respect for virtue, by rendering beauty, the grand tempter, more seductive; if these relaxing feelings are incompatible with the nervous exertions of morality, the sun of Europe is not set; it begins to dawn, when cold metaphysicians try to make the head give laws to the heart.

But should experience prove that there is a beauty in virtue, a charm in order, which necessarily implies exertion, a depraved sensual taste may give way to a more manly one – and *melting* feelings to rational satisfactions. Both may be equally natural to man; the test is their moral difference, and that point reason alone can decide.

Such a glorious change can only be produced by liberty. Inequality of rank must ever impede the growth of virtue, by vitiating the mind that submits or domineers; that is ever employed to procure nourishment for the body, or amusement for the mind. And if this grand example be set by an assembly of unlettered clowns, if they can produce a crisis that may involve the fate of Europe, and 'more than Europe,' you must allow us to respect unsophisticated reason, and reverence the active exertions that were not relaxed by a fastidious respect for the beauty of rank, or a dread of the deformity produced by any *void* in the social structure. [...]

Is hereditary weakness necessary to render religion lovely? and will her form have lost the smooth delicacy that inspires love, when stripped of its Gothic drapery? Must every grand model be placed on the pedestal of property? and is there no beauteous proportion in virtue, when not clothed in a sensual garb?

Of these questions there would be no end, though they lead to the same conclusion; – that your politics and morals, when simplified, would undermine religion and virtue to set up a spurious, sensual beauty, that has long debauched your imagination, under the specious form of natural feelings.

And what is this mighty revolution in property? The present incumbents only are injured, or the hierarchy of the clergy, an ideal part of the constitution, which you have personified, to render your affection more tender. How has posterity been injured by a distribution of the property snatched, perhaps, from innocent hands, but accumulated by the most abominable violation of every sentiment of justice and piety? Was the monument of former ignorance and iniquity to be held sacred, to enable the present possessors of enormous benefices to *dissolve* in indolent pleasures? Was not their convenience, for they have not been turned adrift on the world, to give place to a just partition of the land belonging to the state? And did not the respect due to the natural equality of man require this triumph over Monkish rapacity? Were those monsters to be reverenced on account of their antiquity, and their unjust claims perpetuated to their ideal children, the clergy, merely to preserve the sacred majesty of Property inviolate, and to enable the Church to retain her pristine splendor? Can posterity be injured by individuals losing the chance of obtaining great wealth, without meriting it, by its being diverted from a narrow channel, and disembogued into the sea that affords clouds to water all the land? Besides, the clergy not brought up with the expectation of great revenues will not feel the loss; and if bishops should happen to be chosen on account of their personal merit, religion may be benefited by the vulgar nomination.

The sophistry of asserting that Nature leads us to reverence our civil institutions from the same principle that we venerate aged individuals, is a palpable fallacy 'that is so like truth, it will serve the turn as well.' And when you add, 'that we have chosen our nature rather than our speculations, our breasts rather than our inventions,' the pretty jargon seems equally unintelligible.

But it was the downfall of the visible power and dignity of the church that roused your ire; you could have excused a little squeezing of the individuals to supply present exigencies; the actual possessors of the property might have been oppressed with something like impunity, if the church had not been spoiled of its gaudy trappings. You love the church, your country, and its laws, you repeatedly tell us, because they deserve to be loved; but from you this is not a panegyric: weakness and indulgence are the only incitements to love and confidence that you can discern, and it cannot be denied that the tender mother you venerate deserves, on this score, all your affection.

It would be as vain a task to attempt to obviate all your passionate objections, as to unravel all your plausible arguments, often illustrated by known truths, and rendered forcible by pointed invectives. I only attack the foundation. On the natural principles of justice I build my plea for disseminating the property artfully said to be appropriated to religious purposes, but, in reality, to support idle tyrants, amongst the society whose ancestors were cheated or forced into illegal grants. Can there be an opinion more subversive of morality, than that time sanctifies crimes, and silences the blood that calls out for retribution, if not for vengeance? If the revenue annexed to the Gallic church was greater than the most bigoted protestant would now allow to be its reasonable share, would it not have been trampling on the rights of men to perpetuate such an arbitrary appropriation of the common flock, because time had rendered the fraudulent seizure venerable? Besides, if Reason had suggested, as surely she must, if the imagination had not been allowed to dwell on the fascinating pomp of ceremonial grandeur, that the clergy would be rendered both more virtuous and useful by being put more on a par with each other, and the mass of the people it was their duty to instruct; – where was there room for hesitation? The charge of presumption, thrown by you on the most reasonable innovations, may, without any violence to truth, be retorted on every reformation that has meliorated our condition, and even on the improvable faculty that gives us a claim to the pre-eminence of intelligent beings. [...]

You find it very difficult to separate policy from justice: in the political world they have frequently been separated with shameful dexterity. To mention a recent instance. According to the limited views of timid, or interested politicians, an abolition of the infernal slave trade would not only be unsound policy, but a flagrant infringement of the laws (which are allowed to have been infamous) that induced the planters to purchase their estates. But is it not consonant with justice, with the common principles of humanity, not to mention Christianity, to abolish this abominable mischief? There is not one argument, one invective, levelled by you at the confiscators of the church revenue, which could not, with the strictest propriety, be applied by the planters and negro-drivers to our Parliament, if it gloriously dared to shew the world that British senators were men: if the natural feelings of humanity silenced the cold cautions of timidity, till this stigma on our nature was wiped off, and all men were allowed to enjoy their birth-right – liberty, till by their crimes they had authorized society to deprive them of the blessing they had abused.

The same arguments might be used in India, if any attempt were made to bring back things to nature, to prove that a man ought never to quit the cast that confined him to the profession of his lineal forefathers. The Bramins would doubtless find many ingenious reasons to justify this debasing, though venerable prejudice; and would not, it is to be supposed, forget to observe that time, by interweaving the oppressive law with many useful customs, had rendered it for the present very convenient, and consequently legal. Almost every vice that has degraded our nature might be justified by shewing that it had been productive of *some* benefit to society: for it would be as difficult to point out positive evil as unallayed good, in this imperfect state. What indeed would become of morals, if they had no other test than prescription? The manners of men may change without end; but, wherever reason receives the least cultivation – wherever men rise above brutes, morality must rest on the same base. And the more man discovers of the nature of his mind and body, the more clearly he is convinced, that to act according to the dictates of reason is to conform to the law of God. [...]

It may be confidently asserted that no man chooses evil, because it is evil; he only mistakes it for happiness, the good he seeks. And the desire of rectifying these mistakes, is the noble ambition of an enlightened understanding, the impulse of feelings that Philosophy invigorates. To endeavour to make unhappy men resigned to their fate, is the tender endeavour of short-sighted benevolence, of transient yearnings of humanity; but to labour to increase human happiness by extirpating error, is a masculine godlike affection. This remark may be carried still further. Men who possess uncommon sensibility, whose quick emotions shew how closely the eye and heart are connected, soon forget the most forcible sensations. Not tarrying long enough in the brain to be subject to reflection, the next sensations, of course, obliterate them. Memory, however, treasures up these proofs of native goodness; and the being who is not spurred on to any virtuous act, still thinks itself of consequence, and boasts of its feelings. Why? Because the sight of distress, or an affecting narrative, made its blood flow with more velocity, and the heart, literally speaking, beat with sympathetic emotion. We ought to beware of confounding mechanical instinctive sensations with emotions that reason deepens, and justly terms the feelings of *humanity*. This word discriminates the active exertions of virtue from the vague declamation of sensibility.

The declaration of the National Assembly, when they recognized the rights of men, was calculated to touch the humane heart – the downfall of the clergy, to agitate the pupil of impulse. On the watch to find fault, faults met your prying eye; a different prepossession might have produced a different conviction. [...]

Judgment is sublime, wit beautiful, and, according to your own theory, they cannot exist together without impairing each other's power. The predominancy of the latter, in your endless Reflections, should lead hasty readers to suspect that it may, in a great degree, exclude the former.

But, among all your plausible arguments, and witty illustrations, your contempt for the poor always appears conspicuous, and rouses my indignation. The following paragraph in particular struck me, as breathing the most tyrannic spirit, and displaying the most factitious feelings. 'Good order is the foundation of all good things. To be enabled to acquire, the people, without being servile, must be tractable and obedient. The magistrate must have his reverence, the laws their authority. The body of the people must not find the principles of natural subordination by art rooted out of their minds. They *must* respect that property of which they *cannot* partake. *They must labour to obtain what by labour can be obtained; and when they find, as they commonly do, the success disproportioned to the endeavour, they must be taught their consolation in the final proportions of eternal justice.* Of this consolation, whoever deprives them, deadens their industry, and strikes at the root of all acquisition as of all conservation. He that does this, is the cruel oppressor, the merciless enemy, of the poor and wretched; at the same time that, by his wicked speculations, he exposes the fruits of successful industry, and the accumulations of fortune, (ah! there's the rub) to the plunder of the negligent, the disappointed, and the unprosperous.'

This is contemptible hard-hearted sophistry, in the specious form of humility, and submission to the will of Heaven. – It is, Sir, *possible* to render the poor happier in this world, without depriving them of the consolation which you gratuitously grant them in the next. They have a right to more comfort than they at present enjoy; and more comfort might be afforded them, without encroaching on the pleasures of the rich: not now waiting to enquire whether the rich have any right to exclusive pleasures. What do I say? – encroaching! No; if an intercourse were established between them, it would impart the only true pleasure that can be snatched in this land of shadows, this hard school of moral discipline.

I know, indeed, that there is often something disgusting in the distresses of poverty, at which the imagination revolts, and starts back to exercise itself in the more attractive Arcadia of fiction. The rich man builds a house, art and taste give it the highest finish. His gardens are planted, and the trees grow to recreate the fancy of the planter, though the temperature of the climate may rather force him to avoid the dangerous damps they exhale, than seek the umbrageous retreat. Every thing on the estate is cherished but man; – yet, to contribute to the happiness of man, is the most sublime of all enjoyments. But if, instead of sweeping pleasure-grounds, obelisks, temples, and elegant cottages, as *objects* for the eye, the heart was allowed to beat true to nature, decent farms would be scattered over the estate, and plenty smile around. Instead of the poor being subject to the griping hand of an avaricious steward, they would be watched over with fatherly solicitude, by the man whose duty and pleasure it was to guard their happiness, and shield from rapacity the beings who, by the sweat of their brow, exalted him above his fellows.

I could almost imagine I see a man thus gathering blessings as he mounted the hill of life; or consolation, in those days when the spirits lag, and the tired heart finds no pleasure in them. It is not by squandering alms that the poor can be relieved, or improved – it is the fostering sun of kindness, the wisdom that finds them employments calculated to give them habits of virtue, that meliorates their condition. Love is only the fruit of love; condescension and authority may produce the obedience you applaud; but he has lost his heart of flesh who can see a fellow-creature humbled before him, and trembling at the frown of a being, whose heart is supplied by the same vital current, and whose pride ought to be checked by a consciousness of having the same infirmities.

What salutary dews might not be shed to refresh this thirsty land, if men were more *enlightened!* Smiles and premiums might encourage cleanliness, industry, and emulation. – A garden more inviting than Eden would then meet the eye, and springs of joy murmur on every side. The clergyman would superintend his own flock, the shepherd would then love the sheep he daily tended; the school might rear its decent head, and the buzzing tribe, let loose to play, impart a portion of their vivacious spirits to the heart that longed to open their minds, and lead them to taste the pleasures of men. Domestic comfort, the civilizing relations of husband, brother, and father, would soften labour, and render life contented.

Returning once from a despotic country to a part of England well cultivated, but not very picturesque – with what delight did I not observe the poor man's garden! – The homely palings and twining woodbine, with all the rustic contrivances of simple, unlettered taste, was a sight which relieved the eye that had wandered indignant from the stately palace to the pestiferous hovel, and turned from the awful contrast into itself to mourn the fate of man, and curse the arts of civilization!

Why cannot large estates be divided into small farms? these dwellings would indeed grace our land. Why are huge forests still allowed to stretch out with idle pomp and all the indolence of Eastern grandeur? Why does the brown waste meet the traveller's view, when men want work? But commons cannot be enclosed without *acts of parliament* to increase the property of the rich! Why might not the industrious peasant be allowed to steal a farm from the heath? [...]

In this great city, that proudly rears its head, and boasts of its population and commerce, how much misery lurks in pestilential corners, whilst idle mendicants assail, on every side, the man who hates to encourage impostors, or repress, with angry frown, the plaints of the poor! How many mechanics, by a flux of trade or fashion, lose their employment; whom misfortunes, not to be warded off, lead to the idleness that vitiates their character and renders them afterwards averse to honest labour! Where is the eye that marks these evils, more gigantic than any of the infringements of property, which you piously deprecate? Are these remediless evils? And is the humane heart satisfied with turning the poor over to *another* world, to receive the blessings this could afford? If society was regulated on a more enlarged plan; if man was contented to be the friend of man, and did not seek to bury the sympathies of humanity in the servile appellation of master; if, turning his eyes from ideal regions of taste and elegance, he laboured to give the earth he inhabited all the beauty it is capable of receiving, and was ever on the watch to shed abroad all the happiness which human nature can enjoy; – he who, respecting the rights of men, wishes to convince or persuade society that this is true happiness and dignity, is not the cruel *oppressor* of the poor, nor a short-sighted philosopher – HE fears God and loves his fellow-creatures. – Behold the whole duty of man! – the citizen who acts differently is a sophisticated being. [...]

Is it absolute blasphemy to doubt of the omnipotence of the law, or to suppose that religion might be more pure if there were fewer baits for hypocrites in the church? But our manners, you tell us, are drawn from the French, though you had before celebrated our native plainness. If they were, it is time we broke loose from dependance – Time that Englishmen drew water from their own springs; for, if manners are not a painted substitute for morals, we have only to cultivate our reason, and we shall not feel the want of an arbitrary model. Nature will suffice; but I forget myself: – Nature and Reason, according to your system, are all to give place to authority; and the gods, as Shakespeare makes a frantic wretch exclaim, seem to kill us for their sport, as men do flies.

Before I conclude my cursory remarks, it is but just to acknowledge that I coincide with you in your opinion respecting the *sincerity* of many modern philosophers. Your consistency in avowing a veneration for rank and riches deserves praise; but I must own that I have often indignantly observed that some of the *enlightened* philosophers, who talk most vehemently of the native rights of men, borrow many noble sentiments to adorn their conversation, which have no influence on their conduct. They bow down to rank, and are careful to secure property; for virtue, without this adventitious drapery, is seldom very respectable in their eyes – nor are they very quick-sighted to discern real dignity of character when no sounding name exalts the man above his elbows. – But neither open enmity nor hollow homage destroys the intrinsic value of those principles which rest on an eternal foundation, and revert for a standard to the immutable attributes of God.

PART IV

Federalism and Anti-Federalism:

JAMES MADISON AND MERCY OTIS WARREN

This small company of settlers, after wandering some time on the frozen shore, fixed themselves at the bottom of the Massachusetts Bay. Though dispirited by innumerable discouraging circumstances, they immediately entered into engagements with each other to form themselves into a regular society, and drew up a convenant, by which they bound themselves to submit to order and subordination.[1]

> *Mercy Otis Warren, writing in 1805 about the establishment of an American colony in 1620, in her* History of the American Revolution

Mercy Otis Warren must have felt herself to be very much connected to the "Old Colony" of Massachusetts, which had been the first settlement by whites in New England, for she and her husband were both descendants of *Mayflower* passengers. Her father, James Otis, was a prosperous if uneducated farmer and merchant on Cape Cod, who served in several public positions in the young colony. Focused on the education of his sons, Colonel Otis found it convenient to have an inconvenient daughter educated with her brothers, James and Joseph, at the home of a local minister.[2] Here, Mercy Otis Warren was tutored in the plays and poetry of Milton and Shakespeare, Dryden and Pope, and the political essays of John Locke. She particularly relished Raleigh's *History of the World*, written by the man whose own exploits had led to the first white settlement in Virginia – Massachusetts' rival as intellectual and commercial center of the American colonies.

Later, when the boys were sent away to Harvard College, Warren maintained her close relationship with her brother, James Jr. (Jemmy), marrying his classmate, James Warren of Plymouth. Jemmy Otis became perhaps the best-known patriot of his time on both sides of the Atlantic, when he resigned his position in the General Court rather than defend certain Parliamentary Acts. At issue were the writs of assistance which allowed English soldiers to search houses and seize goods under what amounted to a blanket warrant. Speaking as a citizen rather than as a member of the colonial government, he declared:

I oppose the kind of power the exercise of which, in former periods of English history, cost one king his head, and another his throne[3] in an inspirational oratory before the Superior Court of Massachusetts. This transformative moment in colonial history marked the first public suggestion among colonists that the revered English legal system, with its Acts of Parliament and colonial charters, and which provided the edifice upon which the rationalizations of Empire were built, was subject to a more profound and fundamental system of natural law and unwritten rights. Historian Jean Fritz describes the impact of Jemmy Otis's speech:

> Although most people were well acquainted with John Locke's principles, they had never heard them applied officially in such a practical way to their own specific needs.[4]

The colonists were first and foremost English. They derived their self-perception from the twin Enlightenment notions of reason and rights, concepts derived from the theories of Isaac Newton, John Locke, and many others. They were proud of an English legal history which in their view upheld the rights of individuals. The intention of Parliament to treat colonists on their native ground as inferior to the English (made clear by the Acts of Parliament and the actions of Governor Hutchinson) incensed their eighteenth-century sensibilities. This transgression was made brilliantly clear by James Otis.

Warren's intelligence matched that of her brother, but whereas his included a flair for public oratory and dramatic gesture, the sister's was more controlled and ultimately more productive. Mercy Otis Warren, her brother, and her father were players on a revolutionary stage inhabited by Samuel Adams, John and Abigail Adams, King George III, John Hancock, James and Dolley Madison, and Thomas Jefferson. Many of the revolutionary leaders visited the Plymouth house of Mercy Otis Warren and corresponded with her, most notably John Adams with whom she formed a close, though sometimes troubled, friendship. Her writing reflected and recorded what she viewed as a divinely designed period in world history, when the harmony and virtue of classical republicanism took new form.

Warren wrote numerous letters, poems, and essays, often publishing them in newspapers and broadsheets. Between 1773 and 1779 she wrote and published anonymously several plays, *The Adulateur, The Group, The Defeat*, perhaps *The Blockheads* and *The Motley Assembly*, and two prose poems, *The Ladies of Castile* and *The Sack of Rome*.[5] The plays are political satires, commentaries on public life at the time. Her chief accomplishment was her *History of the Rise, Progress and Termination of the American Revolution*, which constitutes the only major contemporary anti-federalist account of the American Revolution, and it does so from the standpoint of someone concerned with philosophical issues: republicanism versus monarchy, the roles of virtue, of patriotism, and of religion. In time, Warren's political arguments caused her to become estranged from John Adams, but they later reconciled. She died in 1814, shortly after the burning of Washington, D.C. by the British, having witnessed firsthand the major events in the creation of the United States.

PUBLIUS AND THE COLUMBIAN PATRIOT: THE GENTLEMAN FROM VIRGINIA MEETS THE LADY FROM CAPE COD

The world is now viewing America, as experimenting a new system of FEDERAL REPUBLIC, including a territory to which the Kingdoms of Great Britain and Ireland bear little proportion.[6]

James Madison is known as a diminutive man, a person of practical genius, and a chief author of the United States Constitution, a document Mercy Otis Warren thought dangerous (for its monarchical tendencies) and unnecessary (since the Articles of Confederation could be revised instead). The son of a wealthy Virginian landowner, the intellectual Madison was educated at The College of New Jersey (Princeton) and later studied for the ministry. He was a delegate to the Virginia Convention of 1776 where he helped to draft the state's constitution. Madison was several times elected to Congress, intrigued by intricate problems of financing the federal government while honoring the rights of states. Among his early interests were religious freedom (which he had tried to secure in the Virginia constitution) and regulating commerce, a policy which led, later during his time as president, directly to war with Britain.

Political differences among the colonists who became the newly independent Americans had persisted throughout the latter half of the eighteenth century, and became intensely focused during the Constitutional Convention and the campaigns for its ratification in 1787–9. On the one side were the commercial towns, the great planters, the army officers, the creditors and property-holders (such as Alexander Hamilton) along with some genuine political thinkers (such as Madison). On the other were farmers and small businessmen, radical republicans and patriots acutely mindful of the causes of the revolution. Among these were a few southerners: Virginians George Mason and James Monroe, and many Northerners: Otises and Warrens, Patrick Henry, and Governors Eldridge Gerry and George Clinton of Massachusetts and New York. At issue were competing concerns. Federalists desired a sufficiently strong central government to provide stability and commercial protection. They sympathized with the British reaction against the French democratic movement. Some, such as Hamilton, favored a strong presidency and even more central powers than were proposed in the new Constitution. Under the pseudonym "Publius," Madison, together with Alexander Hamilton and John Jay, wrote the *Federalist Papers* designed to promote the new Constitution.

Anti-federalists harbored a deep-seated suspicion of central government, and a conviction that the essence of republicanism lies in small states of individuals holding similar values and interests. Warren opposed the ratification of the new Constitution and saw it as a dangerous replacement for the (admittedly flawed) Articles of Confederation. In her "Observations On the New Constitution, And on the Federal and State Conventions, By A Columbian Patriot," published in 1788, Warren raises numerous specific objections to the proposed Constitution. She despairs the deputation of the powers of taxation to the national government. She is concerned about the failure to specifically secure the liberties of conscience and of the press. She is concerned about the potentially extensive powers of judicial review, the blending of the branches of government, and the fact that there is no clear separation of powers. She fears that a standing army may endanger the freedoms of the states, especially their right to muster militias. She wonders how state governments will support themselves, with the main powers of revenue in the hands of federal government. She despairs at Congress determining their own salaries, and the possibility that the republican principle of rotation in office will be undermined by a lack of "term limits," and excessive term lengths. She reiterates Montesquieu's complaint that republics of too great a size are doomed to failure.

It was a controversy which, in a sense, both sides won. The federalists succeeded in having the Constitution ratified, but only on the promise to honor the arguments of anti-federalists like Warren through the addition of the Bill of Rights. Many ironies attend this compromise. The appended document, the Bill of Rights, rather than the Constitution itself is the one which stands as the outstanding political, philosophical, and legal tract. Yet the federalists had the privilege not only of writing history, but of writing the opposition document as well. Madison, convinced of the necessity of a Bill of Rights to preserve the nation and the Constitution from further anti-federalist attack, took it upon himself to codify and compose the Bill of Rights as a way of controlling its contents and preventing a more radical tract. Thus, a part of Madison's genius was his ability to distill the concerns of Warren and others into an acceptable form.

In her *History* she describes the emotions of some at the signing of the Constitution:

> the philosophic doctor Franklin... signed the instrument for the consolidation of the government of the United States with tears and apologized for doing it at all. Many of the intelligent yeomanry and the great bulk of independent landowners, who had tasted the sweets of... equality and liberty, read every unconditional ratification of the new system in silent anguish.[7]

Warren's objections are of twofold importance. As cogently as any, she consolidates the major meaningful objections to the Constitution. This is no small feat, since the anti-federalists are characterized by their lack of agreement regarding objections, and caricatured for this by Madison (in *The Federalist* 38). Further, the anti-federalist objections are central to political theory and shed light on current politics, particularly in the USA and Europe today, but also in other parts of the world. Certain branches of the conservative position in the United States, including the "militia movement" in its uglier forms, but also reasoned political thinkers, focus on what is perceived as undue national power, for enforcement and taxation, excessive terms in office, and what are perceived as federal encroachments on civil liberties. Coming out of different cultural and national backgrounds, the movement for European Union today is the center for heated debates about the rights of individual nations over and against those of the unified government.

Madison's concerns were practical. He had seen first-hand, and was aware more than most, that the largest threat to union, one which had nearly undone the nation during the War of Independence, was a central government unable to muster funds and governance sufficient to operate. But his approach was intellectual, and his invention ingenious. Although he is seen as chief among the federalists, far more than Hamilton (and Jay) he saw the need to accommodate the states and maintain their power. He painstakingly creates the "federal republic," a concept (and reality) designed to maintain a large sphere of state autonomy while claiming the authority of a national government essential to stability and long-term union. He argues for a blending rather than a strict separation of powers in the branches of government. He argues for a strict construction of the Constitution. He argues that the technology of the day – road and canal construction – will shrink the nation into a manageable size for democracy.

RACE, CLASS, AND GENDER

Though not on the tips of their pens, racial issues were in the forefront of the minds of these writers, and figured prominently in many discussions. Madison himself was the author of the three-fifths Compromise in Article 1, Section 2 of the United States Constitution, whereby three-fifths of slaves were to be counted to determine both representation in Congress and taxation of property, and yet Madison himself was opposed to slavery. He wished to end the importation of slaves immediately, rather than, as had been called for, in 1808. In his own notes made during the Constitutional Convention Madison offered the following observation:

> We have seen the mere distinction of colour made in the most enlightened period of time, a ground of the most oppressive dominion ever exercised by man over man. What has been the source of those unjust laws complained among ourselves? Has it not been the real or supposed interest of the major number?[8]

And yet Madison was a slave holder. Nonetheless, he worked diligently for a particular scheme of gradual emancipation and deportation, under the rubric "colonization," whereby slaves would be bought and sent to Africa. He avers:

> A general emancipation of slaves ought to be 1. gradual, 2. equitable and satisfactory to the individuals immediately concerned, 3. consistent with the existing and durable prejudices of the nation.[9]

Madison's reason for removing Blacks pertains to what he sees as enduring and insurmountable prejudice:

> If the blacks, strongly marked as they are by Physical & lasting peculiarities, be retained amid the Whites, under the degrading privation of equal rights political or social, they must always be dissatisfied with their condition as a change only from one to another species of oppression: always secretly confederated against the ruling and privileged class ...[10]

Madison goes on to adduce that the cost of this plan will be about 600 million dollars, a plan adopted in spirit by Abraham Lincoln, and rejected by political theorist Maria Stewart as a preposterous violation of the rights of Blacks to live in, what was for most, their native country – the United States (see Part V of this volume). That Madison, considered a vigorous foe of slavery, could not even emancipate his own slaves says something of the difficulties of consistency which characterize attitudes toward race in the United States. Yet Madison, in the above passage and elsewhere, also shows a keen awareness of the political disabilities generated by social class as well as race.

Mercy Otis Warren remained astonishingly untouched, even by the feminist arguments of her day. She must have read her brother Jemmy's pamphlet "The Rights of the British Colonies Asserted and Proved," in which he asserts:

> Are not women born as free as men? Would it not be infamous to assert that the ladies are all slaves by nature? If every man and woman born or to be born has and will have a right to be consulted and must accede to the original compact before they can with any kind of justice be said to be bound by it, will not the compact be ever forming and never finished? If upon abdication all were reduced to the state of nature, had not the apple women and orange girls as good a right to give their respectable suffrages for a new King as the philosopher, courtier, and politician?[11]

Far from adopting the notion that women had equal political rights with men, Warren was a devotee of the natural complement theory of Kant and others, which held a separate and complementary sphere for women (a view sometimes held and sometimes attacked by Mary Wollstonecraft). If anyone ever ascribed to the notion of republican motherhood, it was Warren.[12] Her view of the republic was that religion (not prescribed by the state) played a special role in the United States. She believed the country itself to be favored by God, and especially believed that certain virtues attached to republicanism – simplicity, honesty, equality, and liberty. It is clear from her writing that one of her gravest fears was the degeneracy resulting from wealth and privilege. She thought women to be especially suited to the teaching of public and civic virtue to their children.

Warren, therefore, does not seem to see inequality in the male/female political relations of her time. Perhaps this is because she herself was so influential, with her own husband, her father and brothers and sons, and also with John Adams, and other major political figures. She does, however, often wonder if she is overstepping her bounds by writing political theory, and seeks the assurance of Adams and others that she is not. This conundrum reflects the complexity of this important theorist.

Few political theorists today address the issue of the size of the state, yet it was of paramount concern to Enlightenment philosophers. This is not because of a love of "rugged individualism," but because of a profound sense of the importance of community, and a conviction that centralization and an increased scale of government would harm the community on which political governance is based. In this, the concerns of Madison and Warren, at odds in their own time, perhaps seem closer together now than they would have two hundred years ago. Yet they still may reflect the concerns of any group trying to balance community-identified goals that conflict with dominant ideologies with the demands made by the nation-state. As smaller groups identified, for example, by common cultural or religious values reach greater political awareness, it becomes more important for political theory to address ways of honoring their group-identified concerns. The mechanisms advocated by Warren and crafted into the *Bill of Rights* by Madison are eminently useful in this project.

Notes

1   Mercy Warren, *History of the Rise, Progress and Termination of the American Revolution Interpreted with Biographical, Political and Moral Observations*, edited and annotated by Lester H. Cohen (Indianapolis: Indiana University Press (Liberty Classics), 1988, 2 vols), vol. 1, p. 11.
2   Elizabeth Cady Stanton was also educated with her brother, for the same reason.
3   Warren, *History of . . . the American Revolution*, p. 48.
4   Jean Fritz, *Cast for a Revolution: Some American Friends and Enemies, 1728–1814* (Boston: Houghton Mifflin Co., 1972), p. 43.
5   Several other plays are sometimes attributed to Warren. See Joan Hoff, *Law, Gender and Injustice: A Legal History of U.S. Women* (New York: NYU Press, 1991), pp. 68ff, for a brief account of these works.
6   Warren, *History*, vol. 1, p. vii.
7   Ibid., pp. 210–11.
8   James Madison, *Mind of the Founder: Sources of the Political Thought of James Madison*, with an introduction by Marvin Meyers (Boston: University Presses of New England, 1981), p. 314.
9   Ibid.

10 Ibid.
11 Quoted in Joan Hoff, *Law, Gender and Injustice*, p. 79.
12 See Hoff, *Law, Gender and Injustice*, for a description of "republican motherhood."

CHAPTER 7

The Federalist

JAMES MADISON

THE FEDERALIST NO. 10

To the People of the State of New York:

Among the numerous advantages promised by a well-constructed Union, none deserves to be more accurately developed than its tendency to break and control the violence of faction. The friend of popular governments never finds himself so much alarmed for their character and fate, as when he contemplates their propensity to this dangerous vice. He will not fail, therefore, to set a due value on any plan which, without violating the principles to which he is attached, provides a proper cure for it. The instability, injustice, and confusion introduced into the public councils, have, in truth, been the mortal diseases under which popular governments have everywhere perished; as they continue to be the favorite and fruitful topics from which the adversaries to liberty derive their most specious declamations. The valuable improvements made by the American constitutions on the popular models, both ancient and modern, cannot certainly be too much admired; but it would be an unwarrantable partiality, to contend that they have as effectually obviated the danger on this side, as was wished and expected. Complaints are everywhere heard from our most considerate and virtuous citizens, equally the friends of public and private faith, and of public and personal liberty, that our governments are too unstable; that the public good is disregarded in the conflicts of rival parties; and that measures are too often decided, not according to the rules of justice and the rights of the minor party, but by the superior force of an interested and overbearing majority. However anxiously we may wish that these complaints had no foundation, the evidence of known facts will not permit us to deny that they are in some degree true. It will be found, indeed, on a candid review of our situation, that some of the distresses under which we labor have been erroneously charged on the operation of our governments; but it will be found, at the same time, that other causes will not

James Madison. *The Federalist*. Originally published in 1787–8.

alone account for many of our heaviest misfortunes; and, particularly, for that prevailing and increasing distrust of public engagements, and alarm for private rights, which are echoed from one end of the continent to the other. These must be chiefly, if not wholly, effects of the unsteadiness and injustice with which a factious spirit has tainted our public administrations.

By a faction, I understand a number of citizens, whether amounting to a majority or minority of the whole, who are united and actuated by some common impulse of passion, or of interest, adverse to the rights of other citizens, or to the permanent and aggregate interests of the community.

There are two methods of curing the mischiefs of faction: the one, by removing its causes; the other, by controlling its effects.

There are again two methods of removing the causes of faction: the one, by destroying the liberty which is essential to its existence; the other, by giving to every citizen the same opinions, the same passions, and the same interests.

It could never be more truly said than of the first remedy, that it is worse than the disease. Liberty is to faction what air is to fire, an aliment without which it instantly expires. But it could not be less folly to abolish liberty, which is essential to political life, because it nourishes faction, than it would be to wish the annihilation of air, which is essential to animal life, because it imparts to fire its destructive agency.

The second expedient is as impracticable as the first would be unwise. As long as the reason of man continues fallible, and he is at liberty to exercise it, different opinions will be formed. As long as the connection subsists between his reason and his self-love, his opinions and his passions will have a reciprocal influence on each other; and the former will be objects to which the latter will attach themselves. The diversity in the faculties of men, from which the rights of property originate, is not less an insuperable obstacle to a uniformity of interests. The protection of these faculties is the first object of government. From the protection of different and unequal faculties of acquiring property, the possession of different degrees and kinds of property immediately results; and from the influence of these on the sentiments and views of the respective proprietors, ensues a division of the society into different interests and parties.

The latent causes of faction are thus sown in the nature of man; and we see them everywhere brought into different degrees of activity, according to the different circumstances of civil society. A zeal for different opinions concerning religion, concerning government, and many other points, as well of speculation as of practice; an attachment to different leaders ambitiously contending for pre-eminence and power; or to persons of other descriptions whose fortunes have been interesting to the human passions, have, in turn, divided mankind into parties, inflamed them with mutual animosity, and rendered them much more disposed to vex and oppress each other than to co-operate for their common good. So strong is this propensity of mankind to fall into mutual animosities, that where no substantial occasion presents itself, the most frivolous and fanciful distinctions have been sufficient to kindle their unfriendly passions and excite their most violent conflicts. But the most common and durable source of factions has been the various and unequal distribution of property. Those who hold and those who are without property have ever formed distinct interests in society. Those who are creditors, and those who are debtors, fall under a like discrimination. A landed interest, a manufacturing interest, a mercantile interest, a moneyed interest, with many lesser interests, grow up of necessity in civilized nations, and divide them into different classes, actuated by different sentiments and views. The regulation of these various and interfering interests forms the principal task of modern legislation, and involves the spirit of party and faction in the necessary and ordinary operations of the government.

No man is allowed to be a judge in his own cause, because his interest would certainly bias his judgment, and, not improbably, corrupt his integrity. With equal, nay with greater reason, a body of men are unfit to be both judges and parties at the same time; yet what are many of the most important acts of legislation, but so many judicial determinations, not indeed concerning the rights of single persons, but concerning the rights of large bodies of citizens? and what are the different classes of legislators but advocates and parties to the causes which they determine? Is a law proposed concerning private debts? It is a question to which the creditors are parties on one side and the debtors on the other. Justice ought to hold the balance between them. Yet the parties are, and must be, themselves the judges; and the most numerous party, or, in other words, the most powerful faction must be expected to prevail. Shall domestic manufactures be encouraged, and in what degree, by restrictions on foreign manufactures? are questions which would be differently decided by the landed and the manufacturing classes, and probably by neither with a sole regard to justice and the public good. The apportionment of taxes on the various descriptions of property is an act which seems to require the most exact impartiality; yet there is, perhaps, no legislative act in which greater opportunity and temptation are given to a predominant party to trample on the rules of justice. Every shilling with which they overburden the inferior number is a shilling saved to their own pockets.

It is in vain to say that enlightened statesmen will be able to adjust these clashing interests and render them all subservient to the public good. Enlightened statesmen will not always be at the helm. Nor, in many cases, can such an adjustment be made at all without taking into view indirect and remote considerations, which will rarely prevail over the immediate interest which one party may find in disregarding the rights of another or the good of the whole.

The inference to which we are brought is, that the *causes* of faction cannot be removed, and that relief is only to be sought in the means of controlling its *effects*.

If a faction consists of less than a majority, relief is supplied by the republican principle, which enables the majority to defeat its sinister views by regular vote. It may clog the administration, it may convulse the society; but it will be unable to execute and mask its violence under the forms of the Constitution. When a majority is included in a faction, the form of popular government, on the other hand, enables it to sacrifice to its ruling passion or interest both the public good and the rights of other citizens. To secure the public good and private rights against the danger of such a faction, and at the same time to preserve the spirit and the form of popular government, is then the great object to which our inquiries are directed. Let me add that it is the great desideratum by which this form of government can be rescued from the opprobrium under which it has so long labored, and be recommended to the esteem and adoption of mankind.

By what means is this object attainable? Evidently by one of two only. Either the existence of the same passion or interest in a majority at the same time must be prevented, or the majority, having such coexistent passion or interest, must be rendered by their number and local situation unable to concert and carry into effect schemes of oppression. If the impulse and the opportunity be suffered to coincide, we well know that neither moral nor religious motives can be relied on as an adequate control. They are not found to be such on the injustice and violence of individuals, and lose their efficacy in proportion to the number combined together, that is, in proportion as their efficacy becomes needful.

From this view of the subject it may be concluded that a pure democracy, by which I mean a society consisting of a small number of citizens, who assemble and administer the government in person, can admit of no cure for the mischiefs of faction. A common passion or interest will, in almost every case, be felt by a majority of the whole; a communication and concert result from the form of government itself; and there is nothing to check the inducements to sacrifice the weaker party or an obnoxious individual. Hence it is that such democracies have ever been spectacles of turbulence and contention; have ever been found incompatible with personal security or the rights of property; and have in general been as short in their lives as they have been violent in their deaths. Theoretic politicians, who have patronized this species of government, have erroneously supposed that by reducing mankind to a perfect equality in their political rights, they would, at the same time, be perfectly equalized and assimilated in their possessions, their opinions, and their passions.

A republic, by which I mean a government in which the scheme of representation takes place, opens a different prospect, and promises the cure for which we are seeking. Let us examine the points in which it varies from pure democracy, and we shall comprehend both the nature of the cure and the efficacy which it must derive from the Union.

The two great points of difference between a democracy and a republic are: first, the delegation of the government in the latter to a small number of citizens elected by the rest; secondly, the greater number of citizens and greater sphere of country over which the latter may be extended.

The effect of the first difference is, on the one hand, to refine and enlarge the public views, by passing them through the medium of a chosen body of citizens, whose wisdom may best discern the true interest of their country, and whose patriotism and love of justice will be least likely to sacrifice it to temporary or partial considerations. Under such a regulation, it may well happen that the public voice, pronounced by the representatives of the people, will be more consonant to the public good than if pronounced by the people themselves, convened for the purpose. On the other hand, the effect may be inverted. Men of factious tempers, of local prejudices, or of sinister designs, may by intrigue, by corruption, or by other means, first obtain the suffrages, and then betray the interests of the people. The question resulting is, whether small or extensive republics are more favorable to the election of proper guardians of the public weal; and it is clearly decided in favor of the latter by two obvious considerations.

In the first place, it is to be remarked that, however small the republic may be, the representatives must be raised to a certain number in order to guard against the cabals of a few; and that, however large it may be, they must be limited to a certain number in order to guard against the confusion of a multitude. Hence, the number of representatives in the two cases not being in proportion to that of the two constituents, and being proportionally greater in the small republic, it follows that, if the proportion of fit characters be not less in the large than in the small republic, the former will present a greater option and consequently a greater probability of a fit choice.

In the next place, as each representative will be chosen by a greater number of citizens in the large than in the small republic, it will be more difficult for unworthy candidates to practise with success the vicious arts by which elections are too often carried; and the suffrages of the people being more free, will be more likely to centre in men who possess the most attractive merit and the most diffusive and established characters.

It must be confessed that in this, as in most other cases, there is a mean, on both sides of which inconveniences will be found to lie. By enlarging too much the number of electors, you render the representative too little acquainted with all their local circumstances and lesser interest: as by reducing it too much, you render him unduly attached to these, and too little fit to comprehend and pursue great and national objects. The federal Constitution forms a happy combination in this respect; the great and aggregate interests being referred to the national, the local and particular to the State legislatures.

The other point of difference is, the greater number of citizens and extent of territory which may be brought within the compass of republican than of democratic government; and it is this circumstance principally which renders factious combinations less to be dreaded in the former than in the latter. The smaller the society, the fewer probably will be the distinct parties and interests composing it; the fewer the distinct parties and interests, the more frequently will a majority be found of the same party; and the smaller the number of individuals composing a majority, and the smaller the compass within which they are placed, the more easily will they concert and execute their plans of oppression. Extend the sphere, and you take in a greater variety of parties and interests; you make it less probable that a majority of the whole will have a common motive to invade the rights of other citizens; or if such a common motive exists, it will be more difficult for all who feel it to discover their own strength and to act in unison with each other. Besides other impediments, it may be remarked that, where there is a consciousness of unjust or dishonorable purposes, communication is always checked by distrust in proportion to the number whose concurrence is necessary.

Hence, it clearly appears that the same advantage which a republic has over a democracy in controlling the effects of faction is enjoyed by a large over a small republic, – is enjoyed by the Union over the States composing it. Does the advantage consist in the substitution of representatives whose enlightened views and virtuous sentiments render them superior to local prejudices and to schemes of injustice? It will not be denied that the representation of the Union will be most likely to possess these requisite endowments. Does it consist in the greater security afforded by a greater variety of parties, against the event of any one party being able to outnumber and oppress the rest? In an equal degree does the increased variety of parties comprised within the Union, increase this security. Does it, in fine, consist in the greater obstacles opposed to the concert and accomplishment of the secret wishes of an unjust and interested majority? Here, again, the extent of the Union gives it the most palpable advantage.

The influence of factious leaders may kindle a flame within their particular States, but will be unable to spread a general conflagration through the other States. A religious sect may degenerate into a political faction in a part of the Confederacy; but the variety of sects dispersed over the entire face of it must secure the national councils against any danger from that source. A rage for paper money, for an abolition of debts, for an equal division of property, or for any other improper or wicked project, will be less apt to pervade the whole body of the Union than a particular member of it; in the same proportion as such a malady is more likely to taint a particular county or district, than an entire State.

In the extent and proper structure of the Union, therefore, we behold a republican remedy for the diseases most incident to republican government. And according to the degree of pleasure and pride we feel in being republicans, ought to be our zeal in cherishing the spirit and supporting the character of Federalists.

PUBLIUS

THE FEDERALIST NO. 37

To the People of the State of New York:

In reviewing the defects of the existing Confederation, and showing that they cannot be supplied by a government of less energy than that before the public, several of the most important principles of the latter fell of course under consideration. [...]

Among the difficulties encountered by the convention a very important one must have lain in combining the requisite stability and energy in government with the inviolable attention due to liberty and to the republican form. Without substantially accomplishing this part of their undertaking, they would have very imperfectly fulfilled the object of their appointment or the expectation of the public; yet that it could not be easily accomplished will be denied by no one who is unwilling to betray his ignorance of the subject. Energy in government is essential to that security against external and internal danger, and to that prompt and salutary execution of the laws which enter into the very definition of good government. Stability in government is essential to national character and to the advantages annexed to it, as well as to that repose and confidence in the minds of the people, which are among the chief blessings of civil society. An irregular and mutable legislation is not more an evil in itself than it is odious to the people; and it may be pronounced with assurance that the people of this country, enlightened as they are with regard to the nature, and interested, as the great body of them are, in the effects of good government, will never be satisfied till some remedy be applied to the vicissitudes and uncertainties which characterize the State administrations. On comparing, however, these valuable ingredients with the vital principles of liberty, we must perceive at once the difficulty of mingling them together in their due proportions. The genius of republican liberty seems to demand on one side, not only that all power should be derived from the people, but that those intrusted with it should be kept in dependence on the people, by a short duration of their appointments; and that even during this short period the trust should be placed not in a few, but a number of hands. Stability, on the contrary, requires that the hands in which power is lodged should continue for a length of time the same. A frequent change of men will result from a frequent return of elections; and a frequent change of measures from a frequent change of men; whilst energy in government requires not only a certain duration of power, but the execution of it by a single hand. [...]

PUBLIUS

THE FEDERALIST NO. 38

To the People of the State of New York:

It is not a little remarkable that in every case reported by ancient history, in which government has been established with deliberation and consent, the task of framing it has not been committed to an assembly of men, but has been performed by some individual citizen of pre-eminent wisdom and approved integrity....

Whence could it have proceeded that a people, jealous as the Greeks were of their liberty, should so far abandon the rules of caution as to place their destiny in the hands of a single citizen? Whence could it have proceeded that the Athenians, a people who would not suffer an army to be commanded by fewer than ten generals and who required no other proof of danger to their liberties than the illustrious merit of a fellow-citizen, should consider one illustrious citizen as a more eligible depositary of the fortunes of themselves and their posterity than a select body of citizens from whose common deliberations more wisdom, as well as more safety, might have been expected? These questions cannot be fully answered, without supposing that the fears of discord and disunion among a number of counsellors exceeded the apprehension of treachery or incapacity in a single individual. History informs us, likewise, of the difficulties with which these celebrated reformers had to contend, as well as the expedients which they were obliged to employ in order to carry their reforms into effect. Solon, who seems to have indulged a more temporizing policy, confessed that he had not given to his countrymen the government best suited to their happiness, but most tolerable to their prejudices. And Lycurgus, more true to his object, was under the necessity of mixing a portion of violence with the authority of superstition, and of securing his final success by a voluntary renunciation, first of his country, and then of his life. If these lessons teach us, on one hand, to admire the improvement made by America on the ancient mode of preparing and establishing regular plans of government, they serve not less, on the other, to admonish us of the hazards and difficulties incident to such experiments, and of the great imprudence of unnecessarily multiplying them. [...]

A patient who finds his disorder daily growing worse, and that an efficacious remedy can no longer be delayed without extreme danger, after coolly revolving his situation, and the characters of different physicians, selects and calls in such of them as he judges most capable of administering relief, and best entitled to his confidence...

Such a patient and in such a situation is America at this moment. She has been sensible of her malady. She has obtained a regular and unanimous advice from men of her own deliberate choice. And she is warned by others against following this advice under pain of the most fatal consequences. Do the monitors deny the reality of her danger? No. Do they deny the necessity of some speedy and powerful remedy? No. Are they agreed, are any two of them agreed, in their objections to the remedy proposed, or in the proper one to be substituted? Let them speak for themselves. This one tells us that the proposed Constitution ought to be rejected, because it is not a confederation of the States, but a government over individuals. Another admits that it ought to be a government over individuals to a certain extent, but by no means to the extent proposed. A third does not object to the government over individuals, or to the extent proposed, but to the want of a bill of rights. A fourth concurs in the absolute necessity of a bill of rights, but contends that it ought to be declaratory, not of the personal rights of individuals, but of the rights reserved to the States in their political capacity. A fifth is of opinion that a bill of rights of any sort would be superfluous and misplaced, and that the plan would be unexceptionable but for the fatal power of regulating the times and places of election. An objector in a large State exclaims loudly against the unreasonable equality of representation in the Senate. An objector in a small State is equally loud against the dangerous inequality in the

House of Representatives. From this quarter, we are alarmed with the amazing expense, from the number of persons who are to administer the new government. From another quarter, and sometimes from the same quarter on another occasion, the cry is that the Congress will be but a shadow of a representation, and that the government would be far less objectionable if the number and the expense were doubled. A patriot in a State that does not import or export discerns insuperable objections against the power of direct taxation. The patriotic adversary in a State of great exports and imports is not less dissatisfied that the whole burden of taxes may be thrown on consumption. This politician discovers in the Constitution a direct and irresistible tendency to monarchy; that is equally sure it will end in aristocracy. Another is puzzled to say which of these shapes it will ultimately assume, but sees clearly it must be one or other of them; whilst a fourth is not wanting, who with no less confidence affirms that the Constitution is so far from having a bias towards either of these dangers, that the weight on that side will not be sufficient to keep it upright and firm against its opposite propensities. With another class of adversaries to the Constitution the language is that the legislative, executive, and judiciary departments are intermixed in such a manner as to contradict all the ideas of regular government and all the requisite precautions in favor of liberty. Whilst this objection circulates in vague and general expressions, there are but a few who lend their sanction to it. Let each one come forward with his particular explanation, and scarce any two are exactly agreed upon the subject. In the eyes of one the junction of the Senate with the President in the responsible function of appointing to offices, instead of vesting this executive power in the Executive alone, is the vicious part of the organization. To another, the exclusion of the House of Representatives, whose numbers alone could be a due security against corruption and partiality in the exercise of such a power, is equally obnoxious. With another, the admission of the President into any share of a power which must ever be a dangerous engine in the hands of the executive magistrate, is an unpardonable violation of the maxims of republican jealousy. No part of the arrangement, according to some, is more inadmissible than the trial of impeachments by the Senate, which is alternately a member both of the legislative and executive departments, when this power so evidently belonged to the judiciary department. "We concur fully," reply others, "in the objection to this part of the plan, but we can never agree that a reference of impeachments to the judiciary authority would be an amendment of the error. Our principal dislike to the organization arises from the extensive powers already lodged in that department." Even among the zealous patrons of a council of state the most irreconcilable variance is discovered concerning the mode in which it ought to be constituted. The demand of one gentleman is that the council should consist of a small number to be appointed by the most numerous branch of the legislature. Another would prefer a large number and considers it as a fundamental condition that the appointment should be made by the President himself.

As it can give no umbrage to the writers against the plan of the federal Constitution, let us suppose, that as they are the most zealous, so they are also the most sagacious of those who think the late convention were unequal to the task assigned them, and that a wiser and better plan might and ought to be substituted. Let us further suppose that their country should concur, both in this favorable opinion of their merits, and in their unfavorable opinion of the convention; and should accordingly proceed to form them into a second convention with full powers and for the express purpose of revising and remoulding the work of the first. Were the experiment to be seriously made, though it required some effort to view it seriously even in fiction, I leave it to be decided by the sample of opinions just exhibited, whether, with all their enmity to their predecessors, they would in any one point depart so widely from their example, as in the discord and ferment that would mark their own deliberations; and whether the Constitution now before the public would not stand as fair a chance for immortality, as Lycurgus gave to that of Sparta, by making its change to depend on his own return from exile and death, if it were to be immediately adopted, and were to continue in force, not until a BETTER, but until ANOTHER should be agreed upon by this new assembly of lawgivers.

It is a matter both of wonder and regret that those who raise so many objections against the new Constitution should never call to mind the defects of that which is to be exchanged for it. It is not necessary that the former should be perfect: it is sufficient that the latter is more imperfect. No man would refuse to give brass for silver or gold, because the latter had some alloy in it. No man would refuse to quit a shattered and tottering habitation for a firm and commodious building, because the latter had not a porch to it, or because some of the rooms might be a little larger or smaller, or the ceiling a little higher or lower than his fancy would have planned them. But waiving illustrations of this sort, is it not manifest that most of the capital objections urged against the new system lie with tenfold weight against the existing Confederation? Is an indefinite power to raise money dangerous in the hands of the federal government? The present Congress can make requisitions to any amount they please, and the States are constitutionally bound to furnish them; they can emit bills of credit as long as they will pay for the paper; they can borrow both abroad and at home as long as a shilling will be lent. Is an indefinite power to raise troops dangerous? The Confederation gives to Congress that power also; and they have already begun to make use of it. Is it improper and unsafe to intermix the different powers of government in the same body of men? Congress, a single body of men, are the sole depositary of all the federal powers. Is it particularly dangerous to give the keys of the treasury and the command of the army into the same hands? The Confederation places them both in the hands of Congress. Is a bill of rights essential to liberty? The Confederation has no bill of rights. Is it an objection against the new Constitution, that it empowers the Senate with the concurrence of the Executive to make treaties which are to be the laws of the land? The existing Congress without any such control can make treaties which they themselves have declared, and most of the States have recognized, to be the supreme law of the land. Is the importation of slaves permitted by the new Constitution for twenty years? By the old it is permitted forever.

I shall be told, that however dangerous this mixture of powers may be in theory, it is rendered harmless by the dependence of Congress on the States for the means of carrying them into practice; that however large the mass of powers may be, it is in fact a lifeless mass. Then, say I, in the first place, that the Confederation is chargeable with the still greater folly of declaring certain powers in the federal government to be absolutely necessary, and at the same time rendering them absolutely nugatory; and, in the next place, that if the Union is to continue and no better government be substituted, effective powers must either be granted to, or assumed by, the existing Congress; in either of which events, the contrast just stated will hold good. But this is not all. Out of this lifeless mass has already grown an excrescent power, which tends to realize all the dangers that can be apprehended from a defective construction of the supreme government of the Union. It is now no longer a point of speculation and hope that the western territory is a mine of vast wealth to the United States; and although it is not of such a nature as to extricate them from their present distresses, or for some time to come to yield any regular supplies for the public expenses; yet must it hereafter be able under proper management, both to effect a gradual discharge of the domestic debt, and to furnish, for a certain period, liberal tributes to the federal treasury. A very large proportion of this fund has been already surrendered by individual States; and it may with reason be expected that the remaining States will not persist in withholding similar proofs of their equity and generosity. We may calculate, therefore, that a rich and fertile country, of an area equal to the inhabited extent of the United States, will soon become a national stock. Congress have assumed the administration of this stock. They have begun to render it productive. Congress have undertaken to do more: they have proceeded to form new States, to erect temporary governments, to appoint officers for them, and to prescribe the conditions on which such States shall be admitted into the Confederacy. All this has been done; and done without the least color of constitutional authority. Yet no blame has been whispered; no alarm has been sounded. A GREAT and INDEPENDENT fund of revenue is passing into the hands of a SINGLE BODY of men, who can RAISE TROOPS to an INDEFINITE NUMBER, and appropriate money to their support for an INDEFINITE PERIOD OF TIME. And yet there are men who have not only been silent spectators of this prospect, but who are advocates for the system which exhibits it; and, at the same time, urge against the new system the objections which we have heard. Would they not act with more consistency, in urging the establishment of the latter as no less necessary to guard the Union against the future powers and resources of a body constructed like the existing Congress, than to save it from the dangers threatened by the present impotency of that Assembly?

I mean not... to throw censure on the measures which have been pursued by Congress. I am sensible they could not have done otherwise. The public interest, the necessity of the case, imposed upon them the task of overleaping their constitutional limits. But is not the fact an alarming proof of the danger resulting from a government which does not possess regular powers commensurate to its objects? A dissolution or usurpation is the dreadful dilemma to which it is continually exposed.

PUBLIUS

THE FEDERALIST NO. 39

To the People of the State of New York:

The last paper having concluded the observations which were meant to introduce a candid survey of the plan of government reported by the convention, we now proceed to the execution of that part of our undertaking.

The first question that offers itself is, whether the general form and aspect of the government be strictly republican. It is evident that no other form would be reconcilable with the genius of the people of America; with the fundamental principles of the Revolution; or with that honorable determination which animates every votary of freedom, to rest all our political experiments on the capacity of mankind for self-government. If the plan of the convention, therefore, be found to depart from the republican character, its advocates must abandon it as no longer defensible. [...]

The difference between a federal and national government, as it relates to the *operation of the government*, is supposed to consist in this, that in the former the powers operate on the political bodies composing the Confederacy in their political capacities; in the latter, on the individual citizens composing the nation in their individual capacities. On trying the Constitution by this criterion, it falls under the *national*, not the *federal* character; though perhaps not so completely as has been understood. In several cases, and particularly in the trial of controversies to which States may be parties, they must be viewed and proceeded against in their collective and political capacities only. So far the national countenance of the government on this side seems to be disfigured by a few federal features. But this blemish is perhaps unavoidable in any plan; and the operation of the government on the people, in their individual capacities, in its ordinary and most essential proceedings, may, on the whole designate it in this relation, a *national* government.

But if the government be national with regard to the *operation* of its powers, it changes its aspect again when we contemplate it in relation to the extent of its powers. The idea of a national government involves in it, not only an authority over the individual citizens, but an indefinite supremacy over all persons and things, so far as they are objects of lawful government. Among a people consolidated into one nation, this supremacy is completely vested in the national legislature. Among communities united for particular purposes, it is vested partly in the general and partly in the municipal legislatures. In the former case, all local authorities are subordinate to the supreme; and may be controlled, directed, or abolished by it at pleasure. In the latter, the local or municipal authorities form distinct and independent portions of the supremacy, no more subject within their respective spheres to the general authority, than the general authority is subject to them within its own sphere. In this relation, then, the proposed government cannot be deemed a *national* one; since its jurisdiction extends to certain enumerated objects only, and leaves to the several States a residuary and inviolable sovereignty over all other objects. It is true that in controversies relating to the boundary between the two jurisdictions, the tribunal which is ultimately to decide, is to be established under the general government. But this does not change the principle of the case. The decision is to be impartially made, according to the rules of the Constitution; and all the usual and most effectual precautions are taken to secure this impartiality. Some such tribunal is clearly essential to prevent an appeal to the sword and a dissolution of the compact; and that it ought to be established under the general rather than under the local governments, or, to speak more properly, that it could be safely established under the first alone, is a position not likely to be combated.

If we try the Constitution by its last relation to the authority by which amendments are to be made, we find it neither wholly *national* nor wholly *federal*. Were it wholly national, the supreme and ultimate authority would reside in the *majority* of the people of the Union; and this authority would be competent at all times, like that of a majority of every national society, to alter or abolish its established government. Were it wholly federal, on the other hand, the concurrence of each State in the Union would be essential to every alteration that would be binding on all. The mode provided by the plan of the convention is not founded on either of these principles. In requiring more than a majority, and particularly in computing the proportion by *States*, not by *citizens*, it departs from the *national* and advances towards the *federal* character; in rendering the concurrence of less than the whole number of States sufficient, it loses again the *federal* and partakes of the *national* character.

The proposed Constitution, therefore, is, in strictness, neither a national nor a federal Constitution, but a composition of both. In its foundation it is federal, not national; in the sources from which the ordinary powers of the government are drawn, it is partly federal and partly national; in the operation of these powers, it is national, not federal; in the extent of them, again, it is federal, not national; and, finally, in the authoritative mode of introducing amendments, it is neither wholly federal nor wholly national.

PUBLIUS

THE FEDERALIST No. 44

To the People of the State of New York:

A *fifth* class of provisions in favor of the federal authority consists of the following restrictions on the authority of the several States.

1. "No State shall enter into any treaty, alliance, or confederation; grant letters of marque and reprisal; coin money; emit bills of credit; make anything but gold and silver a legal tender in payment of debts; pass any bill of attainder, *ex-post-facto* law, or law impairing the obligation of contracts; or grant any title of nobility."

The prohibition against treaties, alliances, and confederations makes a part of the existing articles of Union; and for reasons which need no explanation, is copied into the new Constitution. The prohibition of letters of marque is another part of the old system, but is somewhat extended in the new. According to the former, letters of marque could be granted by the States after a declaration of war; according to the latter, these licenses must be obtained, as well during war as previous to its declaration, from the government of the United States. This alteration is fully justified by the advantage of uniformity in all points which relate to foreign powers; and of immediate responsibility to the nation in all those for whose conduct the nation itself is to be responsible. [...]

The *sixth* and last class consists of the several powers and provisions by which efficacy is given to all the rest.

1. Of these the first is, the . . . power "To make all laws which shall be necessary and proper for carrying into execution the foregoing powers, and all other powers vested by this Constitution in the Government of the United States, or in any department or office thereof."

Few parts of the Constitution have been assailed with more intemperance than this; yet on a fair investigation of it, no part can appear more completely invulnerable. Without the *substance* of this power the whole Constitution would be a dead letter. Those who object to the article . . . can only mean that the *form* of the provision is improper. But have they considered whether a better form could have been substituted?

There are four other possible methods which the Constitution might have taken on this subject. They might have copied the second article of the existing Confederation, which would have prohibited the exercise of any power not *expressly* delegated; they might have attempted a positive enumeration of the powers comprehended under the general terms "necessary and proper"; they might have attempted a negative enumeration of them by specifying the powers excepted from the general definition; they might have been altogether silent on the subject, leaving these necessary and proper powers to construction and inference.

Had the convention taken the first method of adopting the second article of Confederation, it is evident that the new Congress would be continually exposed, as their predecessors have been, to the alternative of construing the term *"expressly"* with so much rigor as to disarm the government of all real authority whatever, or with so much latitude as to destroy altogether the force of the restriction. It would be easy to show... that no important power delegated by the articles of Confederation has been or can be executed by Congress without recurring more or less to the doctrine of *construction* or *implication*. As the powers delegated under the new system are more extensive, the government which is to administer it would find itself still more distressed with the alternative of betraying the public interests by doing nothing, or of violating the Constitution by exercising powers indispensably necessary and proper, but, at the same time, not *expressly* granted.

Had the convention attempted a positive enumeration of the powers necessary and proper for carrying their other powers into effect, the attempt would have involved a complete digest of laws on every subject to which the Constitution relates; accommodated too, not only to the existing state of things, but to all the possible changes which futurity may produce; for in every new application of a general power, the *particular powers*, which are the means of attaining the *object* of the general power, must always necessarily vary with that object and be often properly varied whilst the object remains the same.

Had they attempted to enumerate the particular powers or means not necessary or proper for carrying the general powers into execution, the task would have been no less chimerical; and would have been liable to this further objection, that every defect in the enumeration would have been equivalent to a positive grant of authority. If, to avoid this consequence, they had attempted a partial enumeration of the exceptions and described the residue by the general terms, *not necessary or proper*, it must have happened that the enumeration would comprehend a few of the excepted powers only; that these would be such as would be least likely to be assumed or tolerated, because the enumeration would of course select such as would be least necessary or proper; and that the unnecessary and improper powers included in the residuum, would be less forcibly excepted, than if no partial enumeration had been made.

Had the Constitution been silent on this head, there can be no doubt that all the particular powers requisite as means of executing the general powers would have resulted to the government by unavoidable implication. No axiom is more clearly established in law or in reason, than that wherever the end is required, the means are authorized; wherever a general power to do a thing is given, every particular power necessary for doing it is included. Had this last method, therefore, been pursued by the convention, every objection now urged against their plan would remain in all its plausibility; and the real inconveniency would be incurred of not removing a pretext which may be seized on critical occasions for drawing into question the essential powers of the Union.

If it be asked what is to be the consequence, in case the Congress shall misconstrue this part of the Constitution and exercise powers not warranted by its true meaning, I answer, the same as if they should misconstrue or enlarge any other power vested in them; as if the general power had been reduced to particulars, and any one of these were to be violated; the same, in short, as if the State legislatures should violate their respective constitutional authorities. In the first instance, the success of the usurpation will depend on the executive and judiciary departments, which are to expound and give effect to the legislative acts; and in the last resort a remedy must be obtained from the people, who can, by the election of more faithful representatives, annul the acts of the usurpers. The truth is that this ultimate redress may be more confided in against unconstitutional acts of the federal than of the State legislatures for this plain reason, that as every such act of the former will be an invasion of the rights of the latter, these will be ever ready to mark the innovation, to sound the alarm to the people, and to exert their local influence in effecting a change of federal represent-atives. There being no such intermediate body between the State legislatures and the people interested in watching the conduct of the former, violations of the State constitutions are more likely to remain unnoticed and unredressed.

2.   "This Constitution and the laws of the United States which shall be made in pursuance thereof, and all treaties made, or which shall be made, under the authority of the United States, shall be the supreme law of the land, and the Judges in every State shall be bound thereby, anything in the Constitution or laws of any State to the contrary notwithstanding."

The indiscreet zeal of the adversaries to the Constitution has betrayed them into an attack on this part of it also, without which it would have been evidently and radically defective. To be fully sensible of this, we need only suppose for a moment that the supremacy of the State constitutions had been left complete by a saving clause in their favor.

In the first place, as these constitutions invest the State legislatures with absolute sovereignty in all cases not excepted by the existing articles of Confederation, all the authorities contained in the proposed Constitution, so far as they exceed those enumerated in the Confederation, would have been annulled, and the new Congress would have been reduced to the same impotent condition with their predecessors. [...]

Several reasons might be assigned for the distinction. I content myself with one, which is obvious and conclusive. The members of the federal government will have no agency in carrying the State constitutions into effect. The members and officers of the State governments, on the contrary, will have an essential agency in giving effect to the federal Constitution. The election of the President and Senate will depend in all cases on the legislatures of the several States. And the election of the House of Representatives will equally depend on the same authority in the first instance; and will probably forever be conducted by the officers and according to the laws of the States.

4.   Among the provisions for giving efficacy to the federal powers might be added those which belong to the executive and judiciary departments; but as these are reserved for particular examination in another place, pass them over in this.

We have now reviewed in detail all the articles composing the sum or quantity of power delegated by the proposed Constitution to the federal government, and are brought to this undeniable conclusion, that no part of the power is unnecessary or improper for accomplishing the necessary objects of the Union. The question, there-fore, whether this amount of power shall be granted or not resolves itself into another question, whether or not a government commensurate to the exigencies of the Union shall be established; or, in other words, whether the Union itself shall be preserved.

PUBLIUS

CHAPTER 8

Observations on the New Constitution, and on the Federal and State Conventions. By a Columbian Patriot

MERCY OTIS WARREN

Sic transit gloria Americana.

Mankind may amuse themselves with theoretick systems of liberty, and trace its social and moral effects on sciences, virtue, industry, and every improvement of which the human mind is capable; but we can only discern its true value by the practical and wretched effects of slavery; and thus dreadfully will they be realized, when the inhabitants of the Eastern States are dragging out a miserable existence, *only* on the gleanings of their fields; and the Southern, blessed with a softer and more fertile climate, are languishing in hopeless poverty; and when asked, what is become of the flower of their crop, and the rich produce of their farms – they may answer in the hapless stile of the Man of *La Mancha*, – "The steward of my Lord has seized and sent it to *Madrid*." – Or, in the more literal language of truth, The *exigencies* of government require that the collectors of the revenue should transmit it to the *Federal City*.

Animated with the firmest zeal for the interest of this country, the peace and union of the American States, and the freedom and happiness of a people who have made the most costly sacrifices in the cause of liberty, – who have braved the power of Britain, weathered the convulsions of war, and waded thro' the blood of friends and foes to establish their independence and to support the freedom of the human mind; I cannot silently witness this degradation without calling on them, before they are compelled to blush at their own servitude, and to turn back their languid eyes on their lost liberties – to consider, that the character of nations generally changes at the moment of revolution. – And when patriotism is discountenanced and publick virtue becomes the ridicule of the sycophant – when every man of liberality, firmness, and

Mercy Otis Warren. *Observations on the New Constitution, and on the Federal and State Conventions, By a Columbian Patriot*. Originally published in 1788.

penetration, who cannot lick the hand stretched out to oppress, is deemed an enemy to the State – then is the gulph of despotism set open, and the grades to slavery, though rapid, are scarce perceptible – then genius drags heavily its iron chain – science is neglected, and real merit flies to the shades for security from reproach – the mind becomes enervated, and the national character sinks to a kind of apathy with only energy sufficient to curse the breast that gave it milk, and as an elegant writer observes, "To bewail every new birth as an encrease of misery, under a government where the mind is necessarily debased, and talents are seduced to become the panegyrists of usurpation and tyranny." He adds, "that even sedition is not the most indubitable enemy to the publick welfare; but that its most dreadful foe is despotism, which always changes the character of nations for the worse, and is productive of nothing but vice, that the tyrant no longer excites to the pursuits of glory or virtue; it is not talents, it is baseness and servility that he cherishes, and the weight of arbitrary power destroys the spring of emulation." If such is the influence of government on the character and manners, and undoubtedly the observation is just, must we not subscribe to the opinion of the celebrated *Abbé Mablé?* "That there are disagreeable seasons in the unhappy situation of human affairs, when policy requires both the intention and the power of doing mischief to be punished; and that when the senate proscribed the memory of *Caesar* they ought to have put *Anthony* to death, and extinguished the hopes of *Octavius.*" Self defence is a primary law of nature, which no subsequent law of society can abolish; this primæval principle, the immediate gift of the Creator, obliges every one to remonstrate against the strides of ambition, and a wanton lust of domination, and to resist the first approaches of tyranny, which at this day threaten to sweep away the rights for which the brave sons of America have fought with an heroism scarcely paralleled even in ancient republicks. It may be repeated, they have purchased it with their blood, and have gloried in their independence with a dignity of spirit, which has made them the admiration of philosophy, the pride of America, and the wonder of Europe. It has been observed, with great propriety, that "the virtues and vices of a people when a revolution happens in their government, are the measure of the liberty or slavery they ought to expect – An heroic love for the publick good, a profound reverence for the laws, a contempt of riches, and a noble haughtiness of soul, are the only foundations of a free government." Do not their dignified principles still exist among us? Or are they extinguished in the breasts of Americans, whose fields have been so recently crimsoned to repel the potent arm of a foreign Monarch, who had planted his engines of slavery in every city, with design to erase the vestiges of freedom in this his last asylum. It is yet to be hoped, for the honour of human nature, that no combinations either foreign or domestick have thus darkened this western hemisphere. – On these shores freedom has planted her standard, [dyed] in the purple tide that flowed from the veins of her martyred heroes; and here every uncorrupted American yet hopes to see it supported by the vigour, the justice, the wisdom and unanimity of the people, in spite of the deep-laid plots, the secret intrigues, or the bold effrontery of those interested and avaricious adventurers for place, who intoxicated with the ideas of distinction and preferment, have prostrated every worthy principle beneath the shrine of ambition. Yet these are the men who tell us republicanism is dwindled into theory – that we are incapable of enjoying our liberties – and that we must have a master. – Let us retrospect the days of our adversity, and recollect who were then our friends; do we find them among the sticklers for aristocratick authority? No, they were generally the same men who now wish to save us from the distractions of anarchy on the one hand, and the jaws of tyranny on the other; where then were the class who now come forth importunately urging that our political salvation depends on the adoption of a system at which freedom spurns? – Were not some of them hidden in the corners of obscurity, and others wrapping themselves in the bosom of our enemies for safety? Some of them were in the arms of infancy; and others speculating for fortune, by sporting with public money; while a few, a very few of them were magnanimously defending their country, and raising a character, which I pray heaven may never be sullied by aiding measures derogatory to their former exertions. But the revolutions in principle which time produces among mankind, frequently exhibits the most mortifying instances of human weakness; and this alone can account for the extraordinary appearance of a few names, once distinguished in the honourable walks of patriotism, but now found on the list of the Massachusetts assent to the ratification of a Constitution, which, by the undefined meaning of some parts, and the ambiguities of expression in others, is dangerously adapted to the purposes of an immediate *aristocratic tyranny*; that from the difficulty, if not impracticability of its operation, must soon terminate in the most *uncontrouled despotism*.

All writers on government agree, and the feelings of the human mind witness the truth of these political axioms, that man is born free and possessed of certain unalienable rights – that government is instituted for the protection, safety, and happiness of the people, and not for the profit, honour, or private interest of any man, family, or class of men – That the origin of all power is in the people, and that they have an incontestible right to check the creatures of their own creation, vested with certain powers to guard the life, liberty and property of the community: And if certain selected bodies of men, deputed on these principles, determine contrary to the wishes and expectations of their constituents, the people have an undoubted right to reject their decisions, to call for a revision of their conduct, to depute others in their room, or if they think proper, to demand further time for deliberation on matters of the greatest moment: it therefore is an unwarrantable stretch of authority or influence, if any methods are taken to preclude this reasonable, and peaceful mode of enquiry and decision. And it is with inexpressible anxiety, that many of the best friends to the Union of the States – to the peaceable and equal participation of the rights of nature, and to the glory and dignity of this country, behold the insidious arts, and the strenuous efforts of the partisans of arbitrary power, by their vague definitions of the best established truths, endeavoring to envelope the mind in darkness the concomitant of slavery, and to lock the strong chains of domestic despotism on a country, which by the most glorious and successful struggles is but newly emancipated from the sceptre of foreign dominion. – But there are certain seasons in the course of human affairs, when Genius, Virtue, and Patriotism, seems to nod over the vices of the times, and perhaps never more remarkably, than at the present period; or we should not see such a passive disposition prevail in some, who we must candidly suppose, have liberal and enlarged sentiments; while a supple multitude are paying a blind and idolatrous homage to the opinions of those who by the most precipitate steps are treading down their dear bought privileges; and who are endeavouring by all the arts of insinuation, and influence, to betray the people of the United States, into an acceptance of a most complicated system of government; marked on the one side with the *dark, secret* and *profound intrigues*, of the statesman, long practiced in the purlieus of despotism; and on the other, with the ideal projects of *young ambition*, with its wings just expanded to soar to a summit, which imagination has painted in such gawdy colours as to intoxicate the *inexperienced votary*, and send *him* rambling from State to State, to collect materials to construct the ladder of preferment.

But as a variety of objections to the *heterogeneous phantom*, have been repeatedly laid before the public, by men of the best abilities and intentions; I will not expatiate long on a Republican *form* of government, founded on the principles of monarchy – a democratick branch with the *features* of aristocracy – and the extravagance of nobility pervading the minds of many of the candidates for office, with the poverty of peasantry hanging heavily on them, and insurmountable, from their taste for expence, unless a generous provision should be made in the arrangement of the civil list, which may enable them with the champions of their cause to "*sail down the new pactolean channel.*" Some gentlemen with laboured zeal, have spent much time in urging the necessity of government, from the embarrassments of trade – the want of respectability abroad and confidence in the public engagements at home: – These are obvious truths which no one denies; and there are few who do not unite in the general wish for the restoration of public faith, the revival of commerce, arts, agriculture, and industry, under a lenient, peaceable and energetick government: But the most sagacious advocates for the party have not by fair discussion, and rational argumentation, evinced the necessity of adopting this many-headed monster; of such motley mixture, that its enemies cannot trace a feature of Democratick or Republican extract; nor have its friends the courage to denominate it a Monarchy, an Aristocracy, or an Oligarchy, and the favoured bantling must have passed through the short period of its existence without a name, had not Mr. *Wilson*, in the fertility of his genius, suggested the happy epithet of a *Federal Republic*. – But I leave the field of general censure on the secrecy of its birth, the rapidity of its growth, and the fatal consequences of suffering it to live to the age of maturity, and will particularize some of the most weighty objections to its passing through this continent in a gigantic size. – It will be allowed by every one that the fundamental principle of a free government, is the equal representation of a free people – And I will *first* observe with a justly celebrated writer, "That the principal aim of society is to protect individuals in the absolute rights which were vested in them by the immediate laws of nature, but which could not be preserved in peace, without the mutual intercourse which is gained by the institution of friendly and social communities." And when society has thus deputed a certain number of their equals to take care of their personal rights, and the interest of the whole community, it must be considered that responsibility is the great security of integrity and honour; and that annual election is the basis of responsibility. – Man is not immediately corrupted, but power without limitation, or amenability, may endanger the brightest virtue – whereas a frequent return to the bar of their Constituents is the strongest check against the corruptions to which men are liable, either from the intrigues of others of more subtle genius, or the propensities of their own hearts, – and the gentlemen who have so warmly advocated in the late Convention of the Massachusetts, the change from annual to biennial elections; may have been in the same predicament, and perhaps with the same views that Mr. *Hutchinson* once acknowledged himself, when in a letter to *Lord Hillsborough*, he observed, "that the grand difficulty of making a change in government against the general bent of the people had caused him to turn his thoughts to a variety of plans, in order to find one that might be executed in spite of opposition," and the first he proposed was that, "instead of annual, the elections should be only once in three years:" but the Minister had not the hardiness to attempt such an innovation, even in the revision of colonial charters: nor has any one ever defended Biennial, Triennial, or Septennial, Elections, either in the British House of Commons, or in the debates of Provincial assemblies, on general and free principles: but it is unnecessary to dwell long on this article, as the best political writers have supported the principles of annual elections with a precision, that cannot be confuted, though they may be darkened, by the sophistical arguments that have been thrown out with design, to undermine all the barriers of freedom.

2. There is no security in the profered system, either for the rights of conscience, or the liberty of the Press: Despotism usually while it is gaining ground, will suffer men to think, say, or write what they please; but when once established, if it is thought necessary to subserve the purposes of arbitrary power, the most unjust restrictions may take place in the first instance, and an *imprimator* on the Press in the next, may silence the complaints, and forbid the most decent remonstrances of an injured and oppressed people.

3. There are no well defined limits of the Judiciary Powers, they seem to be left as a boundless ocean, that has broken over the chart of the Supreme Lawgiver "*thus far shalt thou go and no further,*" and as they cannot be comprehended by the clearest capacity, or the most sagacious mind, it would be an Herculean labour to attempt to describe the dangers with which they are replete.

4. The Executive and the Legislative are so dangerously blended as to give just cause of alarm, and every thing relative thereto, is couched in such ambiguous terms – in such vague and indefinite expression, as is a sufficient ground without any other objection, for the reprobation of a system, that the authors dare not hazard to a clear investigation.

5. The abolition of trial by jury in civil causes. – This mode of trial the learned Judge Blackstone observes, "has been coeval with the first rudiments of civil government, that property, liberty and life, depend on maintaining in its legal force the constitutional trial by jury." He bids his readers pauze, and with Sir Matthew Hale observes, how admirably this mode is adapted to the investigation of truth beyond any other the world can produce. Even the party who have been disposed to swallow, without examination, the proposals of the *secret conclave*, have started on a discovery that this essential right was curtailed; and shall a privilege, the origin of which may be traced to our Saxon ancestors – that has been a part of the law of nations, even in the fewdatory systems of France, Germany and Italy – and from the earliest records has been held so sacred, both in ancient and modern Britain, that it could never be shaken by the introduction of Norman customs, or any other conquests or change of government – shall this inestimable privilege be relinquished in America – either thro' the fear of inquistion for unaccounted thousands of public monies in the hands of some who have been officious in the fabrication of the *consolidated system*, or from the apprehension that some future delinquent possessed of more power than integrity, may be called to a trial by his peers in the hour of investigation?

6. Though it has been said by Mr. *Wilson* and many others, that a Standing-Army is necessary for the dignity and safety of America, yet freedom revolts at the idea, when the Divan, or the Despot, may draw out his dragoons to suppress the murmurs of a few, who may yet cherish those sublime principles which call forth the exertions, and lead to the best improvement of the human mind. It is hoped this country may yet be governed by milder methods than are usually displayed beneath the bannerets of military law. – Standing armies have been the nursery of vice and the bane of liberty from the Roman legions, to the establishment of the artful Ximenes, and from

the ruin of the Cortes of Spain, to the planting the British cohorts in the capitals of America: – By the edicts of authority vested in the sovereign power by the proposed constitution, the militia of the country, the bulwark of defence, and the security of national liberty is no longer under the controul of civil authority; but at the rescript of the Monarch, or the aristocracy, they may either be employed to extort the enormous sums that will be necessary to support the civil list – to maintain the regalia of power – and the splendour of the most useless part of the community, or they may be sent into foreign countries for the fulfilment of treaties, stipulated by the President and two thirds of the Senate.

7. Notwithstanding the delusory promise to guarantee a Republican form of government to every State in the Union – If the most discerning eye could discover any meaning at all in the engagement, there are no resources left for the support of internal government, or the liquidation of the debts of the State. Every source of revenue is in the monopoly of Congress, and if the several legislatures in their enfeebled state, should against their own feelings be necessitated to attempt a dry tax for the payment of their debts, and the support of internal police, even this may be required for the purposes of the general government.

8. As the new Congress are empowered to determine their own salaries, the requisitions for this purpose may not be very moderate, and the drain for public moneys will probably rise past all calculation: and it is to be feared when America has consolidated its despotism, the world will witness the truth of the assertion – "that the pomp of an eastern monarch may impose on the vulgar who may estimate the force of a nation by the magnificence of its palaces; but the wise man, judges differently, it is by that very magnificence he estimates its weakness. He sees nothing more in the midst of this imposing pomp, where the tyrant sets enthroned, than a sumptuous and mournful decoration of the dead; the apparatus of a fastuous funeral, in the centre of which is a cold and lifeless lump of unanimated earth, a phantom of power ready to disappear before the enemy, by whom it is despised!"

9. There is no provision for a rotation, nor any thing to prevent the perpetuity of office in the same hands for life; which by a little well timed bribery, will probably be done, to the exclusion of men of the best abilities from their share in the offices of government. – By this neglect we lose the advantages of that check to the overbearing insolence of office, which by rendering him ineligible at certain periods, keeps the mind of man in equilibrio, and teaches him the feelings of the governed, and better qualifies him to govern in his turn.

10. The inhabitants of the United States, are liable to be dragged from the vicinity of their own county, or state, to answer to the litigious or unjust suit of an adversary, on the most distant borders of the Continent; in short the appelate jurisdiction of the Supreme Federal Court, includes an unwarrantable stretch of power over the liberty, life, and property of the subject, through the wide Continent of America.

11. One Representative to thirty thousand inhabitants is a very inadequate representation; and every man who is not lost to all sense of freedom to his country, must reprobate the idea of Congress altering by law, or on any pretence whatever, interfering with any regulations for the time, places, and manner of choosing our own Representatives.

12. If the sovereignty of America is designed to be elective, the circumscribing the votes to only ten electors in this State, and the same proportion in all the others, is nearly tantamount to the exclusion of the voice of the people in the choice of their first magistrate. It is vesting the choice solely in an aristocratic junto, who may easily

combine in each State to place at the head of the Union the most convenient instrument for despotic sway.

13. A Senate chosen for six years will, in most instances, be an appointment for life, as the influence of such a body over the minds of the people will be coequal to the extensive powers with which they are vested, and they will not only forget, but be forgotten by their constituents – a branch of the Supreme Legislature thus set beyond all responsibility is totally repugnant to every principle of a free government.

14. There is no provision by a bill of rights to guard against the dangerous encroachments of power in too many instances to be named: but I cannot pass over in silence the insecurity in which we are left with regard to warrants unsupported by evidence – the daring experiment of granting *writs of assistance* in a former arbitrary administration is not yet forgotten in the Massachusetts; nor can we be so ungrateful to the memory of the patriots who counteracted their operation, as so soon after their manly exertions to save us from such a detestable instrument of arbitrary power, to subject ourselves to the insolence of any petty revenue officer to enter our houses, search, insult, and seize at pleasure. We are told by a gentleman of too much virtue and real probity to suspect he has a design to deceive – "that the whole constitution is a declaration of rights" – but mankind must think for themselves, and to many very judicious and discerning characters, the whole constitution with very few exceptions appears to perversion of the rights of particular states, and of private citizens. – But the gentleman goes on to tell us, "that the primary object is the general government, and that the rights of individuals are only incidentally mentioned, and that there was a clear impropriety in being very particular about them." But, asking pardon for dissenting from such respectable authority, who has been led into several mistakes, more from his predilection in favour of certain modes of government, than from a want of understanding or veracity. The rights of individuals ought to be the primary object of all government, and cannot be too securely guarded by the most explicit declarations in their favor. This has been the opinion of the Hampdens, the Pyms, and many other illustrious names, that have stood forth in defence of English liberties; and even the Italian master in politicks, the subtle and renowned Machiavel acknowledges, that no republic ever yet stood on a stable foundation without satisfying the common people.

15. The difficulty, if not impracticability, of exercising the equal and equitable powers of government by a single legislature over an extent of territory that reaches from the Mississippi to the western lakes, and from them to the Atlantic ocean, is an insuperable objection to the adoption of the new system. – Mr. *Hutchinson*, the great champion for arbitrary power, in the multitude of his machinations to subvert the liberties of this country, was obliged to acknowledge in one of his letters, that, from the extent of country from north to south, the scheme of one government was impracticable. But if the authors of the present visionary project, can by the arts of deception, precipitation and address, obtain a majority of suffrages in the conventions of the states to try the hazardous experiment, they may then make the same inglorious boast with this insidious politician, who may perhaps be their model, that "the union of the colonies was pretty well broken, and that he hoped never to see it renewed."

16. It is an indisputed fact, that not one legislature in the United States had the most distant idea when they first appointed members for a convention, entirely commercial, or when they afterwards authorised them to consider on some amendments of the Federal union, that they would without any warrant from their

constituents, presume on so bold and daring a stride, as ultimately to destroy the state governments, and offer a *consolidated system*, irreversible but on conditions that the smallest degree of penetration must discover to be impracticable.

17. The first appearance of the article which declares the ratification of nine states sufficient for the establishment of the new system, wears the face of dissention, is a subversion of the union of the Confederated States, and tends to the introduction of anarchy and civil convulsions, and may be a means of involving the whole country in blood.

18. The mode in which this constitution is recommended to the people to judge without either the advice of Congress, or the legislatures of the several states, is very reprehensible – it is an attempt to force it upon them before it could be thoroughly understood, and may leave us in that situation, that in the first moments of slavery the minds of the people agitated by the remembrance of their lost liberties, will be like the sea in a tempest, that sweeps down every mound of security.

But it is needless to enumerate other instances, in which the proposed constitution appears contradictory to the first principles which ought to govern mankind; and it is equally so to enquire into the motives that induced to so bold a step as the annihilation of the independence and sovereignty of the thirteen distinct states. – They are but too obvious through the whole progress of the business, from the first shutting up the doors of the federal convention and resolving that no member should correspond with gentlemen in the different states on the subject under discussion; till the trivial proposition of *recommending* a few amendments was artfully ushered into the convention of the Massachusetts. The questions that were then before that honorable assembly were profound and important, they were of such magnitude and extent, that the consequences may run parallel with the existence of the country; and to see them waved and hastily terminated by a measure too absurd to require a serious refutation, raises the honest indignation of every true lover of his country. Nor are they less grieved that the ill policy and arbitrary disposition of some of the sons of America has thus precipitated to the contemplation and discussion of questions that no one could rationally suppose would have been agitated among us, till time had blotted out the principles on which the late revolution was grounded; or till the last traits of the many political tracts, which defended the separation from Britain, and the rights of men were consigned to everlasting oblivion. After the severe conflicts this country has suffered, it is presumed that they are disposed to make every reasonable sacrifice before the altar of peace. – But when we contemplate the nature of men and consider them originally on an equal footing, subject to the same feelings, stimulated by the same passions, and recollecting the struggles they have recently made, for the security of their civil rights; it cannot be expected that the inhabitants of the Massachusetts, can be easily lulled into a fatal security, by the declamatory effusions of gentlemen, who, contrary to the experience of all ages would persuade them there is no danger to be apprehended, from vesting discretionary powers in the hands of man, which he may, or may not abuse. The very suggestion, that we ought to trust to the precarious hope of amendments and redress, after we have voluntarily fixed the shackles on our own necks should have awakened to a double degree of caution. – This people have not forgotten the artful insinuations of a former Governor, when pleading the unlimited authority of parliament before the legislature of the Massachusetts; nor that his arguments were very similar to some lately urged by gentlemen who boast of opposing his measures, *"with halters about their necks."*

We were then told by him, in all the soft language of insinuation, that no form of government of human construction can be perfect – that we had nothing to fear – that we had no reason to complain – that we had only to acquiesce in their illegal claims, and to submit to the requisitions of parliament, and doubtless the lenient hand of government would redress all grievances, and remove the oppressions of the people: – Yet we soon saw armies of mercenaries encamped on our plains – our commerce ruined – our harbours blockaded – and our cities burnt. It may be replied, that this was in consequence of an obstinate defence of our privileges; this may be true; and when the "*ultima ratio*" is called to aid, the weakest must fall. But let the best informed historian produce an instance when bodies of men were intrusted with power, and the proper checks relinquished, if they were ever found destitute of ingenuity sufficient to furnish pretences to abuse it. And the people at large are already sensible, that the liberties which America has claimed, which reason has justified, and which have been so gloriously defended by the sword of the brave; are not about to fall before the tyranny of foreign conquest: it is native usurpation that is shaking the foundations of peace, and spreading the sable curtain of despotism over the United States. The banners of freedom were erected in the wilds of America by our ancestors, while the wolf prowled for his prey on the one hand, and more savage man on the other; they have been since rescued from the invading hand of foreign power, by the valor and blood of their posterity; and there was reason to hope they would continue for ages to illumine a quarter of the globe, by nature kindly separated from the proud monarchies of Europe, and the infernal darkness of Asiatic slavery. – And it is to be feared we shall soon see this country rushing into the extremes of confusion and violence, in consequence of the proceedings of a set of gentlemen, who disregarding the purposes of their appointment, have assumed powers unauthorised by any commission, have unnecessarily rejected the confederation of the United States, and annihilated the sovereignty and independence of the individual governments. – The causes which have inspired a few men assembled for very different purposes with such a degree of temerity as to break with a single stroke the union of America, and disseminate the seeds of discord through the land may be easily investigated, when we survey the partizans of monarchy in the state conventions, urging the adoption of a mode of government that militates with the former professions and exertions of this country, and with all ideas of republicanism, and the equal rights of men.

Passion, prejudice, and error, are characteristics of human nature; and as it cannot be accounted for on any principles of philosophy, religion, or good policy; to these shades in the human character must be attributed the mad zeal of some, to precipitate to a blind adoption of the measures of the late federal convention, without giving opportunity for better information to those who are misled by influence or ignorance into erroneous opinions. – Literary talents may be prostituted, and the powers of genius debased to subserve the purposes of ambition, or avarice; but the feelings of the heart will dictate the language of truth, and the simplicity of her accents will proclaim the infamy of those, who betray the rights of the people, under the specious, and popular pretence of *justice, consolidation*, and *dignity*.

It is presumed the great body of the people unite in sentiment with the writer of these observations, who most devoutly prays that public credit may rear her declining head, and remunerative justice pervade the land; nor is there a doubt if a free government is continued, that time and industry will enable both the public and private debtor to liquidate their arrearages in the most equitable manner. They wish to see the Confederated States bound together by the most indissoluble union, but without renouncing their separate sovereignties and independence, and becoming tributaries to a consolidated fabrick of aristocratick tyranny. – They wish to see government established, and peaceably holding the reins with honour, energy, and dignity; but they wish for no *federal city* whose *"cloud cap't towers"* may screen the state culprit from the hand of justice; while its exclusive jurisdiction may protect the riot of armies encamped within its limits. – They deprecate discord and civil convulsions, but they are not yet generally prepared with the ungrateful Israelites to ask a King, nor are their spirits sufficiently broken to yield the best of their olive grounds to his servants, and to see their sons appointed to run before his chariots – It has been observed by a zealous advocate for the new system, that most governments are the result of fraud or violence, and this with design to recommend its acceptance – but has not almost every step towards its fabrication been fraudulent in the extreme? Did not the prohibition strictly enjoined by the general Convention, that no member should make any communication to his Constituents, or to gentlemen of consideration and abilities in the other States, bear evident marks of fraudulent designs? – This circumstance is regretted in strong terms by Mr. Martin, a member from Maryland, who acknowledges "He had no idea that all the wisdom, integrity, and virtue of the States was contained in that Convention, and that he wished to have corresponded with gentlemen of eminent political characters abroad, and to give their sentiments due weight" – he adds, "so extremely solicitous were they, that their proceedings should not transpire, that the members were prohibited from taking copies of their resolutions, or extracts from the Journals, without express permission, by vote." – And the hurry with which it has been urged to the acceptance of the people, without giving time, by adjournments, for better information, and more unanimity has a deceptive appearance; and if finally driven to resistance, as the only alternative between that and servitude, till in the confusion of discord, the reins should be seized by the violence of some enterprizing genius, that may sweep down the last barrier of liberty, it must be added to the score of criminality with which the fraudulent usurpation at Philadelphia, may be chargeable. – Heaven avert such a tremendous scene! and let us still hope a more happy termination of the present ferment: – may the people be calm, and wait a legal redress; may the mad transport of some of our infatuated capitals subside; and every influential character through the States, make the most prudent exertions for a new general Convention, who may vest adequate powers in Congress, for all national purposes, without annihilating the individual governments, and drawing blood from every pore by taxes, impositions and illegal restrictions. – This step might again re-establish the Union, restore tranquility to the ruffled mind of the inhabitants, and save America from distresses, dreadful even in contemplation. – "The great art of governing is to lay aside all prejudices and attachments to particular opinions, classes or individual characters; to consult the spirit of the people; to give way to it; and in so doing, to give it a turn capable of inspiring those sentiments, which may induce them to relish a change, which an alteration of circumstances may hereafter make necessary." – The education of the advocates for monarchy should have taught them, and their memory should have suggested that "monarchy is a species of government fit only for a people too much corrupted by luxury, avarice, and a passion for pleasure, to have any love for their country, and whose vices the fear of punishment alone is able to restrain; but by no means calculated for a nation that is poor, and at the same time tenacious of their liberty – animated with a disgust to tyranny – and inspired with the generous feelings of patriotism and liberty, and at the same time, like the ancient Spartans have been hardened by temperance and manly exertions, and equally despising the fatigues of the field, and the fear of enemies," – and while they change their ground they should recollect, that Aristocracy is still a more formidable foe to public virtue, and the prosperity of a nation – that under such a government her patriots become mercenaries – her soldiers, cowards, and the people slaves. – Though several State Conventions have assented to, and ratified, yet the voice of the people appears at present strong against the adoption of the Constitution. – By the chicanery, intrigue, and false colouring of those who plume themselves, more on their education and abilities, than their political, patriotic, or private virtues – by the imbecility of some, and the duplicity of others, a majority of the Convention of Massachusetts have been flattered with the ideas of amendments, when it will be too late to complain – While several very worthy characters, too timid for their situation, magnified the hopeless alternative, between the dissolution of the bands of all government, and receiving the proffered system *in toto*, after long endeavouring to reconcile it to their consciences, swallowed the indigestible panacea, and in a kind of sudden desperation lent their signature to the dereliction of the honorable station they held in the Union, and have broken over the solemn compact, by which they were bound to support their own excellent constitution till the period of revision. – Yet Virginia, equally large and respectable, and who have done honour to themselves, by their vigorous exertions from the first dawn of independence, have not yet acted upon the question; they have wisely taken time to consider before they introduce innovations of a most dangerous nature: – her inhabitants are brave, her burgesses are free, and they have a Governor who dares to think for himself, and to speak his opinion (without first pouring libations on the altar of popularity) though it should militate with some of the most accomplished and illustrious characters.

Maryland, who has no local interest to lead her to adopt, will doubtless reject the system – I hope the same characters still live, and that the same spirit which dictated to them a wise and cautious care, against sudden revolutions in government, and made them the last State that acceded to the independence of America, will lead them to support what they so deliberately claimed. – Georgia apprehensive of a war with the Savages, has acceded in order to insure protection. – Pennsylvania has struggled through much in the same manner, as the Massachusetts, against the manly feelings, and the masterly reasonings of a very respectable part of the Convention: They have adopted the system, and seen some of its authors burnt in effigy – their towns thrown into riot and confusion, and the minds of the people agitated by apprehension and discord.

New-Jersey and Delaware have united in the measure, from the locality of their situation, and the selfish motives which too generally govern mankind; the Federal City, and the seat of government, will naturally attract the intercourse of strangers – the youth of enterprize, and the wealth of the nation to the central States.

Connecticut has pushed it through with the precipitation of her neighbour, with few dissentient voices; – but more from irritation and resentment to a sister State, perhaps partiality to herself in her commercial regulations, than from a comprehensive view of the system, as a regard to the welfare of all. – But New-York has motives, that will undoubtedly lead her to a rejection, without being afraid to appeal to the understanding of mankind, to justify the grounds of their refusal to adopt a Constitution, that even the framers dare not risque to the hazard of revision, amendment, or reconsideration, lest the whole superstructure should be demolished by more skilful and discreet architects. – I know not what part the Carolinas will take; but I hope their determinations will comport with the dignity and freedom of this country – their decisions will have great weight in the scale. – But equally important are the small States of New-Hampshire and Rhode-Island: – New-York, the Carolinas, Virginia, Maryland, and these two lesser States may yet support the liberties of the Continent; if they refuse a ratification, or postpone their proceedings till the spirits of the community have time to cool, there is little doubt but the wise measure of another federal convention will be adopted, when the members would have the advantage of viewing, at large, through the medium of truth, the objections that have been made from various quarters; such a measure might be attended with the most salutary effects, and prevent the dread consequences of civil feuds. – But even if some of those large states should hastily accede, yet we have frequently seen in the story of revolution, relief spring from a quarter least expected.

Though the virtues of a Cato could not save Rome, nor the abilities of a Padilla defend the citizens of Castile from falling under the yoke of Charles; yet a *Tell* once suddenly rose from a little obscure city, and boldly rescued the liberties of his country. – Every age has its Bruti and its Decii, as well as its Caesars and Sejani: – The happiness of mankind depends much on the modes of government, and the virtues of the governors; and America may yet produce characters who have genius and capacity sufficient to form the manners and correct the morals of the people, and virtue enough to lead their country to freedom. Since her dismemberment from the British empire, America has, in many instances, resembled the conduct of a restless, vigorous, luxurious youth, prematurely emancipated from the authority of a parent, but without the experience necessary to direct him to act with dignity or discretion. Thus we have seen her break the shackles of foreign dominion, and all the blessings of peace restored on the most honourable terms: She acquired the liberty of framing her own laws, choosing her own magistrates, and adopting manners and modes of government the most favourable to the freedom and happiness of society. But how little have we availed ourselves of these superior advantages: The glorious fabric of liberty successfully reared with so much labour and assiduity totters to the foundation, and may be blown away as the bubble of fancy by the rude breath of military combinations, and politicians of yesterday.

It is true this country lately armed in opposition to regal despotism – impoverished by the expences of a long war, and unable immediately to fulfil their public or private engagements, have appeared in some instances, with a boldness of spirit that seemed to set at defiance all authority, government, or order, on the one hand; while on the other, there has been, not only a secret with, but an open avowal of the necessity of drawing the reins of government much too taut, not only for republicanism, but for a wise and limited monarchy. – But the character of this people is not averse to a degree of subordination; the truth of this appears from the easy restoration of tranquility, after a dangerous insurrection in one of the states; this also evinces the little necessity of a complete revolution of government throughout the union. But it is a republican principle that the majority should rule; and if a spirit of moderation could be cultivated on both sides, till the voice of the people at large could be fairly heard it should be held sacred – And if, on such a scrutiny, the proposed constitution should appear repugnant to their character and wishes; if they, in the language of a late elegant pen, should acknowledge that "no confusion in my mind, is more terrible to them than the stern disciplined regularity and vaunted police of arbitrary governments, where every heart is depraved by fear, where mankind dare not assume their natural characters, where the free spirit must crouch to the slave in office, where genius must repress her effusions, or like the Egyptian worshippers, offer them in sacrifice to the calves in power, and where the human mind, always in shackles, shrinks from every generous effort." Who would then have the effrontery to say, it ought not to be thrown out with indignation, however some respectable names have appeared to support it. – But if after all, on a dispassionate and fair discussion, the people generally give their voice for a voluntary dereliction of their privileges, let every individual who chooses the active scenes of life, strive to support the peace and unanimity of his country, though every other blessing may expire – And while the statesman is plodding for power, and the courtier practising the arts of dissimulation without check – while the rapacious are growing rich by oppression, and fortune throwing her gifts into the lap of fools, let the sublimer characters, the philosophic lovers of freedom who have wept over her exit, retire to the calm shades of contemplation, there they may look down with pity on the inconsistency of human nature, the revolutions of states, the rise of kingdoms, and the fall of empires.

PART V

Thoughts on Minority Rights and Liberty – From Servitude to Privilege:

MARIA W. STEWART AND JOHN STUART MILL

This is the land of freedom. The press is at liberty. Every man has a right to express his opinion.[1]

Maria W. Stewart, Religion and the Pure Principles of Morality

Maria W. Stewart lived an early life informed by loss, by the unfreedom of domestic service, and by the self-reliance of a life without a family. Born Maria Miller to free Black parents in Hartford, Connecticut, she was orphaned at age five, and "bound out" to service at a clergyman's home until she was fifteen. Her ready intellect must have been developed in her domestic situation and in Sabbath school, but present scholarship on this pivotal figure is so meager that we can only speculate about the nature of her education. In 1826 she married James W. Stewart, a ship's fitter by trade, and she resided on a part of Beacon Hill where many of Boston's middle-class Blacks lived.

What forces prompted her in 1831 to enter the offices of William Lloyd Garrison's *The Liberator*, the foremost abolitionist newspaper, with a manuscript of political and religious writing? Stewart put herself forward at a time when few American women, white or Black, are recorded to have spoken in public on political issues. She must have been galvanized in her actions by several factors. Her education, gained unsystematically and perhaps at some peril, led her to the startlingly contemporary belief that "knowledge is power." She was most likely aware of laws such as the North Carolina Act of 1831 prohibiting the teaching of slaves to read, which was typical of many laws enacted at the time. The institution of slavery and the oppression of free Blacks depended on the systematic imposition of illiteracy, for the nascent Black abolitionist movement would use pamphlets smuggled from North to South to spread the word of rebellion. Throughout her life Stewart believed education to be the enabling condition of freedom.

Stewart's personal losses had a particular impact on her political thinking. She was widowed after only three years of marriage and was cheated by unscrupulous whites out of the relatively substantial wealth of her husband's business. Race, class, and gender oppression converge in the historical practice of using the legal system to deprive the poorer classes of their often meager holdings. In *Bleak House*, Charles Dickens satirizes the practice of legal swindling in England's Chancery courts. In *Maria, Or the Wrongs of Woman*, Mary Wollstonecraft describes how a disaffected husband can have his wife incarcerated and take possession of her property, without any recourse available to her. White professionals and businessmen commonly used the courts to deprive free African Americans of their property, and after two years' litigation and tactics that even the judge deplored, Stewart was deprived of the inheritance from her husband's estate. These examples are important for political theory because they serve as a reminder of the shortcomings of strict legalistic and procedural "solutions" to problems of social justice. In this specific case, Stewart learned at an early age the injustices of the United States' legal and social systems.

Arguably the most profound influence on Maria W. Stewart was David Walker, an African American businessman who was a frequent contributor to *Freedom's Journal*, an early African American abolitionist newspaper. Walker had published his own political tract, *Walker's Appeal*, in which he outlined those elements that were most responsible, in his view, for the wretched condition of African Americans: slavery, ignorance, the contemporary practice of Christian religion, and colonization, a movement to create an African state to which American Blacks could be deported for their own "freedom."[2]

Walker's abolitionist activities were probably at the heart of his mysterious death, killed perhaps by agents of plantation owners. Upon Walker's death, Stewart was alone again: her parents, her husband, and her mentor had all died. Through a religious "rebirth" in 1831 she concluded that death was not to be feared, and that the dangers of advocating freedom from a life enslaved, exploited, and oppressed were worth risking. In the words of her biographer, Marilyn Richardson, "she gave herself over to a secular ministry of political and religious witness."[3]

FROM SERVITUDE TO POLITICAL ACTIVISM

Maria Stewart's public speaking and writing lasted for only three years, during which time she produced a number of works. "Religion and the Pure Principles of Morality" (1831) was published on Garrison's presses and sold for six cents a copy. In this piece she introduces her style, much dependent on the rhetoric of the pulpit and the use of biblical quotations to carry her arguments. Scripture provided a safe source of authority in which to couch her fiery prose. In 1832 she produced "Cause for Encouragement," a comment on the "Second Annual Convention of People of Color" held in Philadelphia, and the "Lecture Delivered at the Franklin Hall to the New England Anti-Slavery Society." In this year she also investigated the issues of gender and race in "An Address Delivered Before the Afric-American Female Intelligence Society of America." This essay anticipates by more than fifty years the work of another Black political thinker, Anna Julia Cooper, who attributes a moral ascendancy to women (see Part VII). According to Cooper:

> Only the BLACK WOMAN can say "when and where I enter, in the quiet, undisputed dignity of my womanhood, without violence and without suing or special patronage, then and there the whole *Negro race enters with me*." ("*Womanhood a Vital Element in the Regeneration and Progress of a Race*")[4]

But Stewart was less enamored of peaceful dignity as a strategy and sympathized greatly with armed uprisings like the American Revolution. In "An Address Delivered at the African Masonic Hall" (*On African Rights and Liberty*) (1833) she forthrightly declares:

> Many powerful sons and daughters of Africa will shortly arise, who will put down vice and immorality among us, and declare by Him that sitteth upon the throne that they will have their rights; and if refused, I am afraid they will spread horror and devastation around.[5]

The liberal language of rights and freedom permeates this text and fuses with the religious language, to make the case for ending the oppression of African Americans, men and women, free and enslaved. This was to be her penultimate public address.

The sexism Stewart encountered finally influenced her to leave public life. In "Mrs. Stewart's Farewell Address to Her Friends in the City of Boston" she developed a more refined set of arguments, based on the historical achievements of women, to demonstrate, *contra* St. Paul, that women are as worthy as men:

> In the 15th century... [we find] women occupying the chairs of Philosophy and Justice; women writing in Greek, and studying Hebrew. Nuns were poetesses, and women of quality Divines; and young girls who had studied Eloquence.... The religious spirit which has animated women in all ages, showed itself at this time. It has made them by turns, martyrs, apostles, warriors, and concluded in making them divines and scholars.[6]

After this speech, she left public life certain that she would shortly die.

Stewart moved to New York, Baltimore, and then to Washington, D.C., teaching thousands of Black students throughout her career. She finally became matron at an institution that is now the Howard University Hospital. That she never wavered from her early convictions about education, liberty, and free speech is demonstrated by an incident late in her career. In 1879 she sued for, and received, a widow's pension for her husband's service in the war of 1812. She used these funds to republish her collected works, along with a biographical sketch. Her teaching was a form of political activism based on her early thought and writings. She died a year after the republication of her works.

> This, then, is the appropriate region of human liberty. It comprises, first, the inward domain of consciousness... liberty of thought and feeling, absolute freedom of opinion and sentiment.[7]
>
> *Mill*, On Liberty

Philosopher, economist, and social reformer, John Stuart Mill is best known for his liberalism and his feminism. His work provides the perfect expression of mid-nineteenth-century progressive thought. He refined the theory of utilitarianism articulated by Jeremy Bentham and Mill's father, James. These men's views were the moral counterparts of Adam Smith's "free market" economics. They developed a moral theory of self-interest and self-development that in principle would simultaneously create the most happiness, or utility, best understood in contemporary terms as *common good*.

The differences between Mill's and Maria Stewart's life could not have been greater. Only three years her junior, Mill was a child of great privilege and astounding intellectual resources. While Maria Stewart was serving in a clergyman's home, devouring scraps of education as they may have been thrown her way, Mill was being prepared an unrivaled intellectual repast. Mill's father and his friend, Bentham, were devising a scheme to test out their utilitarian theories on the experimental subject of young John Stuart Mill. Under their tutelage, Mill studied Greek at the age of three, Latin at eight, and wrote a history of Roman law at ten. His father was severe in his approach, but he put young Mill in the company of the intellectuals of the day, and the lad exhibited tremendous precocity. (Stewart was precocious, too, self-educated, and putting herself forward, as it were, in the infancy of American women's public political speech and presenting her work unbidden at Garrison's office.)

There is another parallel in the lives of this unlikely pair, for within a period of a few years, each underwent a transforming psychological epiphany. In Stewart's case, it was the religious conversion that served as the springboard and inspiration for her political activism. For Mill, it was the revelation that his upbringing had left him barren of feeling and utterly lacking in emotional attachments, along with a disaffection for Benthamite utilitarianism. Despite the pain that his awakening caused him, Mill recovered from his breakdown, mainly through forming an attachment to Mrs. Harriet Taylor, a woman who became his lifelong friend and intellectual companion. Taylor co-authored much of Mill's writing and had a radicalizing influence on him, persuasively arguing for both socialism and feminism. The extent of their collaborations has still not been fully illuminated. We do know that Mill's best work – with Taylor – was only produced after the death of her husband and her subsequent marriage to Mill in 1851. After nearly dying from tuberculosis in 1854, Mill set about writing *On Liberty, Considerations on Representative Government, Utilitarianism,* and *The Subjection of Women.* The help of Taylor and her daughter, Helen, contributed immeasurably to this proliferation of works.

Stewart's career as a political speaker and pamphleteer had virtually ended by the time she was thirty: Mill's major writings did not appear in print until late in his life. Yet their concerns were of a piece – chiefly with the aspects of liberty that allow development of the human spirit – each very much seen through the eyes of their own circumstances and social locations.

POLITICAL THEORY AND MINORITY OPINION

Pairing Mill's *On Liberty* (1859) with Maria Stewart's *On African Rights and Liberty* (1833) juxtaposes the premier political defense of unpopular speech and action with an obscure set of lectures by a little-known political writer. Mill is one of the most renowned and written-about political theorists; Stewart is "hidden in plain sight," with only three printings of her work ever produced.[8] These lectures were first heard and read in the early 1830s. In 1987, Marilyn Richardson compiled the first collection of her work in more than one hundred years. The number of editions of Mill's *On Liberty* are almost too numerous to count. Despite their radical differences, Mill and Stewart are paired as a way of revealing how context, standpoint, and lived experience influence the treatment of the same subject – minority rights and liberty.

Mill delved into the theory and practice of listening to minority opinion. As a youth he disseminated information about birth control and wrote numerous articles for radical causes. He advocated an end to slavery. Late in life Mill, along with Taylor, wrote *The Subjection of Women*, in which they present unpopular views about women's equality. Although sometimes failing to trace the labyrinthine paths followed by truly oppressed speech, Mill was concerned about minority religious opinion and unpopular political expression, such as anti-property and anti-aristocracy speeches. He was also concerned about *individual* acts that may be unpopular, self-damaging, or risky, such as over-imbibing alcohol, or religious practices such as Mormon polygamy.

Mill was more fearful of the censorious character of public opinion than he was of the government, in suppressing unpopular opinion and action:

> Society itself is the tyrant... and if it issues wrong mandates instead of right, or any mandates at all in things with which it ought not to meddle, it practices a social tyranny more formidable than many kinds of political oppression since... it leaves fewer means of escape, penetrating more deeply into the details of life, and enslaving the soul itself.[9]

But whether from naiveté or as an argumentative strategy, he downplays the revolutionary power of minority speech and action. By using examples calculated to make speech seem unthreatening and eminently useful, is Mill writing to influence legislation and practice? Or is he speaking from a world of relative civil freedom, curiously unaware of both the worst suppression of speech and action and of its awesome power?

SILENCING

The contemporary feminist movement has taken as a central theme the silencing of minority speakers, and it has chronicled the multiple ways in which this can happen. Early feminists such as Wollstonecraft and Stewart faced serious structural barriers to being heard, including a lack of formal education, a social stricture against women entering professions, including writing and speaking, and the public's strong predisposition to consider women writers or orators as sexually promiscuous and unworthy. Minority opinions have been subjected to ridicule, denied a forum, and ignored by the press. They have been misrepresented and belittled. Often portrayed as dangerous or trivial, they have most frequently been presented as contrary to the interests of the dominant culture.

Violence and the threat of violence are surely among the most effective ways of silencing non-dominant views; whether it is battering in the home, sanctions threatened through the legal system, or part of a system of publicly condoned crime such as lynching (see, for example, the work of Ida B. Wells), it is a most effective means of censorship. Speaking out against slavery had a treasonous flavor, and a fairly well-established, if loose-knit, code prevailed for murdering those who threatened the system of slavery. Stewart was well aware of this ultimate threat to speech, for her mentor, David Walker, was most likely murdered for his political stance promoting political and civil rights for Blacks. Those obstacles facing most women are considerably multiplied for Black women in the United States. Consider, for example, the work of Frances W. Harper. Although she wrote more than a dozen books and was the most popular woman poet of her time, she is largely unknown today, and her first book of published poetry is completely lost to us. In fact, little is known about many Black women writers, and the authority of their speech is often questioned.

BLACK FEMINIST THOUGHT – HIDDEN IN PLAIN SIGHT

To resurrect a *system* of political thought, and not just put forth a voice in the darkness, Stewart should be studied as part of a continuum of political writers, especially women and Blacks. Among those of importance are Mary Wollstonecraft, Martin Delany, Sojourner Truth, Frederick Douglass, Anna J. Cooper, and Ida B. Wells (Barnett), and contemporary writers such as Angela Davis, bell hooks, June Jordan, Audre Lorde, Joy James, Patricia Hill Collins, and Patricia Williams.[10] Two related themes that emerge from this tradition are the difficulties in being heard and the misportrayals of Black women's speech. Hill Collins and many others focus on the stereotypes that are used to caricature Black women and deprive them of an authentic voice. Williams addresses the problem as well, as a lawyer who has been subjected to illegal racial discrimination, and had her evidence doubted:

> What would it take to make my experience verifiable. The testimony of a white bystander? (a requirement in fact imposed in US Supreme Court holdings through the first part of the century).[11]

One commentator suggests that the testimonial letters by whites that introduce the 1879 edition of Stewart's works are part of an oppressive framing whereby white authority is the only proper conduit for Black speech.[12] Another obstacle to serious research is the spareness of her writing in a field where mainstream writers produced multiple volumes of material. But Stewart's political writing, like the poetry of Frances Harper and Alice Dunbar Nelson, must be viewed in the context of what Audre Lorde calls a "distillation of experience" through which the underheard are able to raise their voices and speak through the most available medium. Works such as Margaret Busby's *Daughters of Africa*, Paula Giddings' *When and Where I Enter*, Darlene Clark Hine's *Black Women in America*, and Gerda Lerner's *Black Women in White America* open the door to the study of these social and political writers.

The contemporary feminist movement, composed of such disparate voices as socialist, radical, and post-colonial, all informed by the work of women of color, endorses the notion that one's particular historical, cultural, and social location create the subject position from which one speaks. Inhabiting that particular social location provides the standpoint for the epistemology which frames their positions. For women, the poor, Blacks, and people of color, the inhabited social location is often one which has been hidden in plain sight from the dominant viewpoint. Unlike speech from the dominant view, which issues with a trumpet blast or with the quiet confidence that it will be heard, the first act of a writer such as Maria W. Stewart must be to make herself heard.

NINETEENTH-CENTURY BLACK FEMINIST THOUGHT AND THE MATRICES OF OPPRESSION

Stewart adopts the radical language of her day, the language of liberalism. But she is also developing the concept of multiple oppression that forms a centerpiece for contemporary Black feminist thought. Current theorists have argued that certain categories, most particularly race, class, and gender, but also age, sexual identity, and ability, may all be sites of oppression, and they interact often in geometrically expanding ways. Rather than focus exclusively on any one form of oppression, these theorists urge scholars and activists to take account of "the simultaneity of oppression," or the matrices of oppression.[13] Stewart is keenly aware of the intersection of race, class, and gender oppression. Among African Americans:

> I have asked several individuals of my sex, who transact business for themselves, if providing our girls were to give them the most satisfactory references, they would not be willing to grant them an equal opportunity with others? Their reply has been – for their own part, they had no objection: but as it was not the custom, were they to take them into their employ, they would be in danger of losing the public patronage.[14]

It is unusual in this period to find the language of equal opportunity being employed, as it is in this passage, and it is particularly striking to find it applied to employment discrimination against girls in the African American community. Even today it is difficult to discuss gender inequities within African American practices, as the charge is often raised that such attention detracts from a focus on race inequities. Yet Stewart perceives the interrelated character of these injustices. She progresses to a class analysis:

> Few white persons of either sex . . . are willing to spend their lives and bury their talents in performing mean, servile labor. And such is the horrible idea that I entertain respecting a life of servitude, that if I conceived of their [sic] being no possibility of my rising above the condition of servant, I would gladly hail death as a welcome messenger.[15]

Stewart shares with Mill a horror of not developing one's talents or intellect, limitations imposed upon the serving class.

Stewart's argument about racism is subtle and interesting. She uses an analogy to make the case for African American rights and liberty. But she does not argue directly that white and Black Americans are the same. She instead makes the case that the liberation struggles of African Americans are the same as those of the Poles, Greeks, and Irish, all of whom were supported by the young American nation, which engaged in a similar struggle for independence. Only then does she argue that African Americans and white Americans share the same political ideals of liberty and equality. Rhetorically, she removes by a step the Black/white analogy. In astonishingly contemporary terms, she is posing the question of *what differences count*. For what do the Poles, the Greeks, and the Americans have in common? Not a language or culture or geographical terrain. Not even a personal familiarity. By using this two-part analogy, she is able to suggest that African Americans and white Americans may have even more in common – language and location, and to some degree, custom and culture. Her argument is couched in the language of rights:

> . . . we will tell you that our souls are fired with the same love of liberty and independence with which your souls are fired . . . it is the blood of our fathers and the tears of our brethren that have enriched your soils. AND WE CLAIM OUR RIGHTS.[16]

She addresses racism through this analogical argument, noting that the United States failed to support the liberation struggle in Haiti. Using an argument that tantalizingly oscillates between the literal and the figurative, she challenges race as a category:

> We tell you that too much of your blood flows in our veins; too much of your color in our skins, for us not to possess your spirits.[17]

Does she mean only that the fiery desire for liberty is as much a part of Black fabric as it is of white longing? Or is she hinting at the miscegenation that has occurred to such a degree as to make genuine biological distinction between the races impossible? Is she suggesting, as some contemporary theorists do, that race is a constructed, not a biological category? In any case, her argument is that the spirit or soul, the quality that makes one a human being – the seat of rationality – is shared by Blacks and whites alike. The gender argument here is fully enthymematic. Since she uses the personal pronoun *we* and includes herself as a Black and a woman, the argument is radically for both race and gender inclusiveness.

Stewart scholar Marilyn Richardson summarizes what she calls "the dynamic elements" of Stewart's ideology as: "the inestimable value of education, the historical inevitability of Black liberation, the need for Black unity and collective action, and the special responsibilities of women."[18] Stewart speaks the language of liberalism, while she is developing a distinct political philosophy from the perspective – the social location – of an African American woman.

ON LIBERTY IN THOUGHT AND ACTION

How tame by comparison is Mill's measured essay, regarded as the strongest argument ever made for freedom of expression, when seen against the fiery exhortations of Maria Stewart. How amazing it is that Mill barely mentions race or sex despite the fact that he was at work with Taylor on *The Subjection of Women*, and that the United States was on the brink of civil war over the issues of race and freedom, causes he supported.

Mill often uses examples from China and India and it is possible that just as Stewart used remoter cultures to make her argument, Mill also saw the wisdom in removing the images from those of the immediate, and perhaps more personally threatening, to those at more of a distance. He does use diversity arguments and often refers to different cultural practices. Mill rarely uses demonstratively strong examples, which is surprising, given the wave of revolutions and uprisings that swept through Europe in the 1840s and 1850s. What are we to make of his claim that:

> An opinion that corn dealers are starvers of the poor, or that private property is robbery, ought to be unmolested when simply circulated through the press, but may justly incur punishment when delivered orally to an excited mob assembled before the house of a corn dealer...[19]

Isn't anti-slavery speech designed to impel rebellion? He often writes as though the worst results of most free speech will be hurt feelings and strange practices. On the other side of his utilitarian calculus, suppressing speech is bad for the common good because it will do violence to – the Truth! Surely Mill must have known the power of speech, but in arguing for its cause, he may have been well served to downplay its effects. Is his rhetorical strategy to pretend that free speech will *not* cause violence? Or in his comfortable world, is strong speech merely a matter of intense arguments between individuals?

What these selections show, then, is the degree to which social location shapes one's political thought. As the descendant of Africans enslaved in America, or as the son of a philosopher and protégé of a legal scholar, these writers had vastly different visions. But they were drawn to the same topic – minority rights and liberties. One writer is almost fully wrapped up in the need for legislation and social opinion not to stifle unpopular views, while the other is focused on truly fomenting a revolution. Perhaps the difference lies in the step from thought to action. They also show the special understanding that viewing from the position of the oppressed can give in illuminating the matrices of oppression. For political theory, the tension between protecting individual rights and furthering the common good remains. Perhaps a contemporary political theory of liberation can contribute a concept of individuals embedded in communities that will allow us to rethink the seeming contradictions and competing needs that are endemic to liberal political theory.

Notes

1 Maria W. Stewart, *Writings and Addresses*, p. 215 of this volume.
2 David Walker, *David Walker's Appeal*, ed. and intro. Charles M. Wiltse (New York: Hill and Wang, 1965).
3 Marilyn Richardson, ed. and intro., *Maria W. Stewart, America's First Black Political Writer* (Bloomington: Indiana University Press, 1987), p. 8.
4 Anna Julia Cooper, *A Voice from the South*, p. 343 of this volume.
5 Stewart, *Writings and Addresses*, p. 229 of this volume.
6 Ibid., p. 231.
7 John Stuart Mill, *On Liberty*, p. 234 of this volume.
8 The phrase "hidden in plain sight" is Marilyn Richardson's, and aptly describes much work by feminists and people of color (p. xv).
9 John Stuart Mill, *On Liberty*, ed. Elizabeth Rapaport (Indianapolis: Hackett, 1978), p. 4.
10 There are so many outstanding contemporary theorists that it is difficult to draw up a list. Here I have named a few in fields related to politics. Many more literary theorists have made substantial contributions to political understanding.
11 Patricia J. Williams, *The Alchemy of Race and Rights: Diary of a Law Professor* (Cambridge, MA: Harvard University Press, 1991), p. 47.
12 N. Stepko quoted in Richardson, *Maria W. Stewart*, p. 80.
13 See Gloria T. Hull et al., *But Some of Us Are Brave: Black Women's Studies* (New York: Feminist Press, 1986), and Patricia Hill Collins, *Black Feminist Thought: Knowledge, Consciousness and the Politics of Empowerment* (New York: Routledge, 1991).
14 Stewart, *Writings and Addresses*, p. 221 of this volume.
15 Ibid., p. 222.
16 Ibid., p. 220.
17 Ibid.
18 Richardson, Introduction to *Maria W. Stewart*, p. 9.
19 Mill, *On Liberty*, p. 238 of this volume.

CHAPTER 9

Writings and Addresses

MARIA W. STEWART

RELIGION AND THE PURE PRINCIPLES OF MORALITY, THE SURE FOUNDATION ON WHICH WE MUST BUILD

Introduction

Feeling a deep solemnity of soul, in view of our wretched and degraded situation, and sensible of the gross ignorance that prevails among us, I have thought proper thus publicly to express my sentiments before you. I hope my friends will not scrutinize these pages with too severe an eye, as I have not calculated to display either elegance or taste in their composition, but have merely written the meditations of my heart as far as my imagination led; and have presented them before you in order to arouse you to exertion, and to enforce upon your minds the great necessity of turning your attention to knowledge and improvement.

I was born in Hartford, Connecticut, in 1803; was left an orphan at five years of age; was bound out in a clergyman's family; had the seeds of piety and virtue early sown in my mind, but was deprived of the advantages of education, though my soul thirsted for knowledge. Left them at fifteen years of age; attended Sabbath schools until I was twenty; in 1826 was married to James W. Stewart; was left a widow in 1829; was, as I humbly hope and trust, brought to the knowledge of the truth, as it is in Jesus, in 1830; in 1831 made a public profession of my faith in Christ.

From the moment I experienced the change, I felt a strong desire, with the help and assistance of God, to devote the remainder of my days to piety and virtue, and now possess that spirit of independence that, were I called upon, I would willingly sacrifice my life for the cause of God and my brethren.

All the nations of the earth are crying out for liberty and equality. Away, away with tyranny and oppression! And shall Afric's sons be silent any longer? Far be it from me to recommend to you either to kill, burn, or destroy. But I would strongly

Maria W. Stewart. Writings and Addresses. Originally published in 1830–3.

recommend to you to improve your talents; let not one lie buried in the earth. Show forth your powers of mind. Prove to the world that

> Though black your skins as shades of night,
> Your hearts are pure, your souls are white.

This is the land of freedom. The press is at liberty. Every man has a right to express his opinion. Many think, because your skins are tinged with a sable hue, that you are an inferior race of beings; but God does not consider you as such. He hath formed and fashioned you in his own glorious image, and hath bestowed upon you reason and strong powers of intellect. He hath made you to have dominion over the beasts of the field, the fowls of the air, and the fish of the sea. He hath crowned you with glory and honor; hath made you but a little lower than the angels; and according to the Constitution of these United States, he hath made all men free and equal. Then why should one worm say to another, "Keep you down there, while I sit up yonder; for I am better than thou?" It is not the color of the skin that makes the man, but it is the principles formed within the soul.

Many will suffer for pleading the cause of oppressed Africa, and I shall glory in being one of her martyrs; for I am firmly persuaded, that the God in whom I trust is able to protect me from the rage and malice of mine enemies, and from them that will rise up against me; and if there is no other way for me to escape, he is able to take me to himself, as he did the most noble, fearless, and undaunted David Walker.

Never Will Virtue, Knowledge, and True Politeness Begin to Flow, till the Pure Principles of Religion and Morality Are Put into Force

My Respected Friends,

I feel almost unable to address you; almost incompetent to perform the task; and at times I have felt ready to exclaim, O that my head were waters, and mine eyes a fountain of tears, that I might weep day and night, for the transgressions of the daughters of my people. Truly, my heart's desire and prayer is, that Ethiopia might stretch forth her hands unto God. But we have a great work to do. Never, no, never will the chains of slavery and ignorance burst, till we become united as one, and cultivate among ourselves the pure principles of piety, morality and virtue. I am sensible of my ignorance; but such knowledge as God has given to me, I impart to you. I am sensible of former prejudices; but it is high time for prejudices and animosities to cease from among us. I am sensible of exposing myself to calumny and reproach; but shall I, for fear of feeble man who shall die, hold my peace? Shall I for fear of scoffs and frowns, refrain my tongue? Ah, no! I speak as one that must give an account at the awful bar of God; I speak as a dying mortal to dying mortals. O, ye daughters of Africa, awake! Awake! Arise! No longer sleep nor slumber, but distinguish yourselves. Show forth to the world that ye are endowed with noble and exalted faculties. O, ye daughters of Africa! What have ye done to immortalize your names beyond the grave? What examples have ye set before the rising generation? What foundation have ye laid for generations yet unborn? Where are our union and love? And where is our sympathy, that weeps at another's woe, and hides the faults we see? And our daughters, where are they? Blushing in innocence and virtue? And our sons, do they bid fair to become crowns of glory to our hoary heads? Where is the parent who is conscious of having faithfully discharged his duty, and at the last awful day of account, shall be able to say, here, Lord, is thy poor, unworthy servant, and the children thou hast given me? And where are the children that will arise and call them blessed? Alas, O God! Forgive me if I speak amiss; the minds of our tender babes are tainted as soon as they are born; they go astray, as it were, from the womb. Where is the maiden who will blush at vulgarity? And where is the youth who has written upon his manly brow a thirst for knowledge; whose ambitious mind soars above trifles, and longs for the time to come, when he shall redress the wrongs of his father and plead the cause of his brethren? Did the daughters of our land possess a delicacy of manners, combined with gentleness and dignity; did their pure minds hold vice in abhorrence and contempt, did they frown when their ears were polluted with its vile accents, would not their influence become powerful? Would not our brethren fall in love with their virtues? Their souls would become fired with a holy zeal for freedom's cause. They would become ambitious to distinguish themselves. They would become proud to display their talents. Able advocates would arise in our defence. Knowledge would begin to flow, and the chains of slavery and ignorance would melt like wax before the flames. I am but a feeble instrument. I am but as one particle of the small dust of the earth. You may frown or smile. After I am dead, perhaps before, God will surely rise up those who will more powerfully and eloquently plead the cause of virtue and the pure principles of morality than I am able to do. O virtue! How sacred is thy name! How pure are thy principles! Who can find a virtuous woman? For her price is far above rubies. Blessed is the man who shall call her his wife; yea, happy is the child who shall call her mother. O woman, woman, would thou only strive to excel in merit and virtue; would thou only store thy mind with useful knowledge, great would be thine influence. Do you say you are too far advanced in life now to begin? You are not too far advanced to instil these principles into the minds of your tender infants. Let them by no means be neglected. Discharge your duty faithfully, in every point of view: leave the event with God. So shall your skirts become clear of their blood.

When I consider how little improvement has been made the last eight years; the apparent cold and indifferent state of the children of God; how few have been hopefully brought to the knowledge of the truth as it is in Jesus; that our young men and maidens are fainting and drooping, as it were, by the way-side, for the want of knowledge; when I see how few care to distinguish themselves either in religious or moral improvement, and when I see the greater part of our community following the vain bubbles of life with so much eagerness, which will only prove to them like the serpent's sting upon the bed of death, I really think we are in as wretched and miserable a state as was the house of Israel in the days of Jeremiah.

I suppose many of my friends will say, "Religion is all your theme," I hope my conduct will ever prove me to be what I profess, a true follower of Christ; and it is the religion of Jesus alone that will constitute your happiness here, and support you in a dying hour. O then, do not trifle with God and your own souls any longer. Do not presume to offer him the very dregs of your lives; but now, whilst you are blooming in health and vigor, consecrate the remnant of your days to him. Do you wish to become useful in your day and generation? Do you wish to promote the welfare and happiness of your friends, as far as your circle extends? Have you one desire to become truly great? O then become truly pious and God will endow you with wisdom and knowledge from on high.

Come, turn to God, who did thee make
And at his presence fear and quake;
Remember him now in thy youth,
And let thy soul take hold of truth.
The devil and his ways defy,
Believe him not, he doth but lie;
His ways seem sweet: but youth, beware!
He for thy soul hath laid a snare.

Religion is pure; it is ever new; it is beautiful; it is all that is worth living for; it is worth dying for. O, could I but see the church built up in the most holy faith; could I but see men spiritually minded, walking in the fear of God, not given to filthy lucre, not holding religion in one hand and the world in the other, but diligent in business, fervent in spirit, serving the Lord, standing upon the walls of Zion, crying to passers by, "Ho, every one that thirsteth, come ye to the waters, and he that hath no money; yea, come and buy wine and milk without money and without price." Turn ye, turn ye, for why will ye die? Could I but see mothers in Israel, chaste, keepers at home, not busy bodies, meddlers in other men's matters, whose adorning is of the inward man, possessing a meek and quiet spirit, whose sons were like olive-plants, and whose daughters were as polished corner-stones; could I but see young men and maidens turning their feet from impious ways, rather choosing to suffer affliction with the people of God than to enjoy the pleasures of sin for a season; could I but see the rising youth blushing in artless innocence, then could I say, now, Lord, let thine unworthy handmaiden depart in peace, for I have seen the desire of mine eyes, and am satisfied. [...]

I have been taking a survey of the American people in my own mind, and I see them thriving in arts and sciences, and in polite literature. Their highest aim is to excel in political, moral and religious improvement. They early consecrate their children to God, and their youth indeed are blushing in artless innocence. They wipe the tears from the orphan's eyes, and they cause the widow's heart to sing for joy! And their poorest ones, who have the least wish to excel, they promote! And those that have but one talent they encourage. But how very few are there among them that bestow one thought upon the benighted sons and daughters of Africa, who have enriched the soils of America with their tears and blood: few to promote their cause, none to encourage their talents. Under these circumstances, do not let our hearts be any longer discouraged; it is no use to murmur nor to repine; but let us promote ourselves and improve our own talents. And I am rejoiced to reflect that there are many able and talented ones among us, whose names might be recorded on the bright annals of fame. But "I can't," is a great barrier in the way. I hope it will soon be removed, and "I will," resume its place. [...]

O, ye mothers, what a responsibility rests on you! You have souls committed to your charge, and God will require a strict account of you. It is you that must create in the minds of your little girls and boys a thirst for knowledge, the love of virtue, the abhorrence of vice, and the cultivation of a pure heart. The seeds thus sown will grow with their growing years; and the love of virtue thus early formed in the soul will protect their inexperienced feet from many dangers. O, do not say you cannot make any thing of your children; but say, with the help and assistance of God, we will try. Do not indulge them in their little stubborn ways; for a child left to himself bringeth his mother to shame. Spare not for their crying; thou shalt beat them with a rod, and they shall not die; and thou shalt save their souls from hell. When you correct them, do it in the fear of God, and for their own good. They will not thank you for your false and foolish indulgence; they will rise up, as it were, and curse you in this world and, in the world to come, condemn you. It is no use to say you can't do this, or you can't do that; you will not tell your Maker so, when you meet him at the great day of account. And you must be careful that you set an example worthy of following, for you they will imitate. There are many instances, even among us now, where parents have discharged their duty faithfully, and their children now reflect honor upon their gray hairs.

Perhaps you will say that many parents have set pure examples at home, and they have not followed them. True, our expectations are often blasted; but let not this dishearten you. If they have faithfully discharged their duty, even after they are dead their works may live; their prodigal children may return to God and become heirs of salvation; if not, their children cannot rise and condemn them at the awful bar of God.

Perhaps you will say that you cannot send them to high schools and academies. You can have them taught in the first rudiments of useful knowledge, and then you can have private teachers who will instruct them in the higher branches; and their intelligence will become greater than ours, and their children will attain to higher advantages, and their children still higher; and then, though we are dead, our works shall live: though we are mouldering, our names shall not be forgotten.

Finally, my heart's desire and prayer to God is that there might come a thorough reformation among us. Our minds have too long grovelled in ignorance and sin. Come, let us incline our ears to wisdom, and apply our hearts to understanding; promote her, and she will exalt thee; she shall bring thee honor when thou dost embrace her. An ornament of grace shall she be to thy head, and a crown of glory shall she deliver to thee. Take fast hold of instruction; let her not go; keep her, for she is thy life. Come, let us turn unto the Lord our God, with all our heart and soul, and put away every unclean and unholy thing from among us, and walk before the Lord our God, with a perfect heart, all the days of our lives: then we shall be a people with whom God shall delight to dwell; yea, we shall be that happy people whose God is the Lord.

I am of a strong opinion that the day on which we unite, heart and soul, and turn our attention to knowledge and improvement, that day the hissing and reproach among the nations of the earth against us will cease. And even those who now point at us with the finger of scorn, will aid and befriend us. It is of no use for us to sit with our hands folded, hanging our heads like bulrushes, lamenting our wretched condition; but let us make a mighty effort, and arise; and if no one will promote or respect us, let us promote and respect ourselves.

The American ladies have the honor conferred on them, that by prudence and economy in their domestic concerns, and their unwearied attention in forming the minds and manners of their children, they laid the foundation of their becoming what they now are. The good women of Wethersfield, Conn., toiled in the blazing sun, year after year, weeding onions, then sold the seed and procured enough money to erect them a house of worship; and shall we not imitate their examples, as far as they are worthy of imitation? Why cannot we do something to distinguish ourselves, and contribute some of our hard earnings that would reflect honor upon our memories, and cause our children to arise and call us blessed? Shall it any longer be said of the daughters of Africa, they have no ambition, they have no force? By no means. Let every female heart become united, and let us raise a fund ourselves; and at the end of one year and a half, we might be able to lay the corner stone for the building of a High School, that the higher branches of knowledge might be enjoyed by us; and God would raise us up, and enough to aid us in our laudable designs. Let each one strive to excel in good housewifery, knowing that prudence and economy are the road to wealth. Let us not say we know this, or we know that, and practise nothing; but let us practise what we do know.

How long shall the fair daughters of Africa be compelled to bury their minds and talents beneath a load of iron pots and kettles? Until union, knowledge and love begin to flow among us. How long shall a mean set of men flatter us with their smiles, and enrich themselves with our hard earnings; their wives' fingers sparkling with rings, and they themselves laughing at our folly? Until we begin to promote and patronize each other. Shall we be a by-word among the nations any longer? Shall they laugh us to scorn forever? Do you ask, what can we do? Unite and build a store of your own, if you cannot procure a license. Fill one side with dry goods, and the other with groceries. Do you ask where is the money? We have spent more than enough for nonsense, to do what building we should want. We have never had an opportunity of displaying our talents; therefore the world thinks we know nothing. And we have been possessed by far too mean and cowardly a disposition, though I highly disapprove of an insolent or impertinent one. Do you ask the disposition I would have you possess? Possess the spirit of independence. The Americans do, and why should not you? Possess the spirit of men, bold and enterprising, fearless and undaunted. Sue for your rights and privileges. Know the reason that you cannot attain them. Weary them with your importunities. You can but die if you make the attempt; and we shall certainly die if you do not. The Americans have practised nothing but head-work these 200 years, and we have done their drudgery. And is it not high time for us to imitate their examples, and practise head-work too, and keep what we have got, and get what we can? We need never to think that anybody is going to feel interested for us, if we do not feel interested for ourselves. That day we, as a people, hearken unto the voice of the Lord, our God, and walk in his ways and ordinances, and become distinguished for our ease, elegance and grace, combined with other virtues, that day the Lord will raise us up, and enough to aid and befriend us, and we shall begin to flourish.

Did every gentleman in America realize, as one, that they had got to become bondmen, and their wives, their sons, and their daughters, servants forever, to Great Britain, their very joints would become loosened, and tremblingly would smite one against another; their countenance would be filled with horror, every nerve and muscle would be forced into action, their souls would recoil at the very thought, their hearts would die within them, and death would be far more preferable. Then why have not Afric's sons the right to feel the same? Are not their wives, their sons, and their daughters, as dear to them as those of the white man's? Certainly God has not deprived them of the divine influences of his Holy Spirit, which is the greatest of all blessings, if they ask him. Then why should man any longer deprive his fellow-man of equal rights and privileges? Oh, America, America, foul and indelible is thy stain! Dark and dismal is the cloud that hangs over thee, for thy cruel wrongs and injuries to the fallen sons of Africa. The blood of her murdered ones cries to heaven for vengeance against thee. Thou art almost become drunken with the blood of her slain; thou hast enriched thyself through her toils and labors; and now thou refuseth to make even a small return. And thou hast caused the daughters of Africa to commit whoredoms and fornications; but upon thee be their curse.

O, ye great and mighty men of America, ye rich and powerful ones, many of you will call for the rocks and mountains to fall upon you, and to hide you from the wrath of the Lamb, and from him that sitteth upon the throne; whilst many of the sable-skinned Africans you now despise will shine in the kingdom of heaven as the stars forever and ever. Charity begins at home, and those that provide not for their own are worse than infidels. We know that you are raising contributions to aid the gallant Poles; we know that you have befriended Greece and Ireland; and you have rejoiced with France, for her heroic deeds of valor. You have acknowledged all the nations of the earth, except Hayti; and you may publish, as far as the East is from the West, that you have two millions of negroes, who aspire no higher than to bow at your feet, and to court your smiles. You may kill, tyrannize, and oppress as much as you choose, until our cry shall come up before the throne of God; for I am firmly persuaded, that he will not suffer you to quell the proud, fearless and undaunted spirits of the Africans forever; for in his own time, he is able to plead our cause against you, and to pour out upon you the ten plagues of Egypt. We will not come out against you with swords and staves, as against a thief; but we will tell you that our souls are fired with the same love of liberty and independence with which your souls are fired. We will tell you that too much of your blood flows in our veins, too much of your color in our skins, for us not to possess your spirits. We will tell you that it is our gold that clothes you in fine linen and purple, and causes you to fare sumptuously every day; and it is the blood of our fathers, and the tears of our brethren that have enriched your soils. AND WE CLAIM OUR RIGHTS. We will tell you that we are not afraid of them that kill the body, and after that can do no more; but we will tell you whom we do fear. We fear Him who is able, after He hath killed, to destroy both soul and body in hell forever. Then, my brethren, sheath your swords, and calm your angry passions. Stand still and know that the Lord he is God. Vengeance is his, and he will repay. It is a long lane that has no turn. America has risen to her meridian. When you begin to thrive, she will begin to fall. God hath raised you up a Walker and a Garrison. Though Walker sleeps, yet he lives, and his name shall be had in everlasting remembrance. I, even I, who am but a child, inexperienced to many of you, am a living witness to testify unto you this day, that I have seen the wicked in great power, spreading himself like a green bay tree, and lo, he passed away; yea, I diligently sought him, but he could not be found; and it is God alone that has inspired my heart to feel for Afric's woes. Then fret not yourselves because of evil doers. Fret not yourselves because of the men who bring wicked devices to pass; for they shall be cut down as the grass, and wither as the green herb. Trust in the Lord, and do good; so shalt thou dwell in the land, and verily thou shalt be fed. Encourage the noble-hearted Garrison. Prove to the world that you are neither ourang-outangs, or a species of mere animals, but that you possess the same powers of intellect as the proud-boasting American.

I am sensible, my brethren and friends, that many of you have been deprived of advantages, kept in utter ignorance, and that your minds are now darkened; and if any one of you have attempted to aspire after high and noble enterprises, you have met with so much opposition that your souls have become discouraged. For this very cause, a few of us have ventured to expose our lives in your behalf, to plead your cause against the great; and it will be of no use, unless you feel for yourselves and then your little ones, and exhibit the spirits of men. Oh then, turn your attention to knowledge and improvement; for knowledge is power. And God is able to fill you with wisdom and understanding, and to dispel your fears. Arm yourselves with the weapons of prayer. Put your trust in the living God. Persevere strictly in the paths of virtue. Let nothing be lacking on your part; and in God's own time, and his time is certainly the best, he will surely deliver you with a mighty hand and with an outstretched arm.

I have never taken one step, my friends, with a design to raise myself in your esteem, or to gain applause. But what I have done, has been done with an eye single to the glory of God, and to promote the good of souls. I have neither kindred nor friends. I stand alone in your midst, exposed to the fiery darts of the devil, and to the assaults of wicked men. But though all the powers of earth and hell were to combine against me, though all nature should sink into decay, still I would trust in the Lord, and joy in the God of my salvation. For I am full persuaded that he will bring me off conqueror, yea, more than conqueror, through him who hath loved me and given himself for me.

Boston, October, 1831

Lecture Delivered at the Franklin Hall to the New England Anti-Slavery Society, Boston, September 21, 1832

Why sit ye here and die? If we say we will go to a foreign land, the famine and the pestilence are there, and there we shall die. If we sit here, we shall die. Come let us plead our cause before the whites: if they save us alive, we shall live – and if they kill us, we shall but die.

Methinks I heard a spiritual interrogation – "Who shall go forward, and take off the reproach that is cast upon the people of color? Shall it be a woman?" And my heart made this reply – "If it is thy will, be it even so, Lord Jesus!"

I have heard much respecting the horrors of slavery; but may Heaven forbid that the generality of my color throughout these United States should experience any more of its horrors than to be a servant of servants, or hewers of wood and drawers of water! Tell us no more of southern slavery; for with few exceptions, although I may be very erroneous in my opinion, yet I consider our condition but little better than that. Yet, after all, methinks there are no chains so galling as those that bind the soul, and exclude it from the vast field of useful and scientific knowledge. O, had I received the advantages of an early education, my ideas would, ere now, have expanded far and wide; but, alas! I possess nothing but moral capability – no teachings but the teachings of the Holy Spirit.

I have asked several individuals of my sex, who transact business for themselves, if providing our girls were to give them the most satisfactory references, they would not be willing to grant them an equal opportunity with others? Their reply has been – for their own part, they had no objection; but as it was not the custom, were they to take them into their employ, they would be in danger of losing the public patronage.

And such is the powerful force of prejudice. Let our girls possess whatever amiable qualities of soul they may; let their characters be fair and spotless as innocence itself; let their natural taste and ingenuity be what they may; it is impossible for scarce an individual of them to rise above the condition of servants. Ah! why is this cruel and unfeeling distinction? Is it merely because God has made our complexion to vary? If it be, O shame to soft, relenting humanity! "Tell it not in Gath! publish it not in the streets of Askelon!" Yet, after all, methinks were the American free people of color to turn their attention more assiduously to moral worth and intellectual improvement, this would be the result: prejudice would gradually diminish, and the whites would be compelled to say, unloose those fetters!

Though black their skins as shades of night,
Their hearts are pure, their souls are white.

Few white persons of either sex, who are calculated for anything else, are willing to spend their lives and bury their talents in performing mean, servile labor. And such is the horrible idea that I entertain respecting a life of servitude, that if I conceived of their being no possibility of my rising above the condition of servant, I would gladly hail death as a welcome messenger. O, horrible idea, indeed! to possess noble souls aspiring after high and honorable acquirements, yet confined by the chains of ignorance and poverty to lives of continual drudgery and toil. Neither do I know of any who have enriched themselves by spending their lives as house-domestics, washing windows, shaking carpets, brushing boots, or tending upon gentlemen's tables. I can but die for expressing my sentiments: and I am as willing to die by the sword as the pestilence; for I am a true born American; your blood flows in my veins, and your spirit fires my breast.

I observed a piece in the Liberator a few months since, stating that the colonizationists had published a work respecting us, asserting that we were lazy and idle. I confute them on that point. Take us generally as a people, we are neither lazy nor idle; and considering how little we have to excite or stimulate us, I am almost astonished that there are so many industrious and ambitious ones to be found; although I acknowledge, with extreme sorrow, that there are some who never were and never will be serviceable to society. And have you not a similar class among yourselves?

Again. It was asserted that we were "a ragged set, crying for liberty." I reply to it, the whites have so long and so loudly proclaimed the theme of equal rights and privileges, that our souls have caught the flame also, ragged as we are. As far as our merit deserves, we feel a common desire to rise above the condition of servants and drudges. I have learnt, by bitter experience, that continual hard labor deadens the energies of the soul, and benumbs the faculties of the mind; the ideas become confined, the mind barren, and, like the scorching sands of Arabia, produces nothing; or like the uncultivated soil, brings forth thorns and thistles.

Again, continual and hard labor irritates our tempers and sours our dispositions; the whole system becomes worn out with toil and fatigue; nature herself becomes almost exhausted, and we care but little whether we live or die. It is true, that the free people of color throughout these United States are neither bought nor sold, nor under the lash of the cruel driver; many obtain a comfortable support; but few, if any, have an opportunity of becoming rich and independent; and the enjoyments we most pursue are as unprofitable to us as the spider's web or the floating bubbles that vanish into air. As servants, we are respected; but let us presume to aspire any higher, our employer regards us no longer. And were it not that the King eternal has declared that Ethiopia shall stretch forth her hands unto God, I should indeed despair. [...]

AN ADDRESS DELIVERED BEFORE THE AFRIC-AMERICAN FEMALE INTELLIGENCE SOCIETY OF AMERICA

The frowns of the world shall never discourage me, nor its smiles flatter me; for with the help of God, I am resolved to withstand the fiery darts of the devil, and the assaults of wicked men. The righteous are as bold as a lion, but the wicked fleeth when no man pursueth. I fear neither men nor devils; for the God in whom I trust is able to deliver me from the rage and malice of my enemies, and from them that rise up against me.

The only motive that has prompted me to raise my voice in your behalf, my friends, is because I have discovered that religion is held in low repute among some of us; and purely to promote the cause of Christ, and the good of souls, in the hope that others more experienced, more able and talented than myself, might go forward and do likewise. I expect to render a strict, a solemn, and an awful account to God for the motives that have prompted me to exertion, and for those with which I shall address you this evening.

What I have to say concerns the whole of us as Christians and as a people; and if you will be so kind as to give me a hearing this once, you shall receive the incense of a grateful heart.

The day is coming, my friends, and I rejoice in that day, when the secrets of all hearts shall be manifested before saints and angels, men and devils. It will be a great day of joy and rejoicing to the humble followers of Christ, but a day of terror and dismay to hypocrites and unbelievers. Of that day and hour knoweth no man, no, not even the angels in heaven, but the Father only. The dead that are in Christ shall be raised first. Blessed is he that shall have a part in the first resurrection. Ah, methinks I hear the finally impenitent crying, "Rocks and mountains! fall upon us, and hide us from the wrath of the Lamb, and from him that sitteth upon the throne!" [...]

It appears to me that there are no people under the heavens so unkind and so unfeeling towards their own, as are the descendants of fallen Africa. I have been something of a traveller in my day; and the general cry among the people is, "Our own color are our greatest opposers;" and even the whites say that we are greater enemies towards each other, than they are towards us. Shall we be a hissing and a reproach among the nations of the earth any longer! Shall they laugh us to scorn forever? We might become a highly respectable people; respectable we now consider ourselves, but we might become a highly distinguished and intelligent people. And how? In convincing the world, by our own efforts, however feeble, that nothing is wanting on our part but opportunity. Without these efforts, we shall never be a people, nor our descendants after us.

But God has said, that Ethiopia shall stretch forth her hands unto him. True, but God uses means to bring about his purposes; and unless the rising generation manifest a different temper and disposition towards each other from what we have manifested, the generation following will never be an enlightened people. We this day are considered as one of the most degraded races upon the face of the earth. It is useless for us any longer to sit with our hands folded, reproaching the whites; for that will never elevate us. All the nations of the earth have distinguished themselves, and have shown forth a noble and gallant spirit. Look at the suffering Greeks! Their proud souls revolted at the idea of serving a tyrannical nation, who were no better than themselves, and perhaps not so good. They made a mighty effort and arose; their souls were knit together in the holy bonds of love and union; they were united, and came off victorious. Look at the French in the late revolution! No traitors among them, to expose their plans to the crowned heads of Europe! "Liberty or Death!" was their cry. And the Haytians, though they have not yet been acknowledged as a nation, yet their firmness of character, and independence of spirit have been greatly admired, and high applauded. Look at the Poles, a feeble people! They rose against three hundred thousand mighty men of Russia; and though they did not gain the conquest, yet they obtained the name of gallant Poles. And even the wild Indians of the forest are more united than ourselves. Insult one of them, and you insult a thousand. They also have contended for their rights and privileges, and are held in higher repute than we are.

And why is it, my friends, that we are despised above all the nations upon the earth? Is it merely because our skins are tinged with a sable hue? No, nor will I ever believe that it is. What then is it? Oh, it is because that we and our fathers have dealt treacherously with one another, and because many of us now possess that envious and malicious disposition, that we had rather die than see each other rise an inch above a beggar. No gentle methods are used to promote love and friendship among us, but much is done to destroy it. Shall we be a hissing and a reproach among the nations of the earth any longer? Shall they laugh us to scorn forever?

Ingratitude is one of the worst passions that reigns in the human breast; it is this that cuts the tender fibres of the soul; for it is impossible for us to love those who are ungrateful towards us. "Behold," says that wise man, Solomon, counting one by one, "a man have I found in a thousand, but a woman among all those have I not found."

I have sometimes thought, that God had almost departed from among us. And why? Because Christ has said, if we say we love the Father, and hate our brother, we are liars, and the truth is not in us; and certainly if we were the true followers of Christ, I think we could not show such a disposition towards each other as we do: for God is all love.

A lady of high distinction among us, observed to me that I might never expect your homage. God forbid! I ask it not. But I beseech you to deal with gentleness and godly sincerity towards me; and there is not one of you, my dear friends, who has given me a cup of cold water in the name of the Lord, or soothed the sorrows of my wounded heart, but God will bless you, not only you, but your children for it. Cruel indeed, are those that indulge such an opinion respecting me as that.

Finally, I have exerted myself both for your temporal and eternal welfare, as far as I am able; and my soul has been so discouraged within me, that I have almost been induced to exclaim, "Would to God that my tongue hereafter might cleave to the roof of my mouth, and become silent forever!" And then I have felt that the Christian has no time to be idle, and I must be active, knowing that the night of death cometh, in which no man can work; and my mind has become raised to such an extent, that I will willingly die for the cause that I have espoused; for I cannot die in a more glorious cause than in the defence of God and his laws.

O woman, woman! Upon you I call; for upon your exertions almost entirely depends whether the rising generation shall be any thing more than we have been or not. O woman, woman! Your example is powerful, your influence great; it extends over your husbands and your children, and throughout the circle of your acquaintance. Then let me exhort you to cultivate among yourselves a spirit of

Christian love and unity, having charity one for another, without which all our goodness is as sounding brass, and a tinkling cymbal. And, O, my God, I beseech thee to grant that the nations of the earth may hiss at us no longer! O suffer them not to laugh us to scorn forever!

An Address Delivered at the African Masonic Hall (On African Rights and Liberty), Boston, February 27, 1833

African rights and liberty is a subject that ought to fire the breast of every free man of color in these United States, and excite in his bosom a lively, deep, decided and heart-felt interest. When I cast my eyes on the long list of illustrious names that are enrolled on the bright annals of fame among the whites, I turn my eyes within, and ask my thoughts, "Where are the names of our illustrious ones?" It must certainly have been for the want of energy on the part of the free people of color, that they have been long willing to bear the yoke of oppression. It must have been the want of ambition and force that has given the whites occasion to say that our natural abilities are not as good, and our capacities by nature inferior to theirs. They boldly assert that did we possess a natural independence of soul, and feel a love for liberty within our breasts, some one of our sable race, long before this, would have testified it, notwithstanding the disadvantages under which we labor. We have made ourselves appear altogether unqualified to speak in our own defence, and are therefore looked upon as objects of pity and commiseration. We have been imposed upon, insulted and derided on every side; and now, if we complain, it is considered as the height of impertinence. We have suffered ourselves to be considered as dastards, cowards, mean, faint-hearted wretches; and on this account (not because of our complexion) many despise us, and would gladly spurn us from their presence.

These things have fired my soul with a holy indignation, and compelled me thus to come forward, and endeavor to turn their attention to knowledge and improvement; for knowledge is power. I would ask, is it blindness of mind, or stupidity of soul, or the want of education that has caused our men who are 60 or 70 years of age, never to let their voices be heard, nor their hands be raised in behalf of their color? Or has it been for the fear of offending the whites? If it has, O ye fearful ones, throw off your fearfulness, and come forth in the name of the Lord, and in the strength of the God of Justice, and make yourselves useful and active members in society; for they admire a noble and patriotic spirit in others; and should they not admire it in us? If you are men, convince them that you possess the spirit of men; and as your day, so shall your strength be. Have the sons of Africa no souls? Feel they no ambitious desires? Shall the chains of ignorance forever confine them? Shall the insipid appellation of "clever negroes," or "good creatures," any longer content them? Where can we find among ourselves the man of science, or a philosopher, or an able statesman, or a counsellor at law? Show me our fearless and brave, our noble and gallant ones. Where are our lecturers in natural history, and our critics in useful knowledge? There may be a few such men among us, but they are rare. It is true our fathers bled and died in the revolutionary war, and others fought bravely under the command of Jackson, in defence of liberty. But where is the man that has distinguished himself in these modern days by acting wholly in the defence of African rights and liberty? There was one, although he sleeps, his memory lives.

I am sensible that there are many highly intelligent men of color in these United States, in the force of whose arguments, doubtless, I should discover my inferiority; but if they are blessed with wit and talent, friends and fortune, why have they not made themselves men of eminence, by striving to take all the reproach that is cast upon the people of color, and in endeavoring to alleviate the woes of their brethren in bondage? Talk, without effort, is nothing; you are abundantly capable, gentlemen, of making yourselves men of distinction; and this gross neglect, on your part, causes my blood to boil within me. Here is the grand cause which hinders the rise and progress of people of color. It is their want of laudable ambition and requisite courage.

Individuals have been distinguished according to their genius and talents, ever since the first formation of man, and will continue to be while the world stands. The different grades rise to honor and respectability as their merits may deserve. History informs us that we sprung from one of the most learned nations of the whole earth; from the seat, if not the parent, of science. Yes, poor despised Africa was once the resort of sages and legislators of other nations, was esteemed the school for learning, and the most illustrious men in Greece flocked thither for instruction. But it was our gross sins and abominations that provoked the Almighty to frown thus heavily upon us, and give our glory unto others. Sin and prodigality have caused the downfall of nations, kings and emperors; and were it not that God in wrath remembers mercy, we might indeed despair; but a promise is left us; "Ethiopia shall again stretch forth her hands unto God."

But it is of no use for us to boast that we sprung from this learned and enlightened nation, for this day a thick mist of moral gloom hangs over millions of our race. Our condition as a people has been low for hundreds of years, and it will continue to be so, unless by true piety and virtue, we strive to regain that which we have lost. White Americans, by their prudence, economy, and exertions, have sprung up and become one of the most flourishing nations in the world, distinguished for their knowledge of the arts and sciences, for their polite literature. While our minds are vacant and starve for want of knowledge, theirs are filled to overflowing. Most of our color have been taught to stand in fear of the white man from their earliest infancy, to work as soon as they could walk, and to call "master" before they could scarce lisp the name of mother. Continual fear and laborious servitude have in some degree lessened in us that natural force and energy which belong to man; or else, in defiance of opposition, our men, before this, would have nobly and boldly contended for their rights. But give the man of color an equal opportunity with the white from the cradle to manhood, and from manhood to the grave, and you would discover the dignified statesman, the man of science, and the philosopher. But there is no such opportunity for the sons of Africa, and I fear that our powerful ones are fully determined that there never shall be. Forbid, ye Powers on high, that it should any longer be said that our men possess no force. O ye sons of Africa, when will your voices be heard in our legislative halls, in defiance of your enemies, contending for equal rights and liberty? How can you, when you reflect from what you have fallen, refrain from crying mightily unto God, to turn away from us the fierceness of his anger, and remember our transgressions against us no more forever? But a god of infinite purity will not regard the prayers of those who hold religion in one hand, and prejudice, sin and pollution in the other; he will not regard the prayers of self-righteousness and hypocrisy. Is it possible, I exclaim, that for the want of knowledge we have labored for hundreds of years to support others, and been content to receive what they chose to give us in return? Cast your eyes about, look as far as you can see; all, all is owned by the lordly white, except here and there a lowly dwelling which the man of color, midst deprivations, fraud, and opposition has been scarce able to procure. Like King Solomon, who put neither nail nor hammer to the temple, yet received the praise; so also have the white Americans gained themselves a name, like the names of the great men that are in the earth, while in reality we have been their principal foundation and support. We have pursued the shadow, they have obtained the substance; we have performed the labor, they have received the profits; we have planted the vines, they have eaten the fruits of them.

I would implore our men, and especially our rising youth, to flee from the gambling board and the dance-hall; for we are poor, and have no money to throw away. I do not consider dancing as criminal in itself, but it is astonishing to me that our fine young men are so blind to their own interest and the future welfare of their children as to spend their hard earnings for this frivolous amusement; for it has been carried on among us to such an unbecoming extent that it has become absolutely disgusting. "Faithful are the wounds of a friend, but the kisses of an enemy are deceitful." Had those men among us who had an opportunity, turned their attention as assiduously to mental and moral improvement as they have to gambling and dancing, I might have remained quietly at home and they stood contending in my place. These polite accomplishments will never enroll your names on the bright annals of fame who admire the belle void of intellectual knowledge, or applaud the dandy that talks largely on politics, without striving to assist his fellow in the revolution, when the nerves and muscles of every other man forced him into the field of action. You have a right to rejoice, and to let your hearts cheer you in the days of your youth; yet remember that for all these things God will bring you into judgment. Then, O ye sons of Africa, turn your mind from these perishable objects, and contend for the cause of God and the rights of man. Form yourselves into temperance societies. There are temperate men among you; then why will you any longer neglect to strive, by your example, to suppress vice in all its abhorrent forms? You have been told repeatedly of the glorious results arising from temperance, and can you bear to see the whites arising in honor and respectability without endeavoring to grasp after that honor and respectability also?

But I forbear. Let our money, instead of being thrown away as heretofore, be appropriated for schools and seminaries of learning for our children and youth. We ought to follow the example of the whites in this respect. Nothing would raise our respectability, add to our peace and happiness, and reflect so much honor upon us, as to be ourselves the promoters of temperance, and the supporters, as far as we are able, of useful and scientific knowledge. The rays of light and knowledge have been hid from our view; we have been taught to consider ourselves as scarce superior to the brute creation; and have performed the most laborious part of American drudgery. Had we as a people received one-half the early advantages the whites have received, I would defy the government of these United States to deprive us any longer of our rights.

I am informed that the agent of the Colonization Society has recently formed an association of young men for the purpose of influencing those of us to go to Liberia who may feel disposed. The colonizationists are blind to their own interest, for should the nations of the earth make war with America, they would find their forces much weakened by our absence; or should we remain here, can our "brave soldiers" and "fellow citizens," as they were termed in time of calamity, condescend to defend the rights of whites and be again deprived of their own, or sent to Liberia in return? Or, if the colonizationists are the real friends to Africa, let them expend the money which they collect in erecting a college to educate her injured sons in this land of gospel, light, and liberty; for it would be most thankfully received on our part, and convince us of the truth of their professions, and save time, expense, and anxiety. Let them place before us noble objects worthy of pursuit, and see if we prove ourselves to be those unambitious negroes they term us. But, ah, methinks their hearts are so frozen toward us they had rather their money should be sunk in the ocean than to administer it to our relief: and I fear, if they dared, like Pharaoh, king of Egypt, they would order every male child among us to be drowned. But the most high God is still as able to subdue the lofty pride of these white Americans as He was the heart of that ancient rebel. They say, though we are looked upon as things, yet we sprang from a scientific people. Had our men the requisite force and energy they would soon convince them by their efforts, both in public and private, that they were men, or things in the shape of men. Well may the colonizationists laugh us to scorn for our negligence; well may they cry: "Shame to the sons of Africa." As the burden of the Israelites was too great for Moses to bear, so also is our burden too great for our noble advocate to bear. You must feel interested, my brethren, in what he under- takes, and hold up his hands by your good works, or in spite of himself his soul will become discouraged and his heart will die within him; for he has, as it were, the strong bulls of Bashan to contend with.

It is of no use for us to wait any longer for a generation of well educated men to arise. We have slumbered and slept too long already; the day is far spent; the night of death approaches; and you have sound sense and good judgment sufficient to begin with, if you feel disposed to make a right use of it. Let every man of color throughout the United States, who possesses the spirit and principles of a man, sign a petition to Congress to abolish slavery in the District of Columbia, and grant you the rights and privileges of common free citizens; for if you had had faith as a grain of mustard seed, long before this the mountain of prejudice might have been removed. We are all sensible that the Anti-Slavery Society has taken hold of the arm of our whole population, in order to raise them out of the mire. Now all we have to do is, by a spirit of virtuous ambition, to strive to raise ourselves; and I am happy to have it in my power thus publicly to say that the colored inhabitants of this city, in some respects, are beginning to improve. Had the free people of color in these United States nobly and freely contended for their rights, and showed a natural genius and talent, although not so brilliant as some; had they held up, encouraged and patron- ized each other, nothing could have hindered us from being a thriving and flourishing people. There has been a fault among us. The reason why our distinguished men have not made themselves more influential, is because they fear that the strong current of opposition through which they must pass would cause their downfall and prove their overthrow. And what gives rise to this opposition? Envy. And what has it amounted to? Nothing. And who are the cause of it? Our whited sepulchres, who want to be great, and don't know how; who love to be called of men "Rabbi, Rabbi;" who put on false sanctity, and humble themselves to their brethren for the sake of acquiring the highest place in the synagogue and the uppermost seat at the feast. You, dearly beloved, who are the genuine followers of our Lord Jesus Christ – the salt of the earth, and the light of the world – are not so culpable. As I told you in the very first of my writing, I will tell you again, I am but as a drop in the bucket – as one particle of the small dust of the earth. God will surely raise up those among us who will plead the cause of virtue and the pure principles of morality more eloquently than I am able to do.

It appears to me that America has become like the great city of Babylon, for she has boasted in her heart: "I sit a queen and am no widow, and shall see no sorrow!" She is, indeed, a seller of slaves and the souls of men; she has made the Africans drunk with the wine of her fornication; she has put them completely beneath her feet, and she means to keep them there; her right hand supports the reins of government and her left hand the wheel of power, and she is determined not to let go her grasp. But many powerful sons and daughters of Africa will shortly arise, who will put down vice and immorality among us, and declare by Him that sitteth upon the throne that they will have their rights; and if refused, I am afraid they will spread horror and devastation around. I believe that the oppression of injured Africa has come up before the majesty of Heaven; and when our cries shall have reached the ears of the Most High, it will be a tremendous day for the people of this land; for strong is the hand of the Lord God Almighty.

Life has almost lost its charms for me; death has lost its sting, and the grave its terrors; and at times I have a strong desire to depart and dwell with Christ, which is far better. Let me entreat my white brethren to awake and save our sons from dissipation and our daughters from ruin. Lend the hand of assistance to feeble merit; plead the cause of virtue among our sable race; so shall our curses upon you be turned into blessings; and though you should endeavor to drive us from these shores, still we will cling to you the more firmly; nor will we attempt to rise above you; we will presume to be called your equals only.

The unfriendly whites first drove the native American from his much loved home. Then they stole our fathers from their peaceful and quiet dwellings, and brought them hither, and made bond-men and bond-women of them and their little ones. They have obliged our brethren to labor; kept them in utter ignorance; nourished them in vice, and raised them in degradation; and now that we have enriched their soil, and filled their coffers, they say that we are not capable of becoming like white men, and that we can never rise to respectability in this country. They would drive us to a strange land. But before I go, the bayonet shall pierce me through. African rights and liberty is a subject that ought to fire the breast of every free man of color in these United States, and excite in his bosom a lively, deep, decided, and heartfelt interest.

MRS. STEWART'S FAREWELL ADDRESS TO HER FRIENDS IN THE CITY OF BOSTON, DELIVERED SEPTEMBER 21, 1833

"Is this vile world a friend to grace,
To help me on to God?"

Ah, no! For it is with great tribulation that any shall enter through the gates of the holy city.

My Respected Friends,
    You have heard me observe that the shortness of time, the certainty of death, and the instability of all things here, induce me to turn my thoughts from earth to heaven.

Borne down with a heavy load of sin and shame, my conscience filled with remorse; considering the throne of God forever guiltless, and my own eternal condemnation as just, I was at last brought to accept of salvation as a free gift, in and through the merits of a crucified Redeemer. Here I was brought to see,

'Tis not by works of righteousness
That our own hands have done,
But we are saved by grace alone,
Abounding through the Son.

After these convictions, in imagination I found myself sitting at the feet of Jesus, clothed in my right mind. For I had been like a ship tossed to and fro, in a storm at sea. Then was I glad when I realized the dangers I had escaped; and then I consecrated my soul and body, and all the powers of my mind to his service, and from that time henceforth; yea, even for evermore, amen. [...]

But to begin my subject: "Ye have heard that it hath been said, whoso is angry with his brother without a cause, shall be in danger of the judgment; and whoso shall say to his brother, Raca, shall be in danger of the council. But whosoever shall say, thou fool, shall be in danger of hell-fire." For several years my heart was in continual sorrow. And I believe that the Almighty beheld from his holy habitation, the affliction wherewith I was afflicted, and heard the false misrepresentations wherewith I was misrepresented, and there was none to help. Then I cried unto the Lord in my troubles. And thus for wise and holy purposes, best known to himself, he has raised me in the midst of my enemies, to vindicate my wrongs before this people; and to reprove them for sin, as I have reasoned to them of righteousness and judgment to come. "For as the heavens are higher than the earth, so are his ways above our ways, and his thoughts above our thoughts." I believe, that for wise and holy purposes, best known to himself, he hath unloosed my tongue, and put his word into my mouth, in order to confound and put all those to shame that have rose up against me. For he hath clothed my face with steel, and lined my forehead with brass. He hath put his testimony within me, and engraven his seal on my forehead. And with these weapons I have indeed set the fiends of earth and hell at defiance.

What if I am a woman; is not the God of ancient times the God of these modern days? Did he not raise up Deborah, to be a mother, and a judge in Israel? Did not queen Esther save the lives of the Jews? And Mary Magdalene first declare the resurrection of Christ from the dead? Come, said the woman of Samaria, and see a man that hath told me all things that ever I did, is not this the Christ? St. Paul declared that it was a shame for a woman to speak in public, yet our great High Priest and Advocate did not condemn the woman for a more notorious offence than this; neither will he condemn this worthless worm. The bruised reed he will not break, and the smoking flax he will not quench, till he send forth judgment unto victory. Did St. Paul but know of our wrongs and deprivations, I presume he would make no objections to our pleading in public for our rights. Again; holy women ministered unto Christ and the apostles; and women of refinement in all ages, more or less, have had a voice in moral, religious and political subjects. Again; why the Almighty hath imparted unto me the power of speaking thus, I cannot tell. "And Jesus lifted up his voice and said, I thank thee, O Father, Lord of Heaven and Earth, that thou hast hid these things from the wise and prudent, and has revealed them unto babes: even so, Father, for so it seemed good in thy sight."

But to convince you of the high opinion that was formed of the capacity and ability of woman by the ancients, I would refer you to "Sketches of the Fair Sex." Read to the 51st page, and you will find that several of the Northern nations imagined that women could look into futurity, and that they had about them, an inconceivable something, approaching to divinity. Perhaps that idea was only the effect of the sagacity common to the sex, and the advantages which their natural address gave them over rough and simple warriors. Perhaps, also, those barbarians, surprised at the influence which beauty has over force, were led to ascribe to the supernatural attraction, a charm which they could not comprehend. A belief, however, that the Deity more readily communicates himself to women, has at one time or other, prevailed in every quarter of the earth; not only among the Germans and the Britons, but all the people of Scandinavia were possessed of it. Among the Greeks, women delivered the Oracles; the respect the Romans paid to the Sibyls is well known. The Jews had their prophetesses. The prediction of the Egyptian women obtained much credit at Rome, even under the Emperors. And in the most barbarous nations, all things that have the appearance of being supernatural, the mysteries of religion, the secrets of physic, and the rites of magic, were in the possession of women.

If such women as are here described have once existed, be no longer astonished then, my brethren and friends, that God at this eventful period should raise up your own females to strive, by their example both in public and private, to assist those who are endeavoring to stop the strong current of prejudice that flows so profusely against us at present. No longer ridicule their efforts, it will be counted for sin. For God makes use of feeble means sometimes, to bring about his most exalted purposes.

In the 15th century, the general spirit of this period is worthy of observation. We might then have seen women preaching and mixing themselves in controversies. Women occupying the chairs of Philosophy and Justice; women writing in Greek, and studying in Hebrew. Nuns were poetesses, and women of quality Divines; and young girls who had studied Eloquence, would with the sweetest countenances and the most plaintive voices, pathetically exhort the Pope and the Christian Princes to declare war against the Turks. Women in those days devoted their leisure hours to contemplation and study. The religious spirit which has animated women in all ages, showed itself at this time. It has made them by turns, martyrs, apostles, warriors, and concluded in making them divines and scholars.

Why cannot a religious spirit animate us now? Why cannot we become divines and scholars? Although learning is somewhat requisite, yet recollect that those great apostles, Peter and James, were ignorant and unlearned. They were taken from the fishing boat, and made fishers of men.

In the 13th century, a young lady of Bologne devoted herself to the study of the Latin language, and of the laws. At the age of twenty-three she pronounced a funeral oration in Latin, in the great church of Bologne. And to be admitted as an orator, she had neither need of indulgence on account of her youth or of her sex. At the age of twenty-six, she took the degree of Doctor of Laws, and began publicly to expound the Institutions of Justinian. At the age of thirty, her great reputation raised her to a chair, where she taught the law to a prodigious concourse of scholars from all nations. She joined the charms and accomplishments of a woman to all the knowledge of a man. And such was the power of her eloquence, that her beauty was only admired when her tongue was silent.

What if such women as are here described should rise among our sable race? And it is not impossible. For it is not the color of the skin that makes the man or the woman, but the principle formed in the soul. Brilliant wit will shine, come from whence it will; and genius and talent will not hide the brightness of its lustre.

But, to return to my subject; the mighty work of reformation has begun among this people. The dark clouds of ignorance are dispersing. The light of science is bursting forth. Knowledge is beginning to flow, nor will its moral influence be extinguished till its refulgent rays have spread over us from East to West, and from North to South. Thus far is this mighty work begun, but not as yet accomplished. Christians must awake from their slumbers. Religion must flourish among them before the church will be built up in its purity, or immorality be suppressed.

Yet, notwithstanding your prospects are thus fair and bright, I am about to leave you, perhaps never more to return. For I find it is no use for me as an individual to try to make myself useful among my color in this city. It was contempt for my moral and religious opinions in private that drove me thus before a public. Had experience more plainly shown me that it was the nature of man to crush his fellow, I should not have thought it so hard. Wherefore, my respected friends, let us no longer talk of prejudice, till prejudice becomes extinct at home. Let us no longer talk of opposition, till we cease to oppose our own. For while these evils exist, to talk is like giving breath to the air, and labor to the wind. Though wealth is far more highly prized than humble merit, yet none of these things move me. Having God for my friend and portion, what have I to fear? Promotion cometh neither from the East or West, and as long as it is the will of God, I rejoice that I am as I am; for man in his best estate is altogether vanity. Men of eminence have mostly risen from obscurity; nor will I, although a female of a darker hue, and far more obscure than they, bend my head or hang my harp upon willows; for though poor, I will virtuous prove. And if it is the will of my heavenly Father to reduce me to penury and want, I am ready to say, amen, even so be it. "The foxes have holes, and the birds of the air have nests, but the Son of man hath not where to lay his head." [. . .]

Farewell. In a few short years from now, we shall meet in those upper regions where parting will be no more. There we shall sing and shout, and shout and sing, and make heaven's high arches ring. There we shall range in rich pastures, and partake of those living streams that never dry. O, blissful thought! Hatred and contention shall cease, and we shall join with redeemed millions in ascribing glory and honor, and riches, and power and blessing to the Lamb that was slain, and to him that sitteth upon the throne. Nor eye hath seen, nor ear heard, neither hath it entered into the heart of man to conceive of the joys that are prepared for them that love God. Thus far has my life been almost a life of complete disappointment. God has tried me as by fire. Well was I aware that if I contended boldly for his cause, I must suffer. Yet, I chose rather to suffer affliction with his people, than to enjoy the pleasures of sin for a season. And I believe that the glorious declaration was about to be made applicable to me, that was made to God's ancient covenant people by the prophet, Comfort ye, comfort ye, my people: say unto her that her warfare is accomplished, and that her iniquities are pardoned. I believe that a rich award awaits me, if not in this world, in the world to come. O, blessed reflection. The bitterness of my soul has departed from those who endeavored to discourage and hinder me in my Christian progress; and I can now forgive my enemies, bless those who have hated me, and cheerfully pray for those who have despitefully used and persecuted me.

Fare you well, farewell.

CHAPTER 10

On Liberty

JOHN STUART MILL

The grand, leading principle, towards which every argument unfolded in these pages directly converges, is the absolute and essential importance of human development in its richest diversity.

Wilhelm von Humboldt, Sphere and Duties of Government

To the beloved and deplored memory of her who was the inspirer, and in part the author, of all that is best in my writings – the friend and wife whose exalted sense of truth and right was my strongest incitement, and whose approbation was my chief reward – I dedicate this volume. Like all that I have written for many years, it belongs as much to her as to me; but the work as it stands has had, in a very insufficient degree, the inestimable advantage of her revision; some of the most important portions having been reserved for a more careful re-examination, which they are now never destined to receive. Were I but capable of interpreting to the world one half the great thoughts and noble feelings which are buried in her grave, I should be the medium of a greater benefit to it, than is ever likely to arise from anything that I can write, unprompted and unassisted by her all but unrivaled wisdom.

CHAPTER I: INTRODUCTORY

The subject of this essay is not the so-called "liberty of the will," so unfortunately opposed to the misnamed doctrine of philosophical necessity; but civil, or social liberty; the nature and limits of the power which can be legitimately exercised by society over the individual. A question seldom stated, and hardly ever discussed in general terms, but which profoundly influences the practical controversies of the age by its latent presence, and is likely soon to make itself recognized as the vital question of the future. It is so far from being new that, in a certain sense, it has divided mankind almost from the remotest ages; but in the stage of progress into which the more civilized portions of the species have now entered, it presents itself under new conditions and requires a different and more fundamental treatment. [...]

The object of this essay is to assert one very simple principle, as entitled to govern absolutely the dealings of society with the individual in the way of compulsion and

John Stuart Mill. *On Liberty.* Originally published in 1859.

control, whether the means used be physical force in the form of legal penalties or the moral coercion of public opinion. That principle is that the sole end for which mankind are warranted, individually or collectively, in interfering with the liberty of action of any of their number is self-protection. That the only purpose for which power can be rightfully exercised over any member of a civilized community, against his will, is to prevent harm to others. His own good, either physical or moral, is not a sufficient warrant. He cannot rightfully be compelled to do or forbear because it will be better for him to do so, because it will make him happier, because, in the opinions of others, to do so would be wise or even right. These are good reasons for remonstrating with him, or reasoning with him, or persuading him, or entreating him, but not for compelling him or visiting him with any evil in case he do otherwise. To justify that, the conduct from which it is desired to deter him must be calculated to produce evil to someone else. The only part of the conduct of anyone for which he is amenable to society is that which concerns others. In the part which merely concerns himself, his independence is, of right, absolute. Over himself, over his own body and mind, the individual is sovereign. [...]

It is proper to state that I forego any advantage which could be derived to my argument from the idea of abstract right as a thing independent of utility. I regard utility as the ultimate appeal on all ethical questions; but it must be utility in the largest sense, grounded on the permanent interests of man as a progressive being. Those interests, I contend, authorize the subjection of individual spontaneity to external control only in respect to those actions of each which concern the interest of other people. If anyone does an act hurtful to others, there is a *prima facie* case for punishing him by law or, where legal penalties are not safely applicable, by general disapprobation. There are also many positive acts for the benefit of others which he may rightfully be compelled to perform, such as to give evidence in a court of justice, to bear his fair share in the common defense or in any other joint work necessary to the interest of the society of which he enjoys the protection, and to perform certain acts of individual beneficence, such as saving a fellow creature's life or interposing to protect the defenseless against ill usage – things which whenever it is obviously a man's duty to do he may rightfully be made responsible to society for not doing. [...]

This, then, is the appropriate region of human liberty. It comprises, first, the inward domain of consciousness, demanding liberty of conscience in the most comprehensive sense, liberty of thought and feeling, absolute freedom of opinion and sentiment on all subjects, practical or speculative, scientific, moral, or theological. The liberty of expressing and publishing opinions may seem to fall under a different principle, since it belongs to that part of the conduct of an individual which concerns other people, but, being almost of as much importance as the liberty of thought itself and resting in great part on the same reasons, is practically inseparable from it. Secondly, the principle requires liberty of tastes and pursuits, of framing the plan of our life to suit our own character, of doing as we like, subject to such consequences as may follow, without impediment from our fellow creatures, so long as what we do does not harm them, even though they should think our conduct foolish, perverse, or wrong. Thirdly, from this liberty of each individual follows the liberty, within the same limits, of combination among individuals; freedom to unite for any purpose not involving harm to others: the persons combining being supposed to be of full age and not forced or deceived.

No society in which these liberties are not, on the whole, respected is free, whatever may be its form of government; and none is completely free in which they do not exist absolute and unqualified. The only freedom which deserves the name is that of pursuing our own good in our own way, so long as we do not attempt to deprive others of theirs or impede their efforts to obtain it. Each is the proper guardian of his own health, whether bodily *or* mental and spiritual. Mankind are greater gainers by suffering each other to live as seems good to themselves than by compelling each to live as seems good to the rest. [...]

Chapter II: Of the Liberty of Thought and Discussion

The time, it is to be hoped, is gone by when any defense would be necessary of the "liberty of the press" as one of the securities against corrupt or tyrannical government. No argument, we may suppose, can now be needed against permitting a legislature or an executive, not identified in interest with the people, to prescribe opinions to them and determine what doctrines or what arguments they shall be allowed to hear. [...] But the peculiar evil of silencing the expression of an opinion is that it is robbing the human race, posterity as well as the existing generation – those who dissent from the opinion, still more than those who hold it. If the opinion is right, they are deprived of the opportunity of exchanging error for truth; if wrong, they lose, what is almost as great a benefit, the clearer perception and livelier impression of truth produced by its collision with error.

It is necessary to consider separately these two hypotheses, each of which has a distinct branch of the argument corresponding to it. We can never be sure that the opinion we are endeavoring to stifle is a false opinion; and if we were sure, stifling it would be an evil still.

First, the opinion which it is attempted to suppress by authority may possibly be true. Those who desire to suppress it, of course, deny its truth; but they are not infallible. They have no authority to decide the question for all mankind and exclude every other person from the means of judging. To refuse a hearing to an opinion because they are sure that it is false is to assume that *their* certainty is the same thing as *absolute* certainty. All silencing of discussion is an assumption of infallibility. Its condemnation may be allowed to rest on this common argument, not the worse for being common. [...]

The truth of an opinion is part of its utility. If we would know whether or not it is desirable that a proposition should be believed, is it possible to exclude the consideration of whether or not it is true? In the opinion, not of bad men, but of the best men, no belief which is contrary to truth can be really useful; and can you prevent such men from urging that plea when they are charged with culpability for denying some doctrine which they are told is useful, but which they believe to be false? Those who are on the side of received opinions never fail to take all possible advantage of this plea; you do not find *them* handling the question of utility as if it could be completely abstracted from that of truth; on the contrary, it is, above all, because their doctrine is "the truth" that the knowledge or the belief of it is held to be so indispensable. There can be no fair discussion of the question of usefulness when an argument so vital may be employed on one side, but not on the other. And in point of fact, when law or public feeling do not permit the truth of an opinion to be disputed, they are just as little tolerant of a denial of its usefulness. The utmost they allow is an extenuation of its absolute necessity, or of the positive guilt of rejecting it.

In order more fully to illustrate the mischief of denying a hearing to opinions because we, in our own judgment, have condemned them, it will be desirable to fix down the discussion to a concrete case; and I choose, by preference, the cases which are least favorable to me – in which the argument against freedom of opinion, both on the score of truth and on that of utility, is considered the strongest. Let the opinions impugned be the belief in a God and in a future state, or any of the commonly received doctrines of morality. To fight the battle on such ground gives a great advantage to an unfair antagonist, since he will be sure to say (and many who have no desire to be unfair will say it internally), Are these the doctrines which you do not deem sufficiently certain to be taken under the protection of law? Is the belief in a God one of the opinions to feel sure of which you hold to be assuming infallibility? But I must be permitted to observe that it is not the feeling sure of a doctrine (be it what it may) which I call an assumption of infallibility. It is the undertaking to decide that question *for others*, without allowing them to hear what can be said on the contrary side. And I denounce and reprobate this pretension not the less if put forth on the side of my most solemn convictions. However positive anyone's persuasion may be, not only of the falsity but of the pernicious consequences – not only of the pernicious consequences, but (to adopt expressions which I altogether condemn) the immorality and impiety of an opinion – yet if, in pursuance of that private judgment, though backed by the public judgment of his country or his contemporaries, he prevents the opinion from being heard in its defense, he assumes infallibility. And so far from the assumption being less objectionable or less dangerous because the opinion is called immoral or impious, this is the case of all others in which it is most fatal. These are exactly the occasions on which the men of one generation commit those dreadful mistakes which excite the astonishment and horror of posterity. It is among such that we find the instances memorable in history, when the arm of the law has been employed to root out the best men and the noblest doctrines; with deplorable success as to the men, though some of the doctrines have survived to be (as if in mockery) invoked in defense of similar conduct toward those who dissent from *them*, or from their received interpretation.

Mankind can hardly be too often reminded that there was once a man named Socrates, between whom and the legal authorities and public opinion of his time there took place a memorable collision. Born in an age and country abounding in individual greatness, this man has been handed down to us by those who best knew both him and the age as the most virtuous man in it; while *we* know him as the head and prototype of all subsequent teachers of virtue, the source equally of the lofty inspiration of Plato and the judicious utilitarianism of Aristotle, "*i maestri di color che sanno*," the two headsprings of ethical as of all other philosophy. This acknowledged master of all the eminent thinkers who have since lived – whose fame, still growing after more than two thousand years, all but outweighs the whole remainder of the names which make his native city illustrious – was put to death by his countrymen, after a judicial conviction, for impiety and immorality. Impiety, in denying the gods recognized by the State; indeed, his accuser asserted (see the *Apologia*) that he believed in no gods at all. Immorality, in being, by his doctrines and instructions, a "corruptor of youth." Of these charges the tribunal, there is every ground for believing, honestly found him guilty, and condemned the man who probably of all then born had deserved best of mankind to be put to death as a criminal.

To pass from this to the only other instance of judicial iniquity, the mention of which, after the condemnation of Socrates, would not be an anti-climax: the event which took place on Calvary rather more than eighteen hundred years ago. The man who left on the memory of those who witnessed his life and conversation such an impression of his moral grandeur that eighteen subsequent centuries have done homage to him as the Almighty in person, was ignominiously put to death, as what? As a blasphemer. Men did not merely mistake their benefactor, they mistook him for the exact contrary of what he was and treated him as that prodigy of impiety which they themselves are now held to be for their treatment of him. [...]

It is a piece of idle sentimentality that truth, merely as truth, has any inherent power denied to error of prevailing against the dungeon and the stake. Men are not more zealous for truth than they often are for error, and a sufficient application of legal or even of social penalties will generally succeed in stopping the propagation of either. The real advantage which truth has consists in this, that when an opinion is true, it may be extinguished once, twice, or many times, but in the course of ages there will generally be found persons to rediscover it, until some one of its reappearances falls on a time when from favorable circumstances it escapes persecution until it has made such head as to withstand all subsequent attempts to suppress it. [...]

Let us now pass to the second division of the argument, and dismissing the supposition that any of the received opinions may be false, let us assume them to be true and examine into the worth of the manner in which they are likely to be held when their truth is not freely and openly canvassed. However unwillingly a person who has a strong opinion may admit the possibility that his opinion may be false, he ought to be moved by the consideration that, however true it may be, if it is not fully, frequently, and fearlessly discussed, it will be held as a dead dogma, not a living truth.

There is a class of persons (happily not quite so numerous as formerly) who think it enough if a person assents undoubtingly to what they think true, though he has no knowledge whatever of the grounds of the opinion and could not make a tenable defense of it against the most superficial objections. Such persons, if they can once get their creed taught from authority, naturally think that no good, and some harm, comes of its being allowed to be questioned. Where their influence prevails, they make it nearly impossible for the received opinion to be rejected wisely and considerately, though it may still be rejected rashly and ignorantly; for to shut out discussion entirely is seldom possible, and when it once gets in, beliefs not grounded on conviction are apt to give way before the slightest semblance of an argument. Waiving, however, this possibility – assuming that the true opinion abides in the mind, but abides as a prejudice, a belief independent of, and proof against, argument – this is not the way in which truth ought to be held by a rational being. This is not knowing the truth. Truth, thus held, is but one superstition the more, accidentally clinging to the words which enunciate a truth. [...]

In politics, again, it is almost a commonplace that a party of order or stability and a party of progress or reform are both necessary elements of a healthy state of political life, until the one or the other shall have so enlarged its mental grasp as to be a party equally of order and of progress, knowing and distinguishing what is fit to be preserved from what ought to be swept away. Each of these modes of thinking derives its utility from the deficiencies of the other; but it is in a great measure the opposition of the other that keeps each within the limits of reason and sanity. Unless opinions favorable to democracy and to aristocracy, to property and to equality, to co-operation and to competition, to luxury and to abstinence, to sociality and individuality, to liberty and discipline, and all the other standing antagonisms of practical life, are expressed with equal freedom and enforced and defended with equal talent and energy, there is no chance of both elements obtaining their due; one scale is sure to go up, and the other down. Truth, in the great practical concerns of life, is so much a question of the reconciling and combining of opposites that very few have minds sufficiently capacious and impartial to make the adjustment with an approach to correctness, and it has to be made by the rough process of a struggle between combatants fighting under hostile banners. [...]

We have now recognized the necessity to the mental well-being of mankind (on which all their other well-being depends) of freedom of opinion, and freedom of the expression of opinion, on four distinct grounds, which we will now briefly recapitulate:

First, if any opinion is compelled to silence, that opinion may, for aught we can certainly know, be true. To deny this is to assume our own infallibility.

Secondly, though the silenced opinion be an error, it may, and very commonly does, contain a portion of truth; and since the general or prevailing opinion on any subject is rarely or never the whole truth, it is only by the collision of adverse opinions that the remainder of the truth has any chance of being supplied.

Thirdly, even if the received opinion be not only true, but the whole truth; unless it is suffered to be, and actually is, vigorously and earnestly contested, it will, by most of those who receive it, be held in the manner of a prejudice, with little comprehension or feeling of its rational grounds. And not only this, but, fourthly, the meaning of the doctrine itself will be in danger of being lost or enfeebled, and deprived of its vital effect on the character and conduct: the dogma becoming a mere formal profession, inefficacious for good, but cumbering the ground and preventing the growth of any real and heart-felt conviction from reason or personal experience. [...]

CHAPTER III: OF INDIVIDUALITY, AS ONE OF THE ELEMENTS OF WELL-BEING

Such being the reasons which make it imperative that human beings should be free to form opinions and to express their opinions without reserve; and such the baneful consequences to the intellectual, and through that to the moral nature of man, unless this liberty is either conceded or asserted in spite of prohibition; let us next examine whether the same reasons do not require that men should be free to act upon their opinions – to carry these out in their lives without hindrance, either physical or moral, from their fellow men, so long as it is at their own risk and peril. This last proviso is of course indispensable. No one pretends that actions should be as free as opinions. On the contrary, even opinions lose their immunity when the circumstances in which they are expressed are such as to constitute their expression a positive instigation to some mischievous act. An opinion that corn dealers are starvers of the poor, or that private property is robbery, ought to be unmolested when simply circulated through the press, but may justly incur punishment when delivered orally to an excited mob assembled before the house of a corn dealer, or when handed about among the same mob in the form of a placard. Acts, of whatever kind, which without justifiable cause do harm to others may be, and in the more important cases absolutely require to be, controlled by the unfavorable sentiments, and, when needful, by the active interference of mankind. The liberty of the individual must be thus far limited; he must not make himself a nuisance to other people. But if he refrains from molesting others in what concerns them, and merely acts according to his own inclination and judgment in things which concern himself, the same reasons which show that opinion should be free prove also that he should be allowed, without molestation, to carry his opinions into practice at his own cost. That mankind are not infallible; that their truths, for the most part, are only half-truths; that unity of opinion, unless resulting from the fullest and freest comparison of opposite opinions, is not desirable, and diversity not an evil, but a good, until mankind are much more capable than at present of recognizing all sides of the truth, are principles applicable to men's modes of action not less than to their opinions. As it is useful that while mankind are imperfect there should be different opinions, so is it that there should be different experiments of living; that free scope should be given to varieties of character, short of injury to others; and that the worth of different modes of life should be proved practically, when anyone thinks fit to try them. It is desirable, in short, that in things which do not primarily concern others individuality should assert itself. Where not the person's own character but the traditions or customs of other people are the rule of conduct, there is wanting one of the principal ingredients of human happiness, and quite the chief ingredient of individual and social progress. [...]

The despotism of custom is everywhere the standing hindrance to human advancement, being in unceasing antagonism to that disposition to aim at something better than customary, which is called, according to circumstances, the spirit of liberty, or that of progress or improvement. The spirit of improvement is not always a spirit of liberty, for it may aim at forcing improvements on an unwilling people; and the spirit of liberty, in so far as it resists such attempts, may ally itself locally and temporarily with the opponents of improvement; but the only unfailing and permanent source of improvement is liberty, since by it there are as many possible independent centers of improvement as there are individuals. The progressive principle, however, in either shape, whether as the love of liberty or of improvement, is antagonistic to the sway of custom, involving at least emancipation from that yoke; and the contest between the two constitutes the chief interest of the history of mankind. [...]

The circumstances which surround different classes and individuals, and shape their characters, are daily becoming more assimilated. Formerly, different ranks, different neighborhoods, different trades and professions lived in what might be called different worlds; at present, to a great degree in the same. Comparatively speaking, they now read the same things, listen to the same things, see the same things, go to the same places, have their hopes and fears directed to the same objects, have the same rights and liberties, and the same means of asserting them. Great as are the differences of position which remain, they are nothing to those which have ceased. And the assimilation is still proceeding. All the political changes of the age promote it, since they all tend to raise the low and to lower the high. Every extension of education promotes it, because education brings people under common influences and gives them access to the general stock of facts and sentiments. Improvements in the means of communication promote it, by bringing the inhabitants of distant places into personal contact, and keeping up a rapid flow of changes of residence between one place and another. The increase of commerce and manufactures promotes it, by diffusing more widely the advantages of easy circumstances and opening all objects of ambition, even the highest, to general competition, whereby the desire of rising becomes no longer the character of a particular class, but of all classes. A more powerful agency than even all these, in bringing about a general similarity among mankind, is the complete establishment, in this and other free countries, of the ascendancy of public opinion in the State. As the various social eminences which enabled persons entrenched on them to disregard the opinion of the multitude gradually become leveled; as the very idea of resisting the will of the public, when it is positively known that they have a will, disappears more and more from the minds of practical politicians, there ceases to be any social support for nonconformity – any substantive power in society which, itself opposed to the ascendancy of numbers, is interested in taking under its protection opinions and tendencies at variance with those of the public.

The combination of all these causes forms so great a mass of influences hostile to individuality that it is not easy to see how it can stand its ground. It will do so with increasing difficulty unless the intelligent part of the public can be made to feel its value – to see that it is good there should be differences, even though not for the better, even though, as it may appear to them, some should be for the worse. If the claims of individuality are ever to be asserted, the time is now while much is still wanting to complete the enforced assimilation. It is only in the earlier stages that any stand can be successfully made against the encroachment. The demand that all other people shall resemble ourselves grows by what it feeds on. If resistance waits till life is reduced *nearly* to one uniform type, all deviations from that type will come to be considered impious, immoral, even monstrous and contrary to nature. Mankind speedily become unable to conceive diversity when they have been for some time unaccustomed to see it.

CHAPTER IV: OF THE LIMITS TO THE AUTHORITY OF SOCIETY OVER THE INDIVIDUAL

What, then, is the rightful limit to the sovereignty of the individual over himself? Where does the authority of society begin? How much of human life should be assigned to individuality, and how much to society?

Each will receive its proper share if each has that which more particularly concerns it. To individuality should belong the part of life in which it is chiefly the individual that is interested; to society, the part which chiefly interests society.

Though society is not founded on a contract, and though no good purpose is answered by inventing a contract in order to deduce social obligations from it, everyone who receives the protection of society owes a return for the benefit, and the fact of living in society renders it indispensable that each should be bound to observe a certain line of conduct toward the rest. This conduct consists, first, in not injuring the interests of one another, or rather certain interests which, either by express legal provision or by tacit understanding, ought to be considered as rights; and secondly, in each person's bearing his share (to be fixed on some equitable principle) of the labors and sacrifices incurred for defending the society or its members from injury and molestation. These conditions society is justified in enforcing at all costs to those who endeavor to withhold fulfillment. Nor is this all that society may do. The acts of an individual may be hurtful to others or wanting in due consideration for their welfare, without going to the length of violating any of their constituted rights. The offender may then be justly punished by opinion, though not by law. As soon as any part of a person's conduct affects prejudicially the interests of others, society has jurisdiction over it, and the question whether the general welfare will or will not be promoted by interfering with it becomes open to discussion. But there is no room for entertaining any such question when a person's conduct affects the interests of no persons besides himself, or needs not affect them unless they like (all the persons concerned being of full age and the ordinary amount of understanding). In all such cases, there should be perfect freedom, legal and social, to do the action and stand the consequences. [...]

The distinction between the loss of consideration which a person may rightly incur by defect of prudence or of personal dignity, and the reprobation which is due to him for an offense against the rights of others, is not a merely nominal distinction. It makes a vast difference both in our feelings and in our conduct toward him whether he displeases us in things in which we think we have a right to control him or in things in which we know that we have not. If he displeases us, we may express our distaste, and we may stand aloof from a person as well as from a thing that displeases us; but we shall not therefore feel called on to make his life uncomfortable. We shall reflect that he already bears, or will bear, the whole penalty of his error; if he spoils his life by mismanagement, we shall not, for that reason, desire to spoil it still further; instead of wishing to punish him, we shall rather endeavor to alleviate his punishment by showing him how he may avoid or cure the evils his conduct tends to bring upon him. He may be to us an object of pity, perhaps of dislike, but not of anger or resentment; we shall not treat him like an enemy of society; the worst we shall think ourselves justified in doing is leaving him to himself, if we do not interfere benevolently by showing interest or concern for him. It is far otherwise if he has infringed the rules necessary for the protection of his fellow creatures, individually or collectively. The evil consequences of his acts do not then fall on himself, but on others; and society, as the protector of all its members, must retaliate on him, must inflict pain on him for the express purpose of punishment, and must take care that it be sufficiently severe. In the one case, he is an offender at our bar, and we are called on not only to sit in judgment on him, but, in one shape or another, to execute our own sentence; in the other case, it is not our part to inflict any suffering on him, except what may incidentally follow from our using the same liberty in the regulation of our own affairs which we allow to him in his. [...]

Whenever, in short, there is a definite damage, or a definite risk of damage, either to an individual or to the public, the case is taken out of the province of liberty and placed in that of morality or law.

But with regard to the merely contingent or, as it may be called, constructive injury which a person causes to society by conduct which neither violates any specific duty to the public, nor occasions perceptible hurt to any assignable individual except himself, the inconvenience is one which society can afford to bear, for the sake of the greater good of human freedom. If grown persons are to be punished for not taking proper care of themselves, I would rather it were for their own sake than under pretense of preventing them from impairing their capacity of rendering to society benefits which society does not pretend it has a right to exact. But I cannot consent to argue the point as if society had no means of bringing its weaker members up to its ordinary standard of rational conduct, except waiting till they do something irrational, and then punishing them, legally or morally, for it. Society has had absolute power over them during all the early portion of their existence; it has had the whole period of childhood and nonage in which to try whether it could make them capable of rational conduct in life. The existing generation is master both of the training and the entire circumstances of the generation to come; it cannot indeed make them perfectly wise and good, because it is itself so lamentably deficient in goodness and wisdom; and its best efforts are not always, in individual cases, its most successful ones; but it is perfectly well able to make the rising generation, as a whole, as good as, and a little better than, itself. If society lets any considerable number of its members grow up mere children, incapable of being acted on by rational consideration of distant motives, society has itself to blame for the consequences. Armed not only with all the powers of education, but with the ascendancy which the authority of a received opinion always exercises over the minds who are least fitted to judge for themselves, and aided by the *natural* penalties which cannot be prevented from falling on those who incur the distaste or the contempt of those who know them – let not society pretend that it needs, besides all this, the power to issue commands and enforce obedience in the personal concerns of individuals in which, on all principles of justice and policy, the decision ought to rest with those who are to abide the consequences. Nor is there anything which tends more to discredit and frustrate the better means of influencing conduct than a resort to the worse. If there be among those whom it is attempted to coerce into prudence or temperance any of the material of which vigorous and independent characters are made, they will infallibly rebel against the yoke. No such person will ever feel that others have a right to control him in his concerns, such as they have to prevent him from injuring them in theirs; and it easily comes to be considered a mark of spirit and courage to fly in the face of such usurped authority and do with ostentation the exact opposite of what it enjoins, as in the fashion of grossness which succeeded, in the time of Charles II, to the fanatical moral intolerance of the Puritans. With respect to what is said of the necessity of protecting society from the bad example set to others by the vicious or the self-indulgent, it is true that bad example may have a pernicious effect, especially the example of doing wrong to others with impunity to the wrongdoer. But we are now speaking of conduct which, while it does no wrong to others, is supposed to do great harm to the agent himself; and I do not see how those who believe this can think otherwise than that the example, on the whole, must be more salutary than hurtful, since, if it displays the misconduct, it displays also the painful or degrading consequences which, if the conduct is justly censured, must be supposed to be in all or most cases attendant on it.

But the strongest of all the arguments against the interference of the public with purely personal conduct is that, when it does interfere, the odds are that it interferes wrongly and in the wrong place. On questions of social morality, of duty to others, the opinion of the public, that is, of an overruling majority, though often wrong, is likely to be still oftener right, because on such questions they are only required to judge of their own interests, of the manner in which some mode of conduct, if allowed to be practiced, would affect themselves. But the opinion of a similar majority, imposed as a law on the minority, on questions of self-regarding conduct is quite as likely to be wrong as right, for in these cases public opinion means, at the best, some people's opinion of what is good or bad for other people, while very often it does not even mean that – the public, with the most perfect indifference, passing over the pleasure or convenience of those whose conduct they censure and considering only their own preference. [. . .]

There is confessedly a strong tendency in the modern world toward a democratic constitution of society, accompanied or not by popular political institutions. It is affirmed that in the country where this tendency is most completely realized – where both society and the government are most democratic: the United States – the feeling of the majority, to whom any appearance of a more showy or costly style of living than they can hope to rival is disagreeable, operates as a tolerably effectual sumptuary law, and that in many parts of the Union it is really difficult for a person possessing a very large income to find any mode of spending it which will not incur popular disapprobation. Though such statements as these are doubtless much exaggerated as a representation of existing facts, the state of things they describe is not only a conceivable and possible, but a probable result of democratic feeling combined with the notion that the public has a right to a veto on the manner in which individuals shall spend their incomes. We have only further to suppose a considerable diffusion of Socialist opinions, and it may become infamous in the eyes of the majority to possess more property than some very small amount, or any income not earned by manual labor. Opinions similar in principle to these already prevail widely among the artisan class and weigh oppressively on those who are amenable to the opinion chiefly of that class, namely, its own members. It is known that the bad workmen who form the majority of the operatives in many branches of industry are decidedly of opinion that bad workmen ought to receive the same wages as good, and that no one ought to be allowed, through piece-work or otherwise, to earn by superior skill or industry more than others can without it. And they employ a moral police, which occasionally becomes a physical one, to deter skillful workmen from receiving, and employers from giving, a larger remuneration for a more useful service. If the public have any jurisdiction over private concerns, I cannot see that these people are in fault, or that any individual's particular public can be blamed for asserting the same authority over his individual conduct which the general public asserts over people in general.

But, without dwelling upon suppositious cases, there are, in our own day, gross usurpations upon the liberty of private life actually practiced, and still greater ones threatened with some expectation of success, and opinions propounded which assert an unlimited right in the public not only to prohibit by law everything which it thinks wrong, but, in order to get at what it thinks wrong, to prohibit any number of things which it admits to be innocent. [. . .]

If civilization has got the better of barbarism when barbarism had the world to itself, it is too much to profess to be afraid lest barbarism, after having been fairly got under, should revive and conquer civilization. A civilization that can thus succumb to its vanquished enemy must first have become so degenerate that neither its appointed priests and teachers, nor anybody else, has the capacity, or will take the trouble, to stand up for it. If this be so, the sooner such a civilization receives notice to quit, the better. It can only go on from bad to worse until destroyed and regenerated (like the Western Empire) by energetic barbarians.

PART VI

Abolitionism, Socialism, and Feminism:

THE RADICAL POLITICAL THEORIES OF FREDERICK DOUGLASS, KARL MARX, AND MATILDA JOSLYN GAGE

A large portion of the slaves *know* that they have a right to their liberty. – It is often talked about and read of, for some of us know how to read, although our knowledge is all gained in secret.[1]

Frederick Douglass, Address, 1841

In the early part of the nineteenth century, many plantation owners of the south and new industrialists of the northern United States prospered. The new nation offered possibilities for pioneers, fur traders, adventurers, and opportunists of all sorts, but it was a less felicitous place for slaves laboring under the oppression of the plantation system, for factory workers, mainly women and children, many of whom worked for credit at company stores, and for Native Americans who were forced off their already reduced land by the Indian Removal Acts. American expansion in the case of each new state raised issues of states' rights and human rights – would they allow slave-holding or would they be free? Trade, tariffs, and other economic concerns reinforced differences between free states and slave and, with the contrasts between prosperity and hardship, tensions increased.

In 1831, Nat Turner's rebellion brought the bloodiest and most important slave revolt in US history. Meanwhile, the abolitionist movement was gaining strength. Fueling the movement in New England were two important anti-slavery newspapers: the revolutionary abolitionist David Walker served as Boston agent for the African American paper *Freedom's Journal*, and the white abolitionist leader, William Lloyd Garrison, published his weekly, *The Liberator*.[2]

Born Frederick Augustus Washington Bailey in Tuckahoe, Maryland, Frederick Douglass (1917–95) was the most influential Black leader of the abolition movement. He was raised by his grandparents, Isaac and Betsey Bailey, until he was almost eight years old. He was then sent to labor on the plantation of Colonel Edward Lloyd, which was managed by Captain Aaron Anthony, who may have been his father. There, hiding in a closet, he witnessed for the first time the brutality of slavery:

I have often been awakened at the dawn of the day by the most heart-rending shrieks of
an own aunt of mine, whom he used to tie up to a joist, and whip upon her naked back
till she was literally covered with blood.[3]

Douglass perceived the injustice, not just of the physical violence, but of the sharp
differences in lifestyle between ante-bellum plantation opulence in food, clothing,
and service for whites and the meager dress and near-starvation rations for slaves.
When he was sent to the family of Hugh Auld in Baltimore, he witnessed first-hand
the dehumanizing effects of slavery on white people. Sophia Auld, perhaps unaccustomed to the norms of slavery, at first treated Douglass with dignity and began
teaching him to read. Once her husband discovered this, he demanded an end to it,
but it was too late, for Douglass had immediately divined that this mysterious skill
was the key to many kinds of freedom, and although his tutor turned against him, he
devised numerous ingenious ways to become literate.

Douglass's first attempt at escape was a failure, but his second was successful,
when he disguised himself as a sailor and escaped by rail to New York City, and then
to New Bedford, Massachusetts. Delivering an anti-slavery speech in Nantucket, he
impressed William Lloyd Garrison, the foremost abolitionist of the day, and soon
became a charismatic orator and political thinker, traveling the lecture circuit for
the Massachusetts Anti-Slavery Society. John W. Blassingame, editor of *The Frederick Douglass Papers*, describes how:

> During his first year on the lecture circuit, Douglass discussed the pro-slavery character
> of American churches, freedom of speech, abolitionists and third parties, nonresistance,
> northern economic support of slavery, the right of petition, northern racial prejudice,
> black suffrage, the imprisonment of fugitive slaves, segregation in northern churches,
> and disunion.[4]

In 1845, Garrison published Douglass' moving personal account of slavery and
escape. Like *David Walker's Appeal*, the *Narrative of the Life of Frederick Douglass*
carried revolutionary implications. In it, Douglass describes an encounter with a
slave-breaker, Covey, whose cruelty drove Douglass to do the unimaginable and
rebel. He conveys at length a physical battle between himself and the slave-breaker
which spanned several hours, and which ended as a sort of draw. But the result was
that Covey never again whipped Douglass:

> This battle with Mr. Covey was the turning-point in my career as a slave. It rekindled
> the few expiring embers of freedom, and revived within me a sense of my own
> manhood.[5]

The publication of his narrative along with other works sent a clear message to those
who could read, and also to those who couldn't, but who knew how to listen to a
story. Nor was the message lost upon slave-owners. Fear of being captured and
returned as a fugitive slave sent Douglass on a brilliant lecture tour to Great Britain
and Ireland, a journey that gave him a broadened understanding of world issues and
also gave him the experience of escaping anti-Black racism for the first time. Here, he
was able to raise the funds to purchase his legal manumission back home – to buy his
freedom. Upon returning to the States, Douglass went on to deliver thousands of
lectures and write hundreds more letters and essays. He broke with Garrison and the
disunionists in the 1850s, traveling west to Rochester to settle and inaugurate his

own newspaper, the *North Star*, later to become *Frederick Douglass' Paper* and then *Douglass' Monthly*.

FREDERICK DOUGLASS AS A HUMANIST

Douglass had intellectual differences both with Garrison and with Black leader Martin Delany. A separatist and advocate of colonization, Delany published his *The Condition, Elevation, Emigration, and Destiny of the Colored People of the United States, Politically Considered* in 1852.[6] He crafted a sophisticated analysis of the European view of social and slave classes. According to political philosopher Bernard Boxill, "Delany... denounced moral suasion as a way for blacks to win their liberty."[7] Assuming that the European enslavement of Africans rested on Hobbesian principles of self-interest and not on moral sensibility, Delany argued that a lack of sympathy by whites for Blacks was important for the maintenance of slavery, and physical difference fed the lack of sympathy. Boxill contrasts Delany's views about sympathy to Scottish philosopher David Hume's. Hume posits contiguity and familiarity as conditions for sympathy, but Boxill holds that Delany "saw every day that white sympathy for black misfortune was faint and weak, though the races were, by that time, no longer strangers to, nor remote from, one another."[8] Delany's views led him to believe that whites and Blacks would never successfully live in the same nation, so he counseled for separatism, and African American emigration to Africa.

In contrast, Douglass was an assimilationist: he believed that people of different social, cultural, and ethnic backgrounds could acquire common attitudes and modes of life. He adopted the viewpoint that skin color was not a significant human difference and that possessing reason and a soul were the key elements of humanity. The proper source of appeal was not self-interest but moral suasion. Based upon Lockean philosophical views, he argues regarding African Americans:

> Adopt any mode of reasoning you please with respect to him, he is a man, possessing an immortal soul, illuminated by intellect, capable of heavenly aspirations, and in all things pertaining to manhood, he is at once self-evidently a man, and therefore entitled to all the rights and privileges which belong to human nature.[9]

Moral suasion was also his lifelong strategy. When turned away from public places, restaurants, or train cars, he would confront the gate-keeping conductor or manager, asking the patrons directly if anyone minded if he joined them. Generally they did not. Moral suasion worked for Douglass, and by extension, it worked as an argument for integration and assimilation generally. Boxill points out that this difference between Douglass and Delany is not just one of strategy but of profoundly different views about human nature.[10]

DOUGLASS' THEORIES OF RACE

[Douglass'] valiant attempt to use a humanist approach to undermine a racialist society reflected his perception of the international quality of both his people's struggle and his leadership. Paradoxically, he functioned as a race leader to help realize a nation where race was insignificant.[11]

Legal theorist Patricia J. Williams underscores the importance of subject position, especially for African Americans, and this is certainly true for Frederick Douglass as a humanist.[12] As Douglass' political thought developed, he became increasingly aware of the complexities of racial difference in society. As he came to work more with Blacks, he understood that uplift and self-reliance might transitionally require separate cultural and educational institutions to promote racial solidarity and social improvement.

In 1881, two decades before the African American intellectual W. E. B. DuBois predicted that the problem of the twentieth century would be the problem of the color line, Douglass pioneered this observation (one taken up by Anna Julia Cooper fifteen years later). In an essay in the *North American Review* he carefully marshals a series of arguments to refute white racialism. He describes the social causes of Black degradation and exposes the faulty reasoning that attributes a natural cause to the admittedly inferior position of Blacks in nineteenth-century society. He recounts the factors of physical abuse and degradation, deprivation of education, the economic conditions, imposed servility, and a host of other contributing circumstances.

> The office of color in the color line is a very plain and subordinate one. It simply advertises the objects of oppression, insult, and persecution. It is not the maddening liquor, but the black letters on the sign telling the world where it may be had.[13]

Thus, as David Hume might say, there is not causation between color and degradation, merely constant conjunction due to social conditions.

Douglass went on to become close to Abraham Lincoln, to be named assistant secretary of the Santo Domingo commission, Marshal and then Recorder of Deeds for the District of Columbia, and the American minister resident and consul-general in the Republic of Haiti. In addition to his theories of humanism, racism, assimilation, and integrationism he developed and articulated views on labor and economics, anti-colonialism, and feminism.

> **Women formed no part of the constituent elements of the moral world. In summoning the friends of the slave from all parts of the two hemispheres... John Bull never dreamed that women, too would answer his call.[14]**
> *Elizabeth Cady Stanton,* A History of Woman Suffrage

Along with abolitionism, various other reform movements captured the imaginations of those who wished to work for progress. An organized effort for "moral reform" was designed to close the brothels in the wake of a world-wide epidemic of syphilis.[15] The Christian-based temperance movement of the early 1840s advocated moderation, and later abstinence, in the use of alcoholic beverages, and gave expression to women's activism against abuses by drunken and violent husbands, fathers, and brothers.[16] Nineteenth-century women's activism was forged in the movements for social reform and spanned the political spectrum.

A World Anti-Slavery Convention, convened in 1840, gathered together western activists against slavery and was pivotal in sowing the seeds for the US and European women's rights movements. As American delegates, including a number of women, set sail for London, the English conveners moved to block the women's participation. When the assembly convened, a floor fight ensued about whether or not to seat the women. Following heated argument, the decision was made not to allow the women to be seated in the main section of the conference hall. They were not to vote or participate in any meaningful way. They could, however, sit behind a curtain in the balcony.[17] The indignity was only marginally mitigated by the fact that the foremost US abolitionist, William Lloyd Garrison, arriving too late for the credentials challenge, opted to sit in the gallery with the women, as protest against the alarming proceedings. This occurrence laid bare that a powerful faction in the anti-slavery movement, in a sentiment expressed by Susan B. Anthony, had never intended to free all the slaves – just the men – and had no intention of working for equality for women. This realization provided a galvanizing moment for many feminists.

At the London conference, where her husband, Henry, was a delegate, Elizabeth Cady Stanton met Lucretia Mott, a Quaker abolitionist, seasoned speaker, and an inspirational leader of the abolition movement. On a trip to the British Museum, Mott and Stanton bypassed the tour, and instead sat and talked about theology, Quakerism, and the social theories of Mary Wollstonecraft. Stanton, whose husband belonged to one of the societies that excluded women from the convention (though he claimed personally to support their cause), was much affected by the older woman's knowledge, poise, and ability to speak in public. Together they hatched a plot for a Women's Rights Convention in the United States.

At the same time, throughout Europe, feminists were creating a literature arguing for women's rights. In Germany, Louise Otto used international examples to argue for socialist feminism and Luise Dittmar launched a feminist journal. In Ireland, Anna Wheeler forged ties with French Fourierists and Saint-Simonians, who united socialist and feminist demands: "By the outbreak of the 1848 revolutions, scores of feminists in Europe and the United States read the same literature, shared a common discourse, and set of expectations, and had woven close personal connections to each other."[18] English feminist Anne Knight was similarly affected by the rejection of female delegates to the Anti-Slavery Convention, and in response she began to lecture, write, and agitate for radical social change. She moved to Paris and "worked closely with the radical French feminists who produced *La Voix des Femmes*: Eugenie Niboyet, Desiree Veret Gay, Jeanne Deroin."[19] Newspaper articles carried news of revolutionary activities in Europe in 1848 across the Atlantic. In the 1850s, some of these articles were written by Karl Marx for Horace Greeley's *New York Tribune*. The cross-fertilization of ideas energized and radicalized progressives involved in the growth of revolutionary change.

THE TRIUMVIRATE

Activism and political theory were entwined in nineteenth-century America. A first precept of feminism is that theory and practice develop together, and this is also true of socialism and anti-racism. The major repository of US feminist history and thought in the nineteenth and early twentieth century is a multi-volume work, *The History of Woman Suffrage*, of which the first three volumes – more than 3,000 pages – were compiled by the movement's major activists and theoreticians: Susan B. Anthony, Elizabeth Cady Stanton, and Matilda Joslyn Gage. Anthony's father was a Quaker, whose Society of Friends suspended him for marrying a non-Quaker without the community's permission. According to Anthony's biographer, sociologist Kathleen Barry, Anthony was permanently affected by, on the one hand, the relatively egalitarian Quaker teachings, and on the other, the lifelong cool retreat which was her mother's response to this religious snub.[20] Further, the Quakers of this time had themselves traded in some of their radical views for a more conventional Victorian acceptance in the new world. In contrast, Stanton was raised for a time as a bright boy might have been. Her father was a prominent attorney and she was educated along with other prospective law students for a time, but he regretted openly that she was not a son, a hurt so deep that she recalled it with bitterness throughout her life. Her studies taught her law, logic, and argumentation, useful tools for political campaigns.

The third member of the triumvirate, as they were called, is far less well known, a casualty of the reception given to her own radical views. Matilda Joslyn Gage was the daughter of a clergyman and a well-situated Scottish woman. Her parents' home was a center of abolitionist activity and a station on the "underground railroad," that is, a safe house for runaway slaves. She was raised to question freely and to think for herself, something she did quite well throughout her life.

CREATING FEMINIST THEORY AND ACTIVISM

As civilization advances there is a continual change in the standard of human rights.[21]

Matilda Joslyn Gage, A History of Woman Suffrage

Stanton had moved, not altogether happily, from urban and social Boston to the tranquility of Seneca Falls, New York, where she spent her time in domestic pursuits and tending her children. Once again encountering Lucretia Mott, the two determined to have the long-promised convention, and set a date. A number of men and women gathered together, and using the Declaration of Independence as a model, wrote a tract outlining a variety of wrongs and demanding a variety of rights for women. In this "Declaration of Sentiments" of 1848, they underscored that women had no role in creating laws and no representation. Under the law, marriage, for women, meant civil death; she had no property rights, including no rights to wages, and few avenues for profitable employment. The divorce laws were unfavorable to women, who were also allotted a subordinate position in the church, and had to adhere to a different code of morals. At the convention, Stanton's insistence on the inclusion of a clause advocating woman suffrage was supported by Frederick Douglass, whose arguments carried enormous moral weight, and whose support won inclusion of the clause against heated opposition.

A process of harassment and ridicule followed. Newspapers were merciless in their scorn, a process often applied to disenfranchised groups.[22] The first casualty of the campaign of ridicule was a new form of dress for women, which came to be called the "Bloomer." The trouser-like clothes provided comfort and mobility to women who were physically hampered by the prescribed clothes of the day, but so great was the ridicule that the costume was abandoned after a few years despite the obvious advantages, a campaign so effective that even today the recollection of "bloomers" is sometimes met with derisive mirth. Here there is an important link to late twentieth-century feminism. in theories which analyze the practical negative effects of masculinist control over the female body in objectification, somatophobia, and various physical disorders.[23]

Despite the ridicule, the women's movement took off and a series of Women's Rights Conventions followed. In the radical times prior to the Civil War, feminists and abolitionists shared beliefs about oppression and worked to support each other, with "Anthony working as a paid organizer for the American Anti-Slavery Society, Stanton penning dynamic anti-slavery tracts, and Gage offering her home as a station on the underground railroad for the use of slaves escaping to Canada."[24] Likewise, Garrison supported women's rights at the London anti-slavery convention and in his paper, *The Liberator.* Douglass threw his powerful support behind women at Seneca Falls, in speeches, and in his newspapers. Lecturer/activist Sojourner Truth joined the fight for women's rights at the national conventions in Worcester (1850) and Akron (1851) and in her many speeches around the country.[25] At a time when the ostensible cause of the Civil War was preserving union, the triumvirate pressured Lincoln to admit that slavery was a major cause of the war, argued that victory for the North could only be assured upon emancipation, and organized war efforts based on emancipation as a prerequisite.

The unity of spirit between feminists and abolitionists leading up to and throughout the Civil War was torn asunder in the post-war reactions, in the reconstruction constitutional amendments, and in divisive politics.[26] Anthony, Stanton, Gage, and other radical feminists formed the National Women's Suffrage Association (NWSA), which supported constitutionally extending the franchise to all citizens. A splinter group, the American Woman's Suffrage Association (AWSA), was content for the present at least to give the vote to Black men, if not to Black or white women. The AWSA, generally more conservative, adopted a states-rights approach to woman suffrage (but a federalist approach to Negro male suffrage), whereas the NWSA favored constitutional challenges and federal protections.[27] The NWSA viewed the franchise as a strategy to achieve power and more radical change. Many women attempted to vote, and when Anthony succeeded, she was arrested and tried. Anthony's trial for the crime of voting represented a concrete example of what Marxism describes as the use of the superstructure of law, economics, religion, and society to prevent a class of people from participating in democratic institutions. Anthony was denied a trial of her peers and she was not permitted to speak in her own defense. The judge directed the jury to return a verdict of "guilty" and made his own summation from notes prepared before he had heard any evidence. Anthony was convicted but the courts never pursued the fine, which Anthony refused to pay.

Gage was the first United States feminist to articulate the theory of pre-historic matriarchies, which she believed were egalitarian, woman-centered, and worshipped a female deity. She was also the first to document the persecution of witches, and analyze it as an attempt by the patriarchy to destroy female culture.[28]

Although Gage is the least well-known, she was the most intellectual of the three and wrote the theoretical portions of the *History,* as well as several books and numerous newspaper articles. Gage's political theory is found in the Introduction and Chapter 1 of Volume 1 and the final chapter of Volume III of the *History of Woman Suffrage* and in her major work, *Woman, Church and the State: The Original Exposé of Male Collaboration Against the Female Sex* (1893). The Introduction of the *History* is essentially a set of replies to objections about women's rights, and resonates with John Stuart Mill's and Harriet Taylor's work on women's rights, particularly *The Subjection of Women.* It provides a systematic argumentative base, addressing "the cause of the universal degradation of women in all periods and nations."[29] She debunks the many standard arguments that attribute a natural source to women's social position. The argument she makes here is quite general, and elements of it are applicable to oppression generally and not just to women. In Chapter 1 Gage reveals her lifelong practice of accruing international historical examples both of women's degradation and of women's achievements, citing among the latter, notable women such as Christine of Pisa, Mary Astell, the Abbess Hilda of Whitby, Mercy Otis Warren ("The first person who counseled separation [of the colonies from England] and pressed those views on John Adams when he sought her advice before opening the first Congress"), Margaret Fuller, Mary Wollstonecraft, Harriet Martineau, Catherine of Russia, Frances Wright, to name only a few.[30] The historical portion of Chapter 1 serves as an excellent source for reclaiming forgotten women of consequence.

A portion of an early version of *Woman, Church and the State* is printed as the final chapter of Vol. 111 of *History* (1881), but the work as a whole – her major work – was published in 1893. This remarkable work provides a comprehensive philosophical argument, supported by historical example, that first, society was originally a matriarchate (Gage's term); second, that the teachings and practices of the established Christian church run counter to the teachings of Christianity itself; and third, that church and state have collaborated to place women in a position of social, legal, and religious inferiority, often through the use of violence.

Gage accumulates evidence for the thesis that society was originally a matriarchy in the ancient societies of Assyria, Babylonia, in Africa, and among the Aztecs: "Every part of the world today gives evidence of the system: reminiscences of the Matriarchate abound everywhere."[31] She cites nineteenth-century sources: Bachofen's *Motherright* and others, as well as native Iroquois culture.[32] Gage's view has some notable adherents in the late twentieth century: poet, novelist, and scholar the late Robert Graves in several works, including the introduction to *The Greek Myths*, Elizabeth Gould Davis in *The First Sex*, and Mary Daly in *Gyn/Ecology*.[33] Her examples are scholarly and impressive.

Exploring the doctrine of original sin, Gage extrapolates a double standard which reveres male celibacy and degrades all sensuality, and marriage as well, due to its association with women, whom, she argues, the church does not see as human. In the next chapters she examines the uses of canon and civil law to oppress women. For example, the feudal practice of marquette dictated that the feudal lord could demand sexual access to a newly married woman for one to three days after marriage. Her chapter on witchcraft and the role of the witch trials in obliterating the transmission and practice of women's forms of knowledge, especially medical knowledge, is a subject that has been explored at some length by current writers. She explores issues of labor. She attacks the notion that self-sacrifice is women's first duty and substitutes self-development as a fitting goal for women.

Anthony's more traditional religious values were offended by Gage's extremism. Late in life their bitter split was enacted through the forced "unification" of the NWSA and the AWSA, a move which curbed the radical platform of the women's movement. Gage's own life and contributions are not well represented in the work she contributed so much to – the *History of Woman Suffrage*. Her contributions and especially her writings on religion have been difficult to obtain. Even the reissuing of *Women, Church and the State* by Gage biographer Sally Roesch Wagner in 1980 did not immediately result in the wide recognition of her work. Only very recently has scholarship on Gage begun to pick up steam, with conferences and the gradual increase of journal articles on her contributions.

The history of all hitherto existing society is the history of class struggles.
Karl Marx, The Communist Manifesto

While abolitionism and feminism were the most pressing social issues in the United States, in Europe, theorists such as Charles Fourier, St. Simon, and Pierre Proudhon were developing forms of socialism to address the class problems which dominated the continent. Best known among these is Karl Heinrich Marx, who was born in 1818 in Treves (Trier), a Prussian city on the Rhine which was much influenced by the French Revolution and the Napoleonic era. Marx's ancestors on both sides were rabbis of some local importance, but the nineteenth century was a period of "assimilation" for many European Jews. As in the seventeenth century when "occasional conformists" were forced for professional reasons nominally to practice Anglicanism, Marx's father, who was an attorney, converted to Lutheranism, partly from an optimistic notion that this religion would provide a better life for his family, and partly to elude laws preventing Jews from engaging in government business.[34]

Of his early life in his family, Marx's biographer, the philosopher Isaiah Berlin, observes that his puzzled father became aware that he had

an unusual and difficult son; with a sharp and lucid intelligence he combined a stubborn and domineering temper, a truculent love of independence, exceptional emotional restraint, and over all, a colossal, ungovernable intellectual appetite.[35]

Given the centrality of religion, especially in early Marxist thought, it would be interesting to know more about Marx's mother, Henrietta Pressberger. Did she share her husband's conversion or did she uphold the laws of the rabbinical tradition in which she herself was raised, in the home where she brought up her eight children? Marx is thought to have grown up with little sense of his Jewish heritage; when he came to understand its meaning as a young man he recommended the abolition of all religion and its replacement with scientific socialism.

Marx had a "conventionally brilliant career" at school.[36] Already as an undergraduate he became associated with left-Hegelian groups and radical causes that were deeply critical of religion. He studied at the Universities of Bonn and Berlin and, having written a thesis on Epicurus and Democritus, received a doctorate from the University of Jena. Under the rule of Frederick William III, nephew of Frederick the Great, Prussia was an absolute monarchy, with no parliament or constitution, and no general rights for its citizens. Marx's radicalism made it impossible for him to find employment in the universities or in any official capacity under this repressive regime.

While working briefly for a socialist newspaper, Marx married Jenny Von Westphalen, a descendant of British aristocrats and the daughter of a Prussian government official.[37] Westphalen's father, Marx's first mentor, urged Marx to go beyond the readings of Goethe, Schiller, and Hölderlin, to read Dante, Shakespeare, Homer, Aeschylus, Cervantes, and others. When the newspaper for which he was writing was dissolved, Marx left for Paris to study socialism and political economy. Here, in 1844 he met the person who was to be his lifelong friend and intellectual colleague, Friedrich Engels. Engels managed his family's textile factories in Manchester which produced cloth from the cotton grown on American plantations, picked by American slaves, and shipped to Britain. But Engels' focus was not on the misery of those who labored an ocean away to produce cotton for his factories; it was on his own laborers, whose working conditions he investigated in *Condition of the Working Class in England*.

In 1847, Marx was expelled from Paris for his political activities and moved on to Brussels, where he composed what is by far the most famous piece of socialist doctrine, *The Communist Manifesto*. Throughout Europe there was great social unrest. A population explosion, urbanization, lack of housing, several famines and food shortages led to rising waves of revolution toward whose goals Marx and Engels worked. For his part, Marx returned to Germany (where Engels had fought in the uprisings) and was arrested and tried for high treason. Once acquitted, he was expelled and moved, more or less permanently, to London, where he spent his life in exile.

Marx spent most of his remaining years studying and writing in the British Museum. He continued his activism for a time, as he deftly led the First International Working Men's Association, founded in 1864, through turbulent times. Eventually, factionalization was too great, in particular between Marx and Bakunin, and Marx dissolved the organization. It was his final foray into social activism.

MARX AND CLASSICAL ECONOMIC THEORY

The theory of capitalism has its roots in Locke's labor theory of property, with its concepts of taking property out of the common, of coming to own it by mixing one's labor, and of increasing its value through improvement, thus benefiting oneself and mankind. Capitalism presupposes the existence of individual natural property rights. Given systematic expression in Adam Smith's *Wealth of Nations* (1776), in capitalism, the economic theory of supply and demand is developed, in which natural forces (the invisible or unseen hand) are thought to regulate production and distribution in the most efficient way possible. The "principle of natural liberty" would provide the lowest price consistent with profit, thereby providing the greatest benefit to all. Thus, *laissez faire* economics would provide, without plan or intention, a system of natural justice. As it often is today, classical economics was viewed as a science separate from politics.[38]

Capitalist economics was refined by David Ricardo in his *Principles of Political Economy* (1817). Relying on Malthusian theories of population, he argued against the state restrictions in England which favored landowners over manufacturers.[39] Using his laws of rent and wages he reasoned that landlords gained profits without contributing to production. He also held that wage labor will always only remain at subsistence level and that for the purposes of economics, society comprised, not individuals but "naturally conflicting classes." Historian of political ideas, George Sabine noted with some irony:

> the extent to which liberal economics was controlled by practical considerations rather than by logic is curiously illustrated by the ease with which Karl Marx turned its arguments to quite a different purpose... Classical economics provided Marx with a ready made picture of the exploitation of labour.[40]

A study of classical economic theory reveals how class conflict was the mortar with which the nineteenth-century capitalist system was built. The project, then, was to articulate this, not from the point of view of capital, but from the point of view of the proletariat.

> The essential condition for the existence, and for the sway of the bourgeois class, is the formation and augmentation of capital.
>
> *Karl Marx,* The Communist Manifesto

Marx exposed a superstructure of politics, economics, law, religion and social custom, a series of institutions designed to control and deceive the workers, keeping from them the substructure of reality – the fact of their virtual enslavement to capitalist forces. Eventually and inevitably class struggle would lead to revolution in which the workers would seize control of capital, and a genuine democracy would occur, not the bourgeois democracy of phony representative government, and meaningless individual rights. Freedoms would be economic first. Others would follow "naturally." Among socialist writers, Marx has had far and away the most profound influence worldwide. His critique of capitalism remains incisive today. Marxism has had a particular influence on feminism: within the United States forms of liberal feminism are most common, but outside the USA socialist feminism is more widely accepted.

In the twenty-first century some of the traditionally less familiar elements of Marxist thought are of special interest, in particular his views of the social character of knowledge. Traditional western epistemologies, especially positivist ones, hold that with the establishment of certain methodological procedures, knowledge can be acquired in a systematic and relatively unproblematic way. Marx is one of the first theorists to change the epistemological equation. Instead of human beings passively acquiring knowledge (learning truth) about a reality that has a basic unchanging nature, knowledge is seen as a social process wherein the knower interacts with the known. In Marxism,

> The truth, i.e., the reality and power, of thought, must be demonstrated in practice. The contest as to the reality or non-reality of thought which is isolated from practice, is purely a scholastic question...Philosophers have only *interpreted* the world in various ways but the real task is to *alter* it.[41]

Connecting with his concept of knowledge is his notion of praxis, a concept of human activity that denies Cartesian mind–body dualism and supplants it with the idea of integrated human behavior where the physical and intellectual elements work in harmony. As political scientist Nancy Hartsock notes, for Marx "consciousness itself is social product" and consciousness and society depend on each other.[42] As developed in twentieth-century Marxism, "the experience of the worker provides the ground on which a standpoint, a specific kind of epistemological device, can be constructed."[43] It carries the assertion that "there are some perspectives on society from which, however well-intentioned one may be, the real relations of humans with each other and with the natural world are not visible."[44] Thus, while capitalists are materially advantaged by their class position, as knowers, they are epistemologically disadvantaged. The struggle involved in oppression means that it is possible for the worker, through struggle, to achieve a more complex level of understanding than is available to the ruling classes whose vision is necessarily "partial and perverse."[45] Standpoint epistemologies take on special importance in political theory as different oppositional epistemologies are emerging.[46] With new insights about the sociality of knowledge, never before has epistemology been identifiably so tied with metaphysics on the one side, and politics on the other.

THE "UNHAPPY MARRIAGE" OF MARXISM AND FEMINISM

Marxism and feminism in the nineteenth century issued from similar revolutionary spirits, but different social conditions on the two continents. Without the historical bonds of strict hierarchical class structures, many North American men of European descent lived in a relative equality of social position and political access.[47] With notable exceptions, vast differentials in wealth had not had the time to accrue, as in Europe, where class distinctions were stark and nearly insurmountable. The starkest contrast in the USA was that of differential race privilege, a set of conditions which led to the nation's most bitter war. The *awareness* of sexism, often a hidden oppression, was largely a by-product of the national dispute over race, a syllogism waiting to be completed by women abolitionists in their thinking about race, and then gender. These configurations of class, race, and gender came to form a complex discussion about oppression which was reproduced a century later in an extensive literature about their relationship.

In the 1960s and 1970s US progressives formed sometimes uneasy coalitions to combat racism, classism, and sexism in society. The theoretical work which correlated with the activism took up the question of the primacy of oppressions, disputing whether class (as Marx and Engels would have it) or sex (as radical feminists were arguing) was more fundamental.[48] In the title essay of a collection entitled *Women and Revolution: A Discussion of the Unhappy Marriage of Marxism and Feminism*, Heidi Hartmann frames the problem showing how historical materialism views women only in relation to economics, and not in relation to men.[49] According to Marxist theory, the revolution of the proletariat will end all sorts of oppression, including gender oppression, since the key to women's emancipation is their participation in the labor force. Feminists argue in response that socialism fails to identify the role of patriarchy as a social and historical structure. From a "dual system" of oppression – the systems of capitalism and patriarchy – theorists wondered how they could find a "unified system" to approach the problem. One possibility, proposed by Iris Marion Young, is to posit a "gender division of labor" and a feminist historical materialism. This project has been carried further by Nancy Hartsock. As a part of the same general discussion, Gloria Joseph uncovers the exclusion of race from the feminist/socialist dialogue, an exclusion which reveals the weaknesses in both types of analysis, in the theories of socialism and feminism, and in the practices of their adherents.[50]

> The categories of Marxism are sex-blind *and* race-blind. Feminist analysis is blind to history and insufficiently materialistic. Both marxist and feminist analysis do a gross injustice to Black women whose historical experiences of slavery have left them with a most peculiar legacy of scars.[51]

Further, "sexual inequality between Black men and women has very different historical and cultural beginnings than the sexual inequality between white men and women."[52] In *Women and Revolution*, Joseph argues for an analysis which takes into account these conditions for African Americans.

Both Marxism and feminism call for a specific cultural analysis, but both tend to restrict that analysis in terms of race, and specific historical and cultural conditions. Many Black women writers have theorized about these exclusions: Audre Lorde, Barbara Smith, Barbara Christian, bell hooks, Patricia Hill Collins, and Rosa Brewer, to name a few.[53] Any political theory that intends to provide an adequate conceptual framework for understanding power and oppression must provide a theoretical mechanism for illuminating and understanding the multiplicity of oppressions. Some of these theoretical mechanisms are further explored in Part VII.

Notes

1 Frederick Douglass, "I Have Come to Tell You Something About Slavery: An Address Delivered in Lynn, Massachusetts, in October 1841," in *The Frederick Douglass Papers*, vol. 1, *1841–46*, ed. John W. Blassingame (New Haven: Yale University Press, 1979), p. 4.
2 See Part V for a discussion of David Walker's abolitionist activities.
3 Frederick Douglass, "Narrative of the Life of Frederick Douglass," in Henry Louis Gates, Jr., ed., *The Classic Slave Narratives* (New York: New American Library, 1987), p. 258. See also Jenny Franchot's analysis in "The Punishment of Esther: Frederick Douglass and the Construction of the Feminine," in *Frederick Douglass: New Literary and Historical Essays*, ed. Eric J. Sundquist (Cambridge: Cambridge University Press, 1990). Other versions of this episode are more graphic.
4 Blassingame, *The Frederick Douglass Papers*, vol. 1, p. lii.
5 Gates, *The Classic Slave Narratives*, p. 298.
6 See Nell Irvin Painter, "Martin R. Delany: Elitism and Black Nationalism," in *Black Leaders of the Nineteenth Century*, ed. Leon Litwack and August Meier (Chicago: University of Illinois Press, 1991) for an account of Delany's life and views.
7 Bernard Boxill, "Two Traditions in African American Political Philosophy," *The Philosophical Forum*, vol. XXIV, 1–3, Fall–Spring 1992–3, p. 120.
8 Ibid., p. 121.
9 Philip S. Foner, *The Life and Writings of Frederick Douglass*, vol. 2 (New York: International Publishers, 1955), p. 130.
10 Boxill, "Two Traditions," p. 132.
11 Waldo E. Martin, Jr., "Frederick Douglass: Humanist as Race Leader," in Litwack and Meier, eds., *Black Leaders of the Nineteenth Century*, p. 59.
12 Patricia Williams, *The Alchemy of Race and Rights: Diary of a Law Professor* (Cambridge, MA: Harvard University Press, 1991).
13 Foner, *Life and Writings*, p. 350.
14 Elizabeth Cady Stanton, Susan B. Anthony, and Matilda Joslyn Gage, eds., *A History of Woman Suffrage* (New York: Fowler and Wells, 1881; reprinted 1969, Arno and the *New York Times*), vol. 1, pp. 53–4.
15 Among the victims of this epidemic may have been English political theorist Harriet Taylor Mill. On the basis of physical symptoms, Taylor's biographer, Jo Ellen Jacobs, suggests that Taylor contracted syphilis from her first husband, John Taylor, who may have frequented the London brothels. It seems likely that Taylor and her second husband John Stuart Mill never consummated their marriage. Psychoanalytic literature explains this by attributing sexual frigidity to Taylor, but Jacobs suggests this physical cause.
16 See Alice Rossi, ed., *The Feminist Papers: From Adams to Beauvoir* (New York: Columbia University Press, 1973) for a treatment of issues of social reform during this period.
17 In the 1970s, 130 years after the World Anti-Slavery Convention, and fifty years after women's enfranchisement in the USA, *New York Times* reporter Nan Robertson and other women reporters were not allowed to be seated on the floor of the National Press Club in Washington, D.C., where heads of state, cabinet ministers, and other powerful

dignitaries deliver important speeches. The women were relegated to cramped balcony quarters while men reporters were seated at dinner tables on the main floor, served food and wine, and given choice positioning for socializing with policy makers and reporting events. She gives her account of these events and describes her discrimination suit against the *NYT* for their treatment of women reporters in her book *The Girls in the Balcony: Women, Men and the New York Times* (New York: Fawcett Books, 1993).

18 Bonnie S. Anderson, "The Lid Comes Off: International Radical Feminism and the Revolutions of 1848," *NWSA Journal*, 10:2, Summer 1998 (Bloomington: Indiana University Press), p. 4.

19 Ibid., p. 2.

20 Kathleen Barry, *Susan B. Anthony* (New York: New York University Press, 1988).

21 *A History of Woman Suffrage*, vol. 1, p. 25.

22 Consider, for example, the depictions and characterizations of African Americans in many mainstream nineteenth- and early twentieth-century magazines and the propaganda depictions and characterizations of Jews in Nazi publications of the 1930s and 1940s.

23 See, for example, Naomi Wolfe, *The Beauty Myth: How Images of Beauty are Used Against Women* (New York: Morrow, 1991) for a popular account, and, for a more scholarly one, *Writing on the Body: Female Embodiment and Feminist Theory*, ed. K. Conboy et al. (New York: Columbia University Press, 1997). For examples of "somatophobia," a term used to designate a hatred of the body, see Elizabeth V. Spelman, *Inessential Women: Problems of Exclusion in Feminist Thought* (Boston: Beacon Press, 1988).

24 Sally Roesch Wagner, Introduction to Matilda Joslyn Gage, *Woman, Church and the State: The Original Exposé of Male Collaboration Against the Female Sex* (1893). (Reprinted 1980, Watertown, MA: Persephone Press, p. xvii.)

25 Stanton et al., *History of Woman Suffrage*, vol. 1, pp. 115–17.

26 The Thirteenth Amendment to the US Constitution abolished slavery. The Fourteenth Amendment was particularly significant on the grounds of gender. It states that all persons are citizens and holds that no state shall "abridge the privileges and immunities of citizens," nor deny them "of life, liberty or property, without due process of law." This amendment introduced for the first time the phrase "male inhabitant," a serious setback for women's rights advocates. The Fifteenth Amendment protects voting rights from discrimination on the basis of "race, color, or previous condition of servitude." As legal historian Joan Hoff suggests in her detailed work, *Law, Gender and Injustice: A Legal History of US Women* (New York: New York University Press, 1991), "positive application of the equal-protection clause of the Fourteenth Amendment to women did not materialize until the last quarter of the twentieth century and is still not complete" (p. 146). The complexities of the Fourteenth Amendment, both historically and constitutionally, are given a lucid treatment by Hoff. An especially important feature of this difficult period for radical politics is the degree to which it pitted – or seemed to pit – pro-women and pro-African American groups against each other. As a result, Anthony especially is often accused of racism. But a closer look, especially at the political maneuverings of Lucy Stone's husband Henry Blackwell, reveals a cynical misuse of Anthony and the movement. After more than thirty years in the forefront of the anti-slavery movement, American feminists were stuck with the charge of racism. The degree to which this charge is true and to which it is manufactured, and the political meanings of this split, are central questions of political theory and practice in the United States, from the country's inception to the present.

27 Among the NWSA strategies were attempting to vote in federal elections. See especially the Supreme Court case of *Minor v Happerset*, 88 U.S. 162 (1875), discussed in Hoff, *Law, Gender and Injustice*.

28 Wagner, Introduction to *Woman, Church and the State*, p. xxvii.

29 Gage, *Woman, Church and the State*, p. 13.

30 Stanton et al., *History of Woman Suffrage*, pp. 31–2.

31 Gage, *Woman, Church and the State*, p. 8.

32 Johann Jacob Bachofen, *Das Mutterrecht* (Stuttgart, 1861). See Gail H. Landsman, "The 'Other' as Political Symbol: Image of Indians in the Woman Suffrage Movement," *Ethnohistory*, 39:3 (Summer 1992), pp. 247–84, for a discussion of how Native Americans were treated by suffragists.

33 Robert Graves, *The Greek Myths* (New York: Penguin, 1955); Elizabeth Gould Davis, *The First Sex* (Baltimore: Penguin, 1973); Mary Daly, *Gyn/Ecology* (Boston: Beacon Press, 1978).

34 See Hannah Arendt, *The Origins of Totalitarianism* (New York: Harcourt, Brace, Jovanovich, 1979), first published in 1948, on assimilation and "pariahs and parvenus," an important discussion relating to anti-Semitism.

35 Isaiah Berlin, *Karl Marx* (Oxford: Oxford University Press, 1939), p. 21.

36 Sidney Hook, *Marx and the Marxists* (Princeton: D. Van Nostrand Company, Inc., 1955), pp. 12–13.

37 Married in 1841, Marx and his wife had six children. Only three reached adulthood. The letters that Marx and Westphalen wrote to friends reporting the deaths of the other three children go beyond conventional sentimentality. The couple appear to have had an unusually close relationship to each other, even though he had an illegitimate son. Richard Schmidt notes that it was also a very unequal relationship. Jenny transcribed her husband's virtually illegible hand into neat copy, went to meetings and collected articles for him, and supported his political and scholarly work in other ways – all in addition to bearing six children and caring for them, often under hard conditions. *Introduction to Marx and Engels: A Critical Reconstruction* (Boulder: Westview, 1987).

38 See John Rawls, *A Theory of Justice* (Cambridge, MA: Harvard University Press, 1971) for an explanation and critique of this view.

39 The tariff on imported corn amounted to a price support for English farmers, and kept prices artificially high, raising food prices for wage-laborers.

40 George Sabine, *A History of Political Theory* (London: Harrap, 1963), pp. 693–4.

41 Karl Marx, *Eleven Theses on Feuerbach* (1845).

42 Nancy C.M. Hartsock, *Money, Sex and Power: Toward a Feminist Historical Materialism* (Boston: Northeastern University Press, 1983), p. 95.

43 Ibid., p. 117.

44 Ibid., p. 117.

45 Ibid., pp. 117–18.

46 See Diane Bell, "Yes, Virginia, There is a Feminist Ethnography: Reflections from Three Australian Fields," in *Gendered Fields: Women, Men and Ethnography*, ed. D. Bell, P. Caplan, and W. Karim (London: Routledge, 1993) and Bell's introduction to that volume; Sandra Harding and Merril Hintikka, eds., *Discovering Reality* (Boston: D. Reidel, 1983); Sandra Harding, *The Science Question in Feminism* (Ithaca: Cornell University Press, 1986); Gloria Anzaldúa, "*La conciencia de la mestiza*: Towards a New Consciousness", in Gloria Anzaldúa, ed., *Making Face, Making Soul, Hacienda Caras: Creative and Critical Perspectives by Feminists of Color* (San Francisco: Aunt Lute Books, 1990); Patricia Hill Collins, *Black Feminist Thought: Knowledge, Consciousness and the Politics of Empowerment* (New York: Routledge, 1991).

47 Alexis de Tocqueville marveled at the relative equality he witnessed in the United States, in his *Democracy in America* (New York: Knopf, 1945).

48 Shulamith Firestone, *The Dialectic of Sex* (New York: Bantam Books, 1971); Susan Brownmiller, *Against Our Will: Men, Women and Rape* (New York: Simon and Schuster, 1975); Mary Daly, *Gyn/Ecology: The Metaethics of Radical Feminism*; Susan Griffin, *Woman and Nature: The Roaring Inside Her* (New York: Harper and Row, 1978).

49 Heidi Hartmann, "The Unhappy Marriage of Marxism and Feminism," in Lydia Sargent, ed., *Women and Revolution: A Discussion of the Unhappy Marriage of Marxism and Feminism* (Boston: South End Press, 1981).
50 Iris Young, "Beyond the Unhappy Marriage: A Critique of Dual Systems Theory," and Gloria Joseph, "The Incompatible Ménage à Trois: Marxism, Feminism and Racism," both in Sargent, *Women and Revolution*.
51 Joseph, in Sargent, *Women and Revolution*, p. 93.
52 Ibid., p. 94.
53 See *This Bridge Called My Back: Writings by Radical Women of Color*, eds. Cherrie Moraga and Gloria Anzaldúa (New York: Kitchen Table/Women of Color Press, 1973); Audre Lorde, *Sister/Outsider: Essays and Speeches* (Freedom, CA: The Crossing Press, 1984); Gloria T. Hull, Patricia Bell Scott, and Barbara Smith, eds., *But Some of Us Are Brave: Black Women's Studies* (New York: Feminist Press, 1986); Rosa Brewer, "Theorizing Race, Class and Gender: The New Scholarship of Black Feminist Intellectuals and Black Women's Labor," in *Theorizing Black Feminisms: The Visionary Pragmatism of Black Women*, ed. Stanlie James and Abena Busia (New York: Routledge, 1993); *Black Feminist Criticism: Perspectives on Black Women Writers*, ed. Barbara Christian (New York: Pergamon Press, 1985); bell hooks, *Feminist Theory from Margin to Center* (Boston: South End Press, 1984).

CHAPTER 11

Writings and Addresses

FREDERICK DOUGLASS

AN APPEAL TO THE BRITISH PEOPLE: RECEPTION SPEECH AT FINSBURY CHAPEL, MOORFIELDS, ENGLAND, MAY 12, 1846

I feel exceedingly glad of the opportunity now afforded me of presenting the claims of my brethren in bonds in the United States to so many in London and from various parts of Britain who have assembled here on the present occasion. I have nothing to commend me to your consideration in the way of learning, nothing in the way of education, to entitle me to your attention; and you are aware that slavery is a very bad school for rearing teachers of morality and religion. Twenty-one years of my life have been spent in slavery – personal slavery – surrounded by degrading influences, such as can exist nowhere beyond the pale of slavery; and it will not be strange, if under such circumstances, I should betray, in what I have to say to you, a deficiency of that refinement which is seldom or ever found, except among persons that have experienced superior advantages to those which I have enjoyed. But I will take it for granted that you know something about the degrading influences of slavery, and that you will not expect great things from me this evening, but simply such facts as I may be able to advance immediately in connection with my own experience of slavery.

Now, what is this system of slavery? This is the subject of my lecture this evening – what is the character of this institution? I am about to answer this inquiry, what is American slavery? I do this the more readily, since I have found persons in this country who have identified the term slavery with which I think it is not, and in some instances, I have feared, in so doing, have rather (unwittingly, I know) detracted much from the horror with which the term slavery is contemplated. It is common in this country to distinguish every bad thing by the name of slavery. Intemperance is slavery; to be deprived of the right to vote is slavery, says one; to have to work hard is

Frederick Douglass. Writings and Addresses. Originally published in 1846–9.

slavery, says another; and I do not know but that if we should let them go on, they would say that to eat when we are hungry, to walk when we desire to have exercise, or to minister to our necessities, or have necessities at all, is slavery.

I do not wish for a moment to detract from the horror with which the evil of intemperance is contemplated – not at all; nor do I wish to throw the slightest obstruction in the way of any political freedom that any class of persons in this country may desire to obtain. But I am here to say that I think the term slavery is sometimes abused by identifying it with that which it is not. Slavery in the United States is the granting of that power by which one man exercises and enforces a right of property in the body and soul of another. The condition of a slave is simply that of the brute beast. He is a piece of property – a marketable commodity, in the language of the law, to be bought or sold at the will and caprice of the master who claims him to be his property; he is spoken of, thought of, and treated as property. His own good, his conscience, his intellect, his affections, are all set aside by the master. The will and the wishes of the master are the law of the slave. He is as much a piece of property as a horse. If he is fed, he is fed because he is property. If he is clothed, it is with a view to the increase of his value as property. Whatever of comfort is necessary to him for his body or soul that is inconsistent with his being property is carefully wrested from him, not only by public opinion, but by the law of the country. He is carefully deprived of everything that tends in the slightest degree to detract from his value as property. He is deprived of education. God has given him an intellect; the slaveholder declares it shall not be cultivated. If his moral perception leads him in a course contrary to his value as property, the slaveholder declares he shall not exercise it. The marriage institution cannot exist among slaves, and one-sixth of the population of democratic America is denied its privileges by the law of the land. What is to be thought of a nation boasting of its liberty, boasting of its humanity, boasting of its Christianity, boasting of its love of justice and purity, and yet having within its own borders three millions of persons denied by law the right of marriage? – what must be the condition of that people?

I need not lift up the veil by giving you any experience of my own. Every one that can put two ideas together must see the most fearful results from such a state of things as I have just mentioned. If any of these three millions find for themselves companions, and prove themselves honest, upright, virtuous persons to each other, yet in these cases – few as I am bound to confess they are – the virtuous live in constant apprehension of being torn asunder by the merciless men-stealers that claim them as their property. This is American slavery; no marriage – no education – the light of the gospel shut out from the dark mind of the bondman – and he forbidden by the law to learn to read. If a mother shall teach her children to read, the law in Louisiana proclaims that she may be hanged by the neck. If the father attempt to give his son a knowledge of letters, he may be punished by the whip in one instance, and in another be killed, at the discretion of the court. Three millions of people shut out from the light of knowledge! It is easy for you to conceive the evil that must result from such a state of things.

I now come to the physical evils of slavery. I do not wish to dwell at length upon these, but it seems right to speak of them, not so much to influence your minds on this question, as to let the slaveholders of America know that the curtain which conceals their crimes is being lifted abroad; that we are opening the dark cell, and leading the people into the horrible recesses of what they are pleased to call their domestic institution. We want them to know that a knowledge of their whippings, their scourgings, their brandings, their chainings, is not confined to their plantations, but that some Negro of theirs has broken loose from his chains – has burst through the dark incrustation of slavery, and is now exposing their deeds of deep damnation to the gaze of the Christian people of England.

The slaveholders resort to all kinds of cruelty. If I were disposed, I have matter enough to interest you on this question for five or six evenings, but I will not dwell at length upon these cruelties. Suffice it to say, that all the peculiar modes of torture that were resorted to in the West India islands are resorted to, I believe, even more frequently in the United States of America. Starvation, the bloody whip, the chain, the gag, the thumb-screw, cathauling, the cat-o'-nine-tails, the dungeon, the blood-hound, are all in requisition to keep the slave in his condition as a slave in the United States. If any one has a doubt upon this point, I would ask him to read the chapter on slavery in Dickens's Notes on America. If any man has a doubt upon it, I have here the "testimony of a thousand witnesses," which I can give at any length, all going to prove the truth of my statement. The blood-hound is regularly trained in the United States, and advertisements are to be found in the southern papers of the Union, from persons advertising themselves as blood-hound trainers, and offering to hunt down slaves at fifteen dollars a piece, recommending their hounds as the fleetest in the neighborhood, never known to fail. Advertisements are from time to time inserted, stating that slaves have escaped with iron collars about their necks, with bands of iron about their feet, marked with the lash, branded with red-hot irons, the initials of their master's name burned into their flesh; and their masters advertise the fact of their being thus branded with their own signature, thereby proving to the world that, however damning it may appear to non-slaveholders, such practices are not regarded discreditable among the slaveholders themselves. Why, I believe if a man should brand his horse in this country – burn the initials of his name into any of his cattle, and publish the ferocious deed here – that the united execrations of Christians in Britain would descend upon him. Yet, in the United States, human beings are thus branded. As Whittier says –

> ... Our countrymen in chains,
>   The whip on woman's shrinking flesh,
> Our soil yet reddening with the stains
>   Caught from her scourgings warm and fresh.

The slave-dealer boldly publishes his infamous acts to the world. Of all things that have been said of slavery to which exception has been taken by slaveholders, this, the charge of cruelty, stands foremost, and yet there is no charge capable of clearer demonstration than that of the most barbarous inhumanity on the part of the slaveholders toward their slaves. And all this is necessary; it is necessary to resort to these cruelties, in order to make the slave a slave, and to keep him a slave. Why, my experience all goes to prove the truth of what you will call a marvelous proposition, that the better you treat a slave, the more you destroy his value as a slave, and enhance the probability of his eluding the grasp of the slaveholder; the more kindly you treat him, the more wretched you make him, while you keep him in the condition of a slave. My experience, I say, confirms the truth of this proposition. When I was treated exceedingly ill; when my back was being scourged daily; when I was whipped within an inch of my life – life was all I cared for. "Spare my life," was my continual prayer. When I was looking for the blow about to be inflicted upon my head, I was not thinking of my liberty; it was my life. But, as soon as the blow was not to be feared, then came the longing for liberty. If a slave has a bad master, his ambition is to get a better; when he gets a better, he aspires to have the best; and when he gets the best, he aspires to be his own master. But the slave must be brutalized to keep him as a slave. The slaveholder feels this necessity. I admit this necessity. If it be right to hold slaves at all, it is right to hold them in the only way in which they can be held; and this can be done only by shutting out the light of education from their minds, and brutalizing their persons.

The whip, the chain, the gag, the thumb-screw, the blood-hound, the stocks, and all the other bloody paraphernalia of the slave system are indispensably necessary to the relation of master and slave. The slave must be subjected to these, or he ceases to be a slave. Let him know that the whip is burned; that the fetters have been turned to some useful and profitable employment; that the chain is no longer for his limbs; that the blood-hound is no longer to be put upon his track; that his master's authority over him is no longer to be enforced by taking his life – and immediately he walks out from the house of bondage and asserts his freedom as a man. The slaveholder finds it necessary to have these implements to keep the slave in bondage; finds it necessary to be able to say, "Unless you do so and so; unless you do as I bid you – I will take away your life!"

Some of the most awful scenes of cruelty are constantly taking place in the middle states of the Union. We have in those states what are called the slave-breeding states. Allow me to speak plainly. Although it is harrowing to your feeling, it is necessary that the facts of the case should be stated. We have in the United States slave-breeding states. The very state from which the minister from our court to yours comes is one of these states – Maryland, where men, women, and children are reared for the market, just as horses, sheep, and swine are raised for the market. Slave-rearing is there looked upon as a legitimate trade; the law sanctions it, public opinion upholds it, the church does not condemn it. It goes on in all its bloody horrors, sustained by the auctioneer's block. If you would see the cruelties of this system, hear the following narrative. Not long since the following scene occurred. A slave-woman and a slaveman had united themselves as man and wife in the absence of any law to protect them as man and wife. They had lived together by the permission, not by right, of their master, and they had reared a family. The master found it expedient, and for his interest, to sell them. He did not ask them their wishes in regard to the matter at all; they were not consulted. The man and woman were brought to the auctioneer's block, under the sound of the hammer. The cry was raised, "Here goes; who bids cash?" Think of it – a man and wife to be sold! The woman was placed on the auctioneer's block; her limbs, as is customary, were brutally exposed to the purchasers, who examined her with all the freedom with which they would examine a horse. There stood the husband, powerless; no right to his wife; the master's right preeminent. She was sold. He was next brought to the auctioneer's block. His eyes followed his wife in the distance; and he looked beseechingly, imploringly, to the man that had bought his wife to buy him also. But he was at length bid off to another person. He was about to be separated forever from her whom he loved. No word of his, no work of his, could save him from this separation. He asked permission of his new master to go and take the hand of his wife at parting. It was denied him. In the agony of his soul he rushed from the man who had just bought him, that he might take a farewell of his wife; but his way was obstructed, he was struck over the head with a loaded whip, and was held for a moment; but his agony was too great. When he was let go, he fell a corpse at the feet of his master. His heart was broken. Such scenes are the every-day fruits of American slavery.

Some two years since, the Hon. Seth M. Gates, an anti-slavery gentleman of the state of New York, a representative in the congress of the United States, told me he saw with his own eyes the following circumstance. In the national District of Columbia, over which the star-spangled emblem is constantly waving, where orators are ever holding forth on the subject of American liberty, American democracy, American republicanism, there are two slave prisons. When going across a bridge, leading to one of these prisons, he saw a young woman run out, bare-footed and bare-headed, and with very little clothing on. She was running with all speed to the bridge he was approaching. His eye was fixed upon her, and he stopped to see what was the matter. He had not paused long before he saw three men run out after her. He now knew what the nature of the case was: a slave escaping from her chains – a young woman, a sister – escaping from the bondage in which she had been held. She made her way to the bridge, but had not reached it, ere from the Virginia side there came two slaveholders. As soon as they saw them, her pursuers called out, "Stop her!" True to their Virginian instincts, they came to the rescue of their brother kidnappers across the bridge. The poor girl now saw that there was no chance for her. It was a trying time. She knew if she went back, she must be a slave forever – she must be dragged down to the scenes of pollution which the slaveholders continually provide for most of the poor, sinking, wretched young women whom they call their property. She formed her resolution; and just as those who were about to take her were going to put hands upon her, to drag her back, she leaped over the balustrades of the bridge, and down she went to rise no more. She chose death, rather than to go back into the hands of those Christian slaveholders from whom she had escaped.

Can it be possible that such things as these exist in the United States? Are not these the exceptions? Are any such scenes as this general? Are not such deeds condemned by the law and denounced by public opinion? Let me read you a few of the laws of the slaveholding states of America. I think no better exposure of slavery can be made than is made by the laws of the states in which slavery exists. I prefer reading the laws to making my statement in confirmation of what I have said myself; for the slaveholders cannot object to this testimony, since it is the calm, the cool, the deliberate enactment of their wisest heads, of their most clear-sighted, their own constituted representatives. "If more than seven slaves together are found in any road without a white person, twenty lashes a piece; for visiting a plantation without a written pass, ten lashes; for letting loose a boat from where it is made fast, thirty-nine lashes for the first offense; and for the second shall have cut off from his head one ear; for keeping or carrying a club, thirty-nine lashes; for having any article for sale, without a ticket from his master, ten lashes; for traveling in any other than the most usual and accustomed road, when going alone to any place, forty lashes; for traveling in the night without a pass, forty lashes."

I am afraid you do not understand the awful character of these lashes. You must bring it before your mind. A human being in a perfect state of nudity, tied hand and foot to a stake, and a strong man standing behind with a heavy whip, knotted at the end, each blow cutting into the flesh, and leaving the warm blood dripping to the feet; and for these trifles. For being found in another person's Negro-quarters, forty lashes; for hunting with dogs in the woods, thirty lashes; for being on horseback without the written permission of his master, twenty-five lashes; for riding or going abroad in the night, or riding horses in the day time, without leave, a slave may be whipped, cropped, or branded in the cheek with the letter R, or otherwise punished, such punishment not extending to life, or so as to render him unfit for labor. The laws referred to may be found by consulting Brevard's Digest; Haywood's Manual; Virginia Revised Code; Prince's Digest; Missouri Laws; Mississippi Revised Code. A man, for going to visit his brethren, without the permission of his master – and in many instances he may not have that permission; his master, from caprice or other reasons, may not be willing to allow it – may be caught on his way, dragged to a post, the branding-iron heated, and the name of his master or the letter R branded into his cheek or on his forehead.

They treat slaves thus, on the principle that they must punish for light offenses in order to prevent the commission of larger ones. I wish you to mark that in the single state of Virginia there are seventy-one crimes for which a colored man may be executed; while there are only three of these crimes which, when committed by a white man, will subject him to that punishment. There are many of these crimes which if the white man did not commit he would be regarded as a scoundrel and a coward. In the state of Maryland there is a law to this effect: that if a slave shall strike his master, he may be hanged, his head severed from his body, his body quartered, and his head and quarters set up in the most prominent places in the neighborhood. If a colored woman, in the defense of her own virtue, in defense of her own person, should shield herself from the brutal attacks of her tyrannical master, or make the slightest resistance, she may be killed on the spot. No law whatever will bring the guilty man to justice for the crime.

But you will ask me, can these things be possible in a land professing Christianity? Yes, they are so; and this is not the worst. No, a darker feature is yet to be presented than the mere existence of these facts. I have to inform you that the religion of the southern states, at this time, is the great supporter, the great sanctioner of the bloody atrocities to which I have referred. While America is printing tracts and Bibles; sending missionaries abroad to convert the heathen; expending her money in various ways for the promotion of the Gospel in foreign lands – the slave not only lies forgotten, uncared for, but is trampled under foot by the very churches of the land. What have we in America? Why, we have slavery made part of the religion of the land. Yes, the pulpit there stands up as the great defender of this cursed institution, as it is called. Ministers of religion come forward and torture the hallowed pages of inspired wisdom to sanction the bloody deed. They stand forth as the foremost, the strongest defenders of this "institution."

As a proof of this, I need not do more than state the general fact, that slavery has existed under the droppings of the sanctuary of the south for the last two hundred years, and there has not been any war between the religion and the slavery of the south. Whips, chains, gags, and thumb-screws have all lain under the droppings of the sanctuary, and instead of rusting from off the limbs of the bondman, those droppings have served to preserve them in all their strength. Instead of preaching the Gospel against this tyranny, rebuke, and wrong, ministers of religion have sought, by all and every means, to throw in the background whatever in the Bible could be construed into opposition to slavery, and to bring forward that which they could torture into its support.

This I conceive to be the darkest feature of slavery, and the most difficult to attack, because it is identified with religion, and exposes those who denounce it to the charge of infidelity. Yes, those with whom I have been laboring, namely, the old organization anti-slavery society of America, have been again and again stigmatized as infidels, and for what reason? Why, solely in consequence of the faithfulness of their attacks upon the slaveholding religion of the southern states, and the northern religion that sympathizes with it. I have found it difficult to speak on this matter without persons coming forward and saying, "Douglass, are you not afraid of injuring the cause of Christ? You do not desire to do so, we know; but are you not undermining religion?" This has been said to me again and again, even since I came to this country, but I cannot be induced to leave off these exposures. I love the religion of our blessed Savior. I love that religion that comes from above, in the "wisdom of God, which is first pure, then peaceable, gentle, and easy to be entreated, full of mercy and good fruits, without partiality and without hypocrisy." I love that religion that sends its votaries to bind up the wounds of him that has fallen among thieves. I love that religion that makes it the duty of its disciples to visit the fatherless and the widow in their affliction. I love that religion that is based upon the glorious principle, of love to God and love to man; which makes its followers do unto others as they themselves would be done by. If you demand liberty to yourself, it says, grant it to your neighbors. If you claim a right to think for yourself, it says, allow your neighbors the same right. If you claim to act for yourself, it says, allow your neighbors the same right. It is because I love this religion that I hate the slaveholding, the woman-whipping, the mind-darkening, the soul-destroying religion that exists in the southern states of America. It is because I regard the one as good, and pure, and holy, that I cannot but regard the other as bad, corrupt, and wicked. Loving the one I must hate the other; holding to the one I must reject the other.

I may be asked why I am so anxious to bring this subject before the British public – why I do not confine my efforts to the United States? My answer is, first, that slavery is the common enemy of mankind, and all mankind should be made acquainted with its abominable character. My next answer is, that the slave is a man, and, as such, is entitled to your sympathy as a brother. All the feelings, all the susceptibilities, all the capacities, which you have he has. He is a part of the human family. He has been the prey – the common prey – of christendom for the last three hundred years, and it is but right, it is but just, it is but proper, that his wrongs should be known throughout the world.

I have another reason for bringing this matter before the British public, and it is this: slavery is a system of wrong, so blinding to all around, so hardening to the heart, so corrupting to the morals, so deleterious to religion, so sapping to all the principles of justice in its immediate vicinity, that the community surrounding it lacks the moral stamina necessary to its removal. It is a system of such gigantic evil, so strong, so overwhelming in its power, that no one nation is equal to its removal. It requires the humanity of Christianity, the morality of the world to remove it. Hence, I call upon the people of Britain to look at this matter, and to exert the influence I am about to show they possess, for the removal of slavery from America. I can appeal to them, as strongly by their regard for the slaveholder as for the slave, to labor in this cause. I am here, because you have an influence on America that no other nation can have. You have been drawn together by the power of steam to a marvelous extent; the distance between London and Boston is now reduced to some twelve or fourteen days, so that the denunciations against slavery, uttered in London this week, may be heard in a fortnight in the streets of Boston, and reverberating amidst the hills of Massachusetts. There is nothing said here against slavery that will not be recorded in the United States.

I am here, also, because the slaveholders do not want me to be here; they would rather that I were not here. I have adopted a maxim laid down by Napoleon, never to occupy ground which the enemy would like me to occupy. The slaveholders would much rather have me, if I will denounce slavery, denounce it in the northern states, where their friends and supporters are, who will stand by and mob me for denouncing it. They feel something as the man felt, when he uttered his prayer, in which he made out a most horrible case for himself, and one of his neighbors touched him and said, "My friend, I always had the opinion of you that you have now expressed for yourself – that you are a very great sinner." Coming from himself, it was all very well, but coming from a stranger it was rather cutting.

The slaveholders felt that when slavery was denounced among themselves, it was not so bad; but let one of the slaves get loose, let him summon the people of Britain, and make known to them the conduct of the slaveholders toward their slaves, and it cuts them to the quick, and produces a sensation such as would be produced by nothing else. The power I exert now is something like the power that is exerted by the man at the end of the lever; my influence now is just in proportion to the distance that I am from the United States. My exposure of slavery abroad will tell more upon the hearts and consciences of slaveholders than if I was attacking them in America; for almost every paper that I now receive from the United States, comes teeming with statements about this fugitive Negro, calling him a "glib-tongued scoundrel," and saying that he is running out against the institutions and people of America.

I deny the charge that I am saying a word against the institutions of America, or the people, as such. What I have to say is against slavery and slaveholders. I feel at liberty to speak on this subject. I have on my back the marks of the lash; I have four sisters and one brother now under the galling chain. I feel it my duty to cry aloud and spare not. I am not averse to having the good opinion of my fellow-creatures. I am not averse to being kindly regarded by all men; but I am bound, even at the hazard of making a large class of religionists in this country hate me, oppose me, and malign me as they have done – I am bound by the prayers, and tears, and entreaties of three millions of kneeling bondsmen, to have no compromise with men who are in any shape or form connected with the slaveholders of America.

I expose slavery in this country, because to expose it is to kill it. Slavery is one of those monsters of darkness to whom the light of truth is death. Expose slavery, and it dies. Light is to slavery what the heat of the sun is to the root of a tree; it must die under it. All the slaveholder asks of me is silence. He does not ask me to go abroad and preach in favor of slavery; he does not ask any one to do that. He would not say that slavery is a good thing, but the best under the circumstances. The slaveholders want total darkness on the subject. They want the hatchway shut down, that the monster may crawl in his den of darkness, crushing human hopes, and happiness, destroying the bondman at will, and having no one to reprove or rebuke him. Slavery shrinks from the light; it hateth the light, neither cometh to the light, lest its deed should be reproved. To tear off the mask from this abominable system, to expose it to the light of heaven, aye, to the heat of the sun, that it may burn and wither it out of existence, is my object in coming to this country. I want the slaveholder surrounded, as by a wall of anti-slavery fire, so that he may see the condemnation of himself and his system glaring down in letters of light. I want him to feel that he has no sympathy in England, Scotland, or Ireland; that he has none in Canada, none in Mexico, none among the poor wild Indians; that the voice of the civilized, aye, and savage world, is against him. I would have condemnation blaze down upon him in every direction, till, stunned and overwhelmed with shame and confusion, he is compelled to let go the grasp he holds upon the persons of his victims, and restore them to their long-lost rights.

THE WAR WITH MEXICO

From aught that appears in the present position and movements of the executive and cabinet – the proceedings of either branch of the national Congress, – the several State Legislatures, North and South – the spirit of the public press – the conduct of leading men, and the general views and feelings of the people of the United States at large, slight hope can rationally be predicated of a very speedy termination of the present disgraceful, cruel, and iniquitous war with our sister republic. Mexico seems a doomed victim to Anglo Saxon cupidity and love of dominion. The determination of our slaveholding President to prosecute the war, and the probability of his success in wringing from the people men and money to carry it on, is made evident, rather than doubtful, by the puny opposition arrayed against him. No politician of any considerable distinction or eminence, seems willing to hazard his popularity with his party, or stem the fierce current of executive influence, by an open and unqualified disapprobation of the war. None seem willing to take their stand for peace at all risks; and all seem willing that the war should be carried on, in some form or other. If any oppose the President's demands, it is not because they hate the war, but for want of information as to the aims and objects of the war. The boldest declaration on this point is that of Hon. John P. Hale, which is to the effect that he will not vote a single dollar to the President for carrying on the war, until he shall be fully informed of the purposes and objects of the war. Mr. Hale knows, as well as the President can inform him, for what the war is waged; and yet he accompanies his declaration with that prudent proviso. This shows how deep seated and strongly bulwarked is the evil against which we contend. The boldest dare not fully grapple with it.

Meanwhile, "the plot thickens"; the evil spreads. Large demands are made on the national treasury, (to wit: the poor man's pockets.) Eloquent and patriotic speeches are made in the Senate, House of Representatives and State Assemblies: Whig as well as Democratic governors stand stoutly up for the war: experienced and hoary-headed statesmen tax their declining strength and ingenuity in devising ways and means for advancing the infernal work: recruiting sergeants and corporals perambulate the land in search of victims for the sword and food for powder. Wherever there is a sink of iniquity, or a den of pollution, these buzzards may be found in search of their filthy prey. They dive into the rum shop, and gambling house, and other sinks too infamous to name, with swine-like avidity, in pursuit of degraded men to vindicate the insulted honor of our Christain country. Military chieftains and heroes multiply, and towering high above the level of common men, are glorified, if not deified, by the people. The whole nation seems to "wonder after these beasts." Grasping ambition, tyrannic usurpation, atrocious aggression, cruel and haughty pride, spread, and pervade the land. The curse is upon us. The plague is abroad. No part of the country can claim entire exemption from its evils. They may be seen as well in the State of New York, as in South Carolina; on the Penobscot, as on the Sabine. The people appear to be completely in the hands of office seekers, demagogues, and political gamblers. Within the bewildering meshes of their political nets, they are worried, confused, and confounded, so that a general outcry is heard –

"Vigorous prosecution of the war!" – "Mexico must be humbled!" – "Conquer a peace!" – "Indemnity!" – "War forced upon us!" – "National honor!" – "The whole of Mexico!" – "Our destiny!" – "This continent!" – "Anglo Saxon blood!" – "More territory!" – "Free institutions!" – "Our country!" till it seems indeed "that justice has fled to brutish beasts, and men have lost their reason." The taste of human blood and the smell of powder seem to have extinguished the senses, seared the conscience, and subverted the reason of the people to a degree that may well induce the gloomy apprehension that our nation has fully entered on her downward career, and yielded herself up to the revolting idea of battle and blood. "Fire and sword," are now the choice of our young republic. The loss of thousands of her own men, and the slaughter of tens of thousands of the sons and daughters of Mexico, have rather given edge than dullness to our appetite for fiery conflict and plunder. The civilization of the age, the voice of the world, the sacredness of human life, the tremendous expense, the dangers, hardships, and the deep disgrace which must forever attach to our inhuman course, seem to oppose no availing check to the mad spirit of proud ambition, blood, and carnage, let loose in the land.

We have no preference for parties, regarding this slaveholding crusade. The one is as bad as the other. The friends of peace have nothing to hope from either. The Democrats claim the credit of commencing, and the Whigs monopolize the glory of voting supplies and carrying on the war; branding the war as dishonorably commenced, yet boldly persisting in pressing it on. If we have any preference of two such parties, that preference inclines to the one whose practice, though wicked, most accords with its professions. We know where to find the so called Democrats. They are the accustomed panderers to slaveholders: nothing is either too mean, too dirty, or infamous for them, when commanded by the merciless man stealers of our country. No one expects any thing honorable or decent from that party, touching human rights. They annexed Texas under the plea of extending the area of freedom. They elected James K. Polk, the slaveholder, as the friend of freedom; and they have backed him up in his Presidential falsehoods. They have used their utmost endeavors to crush the right of speech, abridge the right of petition, and to perpetuate the enslavement of the colored people of this country. But we do not intend to go into any examination of parties just now. That we shall have frequent opportunities of doing hereafter. We wish merely to give our readers a general portrait of the present aspect of our country in regard to the Mexican war, its designs, and its results, as they have thus far transpired.

Of the settled determination to prosecute the war, there can be no doubt: Polk has avowed it; his organs have published it; his supporters have rallied round him; all their actions bend in that direction; and every effort is made to establish their purpose firmly in the hearts of the people, and to harden their hearts for the conflict. All danger must be defied; all suffering despised; all honor eschewed; all mercy dried up; and all the better promptings of the human soul blunted, silenced and repudiated, while all the furies of hell are invoked to guide our hired assassins, – our man-killing machines, – now in and out of Mexico, to the infernal consummation. Qualities of head and heart, principles and maxims, counsels and warnings, which once commanded respect, and secured a nation's reverence, must all now be scouted; sense of decency must be utterly drowned: age nor sex must exercise any humanizing effect upon our gallant soldiers, or restrain their satanic designs. The groans of slaughtered men, the screams of violated women, and the cries of orphan children, must bring no throb of pity from our national heart, but must rather serve as music to inspire our gallant troops to deeds of atrocious cruelty, lust, and blood. The work is thus laid out, commenced, and is to be continued. Where it will end is known only to the Great Ruler of the Universe; but where the responsibility rests, and upon whom retribution will fall, is sure and certain. [...]

We beseech our countrymen to leave off this horrid conflict, abandon their murderous plans, and forsake the way of blood. Peradventure our country may yet be saved. Let the press, the pulpit, the church, the people at large, unite at once; and let petitions flood the halls of Congress by the million, asking for the instant recall of our forces from Mexico. This may not save us, but it is our only hope.

The North Star, January 21, 1848

THE RIGHTS OF WOMEN

One of the most interesting events of the past week, was the holding of what is technically styled a Woman's Rights Convention at Seneca Falls. The speaking, addresses, and resolutions of this extraordinary meeting was almost wholly conducted by women; and although they evidently felt themselves in a novel position, it is but simple justice to say that their whole proceedings were characterized by marked ability and dignity. No one present, we think, however much he might be disposed to differ from the views advanced by the leading speakers on that occasion, will fail to give them credit for brilliant talents and excellent dispositions. In this meeting, as in other deliberative assemblies, there were frequent differences of opinion and animated discussion; but in no case was there the slightest absence of good feeling and decorum. Several interesting documents setting forth the rights as well as the grievances of women were read. Among these was a Declaration of Sentiments, to be regarded as the basis of a grand movement for attaining the civil, social, political, and religious rights of women. We should not do justice to our own convictions, or to the excellent persons connected with this infant movement, if we did not in this connection offer a few remarks on the general subject which the Convention met to consider and the objects they seek to attain. In doing so, we are not insensible that the bare mention of this truly important subject in any other than terms of contemptuous ridicule and scornful disfavor, is likely to excite against us the fury of bigotry and the folly of prejudice. A discussion of the rights of animals would be regarded with far more complacency by many of what are called the *wise* and the *good* of our land, than would a discussion of the rights of women. It is, in their estimation, to be guilty of evil thoughts, to think that woman is entitled to equal rights with man. Many who have at last made the discovery that the Negroes have some rights as well as other members of the human family, have yet to be convinced that women are entitled to any. Eight years ago a number of persons of this description actually abandoned the anti-slavery cause, lest by giving their influence in that direction they might possibly be giving countenance to the dangerous heresy that woman, in respect to rights, stands on an equal footing with man. In the judgment of such persons the American slave system, with all its concomitant horrors, is less to be deplored than this *wicked* idea. It is perhaps needless to say, that we cherish little sympathy for such sentiments or respect for such prejudices. Standing as we do upon the watch-tower of human freedom, we cannot be deterred from an expression of our approbation of any movement, however humble, to improve and elevate the character of any members of the human family. While it is impossible for us to go into this subject at length, and dispose of the various objections which are often urged against such a doctrine as that of female equality, we are free to say that in respect to political rights, we hold woman to be justly entitled to all we claim for man. We go farther, and express our conviction that all political rights which it is expedient for man to exercise, it is equally so for woman. All that distinguishes man as an intelligent and accountable being, is equally true of woman, and if that government only is just which governs by the free consent of the governed, there can be no reason in the world for denying to woman the exercise of the elective franchise, or a hand in making and administering the laws of the land. Our doctrine is that "right is of no sex." We therefore bid the women engaged in this movement our humble Godspeed.

The North Star, July 28, 1848

THE REVOLUTION OF 1848: SPEECH AT WEST INDIA EMANCIPATION CELEBRATION, ROCHESTER, NEW YORK, AUGUST 1, 1848

Mr. President and Friends:

We have met to commemorate no deed of sectional pride, or partial patriotism; to erect no monument to naval or military heroism; to applaud the character or commend the courage of no blood-stained warrior; to gloat over no fallen or vanquished foe; to revive no ancient or obsolete antipathy; to quicken and perpetuate the memory of no fierce and bloody struggle; to take from the ashes of oblivion no slumbering embers of fiery discord.

We attract your attention to no horrid strife; to no scenes of blood and carnage, where foul and unnatural murder carried its true designation, because regimentally attired. We brighten not the memories of brave men slain in the hostile array and the deadly encounter. The celebration of such men, and such deeds, may safely be left to others. We thank Heaven, that is committed a more grateful and congenial task.

The day we have met to commemorate, is marked by no deeds of violence, associated with no scenes of slaughter, and excites no malignant feelings. Peace, joy and liberty shed a halo of unfading and untarnished glory around this annual festival. On this occasion, no lonely widow is reminded of a slaughtered husband; no helpless orphans are reminded of slaughtered fathers; no aged parents are reminded of slaughtered sons; no lovely sisters meet here to mourn over the memory of slaughtered brothers. Our gladness revives no sorrow; our joyous acclamation awakens no responsive mourning. The day, the deed, the event, which we have met to celebrate, is the Tenth Anniversary of West India Emancipation – a day, a deed, an event, all glorious in the annals of Philanthropy, and as pure as the stars of heaven! On this day, ten years ago, eight hundred thousand slaves became freemen. To congratulate our disenthralled brethren of the West Indies on their peaceful emancipation; to express our unfeigned gratitude to Almighty God, their merciful deliverer; to bless the memory of the noble men through whose free and faithful labors the grand result was finally brought about; to hold up their pure and generous examples to be admired and copied; and to make this day, to some extent, subservient to the sacred cause of human freedom in our own land, and throughout the world, is the grand object of our present assembling.

I rejoice to see before me white as well as colored persons; for though this is our day peculiarly, it is not so exclusively. The great fact we this day recognize – the great truth to which we have met to do honor, belongs to the whole human family. From this meeting, therefore, no member of the human family is excluded. We have this day a free platform, to which, without respect to class, color, or condition, all are invited. Let no man here feel that he is a mere spectator – that he has no share in the proceedings of this day, because his face is of a paler hue than mine. The occasion is not one of color, but of universal man – from the purest black to the clearest white, welcome, welcome! In the name of liberty and justice, I extend to each and to all, of every complexion, form and feature, a heartfelt welcome to a full participation in the joys of this anniversary...

We live in times which have no parallel in the history of the world. The grand commotion is universal and all-pervading. Kingdoms, realms, empires, and republics, roll to and fro like ships upon a stormy sea. The long pent up energies of human rights and sympathies, are at last let loose upon the world. The grand conflict of the angel Liberty with the monster Slavery, has at last come. The globe shakes with the contest. – I thank God that I am permitted, with you, to live in these days, and to participate humbly in this struggle. We are, Mr. President, parties to what is going on around us. We are more than spectators of the scenes that pass before us. Our interests, sympathies and destiny compel us to be parties to what is passing around us. Whether the immediate struggle be baptized by the Eastern or Western wave of the waters between us, the water is one, and the cause one, and we are parties to it. Steam, skill, and lightning, have brought the ends of the earth together. Old prejudices are vanishing. The magic power of human sympathy is rapidly healing national divisions, and bringing mankind into the harmonious bonds of a common brotherhood. In some sense, we realize the sublime declaration of the Prophet of Patmos, "And there shall be no more sea." The oceans that divided us, have become bridges to connect us, and the wide "world has become a whispering gallery." The morning star of freedom is seen from every quarter of the globe.

> From spirit to spirit – from nation to nation,
> From city to hamlet, thy dawning is cast;
> And tyrants and slaves are like shadows of night,

Standing in the far West, we may now hear the earnest debate of the Western world. – The means of intelligence is so perfect, as well as rapid, that we seem to be mingling with the thrilling scenes of the Eastern hemisphere.

In the month of February of the present year, we may date the commencement of the great movements now progressing throughout Europe. In France, at that time, we saw a king to all appearance firmly seated on his costly throne, guarded by two hundred thousand bayonets. In the pride of his heart, he armed himself for the destruction of liberty. A few short hours ended the struggle. A shout went up to heaven from countless thousands, echoing back to earth, "Liberty – Equality – Fraternity." The troops heard the glorious sound, and fraternized with the people in the court yard of the Tuilleries. – Instantly the King was but a man. All that was kingly fled. The throne whereon he sat was demolished; his splendid palace sacked; his royal carriage was burnt with fire; and he who had arrayed himself against freedom, found himself, like the great Egyptian tyrant, completely overwhelmed. Out of the ruins of this grand rupture, there came up a Republican Provisional

Government, and snatching the revolutionary motto of "Liberty – Equality – Fraternity," from the fiery thousands who had just rolled back the tide of tyranny, they commenced to construct a State in accordance with that noble motto. Among the first of its acts, while hard pressed from without and perplexed within, beset on every hand – to the everlasting honor of that Government, it decreed the complete, unconditional emancipation of every slave throughout the French colonies. This act of justice and consistency went into effect on the 23d of last June. Thus were three hundred thousand souls admitted to the joys of freedom. – That provisional government is now no more. The brave and brilliant men who formed it, have ceased to play a conspicuous part in the political affairs of the nation. For the present, some of the brightest lights are obscured. Over the glory of the great-hearted Lamartine, the dark shadow of suspicion is cast. – The most of the members of that government are now distrusted, suspected, and slighted. – But while there remains on the earth one man of sable hue, there will be one witness who will ever remember with unceasing gratitude this noble act of that provisional government.

Sir, this act of justice to our race, on the part of the French people, has had a widespread effect upon the question of human freedom in our own land. Seldom, indeed, has the slave power of the nation received what they regarded such bad news. It placed our slaveholding Republic in a dilemma which all the world could see. We desired to rejoice with her in her republicanism, but it was impossible to do so without seeming to rejoice over abolitionism. Here inconsistency, hypocrisy, covered even the brass face of our slaveholding Republic with confusion. Even that staunch Democrat and Christian, John C. Calhoun, found himself embarrassed as to how to vote on a resolution congratulating the French people on the triumph of Republicanism over Royalty.

But to return to Europe. France is not alone the scene of commotion. Her excitable and inflammable disposition makes her an appropriate medium for lighting more substantial fires. Austria has dispensed with Metternich, while all the German States are demanding freedom; and even iron-hearted Russia is alarmed and perplexed by what is going on around her. The French metropolis is in direct communication with all the great cities of Europe, and the influence of her example is everywhere powerful. The Revolution of the 24th February has stirred the dormant energies of the oppressed classes all over the continent. Revolutions, outbreaks, and provisional governments, followed that event in almost fearful succession. A general insecurity broods over the crowned heads of Europe. Ireland, too, the land of O'Connell, among the most powerful that ever advocated the cause of human freedom – Ireland, ever chafing under oppressive rule, famine-stricken, ragged and wretched, but warm-hearted, generous and unconquerable Ireland, caught up the inspiring peal as it swept across the bosom of St. George's Channel, and again renewed her oath, to be free or die. Her cause is already sanctified by the martyrdom of Mitchell, and millions stand ready to be sacrificed in the same manner. England, too – calm, dignified, brave old England – is not unmoved by what is going on through the sisterhood of European nations. Her toiling sons, from the buzz and din of the factory and workshop, to her endless coal mines deep down below the surface of the earth, have heard the joyful sound of "Liberty – Equality – Fraternity" and are lifting their heads and hearts in hope of better days. [...]

I now turn from the contemplation of men and movements in Europe, to our own great country. Great we are, in many and very important respects. As a nation, we are great in numbers and geographical extent – great in wealth – great in internal resources – great in the proclamations of great truths – great in our professions of republicanism and religion – great in our inconsistencies – great in our hypocrisy – and great in our atrocious wickedness. While our boast is loud and long of justice, freedom, and humanity, the slavewhip rings to the mockery; while we are sympathising with the progress of freedom abroad, we are extending the foul curse of slavery at home; while we are rejoicing at the progress of freedom in France, Italy, Germany, and the whole European continent, we are propagating slavery in Oregon, New Mexico, California, and all our blood-bought possessions in the South and South-west. – While we are engaged in congratulating the people of the East on casting down tyrants, we are electing tyrants and men-stealers to rule over us. Truly we are a great nation! At this moment, three million slaves clank their galling fetters and drag their heavy chains on American soil. Three million from whom all rights are robbed. Three millions, a population equal to that of all Scotland, who in this land of liberty and light, are denied the right to learn to read the name of God. – They toil under a broiling sun and a driver's lash; they are sold like cattle in the market – and are shut out from human regards – thought of and spoken of as property – sanctioned as property by cruel laws, and sanctified as such by the Church and Clergy of the country. – While I am addressing you, four of my own dear sisters and one brother are enduring the frightful horrors of American slavery. In what part of the Union, they may be, I do not know; two of them, Sarah and Catharine, were sold from Maryland before I escaped from there. I am cut off from all communication with – I cannot hear from them, nor can they hear from me – we are sundered forever.

My case, is the case of thousands; and the case of my sisters, is the case of millions. I have no doubt, that there are hundreds here to-day, that have parents, children, sisters and brothers, who are now in slavery. Oh! how deep is the damnation of America – under what a load of crime does she stagger from day to day! What a hell of wickedness is there coiled up in her bosom, and what awful judgment awaits her impenitence! My friends, words cannot express my feelings. My soul is sick of this picture of an awful reality. – The wails of bondmen are on my ear, and their heavy sorrows weigh down my heart.

I turn from these horrors – from these God-defying, man imbruting crimes, to those who in my judgment are responsible for them. And I trace them to the door of every American citizen. Slavery exists in this land because of the moral, constitutional, political and religious support which it receives from the people of this country, especially the people of the North. As I stand before many to whom this subject may be new, I may be allowed here to explain. The people of this country are held together by a Constitution. That Constitution contains certain compromises in favor of slavery, and which bind the citizens to uphold slavery. The language of every American citizen to the slave, so far as he can comprehend that language is, "You shall be a slave or die." The history and character of the American people confirms the slave in this belief. To march to the attainment of his liberty, is to march directly upon the bristling bayonets of the whole military power of the nation. About eighteen years ago, a man of noble courage, rose among his brethren in Virginia. "We have long been subjected to slavery. The hour for our deliverance has come. Let us rise and strike for liberty. In the name of a God of justice let us stay our oppressors." What was the result? He fell amid showers of American bullets, fired by *United States* troops. The fact that the Constitution guarantees to the slaveholder the naval and military support of the nation; the fact that he may under that

Constitution, recapture his flying bondman in any State or territory within or belonging to this Union; and the fact that slavery alone enjoys a representation in Congress, makes every man who in good faith swears to support that Constitution and to execute its provisions, responsible for all the outrages committed on the millions of our brethren now in bonds. I therefore this day, before this large audience, charge home upon the voters of this city, county and state, the awful responsibility of enslaving and imbruting my brothers and sisters in the Southern States of this Union. Carry it home with you from this great gathering in Washington Square, that you, my white fellow-countrymen, are the enslavers of men, women, and children, in the Southern States; that what are called the compromises of your glorious Constitution, are but bloody links in the chain of slavery; and that they make you parties to that chain. But for these compromises – but for your readiness to stand by them, "in the fullness of their letter and the completeness of their letter," the slave might instantly assert and maintain his rights. The contest now would be wonderfully unequal. Seventeen millions of armed, disciplined, and intelligent people, against three millions of unarmed and uninformed. Sir, we are often taunted with the inquiry from Northern white men – "Why do your people submit to slavery? and does not that submission prove them an inferior race? Why have they not shown a desire for freedom?" Such language is as disgraceful to the insolent men who use it, as it is tantalising and insulting to us.

It is mean and cowardly for any white man to use such language toward us. My language to all such, is, Give us fair play and if we do not gain our freedom, it will be time to taunt us thus.

Before taking my seat, I will call your attention to some charges and misrepresentations of the American press, respecting the result of the great measure which we this day commemorate. We continually find statements and sentiments like this, in the whirlpool of American newspapers – "The British Colonies are ruined," "The emancipated Negroes are lazy and won't work," "Emancipation has been a failure." Now, I wish to reply to these sentiments and statements – and to say something about laziness in general, as applied to the race to which I belong. By the way, I think I may claim a superior industry for the colored man over the white man, on the showing of the white men themselves. We are just now appropriating to ourselves, vast regions of country in the South-west. – What is the language of white men, as to the best population to develop the great resources of those vast countries? Why, in good plain English this: that white industry is unequal to it, and that none but the sinewy arm of the sable race is capable of doing so. Now, for these lazy drones to be taunting us with laziness, is a little too bad. I will answer the statements respecting the ruined condition of the West India Islands, by a declaration recently made on this very subject by Lord John Russell, present Prime Minister of England, a man remarkable for coolness and accuracy of speech. In regard to the measure of emancipation, he says, and I read from the London Times of the 17th of June, 1848: –

"The main purpose of the act of 1834 was as I have stated, to give freedom to 800,000 persons, to place those then living in a condition of slavery in a state of independence, prosperity, and happiness. That object, I think, every one admits has been accomplished. [Cheers.] I believe a class of laborers more happy, more in possession of all the advantages and enjoyments of life than the Negro population of the West Indies, does not exist. [Cheers.] – That great object has been accomplished by the act of 1834."

"It appears by evidence that the Negroes of the West India colonies since the abolition of slavery had been in the best condition. They had the best food, and were in all respects better clothed and provided for than any peasantry in the world. There was a resolution passed by a committee in 1842 declaring that the measure of emancipation had completely succeeded so far as the welfare of the Negroes was concerned. I believe the noble lord the member for Lynn, moved a similar resolution on a subsequent occasion. We have it in evidence that the Negroes were able to indulge in the luxury of dress, which they carried to an almost ridiculous excess. Some were known to have dress worth 50*l.*"

Now, sir, I call upon the press of Rochester and of this country at large, to let these facts be known, that a long abused and injured race may at last have justice done them.

I must thank you now my friends, for your kind and patient attention: asking your pardon for having trespassed so long upon your hearing, I will take my seat.

The North Star, August 4, 1848

A TRIBUTE FOR THE NEGRO

"A TRIBUTE FOR THE NEGRO; being a vindication of the moral and religious capabilities, of the colored portion of mankind; with particular reference to the African race; illustrated by numerous biographical sketches – facts – anecdotes, &c., and many superior engravings. By Wilson Armistead."

A copy of this long looked for work has reached our table. It is a volume of five hundred and sixty-four pages, neatly bound, well printed and on excellent paper. [...]
The Book under consideration [...] [is] a most valuable work. [...] In proof of the ancient greatness of the Negro race, the testimony of Herodotus and Volney is adduced. In addition to this sort of testimony, we have many extracts from the writings, speeches, poems and narratives of distinguished colored persons. The whole work abounds in evidence of the natural kindness of heart, gentleness, hospitality and honesty of the Negro race. Missionaries, sea-captains, and others, testify that the Negro is peculiarly susceptible of religious impressions. Facts are presented, showing that in many parts of Africa quite a high point of civilization has already been attained. Articles of apparel, manufactured by the natives, prove the skill and ingenuity of the African race. – Instances are referred to, illustrating the readiness and ease with which the colored race assimilate with the habits and customs of a higher civilization. The fact that Negroes are as eager to improve their condition and obtain education as other men, is alleged.
Color is accounted for by climate, food and habits. Various facts are adduced in favor of this position, and we think they are quite conclusive. Haiti, with her heroes, is strongly brought out; and the voice of youthful Liberia is heard in testimony of Negro capabilities. [...]
What a fact to be handed down to coming generations, that the Christian people of England and America had become so hardened by crime, and blinded by pre-judice, that, in the year 1849, they needed the light of a volume of nearly six hundred pages to distinguish their brother man from the beast of the field. The antiquarian of

coming ages will search out this work as one of the literary curiosities of the nineteenth century, and will produce it as evidence of the darkness of this age. What a
commentary upon our enlightenment, that we must have books to prove what is
palpable even to the brute creation – to wit: the Negro is a man!

Here we are plowing, planting, reaping – using all kinds of mechanical tools –
building houses, bridges, ships – working in metals of brass, iron, copper, silver and
gold – living in families as husbands and wives, brothers and sisters, parents and
children – supporting and sustaining week and Sabbath-day schools – reading,
writing, cyphering – acting as clerks, secretaries, merchants – having among us
lawyers, ministers, doctors, poets, authors, editors, orators, teachers – building
ships on land, and navigating them at sea – taming and domesticating animals on
land, and pursuing the huge leviathans of the Pacific, – here we are walking, talking,
acting, feeling, thinking, planning – in a word, engaged in all the professions and
callings into which other men press, and which are open to us, with our minds
grasping in the fulness of manly strength the awfully sublime idea, one Supreme
God, who is the Common Father and Creator of us all; and yet, with these facts
before the Christian world, it requires a book to prove that the Negro is a man and
an equal brother, having equal capabilities with the rest of mankind. Shame on the
hardness of heart and blindness of mind! [...]

We recommend this work especially to the Negro-haters of our own Christian
land; we recommend it to our "Negro pew" churches and our Negro-hating priesthood, and ask them to look at its facts, statements, reasonings, and lay its mighty
truths to heart; remembering that the work is not that of a wild enthusiast who
bends facts, no matter how inconsistent and opposed to his theory, to suit his
purpose; but that of a calm, disinterested Christian and scholar, with a heart alive
to human woe, and whose only aim in these pages, appears to be to befriend the
helpless. We would also commend the work to our own beloved but heart-broken
brethren, the victims of prejudice and slavery. The book should be in all your houses,
and those who can ought to purchase one and possess it. We need and ought to
possess it. We need it, as a means of refuting with their own weapons and on their
own ground, the cruel calumniators of our race, as well as to inspire us with higher
aspirations and a nobler zeal and earnestness in the cause of our own elevation and
improvement.

We observe that one of our exchanges, the *Ram's Horn*, alleges the complaint, that
the work takes too low ground with respect to our abilities as a people. The
complaint is not only unjust, but, in the person who prefers it, immodest. A work
admitting the brilliant talents and genius of many of our number, and vindicating the
capabilities of the whole people, is quite as much as we can ask or justly demand. As
much or more injury is done by an over estimate of our abilities, as by an under
estimation of them. We would be just, though we should thereby pluck wreaths of
glory from the brow of our own people, and consign us to an inferior sphere in the
ranks of human brotherhood. That Africa is behind Europe in the pathway of
improvement it is madness, if nothing worse, to pretend to doubt; and in such
circumstances Africa ought to be thankful for a simple vindication of her capabilities. For our part, as a man, a slave, and an humble advocate for emancipation, and
as a child of Africa, we thank, from the very depth of our heart, Wilson Armistead,
for the faithfulness of this book, and the great good which we believe will result from
its publication on both sides the Atlantic. – F. D.

The North Star, April 7, 1849

COLORPHOBIA IN NEW YORK!

The fifth of May will long be remembered as the most trying day ever experienced by the unfortunate victims of colorphobia in the city of New York. The disease was never more malignant or general than on that day. The streets were literally crowded with persons of all classes afflicted with this terrible malady. Whole omnibus loads were attacked at the same moment, and their hideous and unearthly howls were truly distressing, excruciating. It will be impossible to describe, or give the reader any correct idea either of the extent of the disease or the agony it seemed to occasion. Like most epidemics, its chief havoc was among the baser sort. The suffering here was fearful and intense. If the genteel suffered from the plague, they managed to suppress and control their feelings better than what are called the "lower orders." But, even here, there could be no successful concealment. The strange plague defied all concealment, and would show itself in spite of veils, white pocket handkerchiefs, parasols, hats, bonnets and umbrellas. In the refined the presence of the plague might be seen by a distortion of the countenance, a red and furious look about the cheek, a singular turn up of the nose, and a *"lower me!"* expression of the eyes.

Among the low and vulgar the symptoms were different; – the hand clinched, head shaking, teeth grating, hysteric yells and horrid imprecation, marked the presence of the disease and the agony of the miserable creatures who were its unfortunate victims. Persons who, at a distance of thirty or forty yards, appeared the very pictures of health, were found, on a nearer approach, most horribly cut and marred.

But the effect upon the outward man was not half so strange and dreadful as that upon the mind. Here all was utter ruin. Gough's description of "delirium tremens" would not be much out of place in describing one haunted and afflicted with color-phobia. Monsters, goblins, demons, snakes, lizards and scorpions – all that was foul, strange and loathsome – seized upon their bewildered imaginations. Pointing with outstretched arm towards us, its victims would exclaim, as if startled by some terrible sight – "Look! look!" "Where?" "Ah, what?" "Why?" "Why, don't you see?" "See what?" "Why, that BLACK! black! *black*!" Then, with eyes turned up in horror, they would exclaim in the most unearthly manner, and start off in a furious gallop – running all around us, and gazing at us, as if they would read our very hearts. The whole scene was deeply afflicting and terrible.

But to the cause of this wide-spread plague, or rather the manifestation of it. We think it can all be made plain to the dullest comprehension. There had arrived in New York, a few days previous, two *English* Ladies, from London – friends of Frederick Douglass – and had taken apartments at the Franklin House, Broadway; and were not only called upon at that Hotel by Mr. Douglass, but really allowed themselves to take his arm, and to walk many times up and down Broadway, in broad-day light, when that great thoroughfare was crowded with pure American ladies and gentlemen. Such an open, glaring outrage upon *pure American* tastes had never before been perpetrated. Two ladies, elegantly attired, educated, and of the most approved manners, faultless in appearance and position, actually walking, and leaning upon the arm of a person, with a skin not colored like their own! Oh! monstrous! Was it not enough to cause the very stones to leap up with indignation from the pavement! and to "stir them up to mutiny and rage"? More and worse still, these ladies appeared wholly indifferent to, and oblivious of, all the indignation and fury going on about them; but walked, talked and acted as though nothing unusual was passing. In a word, they seemed to forget that they were in the greatest Commercial Emporium of this, the mightiest Nation in the world, and to act as though they had been in the paltry city of London!! instead of New York. What could they have been thinking about? How strange that they had not made themselves acquainted with the institutions and customs of the great Nation, upon whose sacred soil they were *allowed* to land? How singular that their friends had not warned them against such a monstrous outrage upon the established customs of this, the "*freest*" country in the world? They certainly must have been deceived. It is impossible "that nature so could err." "Charms, conjuration – mighty magic," must have bewildered and misled them. They would have been kindly received and hospitably entertained by some of the most respectable and refined families in the city of New York; but, with a strange hallucination, they preferred to identify themselves with the most despised and injured portion of all the people of America – and thus to make themselves of no reputation, and cut themselves off from all sympathy and attention of the highly favored and accomplished sons and daughters of America. Before quitting this subject, we wish to call attention to certain singular inconsistencies connected with the development of the feeling, called (erroneously) prejudice against color. The first is this. The poor creatures who seemed most disturbed by the fact that these ladies walked through the streets of New York in company with a colored man, felt in no wise shocked at seeing ladies seated in their gilded carriages, with colored persons seated near them, driving their horses and otherwise assisting such ladies. All this was perfectly right. They were in the capacity of servants. Hence New York toadyism is rather pleased than disgusted. It is not with colored servants that New York loafers are displeased; but with colored *gentlemen*. It is with the colored man as a gentleman that they feel the most intense displeasure. They cannot bear it, and they must pour out their pent-up wrath, whenever an opportunity is afforded for doing so.

In this same Franklin Hotel, in which we could not be allowed to dine on account of our color, we saw a large number of colored waiters in the nearest proximity to white gentlemen and ladies, without offence.

We, however, tire of this subject. This prejudice is so unjust, unnatural and irrational, that ridicule and indignation seem to be the only weapons with which to assail it.

Our friends informed us that when they landed, they were assured that they had reached the shores of a free country, and were congratulated upon that fact. But they had scarcely reached the hotel, when they were informed that a friend of theirs, who was not deemed unfit to be associated with in London, and who would have been kindly received at the best hotels in that city, and in Paris, would not be allowed to take dinner with them at the Franklin Hotel, in the city of New York. In this free country one is not permitted to choose and enjoy the society of his friends, without being subjected to innumerable insults and annoyances.

We shall not, however, despair on this point. A marked improvement has already taken place in the manner of treating colored travelers, and the change is going on still. Nothing, however, facilitates this more than such examples of fidelity to principle, and indifference to a corrupt and brutal public opinion, as is presented in the conduct of these two English ladies, and others. This prejudice must be removed; and the way for abolitionists and colored persons to remove it, is to act as though it did not exist, and to associate with their fellow creatures irrespective of all complexional differences. We have marked out this path for ourselves, and we mean to pursue it at all hazards. – F. D.

The North Star, May 25, 1849

THE DESTINY OF COLORED AMERICANS

It is impossible to settle, by the light of the present, and by the experience of the past, any thing, definitely and absolutely, as to the future condition of the colored people of this country; but, so far as present indications determine, it is clear that this land must continue to be the home of the colored man so long as it remains the abode of civilization and religion. For more than two hundred years we have been identified with its soil, its products, and its institutions; under the sternest and bitterest circumstances of slavery and oppression – under the lash of Slavery at the South – under the sting of prejudice and malice at the North – and under hardships the most unfavorable to existence and population, we have lived, and continue to live and increase. The persecuted red man of the forest, the original owner of the soil, has, step by step, retreated from the Atlantic lakes and rivers; escaping, as it were, before the footsteps of the white man, and gradually disappearing from the face of the country. He looks upon the steamboats, the railroads, and canals, cutting and crossing his former hunting grounds; and upon the ploughshare, throwing up the bones of his venerable ancestors, and beholds his glory departing – and his heart sickens at the desolation. He spurns the civilization – he hates the race which has despoiled him, and unable to measure arms with his superior foe, he dies.

Not so with the black man. More unlike the European in form, feature and color – called to endure greater hardships, injuries and insults than those to which the Indians have been subjected, he yet lives and prospers under every disadvantage. Long have his enemies sought to expatriate him, and to teach his children that this is not their home, but in spite of all their cunning schemes, and subtle contrivances, his footprints yet mark the soil of his birth, and he gives every indication that America will, for ever, remain the home of his posterity. We deem it a settled point that the destiny of the colored man is bound up with that of the white people of this country; be the destiny of the latter what it may.

It is idle – worse than idle, ever to think of our expatriation, or removal. The history of the colonization society must extinguish all such speculations. We are rapidly filling up the number of four millions; and all the gold of California combined, would be insufficient to defray the expenses attending our colonization. We are, as laborers, too essential to the interests of our white fellow-countrymen, to make a very grand effort to drive us from this country among probable events. While labor is needed, the laborer cannot fail to be valued; and although passion and prejudice may sometimes vociferate against us, and demand our expulsion, such efforts will only be spasmodic, and can never prevail against the sober second thought of self-interest. *We are here*, and here we are likely to be. To imagine that we shall ever be eradicated is absurd and ridiculous. We can be remodified, changed, and assimilated, but never extinguished. We repeat, therefore, that *we are here;* and that this is *our* country; and the question for the philosophers and statesmen of the land ought to be, What principles should dictate the policy of the action towards us? We shall neither die out, nor be driven out; but shall go with this people, either as a testimony against them, or as an evidence in their favor throughout their generations. We are clearly on their hands, and must remain there for ever. All this we say for the benefit of those who hate the Negro more than they love their country. In an article, under the caption of "Government and its Subjects," (published in our last week's paper,) we called attention to the unwise, as well as the unjust policy usually adopted, by our Government, towards its colored citizens. We would continue to direct attention to that policy, and in our humble way, we would remonstrate against it, as fraught with evil to the white man, as well as to his victim.

The white man's happiness cannot be purchased by the black man's misery. Virtue cannot prevail among the white people, by its destruction among the black people, who form a part of the whole community. It is evident that white and black "must fall or flourish together." In the light of this great truth, laws ought to be enacted, and institutions established – all distinctions, founded on complexion, ought to be repealed, repudiated, and for ever abolished – and every right, privilege, and immunity, now enjoyed by the white man, ought to be as freely granted to the man of color.

Where "knowledge is power," that nation is the most powerful which has the largest population of intelligent men; for a nation to cramp, and circumscribe the mental faculties of a class of its inhabitants, is as unwise as it is cruel, since it, in the same proportion, sacrifices its power and happiness. The American people, in the light of this reasoning, are, at this moment, in obedience to their pride and folly, (we say nothing of the wickedness of the act,) wasting one sixth part of the energies of the entire nation by transforming three millions of its men into beasts of burden. – What a loss to industry, skill, invention, (to say nothing of its foul and corrupting influence,) is *Slavery!* How it ties the hand, cramps the mind, darkens the understanding, and paralyses the whole man! Nothing is more evident to a man who reasons at all, than that America is acting an irrational part in continuing the slave system at the South, and in oppressing its free colored citizens at the North. Regarding the nation as an individual, the act of enslaving and oppressing thus, is as wild and senseless as it would be for Nicholas to order the amputation of the right arm of every Russian soldier before engaging in a war with France. We again repeat that Slavery is the peculiar weakness of America, as well as its peculiar crime; and the day may yet come when this visionary and oft repeated declaration will be found to contain a great truth. – F. D.

The North Star, November 16, 1849

CHAPTER 12

The Communist Manifesto

KARL MARX

1: BOURGEOIS AND PROLETARIANS

The history of all hitherto existing society is the history of class struggles.

Freeman and slave, patrician and plebeian, lord and serf, guild-master and jour-neyman, in a word, oppressor and oppressed, stood in constant opposition to one another, carried on an uninterrupted, now hidden, now open fight, a fight that each time ended, either in a revolutionary reconstitution of society at large, or in the common ruin of the contending classes.

In the earlier epochs of history, we find almost everywhere a complicated arrange-ment of society into various orders, a manifold gradation of social rank. In ancient Rome we have patricians, knights, plebeians, slaves; in the Middle Ages, feudal lords, vassals, guild-masters, journeymen, apprentices, serfs; in almost all of these classes, again, subordinate gradations.

The modern bourgeois society that has sprouted from the ruins of feudal society has not done away with class antagonisms. It has but established new classes, new conditions of oppression, new forms of struggle in place of the old ones.

Our epoch, the epoch of the bourgeoisie, possesses, however, this distinctive feature: it has simplified the class antagonisms. Society as a whole is more and more splitting up into two great hostile camps, into two great classes directly facing each other: Bourgeoisie and Proletariat.

From the serfs of the Middle Ages sprang the chartered burghers of the earliest towns. From these burgesses the first elements of the bourgeoisie were developed.

The discovery of America, the rounding of the Cape, opened up fresh ground for the rising bourgeoisie. The East-Indian and Chinese markets, the colonization of America, trade with the colonies, the increase in the means of exchange and in commodities generally, gave to commerce, to navigation, to industry, an impulse

---

Karl Marx. *The Communist Manifesto*. Originally published in 1848.

never before known, and thereby, to the revolutionary element in the tottering feudal society, a rapid development.

The feudal system of industry, under which industrial production was monopolized by closed guilds, now no longer sufficed for the growing wants of the new markets. The manufacturing system took its place. The guild-masters were pushed on one side by the manufacturing middle class; division of labour between the different corporate guilds vanished in the face of division of labour in each single workshop.

Meantime the markets kept ever growing, the demand ever rising. Even manufacture no longer sufficed. Thereupon, steam and machinery revolutionized industrial production. The place of manufacture was taken by the giant, Modern Industry, the place of the industrial middle class, by industrial millionaires, the leaders of whole industrial armies, the modern bourgeois.

Modern industry has established the world market, for which the discovery of America paved the way. This market has given an immense development to commerce, to navigation, to communication by land. This development has, in its turn, reacted on the extension of industry; and in proportion as industry, commerce, navigation, railways extended, in the same proportion the bourgeoisie developed, increased its capital, and pushed into the background every class handed down from the Middle Ages.

We see, therefore, how the modern bourgeoisie is itself the product of a long course of development, of a series of revolutions in the modes of production and of exchange.

Each step in the development of the bourgeoisie was accompanied by a corresponding political advance of that class. An oppressed class under the sway of the feudal nobility, an armed and self-governing association in the medieval commune; here independent urban republic (as in Italy and Germany), there taxable "third estate" of the monarchy (as in France), afterwards, in the period of manufacture proper, serving either the semi-feudal or the absolute monarchy as a counterpoise against the nobility, and, in fact, corner-stone of the great monarchies in general, the bourgeoisie has at last, since the establishment of Modern Industry and of the world market, conquered for itself, in the modern representative State, exclusive political sway. The executive of the modern State is but a committee for managing the common affairs of the whole bourgeoisie.

The bourgeoisie, historically, has played a most revolutionary part.

The bourgeoisie, wherever it has got the upper hand, has put an end to all feudal, patriarchal, idyllic relations. It has pitilessly torn asunder the motley feudal ties that bound man to his 'natural superiors', and has left remaining no other nexus between man and man than naked self-interest, than callous 'cash payment'. It has drowned the most heavenly ecstasies of religious fervour, of chivalrous enthusiasm, of philistine sentimentalism, in the icy water of egotistical calculation. It has resolved personal worth into exchange value, and in place of the numberless indefeasible chartered freedoms, has set up that single, unconscionable freedom – Free Trade. In one word, for exploitation, veiled by religious and political illusions, it has substituted naked, shameless, direct, brutal exploitation.

The bourgeoisie has stripped of its halo every occupation hitherto honoured and looked up to with reverent awe. It has converted the physician, the lawyer, the priest, the poet, the man of science, into its paid wage-labourers.

The bourgeoisie has torn away from the family its sentimental veil, and has reduced the family relation to a mere money relation.

The bourgeoisie has disclosed how it came to pass that the brutal display of vigour in the Middle Ages, which Reactionists so much admire, found its fitting complement in the most slothful indolence. It has been the first to show what man's activity can bring about. It has accomplished wonders far surpassing Egyptian pyramids, Roman aqueducts, and Gothic cathedrals; it has conducted expeditions that put in the shade all former Exoduses of nations and crusades.

The bourgeoisie cannot exist without constantly revolutionizing the instruments of production, and thereby the relations of production, and with them the whole relations of society. Conservation of the old modes of production in unaltered form, was, on the contrary, the first condition of existence for all earlier industrial classes. Constant revolutionizing of production, uninterrupted disturbance of all social conditions, everlasting uncertainty and agitation distinguish the bourgeois epoch from all earlier ones. All fixed, fast-frozen relations, with their train of ancient and venerable prejudices and opinions are swept away, all new-formed ones become antiquated before they can ossify. All that is solid melts into air, all that is holy is profaned, and man is at last compelled to face with sober senses, his real conditions of life, and his relations with his kind.

The need of a constantly expanding market for its products chases the bourgeoisie over the whole surface of the globe. It must nestle everywhere, settle everywhere, establish connexions everywhere.

The bourgeoisie has through its exploitation of the world market given a cosmopolitan character to production and consumption in every country. To the great chagrin of Reactionists, it has drawn from under the feet of industry the national ground on which it stood. All old-established national industries have been destroyed or are daily being destroyed. They are dislodged by new industries, whose introduction becomes a life and death question for all civilized nations, by industries that no longer work up indigenous raw material, but raw material drawn from the remotest zones; industries whose products are consumed, not only at home, but in every quarter of the globe. In place of the old wants, satisfied by the productions of the country, we find new wants, requiring for their satisfaction the products of distant lands and climes. In place of the old local and national seclusion and self-sufficiency, we have intercourse in every direction, universal inter-dependence of nations. And as in material, so also in intellectual production. The intellectual creations of individual nations become common property. National one-sidedness and narrow-mindedness become more and more impossible, and from the numerous national and local literatures, there arises a world literature.

The bourgeoisie, by the rapid improvement of all instruments of production, by the immensely facilitated means of communication, draws all, even the most barbarian, nations into civilization. The cheap prices of its commodities are the heavy artillery with which it batters down all Chinese walls, with which it forces the barbarians' intensely obstinate hatred of foreigners to capitulate. It compels all nations, on pain of extinction, to adopt the bourgeois mode of production; it compels them to introduce what it calls civilization into their midst, i.e., to become bourgeois themselves. In one word, it creates a world after its own image.

The bourgeoisie has subjected the country to the rule of the towns. It has created enormous cities, has greatly increased the urban population as compared with the rural, and has thus rescued a considerable part of the population from the idiocy of rural life. Just as it has made the country dependent on the towns, so it has made barbarian and semi-barbarian countries dependent on the civilized ones, nations of peasants on nations of bourgeois, the East on the West.

The bourgeoisie keeps more and more doing away with the scattered state of the population, of the means of production, and of property. It has agglomerated population, centralized means of production, and has concentrated property in a few hands. The necessary consequence of this was political centralization. Independent, or but loosely connected, provinces with separate interests, laws, governments and systems of taxation, became lumped together into one nation, with one government, one code of laws, one national class-interest, one frontier and one customs-tariff.

The bourgeoisie, during its rule of scarce one hundred years, has created more massive and more colossal productive forces than have all preceding generations together. Subjection of Nature's forces to man, machinery, application of chemistry to industry and agriculture, steam-navigation, railways, electric telegraphs, clearing of whole continents for cultivation, canalization of rivers, whole populations conjured out of the ground – what earlier century had even a presentiment that such productive forces slumbered in the lap of social labour?

We see then: the means of production and of exchange, on whose foundation the bourgeoisie built itself up, were generated in feudal society. At a certain stage in the development of these means of production and of exchange, the conditions under which feudal society produced and exchanged, the feudal organization of agriculture and manufacturing industry, in one word, the feudal relations of property became no longer compatible with the already developed productive forces; they became so many fetters. They had to be burst asunder; they were burst asunder.

Into their place stepped free competition, accompanied by a social and political constitution adapted to it, and by the economical and political sway of the bourgeois class.

A similar movement is going on before our own eyes. Modern bourgeois society with its relations of production, of exchange and of property, a society that has conjured up such gigantic means of production and of exchange, is like the sorcerer, who is no longer able to control the powers of the nether world whom he has called up by his spells. For many a decade past the history of industry and commerce is but the history of the revolt of modern productive forces against modern conditions of production, against the property relations that are the conditions for the existence of the bourgeoisie and of its rule. It is enough to mention the commercial crises that by their periodical return put on its trial, each time more threateningly, the existence of the entire bourgeois society. In these crises a great part not only of the existing products, but also of the previously created productive forces, are periodically destroyed. In these crises there breaks out an epidemic that, in all earlier epochs, would have seemed an absurdity – the epidemic of over-production. Society suddenly finds itself put back into a state of momentary barbarism; it appears as if a famine, a universal war of devastation had cut off the supply of every means of subsistence; industry and commerce seem to be destroyed; and why? Because there is too much civilization, too much means of subsistence, too much industry, too much commerce. The productive forces at the disposal of society no longer tend to further the development of the conditions of bourgeois property; on the contrary, they have become too powerful for these conditions, by which they are fettered, and so soon as they overcome these fetters, they bring disorder into the whole of bourgeois society, endanger the existence of bourgeois property. The conditions of bourgeois society are too narrow to comprise the wealth created by them. And how does the bourgeoisie get over these crises? On the one hand by enforced destruction of a mass of productive forces; on the other, by the conquest of new markets, and by the more thorough exploitation of the old ones. That is to say, by paving the way for more extensive and more destructive crises, and by diminishing the means whereby crises are prevented.

The weapons with which the bourgeoisie felled feudalism to the ground are now turned against the bourgeoisie itself.

But not only has the bourgeoisie forged the weapons that bring death to itself; it has also called into existence the men who are to wield those weapons – the modern working class – the proletarians.

In proportion as the bourgeoisie, i.e., capital, is developed, in the same proportion is the proletariat, the modern working class, developed – a class of labourers, who live only so long as they find work, and who find work only so long as their labour increases capital. These labourers, who must sell themselves piecemeal, are a commodity, like every other article of commerce, and are consequently exposed to all the vicissitudes of competition, to all the fluctuations of the market.

Owing to the extensive use of machinery and to division of labour, the work of the proletarians has lost all individual character, and, consequently, all charm for the workman. He becomes an appendage of the machine, and it is only the most simple, most monotonous, and most easily acquired knack, that is required of him. Hence, the cost of production of a workman is restricted, almost entirely, to the means of subsistence that he requires for his maintenance, and for the propagation of his race. But the price of a commodity, and therefore also of labour, is equal to its cost of production. In proportion, therefore, as the repulsiveness of the work increases, the wage decreases. Nay more, in proportion as the use of machinery and division of labour increases, in the same proportion the burden of toil also increases, whether by prolongation of the working hours, by increase of the work exacted in a given time or by increased speed of the machinery, etc.

Modern industry has converted the little workshop of the patriarchal master into the great factory of the industrial capitalist. Masses of labourers, crowded into the factory, are organized like soldiers. As privates of the industrial army they are placed under the command of a perfect hierarchy of officers and sergeants. Not only are they slaves of the bourgeois class, and of the bourgeois State; they are daily and hourly enslaved by the machine, by the overlooker, and, above all, by the individual bourgeois manufacturer himself. The more openly this despotism proclaims gain to be its end and aim, the more petty, the more hateful and the more embittering it is.

The less the skill and exertion of strength implied in manual labour, in other words, the more modern industry becomes developed, the more is the labour of men superseded by that of women. Differences of age and sex have no longer any distinctive social validity for the working class. All are instruments of labour, more or less expensive to use, according to their age and sex.

No sooner is the exploitation of the labourer by the manufacturer, so far, at an end, that he receives his wages in cash, than he is set upon by the other portions of the bourgeoisie, the landlord, the shopkeeper, the pawnbroker, etc.

The lower strata of the middle class – the small tradespeople, shopkeepers, and retired tradesmen generally, the handicraftsmen and peasants – all these sink gradually into the proletariat, partly because their diminutive capital does not suffice for the scale on which Modern Industry is carried on, and is swamped in the competition with the large capitalists, partly because their specialized skill is rendered worthless by new methods of production. Thus the proletariat is recruited from all classes of the population.

The proletariat goes through various stages of development. With its birth begins its struggle with the bourgeoisie. At first the contest is carried on by individual labourers, then by the work-people of a factory, then by the operatives of one trade, in one locality, against the individual bourgeois who directly exploits them. They direct their attacks not against the bourgeois conditions of production, but against the instruments of production themselves; they destroy imported wares that compete with their labour, they smash to pieces machinery, they set factories ablaze, they seek to restore by force the vanished status of the workman of the Middle Ages.

At this stage the labourers still form an incoherent mass scattered over the whole country, and broken up by their mutual competition. If anywhere they unite to form more compact bodies, this is not yet the consequence of their own active union, but of the union of the bourgeoisie, which class, in order to attain its own political ends, is compelled to set the whole proletariat in motion, and is moreover yet, for a time, able to do so. At this stage, therefore, the proletarians do not fight their enemies, but the enemies of their enemies, the remnants of absolute monarchy, the land-owners, the non-industrial bourgeois, the petty bourgeoisie. Thus the whole historical movement is concentrated in the hands of the bourgeoisie; every victory so obtained is a victory for the bourgeoisie.

But with the development of industry the proletariat not only increases in number; it becomes concentrated in greater masses, its strength grows, and it feels that strength more. The various interests and conditions of life within the ranks of the proletariat are more and more equalized, in proportion as machinery obliterates all distinctions of labour, and nearly everywhere reduces wages to the same low level. The growing competition among the bourgeois, and the resulting commercial crises, make the wages of the workers ever more fluctuating. The unceasing improvement of machinery, ever more rapidly developing, makes their livelihood more and more precarious; the collisions between individual workmen and individual bourgeois take more and more the character of collisions between two classes. Thereupon the workers begin to form combinations (Trades Unions) against the bourgeois; they club together in order to keep up the rate of wages; they found permanent associations in order to make provision beforehand for these occasional revolts. Here and there the contest breaks out into riots.

Now and then the workers are victorious, but only for a time. The real fruit of their battles lies, not in the immediate result, but in the ever-expanding union of the workers. This union is helped on by the improved means of communication that are created by modern industry and that place the workers of different localities in contact with one another. It was just this contact that was needed to centralize the numerous local struggles, all of the same character, into one national struggle between classes. But every class struggle is a political struggle. And that union, to attain which the burghers of the Middle Ages, with their miserable highways, required centuries, the modern proletarians, thanks to railways, achieve in a few years.

This organization of the proletarians into a class, and consequently into a political party, is continually being upset again by the competition between the workers themselves. But it ever rises up again, stronger, firmer, mightier. It compels legislative recognition of particular interests of the workers, by taking advantage of the divisions among the bourgeoisie itself. Thus the Ten Hours bill in England was carried.

Altogether collisions between the classes of the old society further, in many ways, the course of development of the proletariat. The bourgeoisie finds itself involved in a constant battle. At first with the aristocracy; later on, with those portions of the bourgeoisie itself, whose interests have become antagonistic to the progress of industry; at all times, with the bourgeoisie of foreign countries. In all these battles it sees itself compelled to appeal to the proletariat, to ask for its help, and thus, to drag it into the political arena. The bourgeoisie itself, therefore, supplies the proletariat with its own elements of political and general education, in other words, it furnishes the proletariat with weapons for fighting the bourgeoisie.

Further, as we have already seen, entire sections of the ruling classes are, by the advance of industry, precipitated into the proletariat, or are at least threatened in their conditions of existence. These also supply the proletariat with fresh elements of enlightenment and progress.

Finally, in times when the class struggle nears the decisive hour, the process of dissolution going on within the ruling class, in fact within the whole range of old society, assumes such a violent, glaring character, that a small section of the ruling class cuts itself adrift, and joins the revolutionary class, the class that holds the future in its hands. Just as, therefore, at an earlier period, a section of the nobility went over to the bourgeoisie, so now a portion of the bourgeoisie goes over to the proletariat, and in particular, a portion of the bourgeois ideologists, who have raised themselves to the level of comprehending theoretically the historical movement as a whole.

Of all the classes that stand face to face with the bourgeoisie today, the proletariat alone is a really revolutionary class. The other classes decay and finally disappear in the face of modern industry; the proletariat is its special and essential product.

The lower middle class, the small manufacturer, the shopkeeper, the artisan, the peasant, all these fight against the bourgeoisie, to save from extinction their existence as fractions of the middle class. They are therefore not revolutionary, but conservative. Nay more, they are reactionary, for they try to roll back the wheel of history. If by chance they are revolutionary, they are so only in view of their impending transfer into the proletariat, they thus defend not their present, but their future interests, they desert their own standpoint to place themselves at that of the proletariat.

The 'dangerous class', the social scum, that passively rotting mass thrown off by the lowest layers of old society, may, here and there, be swept into the movement by a proletarian revolution; its conditions of life, however, prepare it far more for the part of a bribed tool of reactionary intrigue.

In the conditions of the proletariat, those of old society at large are already virtually swamped. The proletarian is without property; his relation to his wife and children has no longer anything in common with the bourgeois family relations; modern industrial labour, modern subjection to capital, the same in England as in France, in America as in Germany, has stripped him of every trace of national character. Law, morality, religion, are to him so many bourgeois prejudices, behind which lurk in ambush just as many bourgeois interests.

All the preceding classes that got the upper hand sought to fortify their already acquired status by subjecting society at large to their conditions of appropriation. The proletarians cannot become masters of the productive forces of society, except by abolishing their own previous mode of appropriation, and thereby also every other previous mode of appropriation. They have nothing of their own to secure and to fortify; their mission is to destroy all previous securities for, and insurances of, individual property.

All previous historical movements were movements of minorities, or in the interest of minorities. The proletarian movement is the self-conscious, independent movement of the immense majority, in the interest of the immense majority. The proletariat, the lowest stratum of our present society, cannot stir, cannot raise itself up, without the whole superincumbent strata of official society being sprung into the air.

Though not in substance, yet in form, the struggle of the proletariat with the bourgeoisie is at first a national struggle. The proletariat of each country must, of course, first of all settle matters with its own bourgeoisie.

In depicting the most general phases of the development of the proletariat, we traced the more or less veiled civil war, raging within existing society, up to the point where that war breaks out into open revolution, and where the violent overthrow of the bourgeoisie lays the foundation for the sway of the proletariat.

Hitherto, every form of society has been based, as we have already seen, on the antagonism of oppressing and oppressed classes. But in order to oppress a class, certain conditions must be assured to it under which it can, at least, continue its slavish existence. The serf, in the period of serfdom, raised himself to membership in the commune, just as the petty bourgeois, under the yoke of feudal absolutism, managed to develop into a bourgeois. The modern labourer, on the contrary, instead of rising with the progress of industry, sinks deeper and deeper below the conditions of existence of his own class. He becomes a pauper, and pauperism develops more rapidly than population and wealth. And here it becomes evident, that the bourgeoisie is unfit any longer to be the ruling class in society, and to impose its conditions of existence upon society as an overriding law. It is unfit to rule because it is incompetent to assure an existence to its slave within his slavery, because it cannot help letting him sink into such a state, that it has to feed him, instead of being fed by him. Society can no longer live under this bourgeoisie, in other words, its existence is no longer compatible with society.

The essential condition for the existence, and for the sway of the bourgeois class, is the formation and augmentation of capital; the condition for capital is wage labour. Wage labour rests exclusively on competition between the labourers. The advance of industry, whose involuntary promoter is the bourgeoisie, replaces the isolation of the labourers, due to competition, by their revolutionary combination, due to association. The development of Modern Industry, therefore, cuts from under its feet the very foundation on which the bourgeoisie produces and appropriates products. What the bourgeoisie, therefore, produces, above all, is its own grave-diggers. Its fall and the victory of the proletariat are equally inevitable.

2: PROLETARIANS AND COMMUNISTS

In what relation do the Communists stand to the proletarians as a whole?

The Communists do not form a separate party opposed to other working-class parties.

They have no interests separate and apart from those of the proletariat as a whole.

They do not set up any sectarian principles of their own, by which to shape and mould the proletarian movement.

The Communists are distinguished from the other working-class parties by this only: 1. In the national struggles of the proletarians of the different countries, they point out and bring to the front the common interests of the entire proletariat, independently of all nationality. 2. In the various stages of development which the struggle of the working class against the bourgeoisie has to pass through, they always and everywhere represent the interests of the movement as a whole.

The Communists, therefore, are on the one hand, practically, the most advanced and resolute section of the working-class parties of every country, that section which pushes forward all others; on the other hand, theoretically, they have over the great mass of the proletariat the advantage of clearly understanding the line of march, the conditions, and the ultimate general results of the proletarian movement.

The immediate aim of the Communists is the same as that of all the other proletarian parties: formation of the proletariat into a class, overthrow of the bourgeois supremacy, conquest of political power by the proletariat.

The theoretical conclusions of the Communists are in no way based on ideas or principles that have been invented, or discovered, by this or that would-be universal reformer.

They merely express, in general terms, actual relations springing from an existing class struggle, from a historical movement going on under our very eyes. The abolition of existing property relations is not at all a distinctive feature of Communism.

All property relations in the past have continually been subject to historical change consequent upon the change in historical conditions.

The French Revolution, for example, abolished feudal property in favour of bourgeois property.

The distinguishing feature of Communism is not the abolition of property generally, but the abolition of bourgeois property. But modern bourgeois private property is the final and most complete expression of the system of producing and appropriating products, that is based on class antagonisms, on the exploitation of the many by the few.

In this sense, the theory of the Communists may be summed up in the single sentence: Abolition of private property.

We Communists have been reproached with the desire of abolishing the right of personally acquiring property as the fruit of a man's own labour, which property is alleged to be the ground work of all personal freedom, activity and independence.

Hard-won, self-acquired, self-earned property! Do you mean the property of the petty artisan and of the small peasant, a form of property that preceded the bourgeois form? There is no need to abolish that; the development of industry has to a great extent already destroyed it, and is still destroying it daily.

Or do you mean modern bourgeois private property?

But does wage labour create any property for the labourer? Not a bit. It creates capital, i.e., that kind of property which exploits wage labour, and which cannot increase except upon condition of begetting a new supply of wage labour for fresh exploitation. Property, in its present form, is based on the antagonism of capital and wage labour. Let us examine both sides of this antagonism.

To be a capitalist is to have not only a purely personal but a social *status* in production. Capital is a collective product, and only by the united action of many members, nay, in the last resort, only by the united action of all members of society, can it be set in motion.

Capital is, therefore, not a personal, it is a social power.

When, therefore, capital is converted into common property, into the property of all members of society, personal property is not thereby transformed into social property. It is only the social character of the property that is changed. It loses its class character.

Let us now take wage labour.

The average price of wage labour is the minimum wage, i.e., that quantum of the means of subsistence which is absolutely requisite to keep the labourer in bare existence as a labourer. What, therefore, the wage-labourer appropriates by means of his labour, merely suffices to prolong and reproduce a bare existence. We by no means intend to abolish this personal appropriation of the products of labour, an appropriation that is made for the maintenance and reproduction of human life, and that leaves no surplus wherewith to command the labour of others. All that we want to do away with is the miserable character of this appropriation, under which the labourer lives merely to increase capital, and is allowed to live only in so far as the interest of the ruling class requires it.

In bourgeois society, living labour is but a means to increase accumulated labour. In Communist society, accumulated labour is but a means to widen, to enrich, to promote the existence of the labourer.

In bourgeois society, therefore, the past dominates the present; in Communist society, the present dominates the past. In bourgeois society capital is independent and has individuality, while the living person is dependent and has no individuality.

And the abolition of this state of things is called by the bourgeois, abolition of individuality and freedom! And rightly so. The abolition of bourgeois individuality, bourgeois independence, and bourgeois freedom is undoubtedly aimed at.

By freedom is meant, under the present bourgeois conditions of production, free trade, free selling and buying.

But if selling and buying disappears, free selling and buying disappears also. This talk about free selling and buying, and all the other 'brave words' of our bourgeoisie about freedom in general, have a meaning, if any, only in contrast with restricted selling and buying, with the fettered traders of the Middle Ages, but have no meaning when opposed to the Communistic abolition of buying and selling, of the bourgeois conditions of production, and of the bourgeoisie itself.

You are horrified at our intending to do away with private property. But in your existing society, private property is already done away with for nine-tenths of the population; its existence for the few is solely due to its non-existence in the hands of those nine-tenths. You reproach us, therefore, with intending to do away with a form of property the necessary condition for whose existence is the non-existence of any property for the immense majority of society.

In one word, you reproach us with intending to do away with your property. Precisely so; that is just what we intend.

From the moment when labour can no longer be converted into capital, money, or rent, into a social power capable of being monopolized, i.e., from the moment when individual property can no longer be transformed into bourgeois property, into capital, from that moment, you say, individuality vanishes.

You must, therefore, confess that by 'individual' you mean no other person than the bourgeois, than the middle-class owner of property. This person must, indeed, be swept out of the way, and made impossible.

Communism deprives no man of the power to appropriate the products of society; all that it does is to deprive him of the power to subjugate the labour of others by means of such appropriation.

It has been objected that upon the abolition of private property all work will cease, and universal laziness will overtake us.

According to this, bourgeois society ought long ago to have gone to the dogs through sheer idleness; for those of its members who work, acquire nothing, and those who acquire anything, do not work. The whole of this objection is but another expression of the tautology: that there can no longer be any wage labour when there is no longer any capital.

All objections urged against the Communistic mode of producing and appropriating material products, have, in the same way, been urged against the Communistic modes of producing and appropriating intellectual products. Just as, to the bourgeois, the disappearance of class property is the disappearance of production itself, so the disappearance of class culture is to him identical with the disappearance of all culture.

That culture, the loss of which he laments, is, for the enormous majority, a mere training to act as a machine.

But don't wrangle with us so long as you apply, to our intended abolition of bourgeois property, the standard of your bourgeois notions of freedom, culture, law, &c. Your very ideas are but the outgrowth of the conditions of your bourgeois production and bourgeois property, just as your jurisprudence is but the will of your class made into a law for all, a will, whose essential character and direction are determined by the economical conditions of existence of your class.

The selfish misconception that induces you to transform into eternal laws of nature and of reason, the social forms springing from your present mode of production and form of property – historical relations that rise and disappear in the progress of production – this misconception you share with every ruling class that has preceded you. What you see clearly in the case of ancient property, what you admit in the case of feudal property, you are of course forbidden to admit in the case of your own bourgeois form of property.

Abolition of the family! Even the most radical flare up at this infamous proposal of the Communists.

On what foundation is the present family, the bourgeois family, based? On capital, on private gain. In its completely developed form this family exists only among the bourgeoisie. But this state of things finds its complement in the practical absence of the family among the proletarians, and in public prostitution.

The bourgeois family will vanish as a matter of course when its complement vanishes, and both will vanish with the vanishing of capital.

Do you charge us with wanting to stop the exploitation of children by their parents? To this crime we plead guilty.

But, you will say, we destroy the most hallowed of relations, when we replace home education by social.

And your education! Is not that also social, and determined by the social conditions under which you educate, by the intervention, direct or indirect, of society, by means of schools, &c? The Communists have not invented the intervention of society in education; they do but seek to alter the character of that intervention, and to rescue education from the influence of the ruling class.

The bourgeois clap-trap about the family and education, about the hallowed co-relation of parent and child, becomes all the more disgusting, the more, by the action of Modern Industry, all family ties among the proletarians are torn asunder, and their children transformed into simple articles of commerce and instruments of labour.

But you Communists would introduce community of women, screams the whole bourgeoisie in chorus.

The bourgeois sees in his wife a mere instrument of production. He hears that the instruments of production are to be exploited in common, and, naturally, can come to no other conclusion than that the lot of being common to all will likewise fall to the women.

He has not even a suspicion that the real point aimed at is to do away with the status of women as mere instruments of production.

For the rest, nothing is more ridiculous than the virtuous indignation of our bourgeois at the community of women which, they pretend, is to be openly and officially established by the Communists. The Communists have no need to introduce community of women; it has existed almost from time immemorial.

Our bourgeois, not content with having the wives and daughters of their proletarians at their disposal, not to speak of common prostitutes, take the greatest pleasure in seducing each other's wives.

Bourgeois marriage is in reality a system of wives in common and thus, at the most, what the Communists might possibly be reproached with, is that they desire to introduce, in substitution for a hypocritically concealed, an openly legalized community of women. For the rest, it is self-evident that the abolition of the present system of production must bring with it the abolition of the community of women springing from that system, i.e., of prostitution both public and private.

The Communists are further reproached with desiring to abolish countries and nationality.

The working men have no country. We cannot take from them what they have not got. Since the proletariat must first of all acquire political supremacy, must rise to be the leading class of the nation, must constitute itself *the* nation, it is, so far, itself national, though not in the bourgeois sense of the word.

National differences and antagonisms between peoples are daily more and more vanishing, owing to the development of the bourgeoisie, to freedom of commerce, to the world market, to uniformity in the mode of production and in the conditions of life corresponding thereto.

The supremacy of the proletariat will cause them to vanish still faster. United action, of the leading civilized countries at least, is one of the first conditions for the emancipation of the proletariat.

In proportion as the exploitation of one individual by another is put an end to, the exploitation of one nation by another will also be put an end to. In proportion as the antagonism between classes within the nation vanishes, the hostility of one nation to another will come to an end.

The charges against Communism made from a religious, a philosophical, and, generally, from an ideological standpoint, are not deserving of serious examination.

Does it require deep intuition to comprehend that man's ideas, views and conceptions, in one word, man's consciousness, changes with every change in the conditions of his material existence, in his social relations and in his social life?

What else does the history of ideas prove, than that intellectual production changes in character in proportion as material production is changed? The ruling ideas of each age have ever been the ideas of its ruling class.

When people speak of ideas that revolutionize society, they do but express the fact, that within the old society, the elements of a new one have been created, and that the dissolution of the old ideas keeps even pace with the dissolution of the old conditions of existence.

When the ancient world was in its last throes, the ancient religions were overcome by Christianity. When Christian ideas succumbed in the 18th century to rationalist ideas, feudal society fought its death battle with the then revolutionary bourgeoisie. The ideas of religious liberty and freedom of conscience, merely gave expression to the sway of free competition within the domain of knowledge.

'Undoubtedly,' it will be said, 'religious, moral, philosophical and juridical ideas have been modified in the course of historical development. But religion, morality, philosophy, political science, and law, constantly survived this change.

'There are, besides, eternal truths, such as Freedom, Justice, etc., that are common to all states of society. But Communism abolishes eternal truths, it abolishes all religion, and all morality, instead of constituting them on a new basis; it therefore acts in contradiction to all past historical experience.'

What does this accusation reduce itself to? The history of all past society has consisted in the development of class antagonisms, antagonisms that assumed different forms at different epochs.

But whatever form they may have taken, one fact is common to all past ages, viz., the exploitation of one part of society by the other. No wonder, then, that the social consciousness of past ages, despite all the multiplicity and variety it displays, moves within certain common forms, or general ideas, which cannot completely vanish except with the total disappearance of class antagonisms.

The Communist revolution is the most radical rupture with traditional property relations; no wonder that its development involves the most radical rupture with traditional ideas.

But let us have done with the bourgeois objections to Communism.

We have seen above, that the first step in the revolution by the working class, is to raise the proletariat to the position of ruling class, to win the battle of democracy.

The proletariat will use its political supremacy to wrest, by degrees, all capital from the bourgeoisie, to centralize all instruments of production in the hands of the State, i.e., of the proletariat organized as the ruling class; and to increase the total of productive forces as rapidly as possible.

Of course, in the beginning, this cannot be effected except by means of despotic inroads on the rights of property, and on the conditions of bourgeois production; by means of measures, therefore, which appear economically insufficient and untenable, but which, in the course of the movement, outstrip themselves, necessitate further inroads upon the old social order, and are unavoidable as a means of entirely revolutionizing the mode of production.

These measures will of course be different in different countries.

Nevertheless, in the most advanced countries, the following will be pretty generally applicable:

1. Abolition of property in land and application of all rents of land to public purposes.
2. A heavy progressive or graduated income tax.
3. Abolition of all right of inheritance.
4. Confiscation of the property of all emigrants and rebels.
5. Centralization of credit in the hands of the State, by means of a national bank with State capital and an exclusive monopoly.

6. Centralization of the means of communication and transport in the hands of the State.

7. Extension of factories and instruments of production owned by the State; the bringing into cultivation of waste-lands, and the improvement of the soil generally in accordance with a common plan.

8. Equal liability of all to labour. Establishment of industrial armies, especially for agriculture.

9. Combination of agriculture with manufacturing industries; gradual abolition of the distinction between town and country, by a more equable distribution of the population over the country.

10. Free education for all children in public schools. Abolition of children's factory labour in its present form. Combination of education with industrial production, &c., &c.

When, in the course of development, class distinctions have disappeared, and all production has been concentrated in the whole nation, the public power will lose its political character. Political power, properly so called, is merely the organized power of one class for oppressing another. If the proletariat during its contest with the bourgeoisie is compelled, by the force of circumstances, to organize itself as a class, if, by means of a revolution, it makes itself the ruling class, and, as such, sweeps away by force the old conditions of production, then it will, along with these conditions, have swept away the conditions for the existence of class antagonisms and of classes generally, and will thereby have abolished its own supremacy as a class.

In place of the old bourgeois society, with its classes and class antagonisms, we shall have an association, in which the free development of each is the condition for the free development of all.

[...]

4: POSITION OF THE COMMUNISTS IN RELATION TO THE VARIOUS EXISTING OPPOSITION PARTIES

Section 2 has made clear the relations of the Communists to the existing working-class parties, such as the Chartists in England and the Agrarian Reformers in America.

The Communists fight for the attainment of the immediate aims, for the enforcement of the momentary interests of the working class; but in the movement of the present, they also represent and take care of the future of that movement. In France the Communists ally themselves with the Social-Democrats, against the conservative and radical bourgeoisie, reserving, however, the right to take up a critical position in regard to phrases and illusions traditionally handed down from the great Revolution.

In Switzerland they support the Radicals, without losing sight of the fact that this party consists of antagonistic elements, partly of Democratic Socialists, in the French sense, partly of radical bourgeois.

In Poland they support the party that insists on an agrarian revolution as the prime condition for national emancipation, that party which fomented the insurrection of Cracow in 1846.

In Germany they fight with the bourgeoisie whenever it acts in a revolutionary way, against the absolute monarchy, the feudal squirearchy, and the petty bourgeoisie.

But they never cease, for a single instant, to instil into the working class the clearest possible recognition of the hostile antagonism between bourgeoisie and proletariat, in order that the German workers may straightway use, as so many weapons against the bourgeoisie, the social and political conditions that the bourgeoisie must necessarily introduce along with its supremacy, and in order that, after the fall of the reactionary classes in Germany, the fight against the bourgeoisie itself may immediately begin.

The Communists turn their attention chiefly to Germany, because that country is on the eve of a bourgeois revolution that is bound to be carried out under more advanced conditions of European civilization, and with a much more developed proletariat, than that of England was in the seventeenth, and of France in the eighteenth century, and because the bourgeois revolution in Germany will be but the prelude to an immediately following proletarian revolution.

In short, the Communists everywhere support every revolutionary movement against the existing social and political order of things.

In all these movements they bring to the front, as the leading question in each, the property question, no matter what its degree of development at the time.

Finally, they labour everywhere for the union and agreement of the democratic parties of all countries.

The Communists disdain to conceal their views and aims. They openly declare that their ends can be attained only by the forcible overthrow of all existing social conditions. Let the ruling classes tremble at a Communistic revolution. The proletarians have nothing to lose but their chains. They have a world to win.

WORKING MEN OF ALL COUNTRIES, UNITE!

CHAPTER 13

Woman, Church, and State

MATILDA JOSLYN GAGE

Woman is told that her present position in society is entirely due to Christianity, and this assertion is then made the basis of opposition to her demands for exact equality with man in all the relations of life. Knowing that the position of every human being keeps pace with the religion and civilization of his country, and that in many ancient nations woman had secured a good degree of respect and power, as compared even with that she has in the present era, it has been decided to present this subject from a historical stand-point, and to show woman's position under the Christian Church for the last 1,500 years.

If in so doing we shall help to show man's unwarranted usurpation over woman's religious and civil rights, and the very great difference between true religion and theology, this chapter will not have been written in vain, as it will prove that the most grievous wound ever inflicted upon woman has been in the teaching that she was not created equal with man, and the consequent denial of her rightful place and position in Church and State.

Woman had acquired great liberty under the old civilizations. In Rome she had not only secured remarkable personal and property rights, but she officiated as priestess in the most holy offices of religion. Not only as Vestal Virgin did she guard the Sacred Fire, upon whose preservation the welfare of Rome was held to depend, but at the end of every consular period women officiated in private worship and sacrifice to the *Bona Dea*, with mystic ceremonies which no man's presence was suffered to profane. The Eleusinian mysteries were attributed to Ceres herself, and but few men had the courage to dare initiation into their most secret rites. In ancient Egypt, woman bought and sold in the markets, was physician, colleges for her instruction in medicine existing 1,200 years before Christ; she founded its literature, the "Sacred Songs" of Isis being deemed by Plato literally 10,000 years old; as priestess she performed the most holy offices of religion, holding the Sacred Sistrum and offering sacrifices to the

Matilda Joslyn Gage. *Woman, Church, and State*. Originally published in 1881, in *The History of Woman Suffrage*, eds. Elizabeth Cady Stanton, Susan B. Anthony, and Matilda Joslyn Gage.

gods; she sat upon its throne and directed the civilization of this country at the most brilliant period of its history; while in the marriage relation she held more than equality; the husband at the ceremony promising obedience to the wife in all things, a rule which according to Wilkinson, wrought no harm, but, on the contrary, was productive of lasting fidelity and regard, the husband and wife sitting together upon the same double chair in life, and lying together in the same tomb after death. Crimes against women were rare in olden Egypt, and were punished in the most severe manner. In Persia, woman was one of the founders of the ancient Parsee religion, which taught the existence of but a single God, thus introducing monotheism into that rare old kingdom. The Germans endowed their wives upon marriage with a horse, bridle, and spear, emblematic of equality, and they held themselves bound to chastity in the marital relation. The women of Scandinavia were regarded with respect, and marriage was held as sacred by both men and women. These old Berserkers reverenced their Alruna, or Holy Women, on earth, and worshiped goddesses in heaven.

All Pagandom recognized a female priesthood, some making their national safety to depend upon them, like Rome; sybils wrote the Books of Fate, and oracles where women presided were consulted by many nations. The proof of woman's also taking part in the offices of the Christian Church at an early date is to be found in the very restrictions which were at a later period placed upon her. The Council of Laodicea, A.D. 365, in its eleventh canon forbade the ordination of women to the ministry, and by its forty-fourth canon prohibited them from entering into the altar.

The Council of Orleans, A.D. 511, consisting of twenty-six bishops and priests, promulgated a canon declaring that on account of their frailty, women must be excluded from the deaconship.

Nearly five hundred years later than the Council of Laodicea, we find the Council of Paris (A.D. 824) bitterly complaining that women serve at the altar, and even give to the people the body and blood of Jesus Christ. The Council of Aix-la-Chapelle, only eight years previously, had forbidden abbesses from taking upon themselves any priestly function. Through these canons we have the negative proof that for many hundred years women preached, baptized, administered the sacrament, and filled various offices of the Church, and that men took it upon themselves to forbid them from such functions through prohibitory canons.

A curious old black-letter volume published in London in 1632, entitled "The Lawes and Resolutions of Women's Rights," says, "the reason why women have no control in Parliament, why they make no laws, consent to none, abrogate none, is their Original Sin."

This doctrine of her original sin lies at the base of the religious and political disqualifications of woman. Christianity, through this doctrine, has been interpreted as sustaining man's rights alone. The offices held by her during the apostolic age, she has been gradually deprived of through ecclesiastical enactments. To Augustine, whose early life was spent in company with the most degraded of woman-kind, is Christianity indebted for the full development of the doctrine of Original Sin, which, although to be found in the religious systems of several ancient nations, was not a primitive one of the Christian Church. Taught as one of the most sacred mysteries of religion, which to doubt or to question was to hazard eternal damnation, it at once exerted a most powerful and repressing influence upon woman, fastening upon her a bondage which the civilization of the nineteenth century has not been able to cast off.

To this doctrine of woman's created inferiority we can trace those irregularities which for many centuries filled the Church with shame, for practices more obscene

than the orgies of Babylon or Corinth, and which dragged Christendom to a darkness blacker than the night of heathendom in pagan countries – a darkness upon
which the most searching efforts of historians cast scarcely one ray of light – a
darkness so profound that from the seventh to the eleventh century no individual
thought can be traced. All was sunk in superstition; men were bound by Church
dogmas, and looked only to aggrandizement through her. The priesthood, which
alone possessed a knowledge of letters, prostituted their learning to the basest uses;
the nobility spent their lives in warring upon each other; the peasantry were the sport
and victim by turns of priest and noble, while woman was the prey of all; her person
and her rights possessing no consideration only as they could be made to advance the
interest or serve the pleasure of noble, husband, father, or priest – some man-god to
whose lightest desire all her wishes were made to bend. The most pronounced
doctrine of the Church during this period was, that through woman sin had been
introduced into the world; that woman's whole tendency was toward evil, and that
had it not been for the unfortunate oversight of her creation, man would be dwelling
in the paradisical innocence and happiness of Eden blessed with immortality. The
Church looking upon woman as under a curse, considered man as God's divinely
appointed agent for its enforcement, and that the restrictions she suffered under
Christianity were but parts of a just punishment for having caused the fall of man.
Christian theology thus at once struck a blow at these old beliefs in woman's
equality, broadly inculcating the doctrine that woman was created for man, was
subordinate to him and under obedience to him. It bade woman stand aside from
sacerdotal offices, forbidding her to speak in the church, commanding her to ask her
husband at home for all she wished to know, at once repressing all tendency toward
her freedom among those who adopted the new religion, and by various decretals
taught her defilement through the physical peculiarities of her being. It placed the
legality of marriage under priestly control, secured to husbands a right of divorce for
causes not freeing the wife, and so far set its ban upon this relation as to hold single
women above the wife and mother in holiness. After having forbidden woman the
priestly office, it forbade her certain benefits to be derived therefrom, thus unjustly
punishing her for an ineligibility of its own creation; offices in the Church, learning,
and property rights, freedom of thought and action, all were held as improper for a
being secondary to man, who came into the world, not as part of the great original
plan, but as an afterthought of the Creator.

    While it took many hundred years to totally exclude woman from the priesthood,
the strict celibacy of the male clergy was during the same period the constant effort
of the Church. At first its restrictions were confined to a single marriage with a
woman who had never before entered that relation. A Council of A.D. 347, consisting of twenty-one bishops, forbade the ordination of those priests who had been
twice married, or who had married a widow. A Council of A.D. 395, ruled that a
bishop who had children after ordination, should be excluded from the major orders.
The Council of A.D. 444, deposed Chelidonius, Bishop of Besancon, for having
married a widow; while the Council of Orleans, A.D. 511, consisting of thirty-two
bishops, decided that any monk who married should be expelled from the ecclesiastical order.

    In the sixth century a Council was held at Macon (585), consisting of forty-three
bishops with sees, sixteen bishops without sees, and fifteen envoys. At this Council
the celebrated discussion took place of which it has often been said, the question was
whether woman had a soul. It arose in this wise. A certain bishop insisted that

woman should not be called "homo"; but the contrary was argued by others from the two facts that the Scriptures say that God created man, male and female, and that Jesus Christ, son of a woman, is called the son of man. Woman was, therefore, allowed to remain a human being in the eyes of the clergy, even though considered a very weak and bad one.

The Church held two entirely opposing views of marriage. Inasmuch as it taught that the fall came through marriage, this relation was regarded by many priests with holy horror as a continuance of the evil which first brought sin into the world. It was declared that God would have found some method of populating the world outside of marriage, and that condition was looked upon as one of peculiar temptation and trial. Another class taught its necessity, though in it woman was under complete subordination to man. These views can be traced to the early fathers; through clerical contempt of marriage, the conditions of celibacy and virginity were regarded as those of highest virtue. Jerome respected marriage as chiefly valuable in that it gave virgins to the Church, while Augustine, although he admitted the possibility of salvation to the married, yet spoke of a mother and daughter in heaven, the mother shining as a dim star, the daughter as one of the first magnitude.

In the "Apostolic Constitutions," held by the Episcopal Church as regulations established by the apostles themselves, and which are believed by many to be among the earliest Christian records, there are elaborate directions for the places of all who attend church, the unmarried being most honored. The virgins and widows and elder women stood, or sat first of all. The Emperor Honorius banished Jovinius for asserting the possibility of a man being saved who lived with his wife, even though he obeyed all the ordinances of the Church and lived a good life.

St. Chrysostom, whose prayer is repeated at every Sunday morning service of the Episcopal Church, described woman as "a necessary evil, a natural temptation, a desirable calamity, a domestic peril, a deadly fascination, and a painted ill." The doctrine of priestly celibacy which was early taught, though not thoroughly enforced until the eleventh century, and the general tenor of the Church against marriage, together with its teaching woman's greater sinfulness, were the great causes of undermining the morals of the Christian world for fifteen hundred years. With these doctrines was also taught the duty of woman to sacrifice herself in every way to man. The loss of chastity in a woman was held as a light sin in comparison to the degradation that marriage would bring upon the priesthood, and young girls ruined by some candidate or priest, considered themselves as doing God service by refusing a marriage that would cause the expulsion of their lovers from this order. With woman's so-called divine self-sacrifice, Heloise chose to remain Abelard's mistress rather than destroy his prospects of advancement in the Church.

To the more strict enforcement of priestly celibacy, the barons were permitted to make slaves of the wives and children of married priests. While by common law children were held as following the condition of their fathers, under Church legislation they were held to follow the condition of their mothers. Serf mothers have thus borne serf children to free-born fathers, and slave mothers have borne slave children to their masters; while unmarried mothers still bear bastard children to unknown fathers, the Church thus throwing the taint of illegitimacy upon the innocent. The relations of man and woman to each other, the sinfulness of marriage, and the license of illicit relations employed most of the thought of the Church. The duty of woman to obey, not only her husband, but all men by virtue of their sex, was sedulously inculcated. She was trained to hold her own desires and even her own thoughts in complete abeyance to those of man; father, husband, brother, son, priest, alike held themselves as her rightful masters, and every holy principle of her nature was subverted in this most degrading assumption. A great many important effects followed the full establishment of priestly celibacy. The doctrine of woman's inherent wickedness took new strength; a formal prohibition of the Scriptures to the laity was promulgated from Toulouse in the twelfth century; the canon law gained control of the civil law; the absolute sinfulness of divorce, which had been maintained in councils, yet allowed by the civil law, was established; the Inquisition arose; the persecution of woman for witchcraft took on a new phase, and a tendency to suicide was developed. The wives of priests rendered homeless, and with their children suddenly ranked among the vilest of the earth, were powerless and despairing, and not a few of them shortened their agony by death at their own hands. For all these crimes the Church was directly responsible.

Priestly celibacy did not cause priestly purity of life, but looking upon themselves as especially sanctified and set apart by virtue of that celibacy, priests made their holy office the cover of the most degrading sensuality. Methods were taken to debauch the minds of women as well as their bodies. As late as the seventeenth century it was taught that a priest could commit no sin. This was an old doctrine, but received new strength from the Illumines. It was said that "The devout, having offered up and annihilated their own selves, exist no longer but in God. Thenceforth they can do no wrong. The better part of them is so divine that it no longer knows what the other is doing." The doctrine of some Protestant sects, "Once in grace, always in grace," is of the same character. The very incarnation was used as a means of weakening woman's virtue. An enforcement of the duty of an utter surrender of the soul and the will was taught by the example of the Virgin, "who obeyed the angel Gabriel and conceived, without risk of evil, for impurity could not come of a spirit." Another lesson, of which the present century has some glimpse, was "that sin could be killed by sin, as the better way of becoming innocent again." The result of this doctrine was seen in the mistresses of the priests, known as "The Hallowed Ones."

Under such religious teaching as to woman, naught could be expected but that the laity would closely imitate the priesthood. Although Church and State may not be legally united, it is impossible for any religious opinion to become widely prevalent without its influencing legislation. Among the Anglo-Saxons, the priesthood possessed great influence; but after the Norman Conquest, ecclesiasticism gained greater control in England. Previous to this, a man was compelled by law to leave his wife one-third of his property, and could leave her as much more as he pleased. Under ecclesiastical law he was not permitted to will her more than one-third, and could leave her as much less as he pleased. Glanville laid it down as a law of the kingdom that no one was compelled to leave another person any portion of his property, and that the part usually devised to wives was left them at the dictate of affection and not of law.

Women were not permitted to testify in court unless on some question especially concerning themselves. It is but twenty years since this law was annulled in Scotland, and but three years since, that by the influence of Signor Morelli, the Parliament of Italy repealed the old restriction upon woman's testimony.

Sisters were not allowed to inherit with brothers, the property, according to old ecclesiastical language, going "to the worthiest of blood." Blackstone acknowledges that this distinction between brothers and sisters reflects shame upon England, and was no part of the old Roman law, where the children of a family inherited equally without distinction of sex. It is but two years since the old law of inheritance of sons alone was repealed in one of the Swiss Cantons. Even in this enlightened age its repeal met much opposition, men piteously complaining that they would be ruined by this act of justice done their sisters.

The minds of people having been corrupted through centuries by Church doctrines regarding woman, it was an easy step for the State to aid in her degradation. The system of Feudalism rising from the theory of warfare as the normal condition of man, still further oppressed woman by bringing into power a class of men accustomed to deeds of violence, and finding their chief pleasure in the sufferings of others. To be a woman, appealed to no instinct of tenderness in this class. To be a woman was not to be protected even, unless she held power in her own right, or was acting in place of some feudal lord. The whole body of villeins and serfs were under absolute dominion of the Feudal Lords. They were held as possessing no rights of their own: the Priest had control of their souls, the Lord of their bodies. But it was not upon the male serfs that the greatest oppression fell.

Although the tillage of the soil, the care of swine and cattle was theirs, the masters claiming the half or more of everything even to one-half the wool shorn from the flock, and all exactions upon them were great, while their sense of security was slight, it was upon their wives and daughters that the greatest outrages were inflicted. It was a pastime of the castle retainers to fall upon peaceful villages to the consternation of its women, who were struck, tortured, and made the sport of the ribald soldiery. "Serfs of the Body," they had no protection. The vilest outrages were perpetrated by the Feudal Lords under the name of Rights. Women were taught by Church and State alike, that the Feudal Lord or Seigneur had a right to them, not only as against themselves, but as against any claim of husband or father. The law known as *Marchetta*, or Marquette, compelled newly-married women to a most dishonorable servitude. They were regarded as the rightful prey of the Feudal Lord from one to three days after their marriage, and from this custom, the oldest son of the serf was held as the son of the lord, "as perchance it was he who begat him." From this nefarious degradation of woman, the custom of Borough-English arose, in which the youngest son became the heir. The original signification of the word borough being to make secure, the peasant through Borough-English made secure the right of his own son to what inheritance he might leave, thus cutting off the claim of the possible son of his hated lord. France, Germany, Prussia, England, Scotland, and all Christian countries where feudalism existed, held to the enforcement of Marquette. The lord deemed this right as fully his as he did the claim to half the crops of the land, or to the half of the wool sheared from the sheep. More than one reign of terror arose in France from the enforcement of this law, and the uprisings of the peasantry over Europe during the twelfth century, and the fierce Jacquerie, or Peasant War, of the fourteenth century in France owed their origin, among other causes, to the enforcement of these claims by the lords upon the newly-married wife. The Edicts of Marly securing the Seigneural Tenure in Lower Canada, transplanted that claim to America when Canada was under the control of France.

To persons not conversant with the history of feudalism, and of the Church for the first fifteen hundred years of its existence, it will seem impossible that such foulness could ever have been part of Christian civilization. That the crimes they have been trained to consider the worst forms of heathendom could have existed in Christian Europe, upheld by both Church and State for more than a thousand five hundred years, will strike most people with incredulity. Such, however, is the truth; we can but admit well-attested facts of history how severe a blow soever they strike our preconceived beliefs.

Marquette was claimed by the Lords Spiritual as well as by the Lords Temporal. The Church, indeed, was the bulwark of this base feudal claim. With the power of penance and excommunication in its grasp, this feudal demand could neither have originated nor been sustained unless sanctioned by the Church.

In Scotland, Margaret, wife of Malcolm Conmore, generally known, from her goodness, as St. Margaret, exerted her royal influence in 1057, against this degradation of her sex, but despite the royal prohibition and the substitution of the payment of a merk in money instead, the custom had such a foothold and appealed so strongly to man's licentious appetite it still continued, remaining in existence nearly seven hundred years after the royal edict against its practice. These customs of feudalism were the customs of Christianity during many centuries. These infamous outrages upon woman were enforced under Christian law by both Church and State.

The degradation of the husband at this infringement of the lord spiritual and temporal upon his marital right, has been pictured by many writers, but history has been quite silent upon the despair and shame of the wife. No hope appeared for woman anywhere. The Church, which should have been the great conserver of morals, dragged her to the lowest depths, through the vileness of its priestly customs. The State, which should have defended her civil rights, followed the example of the Church in crushing her to the earth. God Himself seemed to have forsaken woman. Freedom for the peasants was found alone at night. Known as the Birds of the Night, Foxes and Birds of Prey, it was only at these night assemblages they enjoyed the least happiness or security. Here, with wives and daughters, they met together to talk of their gross outrages. Out of these foul wrongs grew the sacrifice of the "Black Mass," with woman as officiating priestess, in which the rites of the Church were travestied in solemn mockery, and defiance cast at that heaven which seemed to permit the priest and lord alike to trample upon all the sacred rights of womanhood in the names of religion and law.

During this mocking service a true sacrifice of wheat was offered to the Spirit of the Earth who made wheat to grow, and loosened birds bore aloft to the God of Freedom the sighs and prayers of the serfs asking that their descendants might be free. We can not do otherwise than regard this sacrifice as the most acceptable offering made in that day of moral degradation, a sacrifice and prayer more holy than all the ceremonials of the Church. This service, where woman, by virtue of her greater despair, acted both as altar and priest, opened by the following address and prayer: "I will come before Thine altar, but save me, O Lord, from the faithless and violent man!" (from the priest and the baron). From these assemblages, known as "Sabbat," or "the Sabbath," from the old Pagan Midsummer-day sacrifice to "Bacchus Sabiesa," rose the belief in the "Witches' Sabbath," which for several hundred years formed a new source of accusation against women, and sent tens of thousands of them to the most horrible death.

Not until canon or Church law had become quite engrafted upon the civil law, did the full persecutions for witchcraft arise. A witch was held to be a woman who had deliberately sold her soul to the Evil One, who delighted in injuring others, and who chose the Sabbath day for the enactment of her impious rites, and who was especially connected with black animals; the black cat being held as her familiar in many countries.

In looking at the history of witchcraft, we see three striking points for consideration:

First. That women were chiefly accused, a wizard being seldom mentioned.

Second. That man, believing in woman's inherent wickedness, and understanding neither the mental nor the physical peculiarities of her being, ascribed all her idiosyncrasies to witchcraft.

Third. That the clergy inculcated the idea that woman was in league with the devil, and that strong intellect, remarkable beauty, or unusual sickness, were in themselves a proof of that league.

Catholic and Protestant countries alike agreed in holding woman as the chief accessory of the devil. Luther said, "I would have no compassion for a witch; I would burn them all." As late as 1768, John Wesley declared the giving up of witchcraft to be in effect giving up the Bible. James I., on his accession to the throne, ordered the learned work of Reginald Scot against witchcraft, to be burned in compliance with the act of Parliament of 1603, which ratified a belief in witchcraft over the three kingdoms. Under Henry VIII., from whose reign the Protestant Reformation in England dates, an act of Parliament made witchcraft felony; this act was again confirmed under Elizabeth. To doubt witchcraft was as heretical under Protestantism as under Catholicism.

Even the widely extolled Pilgrim Fathers brought this belief with them when they stepped ashore at Plymouth Rock. With the "Ducking-Stool" and the "Scarlet Letter" of shame for woman, while her companion in sin went free, they also brought with them a belief in witches. Richard Baxter, the "greatest of the Puritans," condemned those who disbelieved in witchcraft as "wicked Sadducees," his work against it adding intensity to the persecution. Cotton Mather was active in fomenting a belief in this doctrine.

So convinced were those in power of the tendency of woman to diabolism that the learned Sir Matthew Hale condemned two women without even summing up the evidence. Old women, for no other reason than that they were old, were held as most susceptible to the assaults of the devil, and most especially endowed with supernatural powers for evil, to doubt which was equivalent to doubting the Bible. We see a reason for this hatred of old women, in the fact that woman was chiefly viewed from a sensual stand-point, and when by reason of age or debility, she no longer attracted the physical admiration of man, he looked upon her as of no farther use to the world, and as possessing no right to life. At one period it was very unusual for an old woman in the north of Europe to die peaceably in her bed. The persecution against them raged with special virulence in Scotland, where upon the act of the British Parliament in 17—, abolishing the burning and hanging of witches, the assembly of the Calvinistic Church of Scotland "confessed" this act of Parliament "as a great national sin." Looked upon as a sin rather than a crime, the Church sought its control, and when coming under its power, witchcraft was punished with much greater severity than when falling under lay tribunals. It proved a source of great emolument to the Church, which was even accused of fostering it for purposes of gain. A system of "witch finders" or "witch persecutors" arose. Cardan, a famous Italian physician, said of them: "In order to obtain forfeit property, the same persons acted as accusers and judges, and invented a thousand stories as proof."

Witchcraft was as a sin almost confined to woman; a wizard was rare, one writer saying: to every 100 witches, we find but one wizard. In the time of Louis XIII. this proportion was greatly increased; "to one wizard, 10,000 witches," another person declared there were 100,000 witches in France alone. Sprenger, the great Inquisitor, author of "The Witch Hammer," through whose persecutions many countries were flooded with victims, said, "Heresy of witches, not of wizards, must we call it, for these latter are of very small account." No class or condition escaped Sprenger; we read of witches of fifteen years, and two "infernally beautiful" of seventeen years.

The Parliament of Toulouse burned 400 witches at one time. Four hundred women at one hour on the public square, dying the horrid death of fire, for a crime which never existed save in the imagination of those persecutors, and which grew in their imagination from a false belief in woman's extraordinary wickedness, based upon a false theory as to original sin. Not a Christian country but was full of the horrors of witch persecution and violent death. Remy, Judge of Nancy, acknowledged to having himself burnt 800 in sixteen years. Many women were driven to suicide in fear of the torture in store for them. In 1595 sixteen of those accused by Remy, destroyed themselves rather than fall into his terrible hands. Six hundred were burnt in one small bishopric in one year; 900 during the same period in another. Seven thousand lost their lives at Treves; 1,000 in the province of Como in Italy in a single year; 500 were executed at Geneva in a single month. Under the reign of Francis I. more than 100,000 witches are said to have been put to death, and for hundreds of years this superstition controlled the Church. In Scotland the most atrocious tortures were invented, and women died "shrieking to heaven for that mercy denied them by Christian men." One writer casually mentions seeing nine burning in a single day's journey.

When for "witches" we read "women," we shall gain a more direct idea of the cruelties inflicted by the Church upon woman. Friends were encouraged to cast accusations upon friends, and rewards were offered for conviction. From the pulpit people were exhorted to bring the witch to justice. Husbands who had ceased to care for their wives, or in any way found them a burden, or who for any reason wished to dissolve the marriage tie, now found an easy method. They had but to accuse them of witchcraft, and the marriage was dissolved by the death of the wife at the stake. Mention is made of wives dragged by their husbands before the arch-Inquisitor, Sprenger, by ropes around their necks. In Protestant, as in Catholic countries, the person accused was virtually dead. She was excommunicated from humanity; designated and denounced as one whom all must shun, with whom none must buy or sell, to whom no one must give food or lodging or speech or shelter; life was not worth the living.

Besides those committing suicide, others brought to trial, tired of life amid so many horrors, falsely accused themselves, preferring a death by the torture of fire to a life of endless isolation and persecution. An English woman on her way to the stake, with a greatness of soul all must admire, freed her judges from responsibility by saying to the people, "Do not blame my judges, I wished to put an end to my own self. My parents kept aloof from me; my husband had denied me. I could not live on without disgrace. I longed for death, and so I told a lie."

Of Sir George Mackenzie, the eminent Scotch advocate, it was said:

> He went to examine some women who had confessed, and one of them told him "under secrecie" that she had not confessed because she was guilty, but being a poor wretch who wrought for her meat, and being defined for a witch, she knew she would starve, for no person thereafter would give her either meat or lodging, and that all men would beat her and hound dogs at her, and therefore she desired to be out of the world,

whereupon she wept most bitterly, and upon her knees called upon God to witness what she said.

The death these poor women chose to suffer rather than accept a chance of life with the name of witch clinging to them, was one of the most painful of which we can conceive, although in the diversity of torture inflicted upon "the witch," it is scarcely possible to say which was the least agonizing.

Not only was the persecution for witchcraft brought to New England by the Puritans, but it has been considered and treated as a capital offense by the laws of both Pennsylvania and New York. Trials took place in both colonies not long before the Salem tragedy; the peaceful Quaker, William Penn, presiding upon the bench at the time of the trial of two Swedish women accused of witchcraft. The Grand Jury acting under instruction given in a charge delivered by him, found bills against them, and his skirts were only saved from the guilt of their blood by some technical irregularity in the indictment.

Marriage with devils was long one of the most ordinary accusations in witch trials. The knowledge of witches was admitted, as is shown in the widely extended belief of their ability to work miracles. A large part of the women termed witches were in reality the profoundest thinkers, the most advanced scientists of those ages. For many hundred years the knowledge of medicine, and its practice among the poorer classes was almost entirely in their hands, and many discoveries in this science are due to them; but an acquaintance with herbs soothing to pain, or healing in their qualities, was then looked upon as having been acquired through diabolical agency. Even those persons cured through the instrumentality of some woman were ready when the hour came to assert their belief in her indebtedness to the devil for that knowledge. Not only were the common people themselves ignorant of all science, but their brains were filled with superstitious fears, and the belief that knowledge had been first introduced to the world through woman's obedience to the devil. Thus the persecution which for ages raged against witches, was in reality an attack upon science at the hands of the Church.

The entire subordination of the common law to ecclesiasticism, dates in England to the reign of Stephen, who ascended the throne in 1135. Its new growth of power must be ascribed to avarice, as it then began to take cognizance of crimes, establishing an equivalent in money for every species of wrong-doing. The Church not only remitted penalties for crimes already perpetrated, but sold indulgences for the commission of new ones. Its touch upon property soon extended to all the relations of life. Marriages within the seventh degree were forbidden by the Church as incestuous, but those who could buy indulgence were enabled to get a dispensation. No crime so great that it could not be condoned for money.

Canon law gained its greatest power in the family relation in its control over wills, the guardianship of orphans, marriage and divorce. Under ecclesiastical law, marriage was held as a sacrament, was performed at the church door, the wife being required to give up her name, her person, her property, her own sacred individuality, and to promise obedience to her husband in all things. Certain hours of the day were even set aside as canonical after which no marriage could be celebrated. Wherever it became the basis of legislation, the laws of succession and inheritance, and those in regard to children, constantly sacrificed the interests of wives and daughters to those of husbands and sons. Ecclesiastical law ultimately secured such a hold upon family property and became so grasping in its demands, that the civil law interfered, not, however, in the interests of wives and children, but in the interests of creditors. Canon law had its largest growth through the pious fictions of woman's created inferiority. [. . .]

Property is a delicate test of the condition of a nation. It is a singular fact of history that the rights of property have everywhere been recognized before the rights of persons, and wherever the rights of any class to property are attacked, it is a most subtle and dangerous assault upon personal rights. The chief restrictive element of slavery was the denial to the slave of the proceeds of his own labor. As soon as a slave was allowed to hire his time, the door of freedom began to open to him. The enslavement of woman has been much increased from the denial of the rights of property to her, not merely to the fruits of her own labor, but to the right of inheritance.

The great school of German jurists teach that ownership increases both physical and moral capacity, and that as owner, actual or possible, man is a more capable and worthy being than he would otherwise be. Inasmuch as under canon law woman was debarred from giving testimony in courts of law, sisters were prohibited from taking an inheritance with brothers, and wives were deprived of property rights, it is entirely justifiable to say ecclesiastical law injured civilization by its destruction of the property rights of women.

The worst features of canon law, as Blackstone frankly admits, are those touching upon the rights of woman. These features have been made permanent to this day by the power the Church gained over common law, between the tenth and sixteenth centuries, since which period the complete inferiority and subordination of the female sex has been as fully maintained by the State as by the Church. The influence of canon law upon the criminal codes of England and America has but recently attracted the attention of legal minds. Wharton, whose "Criminal Law" has for years been a standard work, did not examine their relation until his seventh edition, in which he gave a copious array of authors, English, German, and Latin, from whom he deduced proof that the criminal codes of these two countries are pre-eminently based upon ecclesiastical law.

Canon law gave to the husband the power of compelling the wife's return if, for any cause, she left him. She was then at once in the position of an outlaw, branded as a run-away who had left her master's service, a wife who had left "bed and board" without consent, and whom all persons were forbidden "to harbor" or shelter "under penalty of the law." The absconding wife was in the position of an excommunicate from the Catholic Church, or of a woman condemned as a witch. Any person befriending her was held accessory to the wife's theft of herself from her husband, and rendered liable to fine and other punishment for having helped to rob the husband (master) of his wife (slave). [. . .]

Although England was Christianized in the fourth century, it was not until the tenth that a daughter had a right to reject the husband selected for her by her father; and it was not until this same century that the Christian wife of a Christian husband acquired the right of eating at table with him. For many hundred years the law entered families, binding out to servile labor all unmarried women between the ages of eleven and forty.

For more than a thousand years women in England were legislated for as slaves. They were imprisoned for crimes that, if committed by a man, were punished by simple branding in the hand; and other crimes which he could atone for by a fine, were punished in her case by burning alive. Down to the end of the eighteenth century the punishment of a wife who had murdered her husband was burning alive; while if the husband murdered the wife, his was hanging, "the same as if he had murdered any stranger." Her crime was petit treason, and her punishment was the same as that of the slave who had murdered her master. For woman there existed no "benefit of clergy," which in a man who could read, greatly lessened his punishment; this ability to read enabling him to perform certain priestly functions and securing him immunity in crime. The Church having first made woman ineligible to the priesthood, punished her on account of the restrictions of its own making. We who talk of the burning of wives upon the funeral pyres of husbands in India, may well turn our eyes to the records of Christian countries.

Where marriage is wholly or partially under ecclesiastical law, woman's degradation surely follows; but in Catholic and Protestant countries a more decent veil has been thrown over this sacrifice of woman than under some forms of the Greek Church, where the wife is delivered to the husband under this formula: "Here, wolf, take thy lamb!" and the bridegroom is presented with a whip, giving his bride a few blows as part of the ceremony, and bidding her draw off his boots as a symbol of her subjugation to him. With such an entrance ceremony, it may well be surmised that the marriage relation permits of the most revolting tyranny. In Russia, until recently, the wife who killed her husband while he was chastising her, was buried alive, her head only being left above ground. Many lingered for days before the mercy of death reached them.

Ivan Panim, a Russian exile, now a student in Harvard College, made the following statement in a speech at the Massachusetts Woman Suffrage Convention, held in February, 1881:

> A short time ago the wife of a well-to-do peasant came to a justice of one of the district courts in Russia and demanded protection from the cruelty of her husband. She proved conclusively by the aid of competent witnesses, that he had bound her naked to a stake during the cold weather, on the street, and asked the passers-by to strike her; and whenever they refused, he struck her himself. He fastened her, moreover, to the ground, put heavy stones and weights on her and broke one of her arms. The court declared the husband "not guilty." "It cannot afford," it said, "to teach woman to disobey the commands of her husband." This is by no means an extreme or isolated case. Few, indeed, become known to the public through the courts or through the press.

Canon law made its greatest encroachments at the period that chivalry was at its height; the outward show of respect and honor to woman keeping pace in its false pretense with the destruction of her legal rights. Woman's moral degradation was at this time so great that a community of women was even proposed, and was sustained by Jean de Meung, the "Poet of Chivalry," in his Roman de la Rose. Christine of Pisa, the first strictly literary woman of Western Europe, took up her pen in defense of her sex against the general libidinous spirit of the age, writing in opposition to Meung.

Under Feudalism, under Celibacy, under Chivalry, under the Reformation, under the principles of new sects of the nineteenth century – the Perfectionists and Mormons alike – we find this one idea of woman's inferiority, and her creation as a subject of man's passions openly or covertly promulgated.

The Salic law not only denied to women the right to reign, but to the inheritance of houses and lands. One of its famous articles was: "Salic land shall not fall to women; the inheritance shall devolve exclusively on the males." The fact of sex not only prohibited woman's inheritance of thrones and of lands, but there were forms in this law by which a man might "separate himself from his family, getting free from all obligations of relationship and entering upon an entire independence." History does not tell us to what depths of degradation this disseverance of all family ties reduced the women of his household, who could neither inherit house or land. The formation of the Salic code is still buried in the mists of antiquity; it is, however, variously regarded as having originated in the fourth and in the seventh century, many laws of its code being, like English common law, unwritten, and others showing "double origin." But our interest does not so greatly lie in its origin, as in the fact that after the conversion of the Franks to Christianity the law was revised, and all parts deemed inconsistent with this religion were revoked. The restrictions upon woman were retained.

Woman's wrongs under the Reformation, we discover by glancing at different periods. The Cromwellian era exhibited an increase of piety. Puritanism here had its birth, but brought no element of toleration to woman. Lydia Maria Child, in her "History of Woman," says:

> Under the Commonwealth society assumed a new and stern aspect. Women were in disgrace; it was everywhere reiterated from the pulpit that woman caused man's expulsion from Paradise, and ought to be shunned by Christians as one of the greatest temptations of Satan. "Man," said they, "is conceived in sin and brought forth in iniquity; it was his complacency to woman that caused his first debasement; let him not, therefore, glory in his shame; let him not worship the fountain of his corruption." Learning and accomplishments were alike discouraged; and women confined to a knowledge of cooking, family medicines, and the unintelligible theological discussions of the day.

A writer about this period, said: "She that knoweth how to compound a pudding is more desirable than she who skillfully compoundeth a poem."

At the time of the Reformation, Luther at first continued celibate, but thinking "to vex the Pope," he suddenly, at the age of forty-two, gave his influence against celibacy by marriage with Catherine Von Bora, a former nun. But although thus becoming an example of priestly marriage under the new order of things, Luther's whole course shows that he did not believe in woman's equality with man. He took with him the old theory of her subordination. It was his maxim that "no gown or garment worse becomes a woman than that she will be wise." Although opposing monastic life, the home under the Reformation was governed by many of its rules for woman.

First. She was to be under obedience to the masculine head of the household.

Second. She was to be constantly employed for his benefit.

Third. Her society was strictly chosen for her by her master and head.

Fourth. This masculine family head was a general father confessor, to whom she was held responsible in thought and deed.

Fifth. Neither genius nor talent could free woman from such control, without consent.

Luther, though free from the lasciviousness of the old priesthood, was not monogamic in principle. When applied to by the German Elector, Philip, Landgrave of Hesse-Cassel, for permission to marry a second wife, while his first, Margaret of Savoy, was still living, Luther called a synod of six of the principal reformers; who in joint consultation decided that as the Bible nowhere condemned polygamy, and as it had been invariably practiced by the highest dignitaries of the Church, the required permission should be granted. History does not tell us that the wife was consulted in the matter. She was held as in general subordination to the powers that be, as well as in special subordination to her husband; but more degrading than all else is the fact that the doctrine of unchastity for man was brought into the Reformation, as not inconsistent with the principles of the Gospel. [...]

When woman interprets the Bible for herself, it will be in the interest of a higher morality, a purer home. Monogamy is woman's doctrine, as polygamy is man's. Backofen, the Swiss jurist, says that the regulation of marriage by which, in primitive times, it became possible for a woman to belong only to one man, came about by a religious reformation, wherein the women, in armed conflict, obtained a victory over men.

In Christian countries to-day, the restrictions on woman in the married relation are much greater than upon man. Adultery, which is polygamy outside of the married relation, is everywhere held as more venial in man than in woman. In England, while the husband can easily obtain a divorce from his wife, upon the ground of adultery, it is almost impossible for the wife to obtain a divorce upon the same ground. Nothing short of the husband's bringing another woman into the house, to sustain wifely relations to him, at all justifies her in proceeding for a separation; and even then, the husband retains control of the wife's property. A trial in England is scarcely ended in which a husband willed his wife's property to his mistress and illegitimate children. The courts not only decided in his favor, but to this legal robbery of the wife, added the insult of telling her that a part of her own money was enough for her, and that she ought to be willing that her husband's mistress and illegitimate children should share it with her.

Milton's "Paradise Lost" is responsible for many existing views in regard to woman. After the Reformation, as women began to waken to literature, came Milton, a patriot of patriots – as patriots were held in those days, a man who talked of liberty for men – but who held man to stand in God's place toward woman. Although it has been affirmed that in his blindness Milton dictated his great epic to his daughters, and a Scotch artist has painted the scene (a picture recently purchased by the Lenox Library), yet this is one of the myths men call history, and amuse themselves in believing. This tale of blind Milton dictating "Paradise Lost" to his daughters, is a trick designed to play upon our sympathies. Old Dr. Johnson said of Milton, that he would not allow his daughters even to learn to write. Between Milton and his wives, we know there was tyranny upon one side and hatred on the other. He could not gain the love of either wife or daughter, and yet he is the man who did so much to popularize the idea of woman's subordination to man. "He, for God; she, for God in him" – as taught in the famous line: "God thy law, thou mine."

That the clerical teaching of woman's subordination to man was not alone a doctrine of the dark ages, is proven by the most abundant testimony of to-day. The famous See trial of 1876, which shook not only the Presbytery of Newark, but the whole Synod of New Jersey, and finally, the General Presbyterian Assembly of the United States, was based upon the doctrine of the divinely appointed subordination of woman to man, and arose simply because Dr. See admitted two ladies to his pulpit to speak upon temperance; which act, Rev Dr. Craven, the prosecutor, declared to have been "an indecency in the sight of Jehovah." He expressed the general clerical and Church view, when he said:

I believe the subject involves the honor of my God. I believe the subject involves the headship and crown of Jesus. Woman was made for man and became first in the transgression. My argument is that subordination is natural, the subordination of sex. Dr. See has admitted marital subordination, but this is not enough; there exists a created subordination; a divinely arranged and appointed subordination of woman as woman, to man as man. Woman was made for man and became first in the transgression. The proper condition of the adult female is marriage; the general rule for ladies is marriage. Women without children, it might be said, could preach, but they are under the general rule of subordination. It is not allowed women to speak in the Church. Man's place is on the platform. It is positively base for a woman to speak in the pulpit; it is base in the sight of Jehovah. The whole question is one of subordination.

Thus, before a large audience composed mainly of women, Dr. Craven stood, and with denunciatory manner, frequently bringing his fists or his Bible emphatically down, devoted a four hours' speech to proving that the Bible taught woman's subordination; one of his statements being that "in every country, under every clime, from the peasant woman of Naples with a handkerchief over her hair, to the women before him with bonnets, every one wore something upon her head in token of her subordination." Dr. Craven's position was fully sustained by many brother clergymen, some of whom enthusiastically shouted "Amen!" [...]

The teachings of the Church that it was sinful for woman to use her own reason, to think for herself, to question authority, thus fettering her will, together with a false interpretation of Scripture, have been the instruments to hold her, body and soul, in a slavery whose depths of degradation can never be fathomed, whose indescribable tortures can never be understood by man.

Not only has woman suffered in the Church, in society, under the laws, and in the family by this theological degradation of her sex, but in science and literature she has met a like fate. Hypatia, who succeeded her father, Theon, in the government of the Alexandrian school, and whose lectures were attended by the wisest men of Europe, Asia, and Africa, was torn in pieces by a Christian mob afraid of her learning.

A monument erected to Catherine Sawbridge Macaulay, as "Patroness of Liberty," was removed from the Church by order of its rector. Harriet Martineau met the most strenuous opposition from bishops in her effort to teach the poor; her day-schools and even her Sunday-schools were broken up by clerical influence. Madam Pepe-Carpentier, founder of the French system of primary instruction, of whom Froebel caught his kindergarten idea, found her labors interrupted, and her life harassed by clerical opposition.

Mary Somerville, the most eminent English mathematician of this century, was publicly denounced in church by Dean Cockburn, of York; and when George Eliot died a few weeks since, her lifeless remains were refused interment in Westminster Abbey, where so many inferior authors of the privileged sex lie buried; the grave even not covering man's efforts toward the degradation of woman.

When Susannah Wesley dared to conduct religious services in her own house, and to pray for the king, contrary to her husband's wishes, he separated from her in consequence. The husband of Annie Besant left her because she dared to investigate the Scriptures for herself, and was sustained by the courts in taking from her the control of her little daughter, simply because the mother thought best not to train her in a special religious belief, but to allow her to wait until her reason developed, that she might decide her religious views for herself. [...]

Not only has woman recognized her own degradation, but the largest-hearted men have also seen it. Thomas W. Higginson, in an address at the anniversary of the Young Men's Christian Union, in New York City, as long ago as 1858, in an address upon women in Christian civilization, said:

No man can ever speak of the position of woman so mournfully as she has done it for herself. Charlotte Brontë, Caroline Norton, and indeed the majority of intellectual women, from the beginning to the end of their lives, have touched us to sadness even in mirth, and the mournful memoirs of Mrs. Siddons, looking back upon years when she had been the chief intellectual joy of English society, could only deduce the hope, "that there might be some other world hereafter, where justice would be done to woman."

The essayist, E. P. Whipple, in a recent speech before the Papyrus Club of Boston, said of George Eliot:

The great masculine creators and delineators of human character, Homer, Cervantes, Shakespeare, Göethe, Scott, and the rest, cheer and invigorate us even in the vivid representation of our common humanity in its meanest, most stupid, most criminal forms. Now comes a woman endowed not only with their large discourse of reason, their tolerant views of life, and their intimate knowledge of the most obscure recesses of the human heart and brain, but with a portion of that rich, imaginative humor which softens the savageness of the serious side of life by a quick perception of its ludicrous side, and the result of her survey of life is, that she depresses the mind, while the men of genius animate it, and that she saddens the heart, while they fill it with hopefulness and joy. I do not intend to solve a problem so complicated as this, but I would say, as some approach to an explanation, that this remarkable woman was born under the wrath and curse of what our modern philosophers call "heredity." She inherited the results of man's dealings with woman during a thousand generations of their life together.

Contempt for woman, the result of clerical teaching, is shown in myriad forms. Wife-beating is still so common, even in America, that a number of the States have of late introduced bills especially directed to the punishment of the wife-beater. Great surprise is frequently shown by these men when arrested. "Is she not my wife?" is cried in tones proving the brutal husband had been trained to consider this relationship a sufficient justification for any abuse.

In England, wives are still occasionally led to the market by a halter around the neck to be sold by the husband to the highest bidder. George Borrow, in his singular narrative, "The Romany Rye," says:

The sale of a wife with a halter around her neck is still a legal transaction in England. The sale must be made in the cattle market, as if she were a mare, "all women being considered as mares by old English law, and indeed called 'mares' in certain counties where genuine old English is still preserved."

It is the boast of America and Europe that woman holds a higher position in the world of work under Christianity than under pagandom. Heathen treatment of woman in this respect often points the moral and adorns the tale of returned missionaries, who are apparently forgetful that servile labor of the severest and most degrading character is performed by Christian women in highly Christian countries. In Germany, where the Reformation had its first inception, woman carries a hod of mortar up steep ladders to the top of the highest buildings; or, with a coal basket strapped to her back, climbs three or four flights of stairs, her husband remaining at the foot, pipe in mouth, awaiting her return to load the hod or basket, that she may make another ascent, the payment for her work going into the husband's hands for his uncontrolled use. Or mayhap this German wife works in the field harnessed by the side of a cow, while her husband-master holds the plough and wields the whip. Or, perhaps, harnessed with a dog, she serves the morning's milk, or drags her husband home from work at night.

In France women act as porters, carrying the heaviest burdens and performing the most repulsive labors at the docks, while eating food of so poor a quality that the lessening stature of the population daily shows the result. In Holland and Prussia women drag barges on the canal, and perform the most repulsive agricultural duties. On the Alps husbands borrow and lend their wives, one neighbor not scrupling to ask the loan of another's wife to complete some farming task, which loan is readily granted, with the understanding that the favor is to be returned in kind. In England, scantily clothed women work by the side of nude men in coal pits, and, harnessed to trucks, perform the severe labor of dragging coal up inclined planes to the mouth of the pit, a work testing every muscle and straining every nerve, and so severe that the stoutest men shrink from it; while their degradation in brick-yards and iron mines has commanded the attention of philanthropists and legislators.

A gentleman recently travelling in Ireland blushes for his sex when he sees the employments of women, young and old. They are patient drudges, staggering over the bogs with heavy creels of turf on their backs, or climbing the slopes from the seashore, laden like beasts of burden with the heavy sand-dripping seaweed, or undertaking long journeys on foot into the market towns, bearing weighty hampers of farm produce. In Montenegro, women form the beasts of burden in war, and are counted among the "animals" belonging to the prince. In Italy, that land which for centuries led the world in art, women work in squalor and degradation under the shadow of St. Peter's and the Vatican for four-pence a day; while in America, under the Christianity of the nineteenth century, until within twenty years, she worked on rice and cotton plantations waist-deep in water, or under a burning sun performed the tasks demanded by a cruel master, at whose hands she also suffered the same kind of moral degradation exacted of the serf under feudalism. In some portions of Christendom the "service" of young girls to-day implies their sacrifice to the Moloch of man's unrestrained passions.

Augustine, in his work, "The City of God," taunts Rome with having caused her own downfall. He speaks of her slaves, miserable men, put to labors only fit for the beasts of the field, degraded below them; their condition had brought Rome to its own destruction. If such wrongs contributed to the overthrow of Rome, what can we not predict of the Christian civilization which, in the twentieth century of its existence, degrades its Christian women to labors fit only for the beasts of the field; harnessing them with dogs to do the most menial labors; which drags them below even this, holding their womanhood up to sale, putting both Church and State sanction upon their moral death; which, in some places, as in the city of Berlin, so far recognizes the sale of women's bodies for the vilest purposes as part of the Christian religion, that license for this life is refused until they have partaken of the Sacrament; and which demands of the "10,000 licensed women of the town" of the city of Hamburg, certificates showing that they regularly attend church and also partake of the Sacrament? [...]

From all these startling facts in Church and State we see that our government and religion are alike essentially masculine in their origin and development. All the evils that have resulted from dignifying one sex and degrading the other may be traced to this central error: a belief in a trinity of masculine Gods in One, from which the feminine element is wholly eliminated. And yet in the Scriptural account of the simultaneous creation of man and woman, the text plainly recognizes the feminine as well as the masculine element in the Godhead, and declares the equality of the sexes in goodness, wisdom, and power. Genesis i. 26, 27: "And God said: let us make man *in our own image, after our own likeness* ... So God created man in His own image; in the image of God created He him; *male* and *female* created He THEM ... And gave them dominion over the fish of the sea, and over the fowl of the air, and over every living thing that moveth upon the earth."

While woman's subordination is taught as a Scriptural doctrine, the most devout and learned biblical scholars of the present day admit that the Bible has suffered many interpolations in the course of the centuries. Some of these have doubtless occurred through efforts to render certain passages clearer, while others have been forged with direct intention to deceive. Disraeli says that the early English editions contain 6,000 errors, which were constantly introduced, and passages interpolated for sectarian purposes, or to sustain new creeds. Sometimes, indeed, they were added for the purpose of destroying all Scriptural authority by the suppression of texts. *The Church Union* says of the present translation, that there are more than 7,000 variations from the received Hebrew text, and more than 150,000 from the received Greek text.

These 7,000 variations in the Old Testament and 150,000 in the New Testament, are very significant facts. The oldest manuscripts of the New Testament are the Alexandrine Codex, known since the commencement of the seventeenth century, and believed to date back to the middle of the fifth century, the Sinaitic, and the Vatican Codices, each believed to have been executed about the middle of the fourth century. The Sinaitic Codex was discovered by Professor Tischendorf, a German scholar, at a monastery upon Mt. Sinai, in fragments, and at different periods from 1848 to 1859, a period of eleven years elapsing from his discovery of the first fragment until he secured the last one. The Vatican Codex has been in the Vatican library since its foundation, but has been inaccessible to scholars until very recently. It is not known from whence it came or by whom executed, but is deemed the oldest and most authentic copy of the Bible extant. As these oldest codices only date to the middle of the fourth century, we have no record of the New Testament, in its present form, for the first three hundred and fifty years of this era.

A commission of eminent scholars has been engaged for the past eleven years upon a revision of the Bible. The New Testament portion is now about ready for the public, but so great and so many are its diversities from the old version, that it is prophesied the orthodox church will be torn by disputes between adherents of the old and the new, while those anxious for the truth, touch where it may, will be honestly in doubt if either one is to be implicitly trusted. Various comments and inquiries in regard to this revision have already appeared in the press. The oldest codices do not contain many texts we have learned to look upon as especially holy. Portions of the Sermon on the Mount are not in these old manuscripts, a proof of their interpolation to serve the purpose of some one at a later date. In the same way additions have been made to the Lord's Prayer. Neither of these manuscripts contain the story of the woman taken in adultery, as narrated John viii. 1–11, so often quoted as proof of the divine mercy of Jesus. A letter upon this so long accepted story, from the eminent scholar, Howard Crosby, D.D., LL.D., a member of the revisory commission, will be read with interest:

MRS. M. J. GAGE:
DEAR MADAME: – The passage in John viii. 1–11, is *not* in the Alexandrian, nor is it in the Sinaitic, Vatican, and Ephraim Codices. It is found in twelve uncials (though marked *doubtful* in five of these) and in over 300 cursives.

Yours very truly,
HOWARD CROSBY.

116 East 19th, N. Y., *March* 14, '81.

The world still asks, What is Truth? A work has recently been published entitled, "The Christian Religion to A.D. 200." It is the fruit of several years' study of a period upon which the Church has but little record. It finds no evidence of the existence of the New Testament in its present form during that time; neither does it find evidence that the Gospels in their present form date from the lives of their professed authors. All Biblical scholars acknowledge that the world possesses no record or tradition of the original manuscripts of the New Testament, and that to attempt to reëstablish the old text is hopeless. No reference by writers to any part of the New Testament as authoritative is found earlier than the third century (A.D. 202). The first collection, or canon, of the New Testament was prepared by the Synod or Council of Laodicea in the fourth century (A.D. 360). It entirely omitted the Book of Revelation from the list of sacred works. This book has met a similar fate from many sources, not being printed in the Syriac Testament as late as 1562.

Amid this vast discrepancy in regard to the truth of the Scriptures themselves; with no Hebrew manuscript older than the twelfth century; with no Greek one older than the fourth; with the acknowledgment by scholars of 7,000 errors in the Old Testament, and 150,000 in the New; with assurance that these interpolations and changes have been made by men in the interest of creeds, we may well believe that the portions of the Bible quoted against woman's equality are but interpolations of an unscrupulous priesthood, for the purpose of holding her in subjection to man.

Amid this conflict of authority over texts of Scripture we have been taught to believe divinely inspired, destroying our faith in doctrines heretofore declared essential to salvation, how can we be sure that the forthcoming version of the Bible from the masculine revisers of our day will be more trustworthy than those which have been accepted as of Divine origin in the past?

PART VII

From Utilitarianism to Womanist Theory:

JOHN STUART MILL AND ANNA JULIA COOPER

The creed which accepts, as the foundation of morals, Utility, or the Greatest Happiness Principle, holds that actions are right in proportion as they tend to promote happiness, wrong as they tend to produce the reverse of happiness.[1]

John Stuart Mill, Utilitarianism

John Stuart Mill's life and work are taken up in Part V, in particular his foremost political tract, *On Liberty*, which defends freedom of expression and action for minority opinions and acts. Always a prolific writer, in his twenties and thirties Mill contributed numerous letters and essays on topical issues to periodicals such as *Westminster Review, Tait's Magazine*, the *Jurist*, and *Monthly Repository*. His first major work was *System of Logic*, a book which, curiously enough, was a popular success. Presenting a challenge to the Aristotelian syllogistic system, this work "makes plain [Mill's] belief that social planning and political action should rely primarily on scientific knowledge, not on authority, custom, revelation, or prescription."[2]

In the *Logic*, Mill laid the groundwork for utilitarian theory and a philosophy of experience. Rejecting the skeptical conclusions of Humean empiricism, he developed a more positive, progressive empirical epistemology. Then, in 1844, he published *Principles of Political Economy*, a work which systematized and analyzed the theories of free-market economists Adam Smith and David Ricardo. Later revisions to this work, largely influenced by his companion and future wife Harriet Hardy Taylor, supported early socialist theory. The years of Mill's marriage to Harriet Taylor, up to her death in 1858, were especially productive and he credited her as co-author of many of these works, including *Utilitarianism, Three Essays on Religion*, and *On Liberty*.[3] In addition, he wrote numerous other works on metaphysics, on social policy, on politics (*Considerations On Representative Government, The Subjection of Women, On Socialism*), as well as letters, essays, and an autobiography.

Along with *On Liberty*, his most influential work is *Utilitarianism*. In this piece he develops a much transformed doctrine from the mechanistic percursor to behaviorism – the utilitarianism of his father and the Benthamites. He defines and defends the principle that one should act so as to produce the greatest happiness – the Greatest Happiness Principle (GHP). By this he means that actions are right insofar as they promote the happiness, or reduce the pain, of society taken as a whole. This view is neither hedonistic nor egoistic; it does not advocate absorption in base pleasures, nor does it advocate personal selfishness. On the contrary, it is a principle with a strong measure of altruism in it, since the well-being of society is placed above individual happiness. Individuals must act, not just for their own pleasure, but for the good of society as well. Unlike Bentham, for whom all pleasures were equal, and "pushpin is as good as poetry," Mill argued that different kinds of pleasures had different values and that:

> It is better to be a human being dissatisfied, than a pig satisfied; better to be Socrates dissatisfied, than a fool satisfied. And if the fool or pig are of a different opinion, it is because they only know their own side of the question. The other party to the comparison knows both sides.[4]

The GHP required empirical calculations along with argumentation regarding what would produce the long-range good for society. Many of Mill's letters and essays contained utilitarian arguments about issues of social policy: the extension of the franchise, the reduction of the national debt, famine and land reform in Ireland. Like many mid-nineteenth-century theories, utilitarianism related to ideas about political economy and was a part of the movement to make social concerns of justice and morals scientific. It was an optimistic approach, reflecting the hope for progress and human perfection.

In *Utilitarianism*, Mill raised and attempted to answer a series of criticisms: about the apparent connections of utilitarianism to a theory of expediency, about problems in performing the required calculations, and about the theory creating too high a standard for morality. The theory functions as a guide to individual moral behavior, but it is also a social theory and a theory of justice. He associates a variety of attributes or correlative concerns with utilitarianism: the fundamental considerations of personal liberty and property, legal rights, a theory of retributive justice based on the concept of desert, or giving each her or his due, a principle of not breaking faith, a principle of impartiality, and a principle of equality.

Mill's utilitarianism is perhaps most famously criticized by John Rawls, whose *A Theory of Justice* (1971) shattered a relative silence about issues in political theory by mainstream philosophers that extended back to the previous century.[5] Rawls argued that the utilitarian principle could, under the right empirical conditions, require a person to enslave herself/himself or others for the overall good of society:

> ... a slaveholder, when confronted by his slaves attempts to justify his position by claiming that, first of all, given the circumstances of their society, the institution of slavery is in fact necessary to produce the greatest ... happiness, and, secondly, that in the initial contract situation he would choose the ... principle even at the risk of its subsequently happening that he is justifiably held as a slave.[6]

Rawls argued that such a possibility was morally unacceptable; no rational individual would choose to live in a society where the underlying system of justice included the possibility that he or she might be enslaved. Instead, using a complex construction of social contract theory called the "original position," he argued that a set of basic principles must be adopted that guarantee fundamental rights and liberties. For the Rawlsians, the perceived failure to establish basic rights in the underlying structure of society poses an insurmountable difficulty for Mill's utilitarianism.

After the publication of Rawls' book, neo-utilitarian responses to Rawls' criticisms became a growth industry, producing an extensive literature.[7] Among the various utilitarian responses to Rawls is the empirical one that insists that slavery, and suppression of speech and action, would never, in the long run, in fact create the greatest happiness. Other supporters of utilitarianism provide a response based on logic instead of fact, taking the position that Mill's strong defense of liberty, of women's rights, and of an equitable distribution of goods amounted to a claim that even consideration of the greatest happiness could not override these fundamental rights. According to this view, the utilitarian principle is used to generate rules to govern society, and not to assess individual acts *per se*. The rule-based approach holds that certain rules or principles strongly tend to promote the public good, among them freedom of expression and action, and the furthering not just of minority *opinion*, but of the *rights* of underrepresented people. This analysis brings the interpretation of *Utilitarianism* more in line with the views expressed in *On Liberty*. Nonetheless, the dispute about the acceptability of utilitarianism as a theory of justice remains unresolved.

Mill took seriously the application of the theoretical to practical circumstances, with varying results. In his work as an official of the East India Co., which administered the civil service in British colonial India, Mill appears to have seen himself as promoting the happiness of subcontinental Indians, a view that would be soundly challenged by current post-colonial literature, for example in Gayatri Spivak's critique of "imperialism's image as the establisher of the good society."[8] Mill's liberal views were aired in the progressive journals of the day: he supported improved conditions for the working class and an end to slavery in the United States. In his and Harriet Taylor's treatise, *The Subjection of Women*, he argued for furthering the rights of women in western society.

> Everything to this race is new and strange and inspiring. There is a quickening of its pulses and a glowing of its self-consciousness. Aha! I can rival that! I can aspire to that! I can honor my name and vindicate my race! Something like this, it strikes me, is the enthusiasm that stirs the genius of young Africa in America; and the memory of past oppression and the fact of the present attempted repression only serve to gather momentum for its irrepressible forces.[9]
>
> *Anna Julia Cooper*

Anna Julia Haywood Cooper (1858–1964) lived from the end of legal slavery in the United States to the civil rights movement of the 1960s – more than 105 years dedicated to every aspect of education, to theoretical analysis, and to practical activism. A voracious learner, Cooper was among the very first African Americans to earn a B.A. (in Liberal Arts, Oberlin 1884), an M.A. (in Mathematics, Oberlin, 1887), and a Ph.D. (from the Sorbonne in Paris at the age of 65). She was also a prodigious teacher, from the age of nine until late in her long life. She was a philosopher and social theorist of education, developing a conception of African American education that influenced the thinking of W. E. B. DuBois. She was an original educational leader who inspired young scholars and later became embroiled in controversy. She was a lecturer, enormously respected by her students and peers and feared by white racists as a living contradiction of the fundamental racist tenet that African Americans were incapable of matching the accomplishments of whites.

Cooper's mother, Hannah Stanley, was one of 271 slaves owned by the family of George Washington Haywood of Raleigh, North Carolina.[10] Domestic slaves such as Hannah Stanley lived with the threat and terror of being sent to one of the several Haywood plantations outside Raleigh, where the physical violence of the lash was commonplace and the field labor itself was punishing.[11] But while life in the fields meant hard labor, poor conditions, and the lash, life at the grand city house carried its own threats, the chief one being the master himself. Anna Julia Cooper writes:

> My mother was a slave and the finest woman I have ever known...Presumably my father was her master, if so I owe him not a sou and she was always too modest and shamefaced ever to mention him.[12]

Scholars agree with her assessment of her paternity, since plantation owners frequently practiced the systematic sexual assault of women slaves, serving the multiple purposes of ready sexual gratification, the structured exercise of power and terror designed to maintain a docile slave-class, and the eugenic production of a crop of light-skinned offspring thought to be more suitable for house service. Thus, the circumstances of Anna Cooper's birth exemplify the problematic confluence of race and gender oppression. Of her own heritage she says, with characteristic humor and irony:

> The part of my ancestors that did not come over in the Mayflower in 1620, arrived, I am sure, a year earlier in the fateful Dutch trader that put in at Jamestown in 1619...I believe that the third source of my individual stream comes...from the vanishing Red Men, which ought...to the manner born and "inheritor of the globe" [make me a] genuine F.F.A. (First Family of America).[13]

Cooper was born on the eve of the Civil War, in the year of the Abraham Lincoln/ Stephen Douglas presidential debates over the future of slavery in the expansion of the nation. Her earliest years coincided with Lincoln's inauguration, the beginning of the Civil War, numerous battles fought in some proximity to her home, and, in 1863, the Emancipation Proclamation. Technically ending legal enslavement, for Cooper, her mother, and her siblings, this document may not have signaled many significant material changes – except perhaps for one. Hannah Stanley was hired out to the Charles Busbee family as a nursemaid, taking her young daughter with her. For thirty years, until 1863, it had been illegal to teach slaves to read, with serious consequences: fines of up to $300 for white people, and possible imprisonment, and for freed Blacks, the same, plus whipping, not more than 39 nor fewer than 20 lashes.[14] Yet, in the Busbee household, Anna acquired not just literacy, but an education. Slave history and literature reveal over and over again that maintaining illiteracy was vital to the maintenance of slavery and that reading became crucial, sometimes even for simple acts of defiance. For thousands of former slaves, the ability to read and the freedom to learn was transformative. By the time she was nine, Cooper had entered, as a pupil-teacher, the St. Augustine Normal School and Collegiate Institute in Raleigh, a school designed for the education of teachers of

Freedmen, and at this early age her feminist understanding was formed, as she recalls in "The Higher Education of Women":

> I constantly felt (as I suppose many an ambitious girl has felt) a thumping from within unanswered by a beckoning from without ... A boy, however meager his equipment and shallow his pretensions, had only to declare a floating intention to study theology and he could get the support, encouragement, and stimulus he needed, be absolved from work and invested beforehand with all the dignity of his far away office, while a self-supporting girl had to struggle on by teaching in the summer and working after school hours to keep up with board and bills, and actually fight her way against positive discouragements to the higher education ... and when at last that same girl announced her desire and intention to go to college it was received with about the same incredulity and dismay as if the brass button of one of those candidate's coats had propounded a new method for squaring the circle or trisecting the arc.[15]

In her later years at the school, Cooper insisted on taking the more classical curriculum intended for the male theology students, and it was here that she developed a close friendship with George A. C. Cooper, a native of Nassau, British West Indies, whom she married in 1877. George Cooper became an ordained minister in the Episcopal Church and assisted with parish duties, both at the school and in the city. Intelligent, dedicated to the service of African Americans and the church, thoughtful and gentle, George Cooper was apparently overwhelmed by the demands of his position, for he died in 1879 at the age of thirty-two. Like Maria W. Stewart, Cooper suffered the emotional hardship of her early loss, but she gained the social position of one who has the maturity of marriage without the subordination that accompanied it.

Determined to pursue her education, Cooper wrote requesting admission to Oberlin College, Ohio, a progressive institution with associations with feminism and abolitionism. She entered the college in 1881. Others in her class were Ida B. Gibbs (Hunt), one of the first African American women to earn a Bachelor's degree, and Mary Eliza Church (Terrell), whose activism ranged from helping to found the National Association for the Advancement of Colored People (NAACP), to campaigning against lynching, and lecturing on the world stage. Open to women since 1833, Oberlin had long since abandoned the separate Gentlemen's and Ladies' curricula in favor of a single course of study for all students. After graduating from Oberlin, she spent a year teaching at Wilberforce College in Ohio, returning to Raleigh the following year to teach at St. Augustine's. Once back in her native community, she also established community education programs and became a member of the North Carolina Teacher's Association.

In 1886 Cooper delivered an address, "Womanhood A Vital Element in the Regeneration and Progress of a Race" in Washington. The following year, on the basis of a strong recommendation from Oberlin, she was hired to teach Math and Science at the M Street School (now the Paul Dunbar School) – the only Black high school in the District of Columbia. This happened at a time when African Americans in the USA were experiencing some of the benefits of emancipation. Young adults were the first generation not born into slavery or a slave-holding nation. Cooper's biographer Louise Daniel Hutchinson describes the 1890s:

> The decade ... was an important period in the fostering of Black intellectual and political thought. In the vanguard of the struggle for human rights, Cooper and the

groups with which she was associated promoted opportunities for academic excellence for Black youth; built groups and clubs of learning and culture for Black women; defended the honor of, and demanded respect for, the reputations and views of Black people.[16]

Cooper and four other Black women were invited to speak at a special session of the 1893 World's Columbian Exhibition. She delivered an address, "The Intellectual Progress of Colored Women of the United States since Emancipation," an oratory praised by Frederick Douglass, who was present at the speech. But the Exhibition itself was problematic, since attempts by activist groups to have more meaningful Black inclusion had been resisted at every turn, and the emphasis in the exhibits that included people of color was on exoticism and not equality. The great intellectual and anti-lynching activist Ida B. Wells staged a protest at the event. Official organizers called the structure that housed the Exhibition "the White City;" Douglass described it as a "whited sepulcher." African American scholar Hazel Carby analyzes the social and cultural implications of the event, which, she argues, "embodied the definitive failure of the hopes of emancipation and reconstruction and inaugurated an age that was to be dominated by 'the problem of the color line.'"[17] This problem, the articulation of which is attributed to DuBois, is designated "the color line" by Cooper in her essay "What Are We Worth?"

In 1900, along with DuBois and others, Cooper helped to organize and addressed the first Pan-African Conference in London. Two years later, Cooper was named principal of the M Street School, a showcase under her direction for Black intellectual achievement. In those times, much of the nation looked to Washington, D. C. for its models of political and social progress. As the only Black high school in the city, M Street was setting national standards for a curriculum that trained for both vocation and industry, and, through its exceptional classical or liberal arts stream, for the professions. The school successfully prepared students for Ivy League colleges such as Harvard and Yale and for other top collegiate institutions. But a policy of containing Negro achievement was afoot. The "accommodation" philosophy of Booker T. Washington of the Tuskegee Institute in Alabama trained African Americans only for working-class employment and was palatable to whites. The more classical approach pioneered by Cooper, and later taken to exemplify the philosophy of W. E. B. DuBois, was set in opposition to the accommodation approach. Historical sources seem to indicate that Cooper's successes were considered dangerous to white supremacy and evidence was marshaled to undermine her tenure as principal. Charges were made that students were drinking and smoking; Cooper's own virtue and suitability were questioned in a controversy that embroiled the District and occupied the newspapers. As a result, Cooper eventually lost her leadership of the school in 1906. Undaunted, she moved on to teach at Lincoln University in Missouri for four years before finally returning to M Street to teach Latin.

Cooper came to preside over the troubled Frelinghuysen University in Washington, D.C., which had as its aim the education of working people, but lacking adequate resources, it was forced to close. Later in life she continued to write and lecture, on topics including education for working people, "Negro Dialect," "The Social Settlement: What It Is, and What It Does" (1913), *Legislative Measures Concerning Slavery in the United States* (her Ph.D. dissertation) (1942), "The Equality of Races and the Democratic Movement" (1942), *Personal Recollections of the Grimké Family and the Life and Writings of Charlotte Forten Grimké* (1951), and *The Third Step* and autobiographical work.

In her fifties, Cooper adopted five children – great-nieces and nephews, whom she cared for, all the while teaching, attending lectures at Columbia University, and studying for her Ph.D. In 1925 she traveled to Paris for her degree. Confirming the pattern revealed in this text that even quite well-known figures who express minority views can be erased from history, when Cooper died, her own relatives had little idea of her achievements.

It is not the intelligent woman vs. the ignorant woman; not the white woman vs. the black, the brown, and the red, – it is not even the cause of woman vs. man. Nay, 'tis woman's strongest vindication for speaking that *the world needs to hear her voice.*[18]
Anna Julia Cooper, "Woman Versus the Indian"

Cooper's essays provide a cornerstone of systematic Black feminist thought, revealing a continuity of Black women's experiences and ideas from the nineteenth century to the present. The very title of her book resonates with contemporary themes. "A Voice From the South" emphasizes the importance of vocality in the women's movements – the theme of oppressive silencing and the effort to be heard. By subtitling the book "By a Black Woman of the South," Cooper goes on to locate herself, racially, geographically, and in terms of gender. In so positioning herself, she authorizes her social location not as an individual, as one in the classical liberal tradition would, but as a representative of a group whose loci, whose positionality, has not previously had epistemological standing. She foreshadows Patricia Hill Collins' more comprehensive articulation of a Black feminist standpoint "that reconceptualizes the social relations of dominance and resistance" and "addresses ongoing epistemological debates . . . Offering subordinate groups new knowledge about their own experiences can be empowering. But revealing new ways of knowing that allow subordinate groups to define their own reality has far greater implications."[19] In asking for an audience to listen to "a voice from the south by a Black woman of the south," Cooper articulates Collins' thesis that "Black women intellectuals have a distinctive standpoint of self, community and society," that constitutes a subjugated knowledge not widely known or understood. Cooper offers a Black feminist theory that does not essentialize the role of Black women, but valorizes the influence of the traditional women's role as the early childhood educator of women and men, and thus as holding the key to moral as well as scholarly and practical education. In "Womanhood a Vital Element in the Regeneration and Progress of a Race," she describes this role:

Only the BLACK WOMAN can say "when and where I enter, in the quiet, undisputed dignity of my womanhood, without violence and without suing or special patronage, then and there the whole *Negro race enters with me.*"[20]

In *Women, Race and Class*, Angela Davis explores the theme that the social conditions of slavery invested Black women with a special role.[21] Whatever efforts women were able to devote to domestic concerns, in the "home" or raising children, these women were laboring for the Black rather than the white community and earning a small degree of autonomy. Davis argues, however, that Black men *also* participated in certain small, life-affirming tasks that strengthened the Black family. Like

Davis, Joyce Ladner, Patricia Hill Collins, and others continue to develop a compelling case that under conditions of severe oppression, African Americans have nonetheless developed strong domestic relations and a legacy of successful struggle against adversity. As Davis says regarding Black women under slavery: "It was those women who passed on to their nominally free female descendants a legacy of hard work, perseverance and self-reliance, a legacy of tenacity, resistance and insistence on sexual equality – in short, a legacy spelling out standards for a new womanhood."[22] Literary critic Hazel Carby points out that Cooper's condemnation of the elitism of medieval chivalry is a thinly veiled critique of plantation society's hypocrisy regarding the cult of true womanhood for whites in contrast to the treatment of Black women.

Carby identifies and theologian Karen Baker-Fletcher develops the thesis that Cooper's consistent use and advocacy of the gospel is best construed as a womanist liberation theology.[23] In *A Singing Something: Womanist Reflections on Anna Julia Cooper*, Baker-Fletcher develops Cooper's concept that vocality provides a link between God and humans; that which comes to voice against injustice is a divine spark moving toward freedom and equality. Domination is the oppression, not just of human beings but also of the divine voice. Similarly, Carby identifies in Cooper's work a strain of argument against American imperialism that lays bare the practices of a nation willing to build on the backs of the "other" – in Asia, with Native Americans, around the world, and at home. Her analysis of colonialism and imperialism at home foreshadows contemporary work in post-colonial theory, such as that of Trinh Minh Ha, Chandra Talpade Mohanty, and Gayatri Chakravorty Spivak.[24]

Ten years before DuBois articulated his theory that "The Talented Tenth" of educated African Americans would form the vanguard of Black achievement, Cooper fought against the Booker T. Washington model of accommodation to whites and asserted a right of access to both classical and vocational education, and to both professional and industrial employment. Just as she had rebelled as a girl against separate gentlemen's and ladies' curricula, she rebelled against separate white and Black curricula nationwide, a position so dangerous as to contribute to her removal as principal of M Street School.

The Utilitarian Philosophies of John Stuart Mill and Anna Julia Cooper

There is a portion of work rendered necessary by the fact of each person's existence: no one could exist unless work, to a certain amount, were done either by or for him.[25]
                                        John Stuart Mill, "The Negro Question"

What is our market value. Are we a positive and additive quantity or a negative factor in the world's elements. What have we cost and what do we come to?[26]
                                        Anna Julia Cooper, "What Are We Worth?"

Both Mill and Cooper adopt a utilitarian approach to the question of the *value* of African Americans to society, a kind of cost–benefit analysis that may seem crass at present, but which signifies the degree to which both Mill and Cooper believed that a kind of scientific analysis could be applied to questions of social policy. In "The

Negro Question," Mill responds to a letter by Thomas Carlyle (author of the *French Revolution*) in which Carlyle asserts the rights of the privileged over the oppressed, and the use of violence in maintaining that privilege. Mill argues against privilege, against the support by religions of unjust social arrangements, and against the functions of tradition. He derides Carlyle's notions that Blacks must be impelled to work, that Blacks are not sufficiently industrious, and that whites, on the contrary, are. He avers regarding a system of commanding people to work for their own support:

> If this experiment is to be tried in the West Indies, let it be tried impartially; and let the whole of the produce belong to those who do the work which produces it. We would not have Black labourers compelled to grow spices they do not want, and white proprietors who do not work at all exchanging the spices for houses in Belgrave Square.[27]

Mill's utilitarian notions of the value of Black labor and contributions to society are extensively developed years later in Cooper's essay "What Are We Worth?" in which Cooper applies a sophisticated utilitarian calculus to the question of the value of Black labor and the contributions of African Americans as a whole. She also uses this trope as a mechanism for social analysis of the condition of Blacks in America, particularly through her "broken plates" analogy and her assessment of the wastefulness of neglected Black humanity in terms of the potential contributions to society as a whole. She refuses to use racism as an excuse, insisting on Black self-reliance rather than philanthropy as the source of "improvement." At the same time she blames racism's wastefulness for the consequent loss of human productivity. She measures the efforts put into education, health, and employment for Blacks and sketches the areas where additional social reform is needed. This essay demonstrates that Cooper is very much in the nineteenth-century tradition of utilitarian hopefulness and belief in human progress. She unites biting criticism with optimistic, hopeful visions of a future in which Blacks will be recognized as a race of good pedigree, strong contributions, and a hopeful future.

MULTIPLE OPPRESSIONS AND SOCIAL POLICY

Mill is distinctive among traditional political theorists in his theoretical and practical work in support of women, minorities, and the working classes. In this element of his thought, as in all of his later work, he was profoundly influenced by Harriet Taylor Mill. Mill's feminism is expressed in his and Taylor's *The Subjection of Women*, using the same libertarian and utilitarian arguments against subjection. Equality would bring the benefits of having justice instead of injustice, doubling the mental abilities available for the service of humanity, making married life more tolerable, bringing about the moral regeneration of mankind, and producing greater happiness overall. He was an active supporter of the abolitionist cause, writing several letters and essays on the topic for *Fraser's* magazine. He viewed the subjection of African Americans as both a violation of the principle of liberty and as a violation of utilitarian mandates to ensure that all members of society are as productive as possible. While most Blacks in America did more than their share of physical labor, the system impeded full intellectual, cultural, scientific social contributions, detracting from the greatest happiness of society as a whole.

Likewise, Taylor moved Mill closer to a socialist position in *On Socialism* and *Political Economy*. He viewed ameliorating the conditions of workers as a primary goal. Mill did not seem to link race, class, and gender oppression to each other; he opposed each because they counteracted the utilitarian goal. He recognized multiple oppressions, but he did not connect them with structures of dominance and submission.

Writing several generations later, and from the perspective of one subjected to multiple oppressions, Cooper makes the links between different kinds of oppressions:

> And when farther on... our train stops at a dilapidated station... I see two dingy little rooms with "FOR LADIES" swinging over one and "FOR COLORED PEOPLE" over the other [and I wonder] under which head I come.[28]

Current literature contains numerous examinations of problems of self-identity for minorities, or the "other" – those who are somehow different from the dominant group. An early identification of this problem is in the title of Gloria Hull's groundbreaking collection, *Some of Us are Brave*, the title of which refers to the phrase "All the Blacks are men, all the women are white but some of us are brave," indicating the erasure of Black women from social analysis.

Cooper's essays provide remarkably rich ground for contemporary thinking about race, class, and gender. Her thought reaches back to Maria Stewart and the many other nineteenth-century African American thinkers and forward to Hull, Barbara Smith, Barbara Christian, Angela Davis, Rosa Brewer, Patricia Hill Collins, bell hooks, and others. Taking up where we left off in Part VI, Black feminist theory can be seen as providing a resolution for the unhelpful polarization generated by the "unhappy marriage of Marxism and feminism." The push and pull of race and class oppressions is replaced by theories about the interactions or matrices of oppressions:

> Black feminist thought fosters a fundamental paradigmatic shift that rejects additive approaches to oppression. Instead of starting with gender and then adding in other variables such as age, sexual orientation, race, social class, and religion, Black feminist thought sees these distinctive systems of oppression as being part of one overarching structure of domination.[29]

Patricia Hill Collins' challenge is to rethink basic social science concepts such as family, community, individual, power, activism, and others. Cooper provides a tool to do this because she herself challenges traditional theoretical frameworks; she provides rich examples from an earlier time. In doing so, she provides material for a longitudinal analysis whereby contemporary and historical examples can be joined so that Black feminist political theory can be viewed as having an analysis that is sustained over time and developed from a range of experiences and ideas. Finally, the innovations of Black feminist thought provide theoretical tools which extend beyond gender, race, and class to the examination of social and political theory as a whole.

Notes

1   John Stuart Mill, *Utilitarianism*, p. 329 of this volume.
2   J. B. Schneewind, "Utilitarianism," in *The Encyclopedia of Philosophy* (New York: Macmillan Publishing Co., 1967).

3   As with Mary Wollstonecraft and other original feminist thinkers, Harriet Taylor was subjected to the most scurrilous kind of assessment, by contemporaries and historical "authorities" up to recent times. The project of sorting out the original thought of Harriet Hardy Taylor Mill has been initiated by her recent biographer, Jo Ellen Jacobs.

4   Mill, *Utilitarianism*, p. 330 of this volume.

5   Richard Tuck, "The Contribution of History," in *A Companion to Contemporary Political Philosophy*, ed. Robert E. Goodin and Philip Pettit (Oxford: Blackwell, 1993).

6   John Rawls, *A Theory of Justice* (Cambridge, MA: Harvard University Press, 1971), p. 167.

7   See, for example, A. K. Sen and B. Williams, eds., *Utilitarianism and Beyond* (Cambridge: Cambridge University Press, 1982), and J. J. C. Smart and B. Williams, *Utilitarianism: For and Against* (Cambridge: Cambridge University Press, 1973).

8   Gayatri Chakravorty Spivak, "Can the Subaltern Speak?" in C. Nelson and M. Grossberg, eds., *Marxism and the Interpretation of Culture* (Urbana: Illinois University Press, 1988). See also Edward Said, *Orientalism* (New York: Random House, 1979).

9   Anna J. Cooper, *A Voice from the South. By a Black Woman of the South* (Xenia, OH: Aldine Printing House, 1892). Reprinted, with an introduction by Mary Helen Washington (Oxford: Oxford University Press, 1988), pp. 144–5.

10 Louise Daniel Hutchinson, ed. and intro., Anna J. Cooper: A Voice from the South (Washington, D.C.: Smithsonian Institution Press, 1981), p. 14.

11 Ibid. Another Haywood slave, Lunsford Lane, describes the conditions on the Haywood plantations slightly earlier in the century, in *Lunsford Lane: Another Helper from North Carolina* (1864). Hutchinson's book, prepared in conjunction with an exhibition about Cooper's life and work, contains a wealth of information sources about Cooper.

12 Hutchinson, *Anna J. Cooper*, p. 4.

13 Ibid., p. 3.

14 Paula S. Rothenberg, *Racism and Sexism: An Integrated Study* (New York: St. Martin's Press, 1988).

15 Cooper, *A Voice from the South*, ed. Washington, pp. 76–8.

16 Louise Daniel Hutchinson, "Anna Julia Cooper," in Darlene Clark Hine, ed., *Black Women in America: An Historical Encyclopedia* (Brooklyn: Carlson Publishing Co., 1993), p. 277.

17 Hazel V. Carby, *Reconstructing Womanhood: The Emergence of the Afro-American Woman Novelist* (New York: Oxford University Press, 1987), pp. 4–6.

18 Cooper, *A Voice from the South*, ed. Washington, p. 121.

19 Patricia Hill Collins, *Black Feminist Thought: Knowledge, Consciousness and the Politics of Empowerment* (New York: Routledge, 1991).

20 Cooper, *A Voice from the South*, p. 343 of this volume.

21 Angela Y. Davis, *Women, Race and Class* (New York: Vintage, 1983).

22 Ibid., p. 29.

23 Karen Baker-Fletcher, *A Singing Something: Womanist Reflections on Anna Julia Cooper* (New York: Crossroad, 1994).

24 See, for example, Trinh Minh Ha, *Woman, Native, Other: Writing Postcoloniality and Feminism* (Bloomington: Indiana University Press, 1989); Chandra Talpade Mohanty, "Under Western Eyes: Feminist Scholarship and Colonial Discourses," *Boundary*, 2: 12(3) (Spring/Fall, 1984); and Gayatri Spivak, *The Spivak Reader: Selected Works of Gayatri Chakravorty Spivak*, ed. Donna Landry, G. McLean, and G. C. Spivak (New York: Routledge, 1995).

25 John Stuart Mill, "The Negro Question," in *The Collected Works of John Stuart Mill*, ed. John M. Robson (Toronto: University of Toronto Press, 1963), p. 91.

26 Cooper, *A Voice from the South*, p. 353 of this volume.

27 Mill, "The Negro Question," pp. 91–2.

28 Cooper, *A Voice from the South*, pp. 347–8 of this volume.

29 Collins, *Black Feminist Thought*, p. 222.

CHAPTER 14

Utilitarianism

JOHN STUART MILL

CHAPTER 1: GENERAL REMARKS

There are few circumstances, among those which make up the present condition of human knowledge, more unlike what might have been expected, or more significant of the backward state in which speculation on the most important subjects still lingers, than the little progress which has been made in the decision of the controversy respecting the criterion of right and wrong. From the dawn of philosophy, the question concerning the *summum bonum*, or, what is the same thing, concerning the foundation of morality, has been accounted the main problem in speculative thought, has occupied the most gifted intellects, and divided them into sects and schools, carrying on a vigorous warfare against one another. And, after more than two thousand years, the same discussions continue, philosophers are still ranged under the same contending banners, and neither thinkers nor mankind at large seem nearer to being unanimous on the subject than when the youth Socrates listened to the old Protagoras, and asserted (if Plato's dialogue be grounded on a real conversation) the theory of utilitarianism against the popular morality of the so-called sophist.

It is true, that similar confusion and uncertainty, and in some cases similar discordance, exist respecting the first principles of all the sciences, not excepting that which is deemed the most certain of them – mathematics; without much impairing, generally indeed without impairing at all, the trustworthiness of the conclusions of those sciences. An apparent anomaly, the explanation of which is, that the detailed doctrines of a science are not usually deduced from, nor depend for their evidence upon, what are called its first principles. [...]

CHAPTER 2: WHAT UTILITARIANISM IS

A passing remark is all that needs be given to the ignorant blunder of supposing that those who stand up for utility, as the test of right and wrong, use the term in that

John Stuart Mill. *Utilitarianism*. Originally published in 1863.

restricted and merely colloquial sense in which utility is opposed to pleasure. An apology is due to the philosophical opponents of utilitarianism for even the momentary appearance of confounding them with any one capable of so absurd a misconception; which is the more extraordinary, inasmuch as the contrary accusation, of referring every thing to pleasure, and that, too, in its grossest form, is another of the common charges against utilitarianism: and, as has been pointedly remarked by an able writer, the same sort of persons, and often the very same persons, denounce the theory "as impracticably dry when the word 'utility' precedes the word 'pleasure,' and as too practicably voluptuous when the word 'pleasure' precedes the word 'utility.'" Those who know any thing about the matter are aware, that every writer, from Epicurus to Bentham, who maintained the theory of utility, meant by it, not something to be contradistinguished from pleasure, but pleasure itself, together with exemption from pain; and, instead of opposing the useful to the agreeable or the ornamental, have always declared that the useful means these, among other things. [...]

The creed which accepts, as the foundation of morals, Utility, or the Greatest-happiness Principle, holds that actions are right in proportion as they tend to promote happiness, wrong as they tend to produce the reverse of happiness. By happiness is intended pleasure and the absence of pain; by unhappiness, pain and the privation of pleasure. To give a clear view of the moral standard set up by the theory, much more requires to be said; in particular, what things it includes in the ideas of pain and pleasure, and to what extent this is left an open question. But these supplementary explanations do not affect the theory of life on which this theory of morality is grounded – namely, that pleasure, and freedom from pain, are the only things desirable as ends; and that all desirable things (which are as numerous in the utilitarian as in any other scheme) are desirable either for the pleasure inherent in themselves, or as means to the promotion of pleasure and the prevention of pain.

Now, such a theory of life excites in many minds, and among them in some of the most estimable in feeling and purpose, inveterate dislike. To suppose that life has (as they express it) no higher end than pleasure – no better and nobler object of desire and pursuit – they designate as utterly mean and grovelling; as a doctrine worthy only of swine, to whom the followers of Epicurus were, at a very early period, contemptuously likened: and modern holders of the doctrine are occasionally made the subject of equally polite comparisons by its German, French, and English assailants.

When thus attacked, the Epicureans have always answered, that it is not they, but their accusers, who represent human nature in a degrading light, since the accusation supposes human beings to be capable of no pleasures except those of which swine are capable. [...] The comparison of the Epicurean life to that of beasts is felt as degrading, precisely because a beast's pleasures do not satisfy a human being's conceptions of happiness. Human beings have faculties more elevated than the animal appetites; and, when once made conscious of them, do not regard any thing as happiness which does not include their gratification. I do not, indeed, consider the Epicureans to have been by any means faultless in drawing out their scheme of consequences from the utilitarian principle. To do this in any sufficient manner, many Stoic as well as Christian elements require to be included. But there is no known Epicurean theory of life which does not assign to the pleasures of the intellect, of the feelings and imagination, and of the moral sentiments, a much higher value as pleasures than to those of mere sensation. [...]

If I am asked what I mean by difference of quality in pleasures, or what makes one pleasure more valuable than another, merely as a pleasure, except its being greater in amount, there is but one possible answer. Of two pleasures, if there be one to which all or almost all who have experience of both give a decided preference, irrespective of any feeling of moral obligation to prefer it, that is the more desirable pleasure. If one of the two is, by those who are competently acquainted with both, placed so far above the other that they prefer it, even though knowing it to be attended with a greater amount of discontent, and would not resign it for any quantity of the other pleasure which their nature is capable of, we are justified in ascribing to the preferred enjoyment a superiority in quality, so far outweighing quantity, as to render it, in comparison, of small account. [...]

Whoever supposes that this preference takes place at a sacrifice of happiness; that the superior being, in any thing like equal circumstances, is not happier than the inferior – confounds the two very different ideas of happiness and content. It is indisputable, that the being whose capacities of enjoyment are low has the greatest chance of having them fully satisfied; and a highly endowed being will always feel that any happiness which he can look for, as the world is constituted, is imperfect. But he can learn to bear its imperfections, if they are at all bearable; and they will not make him envy the being who is indeed unconscious of the imperfections, but only because he feels not at all the good which those imperfections qualify. It is better to be a human being dissatisfied, than a pig satisfied; better to be Socrates dissatisfied, than a fool satisfied. And if the fool or the pig are of a different opinion, it is because they only know their own side of the question. The other party to the comparison knows both sides.

It may be objected, that many who are capable of the higher pleasures, occasionally, under the influence of temptation, postpone them to the lower. But this is quite compatible with a full appreciation of the intrinsic superiority of the higher. Men often, from infirmity of character, make their election for the nearer good, though they know it to be the less valuable, and this no less when the choice is between two bodily pleasures than when it is between bodily and mental. They pursue sensual indulgences to the injury of health, though perfectly aware that health is the greater good. It may be further objected, that many who begin with youthful enthusiasm for every thing noble, as they advance in years sink into indolence and selfishness. But I do not believe that those who undergo this very common change voluntarily choose the lower description of pleasures in preference to the higher. I believe, that, before they devote themselves exclusively to the one, they have already become incapable of the other. [...]

According to the Greatest-happiness Principle, as above explained, the ultimate end, with reference to and for the sake of which all other things are desirable (whether we are considering our own good or that of other people), is an existence exempt as far as possible from pain, and as rich as possible in enjoyments, both in point of quantity and quality; the test of quality, and the rule for measuring it against quantity, being the preference felt by those, who in their opportunities of experience, to which must be added their habits of self-consciousness and self-observation, are best furnished with the means of comparison. This, being, according to the utilitarian opinion, the end of human action, is necessarily also the standard of morality: which may accordingly be defined, the rules and precepts for human conduct, by the observance of which an existence such as has been described might be, to the greatest extent possible, secured to all mankind; and not to them only, but, so far as the nature of things admits, to the whole sentient creation. [...]

I must again repeat, what the assailants of utilitarianism seldom have the justice to acknowledge, that the happiness which forms the utilitarian standard of what is right in conduct is not the agent's own happiness, but that of all concerned; as, between his own happiness and that of others, utilitarianism requires him to be as strictly impartial as a disinterested and benevolent spectator. In the golden rule of Jesus of Nazareth, we read the complete spirit of the ethics of utility. To do as you would be done by, and to love your neighbor as yourself, constitute the ideal perfection of utilitarian morality. As the means of making the nearest approach to this ideal, utility would enjoin, first, that laws and social arrangements should place the happiness or (as, speaking practically, it may be called) the interest of every individual as nearly as possible in harmony with the interest of the whole; and secondly, that education and opinion, which have so vast a power over human character, should so use that power as to establish in the mind of every individual an indissoluble association between his own happiness and the good of the whole – especially between his own happiness, and the practice of such modes of conduct, negative and positive, as regard for the universal happiness prescribes – so that not only he may be unable to conceive the possibility of happiness to himself, consistently with conduct opposed to the general good, but also that a direct impulse to promote the general good may be in every individual one of the habitual motives of action, and the sentiments connected therewith may fill a large and prominent place in every human being's sentient existence. If the impugners of the utilitarian morality represented it to their own minds in this its true character, I know not what recommendation possessed by any other morality they could possibly affirm to be wanting to it; what more beautiful or more exalted developments of human nature any other ethical system can be supposed to foster; or what springs of action, not accessible to the utilitarian, such systems rely on for giving effect to their mandates. [...]

Utility is often summarily stigmatized as an immoral doctrine by giving it the name of Expediency, and, taking advantage of the popular use of that term, to contrast it with Principle. But the Expedient, in the sense in which it is opposed to the Right, generally means that which is expedient for the particular interest of the agent himself; as when a minister sacrifices the interests of his country to keep himself in place. When it means any thing better than this, it means that which is expedient for some immediate object, some temporary purpose, but which violates a rule whose observance is expedient in a much higher degree. The Expedient, in this sense, instead of being the same thing with the useful, is a branch of the hurtful. Thus it would often be expedient, for the purpose of getting over some momentary embarrassment, or attaining some object immediately useful to ourselves or others, to tell a lie. But inasmuch as the cultivation in ourselves of a sensitive feeling on the subject of veracity is one of the most useful, and the enfeeblement of that feeling one of the most hurtful, things to which our conduct can be instrumental; and inasmuch as any, even unintentional, deviation from truth does that much towards weakening the trustworthiness of human assertion, which is not only the principal support of all present social well-being, but the insufficiency of which does more than any one thing that can be named to keep back civilization, virtue, every thing on which human happiness on the largest scale depends – we feel that the violation, for a present advantage, of a rule of such transcendent expediency, is not expedient; and that he, who, for the sake of a convenience to himself or to some other individual, does what depends on him to deprive mankind of the good, and inflict upon them the evil, involved in the greater or less reliance which they can place in each other's word, acts the part of one of their worst enemies. [...]

The remainder of the stock arguments against utilitarianism mostly consist in laying to its charge the common infirmities of human nature, and the general difficulties which embarrass conscientious persons in shaping their course through life. We are told that an utilitarian will be apt to make his own particular case an exception to moral rules; and, when under temptation, will see an utility in the breach of a rule greater than he will see in its observance. But is utility the only creed which is able to furnish us with excuses for evil-doing, and means of cheating our own conscience? They are afforded in abundance by all doctrines which recognize as a fact in morals the existence of conflicting considerations; which all doctrines do that have been believed by sane persons. It is not the fault of any creed, but of the complicated nature of human affairs, that rules of conduct cannot be so framed as to require no exceptions, and that hardly any kind of action can safely be laid down as either always obligatory or always condemnable. There is no ethical creed which does not temper the rigidity of its laws by giving a certain latitude, under the moral responsibility of the agent, for accommodation to peculiarities of circumstances; and under every creed, at the opening thus made, self-deception and dishonest casuistry get in. There exists no moral system under which there do not arise unequivocal cases of conflicting obligation. These are the real difficulties; the knotty points both in the theory of ethics, and in the conscientious guidance of personal conduct. They are overcome practically with greater or with less success according to the intellect and virtue of the individual; but it can hardly be pretended that any one will be the less qualified for dealing with them, from possessing an ultimate standard to which conflicting rights and duties can be referred. If utility is the ultimate source of moral obligations, utility may be invoked to decide between them when their demands are incompatible. Though the application of the standard may be difficult, it is better than none at all: while in other systems, the moral laws all claiming independent authority, there is no common umpire entitled to interfere between them; their claims to precedence one over another rest on little better than sophistry; and unless determined, as they generally are, by the unacknowledged influence of considerations of utility, afford a free scope for the action of personal desires and partialities. We must remember that only in these cases of conflict between secondary principles is it requisite that first principles should be appealed to. There is no case of moral obligation in which some secondary principle is not involved; and, if only one, there can seldom be any real doubt which one it is, in the mind of any person by whom the principle itself is recognized.

CHAPTER 3: OF THE ULTIMATE SANCTION OF THE PRINCIPLE OF UTILITY

The question is often asked, and properly so, in regard to any supposed moral standard, What is its sanction? what are the motives to obey it? or, more specifically, what is the source of its obligation? whence does it derive its binding force? It is a necessary part of moral philosophy to provide the answer to this question; which, though frequently assuming the shape of an objection to the utilitarian morality, as if it had some special applicability to that above others, really arises in regard to all standards. It arises, in fact, whenever a person is called on to *adopt* a standard, or refer morality to any basis on which he has not been accustomed to rest it. For the customary morality, that which education and opinion have consecrated, is the only one which presents itself to the mind with the feeling of being *in itself* obligatory: and, when a person is asked to believe that this morality *derives* its obligation from some general principle round which custom has not thrown the same halo, the assertion is to him a paradox; the supposed corollaries seem to have a more binding force than the original theorem; the superstructure seems to stand better without than with what is represented as its foundation. He says to himself, "I feel that I am bound not to rob or murder, betray or deceive; but why am I bound to promote the general happiness? If my own happiness lies in something else, why may I not give that the preference?" [...]

The principle of utility either has, or there is no reason why it might not have, all the sanctions which belong to any other system of morals. Those sanctions are either external or internal. Of the external sanctions it is not necessary to speak at any length. They are, the hope of favor and the fear of displeasure from our fellow-creatures, or from the Ruler of the universe, along with whatever we may have of sympathy or affection for them; or of love and awe of him, inclining us to do his will independently of selfish consequences. There is evidently no reason why all these motives for observance should not attach themselves to the utilitarian morality as completely and as powerfully as to any other. Indeed, those of them which refer to our fellow-creatures are sure to do so, in proportion to the amount of general intelligence: for, whether there be any other ground of moral obligation than the general happiness or not, men do desire happiness; and, however imperfect may be their own practice, they desire and commend all conduct in others towards themselves by which they think their happiness is promoted. With regard to the religious motive, if men believe, as most profess to do, in the goodness of God, those who think that conduciveness to the general happiness is the essence, or even only the criterion, of good, must necessarily believe that it is also that which God approves. The whole force, therefore, of external reward and punishment, whether physical or moral, and whether proceeding from God or from our fellow-men, together with all that the capacities of human nature admit of disinterested devotion to either, become available to enforce the utilitarian morality, in proportion as that morality is recognized; and the more powerfully, the more the appliances of education and general cultivation are bent to the purpose.

So far as to external sanctions. The internal sanction of duty, whatever our standard of duty may be, is one and the same – a feeling in our own mind; a pain, more or less intense, attendant on violation of duty, which, in properly cultivated moral natures, rises in the more serious cases into shrinking from it as an impossibility. This feeling, when disinterested, and connecting itself with the pure idea of duty, and not with some particular form of it, or with any of the merely accessory circumstances, is the essence of Conscience: though in that complex phenomenon, as it actually exists, the simple fact is, in general, all incrusted over with collateral associations, derived from sympathy, from love, and still more from fear; from all the forms of religious feeling; from the recollections of childhood, and of all our past life; from self-esteem, desire of the esteem of others, and occasionally even self-abasement. This extreme complication is, I apprehend, the origin of the sort of mystical character, which, by a tendency of the human mind of which there are many other examples, is apt to be attributed to the idea of moral obligation, and which leads people to believe that the idea cannot possibly attach itself to any other objects than those which, by a supposed mysterious law, are found in our present experience to excite it. Its binding force, however, consists in the existence of a mass of feeling which must be broken through in order to do what violates our standard of right; and which, if we do nevertheless violate that standard, will probably have to be encountered afterwards in the form of remorse. Whatever theory we have of the nature or origin of conscience, this is what essentially constitutes it.

The ultimate sanction, therefore, of all morality (external motives apart) being a subjective feeling in our own minds, I see nothing embarrassing, to those whose standard is utility, in the question, What is the sanction of that particular standard? We may answer, The same as of all other moral standards – the conscientious feelings of mankind. Undoubtedly this sanction has no binding efficacy on those who do not possess the feelings it appeals to; but neither will these persons be more obedient to any other moral principle than to the utilitarian one. On them, morality of any kind has no hold but through the external sanctions. Meanwhile the feelings exist – a fact in human nature, the reality of which, and the great power with which they are capable of acting on those in whom they have been duly cultivated, are proved by experience. No reason has ever been shown why they may not be cultivated to as great intensity in connection with the utilitarian as with any other rule of morals. [...]

Chapter 4: Of What Sort of Proof the Principle of Utility is Susceptible

It has already been remarked, that questions of ultimate ends do not admit of proof, in the ordinary acceptation of the term. To be incapable of proof by reasoning is common to all first principles; to the first premises of our knowledge, as well as to those of our conduct. But the former, being matters of fact, may be the subject of a direct appeal to the faculties which judge of fact; namely, our senses, and our internal consciousness. Can an appeal be made to the same faculties on questions of practical ends? Or by what other faculty is cognizance taken of them?

Questions about ends are, in other words, questions what things are desirable. The utilitarian doctrine is, that happiness is desirable, and the only thing desirable, as an end; all other things being only desirable as means to that end. What ought to be required of this doctrine – what conditions is it requisite that the doctrine should fulfil – to make good its claim to be believed?

The only proof capable of being given that an object is visible, is that people actually see it; the only proof that a sound is audible, is that people hear it: and so of the other sources of our experience. In like manner, I apprehend, the sole evidence it is possible to produce that any thing is desirable, is that people do actually desire it. If the end which the utilitarian doctrine proposes to itself were not, in theory and in practice, acknowledged to be an end, nothing could ever convince any person that it was so. No reason can be given why the general happiness is desirable, except that each person, so far as he believes it to be attainable, desires his own happiness. This, however, being a fact, we have not only all the proof which the case admits of, but all which it is possible to require, that happiness is a good; that each person's happiness is a good to that person; and the general happiness, therefore, a good to the aggregate of all persons. Happiness has made out its title as *one* of the ends of conduct, and consequently one of the criteria of morality. [...]

Virtue, according to the utilitarian conception, is a good of this description. There was no original desire of it, or motive to it, save its conduciveness to pleasure, and especially to protection from pain. But, through the association thus formed, it may be felt a good in itself, and desired as such with as great intensity as any other good; and with this difference between it and the love of money, of power, or of fame – that all of these may, and often do, render the individual noxious to the other members of the society to which he belongs, whereas there is nothing which makes him so much a blessing to them as the cultivation of the disinterested love of virtue. And consequently the utilitarian standard, while it tolerates and approves those other acquired desires, up to the point beyond which they would be more injurious to the general happiness than promotive of it, enjoins and requires the cultivation of the love of virtue up to the greatest strength possible, as being above all things important to the general happiness.

It results from the preceding considerations, that there is in reality nothing desired except happiness. Whatever is desired otherwise than as a means to some end beyond itself, and ultimately to happiness, is desired as itself a part of happiness, and is not desired for itself until it has become so. Those who desire virtue for its own sake, desire it either because the consciousness of it is a pleasure, or because the consciousness of being without it is a pain, or for both reasons united: as in truth the pleasure and pain seldom exist separately, but almost always together; the same person feeling pleasure in the degree of virtue attained, and pain in not having attained more. If one of these gave him no pleasure, and the other no pain, he would not love or desire virtue, or would desire it only for the other benefits which it might produce to himself or to persons whom he cared for.

We have now, then, an answer to the question, of what sort of proof the principle of utility is susceptible. If the opinion which I have now stated is psychologically true; if human nature is so constituted as to desire nothing which is not either a part of happiness or a means of happiness – we can have no other proof, and we require no other, that these are the only things desirable. If so, happiness is the sole end of human action, and the promotion of it the test by which to judge of all human conduct; from whence it necessarily follows that it must be the criterion of morality, since a part is included in the whole. [...]

CHAPTER 5: ON THE CONNECTION BETWEEN JUSTICE AND UTILITY

In all ages of speculation, one of the strongest obstacles to the reception of the doctrine, that Utility or Happiness is the criterion of right and wrong, has been drawn from the idea of Justice. The powerful sentiment and apparently clear perception which that word recalls, with a rapidity and certainty resembling an instinct, have seemed to the majority of thinkers to point to an inherent quality in things; to show that the Just must have an existence in nature as something absolute, generically distinct from every variety of the Expedient, and, in idea, opposed to it, though (as is commonly acknowledged) never, in the long-run, disjoined from it in fact. [...]

To find the common attributes of a variety of objects, it is necessary to begin by surveying the objects themselves in the concrete. Let us therefore advert successively to the various modes of action, and arrangements of human affairs, which are classed, by universal or widely spread opinion, as Just or as Unjust. The things well known to excite the sentiments associated with those names are of a very multifarious character. I shall pass them rapidly in review, without studying any particular arrangement.

In the first place, it is mostly considered unjust to deprive any one of his personal liberty, his property, or any other thing which belongs to him by law. Here, therefore, is one instance of the application of the terms Just and Unjust in a perfectly definite sense; namely, that it is just to respect, unjust to violate, the *legal rights* of any one. But this judgment admits of several exceptions, arising from the other forms in which the notions of justice and injustice present themselves. For example: the person who suffers the deprivation may (as the phrase is) have *forfeited* the rights which he is so deprived of; a case to which we shall return presently. But also –

Secondly, The legal rights of which he is deprived may be rights which *ought* not to have belonged to him: in other words, the law which confers on him these rights may be a bad law. When it is so, or when (which is the same thing for our purpose) it is supposed to be so, opinions will differ as to the justice or injustice of infringing it. Some maintain that no law, however bad, ought to be disobeyed by an individual citizen; that his opposition to it, if shown at all, should only be shown in endeavoring to get it altered by competent authority. This opinion (which condemns many of the most illustrious benefactors of mankind, and would often protect pernicious institutions against the only weapons, which, in the state of things existing at the time, have any chance of succeeding against them) is defended, by those who hold it, on grounds of expediency; principally on that of the importance, to the common interest of mankind, of maintaining inviolate the sentiment of submission to law. Other persons, again, hold the directly contrary opinion, that any law, judged to be bad, may blamelessly be disobeyed, even though it be not judged to be unjust, but only inexpedient; while others would confine the license of disobedience to the case of unjust laws. But, again, some say that all laws which are inexpedient are unjust, since every law imposes some restriction on the natural liberty of mankind; which restriction is an injustice, unless legitimated by tending to their good. Among these diversities of opinion, it seems to be universally admitted that there may be unjust laws, and that law, consequently, is not the ultimate criterion of justice, but may give to one person a benefit, or impose on another an evil, which justice condemns. When, however, a law is thought to be unjust, it seems always to be regarded as being so in the same way in which a breach of law is unjust – namely, by infringing somebody's right; which, as it cannot in this case be a legal right, receives a different appellation, and is called a moral right. We may say, therefore, that a second case of injustice consists in taking or withholding from any person that to which he has a *moral right*.

Thirdly, It is universally considered just, that each person should obtain that (whether good or evil) which he *deserves*; and unjust, that he should obtain a good, or be made to undergo an evil, which he does not deserve. This is, perhaps, the clearest and most emphatic form in which the idea of justice is conceived by the general mind. As it involves the notion of desert, the question arises, What constitutes desert? Speaking in a general way, a person is understood to deserve good if he does right; evil, if he does wrong: and, in a more particular sense, to deserve good from those to whom he does or has done good, and evil from those to whom he does or has done evil. The precept of returning good for evil has never been regarded as a case of the fulfilment of justice, but as one in which the claims of justice are waived, in obedience to other considerations.

Fourthly, It is confessedly unjust to *break faith* with any one; to violate an engagement, either express or implied; or disappoint expectations raised by our own conduct, at least if we have raised those expectations knowingly and voluntarily. Like the other obligations of justice already spoken of, this one is not regarded as absolute, but as capable of being overruled by a stronger obligation of justice on the other side, or by such conduct on the part of the person concerned as is deemed to absolve us from our obligation to him, and to constitute a *forfeiture* of the benefit which he has been led to expect.

Fifthly, It is, by universal admission, inconsistent with justice to be *partial*; to show favor or preference to one person over another in matters to which favor and preference do not properly apply. Impartiality, however, does not seem to be regarded as a duty in itself, but rather as instrumental to some other duty; for it is admitted that favor and preference are not always censurable, and indeed the cases in which they are condemned are rather the exception than the rule. A person would be more likely to be blamed than applauded for giving his family or friends no superiority in good offices over strangers, when he could do so without violating any other duty; and no one thinks it unjust to seek one person in preference to another as a friend, connection, or companion. Impartiality, where rights are concerned, is of course obligatory; but this is involved in the more general obligation of giving to every one his right. A tribunal, for example, must be impartial, because it is bound to award, without regard to any other consideration, a disputed object to the one of two parties who has the right to it. There are other cases in which impartiality means, being solely influenced by desert; as with those who, in the capacity of judges, preceptors, or parents, administer reward and punishment as such. There are cases, again, in which it means being solely influenced by consideration for the public interest; as in making a selection among candidates for a government employment. Impartiality, in short, as an obligation of justice, may be said to mean being exclusively influenced by the considerations which it is supposed ought to influence the particular case in hand, and resisting the solicitation of any motives which prompt to conduct different from what those considerations would dictate.

Nearly allied to the idea of impartiality is that of *equality*; which often enters as a component part both into the conception of justice and into the practice of it, and, in the eyes of many persons, constitutes its essence. But, in this still more than in any other case, the notion of justice varies in different persons, and always conforms in its variations to their notion of utility. Each person maintains that equality is the dictate of justice, except where he thinks that expediency requires inequality. The justice of giving equal protection to the rights of all is maintained by those who support the most outrageous inequality in the rights themselves. Even in slave countries, it is theoretically admitted that the rights of the slave, such as they are, ought to be as sacred as those of the master, and that a tribunal which fails to enforce them with equal strictness is wanting in justice; while, at the same time, institutions which leave to the slave scarcely any rights to enforce are not deemed unjust, because they are not deemed inexpedient. Those who think that utility requires distinctions of rank do not consider it unjust that riches and social privileges should be unequally dispensed; but those who think this inequality inexpedient think it unjust also. Whoever thinks that government is necessary sees no injustice in as much inequality as is constituted by giving to the magistrate powers not granted to other people. Even among those who hold levelling doctrines, there are as many questions of justice as there are differences of opinion about expediency. Some Communists consider it unjust that the produce of the labor of the community should be shared on any other principle than that of exact equality; others think it just that those should receive most whose wants are greatest; while others hold that those who work harder, or who produce more, or whose services are more valuable to the community, may justly claim a larger quota in the division of the produce. And the sense of natural justice may be plausibly appealed to in behalf of every one of these opinions. [...]

The entire history of social improvement has been a series of transitions, by which one custom or institution after another, from being a supposed primary necessity of social existence, has passed into the rank of an universally stigmatized injustice and tyranny. So it has been with the distinctions of slaves and freemen, nobles and serfs, patricians and plebeians; and so it will be, and in part already is, with the aristo-cracies of color, race, and sex.

It appears, from what has been said, that justice is a name for certain moral requirements, which, regarded collectively, stand higher in the scale of social utility, and are therefore of more paramount obligation, than any others; though particular cases may occur in which some other social duty is so important as to overrule any one of the general maxims of justice. Thus, to save a life, it may not only be allowable, but a duty, to steal, or take by force, the necessary food or medicine, or to kidnap, and compel to officiate, the only qualified medical practitioner. In such cases, as we do not call any thing justice which is not a virtue, we usually say, not that justice must give way to some other moral principle, but that what is just in ordinary cases is, by reason of that other principle, not just in the particular case. By this useful accommodation of language, the character of indefeasibility attributed to justice is kept up, and we are saved from the necessity of maintaining that there can be laudable injustice.

The considerations which have now been adduced, resolve, I conceive, the only real difficulty in the utilitarian theory of morals. It has always been evident that all cases of justice are also cases of expediency: the difference is in the peculiar senti-ment which attaches to the former, as contradistinguished from the latter. If this characteristic sentiment has been sufficiently accounted for; if there is no necessity to assume for it any peculiarity of origin; if it is simply the natural feeling of resentment, moralized by being made co-extensive with the demands of social good; and if this feeling not only does but ought to exist in all the classes of cases to which the idea of justice corresponds – that idea no longer presents itself as a stumbling-block to the utilitarian ethics. Justice remains the appropriate name for certain social utilities which are vastly more important, and therefore more absolute and imperative, than any others are as a class (though not more so than others may be in particular cases), and which therefore ought to be, as well as naturally are, guarded by a sentiment not only different in degree, but also in kind; distinguished from the milder feeling which attaches to the mere idea of promoting human pleasure or convenience, at once by the more definite nature of its commands, and by the sterner character of its sanctions.

CHAPTER 15

A Voice from the South. By a Black Woman of the South

ANNA JULIA COOPER

WOMANHOOD A VITAL ELEMENT IN THE REGENERATION AND PROGRESS OF A RACE

The two sources from which, perhaps, modern civilization has derived its noble and ennobling ideal of woman are Christianity and the Feudal System. [...]

Respect for woman, the much lauded chivalry of the Middle Ages, meant what I fear it still means to some men in our own day – respect for the elect few among whom they expect to consort.

The idea of the radical amelioration of womankind, reverence for woman as woman regardless of rank, wealth, or culture, was to come from that rich and bounteous fountain from which flow all our liberal and universal ideas – the Gospel of Jesus Christ.

And yet the Christian Church at the time of which we have been speaking would seem to have been doing even less to protect and elevate woman than the little done by secular society. The Church as an organization committed a double offense against woman in the Middle Ages. Making of marriage a sacrament and at the same time insisting on the celibacy of the clergy and other religious orders, she gave an inferior if not an impure character to the marriage relation, especially fitted to reflect discredit on woman. Would this were all or the worst! but the Church by the licentiousness of its chosen servants invaded the household and established too often as vicious connections those relations which it forbade to assume openly and in good faith. "Thus," to use the words of our authority, "the religious corps became as numerous, as searching, and as unclean as the frogs of Egypt, which penetrated into all quarters, into the ovens and kneading troughs, leaving their filthy trail wherever they went." [...]

However much then the facts of any particular period of history may seem to deny it, I for one do not doubt that the source of the vitalizing principle of woman's

Anna J. Cooper. *A Voice from the South. By a Black Woman of the South*. Originally published in 1892.

development and amelioration is the Christian Church, so far as that church is coincident with Christianity.

Christ gave ideals not formulæ. The Gospel is a germ requiring millennia for its growth and ripening. It needs and at the same time helps to form around itself a soil enriched in civilization, and perfected in culture and insight without which the embryo can neither be unfolded or comprehended. With all the strides our civilization has made from the first to the nineteenth century, we can boast not an idea, not a principle of action, not a progressive social force but was already mutely foreshadowed, or directly enjoined in that simple tale of a meek and lowly life. The quiet face of the Nazarene is ever seen a little way ahead, never too far to come down to and touch the life of the lowest in days the darkest, yet ever leading onward, still onward, the tottering childish feet of our strangely boastful civilization.

By laying down for woman the same code of morality, the same standard of purity, as for man; by refusing to countenance the shameless and equally guilty monsters who were gloating over her fall, – graciously stooping in all the majesty of his own spotlessness to wipe away the filth and grime of her guilty past and bid her go in peace and sin no more; and again in the moments of his own careworn and footsore dejection, turning trustfully and lovingly, away from the heartless snubbing and sneers, away from the cruel malignity of mobs and prelates in the dusty marts of Jerusalem to the ready sympathy, loving appreciation and unfaltering friendship of that quiet home at Bethany; and even at the last, by his dying bequest to the disciple whom he loved, signifying the protection and tender regard to be extended to that sorrowing mother and ever afterward to the sex she represented; – throughout his life and in his death he has given to men a rule and guide for the estimation of woman as an equal, as a helper, as a friend, and as a sacred charge to be sheltered and cared for with a brother's love and sympathy, lessons which nineteen centuries' gigantic strides in knowledge, arts, and sciences, in social and ethical principles have not been able to probe to their depth or to exhaust in practice. [...]

The position of woman in society determines the vital elements of its regeneration and progress.

Now that this is so on *a priori* grounds all must admit. And this not because woman is better or stronger or wiser than man, but from the nature of the case, because it is she who must first form the man by directing the earliest impulses of his character. [...]

Woman, Mother, – your responsibility is one that might make angels tremble and fear to take hold! To trifle with it, to ignore or misuse it, is to treat lightly the most sacred and solemn trust ever confided by God to human kind. The training of children is a task on which an infinity of weal or woe depends. Who does not covet it? Yet who does not stand awe-struck before its momentous issues! It is a matter of small moment, it seems to me, whether that lovely girl in whose accomplishments you take such pride and delight, can enter the gay and crowded salon with the ease and elegance of this or that French or English gentlewoman, compared with the decision as to whether her individuality is going to reinforce the good or the evil elements of the world. The lace and the diamonds, the dance and the theater, gain a new significance when scanned in their bearings on such issues. Their influence on the individual personality, and through her on the society and civilization which she vitalizes and inspires – all this and more must be weighed in the balance before the jury can return a just and intelligent verdict as to the innocence or banefulness of these apparently simple amusements.

Now the fact of woman's influence on society being granted, what are its practical bearings on the work which brought together this conference of colored clergy and laymen in Washington? "We come not here to talk." Life is too busy, too pregnant with meaning and far reaching consequences to allow you to come this far for mere intellectual entertainment.

The vital agency of womanhood in the regeneration and progress of a race, as a general question, is conceded almost before it is fairly stated. I confess one of the difficulties for me in the subject assigned lay in its obviousness. The plea is taken away by the opposite attorney's granting the whole question.

"Woman's influence on social progress" – who in Christendom doubts or questions it? One may as well be called on to prove that the sun is the source of light and heat and energy to this many-sided little world.

Nor, on the other hand, could it have been intended that I should apply the position when taken and proven, to the needs and responsibilities of the women of our race in the South. For is it not written, "Cursed is he that cometh after the king?" and has not the King already preceded me in "The Black Woman of the South"?

They have had both Moses and the Prophets in Dr. Crummell and if they hear not him, neither would they be persuaded though one came up from the South.

I would beg, however, with the Doctor's permission, to add my plea for the *Colored Girls* of the South: – that large, bright, promising fatally beautiful class that stand shivering like a delicate plantlet before the fury of tempestuous elements, so full of promise and possibilities, yet so sure of destruction; often without a father to whom they dare apply the loving term, often without a stronger brother to espouse their cause and defend their honor with his life's blood; in the midst of pitfalls and snares, waylaid by the lower classes of white men, with no shelter, no protection nearer than the great blue vault above, which half conceals and half reveals the one Care-Taker they know so little of. Oh, save them, help them, shield, train, develop, teach, inspire them! Snatch them, in God's name, as brands from the burning! There is material in them well worth your while, the hope in germ of a staunch, helpful, regenerating womanhood on which, primarily, rests the foundation stones of our future as a race.

It is absurd to quote statistics showing the Negro's bank account and rent rolls, to point to the hundreds of newspapers edited by colored men and lists of lawyers, doctors, professors, D. D's, LL D's, etc., etc., etc., while the source from which the life-blood of the race is to flow is subject to taint and corruption in the enemy's camp.

True progress is never made by spasms. Real progress is growth. It must begin in the seed. Then, "first the blade, then the ear, after that the full corn in the ear." There is something to encourage and inspire us in the advancement of individuals since their emancipation from slavery. It at least proves that there is nothing irretrievably wrong in the shape of the black man's skull, and that under given circumstances his development, downward or upward, will be similar to that of other average human beings.

But there is no time to be wasted in mere felicitation. That the Negro has his niche in the infinite purposes of the Eternal, no one who has studied the history of the last fifty years in America will deny. That much depends on his own right comprehension of his responsibility and rising to the demands of the hour, it will be good for him to see; and how best to use his present so that the structure of the future shall be stronger and higher and brighter and nobler and holier than that of the past, is a question to be decided each day by every one of us.

The race is just twenty-one years removed from the conception and experience of a chattel, just at the age of ruddy manhood. It is well enough to pause a moment for retrospection, introspection, and prospection. We look back, not to become inflated with conceit because of the depths from which we have arisen, but that we may learn wisdom from experience. We look within that we may gather together once more our forces, and, by improved and more practical methods, address ourselves to the tasks before us. We look forward with hope and trust that the same God whose guiding hand led our fathers through and out of the gall and bitterness of oppression, will still lead and direct their children, to the honor of His name, and for their ultimate salvation.

But this survey of the failures or achievements of the past, the difficulties and embarrassments of the present, and the mingled hopes and fears for the future, must not degenerate into mere dreaming nor consume the time which belongs to the practical and effective handling of the crucial questions of the hour; and there can be no issue more vital and momentous than this of the womanhood of the race.

Here is the vulnerable point, not in the heel, but at the heart of the young Achilles; and here must the defenses be strengthened and the watch redoubled.

We are the heirs of a past which was not our fathers' moulding. "Every man the arbiter of his own destiny" was not true for the American Negro of the past: and it is no fault of his that he finds himself to-day the inheritor of a manhood and woman-hood impoverished and debased by two centuries and more of compression and degradation.

But weaknesses and malformations, which to-day are attributable to a vicious schoolmaster and a pernicious system, will a century hence be rightly regarded as proofs of innate corruptness and radical incurability.

Now the fundamental agency under God in the regeneration, the re-training of the race, as well as the ground work and starting point of its progress upward, must be the *black woman*.

With all the wrongs and neglects of her past, with all the weakness, the debase-ment, the moral thralldom of her present, the black woman of to-day stands mute and wondering at the Herculean task devolving upon her. But the cycles wait for her. No other hand can move the lever. She must be loosed from her bands and set to work.

Our meager and superficial results from past efforts prove their futility; and every attempt to elevate the Negro, whether undertaken by himself or through the philan-thropy of others, cannot but prove abortive unless so directed as to utilize the indispensable agency of an elevated and trained womanhood.

A race cannot be purified from without. Preachers and teachers are helps, and stimulants and conditions as necessary as the gracious rain and sunshine are to plant growth. But what are rain and dew and sunshine and cloud if there be no life in the plant germ? We must go to the root and see that that is sound and healthy and vigorous; and not deceive ourselves with waxen flowers and painted leaves of mock chlorophyll.

We too often mistake individuals' honor for race development and so are ready to substitute pretty accomplishments for sound sense and earnest purpose.

A stream cannot rise higher than its source. The atmosphere of homes is no rarer and purer and sweeter than are the mothers in those homes. A race is but a total of families. The nation is the aggregate of its homes. As the whole is sum of all its parts, so the character of the parts will determine the characteristics of the whole. These are all axioms and so evident that it seems gratuitous to remark it; and yet, unless I am greatly mistaken, most of the unsatisfaction from our past results arises from just such a radical and palpable error, as much almost on our own part as on that of our benevolent white friends.

The Negro is constitutionally hopeful and proverbially irrepressible; and naturally stands in danger of being dazzled by the shimmer and tinsel of superficials. We often mistake foliage for fruit and overestimate or wrongly estimate brilliant results.

The late Martin R. Delany, who was an unadulterated black man, used to say when honors of state fell upon him, that when he entered the council of kings the black race entered with him; meaning, I suppose, that there was no discounting his race identity and attributing his achievements to some admixture of Saxon blood. But our present record of eminent men, when placed beside the actual status of the race in America to-day, proves that no man can represent the race. Whatever the attainments of the individual may be, unless his home has moved on *pari passu*, he can never be regarded as identical with or representative of the whole.

Not by pointing to sun-bathed mountain tops do we prove that Phœbus warms the valleys. We must point to homes, average homes, homes of the rank and file of horny handed toiling men and women of the South (where the masses are) lighted and cheered by the good, the beautiful, and the true, – then and not till then will the whole plateau be lifted into the sunlight.

Only the BLACK WOMAN can say "when and where I enter, in the quiet, undisputed dignity of my womanhood, without violence and without suing or special patronage, then and there the whole *Negro race enters with me*." Is it not evident then that as individual workers for this race we must address ourselves with no half-hearted zeal to this feature of our mission. The need is felt and must be recognized by all. There is a call for workers, for missionaries, for men and women with the double consecration of a fundamental love of humanity and a desire for its melioration through the Gospel; but superadded to this we demand an intelligent and sympathetic comprehension of the interests and special needs of the Negro.

I see not why there should not be an organized effort for the protection and elevation of our girls such as the White Cross League in England. English women are strengthened and protected by more than twelve centuries of Christian influences, freedom and civilization; English girls are dispirited and crushed down by no such all-levelling prejudice as that supercilious caste spirit in America which cynically assumes "A Negro woman cannot be a lady." English womanhood is beset by no such snares and traps as betray the unprotected, untrained colored girl of the South, whose only crime and dire destruction often is her unconscious and marvelous beauty. Surely then if English indignation is aroused and English manhood thrilled under the leadership of a Bishop of the English church to build up bulwarks around their wronged sisters, Negro sentiment cannot remain callous and Negro effort nerveless in view of the imminent peril of the mothers of the next generation. "*I am my Sister's keeper!*" should be the hearty response of every man and woman of the race, and this conviction should purify and exalt the narrow, selfish and petty personal aims of life into a noble and sacred purpose.

We need men who can let their interest and gallantry extend outside the circle of their æsthetic appreciation; men who can be a father, a brother, a friend to every weak, struggling unshielded girl. We need women who are so sure of their own social footing that they need not fear leaning to lend a hand to a fallen or falling sister. We need men and women who do not exhaust their genius splitting hairs on aristocratic distinctions and thanking God they are not as others; but earnest, unselfish souls, who can go into the highways and byways, lifting up and leading, advising and encouraging with the truly catholic benevolence of the Gospel of Christ. [...]

A certain Southern Bishop of our Church reviewing the situation, whether in Godly anxiety or in "Gothic antipathy" I know not, deprecates the fact that the colored people do not seem *drawn* to the Episcopal Church, and comes to the sage conclusion that the Church is not adapted to the rude untutored minds of the Freedmen, and that they may be left to go to the Methodists and Baptists whither their racial proclivities undeniably tend. [...] If this be allowed, a *black woman of the South* would beg to point out two possible oversights in this southern work which may indicate in part both a cause and a remedy for some failure. The first is *not calculating for the Black man's personality*; not having respect, if I may so express it, to his manhood or deferring at all to his conceptions of the needs of his people. When colored persons have been employed it was too often as machines or as manikins. There has been no disposition, generally, to get the black man's ideal or to let his individuality work by its own gravity, as it were. A conference of earnest Christian men have met at regular intervals for some years past to discuss the best methods of promoting the welfare and development of colored people in this country. Yet, strange as it may seem, they have never invited a colored man or even intimated that one would be welcome to take part in their deliberations. Their remedial contrivances are purely theoretical or empirical, therefore, and the whole machinery devoid of soul.

The second important oversight in my judgment is closely allied to this and probably grows out of it, and that is not developing Negro womanhood as an essential fundamental for the elevation of the race, and utilizing this agency in extending the work of the Church. [...]

The institution of the Church in the South to which she mainly looks for the training of her colored clergy and for the help of the "Black Woman" and "Colored Girl" of the South, has graduated since the year 1868, when the school was founded, *five young women*; and while yearly numerous young men have been kept and trained for the ministry by the charities of the Church, the number of indigent females who have here been supported, sheltered and trained, is phenomenally small. Indeed, to my mind, the attitude of the Church toward this feature of her work is as if the solution of the problem of Negro missions depended solely on sending a quota of deacons and priests into the field, girls being a sort of *tertium quid* whose development may be promoted if they can pay their way and fall in with the plans mapped out for the training of the other sex. Now I would ask in all earnestness, does not this force potential deserve by education and stimulus to be made dynamic? Is it not a solemn duty incumbent on all colored churchmen to make it so? Will not the aid of the Church be given to prepare our girls in head, heart, and hand for the duties and responsibilities that await the intelligent wife, the Christian mother, the earnest, virtuous, helpful woman, at once both the lever and the fulcrum for uplifting the race.

As Negroes and churchmen we cannot be indifferent to these questions. They touch us most vitally on both sides. We believe in the Holy Catholic Church. We believe that however gigantic and apparently remote the consummation, the Church will go on conquering and to conquer till the kingdoms of this world, not excepting the black man and the black woman of the South, shall have become the kingdoms of the Lord and of his Christ.

That past work in this direction has been unsatisfactory we must admit. That without a change of policy results in the future will be as meagre, we greatly fear. Our life as a race is at stake. The dearest interests of our hearts are in the scales. We must either break away from dear old landmarks and plunge out in any line and every line that enables us to meet the pressing need of our people, or we must ask the Church to allow and help us, untrammelled by the prejudices and theories of individuals, to work aggressively under her direction as we alone can, with God's help, for the salvation of our people.

The time is ripe for action. Self-seeking and ambition must be laid on the altar. The battle is one of sacrifice and hardship, but our duty is plain. We have been recipients of missionary bounty in some sort for twenty-one years. Not even the senseless vegetable is content to be a mere reservoir. Receiving without giving is an anomaly in nature. Nature's cells are all little workshops for manufacturing sunbeams, the product to be *given out* to earth's inhabitants in warmth, energy, thought, action. Inanimate creation always pays back an equivalent.

Now, *How much owest thou my Lord?* Will his account be overdrawn if he call for singleness of purpose and self-sacrificing labor for your brethren? Having passed through your drill school, will you refuse a general's commission even if it entail responsibility, risk and anxiety, with possibly some adverse criticism? Is it too much to ask you to step forward and direct the work for your race along those lines which you know to be of first and vital importance?

Will you allow these words of Ralph Waldo Emerson? "In ordinary," says he, "we have a snappish criticism which watches and contradicts the opposite party. We want the will which advances and dictates [acts]. Nature has made up her mind that what cannot defend itself, shall not be defended. Complaining never so loud and with never so much reason, is of no use. What cannot stand must fall; *and the measure of our sincerity and therefore of the respect of men is the amount of health and wealth we will hazard in the defense of our right.*"

"WOMAN VERSUS THE INDIAN"

In the National Woman's Council convened at Washington in February 1891, among a number of thoughtful and suggestive papers read by eminent women, was one by the Rev. Anna Shaw, bearing the above title.

That Miss Shaw is broad and just and liberal in principle is proved beyond contradiction. Her noble generosity and womanly firmness are unimpeachable. The unwavering stand taken by herself and Miss Anthony in the subsequent color ripple in Wimodaughsis ought to be sufficient to allay forever any doubts as to the pure gold of these two women.

Of Wimodaughsis (which, being interpreted for the uninitiated, is a woman's culture club whose name is made up of the first few letters of the four words wives, mothers, daughters, and sisters) Miss Shaw is president, and a lady from the Blue Grass State *was* secretary.

Pandora's box is opened in the ideal harmony of this modern Eden without an Adam when a colored lady, a teacher in one of our schools, applies for admission to its privileges and opportunities.

The Kentucky secretary, a lady zealous in good works and one who, I can't help imagining, belongs to that estimable class who daily thank the Lord that He made the earth that they may have the job of superintending its rotations, and who really would like to help "elevate" the colored people (in her own way of course and so long as they understand their places) is filled with grief and horror that any persons of Negro extraction should aspire to learn type-writing or languages or to enjoy any other advantages offered in the sacred halls of Wimodaughsis. Indeed, she had not calculated that there were any wives, mothers, daughters, and sisters, except white ones; and she is really convinced that *Whimodaughsis* would sound just as well, and then it need mean just *white mothers, daughters and sisters*. In fact, so far as there is anything in a name, nothing would be lost by omitting for the sake of euphony, from this unique mosaic, the letters that represent wives. *Whiwimodaughsis* might be a little startling, and on the whole wives would better yield to white; since clearly all women are not wives, while surely all wives are daughters. The daughters therefore could represent the wives and this immaculate assembly for propagating liberal and progressive ideas and disseminating a broad and humanizing culture might be spared the painful possibility of the sight of a black man coming in the future to escort from an evening class this solitary cream-colored applicant. Accordingly the Kentucky secretary took the cream-colored applicant aside, and, with emotions befitting such an epoch-making crisis, told her, "as kindly as she could," that colored people were not admitted to the classes, at the same time refunding the money which said cream-colored applicant had paid for lessons in type-writing.

When this little incident came to the knowledge of Miss Shaw, she said firmly and emphatically, NO. As a minister of the gospel and as a Christian woman, she could not lend her influence to such unreasonable and uncharitable discrimination; and she must resign the honor of president of Wimodaughsis if persons were to be proscribed solely on account of their color.

To the honor of the board of managers, be it said, they sustained Miss Shaw; and the Kentucky secretary, and those whom she succeeded in inoculating with her prejudices, resigned.

'Twas only a ripple, – some bewailing of lost opportunity on the part of those who could not or would not seize God's opportunity for broadening and enlarging their own souls – and then the work flowed on as before.

Susan B. Anthony and Anna Shaw are evidently too noble to be held in thrall by the provincialisms of women who seem never to have breathed the atmosphere beyond the confines of their grandfathers' plantations. It is only from the broad plateau of light and love that one can see petty prejudice and narrow priggishness in their true perspective; and it is on this high ground, as I sincerely believe, these two grand women stand.

As leaders in the woman's movement of to-day, they have need of clearness of vision as well as firmness of soul in adjusting recalcitrant forces, and wheeling into line the thousand and one none-such, never-to-be-modified, won't-be-dictated-to banners of their somewhat mottled array.

The black woman and the southern woman, I imagine, often get them into the predicament of the befuddled man who had to take singly across a stream a bag of corn, a fox and a goose. There was no one to help, and to leave the goose with the fox was death – with the corn, destruction. To re-christen the animals, the lion could not be induced to lie down with the lamb unless the lamb would take the inside berth.

The black woman appreciates the situation and can even sympathize with the actors in the serio-comic dilemma.

But, may it not be that, as women, the very lessons which seem hardest to master now, are possibly the ones most essential for our promotion to a higher grade of work?

We assume to be leaders of thought and guardians of society. Our country's manners and morals are under our tutoring. Our standards are law in our several little worlds. However tenaciously men may guard some prerogatives, they are our willing slaves in that sphere which they have always conceded to be woman's. Here, no one dares demur when her fiat has gone forth. The man would be mad who presumed, however inexplicable and past finding out any reason for her action might be, to attempt to open a door in her kingdom officially closed and regally sealed by her.

The American woman of to-day not only gives tone directly to her immediate world, but her tiniest pulsation ripples out and out, down and down, till the outermost circles and the deepest layers of society feel the vibrations. [...]

The American woman then is responsible for American manners. Not merely the right ascension and declination of the satellites of her own drawing room; but the rising and the setting of the pestilential or life-giving orbs which seem to wander afar in space, all are governed almost wholly through her magnetic polarity. [...]

A good citizen may use his influence to have existing laws and statutes changed or modified, but a public servant must not be blamed for obeying orders. A railroad conductor is not asked to dictate measures, nor to make and pass laws. His bread and butter are conditioned on his managing his part of the machinery as he is told to do. If, therefore, I found myself in that compartment of a train designated by the sovereign law of the state for presumable Caucasians, and for colored persons only when traveling in the capacity of nurses and maids, should a conductor inform me, as a gentleman might, that I had made a mistake, and offer to show me the proper car for black ladies; I might wonder at the expensive arrangements of the company and of the state in providing special and separate accommodations for the transportation of the various hues of humanity, but I certainly could not take it as a want of courtesy on the conductor's part that he gave the information. It is true, public sentiment precedes and begets all laws, good or bad; and on the ground I have taken, our women are to be credited largely as teachers and moulders of public sentiment. But when a law has passed and received the sanction of the land, there is nothing for our officials to do but enforce it till repealed; and I for one, as a loyal American citizen, will give those officials cheerful support and ready sympathy in the discharge of their duty. But when a great burly six feet of masculinity with sloping shoulders and unkempt beard swaggers in, and, throwing a roll of tobacco into one corner of his jaw, growls out at me over the paper I am reading, "Here gurl," (I am past thirty) "you better git out 'n dis kyar 'f yer don't, I'll put yer out," – my mental annotation is *Here's an American citizen who has been badly trained. He is sadly lacking in both "sweetness" and "light";* and when in the same section of our enlightened and progressive country, I see from the car window, working on private estates, convicts from the state penitentiary, among them squads of boys from fourteen to eighteen years of age in a chain-gang, their feet chained together and heavy blocks attached – not in 1850, but in 1890, '91 and '92, I make a note on the fly-leaf of my memorandum, *The women in this section should organize a Society for the Prevention of Cruelty to Human Beings, and disseminate civilizing tracts, and send throughout the region apostles of anti-barbarism for the propagation of humane and enlightened ideas.* And when farther on in the same section our train stops at a dilapidated station, rendered yet more unsightly by dozens of loafers with their hands in their pockets while a productive soil and inviting climate beckon in vain to industry; and when, looking a little more closely, I see two dingy little rooms with "FOR LADIES" swinging over one and "FOR COLORED PEOPLE" over the other; while wondering under which head I come, I notice a little way off the only hotel proprietor of the place whittling a pine stick as he sits with one leg thrown across an empty goods box; and as my eye falls on a sample room next door which seems to be driving the only wide-awake and popular business of the commonwealth, I cannot help ejaculating under my breath, "What a field for the missionary woman." I know that if by any fatality I should be obliged to lie over at that station, and, driven by hunger, should be compelled to seek refreshments or the bare necessaries of life at the only public accommodation in the town, that same stick-whittler would coolly inform me, without looking up from his pine splinter, "We doan uccommodate no niggers hyur." And yet we are so scandalized at Russia's barbarity and cruelty to the Jews! We pay a man a thousand dollars a night just to make us weep, by a recital of such heathenish inhumanity as is practiced on Sclavonic soil. [. . .]

The Black Woman has tried to understand the Southern woman's difficulties; to put herself in her place, and to be as fair, as charitable, and as free from prejudice in judging her antipathies, as she would have others in regard to her own. She has honestly weighed the apparently sincere excuse, "But you must remember that these people were once our slaves"; and that other, "But civility towards the Negroes will bring us on *social equality* with them."

These are the two bugbears; or rather, the two humbugbears: for, though each is founded on a most glaring fallacy, one would think they were words to conjure with, so potent and irresistible is their spell as an argument at the North as well as in the South.

One of the most singular facts about the unwritten history of this country is the consummate ability with which Southern influence, Southern ideas and Southern ideals, have from the very beginning even up to the present day, dictated to and domineered over the brain and sinew of this nation. Without wealth, without education, without inventions, arts, sciences, or industries, without well-nigh every one of the progressive ideas and impulses which have made this country great, prosperous and happy, personally indolent and practically stupid, poor in everything but bluster and self-esteem, the Southerner has nevertheless with Italian finesse and exquisite skill, uniformly and invariably, so manipulated Northern sentiment as to succeed sooner or later in carrying his point and shaping the policy of this government to suit his purposes. Indeed, the Southerner is a magnificent manager of men, a born educator. For two hundred and fifty years he trained to his hand a people whom he made absolutely his own, in body, mind, and sensibility. He so insinuated differences and distinctions among them, that their personal attachment for him was stronger than for their own brethren and fellow sufferers. He made it a crime for two or three of them to be gathered together in Christ's name without a white man's supervision, and a felony for one to teach them to read even the Word of Life; and yet they would defend his interest with their life blood; his smile was their happiness, a pat on the shoulder from him their reward. The slightest difference among themselves in condition, circumstances, opportunities, became barriers of jealousy and disunion. He sowed his blood broadcast among them, then pitted mulatto against black, bond against free, house slave against plantation slave, even the slave of one clan against like slave of another clan; till, wholly oblivious of their ability for mutual succor and defense, all became centers of myriad systems of repellent forces, having but one sentiment in common, and that their entire subjection to that master hand.

And he not only managed the black man, he also hoodwinked the white man, the tourist and investigator who visited his lordly estates. The slaves were doing well, in fact couldn't be happier, – plenty to eat, plenty to drink, comfortably housed and clothed – they wouldn't be free if they could; in short, in his broad brimmed plantation hat and easy aristocratic smoking gown, he made you think him a veritable patriarch in the midst of a lazy, well fed, good natured, over-indulged tenantry.

Then, too, the South represented blood – not red blood, but blue blood. The difference is in the length of the stream and your distance from its source. If your own father was a pirate, a robber, a murderer, his hands are dyed in red blood, and you don't say very much about it. But if your great great great grandfather's grandfather stole and pillaged and slew, and you can prove it, your blood has become blue and you are at great pains to establish the relationship. So the South had neither silver nor gold, but she had blood; and she paraded it with so much gusto that the substantial little Puritan maidens of the North, who had been making bread and canning currants and not thinking of blood the least bit, began to hunt up the records of the Mayflower to see if some of the passengers thereon could not claim the honor of having been one of William the Conqueror's brigands, when he killed the last of the Saxon kings and, red-handed, stole his crown and his lands. Thus the ideal from out the Southland brooded over the nation and we sing less lustily than of yore

> "Kind hearts are more than coronets
> And simple faith than Norman blood."

In politics, the two great forces, commerce and empire, which would otherwise have shaped the destiny of the country, have been made to pander and cater to Southern notions. "Cotton is King" meant the South must be allowed to dictate or there would be no fun. Every statesman from 1830 to 1860 exhausted his genius in persuasion and compromises to smooth out her ruffled temper and gratify her petulant demands. But like a sullen younger sister, the South has pouted and sulked and cried: "I won't play with you now; so there!" and the big brother at the North has coaxed and compromised and given in, and – ended by letting her have her way. Until 1860 she had as her pet an institution which it was death by the law to say anything about, except that it was divinely instituted, inaugurated by Noah, sanctioned by Abraham, approved by Paul, and just ideally perfect in every way. And when, to preserve the autonomy of the family arrangements, in '61, '62 and '63, it became necessary for the big brother to administer a little wholesome correction and set the obstreperous Miss vigorously down in her seat again, she assumed such an air of injured innocence, and melted away so lugubriously, the big brother has done nothing since but try to sweeten and pacify and laugh her back into a companionable frame of mind.

Father Lincoln did all he could to get her to repent of her petulance and behave herself. He even promised she might keep her pet, so disagreeable to all the neighbors and hurtful even to herself, and might manage it at home to suit herself, if she would only listen to reason and be just tolerably nice. But, no – she was going to leave and set up for herself; she didn't propose to be meddled with; and so, of course, she had to be spanked. Just a little at first – didn't mean to hurt, merely to teach her who was who. But she grew so ugly, and kicked and fought and scratched so outrageously, and seemed so determined to smash up the whole business, the head of the family got red in the face, and said: "Well, now, he couldn't have any more of that foolishness. Arabella must just behave herself or take the consequences." [...] Still Arabella sulked, – till the rest of the family decided she might just keep her pets, and manage her own affairs and nobody should interfere.

So now, if one intimates that some clauses of the Constitution are a dead letter at the South and that only the name and support of that pet institution are changed while the fact and essence, minus the expense and responsibility, remain, he is quickly told to mind his own business and informed that he is waving the bloody shirt.

Even twenty-five years after the fourteenth and fifteenth amendments to our Constitution, a man who has been most unequivocal in his outspoken condemnation of the wrongs regularly and systematically heaped on the oppressed race in this country, and on all even most remotely connected with them – a man whom we had thought our staunchest friend and most noble champion and defender – after a two weeks' trip in Georgia and Florida immediately gives signs of the fatal inception of the virus. Not even the chance traveller from England or Scotland escapes. The arch-manipulator takes him under his special watch-care and training, uses up his stock arguments and gives object lessons with his choicest specimens of Negro depravity and worthlessness; takes him through what, in New York, would be called "the slums," and would predicate there nothing but the duty of enlightened Christians to send out their light and emulate their Master's aggressive labors of love; but in Georgia is denominated "our terrible problem, which people of the North so little understand, yet vouchsafe so much gratuitous advice about." With an injured air he shows the stupendous and atrocious mistake of reasoning about these people as if they were just ordinary human beings, and amenable to the tenets of the Gospel; and not long after the inoculation begins to work, you hear this old-time friend of the oppressed delivering himself something after this fashion: "Ah, well, the South must be left to manage the Negro. She is most directly concerned and must understand her problem better than outsiders. We must not meddle. We must be very careful not to widen the breaches. The Negro is not worth a feud between brothers and sisters."

Lately a great national and international movement characteristic of this age and country, a movement based on the inherent right of every soul to its own highest development, I mean the movement making for Woman's full, free, and complete emancipation, has, after much courting, obtained the gracious smile of the Southern woman – I beg her pardon – the Southern *lady*.

She represents blood, and of course could not be expected to leave that out; and firstly and foremostly she must not, in any organization she may deign to grace with her presence, be asked to associate with "these people who were once her slaves." [...]

The second fallacy in the objection grows out of the use of an ambiguous middle, as the logicians would call it, or assigning a double signification to the term "*Social equality.*"

Civility to the Negro implies social equality. I am opposed to *associating* with dark persons on terms of social equality. Therefore, I abrogate civility to the Negro. This is like

> *Light is opposed to darkness.*
> *Feathers are light.*
> Ergo, *Feathers are opposed to darkness.*

The "social equality" implied by civility to the Negro is a very different thing from forced association with him socially. Indeed it seems to me that the mere application of a little cold common sense would show that uncongenial social environments could by no means be forced on any one. I do not, and cannot be made to associate with all dark persons, simply on the ground that I am dark; and I presume the Southern lady can imagine some whose faces are white, with whom she would no sooner think of chatting unreservedly than, were it possible, with a veritable "darkey." Such things must and will always be left to individual election. No law, human or divine, can legislate for or against them. Like seeks like; and I am sure with the Southern lady's antipathies at their present temperature, she might enter ten thousand organizations besprinkled with colored women without being any more deflected by them than by the proximity of a stone. The social equality scare then is all humbug, conscious or unconscious, I know not which. And were it not too bitter a thought to utter here, I might add that the overtures for forced association in the past history of these two races were not made by the manacled black man, nor by *the silent and suffering black woman*!

When I seek food in a public café or apply for first-class accommodations on a railway train, I do so because my physical necessities are identical with those of other human beings of like constitution and temperament, and crave satisfaction. I go because I want food, or I want comfort – not because I want association with those who frequent these places; and I can see no more "social equality" in buying lunch at the same restaurant, or riding in a common car, than there is in paying for dry goods at the same counter or walking on the same street.

The social equality which means forced or unbidden association would be as much deprecated and as strenuously opposed by the circle in which I move as by the most hide-bound Southerner in the land. Indeed I have been more than once annoyed by the inquisitive white interviewer, who, with spectacles on nose and pencil and notebook in hand, comes to get some "points" about "*your people*." My "people" are just like other people – indeed, too like for their own good. They hate, they love, they attract and repel, they climb or they grovel, struggle or drift, aspire or despair, endure in hope or curse in vexation, exactly like all the rest of unregenerate humanity. Their likes and dislikes are as strong; their antipathies – and prejudices too I fear, are as pronounced as you will find anywhere; and the entrance to the inner sanctuary of their homes and hearts is as jealously guarded against profane intrusion.

What the dark man wants then is merely to live his own life, in his own world, with his own chosen companions, in whatever of comfort, luxury, or emoluments his talent or his money can in an impartial market secure. Has he wealth, he does not want to be forced into inconvenient or unsanitary sections of cities to buy a home and rear his family. Has he art, he does not want to be cabined and cribbed into emulation with the few who merely happen to have his complexion. His talent aspires to study without proscription the masters of all ages and to rub against the broadest and fullest movements of his own day.

Has he religion, he does not want to be made to feel that there is a white Christ and a black Christ, a white Heaven and a black Heaven, a white Gospel and a black Gospel, – but the one ideal of perfect manhood and womanhood, the one universal longing for development and growth, the one desire for being, and being better, the one great yearning, aspiring, outreaching, in all the heart-throbs of humanity in whatever race or clime. [...]

What Are We Worth?

I once heard Henry Ward Beecher make this remark: "Were Africa and the Africans to sink to-morrow, how much poorer would the world be? A little less gold and ivory, a little less coffee, a considerable ripple, perhaps, where the Atlantic and Indian Oceans would come together – that is all; not a poem, not an invention, not a piece of art would be missed from the world."

This is not a flattering statement; but then we do not want flattery if seeing ourselves as others see us is to help us in fulfilling the higher order, "know thyself." The world is often called cold and hard. I don't know much about that; but of one thing I am sure, it is intensely practical. Waves of sentiment or prejudice may blur its old eyes for a little while but you are sure to have your bill presented first or last with the inexorable "How much owest thou?" What have you produced, what consumed? What is your real value in the world's economy? What do you give to the world over and above what you have cost? What would be missed had you never lived? What are you worth? What of actual value would go down with you if you were sunk into the ocean or buried by an earthquake to-morrow? Show up your cash account and your balance sheet. In the final reckoning do you belong on the debit or the credit side of the account? according to a fair and square, an impartial and practical reckoning. It is by this standard that society estimates individuals; and by this standard finally and inevitably the world will measure and judge nations and races.

It may not be unprofitable then for us to address ourselves to the task of casting up our account and carefully overhauling our books. It may be well to remember at the outset that the operation is purely a mathematical one and allows no room for sentiment. The good housewife's pet chicken which she took when first hatched, fed from her own hand and fondled on her bosom as lovingly as if it were a babe, is worth no more (for all the affection and care lavished on it) when sold in the shambles: and that never-to-be-forgotten black hen that stole into the parlor, flew upon the mantel looking for a nest among those handsome curios, smashed the sèvers vases and picked the buds from the lovely tea rose – so exasperatingly that the good woman could never again endure the sight of her – this ill-fated bird is worth no less. There are sections of this country in which the very name of the Negro, even in homeopathic doses, stirs up such a storm of feeling that men fairly grow wild and are unfit to discuss the simplest principles of life and conduct where the colored man is concerned; and you would think it necessary for the Ethiopian actually to change his skin before there can be any harmonious living or lucid thinking. [...]

Nine-tenths of the mis-called color prejudice or race prejudice in this country is mere sentiment governed by the association of ideas. It is not color prejudice at all. The color of a man's face *per se* has no more to do with his worthiness and companionableness than the color of his eyes or the shades of his hair. You admire the one or think the other more beautiful to rest the gaze upon. But every one with brains knows and must admit that he must look deeper than this for the man. [...]

Sentiment and cant, then, both being ruled out, let us try to study our subject as the world finally reckons it – not certain crevices and crannies of the earth, but the cool, practical, business-like world. What are we worth? not in Georgia nor in Massachusetts; not to our brothers and sisters and cousins and aunts, every one of whom would unhesitatingly declare us worth a great gold-lump; nor to the exasperated neighbor over the way who would be just as ready, perhaps, to write us down a most unmitigated nuisance. But what do we represent to the world? What is our market value. Are we a positive and additive quantity or a negative factor in the world's elements. What have we cost and what do we come to?

The calculation may be made in the same way and on the same principle that we would estimate the value of any commodity on the market. Men are not very unlike watches. We might estimate first the cost of material – is it gold or silver or alloy, solid or plated, jewelled or sham paste. Settle the relative value of your raw material, and next you want to calculate how much this value has been enhanced by labor, the delicacy and fineness, the honesty and thoroughness of the workmanship; then the utility and beauty of the product and its adaptability to the end and purpose of its manufacture; and lastly is there a demand in the market for such an article. Does it meet a want, *will it go and go right?*[...] In both the fundamental item is the question of material, and then the refining and enhancement of that material through labor, and so on through the list.

What then can we say for our raw material? [...]

Now whatever notions we may indulge on the theory of evolution and the laws of atavism or heredity, all concede that no individual character receives its raw material newly created and independent of the rock from whence it was hewn. No life is bound up within the period of its conscious existence. No personality dates its origin from its birthday. The elements that are twisted into the cord did not begin their formation when first the tiny thread became visible in the great warp and filling of humanity. [...]

In estimating the value of our material, therefore, it is plain that we must look into the deeds of our estates and ferret out their history. The task is an individual one, as likewise its application. Certainly the original timber as it came from the African forests was good enough. No race of heathen are more noted for honesty and chastity than are the tribes of Africa. For one of their women to violate the laws of purity is a crime punishable with death; and so strictly honest are they, it is said, that they are wont to leave their commodities at the place of exchange and go about their business. The buyer coming up takes what he wishes to purchase and leaves its equivalent in barter or money. A returned missionary tells the story that certain European traders, when at a loss as to the safe keeping of their wares, were told by a native chief, "Oh just lay them down there. *They are perfectly safe, there are no Christians here.*"

Whatever may be said of its beauty, then, the black side of the stream with us is pretty pure, and has no cause to blush for its honesty and integrity. From the nature of the case the infusions of white blood that have come in many instances to the black race in this country are not the best that race afforded. And if anything further is needed to account for racial irregularities – the warping and shrinking, the knotting and cracking of the sturdy old timber, the two hundred and fifty years of training here are quite sufficient to explain all. I have often thought, since coming in closer contact with the Puritan element in America, what a different planing and shaping this timber might have received under their hands!

As I compare the Puritan's sound, substantial, sanctified common sense with the Feudal froth and foam of the South; the Puritan's liberal, democratic, ethical and at the same time calculating, economical, stick-to-ative and go-ahead-ative spirit, – with the free and easy lavishness, the aristocratic notions of caste and class distinctions, the pliable consciences and unbending social bars amid which I was reared; – I have wished that it might have been ordered that as my race had to serve a term of bondage it might have been under the discipline of the successors of Cromwell and Milton, rather than under the training and example of the luxurious cavaliers. There is no doubt that the past two hundred and fifty years of working up the material we now inherit, has depreciated rather than enhanced its value. We find in it the foolish ideas of aristocracy founded on anything else than a moral claim; we find the contempt for manual labor and the horror of horny palms, the love of lavish expenditure and costly display, and – alas, that we must own it – the laxness of morals and easy-going consciences inherited and imitated from the old English gentry of the reigns of Charles and Anne. But to know our faults is one step toward correcting them, and there are, I trust, no flaws in this first element of value, *material*, which may not be planed and scraped and sand-papered out by diligent and strenuous effort. One thing is certain, the flaws that are simply ingrained in the timber are not our responsibility. A man is to be praised primarily not for having inherited fine tools and faultless materials but for making the most of the stuff he has, and doing his best in spite of disadvantages and poor material. The individual is responsible, not for what he has not, but for what he has; and the vital part for us after all depends on the use we make of our material.

Many a passable article has by diligent workmanship been made even from inferior material. And this brings us to our second item of value – Labor. [...]

It is labor, development, training, careful, patient, painful, diligent toil that must span the gulf between this vegetating life germ (now worth nothing but toil and care and trouble, and living purely at the expense of another) – and that future consummation in which "the elements are so mixed that Nature can stand up and say to all the world, '*This is a man.*'"

It is a heavy investment, requires a large outlay of money on long time and large risk, no end of labor, skill, pains. Education is the word that covers it all – the working up of this raw material and fitting it into the world's work to supply the world's need – the manufacture of men and women for the markets of the world. But there is no other labor which so creates value. The value of the well developed man has been enhanced far more by the labor bestowed than is the iron in the watch springs. The value of the raw material was far below zero to begin with; but this "quintessence of dust" has become, *through labor*, "the beauty of the world, the paragon of animals, – noble in reason and infinite in faculty!"

What a piece of work, indeed!

Education, then, is the safest and richest investment possible to man. It pays the largest dividends and gives the grandest possible product to the world – a man. The demand is always greater than the supply – and the world pays well for what it prizes.

Now what sort of workmanship are we putting on our raw material. What are we doing for education? The man-factories among our people make, I think, a fairly good showing. Figures are encouraging things to deal with, and too they represent something tangible in casting up our accounts. There are now 25,530 colored schools in the United States with 1,353,352 pupils; the colored people hold in landed property for churches and schools $25,000,000. 2,500,000 colored children have learned to read and most of these to write also. 22,956 colored men and women are teaching in these schools. There are sixty-six academies and high schools and one hundred and fifty schools for advanced education taught by colored teachers, together with seven colleges administered by colored presidents and faculties. There are now one thousand college bred Negro ministers in the country, 250 lawyers, 749 physicians; while, according to Dr. Rankin, there are 247 colored students preparing themselves in the universities of Europe. [...]

The world in putting these crucial questions to men and women, or to races and nations, classifies them under two heads – as consumers or producers. The man who consumes as much as he produces is simply *nil*. It is no matter to the world economically speaking whether he is in it or out of it. He is merely one more to count in taking the census. The man who consumes more than he produces is a destroyer of the world's wealth and should be estimated precisely as the housekeeper estimates moths and mice. These are the world's parasites, the shirks, the lazy lubbers who hang around rum shops and enter into mutual relationships with lamp posts to bear each the other's burdens, moralizing all the while (wondrous moralists and orators they often are!) and insisting that the world owes them a living! To be sure the world owes them nothing of the kind. [...]

Now to which class do we belong? The question must in the first place be an individual one for every man of whatever race: Am I giving to the world an equivalent of what it has given and is giving me? Have I a margin on the outside of consumption for surplus production? We owe it to the world to give out at least as much as we have taken in, but if we aim to be accounted a positive value we must leave it a little richer than we found it. [...]

The highest gifts are not measurable in dollars and cents. Beyond and above the class who run an account with the world and merely manage honestly to pay *in kind* for what they receive, there is a noble army – the Shakespeares and Miltons, the Newtons, Galileos and Darwins, – Watts, Morse, Howe, Lincoln, Garrison, John Brown – a part of the world's roll of honor – whose price of board and keep dwindles into nothingness when compared with what the world owes them; men who have taken of the world's bread and paid for it in immortal thoughts, invaluable inventions, new facilities, heroic deeds of loving self-sacrifice; men who dignify the world for their having lived in it and to whom the world will ever bow in grateful worship as its heroes and benefactors. It may not be ours to stamp our genius in enduring characters – but we can give what we are *at its best*.

Visiting the slave market in Boston one day in 1761, Mrs. John Wheatley was attracted by the modest demeanor and intelligent countenance of a delicate looking black girl just from the slave ship. She was quite nude save for a piece of coarse carpet she had tied about her loins, and the only picture she could give of her native home was that she remembered her mother in the early morning every day pouring out water before the rising sun. The benevolent Mrs. Wheatley expended some labor in polishing up this crude gem, and in 1773 the gifted Phillis gave to the world a small octavo volume of one hundred and twenty precious pages, published in London and dedicated to the Countess of Huntingdon. [...] That girl paid her debts *in song*. [...]

Now each can give something. It may not be a poem, or marble bust, or fragrant flower even; it may not be ours to place our lives on the altar of country as a loving sacrifice, or even to devote our living activities so extensively as B. T. Washington to supplying the world's need for strong and willing helpers. But we can at least *give ourselves*. Each can be *one* of those strong willing helpers – even though nature has denied him the talent of endlessly multiplying his force. And nothing less can honorably cancel our debt. Each is under a most sacred obligation not to squander the material committed to him, not to sap its strength in folly and vice, and to see at the least that he delivers a product worthy the labor and cost which have been expended on him. A sound manhood, a true womanhood is a fruit which the lowliest can grow. And it is a commodity of which the supply never exceeds the demand. There is no danger of the market being glutted. The world will always want *men*. The worth of one is infinite. To this value all other values are merely relative. Our money, our schools, our governments, our free institutions, our systems of religion and forms of creeds are all first and last to be judged by this standard: what sort of men and women do they grow? How are men and women being shaped and molded by this system of training, under this or that form of government, by this or that standard of moral action? You propose a new theory of education; *what sort of men does it turn out?* Does your system make boys and girls superficial and mechanical? Is it a producing of average percentages or a rounding out of manhood, – a sound, thorough, and practical development, – or a scramble for standing and marks? [...]

Let us then quietly commend ourselves to this higher court – this final tribunal. Short sighted idiosyncracies are but transient phenomena. It is futile to combat them, and unphilosophical to be depressed by them. To allow such things to overwhelm us, or even to absorb undue thought, is an admission of weakness. As sure as time *is – these mists will clear away*. And the world – our world, will surely and unerringly see us as we are. Our only care need be the intrinsic worth of our contributions. If we represent the ignorance and poverty, the vice and destructiveness, the vagabondism and parasitism in the world's economy, no amount of philanthropy and benevolent sentiment can win for us esteem: and if we contribute a positive value in those things the world prizes, no amount of negrophobia can ultimately prevent its recognition. And our great "problem" after all is to be solved not by brooding over it, and orating about it, but by *living into it*.

Bibliography

Anderson, Bonnie S. "The Lid Comes Off: International Radical Feminism and the Revolutions of 1848," *NWSA Journal*, 10:2, Summer 1998. Bloomington: Indiana University Press.

Antony, Louise and Charlotte Witt, eds. *A Mind of One's Own: Feminist Essays on Reason and Objectivity*. Boulder: Westview Press, 1992.

Anzaldúa, Gloria. "*La conciencia de la mestiza*: Towards a New Consciousness," in G. Anzaldúa, ed., *Making Face, Making Soul, Hacienda Caras: Creative and Critical Perspectives by Feminists of Color*. San Francisco: Aunt Lute Books, 1990.

Arendt, Hannah. *The Origins of Totalitarianism*. New York: Harcourt, Brace, Jovanovich, 1979.

Bachofen, Johann Jakob, *Mutterrecht und Urreligion*. In English: *Myth, Religion and Mother-right: Selected Writings of Johann Bachofen*, trans. George Boas with an introduction by Joseph Campbell. Princeton, NJ: Princeton University Press, 1967. (Bollingen Series.)

Baker-Fletcher, Karen. *A Singing Something: Womanist Reflections on Anna Julia Cooper*. New York: Crossroad, 1994.

Ballard, George. *Memoirs of Several Great Ladies Who Have Been Celebrated for Their Writings of Skill in the Learned Languages, Arts and Sciences*, ed. Ruth Perry. Detroit: Wayne State University Press, 1985 (first published 1752).

Bar On, Bat-Ami, ed. *Modern Engendering: Critical Feminist Readings in Modern Western Philosophy*. Albany: State University of New York Press, 1994.

Barry, Kathleen, *Susan B. Anthony*. New York: New York University Press, 1988.

Bell, Diane, "Yes, Virginia, There is a Feminist Ethnography: Reflections from Three Australian Fields," in *Gendered Fields: Women, Men and Ethnography*, ed. D. Bell, P. Caplan, and W. Karim. London: Routledge, 1993.

Berlin, Isaiah, *Karl Marx*. Oxford: Oxford University Press, 1939.

Bordo, Susan. *The Flight to Objectivity: Essays on Cartesianism and Culture*. Albany: State University of New York Press, 1987.

Boxill, Bernard. "Two Traditions in African American Political Philosophy," *The Philosophical Forum*, vol. XXIV, 1–3, Fall–Spring 1992–3.

Bracey, J. H. Jr., A. Meier, and E. Rudwick. *Black Nationalism in America*. New York: Bobbs Merrill, 1970.

Brewer, Rosa. "Theorizing Race, Class and Gender: The New Scholarship of Black Feminist Intellectuals and Black Women's Labor," in *Theorizing Black Feminisms: The Visionary Pragmatism of Black Women*, ed. Stanlie James and Abena Busia. New York: Routledge, 1993.

Brownmiller, Susan. *Against Our Will: Men, Women and Rape*. New York: Simon and Schuster, 1975.

Busby, Margaret. *Daughters of Africa*. New York: Pantheon Books, 1992.

Carby, Hazel V. *Reconstructing Womanhood: The Emergence of the Afro-American Woman Novelist*. New York: Oxford University Press, 1987.

Christian, Barbara, ed. *Black Feminist Criticism: Perspectives on Black Women Writers*. New York: Pergamon Press, 1985.

Collins, Patricia Hill. *Black Feminist Thought: Knowledge, Consciousness and the Politics of Empowerment*. New York: Routledge, 1991.

—— *Fighting Words: Black Women and the Search for Justice*. Minneapolis: University of Minnesota Press, 1998.

Conboy, K., et al. *Writing on the Body: Female Embodiment and Feminist Theory*. New York: Columbia University Press, 1997.

Cooper, Anna J. *A Voice from the South. By a Black Woman of the South*. Xenia, Ohio: The Aldine Printing House, 1892. Reprinted, with an introduction by Mary Helen Washington, Oxford: Oxford University Press, 1988.

Daly, Mary. *Gyn/Ecology: The Metaethics of Radical Feminism*. Boston: Beacon Press, 1978.

Davis, Angela Y. *Women, Race and Class*. New York: Vintage, 1983.

Douglass, Frederick. "I Have Come to Tell You Something About Slavery: An Address Delivered in Lynn, Massachusetts, in October 1841," in *The Frederick Douglass Papers*, vol. 1, *1841–46*, ed. John W. Blassingame. New Haven: Yale University Press, 1979.

—— "Narrative of the Life of Frederick Douglass," in Henry Louis Gates, Jr., ed., *The Classic Slave Narratives*. New York: New American Library, 1987.

Ebenstein, William. *Great Political Thinkers: Plato to the Present*. New York: Holt. Rinehart, and Winston, 1965.

Ferguson, Ann. "Androgyny as an Ideal for Human Development," in *Feminism and Philosophy*, ed. Mary Vetterling-Braggin et al. Totowa, NJ: Rowman and Allenheld, 1977.

Firestone, Shulamith. *The Dialectic of Sex*. New York: Bantam Books, 1971.

Foner, Philip, ed. and intro. *The Life and Writings of Frederick Douglass*, vols 1–4. New York: International Publishers, 1955.

Franchot, Jenny. "The Punishment of Esther: Frederick Douglass and the Construction of the Feminine," in *Frederick Douglass: New Literary and Historical Essays*, ed. Eric J. Sundquist. Cambridge: Cambridge University Press, 1990.

Fritz, Jean. *Cast for a Revolution: Some American Friends and Enemies, 1728–1814*. Boston: Houghton Mifflin Company, 1972.

Gage, Matilda Joslyn. *Woman, Church and the State: The Original Exposé of Male Collaboration Against the Female Sex*, 1893. Introduction by Sally Roesch Wagner. Reprinted 1980, Watertown, MA: Persephone Press.

Giddings, Paula. *When and Where I Enter: The Impact of Black Women on Race and Sex in America*. New York: Bantam Books, 1988.

Godwin, William. *Memoirs of the Author of a Vindication of the Rights of Woman*. London: J. Johnson and G. G. and J. Robinson, 1798.

Gould, Elizabeth Davis. *The First Sex*. Baltimore: Penguin Books, 1973.

Grant, Judith. *Fundamental Feminism: Contesting the Core Concepts of Feminist Theory*. New York: Routledge, 1993.

Graves, Robert. *The Greek Myths*. New York: Penguin, 1955.

Griffin, Susan. *Woman and Nature: The Roaring Inside Her*. New York: Harper and Row, 1978.

Gross, Elizabeth and Carole Pateman, eds. *Feminist Challenges: Social and Political Theory.* Boston: Northeastern University Press, 1987.

Harding, Sandra. *The Science Question in Feminism.* Ithaca: Cornell University Press, 1986.

—— *Whose Science? Whose Knowledge?* Ithaca: Cornell University Press, 1991.

Harding, Sandra, and Merrill Hintikka, eds. *Discovering Reality: Feminist Perspectives on Epistemology, Metaphysics, and Philosophy of Science.* Dordrecht: D. Reidel, 1983.

Hart, H. L. A. *The Concept of Law.* Oxford: Oxford University Press, 1961.

Hartmann, Heidi. "The Unhappy Marriage of Marxism and Feminism," in Lydia Sargent, ed., *Women and Revolution: A Discussion of the Unhappy Marriage of Marxism and Feminism.* Boston: South End Press, 1981.

Hartsock, Nancy C. M. *Money, Sex and Power: Toward a Feminist Historical Materialism.* Boston: Northeastern University Press, 1983.

Hempel, Carl G. *The Philosophy of Natural Science.* Englewood Cliffs, NJ: Prentice-Hall, 1966.

Hill, Bridget, ed. and intro. *Mary Astell; The First English Feminist: "Reflections Upon Marriage" and Other Writings by Mary Astell.* New York: St. Martin's Press, 1986.

Hine, Darlene Clark, ed. *Black Women in America: An Historical Encyclopedia.* Brooklyn: Carlson Publishing Co., 1993.

Hirschmann, Nancy J., and Christine Di Stefano. *Revisioning the Political: Feminist Reconstructions of Traditional Concepts in Western Political Theory.* Boulder: Westview Press, 1996.

Hoff, Joan. *Law, Gender and Injustice: A Legal History of U.S. Women.* New York: New York University Press, 1991.

Hook, Sidney. *Marx and the Marxists.* Princeton: D. Van Nostrand Company, Inc., 1955.

hooks, bell. *Feminist Theory from Margin to Center.* Boston: South End Press, 1984.

Hubbard, Ruth. *The Politics of Women's Biology.* New Brunswick: Rutgers University Press, 1990.

Hull, Gloria T., Patricia Bell Scott, and Barbara Smith, eds. *But Some of Us Are Brave: Black Women's Studies.* New York: Feminist Press, 1986.

Hutchinson, Louise Daniel, ed. and intro. *Anna J. Cooper: A Voice from the South.* Washington, D.C.: Smithsonian Institution Press, 1981.

Jacobs, Jo Ellen, and P. H. Payne, eds. *The Complete Works of Harriet Taylor Mill*, by Harriet Hardy Mill. Indianapolis: Indiana University Press, 1998.

Jaggar, Alison M. *Feminist Politics and Human Nature.* Totowa, NJ: Rowman and Allenheld, 1983.

James, Stanlie and Abena Busia, eds. *Theorizing Black Feminisms: The Visionary Pragmatism of Black Women.* New York: Routledge, 1993.

Joseph, Gloria. "The Incompatible Ménage à Trois: Marxism, Feminism and Racism," in Lydia Sargent, ed., *Women and Revolution: A Discussion of the Unhappy Marriage of Marxism and Feminism.* Boston: South End Press, 1981.

Keller, Evelyn Fox. *Reflections on Gender and Science.* New Haven: Yale University Press, 1985.

Kinnaird, Joan K. "Mary Astell: Inspired by Ideas," in Dale Spender, ed., *Feminist Theorists: Three Centuries of Key Women Thinkers.* New York: Pantheon, 1983.

Landsman, Gail H. "The 'Other' as Political Symbol: Image of Indians in the Woman Suffrage Movement," *Ethnohistory,* 39:3, Summer 1992.

Lange, Linda. "Women and Rousseau's Democratic Theory: Philosopher Monsters and Authoritarian Equality," in *Modern Engendering: Critical Feminist Readings in Modern Western Philosophy,* ed. Bat Ami Bar On. Albany: State University of New York Press, 1994.

Laslett, Peter, ed. and intro. John Locke, *Two Treatises of Government.* Cambridge: Cambridge University Press, 1960.

Lerner, Gerda. *Black Women in White America.* New York: Random House, 1972.

——*The Creation of Feminist Consciousness: From the Middle Ages to 1870*. Oxford: Oxford University Press, 1993.

Litwack, Leon and August Meier, eds. *Black Leaders of the Nineteenth Century*. Chicago: University of Illinois Press, 1991.

Lloyd, Genevieve. *The Man of Reason: "Male" and "Female" in Western Philosophy*. Minneapolis: University of Minnesota Press, 1985.

Lorde, Audre. *Sister/Outsider: Essays and Speeches*. Freedom, CA: The Crossing Press, 1984.

Lunsford Lane: Another Helper from North Carolina, ed. William George Hawkins, 1864.

MacKinnon, Catharine A. *Feminism Unmodified: Discourses on Life and Law*. Cambridge, MA: Harvard University Press, 1987.

Madison, James. *Mind of the Founder: Sources of the Political Thought of James Madison*, ed. and intro. Marvin Meyers. Boston: University Presses of New England, 1981.

Martin, Jane Roland. *Reclaiming a Conversation: The Ideal of an Educated Woman*. New Haven: Yale University Press, 1985.

Martin, Waldo E., Jr. "Frederick Douglass: Humanist as Race Leader," in *Black Leaders of the Nineteenth Century*, ed. Leon Litwack and August Meier. Chicago: University of Illinois Press, 1991.

Marx, Karl. *Eleven Theses on Feuerbach*, 1845. In Lawrence H. Simon, ed., *Karl Marx: Selected Writings*. Cambridge, MA: Hackett Publishing Co., 1994.

Meis, Maria. *Ecofeminism*. London and Atlantic Highlands, NJ: Zed, 1993.

Merchant, Carolyn. *Death of Nature: Women, Ecology and the Scientific Revolution*. New York: Harper and Row, 1980.

Minh Ha, Trinh. *Woman, Native, Other: Writing Postcoloniality and Feminism*. Bloomington: Indiana University Press, 1989.

Mohanty, Chandra Talpade. "Under *Western* Eyes: Feminist Scholarship and Colonial Discourses," *Boundary*, 2:12, Spring/Fall, 1984.

Moraga, Cherrie, and Gloria Anzaldúa, eds. *This Bridge Called My Back: Writings by Radical Women of Color*. New York: Kitchen Table Women of Color Press, 1973.

Nozick, Robert. *Anarchy, State and Utopia*. New York: Basic Books, 1974.

Okin, Susan Moller. *Women in Western Political Thought*. Princeton: Princeton University Press, 1979.

——*Justice, Gender and the Family*. New York: Basic Books, 1989.

Painter, Nell Irvin. "Martin R. Delany: Elitism and Black Nationalism," in *Black Leaders of the Nineteenth Century*, ed. Leon Litwack and August Meier. Chicago: University of Illinois Press, 1991.

Pateman, Carole. *Participation and Democratic Theory*. Cambridge: Cambridge University Press, 1970.

——*The Sexual Contract*. Stanford: Stanford University Press, 1988.

Perry, Ruth. *The Celebrated Mary Astell: An Early English Feminist*. Chicago: University of Chicago Press, 1986.

——"Mary Astell and the Critique of Possessive Individualism," *Eighteenth Century Studies*, 23:4, 1990.

Potter, Elizabeth. "Locke's Epistemology and Women's Struggles," in Bat Ami Bar On, ed., *Modern Engendering: Critical Feminist Readings in Modern Western Philosophy*. Albany: State University of New York Press, 1994.

Rawls, John. *A Theory of Justice*. Cambridge, MA: Harvard University Press, 1971.

Rhode, Deborah L. "Gender Difference and Gender Disadvantage," *Women and Politics*, 10:2, 1990.

Rich, Adrienne. *Of Woman Born: Motherhood as Experience and Institution*. New York: W. W. Norton & Co., 1976.

—— *On Lies, Secrets and Silence: Selected Prose, 1966–1978*. New York: W. W. Norton & Co., 1979.

Richardson, Marilyn, ed. and intro. *Maria W. Stewart, America's First Black Political Writer.* Bloomington: Indiana University Press, 1987.

Robertson, Nan. *The Girls in the Balcony: Women, Men and the New York Times.* New York: Fawcett Books, 1993.

Rossi, Alice. *The Feminist Papers: From Adams to Beauvoir.* New York: Columbia University Press, 1973.

Rothenberg, Paula S. *Racism and Sexism: An Integrated Study.* New York: St. Martin's Press, 1988.

Russell, Bertrand. *A History of Western Philosophy.* New York: Simon and Schuster, 1945.

Sabine, George. *A History of Political Theory*, 3rd edn. London: George G. Harrap & Co., 1963.

Said, Edward. *Orientalism.* New York: Random House, 1979.

Sandel, Michael, ed. *Democracy's Discontent: America's in Search of a Public Philosophy.* New York: Belnap Press, 1996.

Sapiro, Virginia. *A Vindication of Political Virtue.* Chicago: University of Chicago Press, 1992.

Schmidt, Richard. *Introduction to Marx and Engels: A Critical Reconstruction.* Boulder: Westview, 1987.

Schneir, Miriam, ed. *Feminism: The Essential Historical Writings.* New York: Vintage, 1972.

Sen, A. K. and B. Williams, eds. *Utilitarianism and Beyond.* Cambridge: Cambridge University Press, 1982.

Shanley, Mary Lyndon, and Carole Pateman, eds. *Feminist Interpretations and Political Theory.* State College, PA: Pennsylvania State University, 1991.

Smart, J. J. C., and B. Williams. *Utilitarianism: For and Against.* Cambridge: Cambridge University Press, 1973.

Spelman, Elizabeth V. *Inessential Women: Problems of Exclusion in Feminist Thought.* Boston: Beacon Press, 1988.

Spender, Dale. *Women of Ideas and What Men Have Done to Them.* London: Routledge and Kegan Paul Ltd., 1982.

Spivak, Gayatri. *The Spivak Reader: Selected Works of Gayatri Chakravorty Spivak*, ed. Donna Landry, G. McLean, and G. C. Spivak. New York: Routledge, 1995.

Springborg, Patricia, ed. *The Political Writings of Mary Astell.* Cambridge: Cambridge University Press, 1996.

—— "Mary Astell (1666–1731), Critic of Locke," *American Political Science Review*, 89:3, 1995.

Stanton, Elizabeth Cady, Susan B. Anthony, and Matilda Joslyn Gage, eds. *A History of Woman Suffrage.* New York: Fowler and Wells, vol. 1, 1881. Reprinted 1969, Arno and The New York Times.

Sunstein, Cass, ed. *Feminism and Political Theory.* Chicago: Chicago University Press, 1989.

Tocqueville, Alexis de. *Democracy in America*, ed. Phillips Bradley. New York: Knopf, 1945.

Todd, Janet, and Marilyn Butler. *The Works of Mary Wollstonecraft.* London: Pickering and Chatto Ltd., 1989.

Tuana, Nancy. *The Less Noble Sex: Scientific, Religious and Philosophical Conceptions of Woman's Nature.* Bloomington: Indiana University Press, 1993.

—— *Women and the History of Philosophy.* New York: Paragon House, 1992.

Tuck, Richard. "The Contribution of History," in *A Companion to Contemporary Political Philosophy*, ed. Robert E. Goodin and Philip Pettit. Oxford: Blackwell Publishers, 1993.

Walker, David. *David Walker's Appeal*, ed. and intro. Charles M. Wiltse. New York: Hill and Wang, 1965.

Warren, Mercy Otis. "Observations on the New Constitution, and on the Federal and State Conventions by a Columbian Patriot," 1788, in Herbert J. Storing, ed., *The Complete Anti-Federalist*, vol. 4. Chicago: University of Chicago Press, 1981.

—— *History of the Rise, Progress and Termination of the American Revolution Interpreted with Biographical, Political and Moral Observations*, ed. Lester H. Cohen. Indianapolis: Indiana University Press (Liberty Classics), 1988.

Waters, Kristin. "(Re)turning to the Modern: Radical Feminism and the Post-modern Turn," in Diane Bell and Renate Klein, eds., *Radically Speaking: Feminism Reclaimed*. Melbourne: Spinifex Press, 1996.

—— "Women in Kantian Ethics: A Failure at Universality," in Bat Ami Bar On, ed., *Modern Engendering: Critical Feminist Readings in Modern Western Philosophy*. Albany: State University of New York Press, 1994.

—— *Robert Nozick and the Demands of Libertarianism*. University Microfilms, 1981.

Weiss, Penny A. *Gendered Community: Rousseau, Sex and Politics*. New York: New York University Press, 1993.

Williams, Patricia J. *The Alchemy of Race and Rights: Diary of a Law Professor*. Cambridge, MA: Harvard University Press, 1991.

Williams, Wendy W. "The Equality Crisis: Some Reflections on Culture, Courts, and Feminism," in *Feminist Legal Theory: Readings in Law and Gender*, ed. Katharine T. Bartlett and Rosanne Kennedy. Boulder: Westview Press, 1991.

Wolff, Robert Paul. *A Defense of Anarchism*. Los Angeles: University of California Press, 1998.

Young, Iris Marion. *Justice and the Politics of Difference*. Princeton: Princeton University Press, 1990.

—— "Beyond the Unhappy Marriage: A Critique of Dual Systems Theory," in Lydia Sargent, ed., *Women and Revolution: A Discussion of the Unhappy Marriage of Marxism and Feminism*. Boston: South End Press, 1981.

Index

Women and Men Political Theorists

ENLIGHTENED CONVERSATIONS

"This carefully crafted sourcebook makes available almost forgotten work in political philosophy by women and men authors from the seventeenth to the early twentieth centuries. Set in its historical and intellectual context with substantial introductions, the material reveals an exciting body of critical literature that contests modern liberal theory and demonstrates the need to rethink the canon of Western political theory."

Alison Jaggar, *University of Colorado*

"Kristin Waters' anthology is an egalitarian and inclusive conversation between political theorists of different races, times, and genders. Her thorough introductions to each of the participants and her insightful interpretive suggestions turn *Women and Men Political Theorists* into a unique text and an excellent addition to political theory."

Bat-Ami Bar On, *Binghamton University (SUNY)*

Women and Men Political Theorists is a rich and insightful collection of essays that restores important works to the arena of modern political theory and debate. Organized by theme, the book pairs up lesser-known figures with canonical writers, to produce a unique historical dialogue. The perspectives of Mary Astell and Mary Wollstonecraft, and African American writers such as Maria W. Stewart and Anna Julia Cooper, answer issues raised by Locke, Rousseau, Mill, and other classical theorists. The editor's fresh approach sheds new light on traditional and feminist concepts while her substantial critical introductions, biographical material, and bibliographies provide an indispensable resource for students and researchers.

Kristin Waters

The editor is Associate Professor of Philosophy at Worcester State College. She has published in the areas of social and political philosophy, feminist ethics and epistemology, and the history of ideas.

Cover illustration: Hogarth, *Southwark Fair* (detail), etching and engraving, 1733.

Cover design by Raven Design

Printed in Great Britain

Visit our website at
http://www.blackwellpublishers.co.uk

ISBN 0-631-20980-8

9 780631 209805

90000>

BLACKWELL
Publishers

DATE RETURN			